Unverkäufliches Muster

Heinz Schelle | Roland Ottmann | Astrid Pfeiffer

PROJECT MANAGER

PROJECT MANAGER

Project manager: Roland Ottmann
Editor: Astrid Pfeiffer
Publisher: German Association for Project Management

Design and production: Peter Design, Nuremberg
Cover illustration: Frey Kommunikations-Design, Fuerth/Bavaria

1st English language edition 2006, Nuremberg (Germany)

© GPM German Association for Project Management
All rights reserved.

The moral rights of the authors have been asserted.

The GPM is the German member association of the International Project Management Association.
www.GPM-IPMA.de

No part of this publication may be reproduced, duplicated or published elsewhere without the written consent of the GPM.

ISBN 3-924841-30-6

PREFACE

Roland Ottmann (MBA) | German Association for Project Management

Dear Readers

The development, writing, reviewing and editing of `Project Manager´ was a genuine team effort. Now, at last, we are delighted that we have completed the book and that you are able to hold a copy of it in your hands. The German Association for Project Management (GPM) intends this textbook to be a new national and international benchmark for all project management development activities. `Project Manager´ is part of the GPM´s initiative to update all its teaching and certification programmes. We have specifically streamlined the content of our courses and examinations and, at the same time, integrated new developments. This is evident throughout the textbook.

The content conforms to all the guidelines of the International Project Management Association´s IPMA Competence Baseline (ICB). In the book, we have given strong emphasis to the topics `people in projects´ and `communication´, because we feel that both have been undervalued for a long time and that there is a great deal of ground to make up. This focus also allows us to help fashion an international trend towards the central importance of people in project management.

A core aim is to deliver comprehensible information so that the textbook is easy to read. We have used a punchy, no-frills style to enable the fast communication of essential content. Studying project management and preparing for certification should be enjoyable. Fast reading and comprehension also save time – a significant factor in increasingly demanding working environments.

`Project Manager´ covers all four GPM/IPMA qualification levels (Level D to Level A). To make this possible, we combined two objectives: to provide readers who are taking their first in-depth look at project management with a fast introduction to the subject and, at the same time, to provide project management professionals who are studying for the higher certification levels with advanced learning materials. We want to provide a comprehensive overview of the most important aspects of project management and also guarantee enough details so that readers can put what they learn into practice.

The textbook will be revised, from edition to edition, in a continuous improvement process for which your suggestions are very welcome. This will ensure that `Project Manager´ is regularly updated with new knowledge and experience, which can then be integrated in project management training and certification processes and in the further development of project management in general.

PREFACE

I would like to thank Professor Heinz Schelle for his contributions as author and for his unwavering professional support; Astrid Pfeiffer for her work as editor, coordinator and author; our authors, Guenter Rackelmann and Kurt E. Weber, who each contributed one chapter; as well as Karin Peter and her team for delivering the layout design so quickly. I give my sincere thanks to our `test readers´, Dr Hans Stromeyer (Vesalius Ventures), Frank Bettgenhaeuser (Deutsche Post), Dr Conor John Fitzsimons (Fitzsimons Coaching & Consulting), Uwe Kliche (Dornier Consult) and Erwin Weitlaner (Siemens) for their hard work and helpful annotations. We remain committed to fostering this process of reciprocal exchange. Birgit Wolf´s translation service, with support from Dr Conor John Fitzsimons, who brought a native-speaking project manager´s perspective to the task, have together made a valuable contribution to this English language edition. The PM-ZERT assessors, Sandra Bartsch-Beuerlein and Wulff Seiler, also deserve our thanks for preparing the taxonomy, as does Werner Schmehr, Manager of the GPM certification body, PM-ZERT, Klaus Pannenbäcker, one of the founding fathers of the 4-L-C and the driving force behind the 4-L-C assessment concept, together with everyone else who has supported this publication.

We hope you enjoy reading and studying `Project Manager´ and wish you every success in your project management career.

Roland Ottmann (MBA)
President of the German Association for Project Management
Project manager and co-author of `Project Manager´

PREFACE

Professor Edward G. Krubasik | Siemens AG

Dear Readers

Project management excellence is a vital success factor for all members of the project team. Success is measured in terms of quality, speed and cost-effectiveness. It has been a longstanding personal aim of mine to ensure that all aspects of a project are handled professionally.

Today, projects account for almost 50 percent of Siemens´ group turnover. This clearly shows the crucial importance of successful project management for the overall success of our business. In this age of globalisation and increasingly tough competition, we have to develop excellent products and solutions with short times to market and, at the same time, deliver the quality standards that our customers demand. This means that project management skills are absolutely vital at every level – from top management to the shop floor. Yet we can only achieve this if project teams are provided with the appropriate training, are familiar with standards and best-practice tools, and if management teams insist on proper project management. We introduced the PM@Siemens initiative many years ago with this very aim in mind.

In this context, I strongly welcome the GPM´s objective of improving project management standards with this publication. It addresses all important aspects of project management in detail. The textbook has the potential to become a recognised platform for improving project management and for preparing project managers-to-be for future challenges.

I hope that this book inspires all who read it. It will show them new approaches to successful project management. Project management is a mammoth task that offers many businesses and organisations the chance to release additional profit potential.

I wish you every success in your projects.

Yours sincerely

Professor Edward G. Krubasik

Member of the Corporate Executive Committee of Siemens AG
President of the Central Association of the German Electrical and Electronic Engineering Industry (ZVEI)
Vice-president of the Federation of German Industries (BDI)

CONTENTS

	THE ICB TAXONOMY	17
	1 Introduction	17
	2 Explanation	17
	3 The ICB elements and their allocation to chapters	19
	4 Guidance for self-evaluation	21
A	**PROJECT AND PROJECT ENVIRONMENT**	23
A 1	**PROJECTS AND PROJECT MANAGEMENT**	25
	1 Definition of a project	25
	2 Definition of project management	28
	3 Process coordination	29
	4 Projects in the private and public sectors	31
A 2	**PROJECT TYPES**	33
	1 External and internal projects	33
	2 Investment, organisational and R&D projects	34
	3 Project classification according to McFarlan and Sizemore House	35
	4 Further classifications	37
A 3	**STAKEHOLDER ANALYSIS**	39
	1 Project and stakeholders	39
	2 Systematic classification of stakeholders	40
	3 Stakeholder analysis	40
	4 Dealing with stakeholders	45
	5 Differences between stakeholder and risk analyses	45
	6 Problems associated with stakeholder analyses	45
A 4	**LEGAL ASPECTS**	47
	1 Significance	47
	2 Project contracts	47
	3 Contract administration	68
	4 Claim management	75
A 5	**PROJECT PERFORMANCE AND SUCCESS FACTORS**	87
	1 Definition	87

		2 Stakeholder objectives	88
		3 Priorities	88
		4 Time of performance measurement	89
		5 The performance measurement procedure	90
		6 Project success factors	90
	A 6	**PROJECT ORGANISATION**	**93**
		1 Projects outside standard management structures	93
		2 Incorporation of projects in the base organisation	95
		3 Project boards	96
		4 Basic forms of project organisation	97
		5 Case study of a balanced matrix for development projects	102
		6 Project control and the project's commercial team	106
B		**PROCESS MODELS**	**109**
		1 Benefits	111
		2 Elements	111
		3 Phase breakdowns for various projects	117
		4 Process models and quality management	118
		5 Process models in the IT sector	118
		6 A critical appraisal of process models	122
		7 Advantages	123
		8 Projects that aren't suitable for a process model approach	123
C		**OPERATIONAL PROJECT MANAGEMENT**	**125**
	C 1	**PROJECT START-UP**	**127**
		1 Significance of the start-up phase	127
		2 Tasks in the start-up phase	130
		3 Project start-up workshop	132
		4 Variations on the start-up process	133
	C 2	**PROJECT OBJECTIVES**	**135**
		1 Variables in objective definition	135
		2 Making project objectives measurable	137
		3 Further rules for formulating objectives	139
		4 Graphic representation of project objectives	140
		5 Relationships between project objectives	140
		6 Relationship between project objectives and organisational objectives	142
		7 Customer and contractor specification	142
	C 3	**PROJECT RISKS**	**145**
		1 Typical project risks	145
		2 Types of risks	146
		3 Benefits of systematic risk management	147
		4 Risk identification	148
		5 Analysis and assessment	150
		6 Selection	152

	7 Monitoring	153
	8 Risk response planning strategies	154
	9 Risk management software	155
	10 Problems relating to the acceptance of risk management	156
C 4	**WORK BREAKDOWN STRUCTURE**	159
	1 Definition	159
	2 Tasks	160
	3 Breakdown	161
	4 Creation	163
	5 Work package descriptions	164
	6 Standard work breakdown structures	165
	7 Rules for WBS creation	168
	8 Coding	169
	9 Common mistakes and omissions	170
C 5	**TIME SCHEDULING**	171
	1 Significance	171
	2 Basic principles	172
	3 Network analysis	175
	4 Methods of structuring and processing network diagrams	196
	5 Display formats for the time schedule	203
C 6	**COST AND RESOURCE PLANNING**	205
	1 Estimating resource requirements and project costs	205
	2 Resource planning	213
	3 Project logistics	218
	4 Cost monitoring during the project	219
C 7	**CONFIGURATION AND CHANGE MANAGEMENT**	227
	1 Change control and change management	227
	2 Significance	227
	3 Interaction of the elements	228
	4 Configuration management	229
	5 Document management	232
	6 Change control	234
C 8	**QUALITY MANAGEMENT**	239
	1 Definitions	239
	2 Benefits of a quality management system	239
	3 Development	241
	4 Standards	243
	5 Strategic and operational management	243
	6 Process orientation	243
	7 ´Zero defects´ performance standard	244
	8 Total Quality Management	244
	9 Control systems	248
	10 Establishment of a quality management system for project management	249

	11	Objective evidence on the basis of quality audits	251
	12	Certification	253
	13	Project quality	254
	14	Quality management methods	258

C 9 PERFORMANCE MEASUREMENT AND PROJECT CONTROL 261

1 Performance measurement 261
2 Project control 269

C 10 PROJECT CLOSE-OUT AND PROJECT LEARNING 283

1 Definition 283
2 Arguments in favour of systematic project close-out 284
3 Tasks at the end of the project 285
4 Project closure meeting 288
5 Final report 289
6 Project learning 289
7 Project analysis and learning methods 291

C 11 IT SUPPORT 299

1 Development history 299
2 Trend towards sophisticated software products 300
3 Software purchased as an alibi 301
4 Software – yes or no? 302
5 Selection 303

D PEOPLE IN PROJECTS 305

D 1 PROJECT MANAGER 307

1 Significance 307
2 Problems and solutions associated with project manager recruitment 308
3 Tasks 310
4 Requirements 311
5 Necessary authority 314
6 Selection 314
7 Assessment 316
8 Change of project manager 317

D 2 TOOLS FOR THE PROJECT MANAGER 319

1 Self-organisation 319
2 Meetings 329
3 Negotiations 334
4 Problem solving 337
5 Presentations 344
6 Creativity techniques 351

D 3 BUILDING AND MANAGING COMPETENT TEAMS 357

1 Teamwork 357
2 Management 371

CONTENTS

	3 Motivation	375
	4 Project coaching	377
	5 Training and certification	378
	6 Personnel management	381
	7 Occupational health and safety	385
D4	**COMMUNICATION**	**389**
	1 Significance	389
	2 Basic principles	390
	3 How communication works	390
	4 Influencing the environment through communication	395
	5 Elements of stakeholder communication	399
	6 Risk communication	404
	7 Project marketing	405
	8 Media relations	407
D5	**CONFLICTS AND CRISES**	**411**
	1 Significance	411
	2 Functions	411
	3 Types of conflicts	412
	4 Causes	413
	5 Indicators	416
	6 Conflict dynamics	418
	7 Conflict escalation	418
	8 Approaches to dealing with conflicts	419
	9 Conflict resolution	423
	10 Crises	426
E	**SINGLE PROJECTS AND PROJECT ENVIRONMENT**	**431**
E1	**PROGRAMME AND MULTI-PROJECT MANAGEMENT**	**433**
	1 Parallel projects	433
	2 Definitions	434
E2	**PROJECT SELECTION AND BUSINESS STRATEGY**	**437**
	1 Significance	437
	2 Operational and strategic project management	438
	3 Management by projects	439
	4 Selection of product development projects	440
	5 Selection of investment projects	444
	6 Bid review process	450
	7 Selection process for all project types	453
	8 Advantages and disadvantages of the methods	455
	9 Improving selection decisions	456
E3	**OPERATIONAL MULTI-PROJECT MANAGEMENT**	**459**
	1 Portfolio board	459
	2 Multi-project manager	459

CONTENTS

F   INTRODUCTION AND OPTIMISATION OF PROJECT MANAGEMENT — 465

F 1   INTRODUCTION OF PROJECT MANAGEMENT — 467
  1 Project management 'by decree' — 467
  2 Introduction of project management structures through software — 468
  3 Obstacles to acceptance — 468
  4 Promoting acceptance — 472
  5 Process model — 473
  6 Communication — 477

F 2   PROJECT MANAGEMENT OPTIMISATION — 479
  1 Maturity models — 479
  2 Critical appraisal of maturity models — 489

F 3   PROJECT MANAGEMENT STANDARDS — 491
  1 Significance — 491
  2 Terminology standards in German-speaking countries — 491
  3 Foreign standards — 492

CASE STUDY — 495
  1 Preliminary remarks — 495
  2 Initial situation — 495
  3 Tasks — 497

AUTHORS — 500

GLOSSARY — 503

KEY WORDS — 517

BIBLIOGRAPHY AND FOOTNOTES — 533

THE ICB TAXONOMY

1 Introduction

Qualification and certification programmes offer project management personnel (both project managers and their teams) an incentive to
- expand and improve their knowledge and experience,
- improve their personal attitudes,
- continue with their professional development,
- maintain and improve the quality of project management and
- run projects more effectively while achieving better results.

The criteria used for certification relate to the fundamentals of project management, project management methods, processes and tools, project organisation, interpersonal skills, general management skills, personal attitude and overall impression. These criteria are assessed on the basis of the taxonomy contained in the International Project Management Association (IPMA)´s Competence Baseline (ICB). It comprises 42 fields (or elements) of project management knowledge and experience.

The assessment of project management competence is expressed in terms of
- the certification requirements (target values levels D to A),
- the candidate's self-assessment (target values levels D to A) and
- the assessors' evaluation of the candidate (assessment values levels D to A).

The certification requirements are stated in the taxonomy in terms of the minimum values expected, on a scale of 1 to 10.

As the national member of the IPMA in the Federal Republic of Germany, German Association for Project Management (GPM) has decided to use the ICB as the national competence baseline for the certification of project management personnel.

2 Explanation

Please evaluate your knowledge, competence and experience in respect of each project management element and enter your grades in the relevant table. The meanings of the values on the scale are shown on the next page.

THE ICB TAXONOMY

Key to the evaluation tables

0	No knowledge and/or competence
1 – 3	Low levels of knowledge and/or competence
4 – 6	Medium levels of knowledge and/or competence
7 – 9	High levels of knowledge and/or competence
10	Special expertise

K Knowledge / competence

Low (1 – 3)
I know the element and the success criteria and I can present and explain it/them.

Medium (4 – 6)
I have a solid knowledge of the element and the criteria for its successful application, and am able to apply the knowledge and check the results.

High (7 – 9)
I have special knowledge of the element, I can create and evaluate the criteria for its successful application and I can interpret and evaluate the results of its application.

Special expertise (10)
I am a recognised expert in this element, I command the relevant knowledge and understand the dependencies involved, and I can also coach and manage employees in this element.

E Experience

Low (1 – 3)
I have gained limited experience of this element based on my involvement in a few projects in one economic sector, and have held management functions in one or more phases of these projects.

Medium (4 – 6)
I have gained experience of this element in the course of several projects in at least one important sector of the economy, and have a good track record as a project manager in most areas and phases of these projects.

High (7 – 9)
I have gained broad experience of this element in the course of many diverse projects, and have managed most phases of these projects.

Special expertise (10)
I am a recognised manager and mentor in the element, I can put it into practice effectively and I can also coach and manage employees in the use of the element.

THE ICB TAXONOMY

3 The ICB elements and their allocation to chapters

ICB Element 1: Projects and Project Management (→ A1)

	0	1	2	3	4	5	6	7	8	9	10
W						D	C	B	A		
E				C			B	A			

ICB Element 2: Project Management Implementation (→ F1)

	0	1	2	3	4	5	6	7	8	9	10
W					D	C	B	A			
E				C			B		A		

ICB Element 3: Management by Projects (→ E2, E3)

	0	1	2	3	4	5	6	7	8	9	10
W				DC		B		A			
E		C		B				A			

ICB Element 4: System Approach and Integration (→ E1)

	0	1	2	3	4	5	6	7	8	9	10
W					DC	B	A				
E			C		B		A				

ICB Element 5: Project Context (→ A3)

	0	1	2	3	4	5	6	7	8	9	10
W					D	C	B	A			
E			C		B		A				

ICB Element 6: Project Phases and Life Cycle (→ B)

	0	1	2	3	4	5	6	7	8	9	10
W					D	CBA					
E			C		BA						

ICB Element 7: Project Development and Appraisal (→ E2)

	0	1	2	3	4	5	6	7	8	9	10
W					D	C	B	A			
E			C		B		A				

ICB Element 8: Project Objectives and Strategies (→ C2, E2)

	0	1	2	3	4	5	6	7	8	9	10
W					DC	BA					
E			C		B	A					

ICB Element 9: Project Success and Failure Criteria (→ A5)

	0	1	2	3	4	5	6	7	8	9	10
W					DC	B	A				
E			C			BA					

ICB Element 10: Project Start Up (→ C1)

	0	1	2	3	4	5	6	7	8	9	10
W					DC	B	A				
E			C		B	A					

ICB Element 11: Project Close Out (→ C10)

	0	1	2	3	4	5	6	7	8	9	10
W					DC	B	A				
E			C		B	A					

ICB Element 12: Project Structures (→ C4)

	0	1	2	3	4	5	6	7	8	9	10
W						DC	B	A			
E				C		B		A			

ICB Element 13: Content, Scope (→ C1)

	0	1	2	3	4	5	6	7	8	9	10
W								DCBA			
E					C		B	A			

ICB Element 14: Time Schedules (→ C5)

	0	1	2	3	4	5	6	7	8	9	10
W						A		DCB			
E					C		BA				

ICB Element 15: Resources (→ C6)

	0	1	2	3	4	5	6	7	8	9	10
W						DCA	B				
E					C		BA				

ICB Element 16: Project Cost and Finance (→ C6)

	0	1	2	3	4	5	6	7	8	9	10
W						A		DCB			
E					C		BA				

ICB Element 17: Configurations and Changes (→ C7)

	0	1	2	3	4	5	6	7	8	9	10
W						DC	A	B			
E				C		B	A				

ICB Element 18: Project Risks (→ C3)

	0	1	2	3	4	5	6	7	8	9	10
W						DC	B	A			
E		C				B		A			

ICB Element 19: Performance Measurement (→ C9)

	0	1	2	3	4	5	6	7	8	9	10
W						DCBA					
E				C	B	A					

ICB Element 20: Project Controlling (→ C9)

	0	1	2	3	4	5	6	7	8	9	10
W							CA	DB			
E				C		B		A			

ICB Element 21: Information, Documentation, Reporting (→ A3, C9)

	0	1	2	3	4	5	6	7	8	9	10
W					D		C	BA			
E				C			B	A			

THE ICB TAXONOMY

ICB Element 22: Project Organisation (→ A6)

	0	1	2	3	4	5	6	7	8	9	10
W						D	C	B	A		
E				C			B	A			

ICB Element 23: Teamwork (→ D3)

	0	1	2	3	4	5	6	7	8	9	10
W						A	DB	C			
E						CBA					

ICB Element 24: Leadership (→ D3)

	0	1	2	3	4	5	6	7	8	9	10
W					D		C	BA			
E					C		B	A			

ICB Element 25: Communication (→ D4)

	0	1	2	3	4	5	6	7	8	9	10
W						D	CB	A			
E					C	B	A				

ICB Element 26: Conflicts and Crises (→ D5)

	0	1	2	3	4	5	6	7	8	9	10
W						DC	BA				
E			C		B		A				

ICB Element 27: Procurements, Contracts (→ A4)

	0	1	2	3	4	5	6	7	8	9	10
W					D	CBA					
E				C	B	A					

ICB Element 28: Project Quality (→ C8)

	0	1	2	3	4	5	6	7	8	9	10
W						DC	B	A			
E				C	B		A				

ICB Element 29: Informatics in Projects (→ C11)

	0	1	2	3	4	5	6	7	8	9	10
W						DCB	A				
E				C	B	A					

ICB Element 30: Standards and Regulations (→ F3)

	0	1	2	3	4	5	6	7	8	9	10
W						DCA	B				
E			C	B	A						

ICB Element 31: Problem Solving (→ D2)

	0	1	2	3	4	5	6	7	8	9	10
W				│ A	DCB					
E				C	B	A					

ICB Element 32: Negotiations, Meetings (→ A4, D4)

	0	1	2	3	4	5	6	7	8	9	10
W						DC	B	A			
E			C			B		A			

ICB Element 33: Permanent Organisation (→ A6)

	0	1	2	3	4	5	6	7	8	9	10
W						DC	B	A			
E				C	B	A					

ICB Element 34: Business Processes (→ B)

	0	1	2	3	4	5	6	7	8	9	10
W						D	C	BA			
E					D		BA				

ICB Element 35: Personnel Development (→ D3)

	0	1	2	3	4	5	6	7	8	9	10
W				DC		B		A			
E					B		A				

ICB Element 36: Organisational Learning (→ C10)

	0	1	2	3	4	5	6	7	8	9	10
W					D	C	B	A			
E				C		B		A			

ICB Element 37: Management of Change (→ F1)

	0	1	2	3	4	5	6	7	8	9	10
W				DC			B	A			
E			C		B		A				

ICB Element 38: Marketing, Product Management (→ D4)

	0	1	2	3	4	5	6	7	8	9	10
W					DC	B		A			
E				C	B		A				

ICB Element 39: System Management (→ E1)

	0	1	2	3	4	5	6	7	8	9	10
W							DCB	A			
E				C	B		A				

ICB Element 40: Safety, Health and Environment (→ D3)

	0	1	2	3	4	5	6	7	8	9	10
W						DC		BA			
E				C			B	A			

ICB Element 41: Legal Aspects (→ A4)

	0	1	2	3	4	5	6	7	8	9	10
W					DC		BA				
E			C			B	A				

ICB Element 42: Finance and Accounting (→ C6)

	0	1	2	3	4	5	6	7	8	9	10
W					D	C	B	A			
E				C	B		A				

Self-evaluation in terms of overall project management competence

	0	1	2	3	4	5	6	7	8	9	10
W					D	C	B	A			
E				C		B	A				

4 Guidance for self-evaluation

by certification level

The following classifications show the significance of each chapter for your certification level (D, C, B, A) and therefore the depth of learning required.

1 Awareness

You have heard of the topics involved and you know where you can find further information on them in this textbook and in other literature.
This subject matter is not relevant for the assessment at your certification level.

2 Knowledge

You understand the subject and can interpret and explain dependencies, but you do not yet need to apply this knowledge in practice.
This subject matter is not relevant for assessment at your certification level.

3 Competence

You can apply what you have learned in practical problem-solving.
This subject matter is not relevant for assessment at your certification level.

4 Management

You may not need to carry out the tasks in this subject area yourself any more, but you do delegate such tasks, provide guidance to the staff who are implementing them and check the appropriateness of the solution adopted.
This subject matter is not relevant for assessment at your certification level.

The following overview shows the relevance of the project management subjects covered in each chapter. The relevance of the questions about the content of each chapter can vary within the range shown. Each chapter is categorised according to highest level of its questions.

		Level D	Level C	Level B	Level A
A	PROJECT AND PROJECT ENVIRONMENT				
A1	PROJECTS AND PROJECT MANAGEMENT	2	3	3	4
A2	PROJECT TYPES	2	2	3	4
A3	STAKEHOLDER ANALYSIS	2	3	3	4
A4	LEGAL ASPECTS	2	2	3	4
A5	PROJECT PERFORMANCE AND SUCESS FACTORS	2	2	3	4
A6	PROJECT ORGANISATION	2	3	3	4

		Level D	Level C	Level B	Level A
B	PROCESS MODELS	2	2	3	4

THE ICB TAXONOMY

		Level D	Level C	Level B	Level A
C	**OPERATIONAL PROJECT MANAGEMENT**				
C1	PROJECT START-UP	2	3	3	4
C2	PROJECT OBJECTIVES	3	3	3	4
C3	PROJECT RISKS	2	3	3	4
C4	WORK BREAKDOWN STRUCTURE	3	3	3	4
C5	TIME SCHEDULING	3	3	3	4
C6	COST AND RESOURCE PLANNING	2	3	3	4
C7	CONFIGURATION AND CHANGE MANAGEMENT	2	2	3	4
C8	QUALITY MANAGEMENT	2	2	3	4
C9	PERFORMANCE MEASUREMENT AND PROJECT CONTROL	2	3	3	4
C10	PROJECT CLOSE-OUT AND PROJECT LEARNING	2	3	3	4
C11	IT SUPPORT	2	3	4	4

		Level D	Level C	Level B	Level A
D	**PEOPLE IN PROJECTS**				
D1	PROJECT MANAGER	2	3	3	4
D2	TOOLS FOR THE PROJECT MANAGER	2	3	4	4
D3	BUILDING AND MANAGING COMPETENT TEAMS	2	3	3	4
D4	COMMUNICATION	2	3	4	4
D5	CONFLICTS AND CRISES	2	3	4	4

		Level D	Level C	Level B	Level A
E	**SINGLE PROJECTS AND PROJECT ENVIRONMENT**				
E1	PROGRAMME AND MULTI-PROJECT MANAGEMENT	1	2	2	3
E2	PROJECT SELECTION AND BUSINESS STRATEGY	1	2	2	3
E3	OPERATIONAL MULTI-PROJECT MANAGEMENT	1	2	3	4

		Level D	Level C	Level B	Level A
F	**INTRODUCTION AND OPTIMISATION OF PROJECT MANAGEMENT**				
F1	INTRODUCTION OF PROJECT MANAGEMENT	1	2	2	3
F2	PROJECT MANAGEMENT OPTIMISATION	1	2	3	4
F3	PROJECT MANAGEMENT STANDARDS	1	2	3	4

BLOCK A

PROJECT AND PROJECT ENVIRONMENT

A1 PROJECTS AND PROJECT MANAGEMENT

What is a project? What is project management? The answers to these two questions form the primer on which the project-based delivery of goods and services is based (IPMA Competence Baseline ICB, Element 1). Knowledge of project management is a basic prerequisite for anyone who wants to work with project management concepts in theory and practice. One must be able to distinguish between projects and routine tasks and to judge when is it reasonable to use project management. This can help avoid the increasing tendency to overuse the term project. A project manager must also understand the basic types and mechanisms of project coordination.

1 Definition of a project

Anyone involved in project management should know several fundamental definitions. Many authors have attempted to define the term project – with varying results. In any event, projects are novel and one-off undertakings – in other words, endeavours that are being undertaken for the first time and will not be subsequently repeated. According to the IPMA Competence Baseline (ICB), projects can be categorised as being:
- complex,
- unique,
- novel and
- interdisciplinary, in terms of the tasks involved [1].

This definition has two disadvantages. First, there is no benchmark against which some of these characteristics can be measured. It is, for example, very difficult to establish how complex or unique a project is. Secondly, not all characteristics apply to all project types.

Disadvantages of the ICB definition

Example
The employees of a construction company build several two-bedroom houses every year. This is therefore not a new or unique activity for them anymore. However, the company's management team treats each undertaking as a separate project and applies project-specific management structures, risk management, operation scheduling, project control and other project management methods. The interlinked activities, the need to cooperate with sub-contractors, as well as time and cost pressures make project management necessary in every single construction project.

1.1 Definition according to DIN 69 901

The definition provided in the DIN 69 901 standard [2] doesn't have the above disadvantages because it considers project management in a broader light.

According to this definition, a project is 'an undertaking that is essentially characterised by a unique set of conditions, such as
- objectives,
- constraints of time, finance, human resources and so on,
- differentiation from other undertakings,
- project-specific organisation.'

This standard enables us to establish on a case-by-case basis whether a particular process of producing goods and services is actually a project.

> **Example**
> *There are no time constraints on the production of newsprint. As a result, no budget is specified. Also, the characteristic project-specific organisation does not apply because the outputs are achieved using a standard organisation. Accordingly, the production of newsprint cannot be considered a project. Instead, it comes under the category of mass production. Project management is not applicable in this case.*

In the same way, it is possible to evaluate other goal-oriented processes, such as the mass production of automobiles or the development of an electrical appliance, to establish whether they are projects.

1.1.1 The work-sharing criterion

Projects with several participants

The DIN definition, although useful, has one minor shortcoming – its authors forgot one characteristic of projects, as did the Project Management Institute of America (PMI). Rüsberg [3] quite rightly emphasises this characteristic: projects involve several individuals, teams, companies or organisations. Projects are team-based processes [4]. A composer working on a piece of music or a violin-maker building a violin, does not constitute a project. Neither requires the coordinating function of the management, only that of self-management.

1.1.2 Projects without a project-specific organisation

Line management and project management functions carried out by the same individual

One important aspect of the DIN definition is the fact that it is qualified by the words such as because not every project necessarily requires a project-specific organisation. For instance, the research and development departments in industrial concerns continually plan and carry out activities that are defined by objectives, are clearly differentiated from other activities and are subject to time-related, financial and personnel constraints. However, a project-specific organisation is missing. The head of the department is responsible for managing the activity using standard management techniques, while, at the same time, carrying out the function of project manager. This solution is recommended when the majority of people involved work in one single organisational unit.

1.1.3 Unique set of conditions

Identical processes, despite a high level of innovation

The characteristic `unique set of conditions´ occasionally causes misunderstandings. It not only refers to the individual project activities but also to the project as a whole. This is clarified by DIN 69 901. This states that even if a project is highly novel, it will include processes that take place not just within the current project but which occur or have already occurred in precisely the same way in earlier projects. One example of this is the creation of parts lists for circuits that are developed in a project. A project can also involve a repetitive process of producing goods and services. This is the case, for example, when large quantities of prototypes are produced during aircraft development.

1.1.4 Borderline cases

There are borderline cases when it is debatable whether an undertaking constitutes a project or a batch production process. For example, if numerous factory buildings are built to an identical blueprint at different locations, is this a project? Dülfer [5] suggests a solution to this differentiation problem on the basis of the DIN 69 901 definition. He proposes that, `the characteristic of uniqueness in industrial build-to-order manufacturing […] should not, in every case, relate to the content of the project […], but, to a greater extent, to the implementation of the project under the specific environmental conditions.´

The border between the project-based production of goods and services and batch production processes is often blurred. The greater the similarity in the configuration of individual objects and the more uniform the general framework, the more likely it is that batch production is involved. There are many examples of such borderline cases in the shipbuilding and housing construction sectors.

At the other end of the scale, when goods such as pharmaceuticals or consumer electronics appliances are produced, we always talk about mass or assembly-line production. The production of a TV set, for example, is in no way project-based.

1.2 Differentiation problems and project inflation

Many organisations attach the label of project to every special-purpose undertaking, however small it may be. Yet they don´t employ systematic project management practices. Instead, the people involved simply muddle through as best they can. In fact, this approach is actually called `management by muddling through´ in project management circles.

Another disadvantage of the very general DIN definition becomes evident at this point: it is merely a rudimentary sieve. Some tasks that don´t pass through the sieve are definitely not project-oriented. However, this definition doesn´t answer the following question: How should an organisation differentiate between undertakings that are to be treated as a project and those that aren´t?

DIN definition just a rudimentary sieve

> **Example**
> *A small-scale machine tooling factory describes the development of a new special-purpose machine for a customer as a project, because it is a highly innovative undertaking for the company and the contract value accounts for a large proportion of its total turnover. In contrast, an automotive concern understands the term highly innovative completely differently. The value of the contract that was awarded to the machine tooling factory would only account for a very small portion of the automotive concern´s total sales. This task would therefore never be classified as a project.*

In other words, every organisation must make its own decision as regards which non-routine undertakings are classified as projects. Decision criteria might include contract value, the planned budget or the projected duration of the activity.

It can be risky to pull out all the project management stops for very short-term projects that have to be implemented on a low budget. It is quite possible in such cases that project planning alone will devour so much time and financial resources that there is nothing left for the production of the

Reasonable cost-benefit ratio

project deliverable. Project management costs should therefore be in proportion to the ensuing practical benefits and the size of the project. Comprehensive project planning will only have visible positive effects in longer-term projects with an adequate budget.

1.3 Organisation-specific project definitions

Many organisations simply use their own definitions to decide which activities are to be treated as projects. A firm of management consultants, for example, formulated the following organisation-specific definition of a project: `All non-routine activities that are scheduled to last for more than three calendar months, are associated with a budget of at least 50 person days and involve more than two people are to be planned and carried out in accordance with the basic principles of the company´s Project Management Manual.´

In contrast, a pharmaceuticals company with a strong focus on R&D opted for a very formal definition of project: `Projects are activities in a specific field that are limited in time and for which a development request has been approved.´

2 Definition of project management

The DIN standard is also a good starting point for the definition of project management.

According to DIN 69 901, project management involves the application of `all management functions, structures, techniques and resources for the purposes of implementing a project.´

Different understandings of the term management

However, the standard´s authors have generated controversy and misunderstanding with their definition because the term management applies in very different contexts, e.g. it means something quite different to a psychologist or a social psychologist than to a manager. The ensuing confusion can be eliminated, however, if we turn to Frese´s [6] definition of management as `the process of directing the various separate activities in an organisation with a view to achievement of the overall objective´. It takes place at all hierarchical levels of this organisation.

In parallel, Frese defines management in a project as `the process of directing the various separate activities in a project with a view to achievement of the project objectives´.

2.1 Management in the functional and institutional sense

The above definition isn´t entirely satisfactory since management, and thus project management, can be interpreted in two different ways. Staehle [7], who has thoroughly researched the term management and its usage, distinguishes between
- management from a functional perspective, and
- management from a positional perspective

Different meanings of the term management

He defines management from a functional perspective as the `specific processes and tasks that take place within and between organisations´. In contrast, management from a positional perspective refers to `individuals or groups of individuals who perform management functions´.

Both perspectives can be found in project management literature and in the language used by project managers.

2.1.1 Characteristics of management in the functional sense

In his definition of management in the functional sense, Staehle [8] selected several characteristics that are at least implicitly contained in practically all definitions in the management literature:

Management characteristics

- An individual cannot accomplish complex activities alone. This is why individuals form teams and share work. The result is a socio-technical system that pursues specific objectives. The term socio-technical refers to a combination of a social and a technical system (e.g. man and machine).
- In order to attain the objectives, it is necessary to procure, combine, coordinate and use resources. These are the activities that constitute management. It is not only necessary to plan the structure of the socio-technical system, but also to organise work, communication and decision-making processes, both within and outside the system.
- An organisation based on socio-technical principles offers a framework for management (as a position) to perform its functions (management in the functional sense).

These characteristics also apply to the project-based production of goods and services and to all types of projects, even though the coordination of team-based processes is not taken into account in either the DIN 69 901 definition or that of the PMI in 2000.

3 Process coordination

Business theory distinguishes between two types of process coordination [9]:
1. Advance coordination as a provision for future events
2. Feedback coordination, also known as project control, in response to problems (→ Chapter C9)

3.1 Coordination mechanisms

A practical classification of coordination mechanisms is [10]:
- hierarchy (instructions to individuals)
- self-coordination
- programmes and rules
- plans or planning.

3.1.1 Hierarchical coordination

In coordination by means of hierarchical structures or on the basis of instructions given to individuals, communication is a vertical process. Examples of this are instructions given by the project manager or a specific line manager to project team members. This coordination tool only permits advance coordination over relatively short timescales and can involve only a few planning variables (e.g. project objectives).

Advance coordination for a limited number of planning variables

On the other hand, it is very flexible. Empirical research shows that general managers spend a great deal of time using oral forms of communication – though, of course, not only for coordination but also to obtain information. According to these surveys, this activity takes up 60 to 80 percent of their time. These figures indicate the high significance of coordination by instruction. The same is also likely to be true for project managers [11].

3.1.2 Self-coordination

In the process of self-coordination, a group of individuals is responsible for the decisions on project coordination. They need to be vested with official decision-making authority and the decisions that they make need to be universally binding. Examples of this are project team meetings. Self-coordination can be used by a project team, a steering committee or senior management, using either their own or more general assessment criteria. It can extend to the institutionalised interaction between boards or coordination bodies (e.g. steering committee, senior management).

Mechanisms for highly innovative projects

This coordination mechanism plays a significant role, especially in research and development projects that attach a high value to innovation. It is based on the assumption that under certain circumstances at least, such as the implementation of a pharmaceutical experiment by a small, interdisciplinary team of researchers, self-coordination must take precedence over hierarchical coordination. In project management practice, self-coordination and hierarchical coordination exist side by side.

3.1.3 Coordination by programmes and rules

Project management manual

The term programmes refers to written instructions and rules specifying appropriate forms of conduct. Project management manuals are a good example of such programmes. They can, for example, specify in which projects critical path methods are to be used and can describe how to create a work breakdown structure. These programmes take some pressure off line managers and reduce communication requirements. Their disadvantage is that they are inflexible and can only be used for advance coordination. Programmes also include in-house or external conventions, rules and standards. There are many such programmes in traditional sectors such as construction. Every architect or construction planner knows which method of representation he will use before putting pen to paper on the blueprint.

Software developers, on the other hand, reconsider the issue of which design language to use each time they begin a new project. This relatively new industry still lacks widely-accepted rules and standards. As a result, coordination instruments are used to a greater extent, especially coordination by instruction to individuals and self-coordination.

3.1.4 Coordination by plans or planning

Project management literature puts particular emphasis on coordination by means of plans. One reason why plans are considered so important lies in the significant role traditionally played by the critical path method of planning in project management. This allows future activities to be planned and monitored systematically.

Software manufacturers like to give the impression that project managers depend almost exclusively on computerised planning and information systems. However, empirical surveys show that reports generated in this way play only a subsidiary role in a senior manager´s personal information system. The person at the top is far more likely to use a variety of information sources to obtain an overall picture of whatever problem he or she is dealing with. Most of this information is obtained through personal communication.

Information obtained through personal communication

On the basis of empirical studies, Tushman [12] concludes that verbal communication is a more efficient means of solving complex problems in research and development projects than written and formal media such as management information systems.

Coordination by planning demands considerable time and effort because plans have to be regularly revised and updated. However, it offers significant advantages:
- Plans can incorporate more parameters than in coordination by personal instruction or self-coordination.
- Interdependencies between various processes can be taken into account more effectively. The critical path method of planning is a good example of this.
- Unlike programmes and rules, plans are valid for a shorter period of time and are a more flexible instrument of coordination.

3.1.5 Advance and feedback coordination

Advance coordination is carried out by project managers in the form of plans and programmes. Since problems occur in the majority of projects, feedback coordination is a further essential aspect of project control.

Feedback for project control

4 Projects in the private and public sectors

The project-based production of goods and services tends to predominate in certain sectors, such as the construction and software. However, projects can exist in every sector, including retail, insurance, banking and transport. In the retail and banking sectors, for example, internal projects are often undertaken to implement technical and organisational changes.

The vision of a project-oriented organisation is increasingly widespread in all sectors. As a result, the number of projects carried out by organisations that do not generate revenue or generate only a small proportion of their revenue by means of projects is also likely to increase. In-house projects can be limited to one or a few business units.

> **Example**
> *A manufacturer of TV sets has its own large-scale research and development department. It can incorporate representatives from other business units such as production scheduling or sales and marketing in its R&D projects. Generally, however, project-based production of goods and services is restricted to the research and development business unit.*

A1 PROJECTS AND PROJECT MANAGEMENT

Figure A1-1 shows the different significance that can be attached to project management within an organisation. It also shows the relationship between the frequency of project-based production of goods and services and the involvement of the organisation's business units.

FREQUENCY OF PROJECT-BASED PRODUCTION OF GOODS AND SERVICES	exclusive or predominant	occasional
INVOLVEMENT OF THE COMPANY'S BUSINESS UNITS IN THE PROJECT		
All or the majority of business units	Example Building trade, heavy machine construction, software companies	Example Move from being a function-oriented organisation to a division-based organisation
One or only a few business units	Example Research and development projects at a company with mass-production and assembly-line operations	Example Rationalisation project in a business unit, e.g. installation of a computerised high-bay warehouse

Figure A1-1 Connection between the project-based production of goods and services and the involvement of business units

Framework constraints

Non-profit organisations such as institutions in the healthcare and public sectors have now also discovered project management. However, they seldom apply it due to the constraints imposed by their operating environments, such as the prevalence of legalistic attitudes and the lack of a business-oriented approach. This especially applies in the public sector.

Self-assessment questions for each certification level

No.	Question	D	C	B	A	Self-assessment
A1.1	What steps are involved in a stakeholder analysis?	2	3	3	4	☐
A1.2	What is a project? What characteristics does it have?	2	2	3	4	☐
A1.3	How is a project differentiated from routine tasks in an organisation?	1	1	2	3	☐
A1.4	How can project management be understood?	2	2	2	2	☐
A1.5	In what senses can the term management be used?	1	2	3	3	☐
A1.6	What types and mechanisms of process coordination exist?	1	2	3	3	☐
A1.7	What does organisation-specific project management involve?	2	2	2	3	☐

A2 PROJECT TYPES

Projects can be categorised in various ways. The classifications themselves (ICB Element 1) often provide useful recommendations for day-to-day project work. A clear differentiation between different aspects of projects makes it much easier to gain an overview of a company´s project environment. It also helps decision-makers to apply project management methods in a goal-oriented way and in accordance with the project type. This chapter focuses on the differences between internal and external projects, as well as investment, organisational and research & development projects.

1 External and internal projects

Many attempts have been made to categorise projects. Generally, each classification focuses on one or two aspects of projects. Several significant classifications [1] are presented in this chapter. The differentiation between external and internal projects is determined by the project sponsor.

1.1 External projects

External project sponsors are persons or institutions outside the organisation implementing the project. Projects of this type are also called sponsored projects. The majority are implemented in industry sectors where the project-based production of goods and services prevails. For example, they can be found in the building construction and civil engineering sectors, in the plant and heavy machine construction industries, and also in the software and consulting sectors.

When a company is considering bidding for a project, it is essential that it assesses whether it is worth its while (the `bid review´ process). On the other hand, the project sponsor (or customer) faces the task of finding a suitable contractor.

Bid review process

There are various methods of assessing which bidder is most suitable for the envisaged project. The traditional method is to request references that provide information about the bidder´s competence in both the relevant field and in project management generally. Alternative methods, which have mainly been developed in the USA since the late-1980s, involve project benchmarking and maturity models. These models assist the customer in assessing whether the contractor has systematic project management expertise.

Identification of the most suitable bidder

The very first such model to be developed, the Capability Maturity Model (CMM), is a good example. It describes a framework of five stages of process maturity in project management (→Chapter F2). The US Ministry of Defense, the world´s largest sponsor of software projects, initiated its development; it only awards projects to providers with at least CMM Level 3. Most companies don´t achieve this advanced level of maturity.

If the customer accepts the bid – with or without changes – both parties conclude a contract with each other. This contract then constitutes the basis for implementation of the project.

1.2 Internal projects

No formal contract

With internal projects, the project sponsor is a person or an entity within the organisation implementing the project. Examples of sponsors include senior management, a project steering committee or a departmental manager. However, the initiative for internal projects and funding can also come from people outside the company. Formal contracts are not generally concluded between the customer and contractor if the only people involved in the project are part of the project sponsor´s organisation.

Internal projects are typically implemented in the research and development (R&D) departments of industrial companies or in conjunction with reorganisation measures (e.g. the restructuring of the HR department). R&D usually has a large number of project proposals. However, since capacity and budget constraints make it impossible to implement all such projects at the same time, Portfolio managers often need to prioritise projects (→ Chapter E2).

2 Investment, organisational and R&D projects

Differentiation is made between investment, organisational and R&D projects [2] in terms of the project deliverables.

2.1 Investment projects

In investment projects, fixed assets are built or procured (e.g. buildings or heavy machinery).

2.2 Organisational projects

Impact on project team members and the project environment

In organisational projects [3] structures for managing development and processes are created or changed. These projects are intended to safeguard or improve the efficiency of an organisational unit. Examples of organisational projects include corporate mergers, the introduction of new staff development concepts and the restructuring of the sales team. One frequent characteristic of organisational projects is that the project result has an impact not only on the project team members but also on the other people in the organisation. Often, these people feel threatened and even aggrieved by the project outcome (e.g. changes in their work processes) even though, from an objective point of view, they suffer no negative effects. This is why the individuals who are affected and those who think they will be affected are often opposed to organisational projects.

2.3 R&D projects

R&D projects are all about gaining new knowledge and skills or developing product designs that show improvements in terms of
- condition,
- function,
- design quality,
- efficiency [4] etc.

One important characteristic of R&D projects is that the relationship between inputs and outputs cannot be determined in advance. Nobody can predict with accuracy what will result from particular efforts, except in routine development projects. Software development projects can also be classified as R&D projects.

Relationship between inputs and outputs

2.4 Differences

R&D projects and organisational projects differ from investment projects in one important respect from a project management point of view. In investment projects, project progress is relatively easy to measure in terms of figures, measurements or weights (e.g. the calculation of how much formwork has been installed or the measurement of excavated material). In the other two types of projects, the question of measurement generally causes problems (→ Chapter C9).

Although they come under the category of R&D projects, software development projects have two special characteristics. When physical products are being developed, it is relatively easy to describe the product features in a way that enables them to be measured and verified. However, this is not true for many of the product objectives associated with software (e.g. user-friendliness). Software also has a high level of plasticity compared with physical products. In other words, substantial changes can be and often are made during the development process. This characteristic necessitates extremely high standards of configuration and change management (→ Chapter C7) and quality management (→ Chapter C8).

3 Project classification according to McFarlan and Sizemore House

Some project classifications are direct sources of project management recommendations. This applies to the systems used by McFarlan [5] and Sizemore House [6]. These two authors focus on two dimensions:
1. the contractor's experience in the relevant field of technology,
2. the degree to which the project objectives at the start of the project are binding.

Sizemore House differentiates between
- planning and control methods (formal planning, formal control), i.e. plan-based project coordination,
- methods of internal integration and
- methods of external integration.

Internal integration
External integration

Internal integration refers predominantly to the selection of the project manager and project team members, and also the structure of relationships within the project team. Project conflicts are a specific focus of attention (→ Chapter D5). Sizemore House defines external integration as the systematic structuring of relationships with internal or external customers and also, importantly, with other stakeholders, i.e. individuals, groups and institutions with an interest in the project or the project outcome (→ Chapter A3).

Figure A2-1 shows the activities given special emphasis in each project category. The matrix shows that close liaison with the project sponsor is especially important during the period before the project

Relative importance of activities

objectives are precisely defined (II and IV). When teams are inexperienced, team building (= internal integration) plays an especially important role. In these cases, the project manager must have good social skills and excellent competence in the relevant field.

TECHNOLOGICAL EXPERIENCE	PROJECT OUTCOME	
	Precise specification of objectives to be achieved	Vague specification of objectives to be achieved
The company has broad experience	Focus Area I Methods of formal planning and control*, internal integration	Focus Area II External integration*, methods of formal planning and control*, internal integration
The company has little experience	Focus Area III Internal integration*, methods of formal planning and control	Focus Area IV External integration*, internal integration*
* Activity with high significance; unmarked activities have average significance		

Figure A2-1 Relationship between project outcome and the degree to which project objectives are binding [5]

Technical management tools are particularly significant if a company already has a lot of experience in the relevant project types (I and II). These projects are already routine projects for staff, a high level of adherence to scheduled dates and costs is expected, and failure is out of the question – for example, a construction project that has a similar format to a previous construction project. The planning and control requirements that are used to exert pressure on the team are relatively inflexible. Regular variance analyses in these projects are very informative.

Negative examples

In project type II, the main focus is on change management. Unless strict configuration management methods are used, the outcome of these projects will often be catastrophic. Examples of such projects include the Vienna General Hospital [7] and Aachen Clinic projects. Although they were implemented several decades ago, they have been thoroughly analysed and are still useful today to demonstrate how not to manage a project. Further negative examples are the 1994 Winter Olympics in Lillehammer and the 2000 Sydney Summer Olympics (in terms of their spiralling costs), and the Eurotunnel between France and the UK (doubling of construction costs).

3.1 McFarlan´s contingency model

Intensity with which activities are carried out

McFarlan and Sizemore House´s approach is essentially a contingency model. In other words, the activities and the intensity with which they are carried out depend on the type of project. If necessary, the model can be extended to include several additional dimensions. Although extensive empirical verification is still necessary, this model is a progressive alternative to the many undifferentiated suggestions made in the literature regarding the use of analytical tools.

The recommendations provided here are by no means intended to play down the significance of plan-based coordination. According to Sizemore House, `it's all a question of balance.´

A2 PROJECT TYPES

4 Further classifications

Other classification scenarios can be used. One differentiates between projects with team members coming from different cultural environments and projects where team members have a common cultural background. The project management manuals of various organisations also classify projects according to size. This is generally measured in terms of the projected number of staff required or the duration.

Self-assessment questions for each certification level

No.	Question	Level D	Level C	Level B	Level A	Self-assessment
A2.1	How can a project be classified?	2	2	3	3	☐
A2.2	What are the main differences between R&D and organisational projects on the one hand and investment projects on the other?	2	2	3	3	☐
A2.3	What is the purpose of classifying projects within an organisation?	1	2	2	3	☐
A2.4	What is CMM?	1	1	2	3	☐
A2.5	What are the characteristics of an investment project?	2	2	3	3	☐
A2.6	What are the characteristics of an organisational project?	2	2	3	3	☐
A2.7	What are the characteristics of an R&D project?	2	2	3	3	☐

A2 PROJECT TYPES

A3 STAKEHOLDER ANALYSIS

The influence of a project on its environment and vice versa (ICB Element 5) and the project manager´s ability to deal with these interactions are strong determinants of a project´s success. Every project manager should therefore be familiar with the terms stakeholder and stakeholder analysis. He must be capable of identifying stakeholders, of determining the extent to which they are affected by the project and of establishing their attitudes towards it. Using this information, he can implement measures that involve the stakeholders in the project and encourage them to support it. A useful way of doing this is detailed in this chapter.

1 Project and stakeholders

Every project is firmly located in an environment with its own dramatis personae. Project and environment affect each other. Patzak and Rattay [1] therefore describe projects as action systems.

> According to the ICB, the project context is the environment in which the project is formulated, as-sessed and implemented, and which directly or indirectly affects the project or is affected by the project or both. External environmental influences can include physical, ecological, social, psychological, cultural, political, economic, financial, legal, contractual, organisational, technological and aesthetic factors.

Stakeholder is another term which, like project context, became established many years ago. According to the DIN ISO 10 006 standard, a stakeholder is an interested party.

Definition of stakeholder

> The ICB describes stakeholders as individuals or groups of individuals who `are participating in the project, are interested in the project performance or are constrained by the project. They have a vested interest in the success of an organisation and the environment in which the organisation operates.´

Yet it often happens that there are project stakeholders who wish to see a project fail.

> Example: Stakeholders in a traffic management project
> 1. The local authority as the project owner
> 2. The municipal transport services as future operators
> 3. Participating firms (contractors)
> 4. The project manager and his team
> 5. Institutions contributing to the project funding (especially banks and the regional government of the county, state or region where the town or city is located)
> 6. Technical inspection authorities
> 7. Authorities responsible for protected buildings and conservation of natural habitats
> 8. Affected residents
> 9. Potential users, as well as the companies and organisations that employ them
> 10. Environmental campaigners and other pressure groups

The majority of these stakeholders are likely to want to see the traffic system implemented one day. Environmental campaigners and other pressure groups, on the other hand, may want to block the project.

2 Systematic classification of stakeholders

Various approaches can be used to clarify potential stakeholders in a meaningful way. A clear way of classifying stakeholders is shown below [2]:

An example of a stakeholder classification table

STAKEHOLDER TYPE	CAN APPEAR AS (ROLES)
Customer	Project sponsor (external or internal) Potential beneficiary of the completed project Operator Investor
Staff member	Project manager Project team member Employee not directly involved in the project Senior manager Departmental manager Member of steering committees or of the works council Project controller Commercial project manager
Owner of the company where the project is implemented	Owner Shareholder Consortium member
All types of suppliers and service providers	Consultant Recruitment company Insurance provider
Society	Local resident Local authority Pressure group Media Environmental protection agency Technical inspection institute

Figure A3-1 Classification of stakeholders

3 Stakeholder analysis

In a project start-up phase, a project manager must analyse the project environment and its stakeholders. In some projects, such as those subject to public authority planning approval, the majority of project stakeholders is known well in advance.

3.1 Arguments in favour of stakeholder analyses

Stakeholder analyses are necessary because
- different stakeholders often have very different expectations of one and the same project. For instance, the senior management of a telecommunications provider will be hoping that a restructuring project will improve the company's return on equity. In contrast, the works council and the employees it represents will be hoping to keep their jobs. The objectives of different stakeholders are not always compatible (Conflict of interests → Chapter C2).
- Stakeholders can either jeopardise or contribute to the success of a project. Many infrastructure projects fail as a result of opposition from pressure groups, whose influence and staying power is initially underestimated by the project initiators. However, if a project manager, who has the job of introducing project management to his company, can secure the support of power brokers, the chances of project success are good. In this case, the managing director of

the company would be a good power broker. He can help the project manager by using his influence to promote the project, whatever the opposition.

A systematic stakeholder analysis allows project mangers to identify the opportunities and risks associated with a project in good time. The project manager is then able to draw up appropriate stakeholder policy measures on the basis of this analysis (→ Checklist Figure A3-3). Possible measures include providing specific stakeholders with regular information about the progress of the project in a project newsletter (→ Chapter D4).

Early detection of opportunities and risks

3.2 Analysis of customer expectations

A company can only be successful if it has satisfied customers. This is why the identification and analysis of customer expectations are especially important aspects of stakeholder analysis. However, it is not always easy to evaluate customer requirements correctly. The first question that any company must ask is, `Who is our customer?´

Identification of the customer

Example
A heavy machinery construction firm is commissioned to manufacture a machine for the production of solid fibre board. The customer plays a wide variety of roles, each of which is associated with different expectations. The production director´s overriding aim is to increase output and reduce costs per tonne. The sales director wants to know how flexibly he can respond to changing order sizes and quality requirements with the new machine. The finance director, meanwhile, wants a low-price machine and favourable terms for financing and payment. The machine operators want equipment that is easy to operate and unlikely to fail; noise and heat emissions will also need to be kept within acceptable limits. Lastly, the safety engineer will be eager to ensure that the operators are not in any danger.

Bearing all these different interests in mind, who is the customer in this project? Which expectations must the contractor fulfil and which can he disregard? The answer is simple: it depends on what weighting the customer accords to his objectives.

Weighting of objectives

Example
A project that was implemented at the Landesbausparkasse building society in Baden-Württemberg, Germany, [3] shows just how varied stakeholder requirements can be. This project was initiated to develop a software application for the building society´s sales representatives, the people at the top of the stakeholder list. The building society also identified various other stakeholders and their requirements. However, it could not satisfy all requirements at the same time. This is why a project manager or a project steering committee, as the case may be, needs to weigh up and prioritise stakeholder objectives. The procedure described in this example can be implemented in all project types (→ Chapter A2).

Table A3-2 provides an overview of key stakeholders in this software project and their expectations, as well as the project deliverable (the developed software). The following list does not include all of the 16 identified stakeholders and their expectations, though it suffices to demonstrate the principles involved in stakeholder analysis.

A3 STAKEHOLDER ANALYSIS

Examples of key stakeholders

STAKEHOLDER	EXPECTATIONS
1. Independent representatives (sales force)	Fast advice and application data entry High quality of advice More efficient evaluation of customer and contract data The ability to use the software while on the road User-friendliness
2. Sales force management department	Central coordination of decentralised sales force activities
3. Staff (software developers)	Use of new programming techniques Acquisition of new knowledge with the aim of safeguarding jobs Enhancement of own market value
4. Data processing / general management	More efficient and low-cost software development process Mid-term reduction in external consulting services Creation of standardised software for the sales representatives with low maintenance requirements Development of skills on the part of employees
5. Customer service department (administration)	Optimisation of customer service Consistent customer orientation Optimisation of the process from application to contract
6. Marketing department	Improvement of the company's image
7. Works council	Safeguarding of data processing jobs Comprehensive information and early involvement in the design of new business processes
8. Internal auditing	Audit-compliant production of the software Data security
9. Legal and corporate governance team	Legality of the programs and form of contract
10. Project partners (Sparkasse savings banks)	Database access Online information exchange
11. Other Landesbausparkasse building societies	Standardised software across Germany for advice and application data entry

Figure A3-2 Stakeholders and their expectations

3.3 Impact analysis

In the software project described above, not only the stakeholders but also their specific interests were identified. This provided project managers with a clear idea of stakeholder expectations and of potential risk areas. In many other projects, e.g. reorganisation projects, the interests of the various stakeholders are not nearly as clear. The impact analysis proposed by Hansel and Lomnitz [4] can help in such cases (→ Figure A3-3).

Stakeholders affected by multiple factors

A good example of this would be a project to introduce a new computerised procedure for handling customer complaints. Administrative staff are often key stakeholders in restructuring projects. The following table shows, in fact, how administrators can be affected by many aspects of a project. For example, it is possible that the introduction of the new complaints procedure will change their job and limit their freedom to act. The thought of this makes the administrative staff concerned about the project. As a result, they might publicly or – as is more frequently the case – covertly sabotage the project.

A3 STAKEHOLDER ANALYSIS

Stakeholder: John Smith, administrator

ASPECT AFFECTED	DEGREE OF IMPACT			TYPE OF IMPACT	
	none	low	high	positive	negative
1. Task assignment			x		x
2. Workflow			x		x
3. Freedom to act			x		x
4. Responsibility			x		x
5. Levels of information		x			x
6. Quality of own work	x			x	
7. Workload	x			x	
8. External supervision			x		x
9. Personal status			x		x
10. Influence			x		x
11. Promotion opportunities		x			x
12. Income	x			x	
13. Work satisfaction			x		x
14. Self-esteem			x		x

Figure A3-3 Impact analysis

3.4 Further steps in stakeholder analysis

After a project manager has identified the stakeholders and their expectations, he needs to find out
- whether the stakeholders are positively or negatively disposed towards the project,
- how powerful they are,
- how they are likely to act, and
- what measures will need to be taken to ensure the project´s success.

Collecting information

3.5 Checklist

Checklist A3-4 for conducting stakeholder analyses [5] can help the project manager to establish appropriate measures for dealing with individual stakeholders. Using the + and – ratings in the Attitude/Atmosphere column, likely project supporters and opponents are identified. In the column headed Influence/Power, the project manager appraises the stakeholders´ levels of influence. He then considers strategies and measures that will enable him to win their support. These actions might include information events for local residents or interviews with the administrative staff affected by the project, measures which can also be categorised as risk management activities (→ Chapter C3).

The behaviour of project stakeholders is often difficult to predict. In important and large-scale projects, it may be necessary to use scenario-planning techniques in order to run through potential problem situations. The objective is to identify such problem areas early on so that the correct action can be taken at a later stage of the project.

Scenario-planning techniques

A3 STAKEHOLDER ANALYSIS

STAKEHOLDER GROUP	ATTITUDE / ATMOSPHERE	INFLUENCE / POWER	EXPECTATIONS (+) FEARS (−)	STRATEGIES / MEASURES
	+ 0 −	1 – 5 *	+ 0 −	
General management	+	5	+	Weekly status reports Face-to-face interviews
Project managers	+	3	+	
Project team	+	3	+	Status meetings, suggestion box team activities etc.
Departments affected by the project	+/−	4	+/−	Regular information
Works council	−	4	−	Face-to-face interviews Status reports as per the reporting
Customer in various roles: • Person placing orders • User • Customer representatives in the project team • etc.	 + + +	 4 3 3	 + + +	Regular personal contact Status reports as per the reporting schedule
Partner companies	+	2	+	Regular contact
Suppliers	+	3	+	Visits from sales representatives Joint events Regular requests for reports
Competitors	−	3	−	Monitoring
Authorities	+/−	4	+/−	Continuous, comprehensive dialogue Timely provision of information
Media, general public	+/−	3	+/−	Press releases on a regular basis and when newsworthy events occur
Local residents	+/−	4	+/−	Information events when each milestone is reached
Pressure groups	+/−	4	+/−	Stakeholder dialogue/panel debates
Environmental campaign groups	+/−	4	+/−	Stakeholder dialogue/joint events

* 1 = very low, 5 = very high

Figure A3-4 Checklist for the stakeholder analysis

Figure A3-5 shows the result of a stakeholder analysis [6]. It highlights the groups of individuals that the stakeholder policy measures must target.

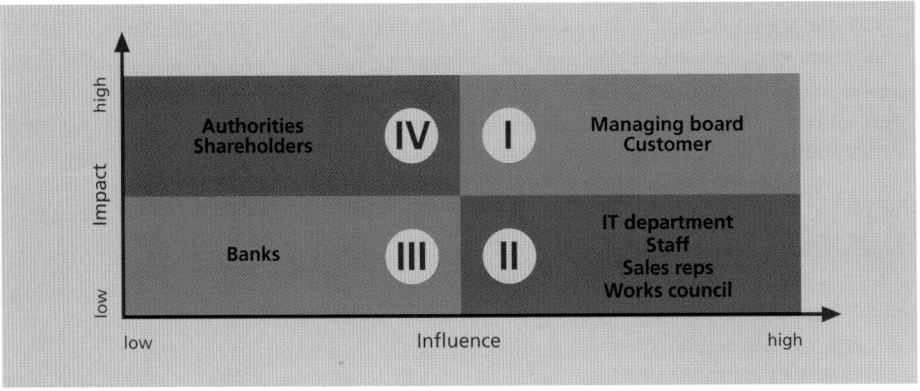

Figure A3-5 Result of a stakeholder analysis

3.6 Changes in the project environment

The results of a stakeholder analysis will never provide more than a snapshot picture. New stakeholders can arrive or depart as the project progresses. In many cases, pressure groups only form after a project has been running for several months. The stakeholders´ attitudes to the project and the balance of power can also change considerably during the course of a project. This means that the project manager regularly needs to review his original analysis and modify the measures to be taken as necessary. He should take stock of the situation at least every time an important milestone is reached.

4 Dealing with stakeholders

As part of the stakeholder analysis process, project managers should draw up prevention plans and establish what immediate-response measures might be adopted. These plans should be used to prevent or alleviate problems with stakeholders, while immediate-response activities can be used in the event that the anticipated problem occurs despite the preventive measures.

Prevention plans and immediate-response measures

> **Example of a prevention plan**
> *In the course of a product development project for an electrical appliance manufacturer, the project manager has identified a rival manufacturer as an important stakeholder. It is difficult to anticipate whether the competitor will launch a similar appliance in the near future, or what features any such appliance might have. Senior management and the project manager will have to take prompt action if they hear of any such plans. Bearing this in mind, the project manager decides to formulate essential and non-essential objectives for the company´s product with the assistance of the project steering committee. In an emergency, the company plans to dispense with the non-essential objectives. This will enable a faster time-to-market and provide it with a lead over its competitors.*

Project marketing is a project management sub-discipline that was developed in recent years to increase the acceptance of a project in its environment (→ Chapter D4).

Project marketing

5 Differences between stakeholder and risk analyses

A powerful stakeholder who opposes a project constitutes a substantial risk. Patzak and Rattay [7] explain, however, how a stakeholder analysis differs from a risk analysis (→ Chapter C3): `A risk analysis delivers facts relating to potential damage caused by individually identified risks and translates them into costs. However, it neither directly addresses nor does it take into account the effects, which are very difficult to quantify, of personal or group attitudes towards the project.´

6 Problems associated with stakeholder analyses

Patzak and Rattay believe that one problem associated with stakeholder analyses is that emotional attitudes and expectations are often not expressed openly and cannot be investigated by means of surveys or questioning. Some of the many possible reasons for this are:

Lack of stakeholder openness

- Employees may fear career setbacks if they openly state their opposition to the project.
- The culture at the organisation in question may not encourage honesty about personal, self-oriented goals.
- If an employee keeps his personal plans and intentions to himself, he runs no risk of losing his existing levels of freedom of action.

These attitudes often lead to situations where stakeholders do not reveal their opposition to a project.

Covert opposition

Some of the many symptoms of covert opposition [8] are:
- Covert opponents fuelling debates about insignificant details instead of discussing the crux of the matter (e.g. at team meetings).
- Good ideas being discussed endlessly until they are eventually abandoned.
- Managers and decision-makers failing to attend important meetings.
- The postponement of necessary decisions.
- Employees working to rule.
- Inefficient staff, who lack motivation, being included in the project team.

If these symptoms appear, the project manager has already made serious mistakes in terms of stakeholder involvement and information policy. This is why it is essential to identify the attitudes of the most important stakeholders and analyse them thoroughly at an early stage of the project. Patzak and Rattay recommend role play as one means of achieving this objective, so that project managers can put themselves in the stakeholders´ shoes.

Self-assessment questions for each certification level

No.	Question	D	C	B	A	Self-assessment
A3.1	What are stakeholders?	2	2	2	2	☐
A3.2	Why is a stakeholder analysis implemented?	2	2	2	2	☐
A3.3	What results does a stakeholder analysis deliver?	2	2	2	2	☐
A3.4	What problems have to be taken into account in a stakeholder analysis?	2	3	3	3	☐
A3.5	What is the definition of a project context/environment?	2	2	2	2	☐
A3.6	What is an impact analysis?	2	2	2	2	☐
A3.7	What is the connection between stakeholder and risk analyses?	2	3	3	4	☐

A4 LEGAL ASPECTS

Project teams have to ensure strict adherence to contracts and statutory provisions (ICB Elements 13, 27, 41) if they wish to implement their project efficiently and successfully. This is the only way to prevent risks such as claims on the part of the customer. The project contract therefore has central significance. It is linked to the management of any claims arising and also with proper contract management, a process by which managers can identify their rights and obligations in respect of project contracts and exercise or discharge these as appropriate. It provides a basis for asserting claims resulting from changes (ICB Element 17) and for achieving revenues over and above those agreed in the contract.

1 Significance

The project contract is the basis for the implementation of practically every project. Its content is binding for all parties to the contract, who – especially the project manager himself – need to be aware of and understand the content of the contract. This requires a basic knowledge of the law.

Contract administration as project management method is helpful, first of all, for the identification of the rights and duties ensuing from the project contract. It also makes the risks associated with the project transparent (→ Chapter C3). The parties can only assert their rights if these are precisely recorded and documented. Contract administration is a means of coordinating contract execution during the project lifecycle to ensure that duties are performed properly in order to minimise risks. Effective contract administration is dependent on the management and project management team´s awareness that contracts must be performed to the letter. This helps them to prevent additional claims on the part of the contractual partner, to control project costs and to ensure that deadlines are met (→ Chapter C9).

Complying with obligations and minimising risks

The claim management process enables contract managers to assist project teams in attaining and in some cases surpassing project objectives, especially financial objectives. It focuses on the rights that exist beyond the actual contract, i.e. rights ensuing from extra work, supplementary orders, and deadlines that are postponed by the parties to the contract. These rights can have considerable economic value. If they are systematically documented and enforced, it is possible to achieve far higher revenues than those agreed in the original contract. At the same time, proper claim management prevents the other party to the contract from making wrongful claims.

Increasing revenues
Claim prevention

2 Project contracts

A project contract is concluded between the project sponsor (= the customer) and the party carrying out the project (= the contractor). It governs the rights and duties of both parties in a specific project. Reflecting the definition of a project as an undertaking that is associated with unique conditions (→ Chapter A1), the project contract is also associated with unique objectives. It is deemed to have been performed when these objectives have been reached.

Example
The planning and construction of a control centre for a power station.

Sometimes, a project contract is only a few pages long. Often, however, it contains hundreds or even thousands of pages.

> **Example**
> *Project contracts for industrial plants are generally substantial. They define the scope of supply and performance for industrial plants. Deadlines and organisational requirements, prices and terms of delivery are additional key parameters for managing the project.*

Representatives with authority to sign

The authorised signatories of each party to the contract must sign the final draft.

2.1 Legal issues after signing

When the contract is signed, a project manager often faces a number of legal questions.
- Has a contract actually been formed?
- What kind of contract is it?
- What statutory provisions have to be observed in connection with this type of contract?

Contract-related pitfalls

First of all, it is necessary to clarify these issues. A project manager also checks whether any of the provisions contain any potential pitfalls. During the course of the project, he is responsible for identifying non-compliance with the contract and establishing the legal consequences – e.g. penalties that are payable if the project team fails to meet contractually agreed deadlines. He must also ensure compliance with contracts that are concluded with sub-contractors and with members of a consortium where appropriate. International contracts have the additional problems of selecting the applicable law and place of jurisdiction, and the need to take national regulations into account.

2.2 Basic legal principles

Throughout A4 we base our discussion on German law, for illustrative purposes. If you manage projects in another country, you need to check what legal principles apply there. Those described here provide a basis for your questions.

Contract law in the BGB
General terms and conditions
Special provisions

In Germany, contract law is governed by Sections 145 ff. and 311 ff. of the German Civil Code (Bürgerliches Gesetzbuch or BGB). Provisions relating to general terms and conditions of business in Sections 305–310 of the BGB and special provisions relating to specific contract types are also relevant, such as Sections 433 ff. (contracts of sale) and 631 ff. (contracts for work and services) of the BGB. The right of impairment of performance pursuant to Sections 280 ff. of the BGB is especially significant for contract execution.

==Contracts are the most frequent manifestation of legal transactions and govern the relationship between two or more parties. A contract defines the actions to be performed by each party, and stipulates the rules that each must observe. Contracts therefore provide legal certainty.==

Definition of parties to the contract

Contracts form a type of law governing the relationship between the contract parties. Therefore, a precise definition of the parties is necessary. Figure A4-1 shows the parties to a contract and their legal relationships.

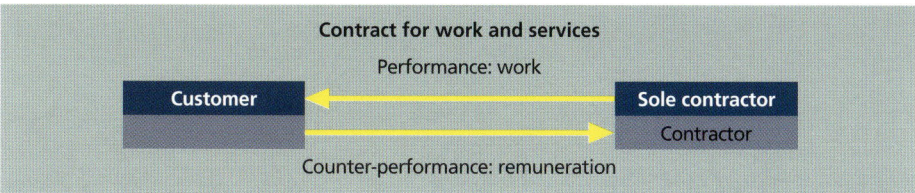

Figure A4-1 The parties to a contract and their legal relationships

2.2.1 Required information

In order to identify the parties to a contract, their precise name, legal status, address and the names of their authorised representatives must be specified in the contract.

> **Example**
> *There are two parties to a contract. These parties are specified on the first page of the contract. Generally, the following wording is used: The following contract has been concluded between Party X Ltd. – the Customer – and Party Y Plc. – the Contractor: ...*

In many cases the names of the parties´ legal representatives (e.g. the managing directors) are specified. Sometimes, several parties are named as representatives of the customer. The names and addresses of each one must be listed separately.

Project contracts are generally reciprocal contracts. One party agrees to perform specific work or services in return for a specific consideration. The work or services to be performed and the consideration received in return must therefore be specified precisely in the contract. For example, the required goods or services (including the exact scope of delivery) can be described in a technical specification. The consideration provided by the customer is generally money. Further details to be specified are price and terms of payment, as well as deadlines, place of delivery, performance guarantees and warranty terms, as well as legal consequences in the event that one of the parties breaches the contractual agreements (= impairment of performance).

Reciprocal contracts

Performance impairment

2.2.2 Entry into force of a contract

A contract becomes legally valid when
- it is signed by all of the parties or their representatives, or
- a written or oral offer is made by one party and unconditionally accepted (i.e. without reservation) by the other party.

> **Example**
> *A turbine supplier A submits an offer in writing to electricity works B, who writes back: `We accept your offer.´ As a result, a valid contract has now been formed. A is bound to provide goods or services to B exactly as described in its offer. On the other hand, if B writes back, `We agree to your offer, but would like the supply lines specified under Item 10 to be larger in size´, he is rejecting A´s original offer. No contract has come into force. A contract only enters into force with legally binding effect when A and B have reached agreement on the payment to be made in respect of those larger supply lines.*

2.2.2.1 Invitations to tender

Invitations to tender

Invitations to tender are sometimes confused with actual orders. These, however, merely constitute a request for bids and do not have the same effect as placing an order.

2.2.2.2 Oral contracts

Although oral contracts have legal force, they are not recommended because it is difficult to prove what has been agreed.

2.2.3 Unambiguousness

Contracts must be clearly and unambiguously formulated. The parties and the subject matter of the contract must be clearly stated.

2.2.4 Invalidity

Freedom of contract

Common decency

In Germany, freedom of contract (= contractual autonomy) prevails, which means all contractual provisions are admissible and valid, subject to limits defined in the German constitution: The parties to the contract must observe effective statutory provisions and the principles of common decency. Contracts that breach these laws and principles are invalid.

2.2.5 Other countries

Check national laws

In other countries, it is necessary to establish on a case-by-case basis whether the conclusion and content of contracts are subject to any national approval procedures. For example, there are restrictions on the admissibility of arbitration agreements in some countries. Even if they are admissible, it is necessary to establish whether an arbitration decision can be enforced in the country in question and whether a claim ensuing from such a decision can actually be collected in the contractual partner´s country. It is also necessary to clarify whether it is admissible under one country´s national law for contracts to be governed by the law of another country.

2.2.6 Standard contracts

Standard form contracts and general terms and conditions

Good faith

If standard contracts with recurring texts (= standard form contacts) or general terms and conditions are used, the provisions of Sections 305 ff. of the BGB apply. Accordingly – and this also applies to contracts between traders – any clauses that unduly disadvantage one party contrary to the requirement of good faith (Section 307 of the BGB) or contain surprising provisions (Section 305c of the BGB) are deemed ineffective.

Undue disadvantage

The author of the general terms and conditions may not invoke ambiguous provisions in the event of doubt. Undue disadvantage exists if a provision
- does not conform to the fundamental ideas behind the law, or if
- fundamental rights or duties ensuing from the spirit of the contract are so restrictive that reaching the objective of the contract is jeopardised.

Examples of invalid contracts are provided below. *Invalid contracts*
The seller of a new engine excludes all warranties in its general terms and conditions.
A customer who purchases an industrial plant includes a provision in its standard contract stipulating a penalty of undefined maximum amount in the event of default.

If the parties to a contract have general terms and conditions that conflict, it is generally assumed that only the non-contradictory provisions form part of the contract. Provisions in the general terms and conditions that conflict are superseded by the relevant provisions of the principal contract or, if the principal contract does not contain any such provisions, by statutory provisions. *Conflicting general terms and conditions*

A protective clause, such as, `terms and conditions to the contrary shall not apply´, is effective as a matter of principle. The other party must therefore veto any such clause in its own general terms and conditions or in a separate document. General terms and conditions must always be discussed in contractual negotiations. Correspondence after the contract has been concluded, or simply printing general terms and conditions on the reverse side of an invoice or delivery note is insufficient. It is admissible, as a matter of principle, to incorporate general terms and conditions in order confirmations. However, if these deviate substantially from oral agreements, they are invalid. *Protective clauses*

2.3 Types of contract pursuant to the BGB

The Civil Code specifies various types of contracts. In projects, the laws governing contracts of sale, service contracts and, especially, contracts for work and services apply.

2.3.1 The law governing contracts of sale

The law governing contracts of sale is regulated in Section 433 of the BGB. The seller is bound to hand over the goods and to transfer ownership of the goods to the buyer. The goods must be free of material defects and defects in title. The buyer is bound to pay the agreed price to the seller and to accept delivery of the purchased item.

Example
The seller delivers 50 mass-produced electric motors.

One-off manufactured non-fixed items are still largely subject to the law governing contracts of sale and not the law governing contracts for work and services. However, the buyer still has a duty to co-operate. *Movable items that are only manufactured once*

Example
The seller manufactures an electric motor to the buyer´s specifications.

2.3.2 The law governing contracts for services

In a contract for services (Section 611 ff. of the BGB) the service provider is bound to perform the agreed service and the customer is bound to make the agreed payment. The billing unit is time, e.g. the time required to train staff members. The service provider makes no undertaking to the customer to deliver a specific result.

Examples
The provision of training to the customer´s staff. The drafting of a specification for an IT system.

2.3.3 The law governing contracts for work and services

Contracts for work and services bind the contractor to perform the agreed work or services and the customer to effect the agreed payment (Section 631 of the BGB). The contractor must deliver a precisely defined result to the customer. Performance must be free of defects and in conformity with the contract. Only then is the customer bound to accept the contractor´s performance, i.e. to confirm the proper execution of the contract (Section 640 of the BGB).

Material defects and defects in title

According to the law governing contracts for work and services, the work or services performed by the contractor for the customer must be free of material defects and defects of title. Performance is free of material defects if the work or service is in accordance with the quality agreed in the contract.

Example
The parties agree to use a make of plaster that does not conform to DIN quality standards. The contractor´s work is free of defects if it applies the agreed plaster.

2.3.3.1 Acceptance

Purpose of acceptance

The act of acceptance is an essential aspect of contracts for work and services. It constitutes confirmation from the customer that the result is free of defects and conforms to the contractual specifications.

Example
An industrial plant contract stipulates the defect-free planning, construction and commissioning of the entire plant.

2.3.3.2 Industrial plant contract

In practice, large-scale industrial plant projects are often awarded as an entire package. An industrial plant contract is a mixed contract that not only includes elements of contracts for work and services, but also of commercial and service contracts. However, the emphasis of the contract is generally on the law governing contracts for work and services, so this law applies.

Classification of project contracts

Project contracts (= contracts for work and services) are generally divided into five large sections:
1. Preamble
2. Definitions
3. Technical specifications
4. Commercial and organisational section
5. Legal section

A4 LEGAL ASPECTS

The sections are generally separated from each other in the form of chapters, making each one easily identifiable and the whole thing more convenient. Whenever a contractual issue arises, the project manager must be able to find the relevant section quickly. The technical specification and the detailed list of suppliers are often appended to the contract. The contract needs to mention specifically that the appendices form part of the contract.

Attachments as part of the contract

The five sections generally contain the following provisions:

1. Preamble

    The preamble briefly describes the situation in which the parties to the contract find themselves and the basic considerations or interests that motivate them to conclude the contract. This information is often helpful for avoiding or amicably resolving disputes that arise during the contract execution phase.

    Basic considerations

    Example
    Country X wishes to increase its electricity supply through the use of hydroelectric power. The customer is the national electricity board. The contractor is an international turbine manufacturing company.
    This information is generally followed by a precise definition of objectives, such as:
    Customer A intends to construct and operate a hydro power station in Town B. Contractor C will supply all the turbines, machines and the necessary know-how. It will also be responsible for the overall management of the project.

    Definition of objectives

2. Definitions

    The inclusion of a section providing definitions is standard international practice, and is also useful in contracts where both or all the parties are from the same country. When contracts are extremely lengthy, it is customary and necessary to define frequently used terms (= contract-specific terms), such as the entry into force of the contract and acceptance. This ensures that all parties have the same understanding of content and – in conjunction with the preamble – provides clarification in the event of any dispute about the parties´ original intentions and purposes when they drafted the contract.

    Contractual terms

3. Technical specification

    The technical specification details the scope of supply and services and is generally written by engineers or technical experts. This, together with all the other services to be rendered, constitutes the contractor´s service package. However, the services or consideration to be provided by the customer are also precisely described for purposes of clarification and limitation.

    Scope of supply and performance

4. Commercial and organisational section

    The commercial and organisational section specifies prices, terms of ordering, delivery and payment, as well as schedules and deadlines. It is the section of the contract that is relevant for the commercial staff, and also for the project and contract management teams (= commercial requirements). It includes provisions relating to cooperation with the customer and also any provisions that are specific to the customer or country.

5. Legal section

    The legal section of the contract regulates the legal consequences that the contractor will face if it defaults on performance – i.e. if it does not supply the agreed item(s) or service(s) in the agreed

    Legal consequences

quantity or quality or on the agreed date, or fails to comply with any other contractual provisions. In other words, this section of the contract includes provisions that could result in project costs and that could therefore jeopardise the project's commercial success. It is particularly important to coordinate the technical specifications with the commercial and organisational section. Legal consequences can also be set down in the commercial section.

2.4 Contract content checklist

It makes sense to create a checklist for the five contract sections and their sub-sections that includes all legally-relevant activities (e.g. bid or quotation structure).

CONTRACT CONTENT CHECKLIST

1. **Preamble and objectives**
2. **Definitions**
3. **Technical specifications**
   - Situation details: raw materials and supplies, geology, climate, water, energy, details on the number of people employed by the customer and their skills, statutory provisions and official regulations
   - Goods to be supplied
   - Services, especially project management services
   - Performance bonds
   - Assembly
   - Human resources
   - Materials to be provided by the customer
   - Duties of the customer to cooperate
4. **Commercial and organisational section**
   - Price
   - Terms of payment
   - Security for payments
   - Inflation clause (to cover cost increases and inflation)
   - Packaging
   - Shipping
   - Insurance
   - Schedules and deadlines
   - Priorities
   - Import formalities, accompanying documents
   - Invoicing
   - Construction and installation progress (verification)
   - Accounting and tax liabilities
   - Costs
   - Test runs
   - Acceptance procedure
5. **Legal section**
   - Order of precedence (of the contractual provisions)
   - Change requests
   - Project manager's authority
   - Existence of official permits
   - Entry into force of the contract, specification of an on-or-before date
   - Breach of contract by way of
     - non-performance or incomplete performance
     - delay and default
     - defective delivery
   - Failed acceptance procedure
   - Liabilities and warranties
   - Supplementary performance, damages, cancellation of contract
   - Penalties
   - Exclusion of liability (= disclaimer and limitation of liability)
   - 'Force majeure'
   - Taxes and levies
   - Applicable law
   - Contract language
   - General terms and conditions
   - Standards, contracting rules for award of public works contracts
   - Statute of limitations
   - Arbitration tribunal or state court for appeals, place of jurisdiction
   - Severability clause (only applies in German-law contracts)

Figure A4-2 Contract content checklist

The checklist for the industrial plant construction project shown in Figure A4-2 includes the most important provisions. It can be used in this format – with some modifications – for all project contracts. The project manager must be able to identify the agreed sanctions, particularly any costs and penalties, on reading through the contract for the first time. These are just as important as the deliverables themselves. Particularly in large-scale projects, delivery delays and occasional quality defects can never be ruled out.

2.5 Special features of project contracts

Project contracts have a number of special features with which project managers need to be familiar.

2.5.1 Acceptance

Acceptance is an important milestone in the project lifecycle. If the contractor has performed the work or services in accordance with the contract, the customer is bound to accept it and the contractor has the right to acceptance (Section 640 of the BGB).

Obligation to accept/right of acceptance

Acceptance of the work or services performed in accordance with a contract generally involves physical acceptance in the form of a transfer of ownership. This is made in the form of a declaration on the part of the customer to the effect that the work or service is in accordance with the contract.

Acceptance is both a de facto act, i.e. the physical acceptance of the work or services, and a legal act. By way of acceptance, the customer confirms that the deliverable conforms in its essentials to the contract.

'De facto' acts
Legal acts

If defects are evident during acceptance, the customer must reserve its rights. If he fails to do this and accepts the service or work, he forfeits his right to assert performance claims. A penalty can only be asserted after acceptance if the customer reserves the right to enforce the penalty in the acceptance protocol or acceptance certificate (→ Figure A4-3). The precise time of acceptance is particularly important owing to the associated legal consequences. The parties should specify the date of acceptance in the joint acceptance protocol.

Reservations
Performance claims

Time of acceptance
Acceptance records

ACCEPTANCE PROTOCOL	
Project	Contract dated
Customer representative	
Contractor representative	
Item being accepted	☐ Overall performance ☐ Following part performance:
The following was ascertained during acceptance	☐ Performance is free of defects. ☐ With the exception of the defects or damage described overleaf, performance is as agreed in the ontract. ☐ We reserve the right to assert the forfeit penalties.
Date of acceptance	(Place, date)
Customer	Contractor

Figure A4-3 Acceptance certificate

A4 LEGAL ASPECTS

2.5.1.1 Legal consequences of acceptance

Legal consequences of acceptance

The legal consequences of acceptance are:
- Passing of the risk (The risk of accidental loss, destruction or deterioration of the deliverable passes to the buyer.)
- Commencement of defect liability periods
- Due date of payments
- The burden of proof shifts to the customer. (The onus is on the customer from this time forward to prove that the contractor is responsible for the defect.)

2.5.1.2 Acceptance procedures

In large-scale projects (e.g. the construction of industrial plants) the parties agree specific acceptance procedures. These regulate the timeframes and conditions that are applicable for pre-acceptance test runs and the conditions under which acceptance is deemed to have taken place. Figure A4-4 shows an example of acceptance procedures and a timeframe.

Semi-commercial operation	Commercial operation		Final hand-over
30	60		365 days
Commencement of service trials			Acceptance

Figure A4-4 Acceptance procedure (example)

2.5.2 Warranty

A warranty is a statement or representation that the goods or services will perform as agreed. German law, for example, specifies quality and durability warranties. A warranty goes beyond statutory guarantee rights (Sections 443, 444, 639 of the BGB).

Exclusion of liability

The scope of rights ensues from the written warranty and the information provided in relevant advertising. These rights can be enforced against the person who issued the warranty (e.g. the retailer or manufacturer). Liability, however, cannot be excluded when warranties are given on the quality for goods or services. The warranty provider is also responsible, without fault, for ensuring that the goods or services are in the warranted quality.

> **Example**
> *A manufacturer warrants that paint will remain weather-proof for four years. The paint, however, peels off after three and a half years. The manufacturer is liable.*

Implied warranty

Another type of warranty is implied warranty. This also includes performance guarantees (e.g. the output from a production plant per unit of time).

2.5.3 Exclusion of liability

The contractor must make an attempt to limit or exclude its liability. If penalties have been agreed, it should ensure that additional liability for damages is excluded. Claims for damages are required to have a fixed upper limit, such as five percent of the contract value.

Limitation of claims for damages

2.5.4 Limitation of defect claims

In the law governing contracts for work and services, which often applies in project contracts, the following periods of limitation apply:
- Five years for construction work or for planning or supervision services rendered in connection with the construction project
- Two years for the manufacture, maintenance or modification of a product and for planning or supervision services rendered in this connection.

The limitation period commences on acceptance. If a defect is repaired within the period of liability for defects, the period automatically extends by two years commencing on the date when the defect was repaired.

2.5.5 Construction contracts, contracting rules for the award of public works contracts

In Germany, the parties to construction contracts generally agree that the contracting rules for award of public works contracts, Part B (VOB/B) apply. These comprise standard contractual terms that form part of the contract when the parties have reached agreement. It is far easier to assert claims on the basis of VOB/B than on the basis of an ordinary contract for work and services because it contains detailed provisions governing the circumstances under which additional rights to remuneration exist. However, this only applies if the standard provisions of the VOB/B are complied with strictly. For example, the customer must be given notification of work and services that are not agreed in the contract before these commence.

2.6 Impairment of performance and legal consequences

In accordance with the contract, the contractor is required to render complete and timely performance to the agreed quality. If he does not do so, its performance is impaired. One central aspect of the law on performance impairment is breach of obligation. If a party to the contract breaches a contractual obligation, the other party is entitled to demand compensation for any resulting damages. It is therefore irrelevant which obligation the party (the obligor) has breached, provided it is established that he has breached an obligation.

Prerequisites

Breaches of obligation

> The term breach of obligation covers all forms of performance impairment:
> 1. Impossibility of performance or inability to perform
> 2. Partial non-performance
> 3. Default
> 4. Defective performance

Examples
A contractor is not able to deliver a replacement part that it has undertaken to supply (= impossibility of performance / inability to perform).
A building contractor constructs a building but doesn´t landscape the grounds (= partial non-performance).
A building owner does not make his lease payments on the agreed date (= default).
A property owner sells land that is contaminated with fuel deposits (= defective performance).

Compensation for damages, cancellation of the contract

In order to obtain damages or cancel the contract, it is only necessary to demand supplementary performance and specify a reasonable date by which performance is to be rendered.

2.6.1 Impairment of performance in project contracts

Customer´s rights

In the event of performance impairment, the customer has the following rights:
1. Contractual penalty
2. Refusal of performance until counter-performance is effected (= retaining lien)
3. Supplementary performance (formerly: rectification of defects – takes precedence over other defect claims)
4. Self-execution (formerly: execution by substitution)
5. Price reduction and cancellation of contract
6. Damages (if the contractor is at fault)
7. Termination for cause

Contractor´s rights

In the event of performance impairment, the contractor has the following rights:
1. Refusal of performance until counter-performance is effected (= retaining lien)
2. Default interest
3. Cancellation of the contract
4. Damages (if the customer is at fault)
5. Termination for cause

To assert the above-mentioned rights, customer and contractor must be aware of them and of the necessary procedures.

Terms and conditions

1. Contractual penalty
   A penalty is only effective if it is agreed in the contract. In standard form contracts, penalty provisions are only admissible and effective if a specific amount is stated.
   Generally, 0.1 to 0.3 percent of the contract value for each working day of delay or default is agreed upon as the penalty. Penalties must also be restricted to a maximum of five percent. If these conditions are not satisfied, the provision is invalid.

(Advance) performance

2. Refusal of performance until counter-performance is effected (= retaining lien)
   Unless bound to do so, a party can refuse to make advance deliveries or payment until counter-performance is effected (Sections 320, 341.3 of the BGB).

Example

A contractor does not repair damage caused by damp that occurred after acceptance. The customer is therefore entitled to withhold at least three times the cost of repairing the defect from a due payment.

3. Supplementary performance
   The customer must notify the contractor of a defect and grant him the opportunity to repair it.

4. Self-execution
   Self-execution is only possible if performance was not rendered within the time granted for supplementary performance. The customer can then demand compensation for costs and an advance payment in respect of these costs. The period of time granted must be reasonable, taking the circumstances into account.

   Expiry of deadline without performance being rendered

5. Price reduction
   Price reductions are also only possible if supplementary performance and performance was not rendered within the time granted. The customer reduces the price by way of a simple declaration to the contractor.

6. Compensation, cancellation of the contract
   Compensation and the cancellation of the contract are also only possible if the time granted for supplementary performance has expired without performance being rendered. If supplementary performance is not successful, it is not necessary to grant a further period of time.

7. Termination for cause
   Termination for cause in accordance with Section 314 of the BGB is only possible if the terminating party cannot be reasonably expected to continue the contractual relationship. The interests of both parties are taken into account when the decision is made. For the termination to be effective, a prior warning must have been issued or a specific period granted to the other party for remedial action. The terminating party must give notice of termination within a reasonable period of time after becoming aware of the cause for termination, i.e. within 14 days of the expiry of the period specified for remedial action. The right to claim damages is not affected by termination.

   Unreasonableness

   Warning

8. Claims for default interest
   Delays result in default. Default is determined on the basis of:
   - Due date of performance
   - Expiry of a calendar-based period of time
   - A letter of reminder when no calendar-based periods of time are agreed
   - In the case of claims for monetary debts: 30 days after the due date and receipt of the invoice or acceptance of counter-performance (Section 286, Paragraph 3 of the BGB)
   - Fault (intent or negligence on the part of the obligor)

   Default

Example

A final payment instalment is due when acceptance takes place. However, the customer does not make the payment, despite having been sent a reminder. Default commences when the customer receives the reminder. The legal consequence is that the supplier can claim damages, in particular for payment of interest.

A4 LEGAL ASPECTS

Interest of 5 percent above the base rate is payable on money debts. If neither of the parties is a consumer, the rate of interest is eight percent above the base rate (Section 288, Paragraphs 1 and 2, of the BGB). The base rate is modified on 1 January and 1 July every year (Section 247 of the BGB). It is published in the business section of the German broadsheets and can also be requested from banks.

> **Example**
> A commercial customer has defaulted of a payment of EUR 100,000 since 1 January. He does not pay until 31 December of the same year. The customer is entitled to demand and assert a claim for default interest of eight percent plus the base rate (= more than EUR 8,000).

2.7 Contractual relationships in a project

Principal contract
Sub-contractors

Figure A4-1 shows the contractual relationship between a customer and a single contractor (= principal contract). When performing the contract, the contractor will often sub-contract work to other companies. Cooperation with external firms (= third parties) is regulated in one of two ways: the contractor either awards sub-contracts to sub-contractors or operates within a consortium of partners, all of whom have the same rights. The contract situation therefore differs, depending on which option is selected.

2.7.1 Contracts with sub-contractors

General contractor

If the contractor awards sub-contracts to sub-contractors, he is the general contractor. The legal relationships are shown in Figure A4-5:

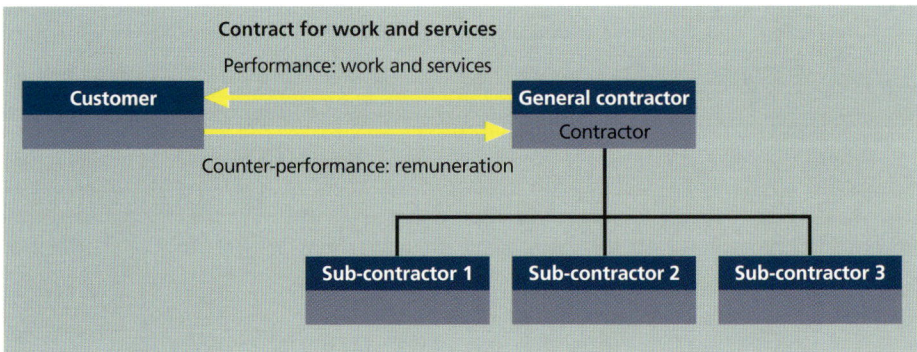

Figure A4-5 General contractor

Figure A4-5 shows that two entirely different contract systems are in place. On the one hand, the (general) contractor has entered into a contractual relationship with the customer. On the other, further contractual relationships exist between the contractor and sub-contractors. One important aspect in this model is that the sub-contractors have no legal relationship with the customer. All relationships with the customer take place via the general contractor.

Vicarious agents

If, as is the case in this model, the general contractor sub-contracts work out to external firms, these are always its vicarious agents in accordance with Section 278 of the BGB. The general contractor is therefore fully liable to the customer for deliveries of goods and services supplied by the sub-contractors.

A4 LEGAL ASPECTS

A general contractor must pay special attention to the interfaces between the various goods and services supplied by sub-contractors. He must also make sure that his own liability and warranty obligations as contractor do not go beyond the total obligations of his sub-contractors. The general contractor also needs to ensure that the sub-contractors' warranties do not expire before the contractor's own warranties to the customer.

Reconciliation of liability and warranty with sub-contractors

2.7.2 Consortium contracts

In many cases, a customer concludes a contract for work and services with not just one but several companies. In such instances, these companies have formed a consortium.

2.7.2.1 External consortium

This model differs from the sub-contractor model because the consortium (= contractor) concludes the contract with the customer. The contract is therefore a single contract with an external party. It also differs from the sub-contractor model because all members of the consortium are the contractual partners of the customer. They are liable for their own obligations and those of the other members of the consortium vis-à-vis the customer (= joint and several liability). Each member of the consortium therefore has a legal relationship with the customer. Figure A4-6 shows the legal relationships in an external consortium.

Joint and several liability

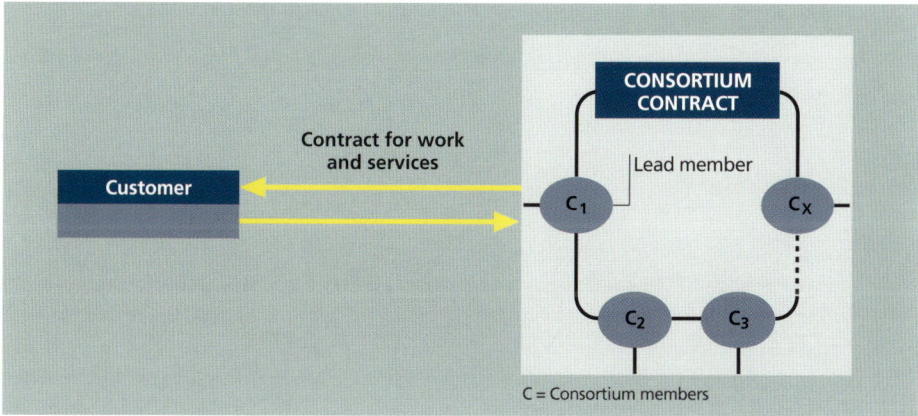

Figure A4-6 External consortium

In order to simplify communication with the customer, one consortium member is generally designated as lead member; he represents the consortium and handles all customer communication. He also coordinates all deliveries, services and decisions within the consortium. In other words, he performs the function of project manager.

Lead member

The relationships of the consortium members with each other (= internal relationships) are governed by a second, separate contract: the consortium contract. First and foremost, this forms the basis for allocating shares of compensation payments among the consortium members when customer liability claims are enforced. The individual consortium members all have equal rights. The consortium has the legal form of a company constituted under civil law.

Consortium contracts

2.7.2.2 Internal consortium

An internal consortium, like an external consortium, has a lead member who represents the consortium as the contractor in contractual relationships with the customer. He concludes the contract externally with the customer in his own name, though internally for the account of the entire consortium. Like the general contractor in the external consortium, he is liable in full towards the customer. However, he forms an internal consortium with other firms (= silent consortium). The individual consortium members' obligations go beyond those of a mere sub-contractor. The general contractor can pass or distribute the risk to the consortium members or among them. The distribution of liability within the consortium is regulated by the consortium contract.

Silent consortia

Distribution of liability

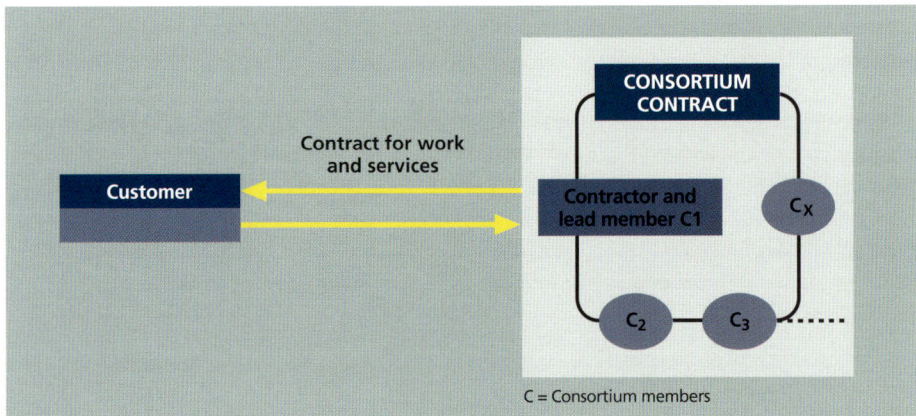

Figure A4-7 Internal consortium

2.7.3 Partnership

A partnership (→ A6) is often formed in the construction industry. It is a consortium whose members are from external firms or the company itself. Basically, it is very similar to a consortium. However, there is one important difference: a partnership has partnership assets. It renders overall performance (of the construction project) by pooling resources such as construction equipment, materials and human resources. The partners participate in overall profits and losses. The partnership is generally awarded contracts in the form of lots (e.g. construction lots).

Partnership assets

2.8 Special risks associated with project contracts

Risks by phase

The various project phases of
1. bidding and contract awarding,
2. development up to acceptance,
3. acceptance and
4. post-acceptance defect liability

have special risks that must be taken into account when designing and executing contracts.

2.8.1 Bidding and contract awarding phase

Entry into force of a contract with condition precedent
A contract with condition precedent only becomes legally valid when the condition occurs (e.g. if a bank grants or refuses funding). It is therefore necessary to ascertain whether the condition precedent affects the start of work only or the validity of the entire contract.

Conditions precedent

Cost estimate
In case of doubt, estimates of costs are not remunerable (Section 632, Paragraph 2 of the BGB).

Definition of performance when work or services overlap
Interfaces are the points of transition when deliveries and services of one contractor pass to another contractor, sub-contractor or the customer. It is necessary both to specify in the contract and precisely to illustrate the point where the performance of one supplier ends and that of another begins. It is recommended that a list of overlapping work or services is drawn up so that the technical aspects, delivery points and deadlines of all deliveries can be coordinated.

List of interfaces

Coordination of defect liability periods
After acceptance, the contractor is liable for the contract deliverable and the sub-contractor for its part of the performance, though the sub-contractor may be liable for a shorter period (due to earlier commencement). If there is no coordination, the contractor is exposed to a higher risk.

Contract assignment
Subject to the consent of the other party.

Nominated sub-contractors
The contractor´s exemption from liability must be agreed.

Operating and maintenance instructions
The contractor is liable for ensuring freedom from defects. This is why limitation of liability is especially important for him.

Exemptions from liability
Should be agreed in the interest of the contractor, especially when turnkey plants are the deliverable (e.g. exemption from liability for defects on parts that are subject to wear and tear).

Briefing the customer´s staff
To be included in a separate contract for services agreement. If this is incorporated in the principal contract, it is possible that liability for results will exist under the law governing contracts for work and services.

Fixed-price contracts, turnkey plant
A precise definition of performance to be rendered by the customer and contractor, plus a list of exemptions, is necessary.

Information procurement provision
Ensures that the contractor cannot plead that its right to receive information has been breached by the customer. If this provision is omitted from a contract, the contractor is always liable for failing to procure information.

Obligation to provide information

A4 LEGAL ASPECTS

Contractual penalty
Lump-sum compensation for damages
Instead of a penalty, in international contracts you should agree a lump-sum amount of compensation. Contractual penalties are not generally admissible in the English-speaking countries.

Development contracts
Formulate these separately in accordance with the law on contracts for services, without accepting liability for results. Proceed phase by phase (e.g. drafting of a specification).

Duties of the customer to cooperate
These must be precisely and comprehensively specified (e.g. procurement of work permits, import and export permits for materials and building site equipment, customs formalities, transfer permits).

Change requests
Formal supplementary orders
Remuneration claims
Formal supplementary orders are necessary (whenever possible in writing). Specify in the contract that every change or additional work or services will be associated with a remuneration claim. Payment should be made on the basis of the specification and schedule of prices or on the basis of a cost estimate made by the contractor.

Cancellation options
Termination with notice
Cancellation should always be excluded and replaced by termination with notice because of the higher risks and costs that are associated with cancellation.

Passing of the risk and transfer of title
This should be precisely regulated. If appropriate, reach separate agreements on transfer of title. Check local laws.

Regulation of legal consequences for failure to render guaranteed performance.
Necessary, for example, in the form of a price reduction as a percentage of reduction in performance.

Liability for defects in title
Infringement of industrial property rights
Impairment of use
Mainly effective when patents or other industrial property rights are infringed. A provision is necessary if it is possible that use may be impaired by third party property rights (e.g. relating to machines or processes used).

Warranties
These go beyond statutory liability for defects. Exclusion of liability is therefore not possible. Warranted performances should therefore be precisely defined in order that liability can be limited.

Force majeure
Duty to renegotiate
Invoicing and payment of performance rendered up to the occurrence of *force majeure*. Agree upon a duty to renegotiate at the end of the incident of force majeure instead of including a termination provision in the contract because the consequences are impossible to foresee.

Arbitration tribunal
Enforceability
The proceedings are faster than regular court proceedings because there is only one sitting. There are no problems relating to international service of process. It is less costly than court proceedings. In some cases, the parties can nominate experts as arbitrators. It is necessary to check in advance whether other countries will recognise and enforce arbitration tribunal decisions.

A4 LEGAL ASPECTS

Choice of law provision
You should select the law of your country whenever possible. If this is not possible, opt for the neutral law of an industrially developed country, as opposed to choosing a law that is influenced by religion (e.g. Saudi Arabia). Agree upon the applicable law, place of jurisdiction and competent arbitration tribunal.

Effectiveness of the chosen law
A *de facto* reference is not necessary. It suffices if the parties have a recognisable interest in the choice of law.

Freedom of choice
Refers to the relationship between the parties under the law of obligations. The issue of transfer of title is regulated at the place where the deliverable is installed in accordance with the mandatory regulations under property law. This also applies for claims under tort law. Due to the applicability of effective regulations at the place of installation, limitation of liability is necessary.

Relationships under the law of obligation / claims under the law of tort

Contract language
If possible, agree upon a language that is standardised and internationally recognised (e.g. English, French, or German). If a contract exists in several language versions, agree which language takes precedence.

Further potential risk areas
Import and export restrictions, local partners, regulations on approvals, customs and foreign currencies, currency risk, transfer risk, cost changes, inflation clause, planning permission.

2.8.2 Development up to acceptance phase

Preliminary acceptance
Acceptance subject to the verification of the promised performance parameters. Preliminary acceptance only pertains to the general condition and basic functional capability of the deliverable. The guaranteed performance parameters can in some circumstances be verified at a later point in time.

Final acceptance
Takes place at the end of the defect liability period. During this period, the contractor performs warranty maintenance. In addition to his statutory liability, e.g. for defects under German law, the contractor must repair every defect at his own expense during the warranty period. Exclude non-acceptance as a result of negligible defects.

Inspections and tests during the construction phase (technical acceptance)
Such inspections and tests do not constitute part acceptance in the legal sense. However, they enable the timely identification of defects and the preservation of evidence (e.g. the inspection of an industrial container on the manufacturer´s premises). If an inspection certificate has been issued in respect of a part, the customer must prove that a subsequently occurring defect was caused by the inspected part.

A4 LEGAL ASPECTS

Contractor's warranty

Warranty maintenance
The contractor repairs any damage that occurs within the warranty period at his own expense. Lump-sum remuneration is possible.

Fictive approval or acceptance
Specify on-or-before dates if applicable. In the event of the customer's non-acceptance of work or services within a reasonable period specified by the contractor, they are nevertheless deemed to have been accepted. When this fictive acceptance occurs, all the legal consequences of acceptance take effect (due date of payment, passing of the risk, commencement of liability for defects, shifting of the burden of proof). Claims in respect of visible defects and penalties can then no longer be asserted, unless the right to assert such claims has been reserved.

2.8.3 Acceptance

Acceptance is one of the customer's main obligations. The contractor has the right to demand the acceptance of any defect-free goods or services that it supplies, and to demand acceptance of goods and services with negligible defects.

2.8.4 Post-acceptance defect liability

Limitation per component

Limitation of liability
Recommended for each delimitable part of the contract deliverable. A contractor aims for low liability, e.g. ten to twenty percent of the value of the delivered item. Liability should never exceed 100 percent of the value.

Direct damage (= consequential damage caused by a defect)
Liability should be fully excluded. Examples of direct damage should be specified (e.g. production stoppages, environmental contamination, unrealised profit).

Neutral instance

Engineer
The engineer is the customer's representative and a neutral legal person with a function similar to that of an arbitrator. However, he only makes decisions after reasonable consultation with the customer and contractor.

Recourse to the arbitration tribunal
This is an option if either the contractor or customer is not satisfied with the engineer's decision. There are three stages in the arbitration tribunal procedure:
1. The engineer reconsiders his decision
2. An attempt is made to reach an amicable settlement
3. The arbitration process commences

2.9 Special risks associated with different project types

Common features

Project contracts can be drawn up for very different types of projects. However, the legal basis is always the same. Project contracts all have the following in common:

- Law governing contracts for work and services
- Defect-free performance of the work or services
- Acceptance
- Contractor's liability for defects within the limitation period
- Obligation of the customer to make payment

Depending on the project field, it is necessary to consider a number of special aspects and potential pitfalls of project contracts.

Pitfalls

2.9.1 Industrial plant contract

Special aspects: it is a contract that is made up of elements found in contracts for work and services, commercial contracts and service contracts.
Potential pitfalls: the contractor's liability, because the major part of the project contract constitutes a contract for work and services.

Example
A provision in a training contract stipulates that the customer's staff must be able to operate the machine without assistance after taking part in the training course.

2.9.2 Research and development

Special aspects: definition of objectives is necessary, long development period.
Potential pitfalls: obligation to deliver a result pursuant to the law governing contracts for work and services without any advance definition of the objective.

Example
A contractor commences work before a specification has been agreed with the customer.

2.9.3 Construction contracts pursuant to the BGB

Special aspects: fictive acceptance, precedence of supplementary performance (over price reduction and compensation for damages).
Potential pitfalls: invalidity of unreasonable provisions in standard-form contracts.

Example
Contractual penalty with no maximum limit.

2.9.4 Construction contracts pursuant to the contracting rules for the award of public works contracts (VOB/B)

Special aspects: supplementary provisions are only effective if incorporated within the contract.

Basis for claim management:	regulation of remuneration for changes and additional work or services (Section 2, Paragraphs 5 and 6).
Potential pitfalls:	amendments to VOB/B provisions.
Legal procedure in case of dispute:	the content of every single VOB/B provision must be checked to establish its validity.

2.9.5 Architect and engineer contract

Special aspects:	they act as representatives of the customer.
Potential pitfalls:	the customer is not liable for orders placed and invoices approved by the architect or engineer. Exception: special authorisation.

2.9.6 Contract with a project manager

Special aspects:	the fee can be freely negotiated in accordance with the Scale of Fees for Architects and Engineers in the relevant country.
Potential pitfalls:	the project manager's liability for work and services in the case of performance-based obligations (e.g. obligation to meet to specific deadlines and cost targets).

2.9.7 Contract with a construction consortium (partnership)

Special aspects:	all partners are fully liable towards third parties. Within the consortium, they are liable to each other in accordance with the internal distribution of liability.
Potential pitfalls:	insolvency or withdrawal of a partner for another reason.

2.9.8 Contract with public sector customers

Threshold values for bidding procedures

Special aspects:	formal bidding procedure if the following threshold values are exceeded:
	Construction EUR 5,000,000
	Drinking water, energy, transport EUR 400,000
	Other goods and services EUR 200,000
Potential pitfalls:	no deviations from the text of the invitation to tender are admissible.

3 Contract administration

Contract administration is the part of project management (→ Figure A4-8) concerned with the coordination of contract design, conclusion, execution with a view to attaining the project objectives, and modification.

Surpassing the project objective

Contract administration allows contracts to be designed, concluded and executed in such a way that the project objective is attained or surpassed. In project contracts, the objective is usually the construction of a facility, in particular a building or an industrial plant. From a contractual perspective, the contract administration team acts to represent the project objectives. This means that it must ensure that the contract deliverable is supplied in a defect-free state. For this, the contract administrator has to identify constraints in terms of time, finances, human resources or other factors and implement appropriate measures. For example, he ensures that contractually-agreed deadlines are met. This also forms the basis for the claim management process. Contract administration is closely related to change and quality management.

The contract administrator must acquire all contractually relevant information and compile it in a format that can be used by the project manager, project team members and senior managers. He oversees contract negotiations between the customer and contractor, contract execution and any contract changes that are necessary for technical, schedule-related or financial reasons. Either the affected and participating business units, a member of the project team, a separate department or, as is more frequently the case nowadays, external experts can assume responsibility for contract administration. The contract administration team members should have interdisciplinary competence. Engineers with commercial knowledge or commercial staff with technical expertise are often perfect for the job. These people also require a basic understanding of the law.

Contract changes

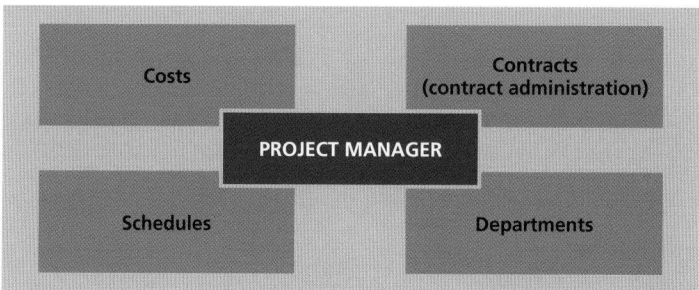

Figure A4-8 The significance of contract administration in project management

3.1 Tools

The contract administration process continues throughout the project. It comprises both factual activities (e.g. preserving evidence for claim management) and legal activities (e.g. contract changes, reminders). The main tools used for contract administration are the various forms of documentation available. These primarily include

- Contracts (e.g. with customers, sub-contractors, consortia)
- Other agreements and change logs
- Correspondence, construction site reports, job records, photos
- Delivery notes, customs certificates, official permits
- Other methods of preserving evidence
- Modern communication media (especially IT)
- Forms and checklists

Documentation tools

3.2 Contract administration phases

Deviation from project phases

Contract administration consists of separate phases and events that are not necessarily identical to the phases and milestones of the project. The lifecycle of a project is divided into three phases from the contract administrator´s viewpoint:
1. Bidding phase
2. Contract conclusion phase
3. Contract execution/project execution phase

3.2.1 Bidding phase

Specifications

Review of outline technical/ commercial bids

The contract administrator is integrated in the project at the earliest possible opportunity – in other words during the bidding phase. Bids are generally submitted in response to invitations to tender, and quotations are sent out in response to direct enquiries. The specification describes what is required of the bidder (`What is to be delivered in return for what?´). The relevant departments then submit a technical and commercial outline bid to the contract administrator. The contract administrator checks the bid to ensure completeness and compliance with any requirements that may be relevant in the subsequent contract execution phase (e.g. entry into force of the contract, deadlines, payment terms, liability and warranty, choice of law, election of an arbitration tribunal). For this he uses a checklist. It is also a good idea for him to consult the project manager. The experience gained by project managers in the customer´s country or in other projects for the same customer should also be considered.

3.2.2 Contract conclusion phase

Eliminate problem sources

This phase occurs when the customer has received a bid in which he is interested. Generally, the two parties then negotiate the specific terms and agree upon the specification (`How is the service to be performed and with what resources?´) When the final version of the contract has been drafted, the contract administrator checks it once again. After lengthy negotiations (in large-scale projects, negotiations can take one, two or even several years) it is possible that the contract will accidentally include conflicting provisions or that important provisions have been omitted. Loopholes and discrepancies can also exist. The contract administrator must ensure that these potential sources of problems are eliminated before the contract is concluded. When ISO 9001 certification is necessary, a quality management element for contract verification will need to be carried out.

3.2.3 Contract performance / project execution phase

As soon as the contract has been legally concluded, a project manager generally assumes responsibility for the project. From then on, the contract administrator´s responsibility is to help the project manager and his team to understand the contract and to execute the project on schedule and within the budget framework.

3.3 Contract administration procedures

The contract administration procedures consist of
1. Contract analysis
2. Entry of keywords in the computerised contract file
3. Contract activity tracking
4. Claim management

3.3.1 Contract analysis

In this procedure, the information relevant for contract execution is identified and put into context. The term contract analysis also covers the process of analysing and evaluating any previous contracts with the same customer or with a customer in the same country before the contract is concluded. It covers all the main activities to be carried out by both the customer and the contractor, contract schedules and deadlines (e.g. for performance, payment and acceptance), legal consequences in the event of performance impairment, contractual penalties and agreements on arbitration tribunals. These aspects can all be included in a summary that makes reference to the relevant provisions of the contract. It is particularly important that performance impairment, delays and the non-attainment of warranted performance should be considered both in relation to one another and in relation to legal sanctions. Even at this stage, it is necessary to consider the contract-related risks. These include

Previous contracts

Summaries

Contract-related risks

- Changes
- Delays
- Warranted performances
- Licences
- Defect elimination periods
- Other liability risks (e.g. relating to product and environmental liability)

The contract administrator then compiles a list of recognised risks, which is either included in the project manual or provided in another format. A written record of the (contract) strategy is also drafted. It provides information on how to minimise these risks and perform the contract to the letter. These documents should be made available to all project team members.

Project manuals / Contract strategy

The content of the contract can be structured on a project-specific basis based on different considerations. Suitable summaries can be drawn up for

Summary by target group

- familiarising the project manager and senior management with the essential aspects of the contract,
- assisting project team members after specific project phases, or
- after key dates (consider penalties!).

It is also important to consider individual performance obligations in relation to the potential legal consequences in the event of performance impairment in these summaries. All project team members should be aware of the consequences of their actions in their field of work. Figures A4-9 to A4-11 show examples of such summaries.

A4 LEGAL ASPECTS

Summary by contract data

CONTRACT DETAILS				
Date	Delivery/service	Legal consequence in event of non-compliant performance	Page in the contract Delivery/service	Legal consequence
30.06.05	Delivery of machine	Penalty	3	27
....	....	....	....	....

Figure A4-9 Summary of basic contract details

Figure A4-10 shows a summary by scheduled dates. The schedule is oriented around the signing of the contract (15.11.2003).

Summary by schedule

SCHEDULE			
Date	Page in the contract	Party involved	Procedure
01.– 05.01.04	15	Consortium	Letter confirming advance payment
01.– 05.01.04	21	Consortium	Notification to the general agent for Greece
13.01.04	13	Consortium	Information to customer
13.01.04	27	Consortium	Performance bond
13.01.04	78	Consortium	Complete thermodynamic calculation for the flue
10.–15.02.04	15	Customer	10% advance payment to the consortium
10.–15.02.04	17	Consortium	Specification of a bank account in Greece
10.–15.02.04	75	Consortium	Engineering work: preliminary plans
10.–15.02.04	29	N.N.	Official approval of the contract
10.02.04	33	All parties	Schedule for supply of goods/services to customer

Figure A4-10 Summary of contractual obligations by scheduled date

Figure A4-11 summarises examples of penalties agreed and the conditions under which they can be imposed.

Summary by contractual penalties

CONTRACTUAL PENALTIES		
1. Default penalties		
0.125 % for each full week during the first eight weeks		
0.250 % for each complete week during the following eight weeks		
0.500 % for each additional complete week		
To a maximum of 5% of the contractually-agreed price for the unit in default. All penalties are calculated from the first day of commercial operation (Unit I: 1.12.2003; Unit II: 14.3.2004)		
2. Contractual penalties for service interruption or service impairment during the period from the commencement of commercial operation until final acceptance.		
Calendar day	0 – 40	0 % per calendar day
Calendar day	41 – 70	0.025 % per calendar day
Calendar day	71 – 100	0.030 % per calendar day
Calendar day	101 – 140	0.035 % per calendar day
Total penalty: to a maximum of 3% per unit		

Figure A4-11 Summary of penalties and the conditions under which they can be imposed

A4 LEGAL ASPECTS

The percentages relate to the total price of the unit. In this case, the unit is a production unit, i.e. a definable part of the total plant. If units cannot be defined, the penalties are based on the total price of the plant.

Reference parameters

3.3.2 Entry of key words in the IT system (contract file)

In this step, an alphabetical key word register is created and entered into the computer system. It contains terms that can appear in more than one contractual provision (e.g. penalty). Summaries of the relevant provision are also included for each term in the file. Reference is also made to relevant provision in the contract (What is regulated, where is it regulated and how is it regulated?).

Key word register

Contract execution instruments are created, at the latest, when the contract file is created. These include forms, work instructions, summaries of overlapping tasks, definitions of the customer and contractor´s performance, as well as graphs and charts. Figure A4-12 shows a list of drawings with a comparison of actual and target dates and an approval date.

Contract execution instruments

LIST OF DRAWINGS							
No.	Index	Content of drawing	Date		Release date	Note	Distributed to
			Target	Actual			

Figure A4-12 List of drawings with variance comparison (sample)

Figure A4-13 shows a sample construction site daily report. The entries relating to impairments, changes and additional work or services are particularly important. These have to be recorded meticulously so that subsequent claims can be asserted or prevented. A tool similar to a daily report could theoretically also be used with other project types. Although the daily report is only one aspect of project reporting, the majority of contractually-relevant events occur on the building site, when machines are being installed, for instance, and in connection with the working relationship between the contractor and its subcontractors.

Job report

A4 LEGAL ASPECTS

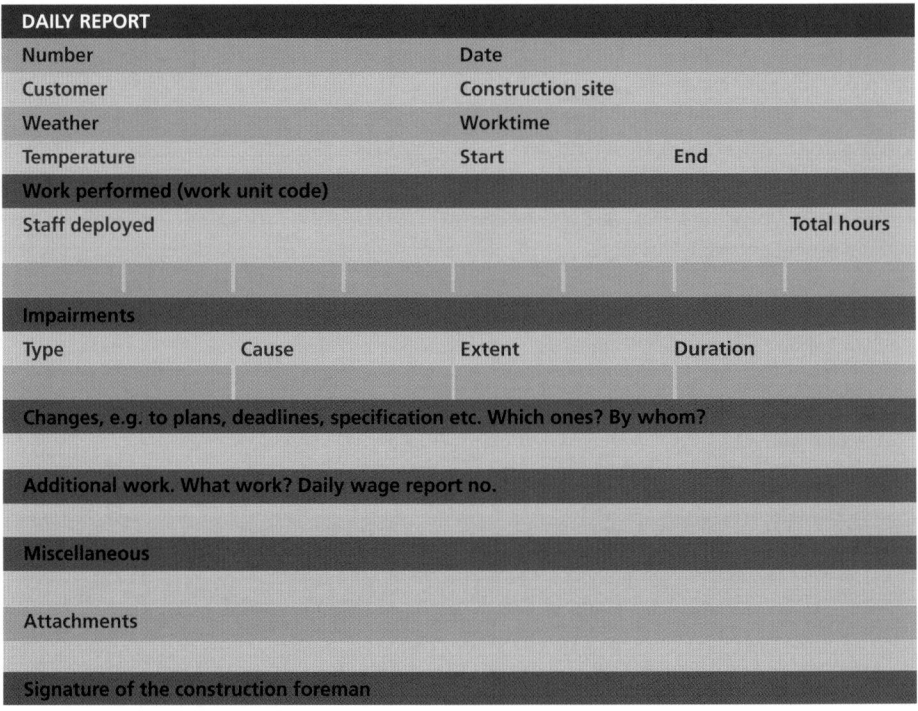

Figure A4-13 Construction site daily report

3.3.3 Contract activity monitoring

The objective of this procedure is to coordinate the workflow from a contractual viewpoint, to issue warnings to parties to the contract in the event of performance impairment (e.g. delays) and to record contract changes. Contract activity tracking includes all contractual correspondence, reports, all registrations and the recording of all contract-related changes and other contract-relevant data using a numerical system that permits simple access to the data and the items of correspondence at all times.

Numerical system

Contract administrator

Preservation of evidence

The contract administrator is responsible for ensuring that the contract is performed to the letter not just in respect of its content but also in respect of the contract formalities involved. In order to enable this, all evidence – i.e. all correspondence, all change logs and minutes of meetings, construction site daily reports, photos, permits, names and statements of witnesses – must be preserved. Comprehensive documentation on contract execution, as well as on goods delivered and services rendered, must exist. The contract administrator is responsible for the collection and archiving of all such documents.

3.3.3.1 Contract changes

Contract changes represent a special aspect of contract activity tracking. For example, they can become necessary if the customer´s requirements change, if new official regulations are introduced or if technical conditions change (→ Chapter C7). Since changes to the original contract can affect essential aspects such as the range of services expected of the contractor, the customer´s obligation to pay, and schedules, they must be negotiated by the individuals responsible on both the customer´s and contractor's sides. These people are often the project managers.

It is then necessary to determine whether a provision governing changes to the contract is included in the principal contract and which persons have the authority to sign for contractual changes with legally-binding effect. If such a provision exists, the parties must ensure precise compliance. If no such provision is included in the contract, the responsible persons on both sides must negotiate how these changes are to be made effective. Their agreement must be set down in writing by the individuals who signed the principal contract. Generally, it is specified that the project managers on both sides need to draw up and sign change logs whenever changes to the contract are necessary. When this document is signed, the change becomes legally effective and forms part of the principal contract.

Change provisions

Change logs

Any agreement between other representatives of the parties (e.g. construction site foremen) is not legally effective. The contract administrator must inform all project team members that change agreements are only effective if they are signed by the project manager.

3.3.4 Claims

Any change to the contract deliverables always affects the contract. In extreme cases, it can actually result in an unwanted or unknowing change to the contract that could constitute grounds for claims.

Inadvertent contract changes

4 Claim management

Claim management is a field of project management that involves the monitoring and appraisal of deviations and/or changes and their economic consequences for the purpose of identifying and asserting claims.

Many companies have introduced claim management processes in response to the globalisation of markets. They often have their own claim management departments because this is such an important field, though many also outsource claim management activities to specialist firms. Claim management is all about identifying deviations from projected values (→ Chapter C9) by way of variance analyses. It involves the pursuit of the claims identified by means of these analyses and taking measures to defend the contractor against counter-claims (= own and third-party claims). The additional revenue generated by the enforcement of claims can be surprisingly significant.

Tasks / activities

Own / third-party claims

Claims can be asserted in respect of
- contract term extensions
- additional remuneration

A claim is a subsequent demand made by one party to a contract to the other when
- change agreements exist
- additional work is performed on the basis of oral instructions
- the other party fails to perform its contractual obligations or performs them defectively
- it can be proven that contract execution has been impaired or interrupted

Differentiation is made between claims ensuing from supplementary contractual agreements and claims resulting from other deviations from planned requirements. The former arise from contract

Types of claim

changes and associated remuneration claims. The latter arise from additional claims above and beyond what was agreed in the contract.

All available documentation tools should be used to record deviations from contractual requirements. They include change requests or logs, correspondence and construction site reports that show evidence of changes to performance or dates. When claims are dealt with promptly, some of the more cost-intensive documentation processes can be dispensed with. It is helpful here if the parties agree upon claim and change management procedures (→ Chapter C7).

Agreement on procedure

Example
The project managers from both parties decide every week, binding for both parties, on the validity of claims and their remuneration.

4.1 The generation of additional revenues through claims

The success of many projects is dependent on a well-structured claim management system. A two-percent profit margin is the norm in large-scale projects. In comparison, potential revenue from claims totals 25 to 30 percent of the project volume. The two-percent margin can easily be wiped out by only marginal cost overruns in the project. Strict claims management not only safeguards this margin, but also offers the chance of additional profit from the claims. As a rule of thumb, around 50 percent of potential claims are actually enforced. The resulting additional revenues from claims can constitute up to 20 percent of the project´s original value.

Total amount of claims

Example
At the time when the electrical equipment for a sewage plant was delivered, the original contract value was approximately EUR 7 million and the profit margin EUR 140,000. Claims amounting to EUR 1.7 million were asserted. EUR 1 million in revenue was obtained from enforced claims, and the resulting profit margin was EUR 20,000. This constitutes more than 14 percent additional profit.

4.2 The interface between contract administration and claim management

The border between project contract administration and claim management is a fluid one. Figure A4-14 clearly shows that the initial focus is on contract administration. Once the contract is signed, however, the emphasis shifts toward claim management. As this shift occurs, the contract administration methods used to ensure the proper execution of the contract increasingly deviate from the profit oriented claim management methods.

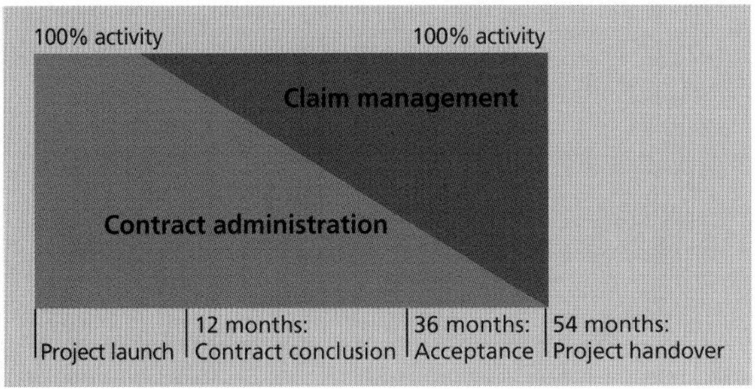

Profit orientation

Figure A4-14 Contract administration and claim management activities during a project

4.3 Procedure

There is no binding or standard claim management procedure because the procedures depend to a great extent on the unique characteristics of the sector of industry or project. However, a number of logical steps and action models have now become established in practice.

4.3.1 Execution phase

Claim management activities commence as soon as the contract is signed. The longer ago an incident took place, the more difficult it is to prove that the incident happened and its cause. This gives rise to unnecessary costs. Therefore, it is important to notify the other party of a claim as soon as a deviation is recorded. This can take the form of a claim notification. The claim manager must make sure that he cannot be accused of failing to notify the other party or of notifying him too late.

Prompt action

Claim notifications

> **Example**
> *If the customer does not make its construction site available on the agreed date, the contractor has to send a letter to the customer reminding him of his contractual obligations without delay. If the customer's missed deadlines cause delays on the contractor's side, the contractor must request that customer reschedules all of his deadlines.*

4.3.1.1 Content of the claim letter
The claim letter must at least include the standard content of a reminder.
- Status
- Claim
- Setting of a deadline

The claim must be precisely formulated.

Warning letter format

> **Example**
> *'Please replace the defective cellar insulation with insulation that conforms to the contractually agreed building specification.'*

This simple format can be supplemented by the following [1]:
- Affected performance, facility, equipment etc.
- Incident with date, facts, causes (proof in the attachment)
- Description of the original contractual agreement
- Description of the effect(s) of the incident
- Demands (dates, costs, performances)
- Specification of a deadline for response and, if appropriate, the consequences in the event of non-response
- Documentation of the incident and causes

4.3.2 Support through configuration management

If configuration management takes place consistently throughout a project (→ Chapter C7), any deviations from the contract during the project, particularly product deviations, will be documented by the change management team (also called: configuration accounting). This includes approvals of

Configuration accounting

changes by the affected parties. The claim manager then only has to request the relevant contractual data from the configuration management team for further processing.

4.3.3 Treatment of adversarial claims

Precautionary measures

The following precautionary measures enable the timely prevention of third party claims [2]:
- Familiarisation of the project team with the contract and with contract changes (e.g. through the use of change forms)
- Timely identification, clarification and documentation of ambiguities
- Regulation of change management (if possible, in contractual form)
- Active project controlling
- Regular checks to ensure conformity by both parties to contract
- Inclusion of claim management on the agenda of project meetings
- Checking of correspondence (especially claims, complaints, changes, orders) and provision of responses in accordance with claim management practices or as otherwise appropriate
- Analysis of behaviour and statements of the other party to the contract in terms of the potential for new claims
- Documentation of all incidents, deviations or unusual occurrences
- Obtaining written confirmation of instructions, decisions, changes and important documents

4.4 Subjective attitudes

Conflicting interests

Personal relationships

Concerns that claim management will mar the positive relationship between the parties to the contract if claims are asserted each time a deviation occurs are unjustified and, in some cases, even dangerous. Foreign customers view such worries as a weakness on the part of German contract partners. The claim management team – especially in international and large-scale projects – must accept from the outset that the customer and contractor will have conflicting interests. At the same time, good personal relationships between the parties´ representatives are obviously useful. They can ensure that the two sides remain objective and continue to communicate with each other even when claim disputes arise. Reciprocal generosity when insignificant incidents occur can help both parties to save costs.

Danger of subsequent claims

In claim management, planning, construction and engineering services are becoming increasingly important. While, in the past, it was mainly deviations in the execution of construction work that gave rise to claims, these now arise principally from deviations from planning, construction and engineering specifications. Since such deviations can have a considerable impact in the early stages of a project, managers should remember that their effect in terms of subsequent claims can be even more dramatic.

> **Example**
> *The accidental back-to-front design of a bridge section goes unnoticed until an attempt is made to put it in place. The result is a lengthy construction stoppage. It is the claim manager´s job to ascertain who is liable here: the construction company, the bridge section manufacturer, the assembly firm (defective preparatory work) or the customer (unprofessional technical acceptance or preliminary tests).*

A4 LEGAL ASPECTS

Engineers should only ever implement technical changes on the basis of explicit written instructions from their own managers. Often, they tend to substitute good solutions with better solutions without any consideration to costs or contractual agreements. However, a better solution can sometimes result in a deviation from the contract. A skilful change manager on the customer´s side will view this as non-performance of the contract and respond by asserting claims.

Written instructions for engineers

4.5 Systematic work processes

Claim management predominantly uses variance analyses to identify deviations from the contract (deviation of the actual status from the target status), (→ Figure A4-15).

Variance analyses

Example
The original contract value (= target value) was 100, the current value is 130 (= actual value). This actual value constitutes a 30 percent deviation from the original contract value. It is the job of the claim manager to realise this 30 percent as additional revenue.

Figure A4-15 Claim management scenario (example)

4.5.1 Procedure when deviations occur

When deviations from the contract occur as a result of accepted change agreements or supplementary agreements, the procedure is simple. The claims resulting from these additional agreements are asserted in the same way as claims resulting from the principal contract. However, if the deviations occur as a result of performance impairment or work carried out outside the terms of the contract, a different procedure is required. The following steps should be taken:
1. Preparation of a list of relevant incidents (non-contracted work, performance impairment)
2. Evaluation (variance analysis)
3. Legal assessment (of individual issues)
4. Incident processing and documentation

Steps

4.5.1.1 List of contractually-relevant incidents
Incidents that are relevant for claims can initially be recorded in a simple list. This list should include a consecutive number, the date, the incident, the provisional value, the partner or supplier (= subcontractor) responsible and a reference to the relevant provision in the contract or documentation. Figure A4-16 shows an example of such a list.

A4 LEGAL ASPECTS

CLAIMS					
Consortium			No. 90		
Date	Description	Costs/ currency	Code, computerised contract file	Supplier/partner	Correspondence, documents, notes
6.3.2004	Cleaning of boiler Nr. III	3,100 EUR	111.3	- / -	Ro 302/98; 2.3.2004

Figure A4-16 List of claims in tabular format

Possible reasons

The main reasons for the documentation of potential claims are
- performance that exceeds or falls below specifications
- defective performance
- changes to scheduled dates
- design changes
- the taking over of tasks by the customer
- delays or interruptions

4.5.1.2 Evaluation (variance analysis)

Initially, lump-sum costs incurred as a result of the variation are included in the list (e.g. non-payment of a deliverable or a contractual penalty due to delay). More precise figures can be obtained when the claims are assessed individually – by making a detailed comparison of contractually-agreed and actual figures (→ Chapter C9). For example, the target schedule will contain the contractually-agreed dates while the actual schedule shows the current status. This comparison provides information about additional requirements in terms of staff and equipment. A cost variance analysis is also carried out. Each performance impairment results in substantial additional costs, especially as a result of the delays before equipment and personnel can be used.

Costs/deadlines/ performance

Recognition of changes to work done/ additional work done

Changes to work done or additional work done can be ascertained by
- comparing documentation on the order and on the actual execution
- comparing the contractual provisions relating to the project processes and constraints with the actual status and
- work required in order to comply with technical standards (e.g. DIN or ISO)

4.5.1.3 Legal assessments

A legal assessment must be obtained before claims can be enforced. A lawyer clarifies whether or not a claim can be asserted on the basis of the contract. If not, he must specify whether a claim formulated on the basis of existing documentation is likely to be enforceable. The assessment is also a means of legally evaluating issues that are not clearly regulated in the contract and for deciding whether a solid basis for the assertion of a claim exists.

4.5.1.4 Incident processing and documentation

When incidents are processed individually, detailed evaluations are obtained in a second procedure that also involves checking existing documentation with regard to the incident under review. It is necessary to ascertain whether firm evidence can be provided of the deviation in question on the basis of existing documentation. Records, construction site reports, photographs and any witness statements available must therefore provide a complete picture of the sequence of events that caused the incident and the counter-measures taken. For example, it is necessary to prove that the customer

Firm evidence

A4 LEGAL ASPECTS

did not complete excavation work on the construction site by the agreed date, that he received a warning and that the contractor was unable to meet his deadlines as a direct result of this delay.

The claim management software available nowadays also simplifies the systematic processing of individual claims.

Software support

4.5.2 Implementation

The preparation of individual claims involves the following steps.

Steps

1. Gathering documents that give the reasons for a change or for the initiation of a change (e.g. builder's instructions, meeting notes, inspection notes)
2. Consecutive numbering of documents
3. Substantiation and clarification of changes by providing timelines
4. Provision of an illustrated comparison of the work agreed in the contract and the subsequent variations
5. Comparison of the contractual position against the work specification and the claim position (a breakdown is necessary for this)
6. Provision of the original calculation as a basis for working out additional remuneration (application of inflation clause)
7. Listing of claim documents gathered pertaining to the incident
8. Provision of a summary showing the original price versus the new price

Figures A4-17 and A4-18 show examples of form-based summaries

No.	Date	Document	Content
\multicolumn{4}{l}{**DOCUMENTS RELATING TO IMPAIRMENTS AND ADDITIONAL COSTS**}
1.	03.02.01	Con. to Cus.	Planning documents, construction specifications missing, machinery not installed
2.	20.02.01	Con. to Cus.	Plans for pipe work and the positioning of metering points
3.	10.11.01	Con. to Cus.	No construction specifications
4.	15.12.01	Cus. to Con.	Completion date changed from 10.11.02 to 31.12.03
5.	13.11.02	Sub-con. to Con.	No construction specifications, travel expenses to be charged
6.	05.05.03	Con. to Cus.	No programming documents
7.	23.05.03	Sub-con. to Con.	No construction specifications – plant component cannot be commissioned
8.	07.06.03	Con. to Cus.	Confirmation of impairment
9.	20.10.03	Sub-con. report	Additional programming activities, changes requested by cus.
10.	15.11.03	Sub-con. report	Reasons for additional costs
11.	18.12.03	Minutes of the meeting	Additional work
12.	22.01.04	Minutes of discussion Sub-con., Con. and Cus.	Changes to tax rates and regulations

Figure A4-17 List of claim documents

A4 LEGAL ASPECTS

CONTRACT PRICE-BASED CLAIMS		
1. Original contract		
Performance specification – Appendix C Total scope, price	EUR (net)	10,574,000.00
2. Claims		
As per list, price	EUR (net)	1,723,673.00
Statement of further justifications for the claims in the attachments: – Facts on which the claims are based – Substantiation of the amount claimed – List of claim documents – Claim documentation file		

Figure A4-18 Details of the contract price and the additional amount claimed

4.5.3 Review of results

Rule of thumb for total enforceable claims

	Σ Higher prices paid by the other party vs. originally agreed prices
–	Σ Accepted price reductions to be paid to the other party
+	Σ Price reductions granted by the sub-contractor
–	Σ Price increases paid to the sub-contractor
+	Σ Cost reductions
–	Σ Cost increases
–	Σ Costs incurred in processing claims
=	**CLAIM-RELATED PROFITS**

As a rule of thumb, around 50 percent of the total volume of claims is enforceable. Figure A4-19 provides an example of how to ascertain the approximate revenue that can be generated by systematic claim management.

Figure A4-19 Example of a calculation to ascertain the financial results achieved through claim management [3]

4.6 Prevention

Early recognition

The following checklist activities can be used to assist with claim prevention and help identify potential claims in good time [4]:

1. Implementation of a project kick-off workshop (→ Chapter C1) with the entire project team
2. Issuing of regular memos about the contract
3. Creation of checklists for typical claim situations
4. Agreements on the procedure to be used in claim situations
5. Regular analyses of the behaviour of the contract partner with regard to potential claims
6. Comprehensive documentation of all changes, incidents of damage, warranty incidents etc.
7. Operation of a change management system
8. Comprehensive minute-taking at relevant meetings
9. Ensuring that detailed daily construction site records are kept
10. If necessary, gathering of photographic documentation
11. Paying attention to witnesses and, if necessary, consulting an expert
12. Recording telephone calls
13. Always obtaining written confirmation of instructions, decisions, changes and important documents

4.7 Costs

Volume of project		Costs of claim management
To	1 MEU	approx. 3.0 %
To	10 MEU	approx. 1.0 %
To	50 MEU	approx. 0.6 %
From	50 MEU	approx. 0.5 %

While the costs of claim management should in principle be allocated to the specific project it is difficult to allocate definitive figures to the costs of claim management. The figures shown here, however, may be useful as a reference.

Reference values for costs

4.8 Errors

The following errors can occur during the claim management process:
- Lack of understanding that a claim expresses a right to remuneration for work performed.
- No precise differentiation between schedule change claims and remuneration claims.
- Lack of communication between the construction site foremen and the decision makers.
- Lack of awareness that claims in respect of planning and engineering work must be asserted in the same way as claims during the contract execution phase.
- No differentiation between claims relating to contractual agreements and claims relating to supplementary work. Claims relating to contractual agreements are associated with an additional order, while claims for supplementary work are not. The contractor must prove that the customer issued instructions for the work to be performed.
- Lack of willingness to pursue an identified claim.
- A failure to analyse the contract from a claims perspective.
- A failure to observe the contractually-agreed claims procedure.
- Inadequate documentation on the claim.
- Imprecise assessment of the claim value.
- Lack of a contractual or legal basis for the claim.
- Inadequate statements of cause and effect.
- Inappropriate claim formats.

Claims should be presented to the opposing party in an easy-to-comprehend format. The person dealing with the claims should not have to search for documents in order to understand and assess a claim.

Presentation

4.9 Relationship to other project management functions

Contract administration and claim management are closely associated with other project management functions.

4.9.1 Configuration and change management

In a project, both the customer and the contractor can propose or request changes ($\rightarrow$ Chapter C7). If they are accepted in accordance with the agreed change procedure, these changes become contractually effective and thereby constitute a change to the contract. The contract administrator is responsible for amending and supplementing the contracts in accordance with the specifications laid down by the change manager. If a change is not formally approved, this could constitute the basis for adversarial claims from both parties.

Agreed change procedures

4.9.2 Risk management

Consequences of performance impairment

Risk management enables the identification and prevention of risks (→ Chapter C3). The timely identification of risks provides a good opportunity to assert claims. In this context, risks constitute the possibility that damaging changes to the situation will occur. These risks are documented and limited within the context of contract administration. The contract administrator identifies all potential performance impairments and their associated effects. The recording and description of risks is a virtually automatic process. Excerpts from the contract and additional comments can serve as evidence. Risks can be allocated to the following categories:

Risk categories

- Predictable risks
- Specific, non-quantifiable risks ensuing from flaws in the contract
- Specific risks in the environment that are not yet quantifiable

Alternative ways of handling risk

There are five alternative ways of handling risk

- Acceptance
- Elimination
- Insurance
- Passing on
- Avoidance

The latter two are particularly significant for contract administration.

Risk reduction options

It is common practice to pass on as many recognised project risks as possible to sub-contractors via contractual provisions, in other words by transferring risks to third parties. When goods are delivered to other countries, the transport risk is often passed on to the supplier, as the sub-contractor, by agreeing upon Free on Board (FOB) delivery.

Further options for limiting or reducing risks are

- precise assessment of the risks,
- the development of possible alternative or counter-measures and
- making case-by-case decisions on specific counter-measures when serious risks occur.

Counter-measures are associated with claim management because recognised risks can always be associated with opportunities. If a risk relating to the timely execution of specific contractual agreements is recognised, a claim can be asserted during this phase if any unscheduled delays occur. It is recommended that the responsible members of the contract administration and risk management teams also cooperate closely on planning out their activities.

4.9.3 Quality management

Cooperation between contract administrators and risk managers

Contract administration and claim management are always elements of a Total Quality Management system (TQM → Chapter C8). The TQM principle of avoiding mistakes by implementing processes correctly from the outset and thereby remaining in control should be applied consistently in project management.

A4 LEGAL ASPECTS

Self-assessment questions for each certification level

No.	Question	Level D	Level C	Level B	Level A	Self-assessment
A4.01	What types of contracts can apply to projects?	2	2	3	3	☐
A4.02	When is a contract considered to be accepted or to have become effective?	1	2	3	3	☐
A4.03	When is a contract invalid?	1	2	3	3	☐
A4.04	What must be taken into account when international contracts are concluded?	1	1	3	3	☐
A4.05	What special features characterise project contracts?	1	2	3	3	☐
A4.06	What rights has a customer in the event of performance impairment?	2	2	3	4	☐
A4.07	What rights has a contractor in the event of performance impairment?	2	2	3	4	☐
A4.08	What is the difference between contracts concluded with contractors, consortia and partnerships?	1	2	3	3	☐
A4.09	What special risks are associated with project contracts?	1	2	3	4	☐
A4.10	What tasks and process steps are involved in contract administration and what are the primary contract administration tools?	1	2	3	4	☐
A4.11	What skills/knowledge should a contract administrator have?	1	2	2	2	☐
A4.12	What is the claim management process and when does it commence?	2	2	3	4	☐
A4.13	Which project management functions are associated with claim management?	1	3	3	4	☐
A4.14	What differences or similarities exist between change management and claim management?	2	3	3	4	☐

A4 LEGAL ASPECTS

A5 PROJECT PERFORMANCE AND SUCCESS FACTORS

Before implementation, an organisation has to establish its own performance parameters for evaluating whether a project is a success. This process not only involves the prioritisation of hard objectives such as deadlines, costs and quality, but also a decision on what significance is accorded to the satisfaction of the various stakeholders. This chapter investigates the traditional definition of project success. It provides project managers with an awareness of the different perspectives and approaches that exist for evaluating project success and explains the evaluation procedures that are available to them.

1 Definition

Many older project management textbooks offer a very simple definition of project success. A project is considered to be a success if the project team satisfies all the customer's requirements by the agreed date and within the agreed budget. To be more precise, a project is a success if
- it meets or surpasses the customer's specifications,
- it is completed on or before the agreed date and
- the budget is adhered to or undercut.

This sounds perfectly plausible at first glance. On closer scrutiny, however, a number of problematic issues relating to this definition become evident. It implies, for example, that a customer is satisfied with the project outcome because his requirements have been met. However, can this really be assumed in every project? What if various parameters change during its course?

Problematic definition

Example
In a software development project, tests reveal that users have difficulty operating some of the functions. As a result, the specification should really be modified. The customer suggests this to the project manager. However, the project manager rejects all change requests, citing the contract with the customer, and postpones them until the next version of the software is developed. He believes that risks associated with such changes for the customer (e.g. lower sales of the software) and for the company executing the project (e.g. customer dissatisfaction) are negligible.

This example shows that the project manager not only has the task of controlling the parameters in the project triangle – costs, time and quality (= performance), but he also has to establish whether the customer is satisfied. More recent approaches to performance measurement include the Project Excellence Model, which was developed by the German Association for Project Management (GPM) (→ Chapter C8).

Customer satisfaction

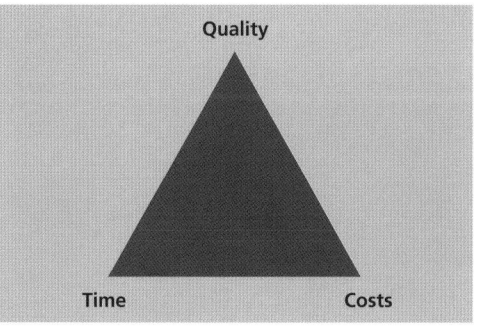

Figure A5-1 The project triangle

2 Stakeholder objectives

The customer is not the only factor to be considered. Other individuals, groups and organisations (= stakeholders, → Chapter A3) are affected by the project. Examples of stakeholders include works councils, company departments, suppliers or even the mayor of the town where a large-scale project is being realised. A project manager has to identify his stakeholders and assess what they think about the project implementation and outcome.

Fixed and variable project stakeholders

Project team members are obviously stakeholders right from the outset of the project, as are senior managers of the company implementing the project – even if they are not directly involved in its implementation. However, the group of `other project stakeholders´ differs in size and composition from project to project. It is, therefore, a project manager´s job in a new project to identify the relevant stakeholder groups. Stakeholders in the same project can have entirely conflicting opinions of it, i.e. their aims (→ Chapter C2) may differ.

> **Example**
> *A retail company has commissioned an advertising agency to produce a new catalogue. The quality of the printed catalogue is excellent, and the company even receives an award for it. The marketing and sales departments are therefore very satisfied with the result. Yet the project is a bone of contention for the financial director because it cost far more than the fixed price that the agency quoted.*

3 Priorities

In recent years, a number of authors have opted for a general definition of project success that takes the project stakeholders into account. For example, as the basis for a study, Lechler [1] defined project success as follows:

> `A project is successful if the persons involved are satisfied and positively evaluate the quality of the technical solution, as well as budget and schedule adherence.´

Subjective view of project success

The term `technical solution´ corresponds to the element of quality in the project triangle of project management. However, this rather generalised definition does not specify who the persons involved are. The phrase, `positively evaluate´ permits a very subjective view of project success.
According to this definition, a project can be considered successful even if it was associated with time and budget overruns, because the quality (= quality of the project deliverable) is evaluated as very good. In other words, if the customer accords higher priority to quality than to time and costs in a project that exceeds both timelines and budget, the project is considered a success.

> **Example**
> *Since the price of electronic components is falling rapidly, a manufacturer must ensure strict schedule adherence in development projects. Development costs are far less important in comparison. An electronics company has calculated annual market growth of 20 percent and an annual decline in price of twelve percent for products with a five-year lifespan. In this scenario, a six-month development delay results in a profit reduction of 45 percent. However, if the R&D budget is overrun by 50 percent, it only depresses the profit margin by 22 percent [2]. This is why adherence to deadlines has higher priority.*

In many cases – at least in the long term – quality is also a priority from the customer's perspective. In time, his consternation about non-compliance with the schedule and budget overruns will abate. However, a defective product that the consumer has to use every day will cause long-term aggravation.

In order to measure project success, it is necessary to allocate priorities to the parameters of the project triangle (T – C – Q).

3.1 Prioritisation of stakeholder satisfaction

Yet this still doesn't answer all the questions. Is the satisfaction of project team members or senior managers just as important as the satisfaction of the customer? After all, it is the customer who finances the project, and the contractor obviously hopes that a follow-up project will be commissioned. The Project Excellence Model (→ Chapter C8) accords lower significance to the satisfaction of employees and other project stakeholders than to the satisfaction of the customer. Anyone using the model can accord project-specific weighting factors to it.

Project Excellence Model

4 Time of performance measurement

When to measure a project's performance must also be considered in any assessment of its success. It is extremely important to distinguish between project management success and product success in this connection.

Project management success and product success

> **Example**
> A company develops a medical diagnostic appliance for which a project team drafts a specification that the managing board (as internal project sponsor) signs. The appliance is developed within the agreed timeframe and budget. The physicians that test it confirm its compliance with all specifications. The project team, managing board and physicians are satisfied. Because the project has been successfully concluded, project management success [3] can be established. Yet the market launch is disappointing. The company does not achieve the forecast sales figures because a rival company has launched an appliance of comparable quality at a lower price during the project lifecycle. This means that product success [4] is low.

The extent of success also depends when performance is measured. Often, it is impossible to reach any conclusions about product success until several years after close-out. For example, a company cannot establish whether its new project management concept really improves the project implementation process efficiency until several projects have been implemented.

A project can also be associated with high product success and low project management success. Products that are developed at high cost and with extensive delays can turn out to be a great success. The teams in research projects don't always attain the desired results, yet an unexpected outcome sometimes provides a point of departure for an extremely successful and innovative product.

> **Example**
> Brightly-coloured Post-It notes can be found in practically every office. Yet they were invented by pure coincidence. A member of an in-house research team was assigned to the task of developing

an extra-strong adhesive. However, the product of his research activities was an adhesive that was so weak, it was easy to pull off again. Nobody knew what to do with the stuff. Years later, one of his colleagues came up with the idea of applying this adhesive to bookmarks because his bookmark was always falling out of the book. It marked the beginning of an incredible success story.

Project as a phase of innovative success

Figure A5-2 illustrates the relationship between the various dimensions of project success [5]. In the scenario shown, the project is only viewed as one phase of an extensive innovation process. The relationship can be effectively illustrated on the basis of the above two examples (medical diagnostics appliance, Post-It notes).

Dimensions of project success

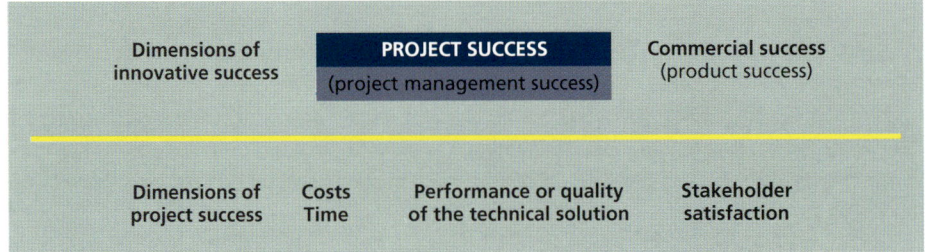

Figure A5-2 Dimensions of project success

5 The performance measurement procedure

Priorities for `hard´ success criteria

Before a project commences, the customer must establish criteria for the subsequent evaluation of its success. Otherwise, there is a risk that a gloss will be put on the project or that excessive project costs will be covered up at some time in the future. In terms of project management success, this means that the customer must give priority to `hard´ success criteria such as time, costs and quality. With quality, it is useful to differentiate between essential and non-essential features.

It is also necessary to identify project stakeholders and establish the weighting that will be accorded to their opinions. The desired product success must also be defined. This is why some project management manuals strongly recommend that the business case is established at the outset of the project. The business case defines the positive long-term effects for the organisation that are anticipated by the stakeholders and the people in charge of the project.

Tracking parameter changes

At regular intervals during the project implementation phase, the customer has to review whether the project´s existence is justified in its current form or whether key parameters have changed. In practice, these reviews and the later assessment of product success are often disregarded. The project is therefore mentally shelved before it has come to a de facto conclusion.

6 Project success factors

Many authors of empirical studies have focused on project success factors. A metastudy by Lechler evaluates 44 empirical analyses comprising more than 5,700 projects of diverse types. He also added one of his own surveys of many different projects in Germany. Lechler defines the term success factor as follows:

A5 PROJECT PERFORMANCE AND SUCCESS FACTORS

'Critical success factors are the few variables that have to be spot-on if the project is to be a success. They represent the areas of management that require specific and continuous attention to increase the project's chances of success.' [6]

These are, therefore, factors that the management can influence itself. Surprisingly, Lechler's findings are unequivocal. He was able to identify eleven success factors (→ Figure A5-3).

FACTORS OF SUCCESS	IMPACT ON SUCCESS			
	++	+	0	−
Objective definition	17	2	1	0
Communication	16	6	0	0
Planning	9	3	1	0
Senior management	9	2	0	0
Controlling	7	1	0	1
Project manager's authority	6	3	0	0
Project team's know-how	6	0	1	0
Project team's motivation	5	3	0	0
Project manager's know-how	4	3	1	2
Planning and control tools	4	1	0	0
Participation	3	4	0	0
(Result of 44 studies)				

Influence of success factors

The table in Figure A5-3 shows how often the various factors were surveyed in the individual studies and how strongly they influenced project success. Two plus signs indicate a very strong positive influence, and one plus sign denotes a significant but weaker level of influence. If a zero is shown next to a factor, no influence could be ascertained. A minus sign indicates negative influence.

Figure A5-3 Lechler's success factors of project management [7]

6.1 Recommendations

Lechler derived the following – abridged and summarised – recommendations [8] from his metastudy and his own analysis:

Recommendations

1. Senior management has a very strong influence on the project outcome. It therefore has to expend a great deal of time and energy on supporting the project.
2. The project manager must have a powerful, formal status with considerable (decision-making) authority.
3. The project manager must have good management skills. This recommendation highlights the significance of appropriate training programmes.
4. The successful implementation of a project depends on the ability of the project team. In real-life projects, departmental managers are often reluctant to part with their most capable employees for selfish reasons.
5. Social and self-organisation skills are crucial. Team development activities and appropriate training for staff are therefore very important.
6. A project manager should have a participative style of management (→ Chapter D3). This means that the team members should be involved in decisions, especially in the idea engineering phase.
7. A project manager must ensure that efficient formal communication structures are in place, that all persons affected by the project are involved at an early point in time and that information is communicated on a selective basis. Recipients won't be able to cope if provided with too much information. Informal communication (→ Chapter D4) can be encouraged if the project manager works in close proximity to the team members.

A5 PROJECT PERFORMANCE AND SUCCESS FACTORS

8. Planning and control tools are key success factors. In the early years of project management, it was a common belief that these were the only tools. They must be responsive and it must be possible to adapt them to the requirements of a specific project.
9. The project manager has to identify and resolve conflicts (→ Chapter D5) as quickly as possible. Preventive conflict management is preferable to reactive conflict management.
10. Special significance is accorded to a detailed time schedule. Lomnitz confirms this by saying: `Tell me how your project will start and I´ll tell you how it will end.´ Adequate time must be provided for the drafting of the project specification. It is important to involve the customer in the early phases of the project, for example in the objective definition phase.

Customer involvement in IT projects

The strong influence of the company´s senior management on the success of the project is also emphasised in later studies, such as those implemented by KPMG, the Standish Group and the Daily Telegraph [9]. Analyses [10] that only cover IT projects emphasise that the involvement of the customer is not only essential in the start-up phase, but also throughout the entire project lifecycle. Projects can involve various groups or individuals with very different objectives. Examples are groups of consumers, the organisation´s IT department, the steering committee and senior management.

Self-assessment questions for each certification level

No.	Question	Level D	Level C	Level B	Level A	Self-assessment
A5.1	When can a project be considered to be a success?	2	3	3	4	☐
A5.2	What are the dimensions of project success?	2	3	3	4	☐
A5.3	What is the difference between project management success and product success in a project?	1	3	3	4	☐
A5.4	What recommendations can be derived from empirical studies on project success factors?	1	2	3	4	☐

A6 PROJECT ORGANISATION

A project organisation can take many forms. The relationship of a project to the base organisation can be structured in various ways (ICB Elements 22 & 23). This chapter describes the key forms of project organisation, their advantages and disadvantages. A balanced matrix for development projects is used as a case study to show the functions, responsibilities and powers of a project manager, project team and steering committee. Project control is an essential aspect of the project organisation. The significance of this function is explained using a project controller's job description.

1 Projects outside standard management structures

A special project organisation is necessary in the following circumstances:
- A project is highly complex in comparison to other projects.
- Resource usage exceeds a for the company critical threshold.
- A project is highly innovative or has high strategic significance from the company's perspective (e.g. entry into a new market segment).
- There is a high risk that the staff involved in the project will not be able to perform project-related tasks (e.g. due to high departmental workloads).

Project-specific organisation structures

In general, at least one of the above circumstances merits a special organisational measure to install a project organisation. Similar suggestions are also found in project management literature: Kummer, Spühler and Wyssen [1] believe that mild organisational interventions only suffice when the criteria listed in Figure A6-1 are satisfied:

Special organisational measures

CRITERION	IMPACT
Significance for the company	Low
Scope of the project	Low
Risk of not attaining targets	Low
Technology	Standard
Pressure of time	Low
Project lifecycle	Short
Complexity	Low
Central control requirements	Low
Employees allocated to the project	Part-time (line management organisation)
Personality of the project manager	Low relevance

Figure A6-1 Criteria for projects with low organisational structure requirements

The base organisation must define the criteria so that they can be applied in practice. For example, it has to establish what constitutes a short project lifecycle and when are central control requirements low. When these criteria have been defined, the people in charge of the project can make prompt decisions, as and when required, about whether special organisational precautions are necessary.

Defining criteria practically

A6 PROJECT ORGANISATION

1.1 Project companies

Projects that are legally and organisationally independent of the base organisation - implemented as a partnership or project company - are an exception to the rule. The Munich Local Authority, the Bavarian State Government and the Federal German Government established a project company for the construction projects for the 1972 Munich Olympics.

Legal independence Project companies [2] are organisations legally independent of the base organisation. Several firms or other organisations often hold stakes in these companies. Project companies with the legal form of a private limited company or a public limited company have identical project and organisational objectives. When the project objective has been reached, the company is liquidated.

International projects Madauss [3] compares three forms of organisation for international projects that make it possible to coordinate the activities of several companies:
- Partnership (a frequent form of organisation in construction projects)
- Integrated project team (IPT)
- Consortium (with one consortium member as general contractor)

Partnerships Based on his many years of experience in the aerospace industry, Madauss believes that partnerships are the wrong choice for complex projects. A partnership doesn't have a lead company with responsibility for the project as a whole.

Integrated project team The integrated project team is a better option if the participating companies can agree to transfer project management authority and responsibility to a project team which they themselves appoint and to which they report. Madauss recommends that the IPT should, in turn, report to a management company.

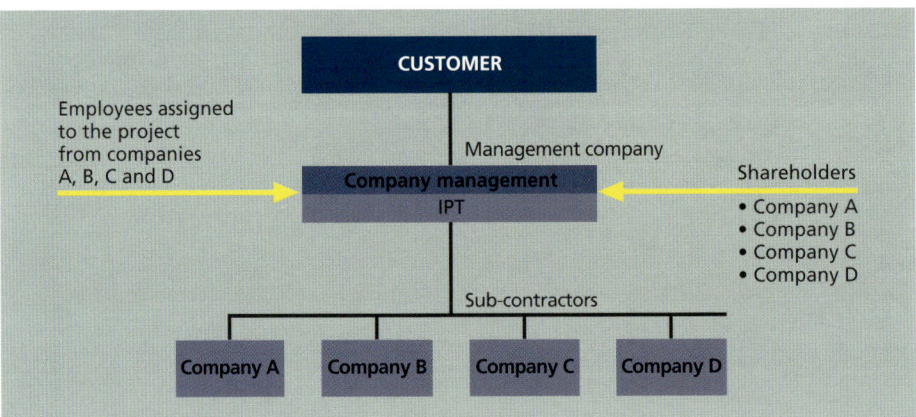

Figure A6-2 Integrated project team [4]

Consortial organisation A consortial organisation is considered to be the best solution [5]. It is governed by a consortial committee made up of representatives of the partners' managing boards. A chairman is appointed for a specific term, after which another chairman is appointed. The consortial committee decides which member will act as the lead company. The remaining members are sub-contractors.

A6 PROJECT ORGANISATION

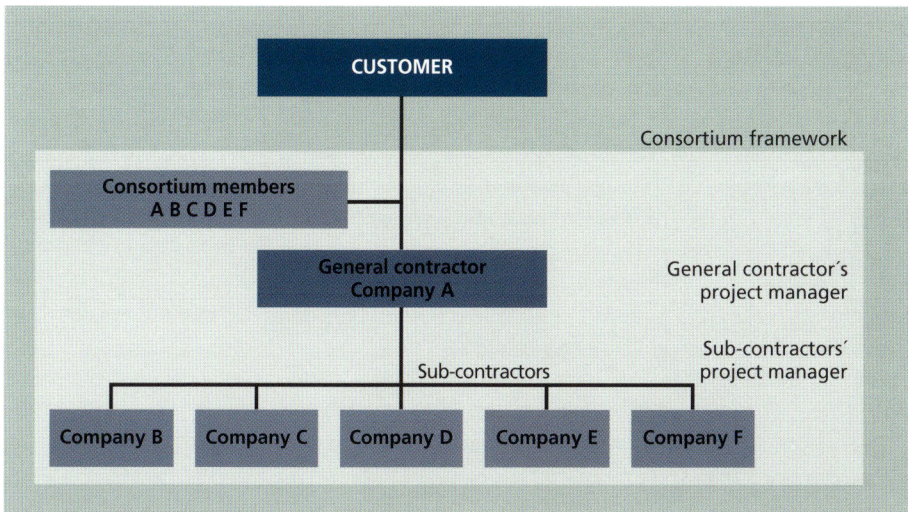

Figure A6-3 Consortial organisation [6]

2 Incorporation of projects in the base organisation

In most cases, projects are incorporated in the base organisation, which the ICB also describes as the line organisation. A base organisation can be a company, an association or an international aid organisation.

As many companies have found out over the years, a function staff-line organisation (→ Figure A6-1) is often unable to cope with a complex project. Such a project involves many separate activities in which specialists or organisational units have to be coordinated.

Complex projects

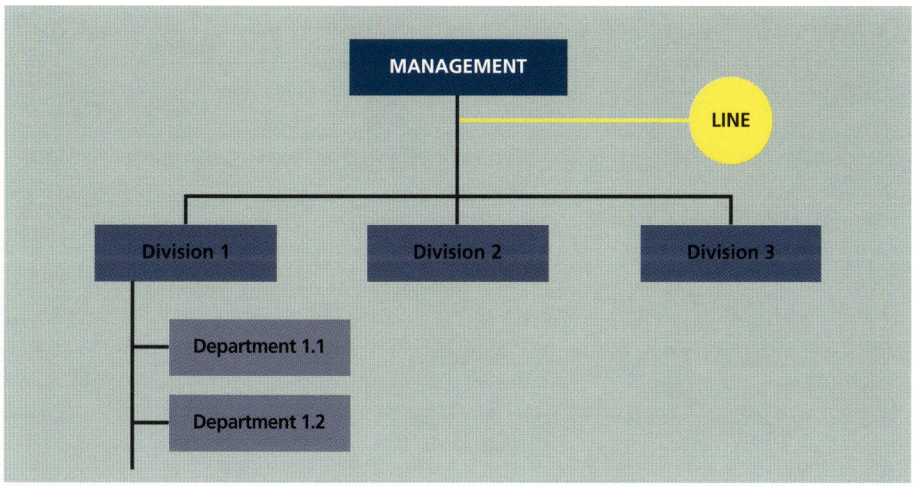

Figure A6-4 Pure line organisation

Sequential processes

Schröder [7] explained the problem of line organisations using the example of an external project that affects several divisions of a company with a function-based organisation. Here is a summary of his comments: A project with no special coordination measures tends to have sequential processes. This means that the individual steps are performed in sequence, as if linked together in a chain. After it has completed a task, a department passes on the documents and results to the next one. This second department, in turn, completes its tasks and passes on the results to yet another department. This process means that it is difficult to view the project as an integrated whole. However, if someone were to keep track of the project as a whole and optimally coordinate the sub-processes, it would be possible to reduce throughput times and costs.

Nevertheless, projects can be executed in the line. Research and development (R&D) projects often use this type of organisation. This works as long as
- in principle, only one organisational unit is responsible for the implementation of the project (e.g. a laboratory team),
- there are few interfaces to other organisational units and no shared resources,
- other departments only provide service functions and
- the project team is relatively small in size.

Control range

In this case, no special organisational measures are necessary within or outside the line organisation. For example, the laboratory manager automatically manages R&D projects in his lab without being formally appointed as project manager. It is important to ensure that the control range does not become too large. In other words, it is important that one manager is not responsible for too many projects at the same time.

3 Project boards

Many organisations install superordinate project boards or project steering committees in addition to the project manager, the project team and the departments. They are often called portfolio boards [8]. They are responsible for all projects in the company, or specific subsets, such as all R&D projects or development projects associated with a specific product line. The members of the project board are drawn from the company´s senior management and often hold positions at a higher management level than those involved in the project.

Tasks

A project board initiates a project, sets its approximate objectives and appoints its manager. It arbitrates in any disputes between project and departmental managers or in disputes between project managers. Its most important function is strategic project management. In contrast, a project manager is responsible for operational project management. He reports to the project board ($\rightarrow$ Chapter E3).

In simple terms, strategic project management is about making sure that the right projects are implemented. The project steering committee decides which of the many projects suggested are viable, vetoes the implementation of projects that have no prospect of success, and prioritises the selected projects. These important decisions can only be made by people who are familiar with the company´s business strategy and its entire project portfolio. A project manager would be unable to cope with this task.

3.1 Project-specific steering committees

A steering committee should be installed for any projects that involve major reorganisation measures. Its members are also the project´s superordinate managers and, in some cases, the project owner. The committee disbands when the project objective has been attained. It has the following functions and powers:
- to monitor project progress
- to decide on the acceptance or rejection of milestone results
- to clarify authority disputes between the project manager and departmental managers

4 Basic forms of project organisation

Project management literature (e.g. [9]) generally differentiates between three basic forms of project management organisation:
- Functional (or staff) project organisation
- Pure (or autonomous or projectised) project organisation
- Matrix organisation

4.1 Functional project organisation

In a functional project organisation [10], a project manager holds a staff position. He does not have any authority to issue instructions to other units, only the authority to coordinate. He can only influence the project on the basis of his technical ability and negotiating skills. He does not make any important project decisions. Therefore, he also has no responsibility for project deadlines, costs or outcome.

Project manager´s role in a functional unit

The project manager´s task in a functional organisation is to collect and distribute information. He must have unrestricted access to all project information. His job involves drawing attention to delays, preparing decisions, making recommendations to project team members and suggesting activities. He has low resource autonomy and low independence from the base organisation.

Resource autonomy is the power over the human and material resources that are required in the project. A high level of autonomy exists if resources are specifically reserved for a project and the project manager has the authority to use them as he sees fit. It is low if other project managers or the base organisation have access to the same resources. A project is only independent if it is realised outside standard management structures and a project manager is appointed. In extreme cases, the project can be completely spun-off from the base organisation [11].

Resource autonomy

The installation of a functional project management structure only constitutes a low level of organisational intervention. This organisation structure is often selected if a project will have an impact on many areas of a company (e.g. organisational projects such as the introduction of a company-wide software system or the installation of a quality management system) and on many or all of the company´s employees.

4.1.1 Use of authority

Project manager's authority

Functional project management can also be effective in large-scale projects which involve many departments and necessitate extensive coordination activities, if a project manager possesses a high level of personal and professional authority. Frese [12] reports similar experiences: `Based on their close collaboration with the departments involved in the project, their high level of being informed and their technical competence, project coordination units have a much stronger influence on project activities than would be expected in a functional organisation structure.´ However, it is not advisable to depend solely on them. It is better to not only assign tasks, but also authority, to the project manager.

Excessive workloads for formal decision-makers

A project coordination unit with formal decision-making powers that reports directly to the board can quickly be overloaded so that it is unable to translate its decision-making powers into decisions. This often happens when the unit is responsible for the coordination of several projects at once. Many project managers simply assume unofficial powers in such situations so that they can keep the project going. They act pragmatically and make urgent decisions for which they do not have the formal authority (e.g. postponement of a milestone).

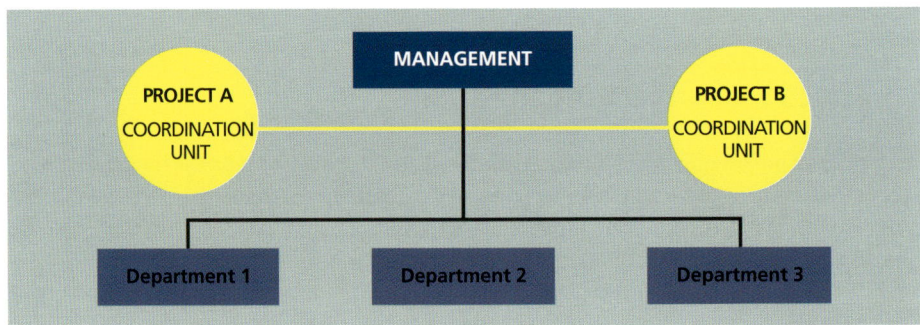

Figure A6-5 Functional project organisation

4.1.2 Advantages and disadvantages of functional project organisation

Functional project organisations require a relatively low level of organisational intervention, which is why they meet with little resistance from departmental managers – partly because the employees remain in their departments.

As already mentioned, the project manager is only able to exert informal influence (e.g. in one-to-one discussions). The departments themselves have sole responsibility for decisions. Fast responses are not possible if a project runs into problems. In some cases, the project coordinator is largely isolated from the project processes.

4.2 Pure project organisation

Project manager in charge

In a pure project organisation, the project manager is responsible for project decisions. He is in charge of the organisational unit where all project team members, who can be recruited from various company departments or externally, work. In the past, such structures have often been used in large-scale,

A6 PROJECT ORGANISATION

long-term armament projects. In extreme cases, they take the form of project-specific single-purpose companies [13], or project companies.

A great deal of project management literature alleges that project team members only receive instructions from the project manager, who is their technical and disciplinary superior. However, this does not apply in every case because an organisational hierarchy often exists below the level of the person in charge of the project in a project organisation. In large-scale projects, horizontal and vertical organisational sub-units are often established, such as sub-projects with sub-project managers (= internal structure). The project manager is responsible for the project schedule, costs and quality. He has the authority to make use of the human and material resources allocated to the project. The base organisation does not have free access to these resources. Resource autonomy is high, as is the level of independence from the base organisation.

Internal structure

In software development projects, the chief programmer concept can be viewed as a form of project organisation, though at a lower hierarchical level. In this case, the project manager is the chief programmer, and the organisation of the project teams is tailored to his needs [14]. This means there is no rivalry between project managers for scarce resources in the line.

Chief programmer concept

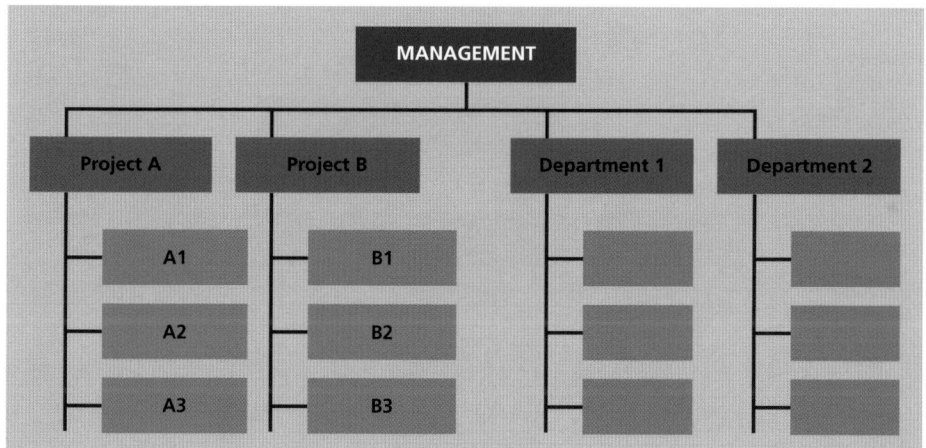

Figure A6-6 Pure project organisation

4.2.1 Advantages and disadvantages of a pure project organisation

In a pure project organisation, resources are allocated on a dedicated basis to the project. There are very few conflicts between project and functional units. The project manager is also the disciplinary superior of the project team members. He can respond promptly to any project problems.

In a pure project organisation, it is difficult to adapt staff levels to reflect changing requirements. Since projects generally require fewer personnel in the start-up, concept and close-out phases than in the implementation phase, some project personnel may not have enough work to do in these phases. As a result, there is a risk that project capacities will not be used fully. In some circumstances, expensive resources may be procured several times. At the beginning and end of the project, the establishment and dissolution of organisational units is generally expensive. Uncertainty about their future position in the company can depress employees' motivation and productivity during the project.

4.3 Matrix organisation

Definition of the distribution of authority

The matrix organisation was used extensively by the aviation and aerospace industry in the early 1960s. Since there are many forms of matrix organisation, it is necessary to define the distribution of authority between the project manager and departmental managers on a project-by-project basis. An IPMA study [15] differentiates between three forms of matrix organisation: dominant-base, balanced-matrix, and dominant-project organisations.

4.3.1 Distribution of authority

Multiple command system

In a matrix organisation, authority and responsibility are distributed between the departments (functional units) and the project organisation units. Project team members receive instructions from at least two units. If an employee is involved in several projects, a multiple command system exists which goes against the principle of single command. The conflict between departments and project manager, which is inevitable in such structures, is intentional. Supporters of the matrix organisation argue that it can actually be constructive because both viewpoints are taken into consideration when dealing with project problems. However, conflicts can cause considerable problems for a project manager, for instance, if they demotivate the project team (→ Chapter D5).

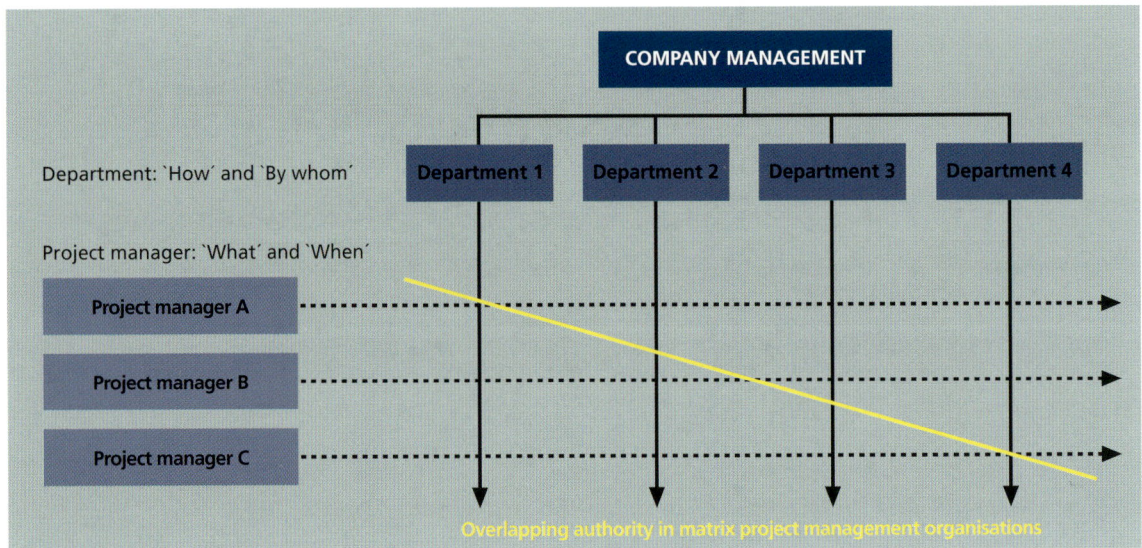

Figure A6-7 Matrix organisation

Problems associated with the inflexible distribution of authority

The distribution of authority between the departments and the project manager can be simplified as follows: The project manager controls the What and When in the project, while the department head controls the How and By Whom. However, this inflexible distribution of authority is not always practical. In development projects that involve highly-skilled personnel, the quality of work performed and the time required (i.e. the What and When) depend to a great extent on which member of staff (By Whom) performs the work. Departments only make competent staff available for projects if they derive direct benefit. This is why project managers need strong powers of persuasion to ensure that the departments assign their best staff to a project. Several project managers often compete for scarce departmental resources.

A6 PROJECT ORGANISATION

Daenzer´s [16] description of the distribution of authority is more precise and closer to reality: `A project manager has considerable influence on the What, When and Where, while departmental managers influence the How, With What, Where From and Where To. Daenzer also takes a more differentiated view of establishing By Whom than most project management literature: He concedes that a project manager can have considerable influence on the staff selection, at least in the later stages of the project.

Practical distribution of authority

The meaning of the individual questions is detailed below:
- What relates to the content of the activity from a qualitative and quantitative viewpoint
- When is the time scheduled for the implementation of the activity
- Where is the place of implementation
- How is the process used
- With What refers to the materials used
- Where From is the place where human resources and materials are procured
- Where To relates to the assignment of human resources and materials when the work or services have been performed

In order to describe and categorise the different types of matrix organisation, it is a good idea to investigate the distribution of authority between departmental and project managers. The following questions help [17]:

Questions on the distribution of authority

DEPARTMENTAL MANAGEMENT AND PROJECT MANAGEMENT AUTHORITY	Departments	Project management
1. Who has the authority to set deadlines for each project phase (= WHEN)?		
2. Who establishes the conditions under which the objectives will be deemed to have been achieved (= WHAT)?		
3. Who decides whether a member of staff is to be assigned to a project or not (= WHO)?		
4. Who has the authority to remove a member of staff from a project (= WHO)?		
5. Who decides on recruitment (= WHO)?		
6. Who has influence, based on a performance evaluation, on the salary paid to and the promotion of staff (= WHO)?		
7. Who selects sub-contractors (= WHERE FROM)?		
8. Who selects suppliers (= WHERE FROM)?		

Figure A6-8 Questions relating to the distribution of authority between the project manager and the departmental managers

The more of these questions are answered with Yes, the more formal is the project manager´s status.

4.3.2 Advantages and disadvantages of the matrix organisation

Overlapping authority can lead to productive conflicts between departments and project managers in a matrix organisation. Very few organisational switch-over costs are incurred. The staff remain in their departments, where they can continue to develop their skills. Staffing levels can easily be adjusted to match the changing needs of different projects. Since a matrix organisation is not needed in every project, responsibility for smaller projects can remain with the departments. The project manager has undisputed responsibility for the project objectives.

Communication requirements

Matrix organisations are communication-intensive. An imprecise definition of authority and tasks can lead to conflicts and confusion among staff and can jeopardise a project's success.

Staehle [18] discovered that 'it is necessary to remember [...] the vast gap that still exists between the theory on matrix organisations in project management literature and their application in practice.' Empirical studies show that the formal authority of a project manager has considerable influence on the project's success. Gmünden's [19] survey is representative of many such analyses, as shown in Figure A6-9:

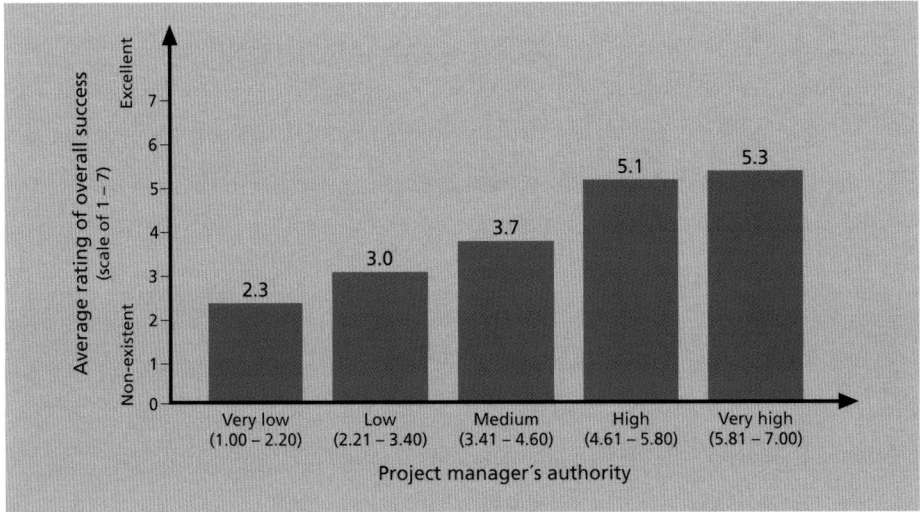

Figure A6-9 The effects of the project manager's formal authority on the project's success

5 Case study of a balanced matrix for development projects

The following definition of authority was made for hardware development projects and constitutes a balanced matrix organisation. It provides an example of the responsibility, tasks and authority of project managers, departmental managers and the project steering committee in development projects.

1. Preliminary remarks

This concept applies for all computer hardware development projects. Projects in our organisation are activities in a specific field that are limited in time and for which a development request has been approved.

2. Management principles in product development projects

The following principles apply for the management of our product development projects:
A person with overall responsibility is assigned to every project (project manager). Project responsibility is personified. The project manager must have the necessary authority to perform his function and to assume responsibility for the project. A differentiation is made between operational and strategic project management tasks. Operational tasks are performed by the project manager and his team, while strategic tasks are performed by the project steering committee. Both strategic and operational project management tasks are inter-departmental, i.e. various departments must cooperate in the project according to the principles of the matrix organisation, which differentiates between project and departmental responsibility.

3. Project organisation structure

The following project-specific individuals/groups/committees exist:
- Project manager and team
- Project steering committee

The functions, responsibility and authority of the project manager, team and steering committee are:

3.1 Project Manager
A project manager is assigned to each project. He coordinates the project throughout its entire lifecycle as far as the pilot series and in all participating departments. He should be a member of the development team.

For his function, he needs (→ Chapter D1)
- several years of professional experience,
- leadership skills, and
- the ability to assert himself.

Essentially, the project manager must
1. Clarify the project objectives and be involved in the definition of the project.
2. Prepare the work breakdown structure, issue work package instructions to all relevant teams and approve the appropriation of project budget funds.
3. Coordinate the project.
4. Enlist and manage the project team.
5. Plan and monitor the project schedule.
6. Plan and track the development of project costs.
7. Monitor project progress (based on milestones and project review dates).
8. Promptly identify deviations from schedule and implement counter measures.
9. Verify and coordinate changes and incorporate them in project planning and implementation activities (product and project-specific).
10. Report to the project steering committee (at milestones and fixed reporting dates).
11. Use the project management tools that the organisation has at its disposal.
12. Ensure the efficiency of project information channels.
13. Establish appropriate structures for managing project development and processes.
14. Represent the project internally and externally.

The project manager is responsible for the reaching the project objectives as specified in the project definition: deadlines, costs and (product) quality. He is responsible for coordinating project team members and their work packages in accordance with the project definition during the project. The departments involved in the project, in contrast, are only responsible for activities that affect them.

So that he can fulfil his project management functions, he has the following powers:
1. The right to participate in the definition of the project objectives relating to the product, costs and deadlines.
2. The right to receive project-specific information in addition to the obligatory reports from project participants.
3. The right to issue project-specific instructions: the project manager is entitled to issue project-specific instructions to the departments relating to the work packages that are allocated, but not on how to perform the activities. The How is the sole responsibility of the departments. The main project-specific instructions are
    - the definition of work packages
    - the duty of departments to coordinate interfaces
    - passing on work results and
    - the provision of project-related information.
4. Internal disputes should be resolved amicably. If this is not possible, the project manager contacts the staff involved with the aim of helping them resolve it.
5. The right to make project-specific decisions: if the project group members do not find a mutually acceptable solution, the project manager decides.
6. The right to have a say in the people who are nominated by the departments to take charge of work packages.
7. The right to make suggestions when work packages are awarded to external firms.
8. The entitlement to agree binding work packages with the departments participating in the project in accordance with the project definition.
9. The approval of work packages based on the participating departments´ permission to charge costs to the relevant work package.
10. Entitlement to accept or reject sub-project results (e.g. when milestones are reached).
11. The right to listen to and comment on project strategy decisions.
12. The right to enlist and manage the project team.

The project manager should exercise his authority in cooperation with the other departments involved in the project.

3.2 Project team
A project team is formed for every project. Its members are representatives of the most important departments involved (e.g. development lab, prototype construction, testing, process engineering). The team can be supplemented with external individuals who only work on the project from time to time in accordance with the project requirements. Additional department representatives can be called in as necessary.

The team supports the project manager in the realisation of his project management function. It also ensures that he receives the information needed for the project´s planning and reporting system in good time. Although the team members represent their department in the project, they do act as lobbyists for these departments. They must always keep track of the project´s overall objectives, including those outside their own field of specialisation. They carry out their project tasks in their departments as agreed in the project group meetings.

3.3 Project steering committee

The members of the project steering committee are the representatives of the most important departments involved (central departmental managers). The committee only realises project strategy tasks. It is not involved in project operations and consults the project manager before making decisions. The committee nominates a spokesperson who reports to senior management. The project steering committee must be kept up-to-date on the project's progress through regular reports. The following list only includes project-specific tasks. It does not include tasks that are associated with a central departmental manager's line function:

- Acceptance of project charters from senior management.
- Appointment of project managers.
- Decisions on project strategy.
- Checking and signing of project definitions.
- Involvement in the initiation of new projects.
- Setting priorities for project strategy implementation. These include plans for the subsequent year and mid-term planning.
- Planning and monitoring of the number of staff involved in the project and the development of costs in the relevant company division.
- Decisions regarding the outsourcing of project tasks to external parties (at the project manager's suggestion).
- Supervision of project deadlines, costs and progress (superordinated monitoring function).
- Preparation of decisions for senior management.
- Solving project-related conflicts if the project manager is not able to do so.

4. Project-related functions and responsibilities of the departments

Departments are responsible for implementing project tasks. Their responsibility extends to the professional and efficient fulfilment of project objectives (the How) and the timely completion, within budget, of the work packages assigned to them. They participate in the planning and monitoring of those aspects of the project that affect them. If deviations from the plan are likely, the project manager informs the departments without delay. Each department nominates one or more project team representatives. Such representatives function as an interface between the departments and project management. Departments are consulted about and agree to the project definition (product and process-related) and with regard to any changes that are made to this definition over the course of the project. This agreement is a declaration that they view the plans as binding for their departments.

The departments should cooperate with the project manager and project team. They must report anything that affects their work, their results or the workload of other project team members to the project manager. They should attempt to ensure compliance with product specifications, and to adhere to the project schedule and budget. On the other hand, the project manager takes departmental needs into account when planning and managing the project.

The roles of sub-project or technical project managers are often defined in addition to that of the project manager, especially in plant construction projects. The technical project manager's main function is to ensure that the project's technical and commercial objectives are attained in accordance with the work package agreements reached between departmental managers and the project manager [20]. In this connection, a technical project is a smaller project within a larger one.

Sub-/technical project manager

6 Project control and the project's commercial team

Service provider to the project manager

Whereas the project manager ensures adherence to cost, deadline and quality requirements, a project controller is the person who ensures transparency in the project. He is therefore a service provider to the project manager. Many attempts to establish permanent project management in an organisation fail because senior management refuses to fund the set-up and running of a project office. This results in a project manager having too high a workload and not making comprehensive use – for lack of time and other reasons – of the range of project management tools available to him. This is where the project controller comes in.

Over the years, various special control disciplines have evolved for specific fields such as research and development, marketing, procurement and project management.

Rule of thumb

It is important to define the location of project control in the organisation. Horvath's [21] rule of thumb is useful as a decision-making tool in this respect: `The coordination tasks forming the systems that affect the organisation as a whole [...] are generally centralised (e.g. strategic planning, IT issues, auditing). Information supply work packages which necessitate a close proximity to project activities [...] are decentralised.´ Project controlling therefore tends to be decentralised. However, the project controller does not replace the project manager and cannot assume the project manager's responsibility for the success of the project. Project control functions are perceived in different ways by different people. Project assistants are a `weak´ source of support for the project management team. In many cases, their work only involves the collection, processing and distribution of project data. Project offices, on the other hand, are a source of strong support and often have extensive powers. They are `in-company providers of a comprehensive range of project management services´ [22] (→ Chapter E3).

Different forms of control

6.1 Job description for a project controller

The following, modified, job description [23] is that of a project controller in a plant construction project. It shows his authority, tasks and responsibility.

1. The project controller's powers

The project controller issues instructions to the project manager and sub-project managers,
- uses certain project management instruments and
- delivers information about the status and trends in activities and work packages unless another party is already under obligation to deliver this information.

2. Main tasks

Projects have to be commercially planned, supervised and managed. Project control offers suitable, user-friendly systems for project planning and control. These are only fully effective if a suitably structured, fast information and reporting system has been installed for the project.

3. Specific responsibilities

1. The project controller is assigned to a (sub-)project to ensure that it is implemented in a structured, cost-effective, transparent and complete way.
2. He therefore provides project-specific support to the (sub-/technical) project managers, the relevant steering committee and the divisional manager.
3. He ensures the standardisation of project network and bar-chart activities (processes) in representative project types.
4. He provides support in specific planning tasks.
5. He is in charge of overall project planning and control (in conjunction with sub-project and technical project managers).
6. He installs a well-structured and comprehensive documentation system.
7. He is the contact for information about the status and trends in all projects that he controls.
8. He develops and updates a standardised project information system (forms, screen mask layout, reports, PC support) that is suitable for all the projects in a division.
9. He prepares forecasts, target-current variance analyses and target-projected variance analyses [see explanation at the end of the job description] and implements trend analyses for specific projects with regard to deadlines, work progress, the employment of budget resources and costs.
10. He ensures that senior managers involved in the project make a timely analysis of the initial situation when plans are defined (customer enquiry/instructions in respect of project structure planning, organisational structures, scheduling, use of budget resources, costs, and liquidity). If necessary, he implements corrective measures.
11. He supports (sub-/technical) project managers and departmental managers in (the structuring of) quotation, order and in-project costing.
12. He monitors the use of the necessary methods/tools for the structured implementation of the project by the (sub-)project managers. He thereby ensures that the project status is transparent at all times, and that the latest data on the deadline situation, project progress and cost position are available. The performance status of sub-contractors and consortium partners is also monitored.

4. Responsibility

The project control team is responsible for ensuring that the project management tools made available are used as effectively as possible and that project processes are transparent at all times.

The term `target-projected´ variance analysis mentioned in Item 9 of the job description can be most effectively explained.

Example

Let´s assume that the initially projected costs of a project or work package (target costs) are EUR 100,000. Based on costs incurred to date of EUR 50,000 and an estimate of residual costs by the person responsible for the work package of EUR 70,000, the projected costs are therefore EUR 120,000.

6.2 Commercial project manager

Commercial project manager

Large-scale building and plant construction projects, and some industrial research and development projects, also have a commercial project manager. His main responsibility is to 'ensure the cost-effective implementation of specific commercial aspects of a project by the agreed date and in accordance with contractual agreements, taking special arrangements into account' [24].

Self-assessment questions for each certification level

No.	Question	Level D	Level C	Level B	Level A	Self-assessment
A 6.01	What basic forms of project organisation exist?	2	2	3	4	☐
A 6.02	What criteria differentiate the basic forms of project organisation?	2	3	3	4	☐
A 6.03	When can projects be realised within the scope of standard management structures?	1	2	2	3	☐
A 6.04	When are project-specific organisation structures advisable?	2	2	3	4	☐
A 6.05	What do project steering committees do?	2	2	2	3	☐
A 6.06	What are the functions of the project controller and project control?	2	3	3	4	☐
A 6.07	What are the functions of the project manager?	2	3	3	4	☐
A 6.08	What responsibilities does the project manager have?	2	3	3	4	☐
A 6.09	What are the functions of a project steering committee?	2	2	2	3	☐
A 6.10	What are the differences between a project board and a project steering committee?	2	2	2	3	☐

BLOCK B

PROCESS MODELS

B PROCESS MODELS

Process models help project managers to plan systematically and execute the entire lifecycle of a project (ICB Element 6). Numerous company-specific, sector-specific, project type-specific and also sector neutral models have been developed. Since process models of various types are commonly used in IT projects, this chapter focuses on the IT sector and the elements of these models. Another topic covered is, what to do when it is impossible to construct a process model for a heterogeneous project environment.

1 Benefits

`You can do it. Just get started!´ Project managers hear these or similar words on a daily basis when their organisations send them off to start a project - without experience, project management training or even a coach or any project office support. They are expected to plan projects systematically, even if they have never had any training for this task. Often, they have no option but to muddle through somehow. Ironically, this approach is called situational project management and often leads to chaos.

In order to prevent this happening, numerous process models have been developed over recent decades as orientation for project managers. There are company-specific and sector-specific models (phase or process models, stage gate models). Each is suitable for a specific type of project, such as IT or plant construction. However, some process models, such as PRINCE 2 [1], developed in the UK, are so general in nature that they can be adapted to whatever type of project is being implemented.

Process model types

Versteegen´s [2] definition is: `A process model describes a coordinated approach to project implementation. It defines the input required to implement the activity and the output that the activity produces.´

2 Elements

Process models have several elements in common [3], such as project phases, activities, milestones and milestone results.

2.1 Project phases

According to the ICB, a project phase is a timeframe within a project that is objectively separate from other project timeframes (e.g. concept definition phase). Process models consist of different project phases. The linking together of individual standardised project phases enables even an inexperienced employee to recognise immediately the sequence of activities to which he must adhere when planning and implementing the project. In practice, project phases are not always in sequence, they can sometimes overlap.

Sequence in planning and realisation phases

B PROCESS MODELS

A general example taken from the ICB of the sequence of project phases is shown in Figure B1:

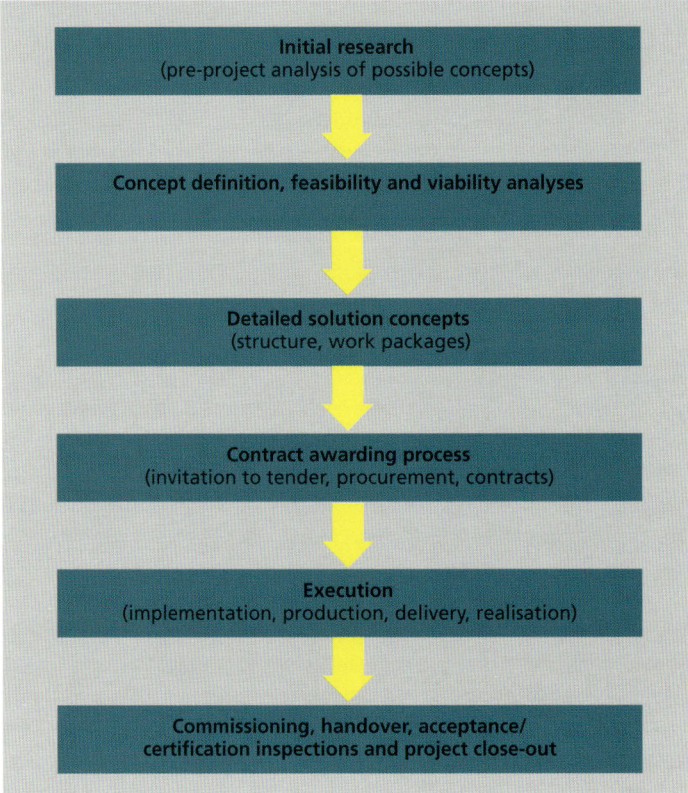

Figure B1 Example of the sequence of project phases

2.2 Activities

Attainment of specific partial results

A project manager receives additional information because – as emphasised by Versteegen – activities are defined for individual project phases and must be implemented in these phases in order to achieve specific partial results. For example, patent research is an activity performed in the concept definition phase of a product development project. Predefined activities are sometimes linked in the critical path method of planning (→ Chapter C5). In other words, a complete project schedule already exists and it is only necessary to allocate timeframes to the individual activities. The project team has to adapt the activity schedule to the specific project by either adding or eliminating activities.

The example [4] in Figure B2 shows the necessary activities and the organisational units responsible for carrying them out in the planning phase for a physical product.

B PROCESS MODELS

PHASE/ ACTIVITIES	STEERING COMMITTEE	PROJECT MANAGER	SALES	R&D	PRODUCTION	QUALITY	CONTROLLING
1. Product planning							
Appoint project manager and core team	■	○					
Prepare requirement list		■	○	○	○	○	
Cost estimate, date overview		■	○	○	○	○	○
Sales estimate		○	■				○
First business case analysis		○		○			■
Drafting of the development order		■	○	○	○	○	○
Development approval	x	○					

x Authorisation
■ Responsible
○ Participation

Figure B2 Activities and organisational units for planning a material product

2.3 Milestones and milestone results

According to the ICB, milestones are `significant events in the project, often indicating change of phases with the decision to repeat the phase or a previous one , to terminate the project, or to start the next phase.´ (→ Chapter C5)

Milestones occur generally at the start or end of a phase, though they can be set in-between. They are not only associated with scheduled and actual dates – and in some cases with projected and incurred cumulative costs – but also with the targeted milestone results (= products). A milestone defines a physical result (milestone content) that is linked to a completion date (= milestone deadline). *Characteristics of milestones*

Milestone results are generated by way of activities. Examples of milestone results are:
- The customer´s specification
- The specification approved by the project steering committee
- The test bed report in respect of a prototype
- Report on patent research
- Official planning permission
- Market survey on the commercial viability of a product to be developed
- Revised work breakdown structure
- Revised schedule

Many process models also stipulate the make-up of the milestone result. For example, minimum content for specifications (→ Chapter C2) or precise regulations for other planning documents (e.g. distribution plan) may be defined.

According to the ICB, a project manager must verify the phase deliverable. However, based on experience, it is often better to allocate this task to people who are not involved in the project. If the phase deliverable does not satisfy the quality required, the project manager must issue instructions for a phase to be repeated in order to revise or produce an entirely different milestone deliverable. Only *Repeating a phase after checking the phase result* then can the next phase commence. If it turns out that the targeted milestone result cannot be attained – perhaps for technical reasons – or that the product´s market outlook has deteriorated considerably since the project commenced, it is possible that the project will have to be abandoned.

2.4 Skills and roles

Responsibility, duties and authority

Some process models describe the skills necessary for the activities to be performed by specific role holders. These also require the allocation of responsibilities, duties and powers. Examples of project roles are
- project manager
- project controller
- steering committee member
- quality manager
- user or customer representative
- system analyst

2.5 Additional detailed instructions

Establishing commercial viability

The more in-depth process models provide a higher level of standardisation and prescribe detailed activities for the project teams. For example, some process models for IT projects stipulate the tools to be used by the team when defining user requirements or user documentation. They often also specify the anticipated marginal return or capital value when physical products are being developed, i.e. parameters that can be used to evaluate the product´s commercial viability.

Formal completeness check

Figure B3 shows an excerpt from a software project process model [5] that includes the elements phases, milestones and milestone results. At the end of the phase study (Milestone A 20), a specification (→ Chapter C2) must have been prepared. In order to simplify this task for the project team members and stop them defining the specification´s content arbitrarily, the process model stipulates a breakdown. When the milestone result is accepted at a milestone meeting, it is possible to check whether all items in the specification have been covered. However, this more formal completeness check does not replace the precise inspection of the document´s content.

B PROCESS MODELS

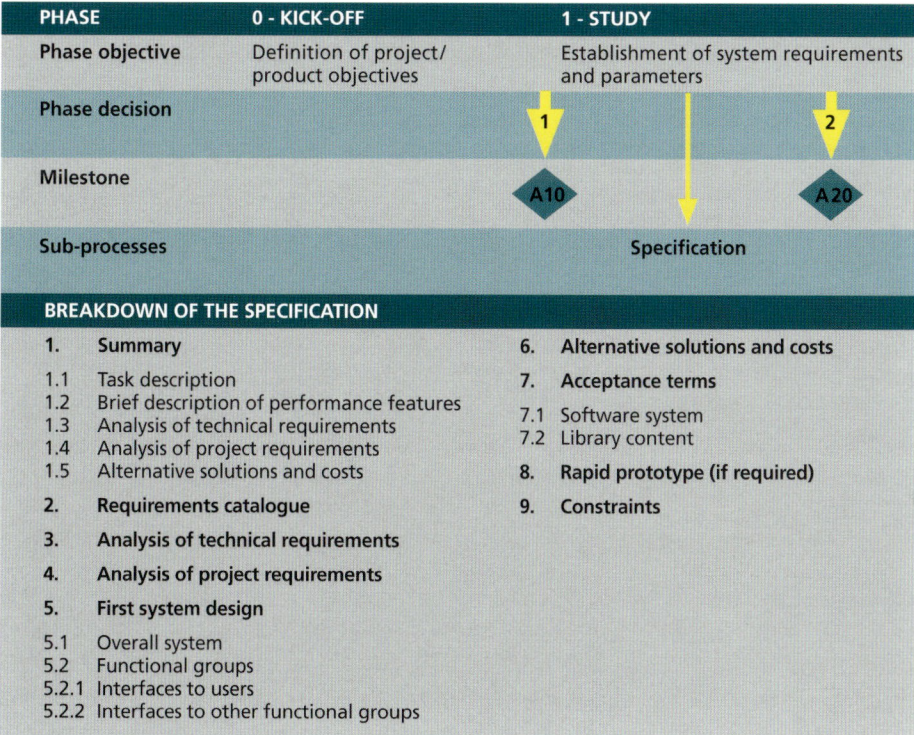

Figure B3 Excerpt from a process model

The process model also contains content-checking aids. One example [6] is the design verification checklist in Figure B4.

Inspection of content

QUESTIONS	YES	NO	NOT APPLICABLE
1. Does the specification include all the customer's requirements?			
2. Does the design satisfy all functional requirements?			
3. Does the design take all ambient conditions into consideration (temperature, vibration, corrosion etc.)?			
4. Were existing information and similar designs inspected and incorporated?			
5. Whenever possible, were standard components used?			
6. Can the required tolerances be adhered to in the production process?			
7. Does the design lead to an optimum installation scenario?			
8. Does the design lead to an optimum maintenance scenario?			
9. Was a thorough value analysis implemented?			
10. Were all safety requirements taken into account?			

Figure B4 Excerpt from a design verification checklist

B PROCESS MODELS

Figure B5 shows the entire process model [7] from which the excerpt in Figure B3 was taken.

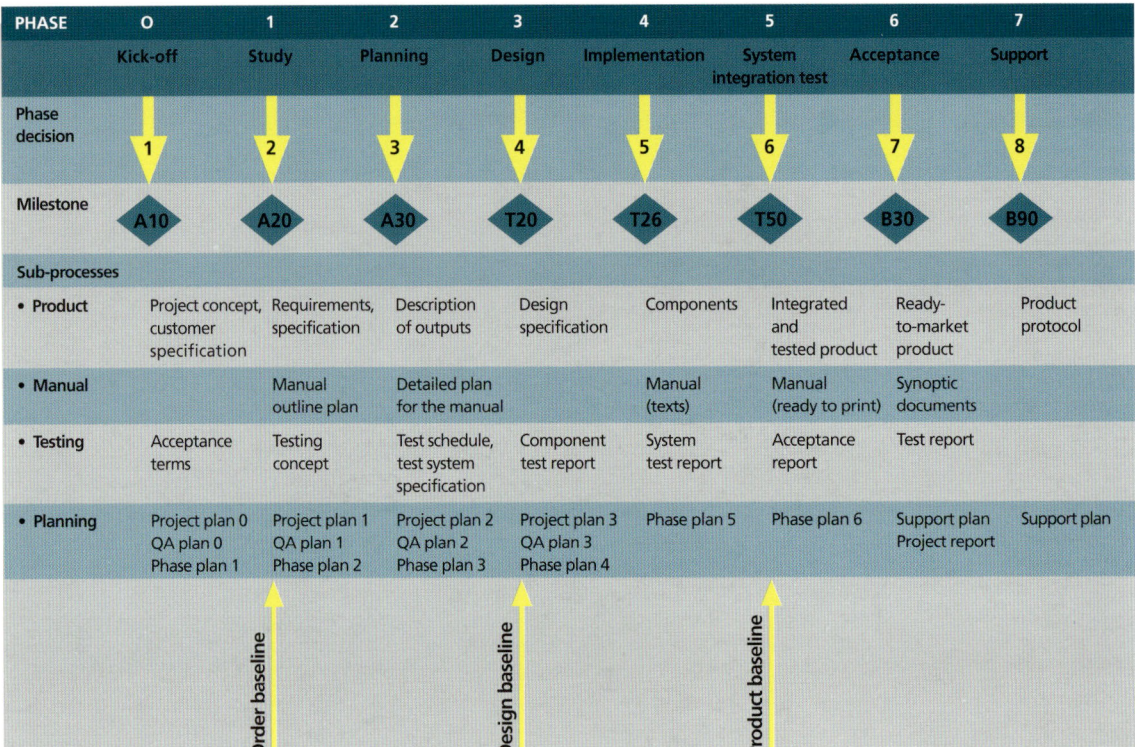

Figure B5 Example of a process model for the IT sector

Four different processes

Figure B5 shows another detail. The developers of this process model differentiate between four different processes:
- Process in which the product is manufactured (the ready-to-market software system)
- Process in which the necessary documentation is prepared
- Process in which the software is tested (= quality management process)
- Project management process in which the other processes are planned and managed

Milestone result categories

The four different processes correspond to the milestone result categories. Milestone meetings are held in respect of milestones A 10, A 20 and so on. At these meetings, a review team (assembled according to the project being implemented) verifies the milestone results and discusses how to proceed. For example, they may decide to backtrack to the previous phase, to modify the project objective extensively or, in extreme cases, to abandon the project.

Reference configuration

The arrows denoting the order baseline, design baseline and product baseline in conjunction with milestones A 20, T 20 and T 50 refer to the process of configuration management (→ Chapter C7). The order, the system design or the finished product is frozen when the relevant milestone is reached, providing a fixed point of reference. Changes are always described in relation to this point (= reference configuration). The project team can only implement changes in a controlled process which, among other things, takes into account their effect on the project schedule and costs.

B PROCESS MODELS

3 Phase breakdowns for various projects

Process models are very common in the IT sector, though they also play an important role elsewhere Figures B6 to B8 show phase breakdowns for various project types [8].

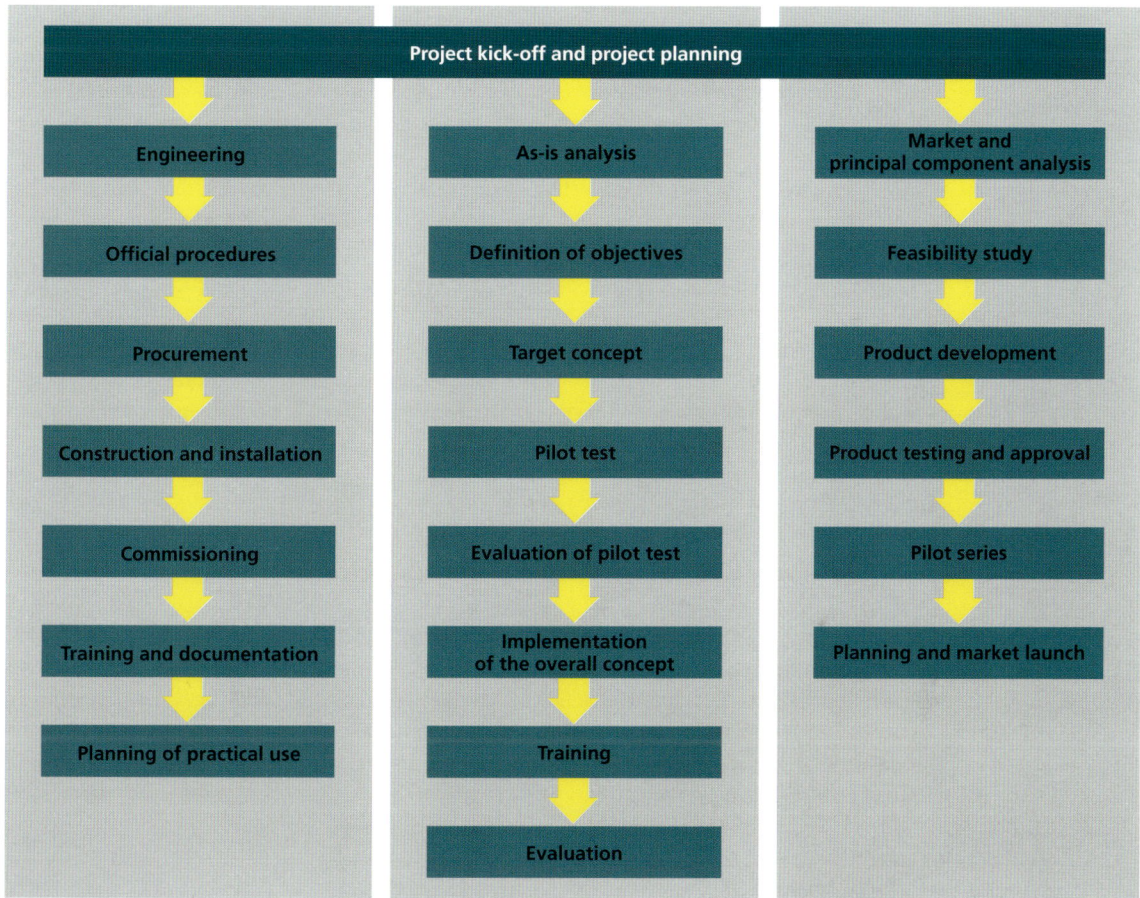

Figure B6 A breakdown of phases in investment projects

Figure B7 A breakdown of phases in organisational projects

Figure B8 A breakdown of phases in the development of physical products

3.1 Overlapping phases

All the above examples are based on a strictly sequential approach. A phase must be completed and the relevant milestone result delivered and approved before the next phase can commence. It is not always possible to do this in practice.

Sequential approach

> **Example**
> *A component with a long lead-time is required for a mass-produced complex circuit. It cannot be ordered until a prototype circuit has been successfully tested. In order to reduce the total project lifecycle, the team orders it `on spec´ before the tests have been completed. They deliberately take the risk that the component may not be used.*

Caution when phases overlap

The project manager has to plan overlapping phases very carefully and make a realistic evaluation of the associated risk.

3.2 Parallel implementation of phases

Many projects involve several phases that are implemented concurrently. This happens in IT projects, for instance, when the hardware and software components for a product are developed at the same time. When the system as a whole is tested, the project team merges the phases again.

Milestone functions

Milestones perform an important function in such processes. Buttermilch and Schmelzer [9] emphasise: `The concurrent implementation of development activities necessitates an even higher level of synchronisation. The planning and monitoring of milestones as synchronisation and control points is therefore more significant in parallel-phase development processes than in sequential ones.´

Simultaneous engineering

Parallel implementation plays an important role in the simultaneous engineering [10]. According to Schmelzer´s [11] definition: `Simultaneous (or concurrent) engineering is a process concept for the simultaneous development of products and production resources.´ Interdisciplinary teams simultaneously or concurrently plan and develop products and production resources. The aim is to speed up development activities through overlapping.

4 Process models and quality management

The relationship between process models and quality management is particularly clear in the design management element of the old ISO 9001:1994 standard [12]. A textbook [13] states: `In complex development projects, the punctual completion of development and construction activities [...] should be ensured with the assistance of a milestone schedule. [...] Review your development schedule after the completion of interim milestones and at the end of the development and construction phases to evaluate the results.´

5 Process models in the IT sector

Process models are particularly common in IT projects. The various models [14] are also a topic of intense debate in the IT sector.

5.1 Waterfall model

The waterfall model is the most well-known process model in which software development is partitioned into several distinct sequential phases. Each phase must be completed before the next one can begin. The model therefore corresponds to the phase processes shown in this chapter for other types of projects.

Document-driven model

Precisely defined documents must exist at the end of each phase. This is why the model is said to be document-driven. The user is only involved in the phases where the requirements are defined, i.e. early on in the project. He does not see the software until it goes into testing. It is only envisaged to backtrack one phase to eliminate, for example, a product defect. It is not possible – at least theoretically – to backtrack several phases.

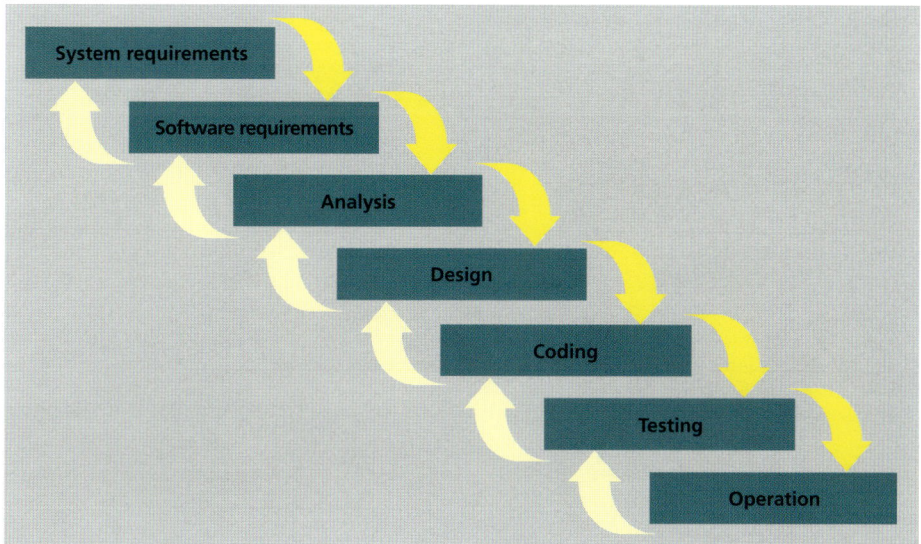

Figure B9 Waterfall model

The simple waterfall model has enabled many organisations to introduce disciplined development processes. However, its critics say [15]:
- The strict orientation on documents is associated with the risk that they will be overrated compared to the system itself.
- Users cannot test the software until it is completely finished. This means that feedback to the developers before completion is almost impossible. As a result, mistakes are often identified too late.
- It isn´t necessary or practical in all cases to realise the development phases in sequence.

Disciplined development

Versteegen [16] comments on criticism of the waterfall model: `If all requirements are established at the outset, the waterfall model is an engineering process that guarantees optimum project implementation.´ However, the gap between theory and practice is often large.

5.2 V-model

The V-model [17] is described in literature as an extension of the waterfall model. It was initially developed for the German armed forces and is now used in the entire German public sector. The current version is from 1997 and incorporates four sub-models:
- a project management model (= PM)
- a quality assurance model (= QA)
- a system development model (SD) and
- a configuration management model (CM) (→ Chapter C7).

Sub-models

The interplay of the four components with which the processes are modelled is shown in Figure B10 [18]:

B PROCESS MODELS

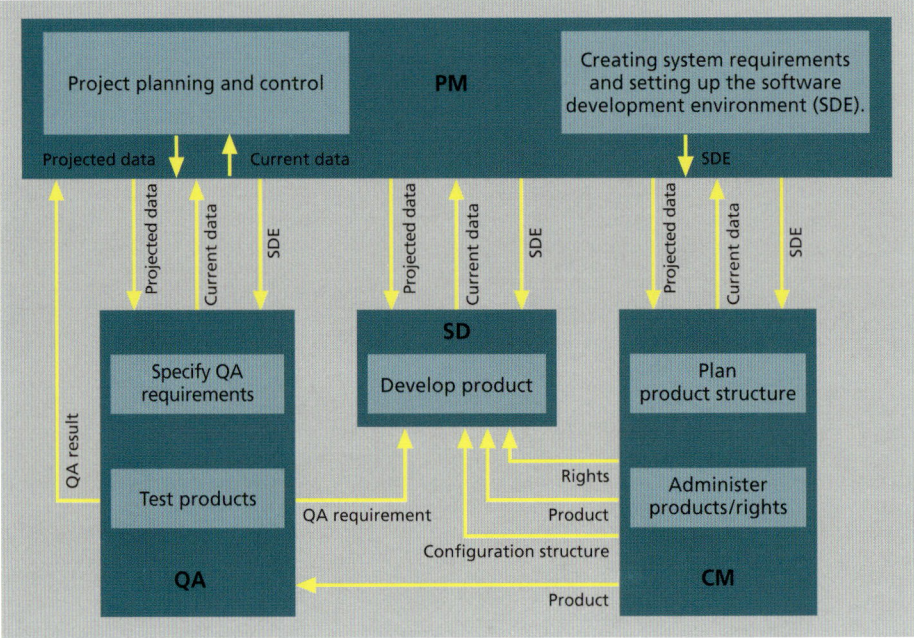

Figure B10 Interrelationships between the four sub-models in the V-model

One remarkable thing about the V-model is that it can be adapted for product-specific requirements (= tailoring). More importantly, however, it expands upon the waterfall model in the area of quality, differentiating between verification and validation:

Verification and validation

- In verification, the team checks whether the software product conforms to the specification. It asks the question: 'Is the product the way it is supposed to be?'
- In validation, the team checks whether the software is suitable for the job it will perform. It asks the question: 'Have we developed the right product?'

The V-model is generally suitable for large-scale projects [19].
However, in smaller and mid-sized projects it can in some cases lead to unnecessary product variety and project bureaucracy.

5.3 Prototyping approach

Criticism that the waterfall model only involves users during the initial development phase (definition of requirements) led to the prototyping approach. It has always been the standard model for the development of physical products. First and foremost, this approach takes into account

Physical products

- that users are often not able to formulate precisely and completely what they require from a new system, and
- there are generally various options for the implementation of each requirement. This is evident by the long menus in project management software packages.

Disposable prototype

The IT sector differentiates between different kinds of prototypes [20]. Here, we only discuss disposable ones. They are created during the project definition phase and help the project team and subsequent users to clarify the requirements and implementation options. A prototype is generally produced quickly (= rapid prototyping) and thrown away when it has satisfied its purpose. Such prototyping can be integrated in the waterfall and other process models.

Involvement of users

5.4 Evolutionary and incremental process models

The waterfall model and V-model are based on the assumption that user requirements can be more or less fully defined during the initial project phases and that the entire system will then be developed in one go. However, this process is associated with the disadvantage that the customer often has a lengthy wait before he gets an operational system. Also, users may find that they have additional requirements once they have used the system.

5.4.1 Evolutionary model

The evolutionary model takes the above scenario into account. First, the software's core functionality is implemented. Then, it is further developed version-by-version. Feedback from users of a specific version helps the team to develop the next version. From the user's perspective, the motto of this approach could be: `I can't say what I want, but I'll know it when I see it.´ Some critics say it is development according to the banana principle – deliver it green and let to ripen with the customer.

Version-by-version development

One disadvantage of the evolutionary model is that, in some circumstances, the entire system architecture has to be revised for subsequent versions of the software because core requirements escaped notice when the pilot version was produced [21].

5.4.2 Incremental model

This is why the incremental model attempts to make the most comprehensive possible definition of system requirements. However, like the evolutionary model, itl initially only defines and realises some of these requirements.

Complete definition

5.5 Other process models in the IT sector

In addition to the above models, the IT sector has developed
- the object-oriented model, which is based on object-oriented software development and focuses on the aspect of reusing software components.
- the concurrent model, which is comparable to the simultaneous engineering approach when developing physical products, and in which as many activities as possible are realised concurrently or overlap greatly.
- the spiral model, also called the meta model, which focuses on minimising development risk.

5.6 Agile project management

Newest process model (iterative)

Agile project management is the most recent process model. While the other models focus on coordination by planning, it centres on self-coordination (→ Chapter A1) and is highly iterative. The project manager approves consecutive versions of product components at short intervals to obtain fast and regular feedback from users. Documents play a subordinate role. The focus is on the code. Only a few project roles are defined (e.g. project manager, project controller).

Agile Manifesto

The Agile Manifesto [22] defines the following basic principles of agile project management:
- Individuals and interactions over processes and tools
- Working software over comprehensive documentation
- Customer collaboration over contract negotiation
- Responding to change over following a plan

6 A critical appraisal of process models

Objections to specific process model types are often voiced in the IT sector. IT people mainly object to models with strictly sequential processes. These criticisms, some of which are justified, led to the development of alternative models. In other sectors, particularly those where physical products are developed (e.g. pharmaceuticals, consumer electronics, automobiles and automobile parts), and in the plant and building construction industries, they are widely accepted and in common use. Generally, it isn´t the process models themselves that are criticised, but their bureaucratic nature and the high volume of non-essential documents.

Bureaucracy

Adaptation to project size

The objection that process models are only suitable for large-scale rather than small projects is based on a misinterpretation. Good process models are flexible and can be tailored to any project size at any time. In some less complex and extensive projects, it can be sufficient merely to use some of the milestones. Individual activities are not defined and a detailed project schedule is dispensed with. Since the project is not considered to be complex, it is assumed that the project manager and his team know precisely how to attain the planned milestones. This approach puts strong constraints on coordination by planning and focuses on self-coordination. It is comparable with order tactics in the military sector. The objective is specified, but not the means of achieving it.

6.1 Setting milestones

Significance for project success

Whatever the sector of industry or the process model, a project manager should always set milestones at close intervals and describe the required milestone results as precisely as possible. This ensures that project team members always have points of reference. Even strong opponents of process models approve of this. Weltz, who is one of the main opponents of the waterfall model, writes: `There is a lot to be said against the old-fashioned phase models. Their advantage is you know where you stand. That´s ideal for project tracking.´ [23]

Yet at what intervals should the milestones be set? There is no universal answer to this question. Examples [24] of projects in the IT sector show that, in some cases, milestones can be just three weeks apart. Generally, the shorter the project life cycle is, the shorter the intervals between the milestones. Also, they should be relatively evenly distributed over the project term. A study [25] implemented by the

Standish Group in 1995 actually points out that closely set milestones in IT projects are a key success factor.

7 Advantages

Process models enjoy many advantages:
- They make it possible to cope with complexity by structuring the project in defined and manageable periods of time.
- They promote a common understanding of project management and standard procedures in the organisation.
- They give a project manager clear instructions on how to proceed in a project, and offer him a range of tools - especially tools for the definition, production and testing of interim results.
- They reduce project development risk because they define project reviews at the transition points between phases. At these milestones, the people in charge decide whether to continue or abandon the project.
- A process model with precisely defined and verified milestone results makes project progress transparent to the controller and is an important quality management tool.
- Predefined interim results are points of reference for project team members. New staff can be quickly incorporated in a project.
- Processes involving sequential phases correspond to human behaviour when solving complex tasks.
- Since a phase cannot commence until the previous phase has been entirely concluded and the correct interim results have been attained, mistakes are identified earlier. Fewer defects are carried over into later phases. This reduces subsequent costs for defect elimination.

7.1 Theory versus practice

In practice, project managers often don´t take a process model approach to project implementation. They
- don´t adequately coordinate concurrent sub-projects
- don´t give adequate consideration to milestone results and approve the next phase for corporate policy reasons, even when the previous phase should really be repeated
- forget to review the original reasons for initiating the project (e.g. favourable sales forecasts, low development risk) from time to time in development meetings.

8 Projects that aren´t suitable for a process model approach

In a heterogeneous project environment, such as a research and development department, it is sometimes impossible to develop a binding process model for all projects. Despite this, milestones are necessary so that the project manager and his team can provide interim reports to the project sponsor and controller. In such cases, the use of examples from similar projects has proven useful to the project manager and his team. The milestones should be described in as much detail as possible, as they would be in a process model, so that external experts can check whether they have been attained.

Examples from similar projects

B PROCESS MODELS

The table in Figure B11 includes examples of well and badly formulated milestones.

BAD	GOOD
Technical and commercial product plan elaborated by the project team.	Technical and commercial product plan prepared as per the in-house product planning guideline, signed and approved by the project steering committee.
Attributes to be realised defined in the databases.	The attributes to be modified in the databases and the keys to be extended have been identified, and the type of switch-over has been defined. The classification of software elements in 'delete', 'definitely not to be changed' and 'to be replaced' is reliable and binding. It initiates the relevant deletion [26].
Test scenarios developed for testing module A	Ten test scenarios for testing module A have been elaborated on the basis of the module specification.
The questionnaire has been outlined.	It has been established how many questionnaires are to be produced for the various recipients and how many paths through the questionnaire exist. The approximate structure (sequence of topics) and the general layout have been defined and approved by the project sponsor.
Cooperation agreement with university institute has been drafted.	Co-operation agreement with university institute has been drafted, checked by the legal department, signed and released by an executive manager.

Figure B11 Examples of well and badly formulated milestones

Self-assessment questions for each certification level

No.	Question	D	C	B	A	Self-assessment
B 01	What types of process models are widely known?	2	2	2	3	☐
B 02	What common elements have the known process models?	2	2	2	3	☐
B 03	What is agile project management?	2	2	2	3	☐
B 04	What advantages and disadvantages have the recognised process models?	2	2	2	3	☐
B 05	How is quality management incorporated into the process models?	2	2	2	3	☐
B 06	How is a milestone defined?	2	2	3	4	☐
B 07	When is simultaneous engineering used?	1	2	2	3	☐
B 08	What is a waterfall model?	1	2	3	4	☐
B 09	When is a V-model used?	1	2	2	4	☐
B 10	What advantage does prototyping provide?	1	2	2	4	☐
B 11	What are evolutionary and incremental process models?	1	2	2	4	☐

BLOCK C

OPERATIONAL PROJECT MANAGEMENT

C1 PROJECT START-UP

The start-up phase (ICB Element 10) is of crucial significance for the rest of the project. This is where the future course is set, especially in terms of defining the project objectives. It is important to dedicate adequate time to this phase. The project manager needs to be aware of the significance of the start-up phase, of the common mistakes to be avoided and of the typical tasks to be performed. This chapter also provides the information necessary for the planning and conduct of the project start-up workshop and describes some alternative tried-and-tested variations on the start-up process.

1 Significance of the start-up phase

The conditions that ensure project success are established in its initial phases. Lomnitz puts it very aptly: `Tell me how your project starts and I´ll tell you how it ends.´ According to Gareis [1], the project start-up phase is the most important project management sub-process of all because it is the project phase in which the foundations for the subsequent sub-processes are put in place (e.g. the formulation of project objectives).

Numerous empirical studies demonstrate the need to dedicate adequate time and resources to the start-up phase.

Time and resources

- According to Anders [2], in the development of physical products, around 90 percent of the functional features of the ultimate finished product, approximately 70 percent of the quality standards and around 60 percent of product costs are determined very early in the process.
- In the experience of the German Ministry of Defence [3], when a weapons system concept is set down in writing, approximately 85 percent of the anticipated costs (development, production, maintenance and operating costs) have already been determined and can then only be modified minimally. In contrast, the proportion of total system costs that have actually been incurred up to that point is still very low.
- A whole series of surveys in the IT sector [4] show that design errors that are not discovered until the software has been developed are very expensive to remedy. As Möller [5] warns, `The costs involved in remedying errors are dependent not just on the time at which they were discovered, but also on the time at which they occurred. The rule of thumb is that the earlier a mistake occurs and the longer it remains unrecognised, the more expensive it is to remedy.´

Errors

- Lechler [6] systematically analysed 444 German projects. He notes that `The initial phase of the project´ in which key parameters are established, `is extremely relevant for the project´s overall success.´
- An experienced manager [7] of construction projects emphasises that `the biggest impact on a project´s results in terms of quality, costs and deadlines can be achieved only during the early phase of a project.´

1.1 Common mistakes

Unfortunately, however, many project managers have learned little from these unequivocal findings. Three common, serious mistakes are:

- Executives provide staff with an imprecise assignment (`Just do it!´ projects) and then expect fast results.
- Owing to a lack of time and funds, no pre-project feasibility study is carried out to clarify objectives.
- Managers fail to involve end users of the project deliverable in the process of formulating objectives due to a shortage of time.

In the USA, this impatient behaviour is attributed to the `WHISCY´ principle. This is an acronym for `Why isn´t Sam coding yet?´ In other words, `Why is that guy still formulating the concept instead of getting on with programming?´

Japan: timely implementation of changes

Project management literature explains the entirely different approach taken by project planners in Japan. They dedicate a great deal of time to the start-up process, measured in terms of the total project lifecycle, in order to obtain as much information as possible and eliminate risks. Studies show that in Japanese companies 90 percent of all changes are made at the concept development stage. In contrast, western companies most often make changes only shortly before large-scale production begins – at which time changes are very expensive to make [8].

The Japanese are rewarded for their patience in that they have much less need than their western counterparts to eliminate faults or make improvements later on. They thereby benefit from a shorter project lifecycle.

1.2 Differentiation between project launch and the end of the start-up phase

When does a project begin and when does the start-up phase end? It is impossible to answer this question precisely since many projects have a long lead-in:
- Various people generate project ideas and then discard them.
- Initial talks between project stakeholders and potential customers take place, fail to make progress, and are then put on the back burner.
- Preliminary concepts that have been discarded are sometimes reinstated in a modified form at a later date.

Information about the project´s history

Gareis [9] rightly emphasises how important it is that the people and organisations involved in the start-up phase of a project are familiar with its often long history. The project manager needs to ensure a relevant knowledge transfer. However, he often encounters unpleasant surprises at the beginning of the project: As Lomnitz [10] points out, `In some projects, important decisions are made well in advance of the official project start-up phase, at a time when the project manager is not even aware of his ¨good fortune¨. The management team establishes completion dates and, in some cases, the budget framework, without being aware of the technical and organisational costs involved in carrying out the project. In many cases, a lot of wishful thinking goes on.´

1.2.1 Consensus and budget

According to Platz [11], the project starts when `consensus is reached within the company to act on this topic and that resources are made available to clarify the further procedure´. If this consensus has been documented – a procedure we recommend – and a first budget has been approved, it is possible pretty much to pinpoint the project launch date.

1.2.2 Feasibility study and product planning

If the parties concerned are unsure of how they can change an unsatisfactory situation through a project, a feasibility study may be necessary. This checks whether the roughly-formulated objectives can be reached on the basis of existing know-how. Some companies have been using the following procedure for many years [12]:

A planning team, consisting of representatives of various departments such as development, design, production, marketing, sales and the commercial department, develops a technical and commercial product plan for the proposed product. Development work can commence only when these planning documents have been examined and approved by a higher-level product committee. If no approval is given, the start-up process is discontinued.

Procedure in a feasibility study

The time of project launch in the above case is further to the left (i.e. earlier) on the time axis (→ Figure C1-1) than in projects where the internal or external customer already has relatively precise ideas on the schedule and outcome of the project.

Figure C1-1 [13] shows a `best-case´ scenario where uncertainties are gradually eliminated and objectives become increasingly clear during the start-up process. Depending on the type, the project can start at different milestones. For example, if there is a complete customer specification (→ Chapter C2) containing his requirements, the project launch shifts towards the right to milestone M2.

Growing clarity in the start-up process

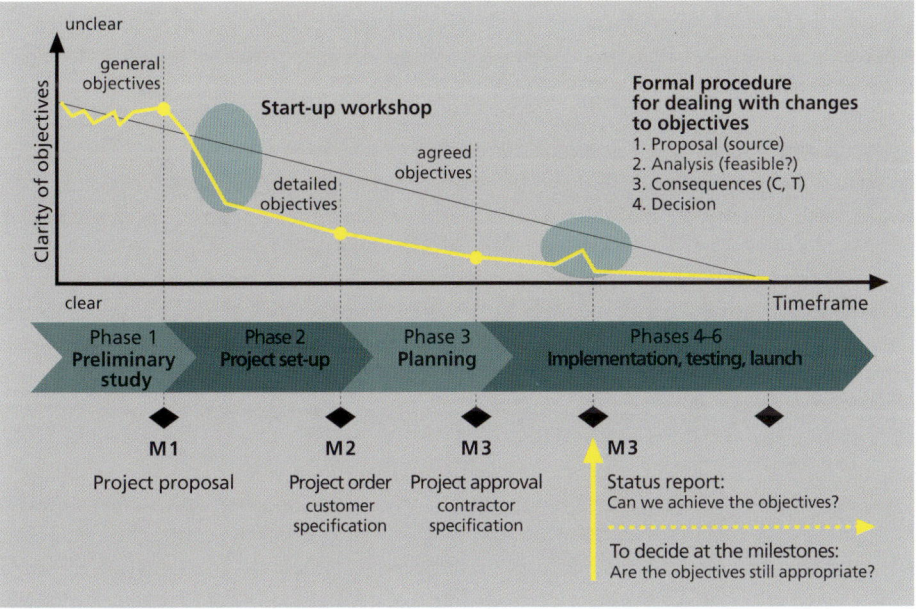

Figure C1-1 `Best case´ scenario for the start-up phase

According to Platz the start-up phase ends when `sufficient information exists for firm agreements to be reached between the project team – represented by the project manager – and key task owners regarding the tasks to be carried out in the project´. In Figure C1-1, the project start-up process ends as soon as the contractor specification is signed by the contractor and the customer (→ Chapter C2).

2 Tasks in the start-up phase

In the start-up phase, the people involved in the project – especially the project manager and his team – need to
- define the project objectives and project content (in collaboration with the customer),
- clarify and establish the overall availability of human, financial and other resources (e.g. operating resources),
- form the project team and establish rules governing co-operation among team members, with line managers and with the customer,
- set up the project management structures,
- prepare the first project plan, and
- undertake an initial risk analysis (→ Chapter C3).

Compatibility with the business strategy

It is the task of the executive management team or a steering committee to analyse whether the project is compatible with the organisation´s business strategy and whether it will contribute to attaining the organisational objectives (e.g. increasing return on investment, improving image). On the basis of this analysis, it will decide on the priority of the project (→ Chapter E2).

2.1 Definition of project stakeholders and project objectives

The stakeholders´ different expectations of the project should, to the greatest extent possible, be reflected in its objectives. Therefore, the project manager needs to define the project stakeholders and their expectations at the outset (→ Chapter A3).

Communication with end users

The most important stakeholder is generally the person financing the project. Their representatives will introduce their technical requirements on the project. The project manager´s role is to document the roles of these various representatives (→ Chapter A3) and their associated expectations. Intensive communication at the outset of the project with the end users of the project deliverable is rightly believed to be a critical success factor. This is particularly important in IT projects where failure to include the end users early-on can jeopardise their approval of a complex, technical system that may require adjustments to working processes and intensive training. However, particularly in software projects, communication between developers and end users is often problematic because the experts use technical terms that the users do not understand. In return, the users find it difficult to express their requirements, concerns and problems clearly.

Opposition to the project

The following recommendation applies to all sectors of industry, though it is often difficult to put into practice – especially if there is strong resistance to the project within the organisation: `End users who are intended to represent their departments in the project team must be chosen with care: they should have a sufficient knowledge of the organisation and their department to have a clear idea of the details and content of the project as a whole, they should demonstrate interest in project activities and they should enjoy communicating. This is important because they´ll be returning to their departments and keeping them up to date on project progress and content.´ [14]

C1 PROJECT START-UP

Once the project stakeholders have been identified, it is necessary to define and prioritise the project objectives step by step. These objectives are then documented in the contractor specification (→ Chapter C2).

2.2 Formation of the project team and rules for project team work

In many projects, the project manager has little authority when it comes to selecting team members. Often, in matrix organisations, he has to make do with employees who are allocated by line managers. While he may sometimes have a right to a say when project team members are selected, he seldom has a veto.

In the start-up phase, the project manager needs particularly to demonstrate his leadership. He must start the team-building process (→ Chapter D3) and ensure that
- a positive project culture is created,
- latent conflicts are brought out into the open and discussed,
- team members can identify with the project, and
- they are familiar with and accept the project objectives.

Team-building process

In the start-up phase every single project group member needs to be especially creative – particularly in defining the project objectives. During this, the project manager is best advised to employ a co-operative management style (→ Chapter D3). In other words, the team members should have the opportunity to contribute their knowledge and participate in decisions.

During this phase, the project manager is responsible for establishing communication channels (→ Chapter D4) with line managers and with the customer to enable proactive stakeholder management. It is especially important to provide regular information via the formal reporting system and in status meetings. The project manager also has to create the basis for effective informal communication, where possible. For example, this can happen if people´s workplaces are close to each other, or through joint activities.

Proactive stakeholder management

2.3 Clarification of key parameters

Some of the most important parameters are the human and financial resources involved in the project. It is necessary to clarify whether
- the necessary funding for the project is available and
- qualified staff can be provided.

The first task requires at least a rough estimate of costs, and the second a rough staff deployment plan for the project (→ Chapter C6). This plan must take into account other running projects and work unrelated to the project.

2.4 Establishment of project management structures

Many companies have mandatory guidelines for establishing the project management structures.

For example, in a matrix organisation, job descriptions generally exist for the project manager (→ Chapter A6), the team members, the project controller and the steering committees. These descriptions specify the responsibilities, tasks and powers associated with each position. In such cases, the project manager has little scope for influencing the structure. This restricts the options available for designing the project-specific organisational structures suggested in some of the literature. Despite this, he should ascertain whether some modifications for the purposes of the project are necessary – even if he is not authorised to implement these himself. In any event, he can, however, allocate roles to team members. He can, for instance, assign a team member to take minutes at project status meetings or to act as a facilitator in a project group.

Adaptation of the management structure

Whatever happens, it is recommended that the following points are documented in writing at the project outset:
- the duties of the project sponsor (e.g. to release a member of staff from regular duties to work on the project),
- the delivery of the necessary data and
- the review of milestone results.

2.5 Creation of the initial project plans

The most important planning documents that the team has to prepare include
- an initial work breakdown structure (→ Chapter C4),
- a milestone plan containing deadlines and interim results (→ Chapter B) and
- a detailed plan of activities and timelines, at least for the next phase of the project (→ Chapter C5).

If the organisation has a suitable standard procedural model, it should be used and, if necessary, adapted to the project.

Work breakdown structure

Opponents of systematic project management often object to the drafting of a work breakdown structure (→ Chapter C4) in the start-up phase for the following reason: `A work breakdown structure cannot be prepared in the start-up phase because managers are not yet aware of the precise work packages that will probably have to be carried out and, with regard to others, they won´t have got much further than naming them.´ On the other hand, a work breakdown structure is a planning document that is very rarely drafted in one go and, in most cases, it can be modified in the course of the project. The plan changes as increasing knowledge is gained.

3 Project start-up workshop

In literature and in practice, the terms `project start-up workshop´ or `project start-up meeting´ and `kick-off meeting´ are used synonymously. However, it has proven advantageous to differentiate between the two types of meeting.
1. Kick-off meetings are used for providing stakeholders with information about the project. They therefore mainly involve one-way communication.
2. In project start-up meetings, the participants establish the basis for subsequent project phases. It is difficult to determine the best time for holding a workshop of this type. Platz positions it in Figure C1-1 between the milestones M1 and M2. If the process of clarifying objectives is a lengthy one, it may be necessary to call several meetings.

Gareis [15] recommends that the start-up workshop should last from one to three days, depending on the project size. This is realistic. However, it is unlikely that all tasks can be completed at a single meeting. Often, it is difficult to arrange for all participants to attend meetings held on several different days. This is why the project team should prepare the workshops so that their results only have to be presented, approved or modified there. Standard work breakdown structures and process models (→ Chapter B) simplify these preparations considerably.

Realistic duration

3.1 Participants

In addition to the project manager and his team, the project start-up workshop should be attended by representatives from the customer´s or project sponsor´s organisation. It is also necessary to invite other key stakeholders if they have been identified. In restructuring projects, these consist of the works or staff council and representatives of the affected organisational units. The first step towards gaining acceptance for the project is taken when key project stakeholders are involved in and are able to contribute to the definition of objectives. The following agenda has proven to be useful:

Key stakeholders

AGENDA
1. Greeting and introduction of the participants
2. Presentation of the agenda and agreement of rules for co-operation at the start-up meeting and during the project
3. Establishment of participants´ expectations in respect of the start-up meeting
4. Collection of information
5. Overview of the existing project management plans
6. Identification of stakeholders and definition of general project objectives
7. Drafting of an initial work breakdown structure
8. First cost estimate
9. Definition of project phases and key milestones
10. Detailed planning for the next project phase
11. Project management structures, information and communication system
12. Project risks
13. Next steps, especially the next deadlines and tasks
14. Feedback round

4 Variations on the start-up process

This chapter describes an `ideal´ start-up process. In practice, the process can take many forms. Particularly in the capital goods sector, for example, the start-up phase differs from that shown in Figure C1-1[16]. Projects in this industry are generally initiated in response to a customer enquiry. Since detailed bids are often associated with high costs and the bid success rate is low, particularly when economic conditions are poor, each bid is subjected to a review process which takes into consideration the customer´s creditworthiness, the expertise and skills available within the bidding company´s own organisation, as well as technical, commercial and political risks (→ Chapter E2).

Capital goods industry

Based on this evaluation, the management decides whether or not to submit a bid. If it decides to submit, a team sets about preparing the tender documents. For large-scale orders this can be viewed as a project in its own right. For example, if the company develops a technical concept for a potential customer, this will form the basis for determining the delivery date and working out the financial aspects of the bid. After the terms of delivery, payment and warranty, and a quote for financing have been worked out, the bid is submitted to the customer.

In some projects, the process of defining objectives needs to be structured with particular care. For example, in aerospace projects, a review team checks the technical concept at several pre-defined control points [17].

Self-assessment questions for each certification level

No.	Question	Level				Self-assessment
		D	C	B	A	
C1.1	What tasks are associated with the project start-up phase?	2	3	3	4	☐
C1.2	What would be a practical agenda for a project start-up workshop?	2	3	3	4	☐
C1.3	How can the end of the start-up phase be distinguished from the project launch?	2	3	3	4	☐
C1.4	What significance does the start-up phase have and what potential mistakes can be made?	2	3	3	4	☐
C1.5	When does a project commence?	2	3	3	4	☐
C1.6	What are the tasks of the executive management team or the steering committee in the start-up phase?	2	2	2	4	☐

C2 PROJECT OBJECTIVES

The definition of project objectives doesn´t sound like a particularly difficult task. However, on closer inspection, it becomes clear that a great deal of work is involved (ICB Elements 8, 13): How do the project objectives look in detail? How can they be made measurable? These and similar issues need to be dealt with by the project manager in the objective definition process. He has to be familiar with the main rules for defining objectives and be aware of their relationship to organisational objectives. He also needs to be able to analyse the inter-relationships between objectives and to set priorities when they are in conflict. When defining objectives, it is necessary to take the expectations of the different stakeholders into account.

1 Variables in objective definition

The ICB differentiates between three variables when objectives are defined:
1. Expenditure (hours and costs)
2. Time (duration and deadlines)
3. Result (work and services of the required quality)

This classification, which only covers the `hard´ objectives (= in terms of costs, time and quality), is too simple. A suitable classification for software development and organisational projects will be provided later on in the chapter. Recently, key stakeholder satisfaction (→ Chapter A3) has also been included as a variable – especially that of customers, project team members and executives. In restructuring projects, the works council and the employees affected by the project result are also stakeholders.

Satisfaction of key stakeholders

Accordingly, the `Benchmarking Model for Project Excellence´ developed by the German Association for Project Management (GPM) requires clear evidence from teams competing for the German and International Project Management Awards of how the project manager formulated, developed, reviewed and implemented project objectives. Above all, they are required to demonstrate
- which stakeholders were identified,
- how they were identified and
- how the various objectives of these stakeholders were ascertained and taken into account in the project objectives [1].

Evidence required for the PM Award

1.1 Cost objectives

Often the estimated project costs only include those for the development or production of a system, but not those that will be incurred when the system is in productive use. Recently, some sectors of industry have begun to realise that all costs incurred during the system´s lifecycle need to be taken into consideration when cost objectives are defined. It is therefore necessary not only to keep development and production costs or their sum to a minimum, but also total lifecycle costs. These include development, production, maintenance and operating costs [2] as well as costs that are incurred in connection with decommissioning and disposing of the system.

Total lifecycle costs

Fixed net cost price

Cost reimbursement price

The significance of the cost objective becomes clear when the situation is simplified and a specific sales revenue target is defined that is to be achieved by the project. A fixed net cost price is one example of this. In this case, the profit or profit margin (= difference between sales revenue and variable costs) achieved by the project can only be maximised if costs that can be influenced are minimised. This does not apply for a cost reimbursement price when an absurd economic scenario occurs: Here, the company´s profit is maximised if the costs are as high as possible, since it receives a certain percentage of reimbursable costs in the form of profits.

In development projects leading to serial or mass production, project costs constitute only a small portion of total costs – even if a high proportion of future production, operating and maintenance costs have already been established during the development process on the basis of the product design.

1.1.1 Design-to-cost approach

Priority for cost objective

With a design-to-cost approach the cost objective takes priority. Supporters of this model assume that a pre-defined, largely technical task can be carried out in ways that result in very different costs. A more or less fixed proportion of costs is specified for development activities. The requirements for the system being developed need to be formulated in line with this cost model and the most important functions are accorded priority.

This approach differs from the conventional approach because the anticipated costs are not derived from the system requirements and specifications. Rather, the specification is adapted to the available resources. This design-to-cost approach has a good deal in common with the target costing methodology ($\rightarrow$ Chapter C6) [3].

1.2 Time objectives

Priority for time objective

The critical path method of planning, which was initially developed as a time scheduling and management tool, makes clear the high priority once accorded to time-related objectives by military customers and by NASA in the United States. Recently, short project lifecycles (based around the concept of `time to market´) have been accorded special significance particularly in research and development projects.

1.3 Quality objectives

Quality objectives can be categorised from a variety of different perspectives. The US Department of Defense [4] has developed a good classification for the development of physical products, and also for investment projects in the plant construction industry.

It specifies four categories of technical project objectives or technical requirements:

Technical project objective categories

1. Performance or effectiveness objectives (e.g. applicability, accuracy, duration, maximum speed, output in units produced per unit of time)
2. Operational objectives (e.g. the requirement that a specific period of total downtime may not be exceeded when the system is in productive use)
3. Design or construction-related objectives (e.g. weight, dimensions)

4. Production and cost-efficiency objectives or productivity objectives (e.g. requirements in terms of costs per unit of output generated by the system)

This classification of quality objectives cannot be used in software development and organisational projects.

1.4 Quantitative and qualitative result and process objectives

Four examples drawn from software development can help to explain the differences between quantitative and qualitative result and process objectives [5]:
- Quantitative result objectives
  - Reduce subscriber administration costs by 25 percent per transaction
  - Reduce the time the business spends on processing orders by ten percent
- Quantitative process objectives
  - Develop software within 12 months
  - Generate a marketing concept within 12 months
- Qualitative result objective
  - Improve the working conditions for school staff
- Qualitative process objective
  - Provide career opportunities for the testing personnel

2 Making project objectives measurable

The project manager should define performance and process objectives in such a way that when the project ends it is possible to ascertain whether and to what extent they have been achieved. In short, every objective should be measurable and therefore verifiable (= operationalisation). For example, the formulation of the qualitative objective `Improve the working conditions for school staff´ is too vague.

Verifiability

The operationalisation of the cost and time objective is basically a simple process. However, problems occur if estimates of project lifecycle and costs are revised too often during the early project phases.

Generally, the following metrics are specified for evaluating adherence to costs and deadlines:

Measuring adherence to deadlines and costs

$$\text{Adherence to deadlines} = \frac{\text{actual time taken to implement the project}}{\text{originally estimated project duration}}$$

$$\text{Adherence to costs} = \frac{\text{actual project costs}}{\text{originally planned project costs}}$$

Von Wasielewski [6] details some far more complex performance indicators for measuring adherence to costs and deadlines. He takes into account the fact that estimated values will be revised during the course of the project. As a result, the ultimate measurements taken are more precise.

Quality objectives can be expressed in the form of technical performance indicators or characteristic curves. Chestnut [7] provides several examples:

Performance indicators and characteristic curves

- Dimension-free quality indicators, such as attenuation factors or the ratio of torque to moment of inertia
- Curves that show efficiency relative to load factor
- Implementation ratios, such as substance output relative to substance input
- Productivity per unit of time, i.e. usable products per unit of time relative to total production per unit of time
- Thermal efficiency
- Transport efficiency (total weight of the vehicle relative to the installed drive power)

Sometimes several years pass before it is possible to ascertain whether a system has satisfied the quality requirements. This applies, for example, to certain reliability values. The result of time-staggered laboratory tests is generally not an adequate substitute for practical tests.

2.1 Problems associated with operationalisation

Social objectives

It is sometimes difficult to operationalise project objectives. When social objectives are formulated, for instance, project managers often have to make do with reference values. For example, to make the objective of `increasing employee satisfaction´ measurable, the project manager has to use the rate of employee turnover as the metric. This is because the measurement of employee satisfaction using a standardised questionnaire is extremely time-consuming. It is, however, very difficult to establish whether a reduced rate of employee turnover is really an indicator of project success. The rate of turnover could, for example, have declined because of a downturn in the labour market.

Software projects

In software projects, particular problems arise in association with operationalisation. How, for example, can abstract objectives such as `user-friendliness and ease of maintenance´ or `software flexibility´ be measured with precision at the end of a project? Over the years, many attempts have been made to make quality objectives in software projects measurable. These include the ISO 9126 quality model. Balzert [8] provides an overview of these attempts.

F-C-M Model

At this point, it is worth describing the Factor Criteria Metric (F-C-M) model briefly. First, quality attributes such as functionality, reliability, usability and correctness are defined. Then, these attributes are broken down into sub-characteristics or criteria. These can then be made measurable by means of quality indicators or metrics.

> **Example**
> *The quality feature of correctness (does the software meet user requirements?) is sub-divided into the criteria of*
> - *completeness,*
> - *consistency and*
> - *traceability of software components in terms of user requirements (i.e. being able to trace how these requirements were met).*

Then, for example, customers or suppliers check whether the criterion of completeness is satisfied with the assistance of a checklist that includes all key functions.

Organisational projects

In organisational projects, those responsible are often reluctant to give a precise definition of objectives against which the final success of the project can be evaluated. They fear that their performance will be measured on the basis of these objectives. The controller, who is responsible for project transparency, should insist on verifiable objectives in such cases.

To see how objectives definitely should not be formulated, we take the example of a project for the 'planning and implementation of a conference'. The first version of the objective is bad as it is incomplete:

> `The congress should be attended by at least 400 people and should achieve a profit margin of at least Euro 50,000.´

It would be far better to formulate this objective including a quality criterion:

> `At least 75 percent of the delegates must evaluate the organisation and content of the event as ``very good´´ or ``good´´ .

3 Further rules for formulating objectives

In addition to the requirement of formulating measurable and therefore verifiable objectives, there are several other rules that the project manager should observe. The table provided by Platz [9] (→ Figure C2-1) shows each of these rules in conjunction with a negative example. The table also makes clear the importance of operationalising project objectives.

INCORRECT FORMULATION	RULES FOR PROJECT OBJECTIVES
1. `The known infrastructure-related temperature problems are to be avoided.´	Project objectives should be formulated understandably and positively.
2. `The throughput of the A3 module is to be substantially increased.´	Project objectives should be quantified wherever possible.
3. `The weight should not be more than 16 kilograms.´	The variables should be precisely specified. Expressions such as `could´ and `ought to´ should be avoided. The use of `must´ or `can´, on the other hand, enables prioritisation.
4. `The product must offer a high degree of user-friendliness.´	Complex terms such as user-friendliness should be broken down into individual components.
5. `The necessary 12 percent reduction in weight of the T 311 must be attained by the use of aluminium and of hollow parts.´	Project objectives should be formulated in a solution-neutral way, so that they do not rule out potential solutions from the outset.
6. `Maximum functionality and complete coverage of all the functions provided by competitor products must be achieved.´	Project objectives should be examined to ascertain whether they are really necessary.
7. `The display, which is powered with 3.3 volts and requires a precision tolerance of at least one percent of the final value, must be designed so that the operator can read it from a distance of three metres.´	Project objectives must be formulated individually as separate statements – i.e. as requirements.
8. `The project objectives are contained in the letter of 3 April, the discussion report of 16 April, the quotation of 18 April and the quality guideline QS03.´	Project objectives should all be documented in one place. Only then can they be revised and updated.
9. `Despite the concerns of the marketing team, it has been decided that the development team´s proposal to use batteries instead of solar cells is binding.´	Project objectives should be accepted by all persons affected.

Figure C2-1 Rules for the formulation of objectives and negative examples according to Platz [9]

4 Graphical representation of project objectives

Hierarchical structure

Project objectives can be shown in a hierarchical structure. Figure C2-2 shows the overall or global objective in a transport project, four objective categories, the specific objectives, their operationalisation and finally, at the bottom, the degree to which the objectives have to be achieved.

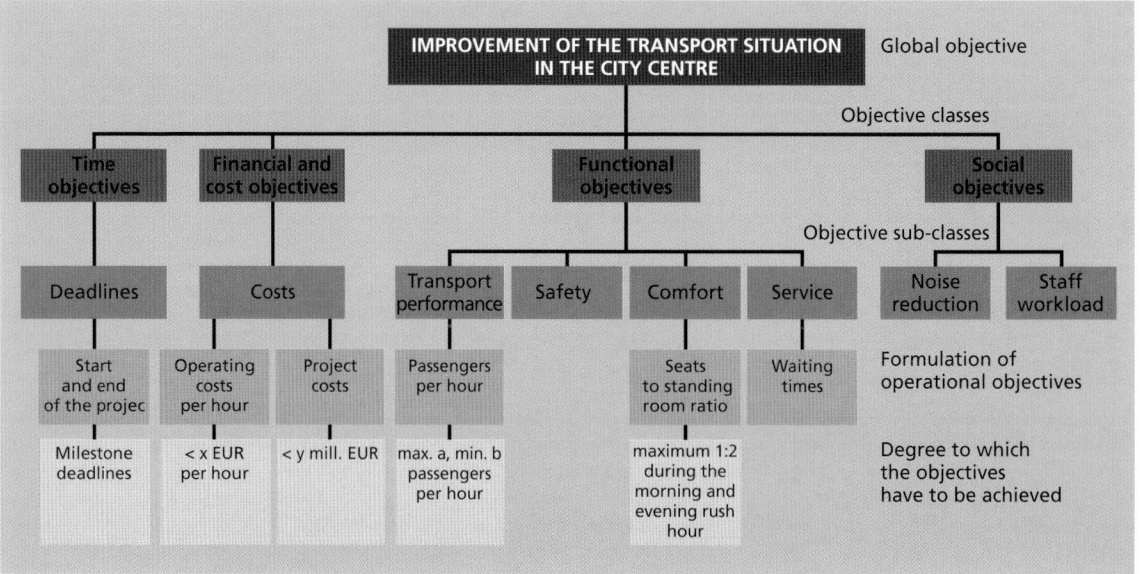

Figure C2-2 Example of the graphical representation of objectives [10]

5 Relationships between project objectives

Competitive and complementary relationships

Competitive or complementary relationships can exist between two project objectives. The second type of relationship is unproblematic since the more fully one objective is attained, the more completely the second objective is also achieved. However, competitive relationships (= conflicts of interest) often exist. In other words, the more fully one objective is attained, the less completely the other is. For example, the shortening of a project lifecycle is often only possible in conjunction with an increase in costs. Higher requirements made of the system to be developed that become evident during the project lifecycle will generally need to be paid for either by extending the project lifecycle or accepting higher costs. Competitive relationships can also exist within a quality objective, which generally consists of several sub-objectives. For instance, increasing the maximum transport load of an aircraft will have a negative effect on the distance it can fly.

The classic experiment by Weinberg [11] demonstrates this problem clearly. The researchers gave five programming teams the same task to perform. However, a different project objective was specified for each group on which to concentrate. Team 1 was required to keep programming hours to a minimum, Team 2 was to minimise program lines, Team 3 was to use as little memory as possible, Team 4 was to aim for maximum program clarity to ensure ease of maintenance and Team 5 was to produce a user-friendly product. Independent experts evaluated and accorded school grades to the project outcome.

C2 PROJECT OBJECTIVES

The matrix in figure C2-3 shows that all teams with the exception of Team 4 received grade A in respect of the objective to which they were required to accord highest priority. However, the matrix also shows many conflicts of interest. For example, Team 1 received grade E for the criterion `program clarity´ and grade D for `minimisation of the number of program lines´ and `minimisation of memory´. In other words, a conflict of interests exists between, on the one hand, the project objective of minimising expenditure or costs and the other three objectives, on the other. It is impossible to optimise all objectives at the same time.

GRADES ACHIEVED BY THE TEAMS IN RESPECT OF THEIR ACHIEVEMENT OF EACH PROJECT OBJECTIVE					
Team objective	Minimisation of effort	Minimisation of program lines	Minimisation of memory	Optimum program clarity	Optimum output clarity
Minimisation of effort	A	D	D	E	C
Minimisation of program lines	B – C	A	B	C	E
Minimisation of memory	E	B	A	D	D
Optimum program clarity	D	C	C	B	B
Optimum output clarity	B – C	E	E	A	A

Figure C2-3 Results of Weinberg´s [11] experiment

In real life projects, conflicts of interest mean that the project manager or customer has to compromise on objectives. In the design-to-cost approach, for example, low project costs are the main objective. The project managers therefore consciously accept a reduction in performance parameters.

Conflicts of interest and compromises

Conflicts between objectives should also be taken into account when managing the project. Every control measure has side effects and long-range effects. In their day-to-day work, project managers generally find that if the requirements of a project deliverable increase during the course of a project, they can only be satisfied at higher cost or by extending the project lifecycle. The procedures for change or configuration management (→ Chapter C7) therefore make it absolutely necessary that the previously valid costs and schedules are checked and – if necessary – revised when changes are made to the specification.

In practice, there are numerous examples of conflicts of interest. If the amount of time spent on testing software or hardware systems is reduced in order to meet a deadline, the negative consequences are generally experienced later on, as there is a risk of impaired product quality and additional costs for reworking incurred by the customer. The growing number of product recalls in the automotive industry also suggests that conflicts of interest between time and quality objectives may have been ignored. When vehicles are developed, the development team often dispenses with sufficient tests under real-life conditions in order to save time and reduce costs. As a result, the vehicles often have to be recalled shortly after delivery and repaired at the manufacturer´s expense.

Brooks´ Law   Brooks, who was responsible for the development of the OS 360 operating system at IBM, formulated the following law: `Adding manpower to a late software project makes it later.´

6 Relationship between project objectives and organisational objectives

It is easy to see how project objectives and organisational objectives are related if a company completes only one project in an accounting period. As an example, consider a shipbuilding company that builds a ship for a customer. The profit generated by the project will then directly correspond to the company´s profit for the period.

Pooled resources   In most cases, however, the relationships are far more complex. Usually, several projects are implemented in parallel and, at least to some extent, they draw on a common pool of scarce resources. Often, a department that is not involved in projects shares resources with the project departments.

In order that management can prioritise project objectives, it has to clarify the following type of issue in advance: `What effect will shortening the lifecycle of Project A by assigning Project B personnel to it have on the profit for the period and on the company´s sales?´

A model that can provide the data for making decisions of this type currently exists only in draft form. When assessing project viability, managers are paying increasing attention to ensuring that the projects they select are in line with the company´s business strategy ($\rightarrow$ Chapter E2).

7 Customer and contractor specification

Depiction of quality objectives   The customer´s requirements of the project and a detailed explanation of the ensuing quality objectives should be laid down in writing and – where necessary – revised during the project lifecycle. This is the purpose of the customer and contractor specifications.

Customer specification   DIN 69 905 defines the two terms. A customer specification includes `all of the customer´s requirements in respect of the supplier´s work and services´. It stipulates what is to be done and why.

Contractor specification   The contractor specification contains `the supplier´s strategy for implementing the customer specification´.

It describes the methods and resources to be used in fulfilling the customer´s requirements. This specification is the basis for further work on the project. In highly innovative projects with objectives that are vague initially, it is necessary to update and add more details to the specification during the project lifecycle.

Figure C2-4 illustrates a customer specification for a small-scale study. Figure C2-5 shows the rough breakdown of a contractor specification for software development. The contractor specification has to have been drafted and approved by the end of the study phase. Figure C2-6 shows the content headings of a contractor specification for a physical product (e.g. mobile phone).

C2 PROJECT OBJECTIVES

PROJECT ORDER 'SOFTWARE AS AN ECONOMIC FACTOR' STUDY	
Project Manager	Mr X
Objectives	The study is intended to provide information about the value currently attached to information technology (IT) particularly by medium-sized enterprises, about trends in IT development, and about options for optimising the value added by IT.
Tasks	The study should provide answers to the following questions: • What significance do the companies attach to information technology? • Where do the IT systems in use today, and those to be procured in the near future, come from? • What value is attached to the IT training that is currently provided to employees? • From where do the companies obtain information on IT-related themes and how do they rate the relevant state support policies?
Required project outcomes:	• Literature study • Tested questionnaire • Evaluation of the questionnaire
Budget	....
Constraints	The majority of respondents will be medium-sized industrial enterprises.
Deadlines, milestones	First interim report in mid-September this year. The interim report must contain the results of the pilot study, the questionnaire and the results of the pre-test. Conclusion of the study at the end of next March Please refer to the detailed milestone plan for details of further milestones and milestone results.
Customer	Institute Y

Figure C2-4 Customer specification for a study

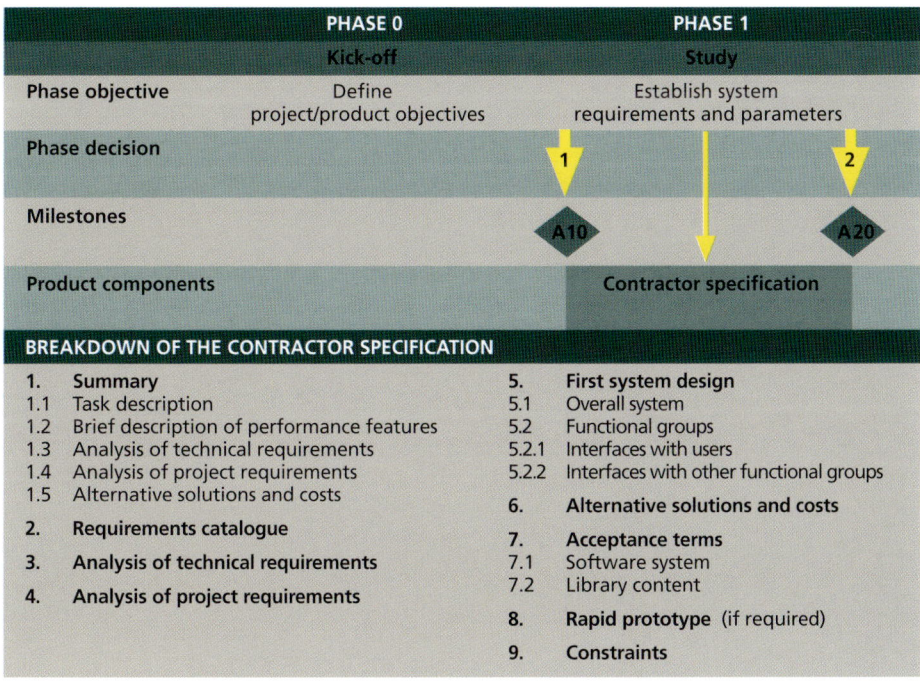

Figure C2-5 Breakdown of a contractor specification for software development [12]

143

C2 PROJECT OBJECTIVES

CONTENT HEADINGS IN A CONTRACTOR SPECIFICATION

1.	Product identification	Name, ID code, number, if appropriate with brief explanation of type and purpose, use, consumption, if appropriate related products (in-house/external), membership of product groups
2.	Marketing objectives	to be attained • User/consumer groups • Target markets (sectors and regions) • Image, aspiration level
3.	Envisaged price and costs	Negotiation parameters
4.	Functional requirements	Technical concept • Principle, mode of operation, fields of application • Performance data, limit values, tolerances • Terms of acceptance
5.	Dimensions and weights	• Shape, overall dimensions, position and function of power supply • Connections for power, exhaust air and waste water
6.	Operating requirements	including environmental requirements, if appropriate in the country of exportation
7.	Construction requirements	• Operability, accessibility • Maintenance requirements, repair options • Scrapping • Control systems
8.	Safety regulations	• Occupational safety, prevention of accidents at work • Damage protection, noise protection • Disposal, environmental protection

Figure C2-6 Content headings in a contractor specification

Self-assessment questions for each certification level

No.	Question	Level				Self-assessment
		D	C	B	A	
C2.1	What variables are commonly used in defining objectives?	3	3	3	4	☐
C2.2	To what constraints can project objectives be subject?	2	3	3	4	☐
C2.3	How can project objectives be operationalised?	2	3	3	4	☐
C2.4	What rules should the project manager observe when formulating objectives?	2	3	3	4	☐
C2.5	What relationships can exist between project objectives?	2	3	3	4	☐
C2.6	Where are the quality objectives for the project generally documented?	3	3	3	4	☐
C2.7	Why is it important to establish how project objectives and organisational objectives are related?	2	2	3	4	☐

C3 PROJECT RISKS

Projects harbour higher levels of risk (ICB Element 18) than routine activities. Therefore, there are many convincing reasons for systematic project risk management systems. Project managers should know how to deal with the processes of risk identification, analysis and assessment, and how to ascertain the key risks that are associated with a project so that these can be taken into account and monitored. They should also be aware of the various options for risk re-sponse planning that are available. Furthermore, they also need to know why systematic risk management systems can sometimes meet with a lack of acceptance in organisations.

1 Typical project risks

Projects are associated with far higher levels of risk than routine activities, since projects are, by definition, undertakings being carried out for the first time (→ Chapter A1). For example, organisations planning to enter new markets and acquire new customers inevitably have to undertake innovative and risky activities.

The need for risky activities

Example 1
A customer who has commissioned the development of a sales-planning software system is not satisfied with the user interface. The employees who have to work with the programme complain about it constantly. It is now doubtful whether the software provider will receive a follow-up order from this customer.

Example 2
In a hardware development project, a lengthy test in the climatic chamber is interrupted when a storm causes a power failure lasting several hours. The test then has to be restarted from scratch when power is restored and, as a result, the project finish date is jeopardised.

Example 3
A new SUV model has to be recalled for repair in authorised workshops because of serious defects in the gearbox.

The outcome of all three examples would have been different if adequate risk-response planning activities had been carried out. In the first example, the supplier could have developed what is known as a `rapid prototype´ (the `rapid prototyping´ process) for evaluation by the subsequent users of the software. In the second example, an emergency power supply could have been made available in good time. In the third example, the manufacturer of the vehicle could have carried out more road tests instead of focusing on vehicle simulations with the aim of achieving the fastest possible time to market. In many cases, a process of systematic risk-response planning can help avoid nasty surprises. Then, if an event of damage or loss occurs, the person responsible is not caught unawares.

Risk response planning

==According to the ICB, project risks are `events with an uncertain outcome or situations that can have potentially negative (detrimental) effects on the success of the project as a whole, individual project objectives, results or events. They are defined in terms of the probability of the occurrence of the event and the impact if it does occur (…)´.==

In this definition, occurrence of the event refers to a situation where the risk actually comes to pass.

2 Types of risks

Versteegen's categorisation

Many attempts to classify risks can be found in project management literature. Versteegen [1] makes a workable distinction between commercial, technical, time-related, resource-related and `political´ risks.

2.1 Commercial risks

Example
A customer who has ordered a large-scale piece of equipment runs into cashflow problems during the course of the project. As a result, he is no longer able to fulfil his contractually agreed payment obligations.

2.2 Technical risks

Example
Flooding suddenly occurs during the construction of a road tunnel, despite a positive geological report.

2.3 Time-related risks

Example
A supplier does not deliver in time an important tool for a new injection-moulded part that is needed in a product development project.

2.4 Resource-related risks

Example
The manager of a product development project has counted on specific employees for his project team. However, these employees are not now available because a customer has found a defect in another product that has already been delivered. This defect has to be remedied as quickly as possible.

2.5 `Political´ risks

Example
In a large-scale plant construction project, an executive selects a supplier with a reputation for sub-standard product quality, despite concerns expressed by the project manager. The reason is that the executives of both companies are old school friends.

2.6 Dependencies between various risk types

Dependencies exist between the various risk types. Here are some examples:
- If a competitor headhunts a highly-qualified member of the project team during an R&D project (= resource-related risk), this can have a considerable impact on meeting deadlines (= time-related risk) and achieving agreed quality levels (= technical risk).
- Flooding during the construction of a tunnel (= technical risk) leads to cost overruns (= commercial risk).
- If an organisation fails to meet a contractually-agreed deadline (= time-related risk), it will have to pay a contractual penalty (= commercial risk).
- In order to make up delays in meeting deadlines (= time-related risk), additional assembly workers are necessary in a plant construction project. However, they are not available at short notice due to the amount of time required to train them (= resource risk).

3 Benefits of systematic risk management

According to the ICB, project risk management comprises `the processes of identification, categorisation and quantification, as well as the management of risk response measures of all project risks. Project risk analysis and management recognises a formal approach to the process as opposed to an intuitive approach. Risk management occurs in all phases of the project life cycle´. [2]

The very definition of the word risk makes it clear that risk management is never a reactive process, but always a proactive one. This means that `risk management involves dealing with risks before they occur.´ [3] Project managers can defend themselves against unidentified risks only by including contingency time in the project schedule, by ensuring that cost estimates are accurate, or by taking out insurance.

Risk-response planning is generally much less costly than resolving the losses incurred if the risk actually comes to pass. A number of commentators in the IT sector make reference to the many projects that have failed owing to the lack of risk response planning. The annual `chaos studies´ published by the Standish Group [4] always include a whole series of such projects.

For this reason, many of the models used for assessing the maturity of IT projects also include a check on whether a risk management system has been set up at the organisation being assessed. In the Capability Maturity Model (CMM) (→ Chapter C9), risk management is mandatory at maturity level 3. [5] The US Ministry of Defense, for example, awards contracts to software suppliers only if they can provide evidence that their project management systems have CMM level 3 certification.

Maturity model

In many cases, risk management is regulated by statutory provisions. The IAS International Accounting Standards (which are mandatory in the European Union) specify that joint-stock companies and other enterprises whose balance sheet total, turnover and number of employees exceed a certain limit must install a monitoring system for the `timely detection of any developments that could jeopardise the company´s continued existence´.

Legislation

The `New Basel Capital Accord´ (Basel II) imposes tougher requirements on banks in respect of risk management – not only for real estate projects, but also for IT projects. [6] A working group of the German Association of Public Banks has devised a proposal for categorising operational risks [7], one of which is `Process and Project Management´.

Many risks can jeopardise the continued existence of an organisation (e.g. currency or environmental risks), and these also include the risks associated with large-scale projects.

Sustainability management An increasing number of organisations are now committed to sustainability management. This means that they operate risk management systems in the areas of economy, environmental protection and social policy (e.g. employee working conditions) to ensure that their corporate development is sustainable. Not only do they publish business data, but also environmental and social data (e.g. data on CO_2 emissions or redundancies) with the aim of mitigating risks (e.g. the risk of damage to their reputation) by increasing the transparency of their operations. This is a sign of their desire to convince the capital markets of their sustainability, build confidence and improve their image.

3.1 Weighing up the costs of risk response planning against the potential loss

Acceptable risks Project managers need to examine each identified risk to ascertain whether preventive measures would actually cost less than the potential loss. There are, for example, some minor areas of potential damage or loss that can simply be accepted, since their potential impact on the budget is actually lower than the cost of introducing measures to prevent their occurrence.

> **Example**
> A construction manager who deviates from the approved construction plan by increasing the height of the attic walls with the aim of benefiting the future users of the building's exposes himself to the risk of being caught out by the building's inspector. However, he deliberately accepts this risk, which he could easily avoid by adhering to the construction plan (= costs of risk response planning), because the anticipated fine is significantly lower than the value of the advantages gained.

4 Risk identification

Risk dynamics over the course of the project In project management practice [8] people often imagine that it is sufficient to identify risks at the outset of the project. Many project managers do not take into account that the project is exposed to different risks during different phases, and that their significance or weighting can change during the project. The ICB therefore emphasises that risk management should be practised in all phases of a project.

4.1 Checklists

Example in the start-up phase In this section we focus on the identification of risks during the start-up phase (→ Chapter C1). Checklists are an important tool for risk identification. Every organisation should systematically analyse projects that have already been completed (→ Chapter C10) and prepare checklists on the basis of their findings.
The VDMA checklist [9] shown in Figure C3-1 only differentiates between technical and commercial risks. These general checklists should be adapted to the requirements of the organisation implementing the project, and extended if necessary. Franke [10] provides a comprehensive checklist for plant construction projects.

C3 PROJECT RISKS

Very few standardised checklists currently exist for other types of projects. Checklists for IT projects that have been issued by the US Ministry of Defense are one exception.

Risk checklists should not be filled in by the project manager or nominated risk manager alone. They support the work of the entire project team. The best way of guaranteeing that a wide range of risks is identified is to involve representatives of all departments concerned, including the commercial departments. According to Versteegen [11], 'One important aspect of team-oriented risk management is the pooling of the knowledge of all project team members – as a type of knowledge management'.

Inclusion of the project team

	VDMA CHECKLIST
1.	**Technical risks**
1.01	Risks relating to the development of a new product
1.02	Risks relating to the planning of a new application
1.03	Risks relating to the testing of a new production process
1.04	Risks relating to the use of a new technology
1.05	Failure to deliver assured (product) characteristics
1.06	Failure to deliver assured performance (e.g. output)
1.07	Failure to deliver a system that functions reliably overall (availability)
1.08	Failure to ensure the functional reliability of the sub-systems
1.09	Interface risk during the implementation of the project
1.10	System interface risk as a result of
	1.10.1 outsourcing
	1.10.2 sub-standard engineering
	1.10.3 inadequate description of performance requirements
	1.10.4 defective local production
1.11	transport and packaging
2	**Commercial risks relating to technical performance**
2.01	Contractual penalties as a result of missed deadlines, defective/incorrect characteristics and system performance
2.02	Supplier-related risks (contract, deadline, quality, costs)
2.03	Product liability/consequential damage or loss
2.04	Risks arising from the customer's requirement for local production (lower quality etc.)
2.05	Unclear definition of assembly procedures
2.06	Force majeure
3	**Commercial risks (internal risks)**
3.01	High order value relative to capital employed
3.02	Risks associated with cost estimates, especially in respect of completeness, correctness, price structure etc.
3.03	Financing risks (internal, especially liquidity)
3.04	Warranty (scope, liability limitation options, time limits, settlement of claims for consequential damage or loss)
3.05	Provision of security for payment obligations
3.06	Definition of performance for assembly work (contractual provisions)
3.07	Definition of acceptance terms and dates
3.08	Risks resulting from compensation transactions
3.09	Risks related to management structure or staffing
4	**Commercial risks, risks ensuing from the organisation's environment**
4.01	Political or economic risks
4.02	Currency risk
4.03	Lack of agreement on applicable law
4.04	Public authority risk (delay in authorisation processes)
4.05	Consortium-related risks
4.06	Financing risks (external)
4.07	Taxes and duties in foreign countries
4.08	Force majeure (e.g. industrial action)
4.09	Arbitration tribunal clause
4.10	Language risk (e.g. instruction of the customer's staff)

Figure C3-1 Risk identification checklist

4.2 Risk workshop

Many organisations fail to introduce project checklists even if they have regularly implemented similar projects. Instead of dispensing entirely with risk analysis – a situation that often happens – it is a good idea for these companies to hold a risk workshop both in the start-up phase and the later phases of the project. A risk workshop can be combined with the start-up workshop (→ Chapter C1). The project team should also take advantage of experience gained in similar projects at other organisations.

Experiences from other organisations

A risk workshop is also a good idea if an organisation is planning an entirely new project (e.g. a company merger).

Füting [12] provides detailed instructions on how to implement a risk workshop. They can be summarised as follows:
- First of all, the project manager presents his project and distributes documents such as the work breakdown structure, milestone plan, customer specification or preliminary supplier specification.
- In a kind of brainstorming session (Metaplan meeting → Chapter D2), people from all the departments involved in the project write down on cards all the things that they believe could go wrong in the project.
- In a third stage, an assessment is made of the probability that the various risks could occur, the financial consequences and the measures to be implemented in the worst-case scenario of the risk actually occurring.

5 Analysis and assessment

Risk list

Generally, the risk identification process produces an extensive list of risks, irrespective of the method used to identify them (checklist, workshop etc.). It is then necessary to assess these risks so that the management can set priorities and create appropriate risk response planning structures.

Controversial mathematical processes

In recent decades, the US armed forces have developed an abundance of complex risk analysis and assessment tools, all of which necessitate mathematical skills. However, their usefulness is debatable. This is why they have not become popular in project management practice. The US Ministry of Defense has now switched back to using checklists and simple risk assessment procedures.

5.1 Monetary assessment

Impact and extent of loss

Monetary assessments are frequently used as a method of risk quantification. The question is, what monetary loss will the organisation incur (impact, or extent of the losses) if the risk event actually occurs? More specifically, what contractual penalty would have to be paid if the agreed project finish date were delayed by four weeks? What effect would a three-month delay in the market launch of a product have on the project's profit margin?

If the worst-case scenario is associated with loss of life, however, assessments based on a purely monetary criterion cannot, of course, be applied. This is also the case for serious risks, such as the damage to reputation resulting from an accident at a chemicals plant, vehicle recalls by car manufacturers, or serious planning mistakes made by a public authority.

5.2 Assessment of probability

The most commonly used textbooks recommend both a quantitative assessment and an assessment of the probability of the risk event occurring. The DIN 62 198 standard [13] defines `project risk´ as a `combination of the probability of a specific event occurring and its impact on the project objectives´.

In many cases, probability of occurrence – which is a subjective probability – is expressed in terms of a range extending from zero percent to 100 percent. Zero percent means that the assessor is absolutely certain that the risk event will not occur. 100 percent means that the risk event will definitely occur. It is therefore no longer a risk.

Subjective probability as a percentage

Both figures – loss (in this case measured in Euro) and probability (measured as a percentage) – can now be multiplied together to provide a risk value. The formula is:

> risk value = probability of an event occurring (%) x impact if it does occur (EUR)

Risk value

Example
The members of a project team estimate that there is a 20 percent probability of the project finish date being delayed by four calendar weeks. If the team delays the date beyond this period, a contractual penalty of € 50,000 will have to be paid. The value of this risk is 0.20 x € 50,000 = € 10,000 penalty.

5.2.1 Modified form of the Delphi method

Franke [14] also commissioned experts to develop a modified form of the Delphi method (→ Chapter C6) for risk assessment. Here, the person chairing a risk workshop first explains the risk to be assessed. Next, the group discusses it. The experts at the workshop then state subjectively the probability that various events will occur. The person chairing the workshop then evaluates the results using a statistical simulation method. Although this approach provides more information than just a simple calculation of the arithmetical mean, based on the workshop participants' statements, it is more time consuming.

Statistical simulation

6 Selection

Assessment by experts

The diagram shown in Figure C3-2 [15] is the result of a risk assessment by experts. The risks are already categorised as A, B and C risks in an ABC analysis.

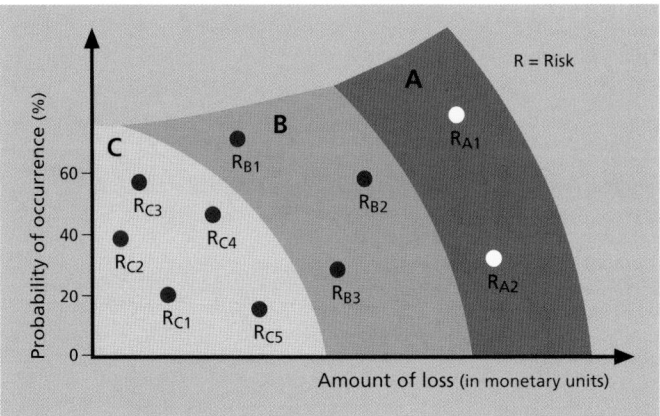

Figure C3-2 Categorisation of risks into A, B and C risks

'A', 'B' and 'C' risks

'A' risks have the most influence on the project risk situation because the estimated probability of occurrence and the assumed impact, and therefore the product of both variables, are high. 'B' risks lie somewhere between 'C' and 'A' risks in terms of probability of occurrence and impact. They should definitely be taken seriously by the project management. 'C' risks, however, are associated with only a low probability of occurrence and financial impact. They can therefore be disregarded in the first stage of the risk response planning process. However, the project manager must still keep an eye on 'C' risks during the course of the project because they can develop into 'B' or even 'A' risks. The project manager must always give priority to taking action with respect to 'A' risks.

6.1 Loss category approach

Loss categories

Since it is sometimes difficult to measure the anticipated loss in monetary terms, several authors have developed other approaches.

Versteegen [16] uses 'loss categories' by selecting an ordinal benchmark (ordinal numbers such as rankings in a sports competition). Figure C 3-3 shows an example of this.

LOSS CATEGORY	TIME	COSTS	FUNCTIONALITY
3 Maximum feasible loss	Considerable time delay	Budget overrun of more than 10 percent	Priority 1 requirements not fully implemented
2 Mid-scale loss	Slight time delay	Budget overrun of up to ten percent	Priority 1 requirements complete, but incorrectly implemented
1 Small-scale loss	Hardly any time delay	Budget overrun of less than five percent	Priority 1 requirements complete, but implemented with minor defects

Figure C3-3 Loss categories according to Versteegen

An ordinal scale is also used for the probability that risk events will occur, with 1 standing for relatively low probability and 5 for high probability. The risk value is obtained by multiplying the two ordinal numbers together. The highest loss value using the above ordinal scales is 15 (3 times 5).

Risk value

6.2 Simple approach used in project management practice

In practice, many project managers – at least those who actually use risk management systems – are happy to use a straightforward assessment scale of `high´, `medium´ and `low´. The example shown in Figure C3-4 [18], which already includes risk response planning measures, was used in an IT project.

Simple risk assessment scale

RISK	CAUSE OF RISK	CONSEQUENCES	MEASURES
(H)igh, (M)edium, (L)ow			
Fixed go-live date (H)	The external computer for the previous application is switched off on the go-live date.	The new application must be installed by this date. Otherwise, a substantial impairment of the organisation´s day-to-day operations is likely to occur.	Strict project management, implementation of the core functions that are absolutely essential.
Impairment of core business as a result of software errors during system start-up (M/H)	Extensive software modifications are expected. Complex interfaces to the PSC (production scheduling and control) application exist.	As a result of time pressure, the software is inadequately tested and defective, impairing core business processes. Financial losses.	Consistent implementation of the projected test plan. Intensive implementation support during the start-up phase.
Poor response times (H)	In the past, the customer has used the software with much lower volumes of data. Complex online interfaces to systems on other computers exist. Use of tried and tested hardware, but decentralised printer structure.	Impairment of day-to-day business processes (e.g. when taking orders by telephone, or printing out shipping instructions).	Performance analysis throughout the project: simulations of actual operation in the user test. Use of a tool to measure and monitor system performance.

Figure C3-4 Risk analysis and countermeasures

7 Monitoring

Risks need to be permanently monitored during the course of the project. Depending on the phase during which risk identification and assessment take place, different phase-typical risks become apparent [18]. Risks that have already been assessed and identified can differ in terms of their impact. For example, the risk that a rival company will launch a product on the market first can be assessed as relatively low during the project start-up phase. However, if the marketing department has gained new information about such activity, it must be assessed as a higher risk in the implementation phase. The main project milestones (→ Chapter B) are very good times for assessing the risk situation.

Change of risk assessment

The table [19] shown in Figure C3-5 contains an example of an ongoing risk monitoring process, which also includes assessment of the effectiveness of the measures implemented. This process was first

Effectiveness check

developed in the IT sector. The priority code numbers indicate which risks the project manager has to focus on during the month.

PRIORITY this month	PRIORITY last month	RISK	RISK POLICY MEASURES (current status)
1	1	Adherence to the agreed finish date.	Commencement of negotiations with the customer about the programme's functions, which will not be available until version 2 is produced.
4	2	The 'what you see is what you get' characteristic is not implemented.	A freelance employee, with whose work the company has been satisfied in the past, will deal with the problem from next week onwards.
2	3	The user interface does not match the customer's expectations.	The team develops two prototype user-interfaces at short notice. As soon as they are finished, the customer will dispatch potential users for testing.
3	4	Some modules exist in different versions. At the moment, it is not clear which version the project team should continue working on or which module – and which version of that module – should be delivered to the customer.	The programme package for configuration management is used consistently. An employee is assigned to develop the reference configuration and to document the implicit changes that have been made.
5	5	The quoted price is a 'political' price. There is a risk that the costs actually incurred will be higher.	The software provider supplying the software adapts the program to the project's cost schedule so that costs can be charged at work package level. The project is subsequently structured into work packages. The commercial department ensures that cost information is available more quickly. The project manager obtains monthly residual cost estimates, measured in terms of person hours.

Figure C3-5 Permanent risk monitoring with checks to ascertain the effectiveness of measures

8 Risk response planning strategies

In the process of risk response planning, a distinction is made between risk avoidance, risk reduction, risk mitigation, risk transfer and risk acceptance.

8.1 Risk avoidance

The bid review process

The priority aim of this strategy is to avoid risk exposure entirely. In extreme cases, this can mean that the organisation decides, after a detailed bid review process (→ Chapter E2), not to submit a bid to a potential customer. Another option would be to delete certain requirements from the customer specification that are associated with high risks.

8.2 Risk reduction

Prevention

This strategy reduces the probability of identified project risks occurring by implementing preventive measures. For example, the risk of cost overruns can be considerably reduced by making regular residual cost estimates and calculating anticipated cost at completion (→ Chapter C6).

8.3 Risk mitigation

Risk mitigation is intended to allow the project team to mitigate the impact of an event. They therefore take effect when a risk event has already occurred. One means of mitigating damage is to allow for redundant activities.

Mitigation of consequences

> **Example**
> *A second computer is provided at the appropriate time so as to minimise the impact of lengthy computer downtime on the project finish date and project costs.*

8.4 Risk transfer

An organisation implements risk transfer measures to transfer project risks to other organisations. For example, it can take out an insurance policy when project work commences. Obviously, risks can only be insured if they are associated with a low probability of occurrence but high potential losses. An appropriate contract structure (→ Chapter A4) can also enable a contractor to transfer the risk to the customer. The degree to which risk transfer will be successful depends, first and foremost, on the contractor´s market position.

Insurance and contracts

8.5 Risk acceptance

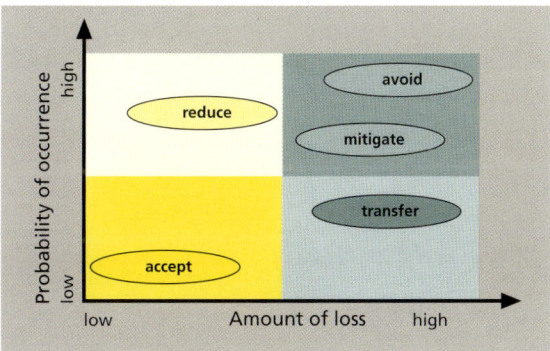

Some risks in a project will be accepted by the management team, which is why no risk response planning measures will be implemented to deal with them. These risks are generally associated with only small-scale losses and are unlikely to occur. Figure C3-6 gives a general overview of the measures that are appropriate for various risks. [20]

Figure C3-6 Range of suitable risk response planning measures

9 Risk management software

In a study implemented by the Fraunhofer Institute for Information and Data Processing [21], several organisations stated that they would be happy to implement risk management but they lacked the appropriate software. However, other than a spreadsheet and word processing programme for creating checklists, software is not essential for risk response planning. Versteegen [22] recommends that `a tool should only ever play a subsidiary role´.

10 Problems relating to the acceptance of risk management

It is not always easy to introduce risk management systems in an organisation. For example, organisations where project team members conceal problems for as long as possible and where people bearing bad news are penalised find it difficult to ensure that risks are identified and assessed honestly and in good time. While such organisations occasionally use risk checklists, these are generally only filled out cursorily by the project manager to comply with the formal requirements of the project manual and to appease the project controller.

Risk checklist with an alibi function

DeMarco and Lister provide a realistic description of this problem [23]: If you work in an organisation that does not have a comprehensive risk management system, you can use risk management tools and methods in your project, but you cannot make public the knowledge that you gain through using them. Anyone who tells the truth in an environment where optimism prevails will be putting himself in a difficult position. If you say that the chance of meeting a proposed deadline is only ten percent, you are likely to encounter an ambitious rival who will take advantage of the situation by saying to your boss, `Give me the job and I´ll make sure we meet the deadline´.

Concealing risks

Dymond made the following observation about concealing risks: `Based on experience in the field of risk management since the appearance of CMMs (→ Chapter C8), it is evident that a lack of communication about risks is one of the biggest obstacles to risk management. Concealing potential problems or risks leads to an escalation of crisis situations as soon as they occur.´ [24]

Corporate culture

If you are serious about risk management, you must therefore foster a corporate culture conducive to risk management, where bad news is not penalised and employees have the opportunity to discuss risks openly.

Hall´s [25] CMM model for project management (shown in Figure C3-7) describes how an organisation can move from ignoring risks towards introducing a reliable risk management system.

	STAGE 1 Problem	STAGE 2 Reduction	STAGE 3 Prevention	STAGE 4 Anticipation	STAGE 5 Opportunity
Desire	I´m sick of fire fighting.	I want to know what might go wrong.	I want to do the right thing so that I don´t have to reproach myself afterwards.	I want to know what our chances of success are.	I want to surpass my own targets.
Identification	I´m too busy to think about the future.	I´m aware of the risks associated with the project, I just don´t know how to explain them to my boss.	I try to discover the causes for potential problems facing me.	I believe that by holding regular project status reviews I can predict when project objectives will be at risk.	I identify project opportunities so that things turn out better than planned.
Planning	I´m too busy to make contingency plans.	I make contingency plans.	I plan ahead to avoid problems.	I try to quantify risks in as much detail as possible so that I can focus on the essential things.	I revise my plans so that I can derive maximum benefit from existing information.

Figure C3-7 Maturity model for project risk management (1)

C3 PROJECT RISKS

	STAGE 1 Problem	STAGE 2 Reduction	STAGE 3 Prevention	STAGE 4 Anticipation	STAGE 5 Opportunity
Behaviour in the project	I'm not afraid.	I don't want to tell people about my problems.	I share my fears with other people if they ask me about them.	If a risk can be quantified, we can keep it under control.	We try to counteract identified risks.
Measurement	I believe that risk management is too vague a concept to be of any use.	I always monitor the most important risks.	I have developed my own procedure and I collect project status data on an ongoing basis.	I use information about the project status to initiate risk planning.	I factor missed opportunities into the equation.
Improvement	I'm too busy to make any improvements.	I avoid mistakes that could jeopardise my career.	I try to avoid problems and prevent surprises for the project team.	When things go wrong, I try to put them right so that I can still achieve the project objectives.	My good ideas are what enable us to deliver excellent work.

Figure C3-7 Maturity model for project risk management (2)

Self-assessment questions for each certification level

No.	Question	Level D	C	B	A	Self-assessment
C3.01	What types of risks are relevant for projects?	2	2	2	2	☐
C3.02	What interdependencies can exist between different types of risks?	2	3	3	4	☐
C3.03	Why should risk management be carried out?	2	2	2	2	☐
C3.04	When should a risk management workshop be held during the project start-up phase?	2	3	3	4	☐
C3.05	How are risks assessed?	2	3	3	4	☐
C3.06	When and why are risks monitored?	2	3	3	4	☐
C3.07	What strategies are suitable for risk management?	2	3	3	4	☐
C3.08	What are the prerequisites for the acceptance of risk management in an organisation?	1	2	2	4	☐
C3.09	How are risk analysis and risk response defined?	2	2	2	2	☐
C3.10	What methods can be used for identifying risks?	2	3	3	4	☐
C3.11	What is the difference between risk analysis and risk management?	2	2	2	2	☐

C3 PROJECT RISKS

C4 WORK BREAKDOWN STRUCTURE

What work does our project involve? In professionally managed projects, the work breakdown structure (WBS) provides the answer to this question. This hierarchically-structured overview of the project (ICB Element 12) performs a range of functions of which the project manager needs to be aware: what structuring options are available, which ones are suitable for his project and how can these be systematically created and coded in the WBS? Detailed work package descriptions represent an important tool for assisting him in this process. In many cases, standard breakdown structures help to reduce the time and expense involved in planning and to ensure that the project manager takes all important project tasks into account. A description is provided of common mistakes and omissions to be avoided.

1 Definition

Conscientious people often write a checklist containing all the tasks to be performed before any major personal project (e.g. a holiday, a family celebration). In the same way, project managers and their teams should prepare a similar list at the earliest opportunity (→ Chapter C1): in other words, a work breakdown structure containing the activities that a project involves. In contrast to personal checklists, a WBS generally consists of several levels, i.e. it has a hierarchical structure. There are a number of rules to be observed when developing a WBS.

Hierarchical structure

According to the ICB, project structuring is the process of breaking down a project into work units and tasks. The WBS is a chart or table showing the structure of the project and a systematic answer to the question: 'What work does our project involve?'

It is a hierarchical representation of the project, broken down into several levels. The structure can be based around objects, sub-tasks or business units.

1.1 Work packages

The lowest hierarchical classifications in each branch of a WBS are known as work packages (WPs). They cannot be sub-divided any further. On the other hand, tasks that are sub-divided are called sub-tasks. This is illustrated in Figure C4-1, which is based on the content of the DIN 69 901 standard.

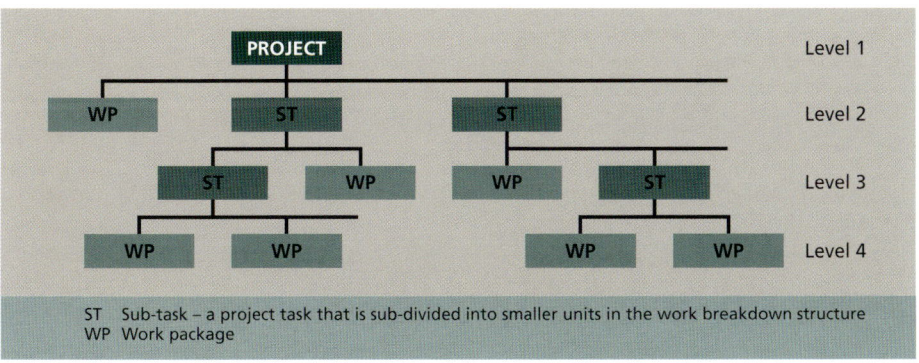

Figure C4-1 Chart showing sub-tasks and work packages in a WBS according to DIN 69 901

Originally, work packages were simply considered to be groups of processes or a single process in a project network diagram. They represented the link between the WBS and project network diagram, because they are shown in both.

> In contrast, DIN 69 901 defines a work package as 'an aspect of the project that is not broken down any further in the WBS and can be located at any of the hierarchical levels.'

2 Tasks

Work breakdown structures perform a wide range of tasks. The most important of these is described by the ICB as follows: 'The WBS is a central instrument of order and communication in the project.' If it is jointly prepared by the project manager and his team, it ensures that everyone has the same understanding of project tasks and procedures.

Simplified expenditure and cost estimation

The WBS is also extremely significant for project-specific cost planning and management. In many project cost management systems, work packages are the lowest elements in the cost centre hierarchy [1] (→ Chapter C6). Experience shows that it is much easier to estimate costs if a complex project is broken down into sub-tasks and work packages than it is if the overall project is not sub-divided further.

Basis for documentation and contractor specification

Often, the WBS and its numbering system are taken as the basis for project reports and technical documentation. The structure of the contractor specification, which documents project requirements, is often identical to that of the WBS. Finally, the individual items in the WBS can also function as information objects in cost databases provided that they form part of a standard structure (→ Chapter C6).

Other tasks

The WBS is the basis
- For allocating tasks and responsibilities.
- For project-specific order management. The project manager, acting as an 'entrepreneur within the enterprise', allocates the various work packages as internal orders to specific departments within the organisation. In some companies, the people responsible for the work package also sign off the work package description.
- In risk analyses, the planners can check which work packages are associated with a particularly high risk of missing deadlines or cost overruns, or of not achieving the desired results. The project manager needs to keep an eye out for early warning signs and implement preventive measures for high-risk work packages.
- In time scheduling, the work packages can be linked together in the schedule of activities according to the principles of the network analysis method of planning (→ Chapter C5). If the planning requires a particularly high degree of detail, the team will break down the work packages in the project network diagram into several processes.

The following description of rules for creating a WBS is an example taken from the plant construction industry [2]:
- Only one WBS may be prepared and used in any one project [in practice, different WBSs for different purposes can sometimes exist within a single project]. A standard structure should be created and kept up to date as the basis for every project.
- The project management team is responsible for project-specific application of the WBS and for updating it in liaison with the departments involved.
- The WBS should remain valid for the entire project lifecycle.

- The content and numbering system of the WBS must be used by all persons involved in the project, as well as the central service departments (e.g. purchasing, accounting).
- The work packages in the WBS should be defined by the people responsible at the instigation and under the supervision of the project manager.

3 Breakdown

The ICB gives the following break-down principles for orientation
- the product to be produced (= object),
- the functions required in the project (= performance),
- the responsible organisational units and
- the place where a task is to be performed.

In practice, projects are most commonly broken down by object and by performance (= breakdown by function). Two textbook examples [3], which refer to the same project, help to explain these two breakdown principles (Figures C4-2 and C4-3).

Object and function-oriented breakdown

3.1 Object-oriented breakdown

When an object-oriented approach is taken to project breakdown, the planners divide up the project deliverable – in this case a camera – into its components, modules and any individual parts. If the breakdown process is purely object-oriented, the product structure and the product structure plan is identical to the WBS [4]. However, this type of structure does not cover all tasks (functions) that are necessary for achieving the project objective. For example, the project team members also have to make sure that the camera being developed is commercially viable (= marketing preparations). They also have to manage the project. This necessitates a function-oriented breakdown.

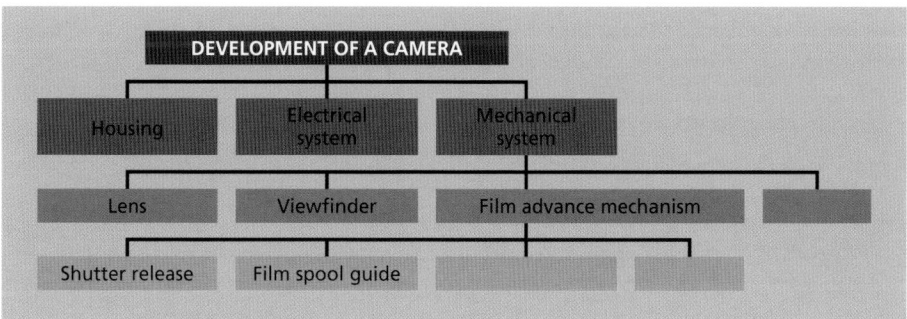

Figure C4-2 Object-oriented WBS (excerpt)

3.2 Function-oriented breakdown

Every project includes a wide variety of functions, such as
- Analysis of customer requirements
- System design
- Quality management

- Planning and monitoring of the project
- Change management
- Production planning
- Marketing and sales preparations
- Staff training
- Support in the product launch phase
- Documentation
- Project hand-over and capturing knowledge

Different WBSs for a project

Breaking the project down by function produces a very different WBS for the camera than an object-oriented approach does.

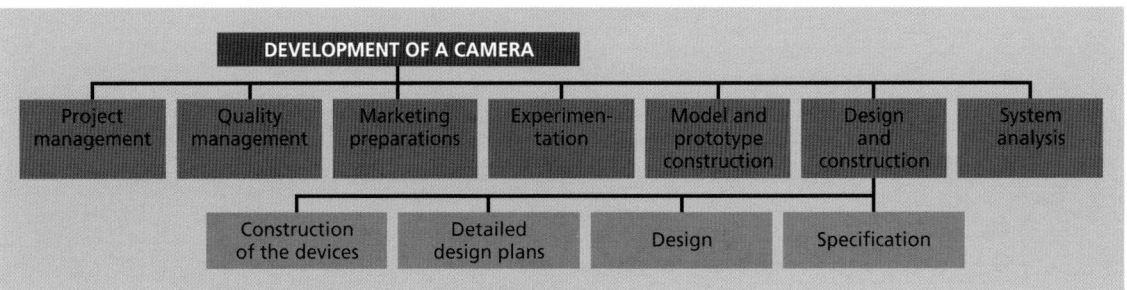

Figure C4-3 Performance-oriented WBS (excerpt)

Even the function-oriented WBS omits one aspect: the camera's component structure. This has been ignored in the higher levels of the WBS as a result of using this breakdown principle.

3.3 Combining breakdown principles

Combined WBS

In order to ensure an integrated view of the project, the team needs to adopt both a function-oriented and an object-oriented approach. This is why, in practice, most WBSs combine both. Often, from level to level, planners will alternate between object-oriented and function-oriented structures. Sometimes, both principles are applied on the same level. Planners generally ignore Platz's recommendation [5] that only one structuring principle should be used on each level.

There are no firm rules about when to apply the different principles. However, it can be ascertained at a very early stage of a project – before the project deliverable has been structured to any significant degree – that a function-oriented approach will prevail – for example in development projects requiring high levels of innovation. Later, at the higher levels of the WBS, sub-tasks should be mainly object-oriented. It is therefore vital to combine the breakdown principles in the correct way.

The example shown in Figure C4-4 demonstrates this on the basis of the camera project.

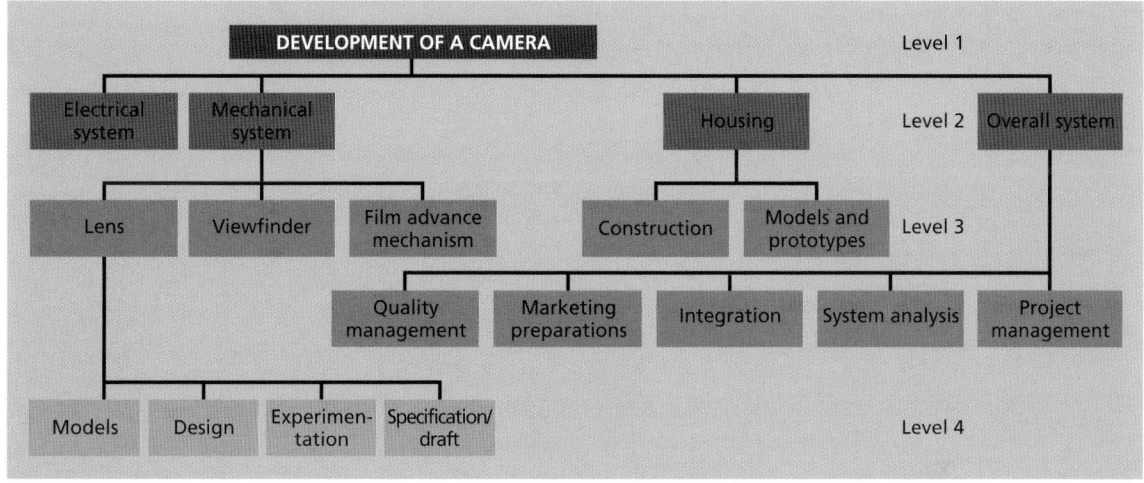

Figure C4-4 Combination of object and function-oriented breakdown approaches (combined WBS, excerpt)

The items on Level 4 are work packages. As specified by the DIN standard, they are not sub-divided any further. The breakdown should end as soon as a set of tasks can be allocated to a particular employee, who can be designated as being responsible for that work package.

End of the breakdown

4 Creation

If the organisation has already implemented similar projects or is familiar with the principles of how to structure a project, the planners can generally develop the project structure by taking a top-down approach.

Example
The planners prepare a WBS for the development project for a new car. They can base this on a known product structure for a car (body, chassis, engine block etc.). The team members are already aware of the main functions required, such as the marketing preparations, application for registration documents, preparation of maintenance and servicing documentation, and training of service technicians, since these are the same in every automotive development project. These large blocks of tasks can be sub-divided across various levels right down to the work package level. This also applies if the vehicle being planned incorporates a series of new features.

The WBS will be developed in a different way if the project is highly innovative for the organisation. In such projects – a PR project at a school for example – the project manager is best advised to hold a workshop with his team in order to define the necessary activities, bundle them into work packages and, by taking a bottom-up approach, combining them into sub-tasks.

High level of innovation

4.1 Creation of a WBS using a reference structure

R&D projects

Instead of directly creating work breakdown structures, where objects or functions are identified and directly incorporated into a WBS, R&D project managers use a more complex procedure. Platz [6] describes this procedure using IT projects.

1. Initially, a product structure is developed that graphically shows all the components of a project in a hierarchical structure. It corresponds to the parts list in a mechanical production process and is identical to a purely object-oriented WBS. Mapping the product structure is a technical planning task.
2. A reference structure is then developed on the basis of the product structure plan, a type of plan that represents an interim step and interface between the product structure and the project structure. This not only includes the product structure, but also all design documents, prototypes, research, equipment, tools and similar. This structure also contains results (e.g. of market surveys or of value analyses) that are not intended for the customer or the market, but must be collected over the course of the project in order to achieve the project objectives.
3. The planners then identify which work packages are needed to obtain the defined final and interim results. This is how they derive a WBS from the reference structure that includes all work packages necessary for the project´s success. At the work package level, it is exclusively function-oriented.

Multi-dimensional WBS

Recent efforts have been made to expand upon project structuring methods and to include several breakdown principles alongside each other (for example, sub-dividing the project on the basis of product components and place of manufacture or development). This leads to multi-dimensional work breakdown structures [7]. However, these approaches have not yet been tried out in practice to any significant degree.

4.2 Changes during the project lifecycle

'Dynamic' WBS

The first WBS is not the end of the story. Particularly in projects involving a high degree of innovation and initially unspecific objectives, the team will often have to add or delete work packages during the course of the project. Also, it is sometimes impossible to provide detailed work package descriptions at the outset of the project. In those cases, work packages are often only given a name, without any detailed explanation. A WBS is therefore dynamic and not static.

5 Work package descriptions

Minimum content

Routine work packages must always be included in the WBS, since they also have to be performed and will consume resources. If work packages are non-routine, it is necessary to provide a detailed description of them according to a specific scheme. There are no firm rules, however, for formulating such descriptions. Each organisation can define them in accordance with its own requirements. As a minimum, however, the descriptions should always include:

- Name, number, version and status (planned, tested, released) of the work package
- Brief description of content
- Projected results to be obtained
- Prerequisites for performance (e.g. deliveries required)
- Projected commencement and completion dates or projected duration

- Projected costs (generally unit costs, e.g. person days)
- Person responsible for the work package

Often, further information is given, such as
- Regulations that staff must observe when performing the work packages (e.g. safety regulations or the organisation´s quality management manual)
- Specific activities to be performed by the person responsible for the work package so that the work package can be executed.

Additional content

Figure C4-5 shows an example work package sheet. The organisational unit with responsibility for the work package is responsible for preparing a detailed description. If the person or unit responsible for the work package has already been nominated by the time that the work package is to be described, they provide the description. The project manager is required to check their description. After all, he is responsible for the timely implementation of the project within budget and in compliance with the agreed quality standards.

Responsibilities

WORK PACKAGE SHEET	
Date	
Project	Work package no.
Project phase	Version
Work package description	
Result	
Activities	
Prerequisites and deliveries required	
Person responsible	
Deadlines	
Target, current	
Start date	
Finish date	
Resource requirements (e.g. in person days)	
Employees involved	

Figure C4-5 Work package sheet

6 Standard work breakdown structures

Up to now, we have only discussed stand-alone work breakdown structures, prepared from scratch for every project. However, companies and other organisations have been creating standard work breakdown structures for certain types of projects for many years. In such cases, the planners then simply have to adapt the work breakdown structure to their specific project by deleting unnecessary subtasks and work packages or by adding new ones. The constituent elements of a standard work breakdown structure can also serve as information objects in a project cost database. These structures offer a range of advantages: They

Project-specific adaptation

- guarantee some degree of consistency in project planning,
- save team members the time and effort of having to prepare an entirely new WBS for each project,
- act as a checklist that ensures that important items and work packages are not forgotten, and
- reduce the time and expense involved in planning, thereby contributing to more cost-effective project management.

Standard structures are often used in power station, plant and communications satellite construction projects, for example. Figure C4-6 shows a standard work breakdown structure created by Madauss [8] for the European Space Agency (ESA). This example shows that standardisation is often also possible in projects that involve a high degree of innovation.

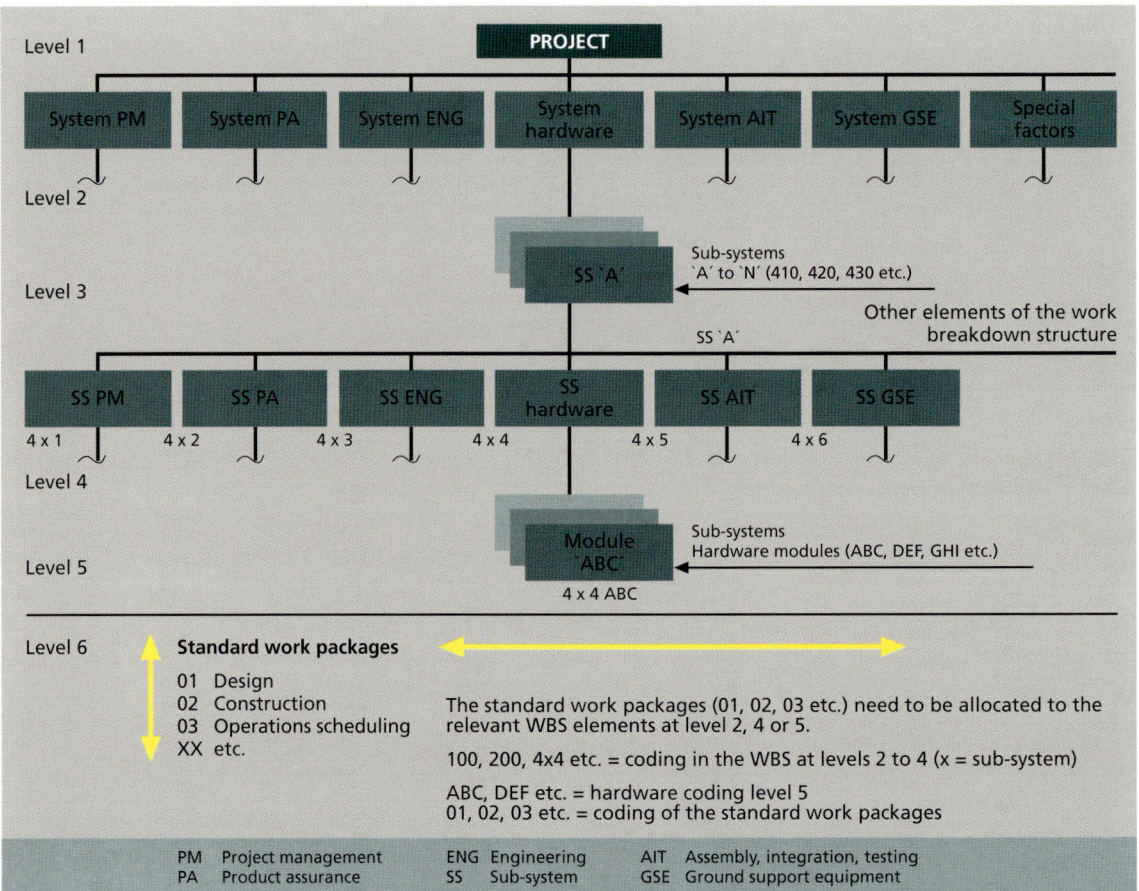

Figure C4-6 Standard work breakdown structure for the ESA

Figure C4-7 shows an excerpt from a standard structure at the work package level [9]. The work packages have already been sub-divided into processes, which are now elements in a standard WBS. These can be linked together in a project network diagram.

C4 WORK BREAKDOWN STRUCTURE

Level 2 sub-task: Market launch				
Level 3 sub-task: Sales promotion				
WP no.	Work package	Process	Person responsible	Result
...	...	...	...	Brief description
				of the projected result
...	...	...	...	Brief description
...	Sales force training	...	PE	of the individual processes
...	...	Concept	...	
...	...	Management structure	...	
...	...	...	...	
Level 2 sub-task: Drive unit				
Level 3 sub-task: Engine				
WP no.	Work package	Process	Person responsible	Result
...	...	Design	...	Brief description
...	Engine development	...	EL	of the projected result
...	...	Breakdown of the individual processes		
...		...	...	
...	...	Sample	...	
...	...	...	...	

Source: Hirzel, M.: Durch Standardisierung Innovationspakete beschleunigen. In: Hirzel, Leder & Partner (publisher): Speed-Management. Geschwindigkeit zum Wettbewerbsvorteil machen. Wiesbaden 1992, pp. 81–101

The terminology used in the chart has been slightly modified.

Figure C4-7 Excerpt from a standard work breakdown structure at work package level

Figure C4-8 shows a standard work breakdown structure for software projects [10].

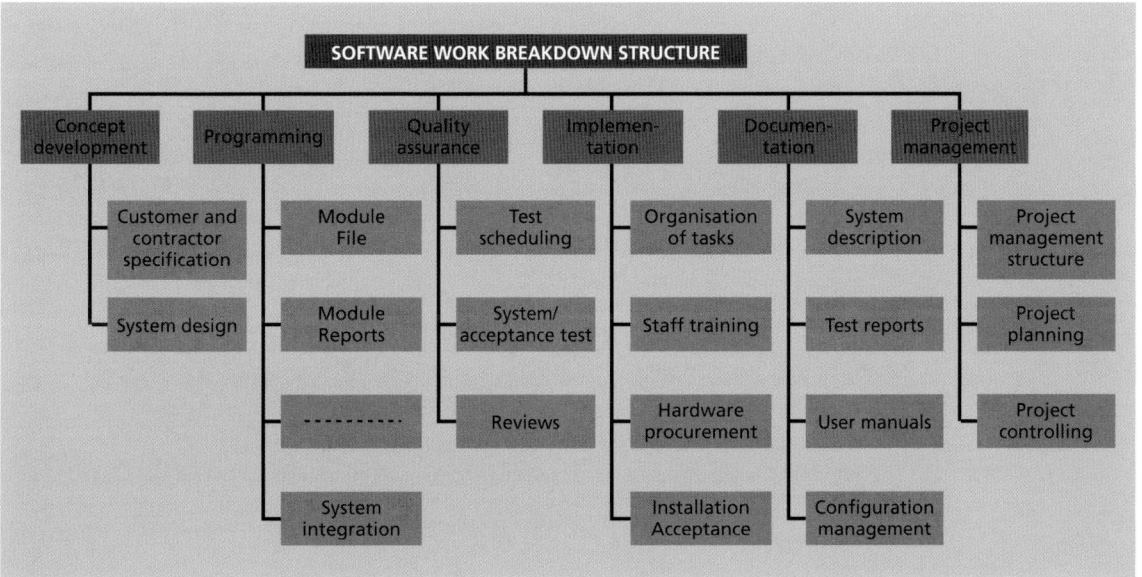

Figure C4-8 Standard work breakdown structure for software projects

7 Rules for WBS creation

Anyone who prepares a new work breakdown structure for every new project is making more work for himself than necessary. Furthermore, many organisations lack the standards and rules that might ensure some degree of standardisation in the project planning process.

It is, however, impossible to give recommendations that are effective in all circumstances and sectors in respect of the procedures to be used for creating a WBS. For example, it is not generally possible to state firmly how many levels should be used for sub-dividing the plan. Even so, various authors have provided some useful suggestions, such as the following one: `The process of breaking down a project into sub-tasks and work packages should end when work packages have been identified that can be handed over to one single organisational unit (company department or external customer) that has full responsibility for their execution. The required co-ordination activities need no longer be carried out by the project manager. Instead, they can be performed by the manager of the unit responsible for the work package.´ [11]

Oversized work packages
If this recommendation is followed consistently, some work packages may result that are too large in relation to the projected budget or time allocation. This can therefore undermine the successful planning and management of the project.

The following general guidelines can be formulated for the creation of a WBS:
- Only one person should be accorded responsibility for each work package – irrespective of how many people will be working on it.
- In phase-oriented project management, it should be possible to assign each work package to one specific phase. Exceptions are multi-phase tasks, such as the ongoing monitoring of costs.
- Tasks that are outsourced should be labelled as stand-alone sub-tasks or work packages.
- A clear specification should be formulated for each element of the WBS so that third parties can easily see whether the work package or sub-task has already been carried out. Otherwise, the project manager will not be able to track the project's progress. Work packages, the project manager´s `micro-milestones´, simplify the project´s supervision.

Example
Formulating a task simply as `Draft contractor specification´ is not useful because it allows the person responsible to decide the extent of detail and care with which this task is performed.
The following formulation is better since it refers to a standard and includes a quality assurance measure: `The contractor specification is to be drafted in line with the standard specified in the project management manual and then sent for approval to the customer.´

Boundaries and links between project activities
A work package should, if possible, be defined as a closed-end performance element that is differentiated from and linked to other work packages in a clear and straightforward way [12].
- The time allocated for completing the work package should be appropriately short in comparison to the overall project lifecycle. Otherwise, there is a risk that the project manager identifies a delay too late to implement effective counter measures. Work packages that are performed throughout the entire project, such as `planning and monitoring time schedules´ are exceptions.

Example
If a work package runs from January 2nd to the end of October, it will miss nine monthly deadline checks. The person responsible for the work package doesn´t have to `show his cards´ until the end of October. If work packages of a shorter duration are bundled together, the project manager can identify delays sooner.

- The target cost (→ Chapter C6) for a work package needs to be sufficiently generous, as otherwise it will be difficult to monitor and control costs during the course of the project.

7.1 Defining the appropriate size for work packages

Reschke and Svoboda [13] suggest that between one and five percent of total project costs should be set as a reference value when establishing the size of a work package. Based on experience, the accuracy with which costs can be allocated to sub-tasks and work packages tends to decline exponentially beyond a threshold, as the number of planning and control units increases [14]. On the other hand, too little detail (i.e. reviews too far apart), reduces the informativeness of the variance analyses carried out and makes cost management more difficult. The level of precision that is practical depends, to a great extent, on the system of data acquisition used.

Effects on cost allocation and management

Burghardt [15] gives different recommendations for different sizes of development projects. In large-scale projects with budgets of several million euros, he specifies a lower limit of two person-months, and for smaller projects a lower limit of one person-week. This recommendation implies a far higher level of precision than that proposed by Reschke and Svoboda. The discrepancy between the two recommendations can be explained in terms of the different levels of efficiency with which the data acquisition is managed.

In both cases, the project manager must ensure that the work packages are neither too large nor too small. This however leads them to a conflict of interests (→ Chapter C2) with respect to project objectives. On the one hand, they need to keep track of deadlines and, on the other – in parallel – monitor costs. These two requirements necessitate different approaches to defining the ideal size of work packages. In practice, compromises need to be made.

Conflict of interests

8 Coding

Every organisation can make its own decision on the system of numbering to be used for sub-tasks and work packages in the WBS. Often, the numbers that are allocated indicate the level of the WBS to which the element belongs (= identification key).

Identification key

A classification key also exists. This indicates the organisational unit responsible for the element or the project phase where it occurs.

Classification key

Since the sub-tasks and work packages generate costs during the course of the project, the coding also needs to satisfy the requirements of the organisation´s accounting department.

9 Common mistakes and omissions

Resource issues Many project managers are reluctant to spend the time on creating a WBS. They prefer to go straight to time scheduling. This is dangerous – especially since some sub-tasks and work packages use up resources even though they are not included in the time schedule. Examples of this are the various project management tasks that have to be done again and again, such as deadline and cost monitoring.

Changes Problems also occur if the team actually creates a WBS in their initial planning euphoria, but then fails to integrate necessary changes during the course of the project.

Forgotten sub-tasks Sometimes, the planners forget important sub-tasks, such as systematic project hand-over. Often, they will make the excuse that they know it anyway, but later on, of course, no one remembers to do the tasks concerned.

Self-assessment questions for each certification level

No.	Question	Level D	Level C	Level B	Level A	Self-assessment
C4.1	What is a WBS used for?	3	3	3	4	☐
C4.2	How can a WBS be broken down?	3	3	3	4	☐
C4.3	What principles for breaking down a WBS are frequently used in practice?	2	2	2	4	☐
C4.4	What minimum content should the work package description include?	3	3	3	4	☐
C4.5	What rules for creating WBSs have proven to be useful?	2	3	3	4	☐
C4.6	Why is it important not to skip the WBS creation stage and start off directly with time scheduling?	2	2	2	2	☐
C4.7	What advantages can be gained from using standard work breakdown structures?	2	2	3	4	☐
C4.8	What are the advantages and disadvantages of multi-dimensional work breakdown structures?	1	2	2	4	☐

C5 TIME SCHEDULING

Time scheduling (ICB Element 14) is the key to the detailed planning and monitoring of project time, cost and quality objectives. It enables planning ahead and offers the opportunity to consider several alternatives. Time scheduling involves regular variance analyses on the basis of regularly updated data records. These variance analyses are the basis for successful project management. The most important time scheduling tool is network analysis. A network diagram shows the interdependencies of the individual processes in a project and enables the calculation of realistic finish dates and milestones.

1 Significance

A project manager needs a toolbox for planning, control and monitoring to implement the project, taking technical and economic considerations into account,
- within a specific timeframe (= deadlines),
- with a limited budget or resources (→ Chapter C6) and
- bearing in mind the objectives to be achieved (Quality → Chapter C8)

(= the iron triangle of time, costs and quality). The methods and processes of time scheduling are the key to the operational realisation of these objectives.

Process scheduling is a valuable aid to project planning in the early phase of the project, and it enables the project manager to consider alternative schedules and solutions taking deadlines, costs and resources into account. It supports the project planners and coordinators, because it enables them to clarify the critical interfaces between individual parts of the project well in advance. It is based on project structuring (→ Chapter C4). If necessary, the planner breaks down the work packages into even smaller units (= activities). This simplifies the process of estimating implementation times and resource requirements, thereby creating the basis for cost estimates.

Planning methods and alternative solutions

When the process sequences have been established and times have been allocated to the tasks to be performed, the process schedule becomes the time schedule – and therefore the timetable for the project. Time scheduling delivers targets and, based on the cyclical acquisition of feedback data, provides an on-going record of the project´s current status. This provides a platform for the monitoring and management of deadlines, resources, costs and activities (→ Chapter C9).

Time schedule

Network analysis plays a central role in time scheduling. With the assistance of the network diagram it is possible to map interdependencies between processes and deadlines, and calculate the scope available for time scheduling and deadline management. If deviations from the planned project lifecycle are ascertained, the project team can use the network diagram to forecast possible consequences for subsequent work packages, sub-projects or project close-out, as well as test countermeasures. This acts as an early warning system so that the team can implement timely corrective measures.

Network analysis

The network diagram is an indispensable tool for the scheduler. However, the results should be presented to the customer in an appropriate format, such as a networked bar chart.

2 Basic principles

Work breakdown structure

Project scheduling cannot be carried out in a complex project until the project has been broken down into sub-tasks and work packages in the project structuring process (→ Chapter C4). The work breakdown structure provides transparency with regard to the functional, organisational or technical breakdown of the project. It shows all tasks (as the total number of work packages), but it does not provide any information about
- the sequence in which the project team processes the work packages,
- interfaces betweens sub-projects/sub-tasks and work packages or
- the precise order and time of implementation.

2.1 Time scheduling steps

Time scheduling is a step-by-step approach to obtaining this information.

Step 1: Specify work packages
In order to plan, monitor and control the project lifecycle, it is generally necessary to break down the individual work packages into smaller units (= activities).

Step 2: Define processes and create of a process schedule
In the second step, the work packages and/or activities are linked logically to one another. In most cases, this is initially done without taking resources into account. The information is transferred to a process schedule (= project network diagram), which clearly defines
- the interdependencies that exist between the activities,
- the activities that can take place in sequence, concurrently or independently of one another and
- the necessary time lags between the individual activities.

Identifying activities and interfaces

Process scheduling performs one of its main functions in this step: it ensures that the project team members specifically define the planned processes at an early stage in the project. This enables the project manager to identify and clarify the interfaces in good time.

Step 3: Integrate the process schedule in the time schedule
In the third step, the project team members estimate realistic implementation times for the activities.

Hidden float

Here, the project manager must ensure that the individual assessors do not include (hidden) float time for their own security. He alone has the authority to establish the total float for the project. If the project team has estimated realistic implementation times for the work packages and activities, taking into account existing resources, the earliest and latest dates for each activity can be calculated and time-critical processes and extra time (= float time) can be charted. This concludes the (preliminary) transition from process schedule to time schedule.

Step 4: Optimise the time schedule
Even if the processes have been carefully defined and the estimated implementation times are realistic, the deadlines that are initially calculated often show that the project team is unlikely to meet

Iterative process

the desired or required project finish date. In this case, the iterative process of schedule optimisation commences in conjunction with all accountable project personnel. The planners can attempt to shorten the project lifecycle, for example by changing the process structure (e.g. by overlapping activities) or reducing the implementation times (e.g. by increasing capacity).

At this stage of scheduling, the project manager can also simulate alternative scenarios and consider their effects on the project finish date or other objectives (e.g. costs or resource requirements).

Alternative scenarios

Step 5: Approve the project schedule
The individuals or units responsible for the project (e.g. customer, executive management, project manager, suppliers) must approve the time schedule after its optimisation. The dates in the project schedule are therefore target dates and form the basis of time management. They are binding on all persons involved. Often, they are important elements of the contract with the project sponsor. There may be penalties for non-conformity with contractually-agreed deadlines (Contractual penalties → Chapter A4).

Step 6: Manage the schedule
Time management is an aspect of time scheduling. It commences with recording deadlines and activities to monitor adherence to deadlines. Variance analyses enable the identification and analysis of deviations from the time schedule – especially delays or changes to the process structure.

Target deviation

Based on the analysis results and provided that network analysis is consistently applied, it is possible to forecast the effects of deviations on specific areas of the project or the project close-out. As in the optimisation phase, the project manager can consider alternative scenarios in order to identify suitable countermeasures.

Whatever the case, time management delivers an early warning to the project manager to indicate when corrective measures (→ Chapter C9) are necessary.

2.2 Regular time schedule updates

The time schedule is not just updated once, but at regular intervals throughout the project. This process comprises:
- Recording of current dates
- Comparison of current and target dates
- Variance analysis
- Planning corrective measures
- Revision of the time schedule

Project control function
The broader concept of project control not only includes time scheduling, but also the scheduling of costs, quality and resources. Consequently, the explanations of variance analyses also apply for resources, costs and quality (→ Chapter C9).

Project control

2.3 Tasks and objectives

The most important tasks and objectives of time scheduling are shown in Figure C5-1.

STEP	OBJECTIVE	TASK	RESULT
1	Breaking complexity down, definition of tasks	Specification of work packages	Activities
2	Timely coordination and planning of processes	Definition of processes • Definition of interdependencies and time lags • Clarification of interfaces	Process schedule (network diagram)
3	Establishment of the preliminary project lifecycle	Incorporation of the process schedule in the time schedule • Estimation of activity duration • Initial calculation of deadlines	Preliminary time schedule
4	Shortening of the project lifecycle	Optimisation of the time schedule • Consideration of alternative scenarios • Step-by-step optimisation	Optimised time schedule
5	Binding specification for all project participants	Approval of the project schedule	'Target' time schedule
6	Monitoring and control of the project lifecycle	Time management • Recording of target dates • Comparison of current and target dates • Variance analysis • Planning of corrective measures • Revision of the time schedule	Updating of the time schedule at each revision date

Figure C5-1 Tasks and objectives of the sequencing and time scheduling

2.4 Transfer of the work breakdown structure to the process schedule

Figure C5-2 illustrates how the work breakdown schedule (→ Chapter C4) is incorporated in the process schedule.

Transition from work package to activity

In the work breakdown structure, a work package is the smallest unit. In the process schedule, the transition from work package to activity is generally a fluid one.
- Individual, manageable work packages do not have to be described in any further detail and are included in the process schedule as an activity (1:1 relationship).
- Generally, a work package contains a series of independent activities (1:n relationship), which have to be planned and monitored as individual activities. In this case, a work package is shown as a subnetwork in the process schedule.
- For specific purposes, such as summarising information relating to deadlines (general project network diagram, framework time schedule), several work packages can be grouped together as one activity (n:1 relationship).

Linking subnets

The linking together of subnetworks necessitates the detailed clarification of interfaces between the work packages. For example, the activities between the various subnetworks are often activities such as coordination tasks, sub-system tests, end-of-phase reviews or technical activities (e.g. test equipment set-up, machine transportation). These processes can be part of other work packages that are impossible to map as closed subnetworks (e.g. work packages such as project management, quality assurance or acceptance).

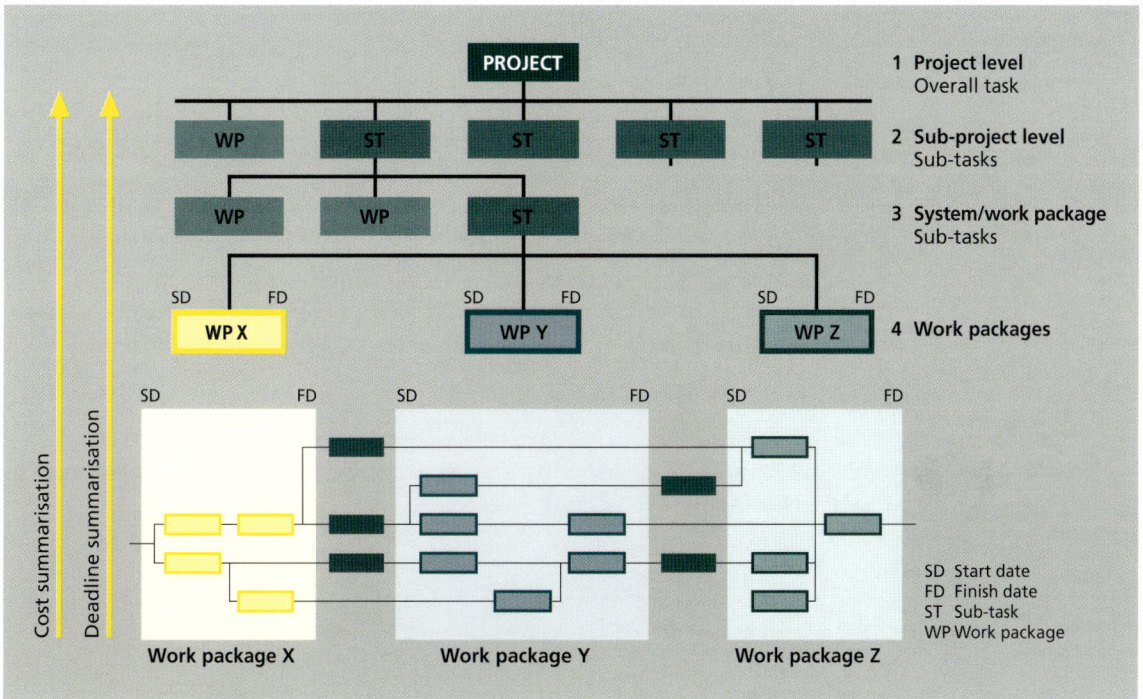

Figure C5-2 From work breakdown structure to process schedule

2.5 Methods of time scheduling

There are many software tools for the practical realisation of time scheduling which support both project planning and the time schedule. These tools deliver process documentation and results in diverse formats, e.g.
- Work breakdown structures
- Activity and deadline lists
- Feedback lists
- (Networked) bar charts
- Network diagrams
- Milestone plans
- Variance analyses
- Milestone trend analyses (MTA → Chapter C9)
- Time-path diagrams

3 Network analysis

3.1 Basic terms

Network analysis has become firmly established as the most important project scheduling tool in practice. It is essential if the project lifecycle is longer than six months and the project team has more than

Criteria for use

five members, and it is also practical in smaller-scale projects. In order to use this method of planning, the project personnel must be familiar with the basic terms.

Network analysis
Network analysis comprises `all processes for the analysis, planning, control and monitoring of processes on the basis of the graph theory´, whereby `time, costs, resources and other factors of influence can be taken into account´ [1].

Network diagram
The network diagram is a `graph or table showing processes and their interdependencies´ [1].
In order to describe the network analysis method, it is necessary to explain the elements of `activity´, `event´ and `precedence relationship´, as well as the representation elements of nodes and arrows.

Activity
Duration

`An activity is a procedural element that represents something specific taking place´ [1]. In practice, it is synonymous with process, procedure, work step or job. An activity starts and ends at a defined point in time and therefore has a specific duration.

Event
Milestone

`An event is a procedural element that represents the incidence of a specific status´ [1]. An event occurs at a specific point in time (= time of occurrence) or is attained at a specific point in time, but does not have any duration. Events of special significance during the project are called key events or milestones.

Precedence relationship (= PR)
`A precedence relationship is a quantifiable relationship between events or activities´ [1]. They are used to define the technical or contextual interrelationships. They can answer the following questions:
- Which activity is a prerequisite (predecessor activity) for the start of the next activity (successor activity)?
- What event must occur before the next project phase can commence?
- What time interval must exist between two activities?
- Can two or more activities (to a certain extent) take place concurrently?

3.2 Graphic representation of network diagrams

Graph theory

The Graph theory delivers the elements and terms for the graphic representation of project network diagrams.

Nodes
Depending on the type of network diagram used, the nodes symbolise either an event or an activity. Nodes are generally shown as boxes and, in some network diagrams, as circles.

Arrow
Depending on the type of network diagram used, the arrows symbolise activities and/or precedence relationships. Arrows are directional, i.e. they show the process direction. In network diagrams, they show the path from a start event/activity to a finish event/activity. Cycles (= loops) are not used.

3.3 Network analysis and methods of network analysis

A differentiation is made between the following network analysis methods [1]:
- Event-on-node (= EON)
- Activity-on-arrow (= AOA)
- Activity-on-node (= AON)
- Conditional network diagram (= CND)

3.3.1 Event-on-node network diagram

The event-on-node network diagram only contains events and precedence relationships. Boxes are used to depict events, and arrows are used to show precedence relationships. Since the EON does not include any activities (= procedures to be carried out), it is not suitable for the planning, management and monitoring activities by the project controller. Milestones can be defined in this network, as well as with the other network analysis methods. The most well-known event-on-node project network diagram method is the Program Evaluation and Review Technique (PERT) developed by the US Navy and Lockheed in 1958.

PERT

3.3.2 Activity-on-arrow network diagram

The activity-on-arrow network diagram is an activity-oriented network diagram in which the activities are depicted by arrows. At the same time, these arrows indicate precedence relationships. As in the event-on-node network diagram, the nodes represent events.

The most common AOA network diagram method is the Critical Path Method (CPM). The Du Pont de Nemours chemicals group developed CPM in 1956/57 in collaboration with the Sperry Rand Corporation. The activity-on-arrow network diagram method is widely used in the USA and in other English-speaking countries. This is why many foreign consortium members demand that CPM network diagrams are used in multinational projects. However, few project management systems allow a switch from AOA to AON or vice-versa.

Critical Path Method

3.3.3 Activity-on-node network diagram

In the activity-on-node network diagram, the activities are shown as boxes (nodes) and the precedence relationships as arrows. It is therefore an activity-oriented network diagram. However, because events (milestones) and activities can be mapped, it is also possible to create a combined process schedule.

Figure C5-4 shows a network diagram with standard AON elements. This example, which is explained in more detail later on in the chapter, contains both activities and events.

In German-speaking countries, the Metra Potential Method (MPM) is the most prevalent network analysis method for creating arrow-on-node network diagrams. The SEMA Company developed it in France in 1958, and it was used for the first time in the time scheduling of a reactor construction project.

Metra Potential Method

MPM focuses on the activity to be planned, implemented and monitored. It is also possible to map all interdependencies between activities and events which can occur in practice with the assistance of precedence relationships.

Figure C5-3 shows a summary of the differences between the various methods in terms of their process and representation elements.

3.3.4 Conditional network diagram

Conditional events and activities

Conditional network diagrams are based on the activity-on-arrow network analysis method and include the stochastic element of additional conditional nodes with optional inputs and outputs. Accordingly, there are conditional events where alternative paths exist for the further course of the project, and conditional activities which on completion offer alternative paths for the further course of the project. Probability values can be allocated to the onward paths at the outputs [1].

Estimated activity durations

Another option for mapping and taking variables into account when scheduling deadlines is to estimate the duration of activities. Instead of defining one single value for the duration of the activity, the planner provides three time estimates:
- Optimistic time estimate
- Most likely time estimate
- Pessimistic time estimate

These are the basis for the calculation of the most probable value or mean activity time [1].

Ascertainment of risks in an early phase

Conditional network diagrams are used to ascertain risks in the early phase of research and development projects (e.g. in the pharmaceuticals sector). However, they are less suitable for project scheduling, mainly because of the considerable workload associated with them. We refer the interested reader to Elmaghraby [3].

C5 TIME SCHEDULING

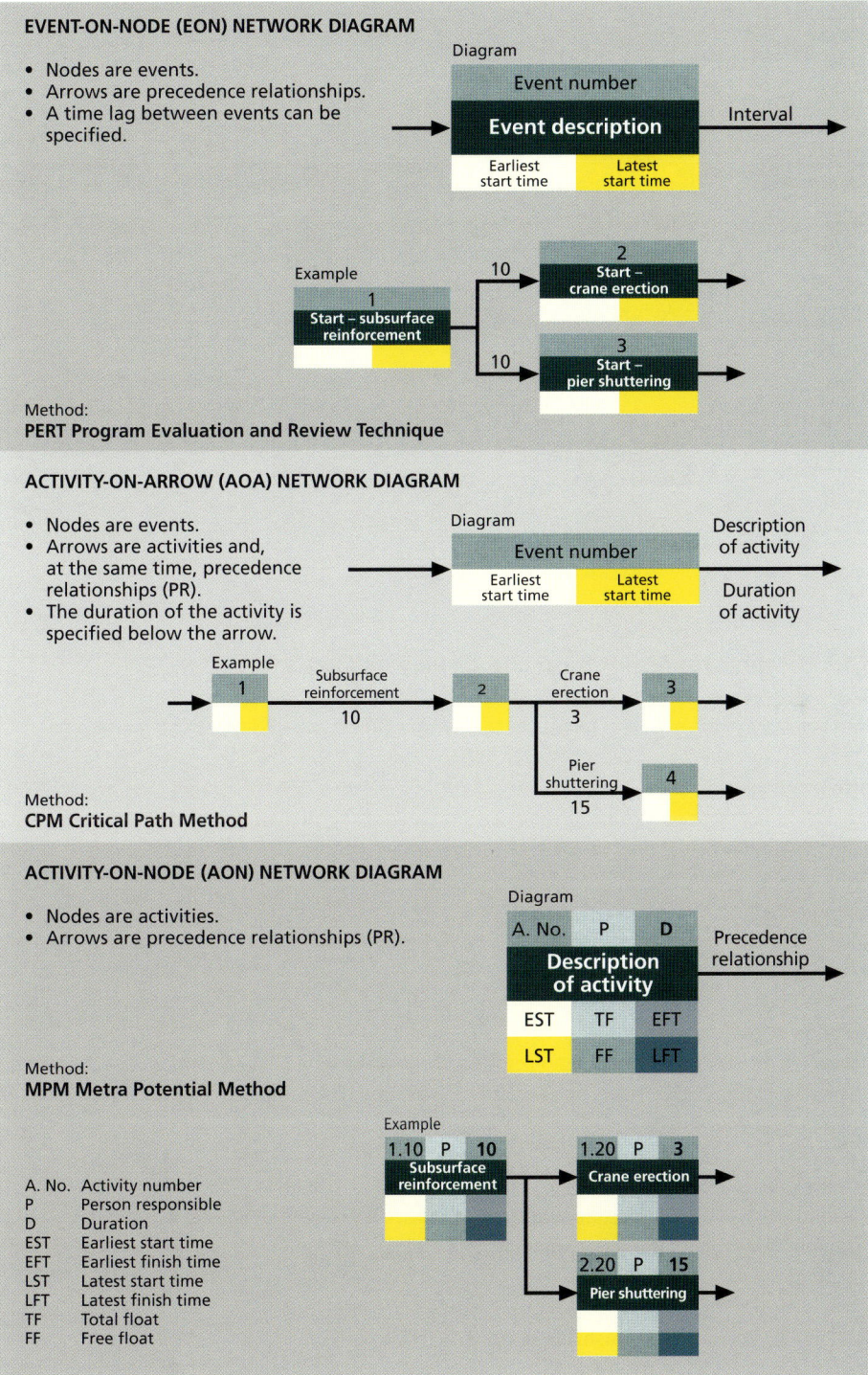

Figure C5-3 Overview of network analysis methods

3.4 Time scheduling with network analysis

Figure C5-4 shows the sample network diagram [2].

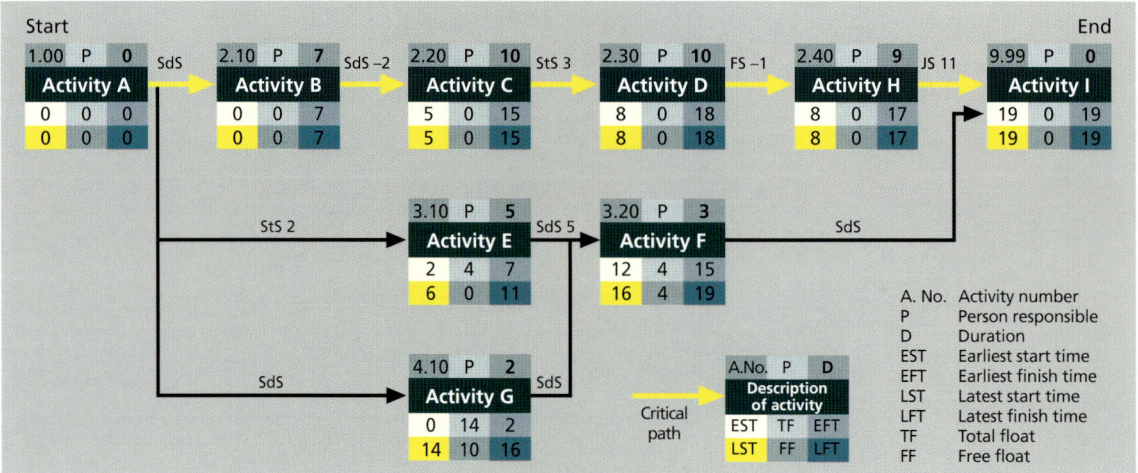

Figure C5-4 Example of an activity-on-node (AON) network diagram

3.4.1 Graphic representation and display elements

Information per activity

Each box represents an activity. It includes the following information (see key to Figure C5-4):

Activity number
The activity number can be constructed as an `informative key´ derived, for example, from the numbering system (= coding) used for the work breakdown structure.

Person responsible
Responsibility for the performance of each activity is allocated to an individual, department or other unit.

Duration of the activity
Depending on the project, the duration of the activity can be stated in time units such as days, weeks or months. In some cases, hours or minutes are used. To simplify the sample network diagram, the unit of time is one workday.

Activity description
The description of an activity states briefly what the activity comprises. The persons responsible provide more details about the activity in their work package descriptions and sometimes in the activity descriptions.

Start event, start activity, finish event, finish activity
The fictive project shown in the example commences with a start event (Event A) and ends with a finish event (Event I). Project start-up and close-out can be interpreted as project milestones.
The activity descriptions are neutral in this example (e.g. Activity A) in order to provide an application

C5 TIME SCHEDULING

and sector-independent introduction to network analysis. For simplification purposes, the brief texts in the sample network diagram refer to both events and activities as activities.

Predecessor activity, successor activity
Basically,
- with the exception of the start event or start activity, all activities can be associated with one or more predecessor activities,
- with the exception of the finish event or finish activity, all activities can be associated with one or more successor activities.

The earliest and latest times or deadlines, total float and free float are ascertained in the network diagram planning process and shown in the network diagram.

3.4.2 Precedence relationships in the activity-on-node network diagram

The precedence relationships (depicted by arrows) determine the logical sequence in which the project team realises the individual activities. The tip of the arrow points in the direction of the process sequence. Network diagrams do not contain any loops (cycles).
Figure C5-5 shows the four types of precedence relationships in an AON network diagram.

Logical processing sequence

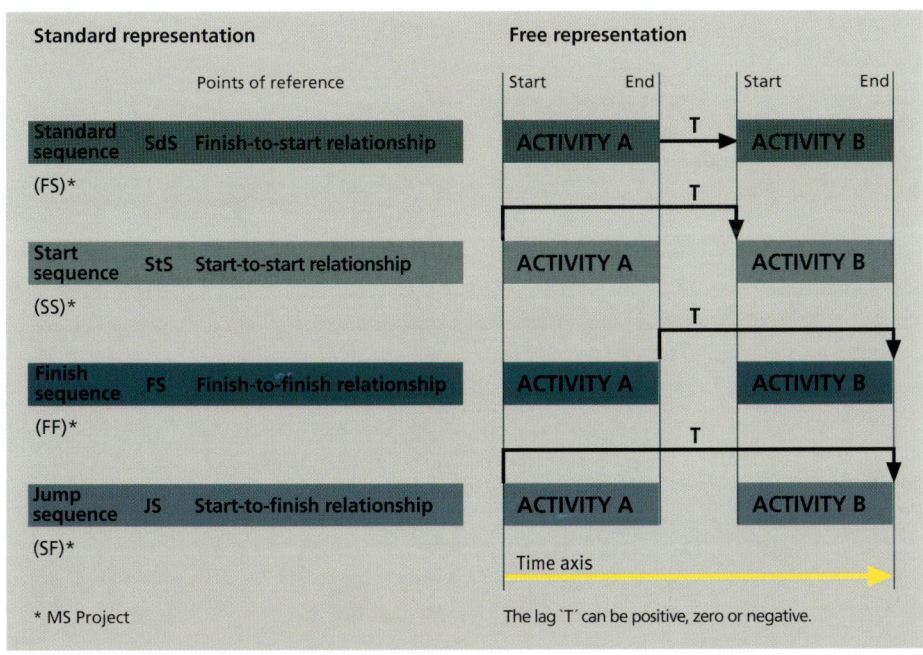

Figure C5-5 Precedence relationships in an activity-on-node network diagram

In the standard diagram, the arrow always starts at the end of the predecessor activity and its tip is always positioned at the start of the successor activity. The type of precedence relationship is described by the abbreviations SdS, StS, FS or JS. In a standard sequence, the abbreviation SdS can also be omitted. In Figure C5-6, a free representation is shown in addition to demonstrate the relationship between the start and finish times of the predecessor activities and successor activities.

Standard and flexible diagrams

Standard sequence (SdS) or finish-to-start relationship
This precedence relationship exists between the finish of the predecessor activity and the start of the successor activity.

Example
Assembly (= predecessor activity) must be concluded before commissioning (= successor activity) can begin.

Start sequence (StS) or start-to-start relationship
This precedence relationship exists between the start of the predecessor activity and the start of the successor activity.

Example
In a printing machine, the insertion of paper and filling of ink can commence at the same time.

Finish sequence (FS) or finish-to-finish relationship
This precedence relationship exists between the finish of the predecessor activity and the finish of the successor activity.

Example
Before the acceptance of a detached house with garden can take place, all cleaning work in the house and landscaping work in the garden must be finished.

Jump sequence (JS) or start-to-finish relationship
This precedence relationship exists between the start of the predecessor activity and the finish of the successor activity.

Example
In a public call for tenders, there is a binding period of 30 days between the 'bid submission' event and the 'contract awarding' event. Within this period, the authority issuing the call for tenders must conduct the activities of 'selection of bidder' and 'preparations for contract awarding'. In this example, the jump sequence JS30 from the start of 'bidder selection' to the 'end of preparations for contract awarding' can be 'parenthesised' because it is binding.

3.4.3 Minimum and maximum lags

Overlapping

In practice it is often necessary – e.g. for technical reasons – to adhere to a minimum or maximum lag between activities. The project team also has to implement some activities concurrently or with partial time overlaps. In order to take the lags between the activities into account, the planners can define a minimum lag MINT or a maximum lag MAXT.

Networked bar chart

Figures C5-6 and C5-7 show all theoretically possible combinations of precedence relationships with MINT and MAXT. Both figures include a standard diagram [2] and a free representation in the form of a networked bar chart. The German DIN standard specifies that minimum lags must be shown above the arrow, and maximum lags below.

C5 TIME SCHEDULING

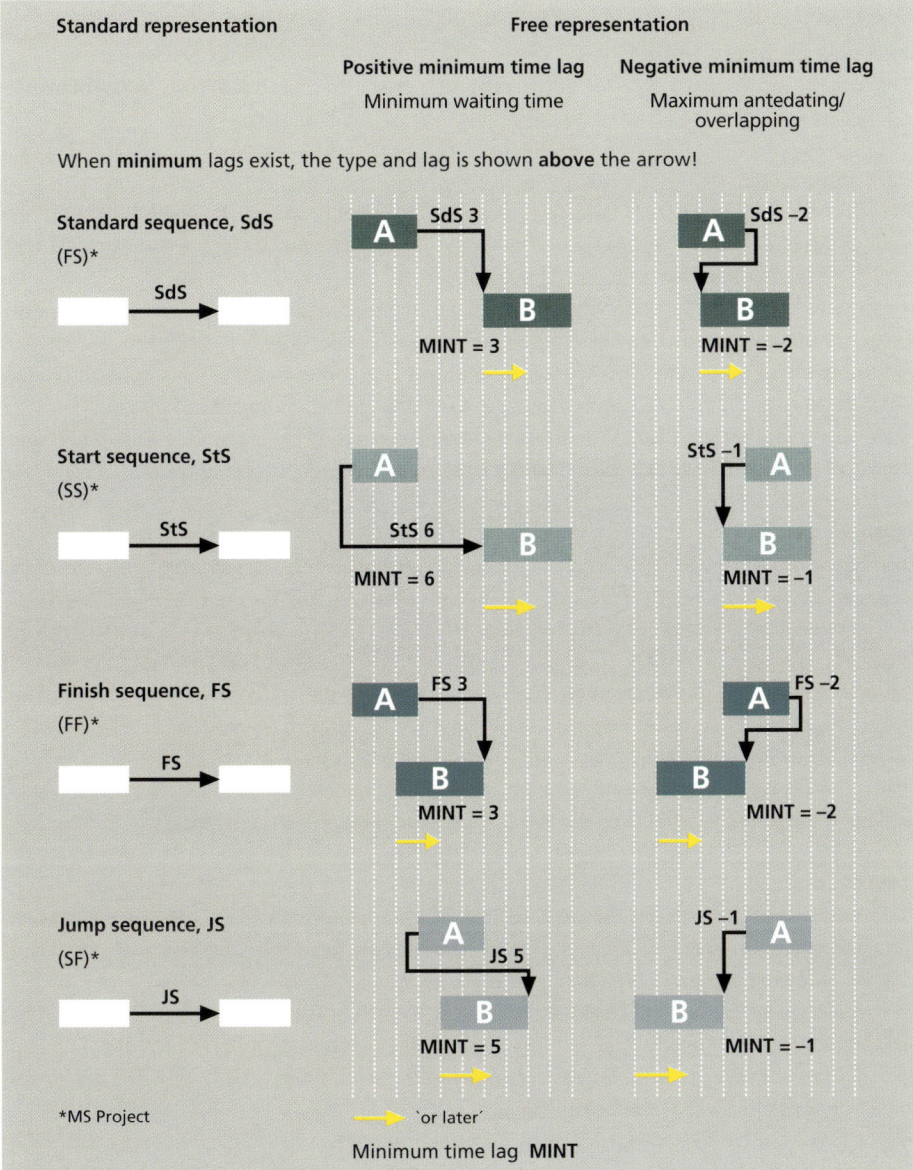

Figure C5-6 Positive and negative minimum lags (=MINT)

Standard sequence SdS

The positive minimum lag MINT between the finish of the predecessor activity A and the start of the successor activity B may not be undercut. The successor activity B can begin, at the earliest, MINT time units or more after the finish of the predecessor activity A. A positive MINT therefore shows the minimum waiting time between activities.

The negative minimum lag MINT between the finish of the predecessor activity A and the start of the successor activity B may not be undercut. The successor activity B can start, at the earliest, MINT time

units before the finish of the predecessor activity A. The successor activity could also start at a later point in time. A negative MINT therefore shows the maximum antedating time (= overlapping) for the successor activity.
MINT = 0: The successor activity B can start immediately after the predecessor activity A finishes. Antedating/overlapping of the activities is not possible. No time lag is necessary.

Start sequence StS

The positive minimum lag MINT between the start of the predecessor activity A and the start of the successor activity B may not be undercut. The successor activity B can start, at the earliest, MINT time units or more after the start of the predecessor activity A.

The negative minimum lag MINT between the start of the predecessor activity A and the start of the successor activity B may not be undercut. The start of the successor activity B can be brought forward by a maximum of MINT time units before the start of the predecessor activity A. However, the successor activity B could also start at an earlier point in time.

MINT = 0: Predecessor activity A and successor activity B could start simultaneously. Antedating/overlapping of the activities is not possible. No lag is necessary between the two processes.

Finish sequence FS

The positive minimum lag MINT between the finish of the predecessor activity A and the finish of the successor activity B may not be undercut. The successor activity B can finish, at the earliest, MINT time units or more after the finish of the predecessor activity A.

The negative minimum lag MINT between the finish of the predecessor activity A and the finish of the successor activity B may not be undercut. The maximum antedating time (= negative overlapping) of the finish time for successor activity B to before the finish time of predecessor activity A is MINT time units. However, the successor activity could finish at a later point in time.

MINT = 0: Predecessor activity A and successor activity B could finish simultaneously. Antedating/overlapping of the activities is not possible. No lag is necessary between the two processes.

Jump sequence JS

The positive minimum lag MINT between the start of the predecessor activity A and the finish of the successor activity B may not be undercut. The successor activity B can finish, at the earliest, MINT time units or more after the start of the predecessor activity A.

The negative minimum lag MINT between the start of the predecessor activity A and the finish of the successor activity B may not be undercut. The finish of the successor activity B can be brought forward by a maximum of MINT time units before the start of the predecessor activity. However, the successor activity B can finish at a later point in time.

MINT = 0: The finish of the successor activity B corresponds to the start of the predecessor activity A. Antedating/overlapping of the activities is not possible. No lag is necessary between the two processes.

Even if the successor activity can start or finish at a later point in time, this does not mean that it can be arbitrarily shifted on the time axis during the scheduling phase. If a successor activity is associated with other predecessor activities, these predecessor activities can result in the successor activity starting or finishing at a later point in time.

Software deficits   In many network analysis software packages, it is not possible to define maximum lags for precedence relationships. Since they are seldom used in practice, this chapter only includes a description of the standard sequence.

C5 TIME SCHEDULING

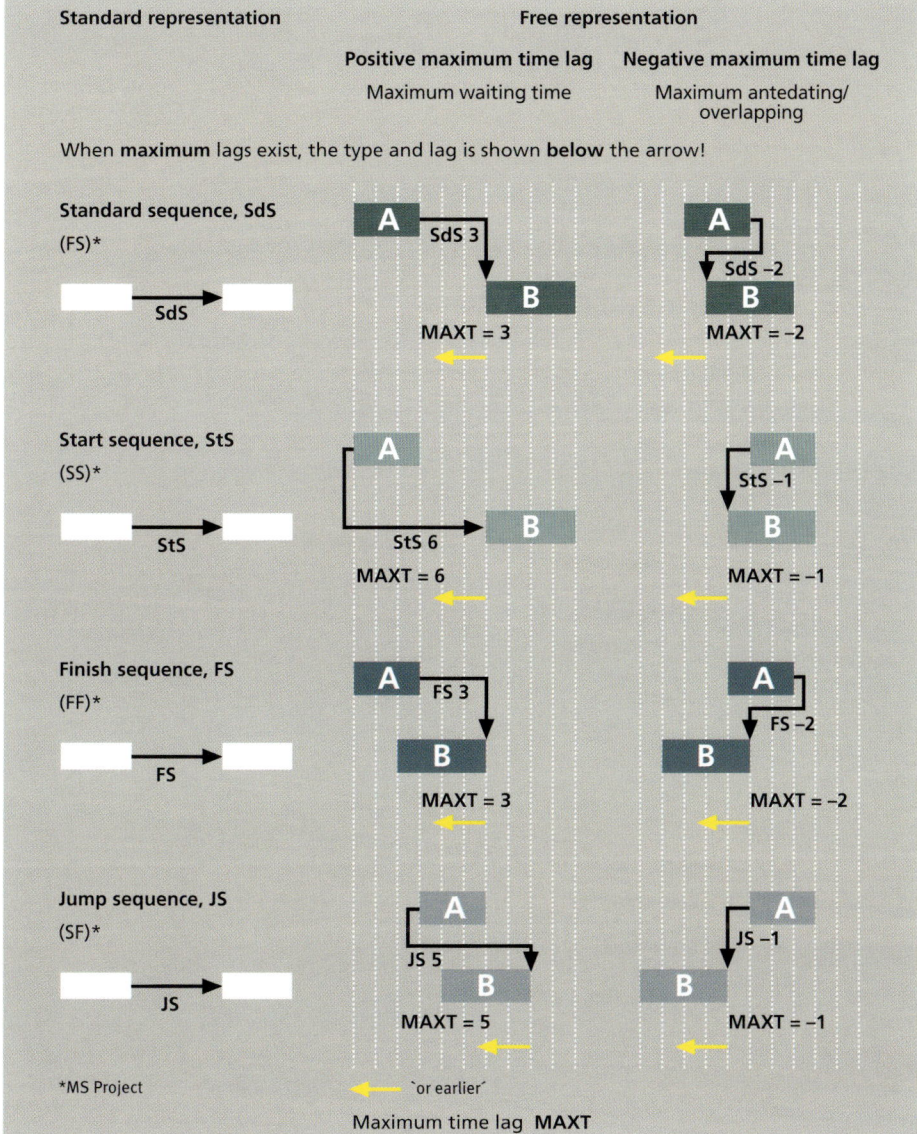

Figure C5-7 Positive and negative maximum lags (=MAXT)

In the standard sequence SdS the following applies:
The positive maximum time lag MAXT between the finish of the predecessor activity A and the start of the successor activity B may not be exceeded (= maximum waiting time). The successor activity B must start MAXT time units at the latest after the finish of the predecessor activity A, although it can start earlier.

Standard sequence

The negative maximum lag MAXT between the finish of the predecessor activity A and the start of the successor activity B may not be exceeded. The successor activity B must start MAXT time units at the latest before the finish of the predecessor activity A (= minimum antedating). However, it can start at an earlier point in time.

If only MAXT is stated, but no specific time value is given under the arrow, there are no limits on the size of MAXT. In other words, the antedating/overlapping of activities is not necessary. Vice-versa, there are no restrictions on the interval between the predecessor and successor activities.

3.4.4 Several precedence relationships between predecessor and successor activities

Rigid and flexible links

In some cases, it is a good idea to either establish fixed links between activities or to space them flexibly within specific limits. This can be done by combining several precedence relationships between two activities. The examples described below are shown in Figure C5-8.

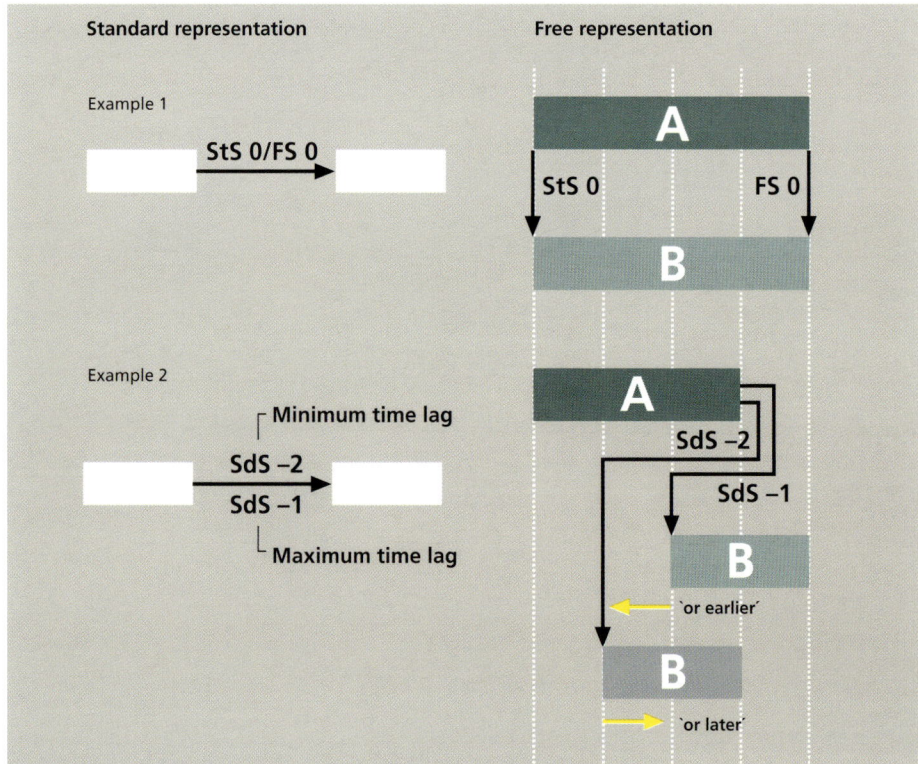

Figure C5-8 Several precedence relationships between predecessor and successor activities

Barrier

Example 1 shows the precedence relationship StS 0, which necessitates the simultaneous start of activities A and B. The relationship FS 0 necessitates that both activities also finish simultaneously. In this combination, the minimum waiting time acts as a solid barrier between the predecessor and successor activity. If the planner alters the start or finish time of one activity, the start or finish time of the other activity is automatically altered, too.

If the project planner specifies a maximum lag MAXT, it is also a good idea to specify a minimum time lag. MINT < MAXT applies. In this situation, the planner requires a `rope´ of the right length to prevent the successor activity being brought forward to the project start time, unless this is already prevented by another precedence relationship.

Rope

In Example 2, the successor activity B must start at the latest one time unit after the finish of the predecessor activity (standard sequence SdS with MAXT = -1). However, activity B could start earlier without affecting the required (negative) maximum lag. On the other hand, the standard sequence SdS with MINT = -2 means that activity B cannot start until at least two time units before the finish of activity A. As a result of these preconditions, there is only one time unit of float before activity B starts.

3.4.5 Definition of dates and float

In the next step, the sample network diagram (→ Figure C5-4) is translated from a process schedule into a time schedule by the calculation of the deadlines. Normally, this calculation is made with the assistance of computer programs. However, the project network diagram example shown in this chapter is calculated manually in order to demonstrate how algorithms work. The time scheduler should be familiar with the basic aspects of time scheduling in order to interpret the results and check their plausibility. The best software available doesn´t absolve him from thinking about the schedule´s logic. First of all, an understanding of basic scheduling terms is necessary.

Basic scheduling terms

Duration
The duration of an activity is the time between the beginning and end of the activity. Time units can be months, weeks, days or hours and, in extreme cases, minutes.

Reference Date
A reference date is a specific point in a process defined in terms of time units (e.g. days, weeks) that is referenced to a specific point in time (e.g. the project start or finish time). In the sample calculations shown in this chapter, the project start time is zero.

Time relationships

Date
A date is a point in time that is expressed by a calandar date and/or a time of the day.

Calendarisation
Scheduling on the basis of calendar dates is called calendarisation.

Scheduled Date
As soon as events or activities are allocated to a (calculated) reference date or date, they have a temporal relationship to one another and occupy a specific position in a schedule. The time at which events and activities are scheduled to take place is shown in a bar chart.

Bar chart

The dates are calculated in a three-step process:
1. Progressive calculation (= forward pass)
2. Reverse calculation (= backward pass)
3. Calculation of slack (= float)

Time scheduling

The duration (= D) of all activities must be known. The example shown is based on relative time units (= TU). So that the calculation processes can be demonstrated, the precedence relationships selected

Calculation of activity duration

C5 TIME SCHEDULING

do not relate to any specific project. In a real project, it is advisable to define the precedence relationships so that they are logically linked in the simplest possible way.

Forward-pass calculation

Earliest times EST and EFT

This is the calculation of the earliest points in time or deadlines for all events and activities in the project network diagram. The forward-pass calculation for the sample project network diagram (→ Figure C5-4) is shown in Figure C5-9.

The earliest start time (= EST) and earliest finish time (= EFT) has been calculated for each activity. The project close-out date is Date 19. In other words, the calculated project duration (= project lifecycle) is 19 time units (days).

FORWARD-PASS CALCULATION			
Activity	Calculation	Precedence relationship with the predecessor activity	Reference points for calculation Minimum lag: **MINT**
Activity A	EST(A) = 0 EFT(A) = EST(A) + D(A) = 0 + 0 = 0		The calculation always starts with ´zero´ ´Activity A´ is an event that does not consume time
Activity B	EST(B) = EFT(A) = 0 EFT(B) = EST(B) + D(B) = 0 + 7 = 7	StS 0 to A	from finish of A to start of B, MINT = 0
Activity C	EST(C) = EFT(B) + MINT = 7 + (–2) = 5 EFT(C) = EST(C) + D(C) = 5 + 10 = 15	StS -2 to B	from finish of B to start of C, minus MINT = -2
Activity D	EST(D) = EST(C) + MINT = 5 + 3 = 8 EFT(D) = EST(D) + D(D) = 8 + 10 = 18	SS 3 to C	from start of C to start of D, plus MINT = 3
Activity H	EFT(H) = EFT(D) + MINT = 18 + (–1) = 17 EST(H) = EFT(H) – D(H) = 17 – 9 = 8	FS -1 to D	from finish of D to finish of H, minus MINT = -1
Activity I			cannot be calculated until activities E, F and G have been calculated
Activity E	EST(E) = EST(A) + MINT = 0 + 2 = 2 EFT(E) = EST(E) + D(E) = 2 + 5 = 7	SS 2 to A	from start of A to start of E, plus MINT = 2
Activity F			cannot start until activities E and G have finished
Activity G	EST(G) = EFT(A) = 0 EFT(G) = EST(G) + D(G) = 0 + 2 = 2	StS 0 to A	from finish of A to start of G, MINT = 0
Activity F	EST(F) = EFT(E) + MINT = 7 + 5 = 12 or EST(F) = EFT(G) = 2	StS 5 to E and/or StS 0 to G	from finish of E to finish of F, plus MINT = 5 from finish of G to finish of F, plus MINT = 0
	In **forward-pass calculations, the maximum of all earliest finish times** of all directly associated previous activities must be selected (taking MINT into consideration). EST(F) = Max (12, 2) = 12 EFT(F) = EST(F) + D(F) = 12 + 3 = 15		
Activity I	EFT(I) = EST(H) + MINT = 8 + 11 = 19 EST(I) = EFT(I) – D(I) = 19 – 0 = 19 or EST(I) = EFT(F) = 15 EST(I) = Max (19, 15) = 19 EFT(I) = EST(I) + D(I) = 19 + 0 = 19	JS 11 to H and SdS 0 to F	from start of H to end of I, plus MINT = 11 and/or from finish of F to start of I, MINT = 0
Result of the calculation: the earliest project finish time ET = 19			

ET   Earliest time of an event
EST Earliest start time
EFT Earliest finish time
D   Duration of the activity
MINT Minimum lag

Figure C5-9 Forward-pass calculation for the sample network diagram

Backward-pass calculation

The objective of the backward-pass calculation is to determine the latest reference dates or dates for all events and activities in the network diagram.

The backward-pass calculation for the sample project network diagram ($\rightarrow$ Figure C5-4) is shown in Figure C5-10. The starting point for the backward-pass calculation is the earliest project duration of 19 time units calculated in the forward pass.

Latest times
LST and LFT

BACKWARD-PASS CALCULATION			
Activity	Calculation	Precedence relationship to the successor activity	Reference points for the calculation Minimum lag: **MINT**
Activity I	LFT(I) = EFT(I) = 19 LST(I) = LFT(I) – D(I) = 19 – 0 = 19		Starting point for the backward-pass calculation: assuming EFT(I) as equal to LFT(I), `Activity I´ is a non-time consuming event
Activity H	LST(H) = LFT(I) – MINT = 19 – 11 = 8 LFT(H) = LST(H) + D(H) = 8 + 9 = 17	JS 11 to I	from finish of I to start of H, minus MINT = 11
Activity D	LFT(D) = LFT(H) – MINT = 17 – (–1) = 18 LST(D) = LFT(D) – D(D) = 18 – 10 = 8	FS –1 to H	from finish of H to finish of D, minus MINT = -1
Activity C	LST(C) = LST(D) – MINT = 8 – 3 = 5 LFT(C) = LST(C) + D(C) = 5 + 10 = 15	StS 3 to D	from start of D to start of C, minus MINT = 3
Activity B	LFT(B) = LST(C) – MINT = 5 – (–2) = 7 LST(B) = LFT(B) – D(B) = 7 – 7 = 0	SdS –2 to C	from start of C to finish of B, minus MINT = -2
Activity A			cannot be calculated until activities E, F and G have been calculated
Activity F	LFT(F) = LST(I) = 19 LST(F) = LFT(F) – D(F) = 19 – 3 = 16	SdS 0 to I	from finish of I to start of F, MINT = 0
Activity E	LFT(E) = LST(F) – MINT = 16 – 5 = 11 LST(E) = LFT(E) – D(E) = 11 – 5 = 6	SdS 5 to F	from start of F to finish of E, minus MINT = 5
Activity G	LFT(G) = LST(F) = 16 LST(G) = LFT(G) – D(G) = 16 – 2 = 14	SdS 0 to F	from start of F to finish of G, MINT = 0
Activity A	LFT(A) = LST(B) = 0 LST(A) = LFT(A) – D(A) = 0 – 0 = 0 or LST(A) = LST(E) – MINZ = 6 – 2 = 4 or LFT(A) = LST(G) = 14 LST(A) = LFT(A) – D(A) = 14 – 0 = 14	SdS 0 to B and StS 2 to E and SdS 0 to G	from start of B to finish of A, MINT = 0 from start of E to start of A, minus MINT = 2 from start of B to finish of A, MINT = 0
	In **backward-pass calculations**, the **minimum of the latest start times of all directly associated successor activities** must be selected (taking MINT into consideration). LST(A) = Min (0, 4, 14) = 0 LFT(A) = LST(A) + D(A) = 0 + 0 = 0		
	Result of the calculation: latest project start time LT = 0		
	LT Latest time of an event LST Latest start time LFT Latest finish time	EFT Earliest finish time D Duration of the activity MINT Minimum lag	

Figure C5-10 Backward-pass calculation for the sample network diagram

Forward and backward pass calculations are prerequisites for the definition of the critical path and reserve (= float).

Critical path

Calculation of float

A comparison (→ Figure C5-4) of the earliest and latest times for each individual activity shows that
- In the top activity chain, there is no difference between EST and LST or EFT and LFT within an activity. The postponement or extension of an activity would extend the entire project life-cycle.
- In the activity chain E-F, the difference between the earliest and latest times within each activity is four time units. For example, Activity F could be extended by two time units without changing the start of Activity I.
- In activity G, the difference between EST and LST or EFT and LFT is 14 time units. This means that a slack of 14 time units exists before Activity I has to commence.

The slack shown is called the total reserve (= total float).

Total float

Total float

Total float (TF) is the `time between the earliest and latest position of an event or activity´. In other words, the predecessor activity is at the earliest position and the successor activity is at the latest position [1].

Calculation of TF

TF can be calculated using the following formula:

$$TF = LST - EST \quad \text{or} \quad TF = LFT - EFT$$

Figure C5-11 shows a different logical calculation based on the above definition of TF. The predecessor activities are always in the earliest position and the successor activities are always in the latest position. A simple calculation for selected activities is shown below:

$$TF(C) = LST(C) - EST(C) = 5 - 5 = 0 \quad \text{or} \quad TF(C) = LFT(C) - EFT(C) = 15 - 15 = 0$$

Critical path

The same formula is used to calculate TF = 0 for all activities in the top chain. The path A-B-C-D-H-I is the critical path in this network diagram. The critical path contains all activities for which the earliest and latest start and finish times agree. If they shift on the time axis, the project finish date changes. For the activity chain E-F, the TF is as follows:

$$TF(E) = LST(E) - EST(E) = 6 - 2 = 4 \qquad TF(F) = LST(F) - EST(F) = 16 - 12 = 4$$
$$TF(G) = LST(G) - EST(G) = 14 - 0 = 14$$

In the activity chain E-F, each activity has a total float of four time units. This float is only available once. For example, if an activity in the chain uses up the entire float, it is no longer available for another activity. If activity F were extended by six time units, a new critical path would result (A-E-F-I) and the project finish would be delayed by two time units.

Jeopardy of project finish

In other words, total float is the time by which a predecessor activity can be displaced until it reaches the critical limit of `latest start time for the successor activity´. The finish of the predecessor activity therefore comes dangerously close to the start of the successor. In project management practice, float is often soon used up, which jeopardises the scheduled project finish.

Another type of float with more advantages from a project scheduler´s viewpoint is free float.

C5 TIME SCHEDULING

Free float

> Free float (FF) is the 'time by which an event or activity can be delayed beyond its earliest start time without altering the earliest start time of other events or activities' [1].

Free float

There is therefore always a specific time interval between the predecessor and successor activity. Free float can be used without jeopardising the project finish. Unfortunately for schedulers, free float is seldom available.

In network diagrams with standard sequences and no time lags, the following applies:

$$FF(P) = EST(S) - EFT(P)$$

whereby P is the predecessor activity and S the successor activity.

It is not possible to calculate free float for the various kinds of precedence relationships with a simple formula if minimum lags are taken into account. Figure C5-12 shows the solution.

Activity E is associated with free float FF = 0. If the planner were to delay the earliest finish time (EFT = 7) by only one time unit, he would also have to delay the earliest start time of the successor activity F by one time unit.

Calculation of TF

TOTAL FLOAT		
Simple calculation	TF = LST − EST = LFT − EFT	
Type of precedence relationship	**Alternative: Logical calculation of a sample network diagram Reference points**	**Sample network diagram**
Standard sequence SdS	TF(P) = (LST[S] − MINT) − EFT(P)	TF(E) = (16 − 5) − 7 = 4 TF(F) = (19 − 0) − 15 = 4, because MINT = 0 TF(G) = (16 − 0) − 2 = 14, because MINT = 0
Start sequence StS	TF(P) = (LST[S] − MINT) − EST(P)	TF(C) = (10 − 5) − 5 = 0
Finish sequence FS	TF(P) = (LFT[S] − MINT) − EFT(P)	TF(D) = (17 − [−1]) − 18 = 18 − 18 = 0
Jump sequence, JS	TF(P) = (LFT[S] − MINT) − EST(P)	TF(H) = (19 − 11) − 8 = 0
	Basically, it is the case that **total float TF = 0 for all activities on the critical path.** If an activity is associated with several successor activities, it is allocated the smallest float time of all relationships.	
	TF Total float P Predecessor S Successor EST Earliest start time	EFT Earliest finish time LST Latest start time LFT Latest finish time MINT Minimum lag

Figure C5-11 Calculation of total float

Calculation of FF

FREE FLOAT

Type of precedence relationship	Calculation Reference points		Sample network diagram
Standard sequence SdS	FF(P) = (EST[S] − MINT) − EFT(P)		FF(B) = (5 − [−2]) − 7 = 0 FF(E) = (12 − 5) − 7 = 0 FF(F) = (19 − 0) − 15 = 4, because here MINT = 0 FF(G) = (12 − 0) − 2 = 10, because here MINT = 0
Start sequence StS	FF(P) = (EST[S] − MINT) − EST(P)		FF(C) = (10 − 5) − 5 = 0
Finish sequence FS	FF(P) = (EFT[S] − MINT) − EFT(P)		FF(D) = (17 − [−1]) − 18 = 18 − 18 = 0
Jump sequence, JS	FF(P) = (EFTZ[S] − MINT) − EST(P)		FF(H) = (19 − 11) − 8 = 0
Basically, it is the case that **free float FF = 0 for all activities on the critical path.** If an activity is associated with several successor activities, it is allocated the smallest float time of all relationships. For all activities ending on the critical path, TF = FF.			
FF Free float TF Total float P Predecessor S Successor			EST Earliest start time EFT Earliest finish time MINT Minimum lag

Figure C5-12 Calculation of free float

All calculations for the sample network diagram have now been completed. A bar chart is a suitable means of illustrating the results.

In Figure C5-13, the earliest and latest positions of all activities in the sample network diagram (→ Figure C5-4) are shown chronologically and linked via precedence relationships (arrows). Total float and free float are also shown.

Further float types

There are two other kinds of float that are seldom used in practice. They are [1]:

Independent float

Independent float (= IF) is the degree of flexibility which an event or activity has when the predecessor activities are at the latest position and the successor activities at the earliest position.

Free reverse float

Free reverse float (FRF) is the time by which an event or an activity can be delayed from its latest position without altering the latest position of other events or activities.

3.4.6 Critical chain project management

Critical chain

By definition, there is no float on the critical path. Delays on this path inevitably result in the extension of a project, unless it is possible to compensate for the delay by using additional resources or by other measures. Goldratt [4] suggests a different approach, called the critical chain. This is the longest possible chain and includes all work packages/activities to be carried out using existing resources and taking interdependencies into account. The time schedules are therefore based on (critical) resources.

C5 TIME SCHEDULING

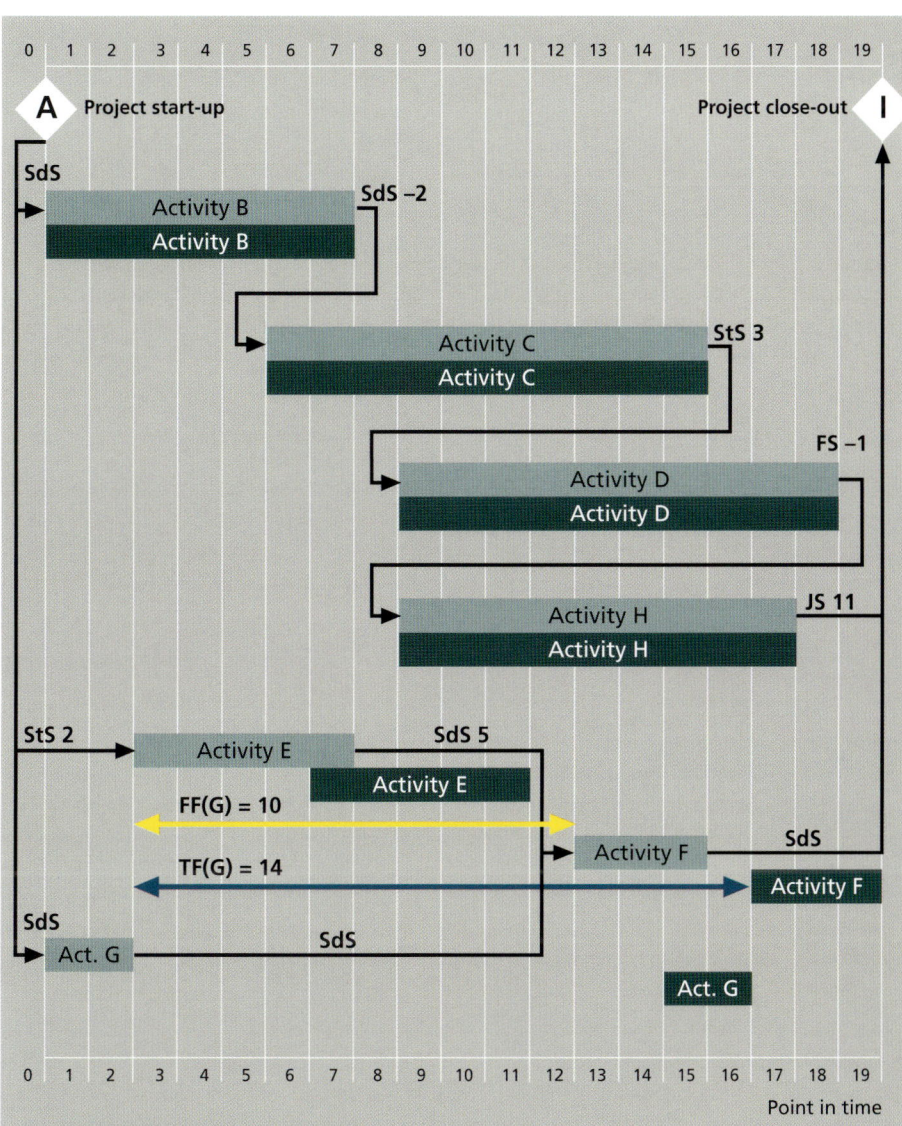

Bar chart display format

Figure C5-13 Bar chart for the sample network diagram

Example
If a project team member is indispensable, but only available to work on the project at specific times because he also has to work on other projects, the schedule must take this scarce resource into account. In this case, for example, work that was originally to have been carried out concurrently has to be scheduled in sequence.

Goldratt also suggests that project team members should make a realistic time estimate without personal float. This allows the project manager to schedule a project float at the end of the project. This

Personal float

reverses the trend of project team members with personal float starting work as late as possible and often not finishing on schedule. Everyone should start their task immediately, including when their predecessor finishes ahead of schedule.

3.4.7 Calendarisation

Calculations on the basis of time units make it easier to show the calculation steps and are the basis for network diagram scheduling. Normally, the scheduler is not interested in a specific reference date, but rather a precise calendar date or sometimes the time of day when an activity finishes.

Individual project calendar

Computerised project planning systems that enable the definition of project-specific calendars are based on the Gregorian calendar, which contains all the days of the year. Users can adapt it to their requirements by eliminating non-workdays. In most cases, the definition of a calendar is a basic activity that precedes all other planning steps.

> **Examples**
> **Company calendar** with consecutively numbered working days, commencing on the first day of the calendar year
> **Project calendar** which differs from the company calendar in that it only contains the real project workdays
> **Shift calendar** which takes two or three work shifts per working day into account
> **Personal work calendar** which contains the specific work times of a project team member

Several calendars for one project
If project work is distributed over several regions or countries, or project work can only be carried out at specific times of the year, it may be necessary to use several calendars in a network diagram.

> **Example**
> The planning and production activities for a plant are carried out in Bavaria (exact dates possible as every German State has different public and school holidays), but assembly work is in Saudi Arabia. In this case, the planner creates a `Bavarian calendar´ for planning and production activities and a `Saudi calendar´ for the assembly work.

Scheduling using the Gregorian calendar
The sample network diagram (→ Figure C5-4) is scheduled on the basis of the Gregorian calendar. The result is shown in Figure C5-14. The selected planning unit is the working day. The planner has established 01.01.YY as the project start date. In order to simplify the example shown, it is assumed that the team works a seven-day week. Certain special attributes can be explained using the example.

C5 TIME SCHEDULING

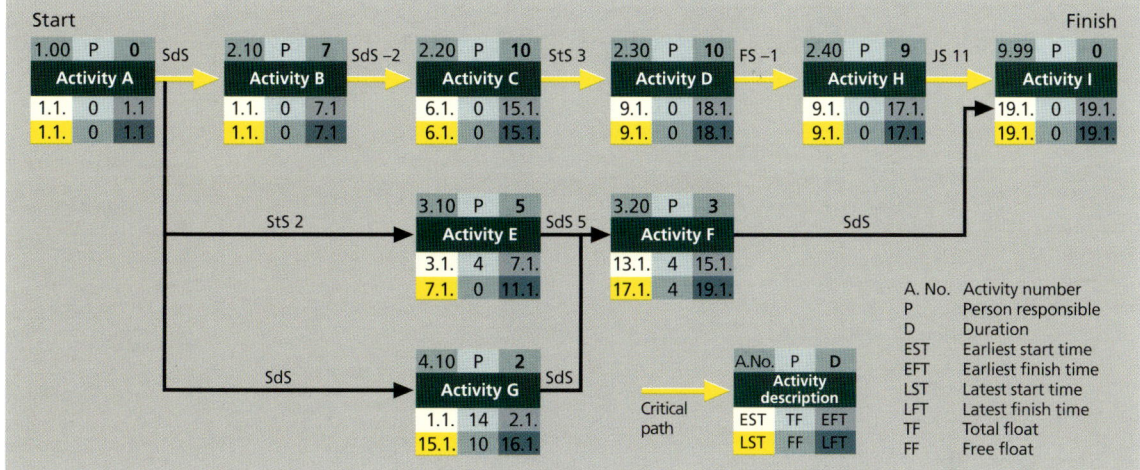

Figure C5-14 Sample network diagram (scheduled using the Gregorian calendar)

Handling of events
The event (Event A) starts on 01.01.YY. An event does not consume time (duration = 0). Event A therefore also ends on 01.01.YY.

Handling of activities
Since the first activity A does not consume any time, the first project activity, Activity B, also starts on 01.01.YY. An activity always begins at 0:00 hours on any one day and ends at 24:00 hours, irrespective of whether or not the planner implicitly assumes an 8-hour working day.
Accordingly, Activity B ends on 07.01.YY and Activity C would start on the next day, 08.01.YY. However, as a result of the precedence relationship StS -2, the start of Activity C is brought forward to two days before the finish of Activity B. Activity C therefore starts on 06.01.YY.

Setting deadlines
Fixed earliest start dates (= ESD) or latest start dates (= LSD) can be specified for every activity in the network diagram not only for the first activity. A fixed start date is always taken into account in forward pass calculations. It takes precedence over a start date calculated on the basis of the deadlines for predecessor activities.
By analogy, fixed earliest finish dates (= EFD) and fixed latest finish dates (= LFD) can be defined for each activity. The activity must finish on this date, even if a standard calculation would lead to a later finish date.

Fixed and preferred dates

A fixed latest finish date (e.g. a contractual deadline) set for the project finish D (= duration) (LFD = 12.04.YY) is at an earlier point in time than the earliest finish date (EFD = 15.04.YY) resulting from the forward-pass calculation (→ Figure C5-15). The project finish must therefore occur at an earlier date than is possible owing to deadline specifications and the precedence relationships associated with the various activities. In the backward-pass calculation, the fixed finish date is taken into account. This leads to an earlier project start than originally planned. The latest dates are positioned before the earliest dates. At the same time, all activities have a negative total float. The project team can therefore only complete the project on schedule if they start earlier than originally planned or if they attempt to save at least three days on the path A-B-C-D.

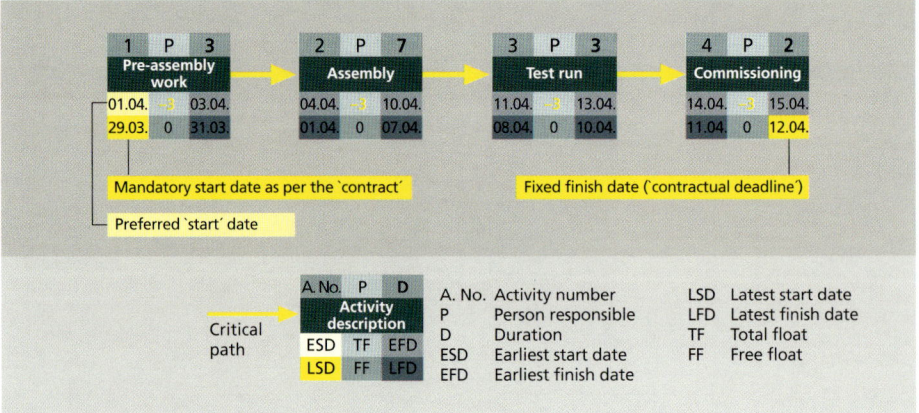

Figure C5-15 Fixed start and finish dates, preferred dates (example)

Negative float

In practice, negative float is the clearest indicator that countermeasures are necessary if the activities with negative total float are in the past. Conversely, the planner can investigate potential critical processes before the project commences by setting fixed dates. He can also simulate alternative date scenarios during the project.

Preferred deadlines
In the same way that fixed dates can be set, the planner can specify preferred dates (EST, EFT, LST, LFT) for each activity in the project network diagram. These dates are taken into account in a forward-pass calculation – if the predecessor activities permit this – taking precedence relationships into consideration. Otherwise they are overwritten.

4 Methods of structuring and processing network diagrams

This part of the chapter provides practical tips on how to create simple network diagrams and methods for the structuring and processing of complex network diagrams.

4.1 Basic procedure for network diagram creation

4.1.1 Step-by-step procedure

When we consider the process of creating a process schedule on the basis of a work breakdown structure, it is clear that the transition from work package to activity is a fluid one (1:1 relationship, 1:n relationship) and depends on the network diagram owner´s interpretation. Basically, it is the case that the network diagram should be as general as possible and as detailed as necessary. The essential criteria to determine the degree of detail necessary, are the level of knowledge about project processes, phase-oriented process definition, simplicity, ease-of-use and the objectives and purpose of the network diagram.

Level of knowledge about project processes

Usually, only general information about project processes is available at the outset of the project. As a result, the first time schedule is only an outline that is gradually filled in as more knowledge is gained. If details are added prematurely on the basis of vague assumptions, too many changes will be necessary over the course of the project.

General schedule

Phase-oriented process definition

In long-term projects (e.g. with a lifecycle of more than one year) that are also phase-oriented, the first step is to plan the first-phase processes in detail. Shortly before the second phase commences, the project manager begins with the detailed planning of the second-phase processes, and so on. This procedure is oriented towards the level of knowledge over the course of the project. It prevents the network diagram from getting 'cluttered' at an early stage of the project and also prevents unnecessary work in the early project phases.

Simplicity and ease of use

According to the principle of 'as general as possible and as detailed as necessary', it is necessary to ensure that the project does not get too complex or bogged down with details. Unless the network diagram owner shows self-discipline, the number of activities and precedence relationships can soon multiply, which makes the network diagram difficult to use (e.g. time expended on updating).

Excessive detail

Objectives of the network diagram

The planner must ask himself why he is preparing a network diagram because
- a high degree of detail is necessary for the monitoring and management of operational deadlines, resources and costs (= detailed network diagram)
- whereas summarised information (master plan, general network diagram, outline network diagram) suffices for the project manager, executive management and project sponsor/customer.

Detailed schedule

Outline network diagram

Purpose of the network diagram

The most practical degree of detail can also depend to a great extent on its purpose.

Purpose of 'time scheduling, monitoring and management'
In this case, the motto is: if you can't monitor it, don't specify it in detail. The content of activities must be defined in such a way that the activity duration is manageable, i.e. as short as possible. Activities that take months or years to complete are split up into manageable timeframes.

Purpose of 'scheduling'
If – especially in the project planning phase – the project manager pursues the objective of precisely analysing and mapping activities, he will have to cope with a vast amount of details. In most cases, the activities have to be summarised again in the time schedule in order that they can be monitored.

Purpose of 'planning, monitoring and management of resources and/or costs'
If the network diagram is not only used for scheduling, but also for resource and cost management and tracking (→ Chapter C6), the following motto applies to the degree of detail: never mix apples with oranges. For example, an activity should not involve both decorators and bricklayers if the project manager is using a separate resource plan based on the different qualifications of the two.

Activity definition   Whenever possible, an activity should be defined in such a way that
1. It is only associated with one specific type of resource (e.g. employee qualification). However, the planner can also (theoretically) split up a resource type into as many activities as he wants.
2. Only costs of a specific type, cost centre, etc. are associated with an activity. As in the case of resources, it is also possible to split up costs among several activities.
3. Activities can be selected or summarised on the basis of specific assessment criteria.

Definition of purpose and objective   A list of the detailing criteria shows that the procedure essentially depends on the purpose and objectives of the network diagram and that priorities must be considered before the project team defines the activities.

4.1.2 Simple work methods for network diagram creation

An inexperienced project manager often finds it difficult to create a network diagram on paper or on the computer. The following information simplifies this task.

Work package description

Breakdown of the project structure   In a consistent project structure ($\rightarrow$ Chapter C4) the work package descriptions are provided in conjunction with activity descriptions (1:1 relationship). The more detailed the work breakdown structure, the easier it is to determine activity content and thus define the activities.

Cooperation with project participants
The project manager should create the process schedule in close cooperation with the other project participants (e.g. sub-project managers, project team members, planners, company departments, suppliers/sub-contractors). In order to ascertain the precedence relationships, he must take advantage of the professional skills of the other people involved in the project. The easiest way to clarify critical interfaces between sub-projects, sub-systems, work packages etc. is to discuss them with the other people who are responsible for their implementation. The incorporation of internal and external project participants is not just a basic prerequisite for a realistic time schedule, but also for the acceptance of the ensuing target schedule.

Activity list
Before a process schedule can be prepared, it is a good idea to create an activity list. It contains all activities in a logical sequence, each referenced to the successor and/or predecessor activity, precedence relationships and lags. The planners can extend the list at a later point in time to record resources and incorporate costs. Figure C5-16 shows an example of an activity list.

C5 TIME SCHEDULING

ACTIVITY NUMBER	ACTIVITY DESCRIPTION	DURATION	PREDECESSOR ACTIVITY PRECEDENCE RELATIONSHIP/ FLOAT	SUCCESSOR ACTIVITY PRECEDENCE RELATIONSHIP/ FLOAT	FURTHER DETAILS ABOUT COSTS AND RESOURCES IF NECESSARY
1	Overall planning	10 days		2	
2	Detailed planning	15 days	1	3	
3	Negotiation	5 days	2	4	
4	Implementation planning	15 days	3	5	
5	Procurement	10 days	4	6 SdS –5	
6	Manufacturing – part 1 + part 2	20 days	5 SdS –5	7 StS 10	
7	Mechanical assembly – part 1	20 days	6 StS 10	8	
8	Electrical assembly – part 1	10 days	7	9	
9	Commissioning – part 1	15 days	8	13	
10	Mechanical assembly – part 2	20 days	6	11 SdS 5	
11	Electrical assembly – part 2	10 days	10 SdS –5	12	
12	Commissioning – part 2	15 days	11	13	
13	Integration test – part 1 + part 2	20 days	12, 9	14, 15	
14	Training	15 days	13	16	
15	Operational test	20 days	13	16	
16	Acceptance	0 days	15, 14		

List of resources and costs

Figure C5-16 Example of an activity list

Metaplan method
The project team can write all activities on metaplan cards (→ Chapter D2) and sort them according to the process logic either on a pin-board or a table. At a meeting, the project team members can vary the processes or add new activities until the final network diagram is approved.

Testing network diagram options

Bar chart method
If a network diagram is to be created with pencil and paper, many people find it easier to draw and link the activities in a bar chart with a time axis instead of using an abstract network diagram structure. Because bar charts are merely a different form of network diagram, this more plausible procedure is recommended.

Simpler methods

Software support
Numerous software tools (→ Chapter C11) are available to support project structuring and to map the planning process. For example, the activity list can initially be entered as structured text. When the activity durations have been entered, the program creates bars of the relevant length along a time axis and the user can link them using the drag-and-drop function and mouse click.

4.2 Subnet method

Complex projects

If a project only involves a few employees and has a duration of only a few months, the planners can create the schedule at the outset of the project using the simple methods outlined above. However, in complex projects, it is advisable to divide the network diagram into subnets.

A subnet plan (= SNP) only shows a sub-project and is structurally linked to other subnet plans for the same project [1].

The subnet method comprises two steps:
- Step 1: Create subnets separately
- Step 2: Link subnets into an overall network diagram

Structuring principles

The subnets are structured according to the principles of project structuring according to
- sub-tasks or work packages,
- project phases,
- organisational units and
- functional aspects.

Example
The project network diagram for the development of a software package is phase-oriented and includes, inter alia, the subnets of analysis, general IT concept, detailed IT concept, realisation, installation, integration test and acceptance.

Benefits of the subnet method
The subnet method offers several advantages:

Separate preparation
- Subnets can (initially) be created, processed and calculated independently of one another. However, the planner must account for the links (= interfaces) with other subnets. These must be kept as simple as possible in order to avoid unnecessary complexity. If the interfaces are clearly defined, it is possible to optimise the individual subnets at a later point in time without impairing the others.

Information gain
- The subdivision of a project network diagram into subnets enhances transparency in a complex project.
- Subnets make it possible to filter out information from the network diagram. Every individual or organisational unit with (partial) responsibility for the project receives specific information for his department or unit.

Network diagram hierarchies
- Subnets simplify the creation of network diagram hierarchies (detailed network diagram for each sub-task, general network diagram for the project as a whole) and support the summarisation of information.

Recurrent activities
- Frequently recurring activities in the individual subnets can be standardised.

4.3 Standard network analysis

Projects are `in principle characterised by the uniqueness of conditions´ [1]. In practice, however, many of a company´s projects or specific processes within a project are repetitive. Analogously to standard work breakdown structures (→ Chapter C4), companies can develop new standard network diagrams after the project starts or modify existing ones from completed projects. These diagrams allow projects to gain from experience from previous projects, and also considerably reduce the scheduling workload.

Example
In large-scale construction projects, a separate contract awarding procedure exists for each construction phase/work package. The process of invitation to tender and contract awarding is generally always the same and can therefore be standardised.

Figure C5-17 outlines the principle of standard network analysis and subnets.

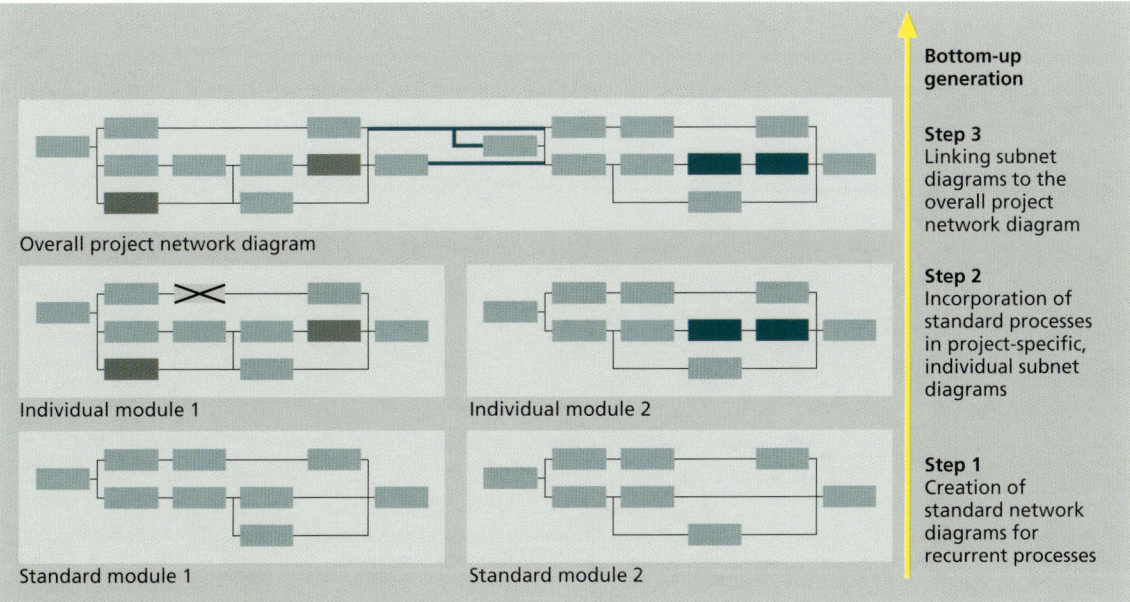

Figure C5-17 Subnets and standard network analysis

In Step 1, standard subnet diagrams are developed. In a second step, the project manager adapts the standard processes to the project's specific requirements by splitting up some activities or adding non-standard project-specific activities. In the third step, the project-specific, individual subnets are linked to the overall project network diagram.

Development steps

The procedure for linking project-specific and/or standardised subnets to an overall project network diagram uses the bottom-up generation principle. It is also possible to take a top-down approach to the generation of a project-specific schedule from a standard network diagram which – like a variant configurator list – contains an abundance of standardised processes.

Bottom-up and top-down generation

Example
In the development phase of the `Airbus Equipment Assembly´ project, the project team developed a process schedule for assembly operations in respect of each aircraft type that contains all possible equipment configurations. If an airline orders one of the aircraft, the project schedule only contains the activity chains for the equipment configuration that the customer requests. This enables the operations scheduling team to produce a complex process schedule in only a short time.

4.4 Network diagram levels and consolidation

Filtering options Depending on requirements, it is possible to filter different levels and information from the network diagrams.

4.4.1 General and detailed schedules

The motto `first general, then detailed´ normally applies to the degree of detail. On the other hand, the project team requires summarised information (e.g. scheduled dates, capacity requirements, costs) to prepare reports – especially reports for executives.

Network diagram levels If the network diagram consistently reflects the project structure, it automatically includes several network diagram levels (e.g. sub-projects, sub-tasks, work packages, activities). Modern network diagram software enables the user to search for and print out specific levels.

> **Example**
> *Level 1*
> *The detailed schedule for the project team contains all scheduled dates for activities, work packages and sub-projects.*
> *Level 2*
> *The outline schedule for the project manager contains all scheduled dates for work packages, sub-tasks and sub-projects.*
> *Level 3*
> *The master plan for the executive management and customer contains all scheduled dates for sub-projects and sub-tasks.*

4.4.2 Milestone scheduling

Key events Milestones are `key events´ [2] that denote important points in the project, such as the start or conclusion of a work package or a project phase, or a review point for decision-making bodies.

Milestone schedules
The milestones integrated in the activity-on-node network diagram can be extracted and linked into a milestone schedule. This gives rise to the problem that the links or precedence relationships between what are often complex logical relationships in the detailed network diagram can only be mapped approximately. They are a substitute for precedence relationships `between ... events that no longer represent specific paths in the consolidated network diagram´ [2].

Milestone list
Milestone trend analysis If the interdependencies are not shown, the milestones can be simply selected (on the computer) and printed out as a milestone list. The selected milestones are the basis for the milestone trend analysis (→ Chapter C9).

5 Display formats for the time schedule

Modern computer tools offer a variety of possibilities for graphic and tabular display. The most important are network diagrams and bar charts.

5.1 Network diagram

The network diagram (→ Figure C5-4) is an important working document for the scheduler. Many project participants (project manager, project sponsor, customer, executive management) who are not familiar with network diagrams reject them as abstract and complex. The planner should therefore ensure that he does not pass on his network diagram prematurely or use it in meetings or reports as a method of illustrating the schedule.

Rejection by project participants

5.2 Bar chart

The bar chart enables the visualisation of activities and deadlines. Simple bar charts or Gantt diagrams are often prepared manually without using network analysis techniques. The objective is to map the sequence of activities over time. In this case, the project manager does not explicitly take the interdependencies between the activities into account, and dispenses with the benefits of network analysis.

Gantt diagram

Network analysis
- ensures that the project interrelationships are thought through systematically.
- enables the reliable scheduling of activities.
- indicates where time reserves exist, where time is lacking and where measures to speed up the activity are necessary.
- is a flexible information medium enabling data exchange between the project manager and the department managers, as well as the executive managers.
- Enables the management of project processes and project deadline monitoring.

Benefits of network analysis

Network analysis software offers many options for displaying the results of time scheduling - i.e. the content of network diagrams - as networked bar charts. The following display options are available:
- predecessor activity in the earliest and latest position, plus float,
- critical path at the time of updating,
- `completed´, `in process´ and `not yet started´ activities, and
  activities with target and actual deadlines

However, the mapping of all precedence relationships as networked bar charts can become too complex in large project schedules. In this case, the project manager or project controller must consider whether he should only display the most important relationships or mask them entirely. The example shown in Figure C5-18 is a combination of an activity list (→ Figure C5-16) and a networked bar chart. The description of precedence relationships deviates from the standard (FS = finish-to-start, SS = start-to-start).

Selective display

C5 TIME SCHEDULING

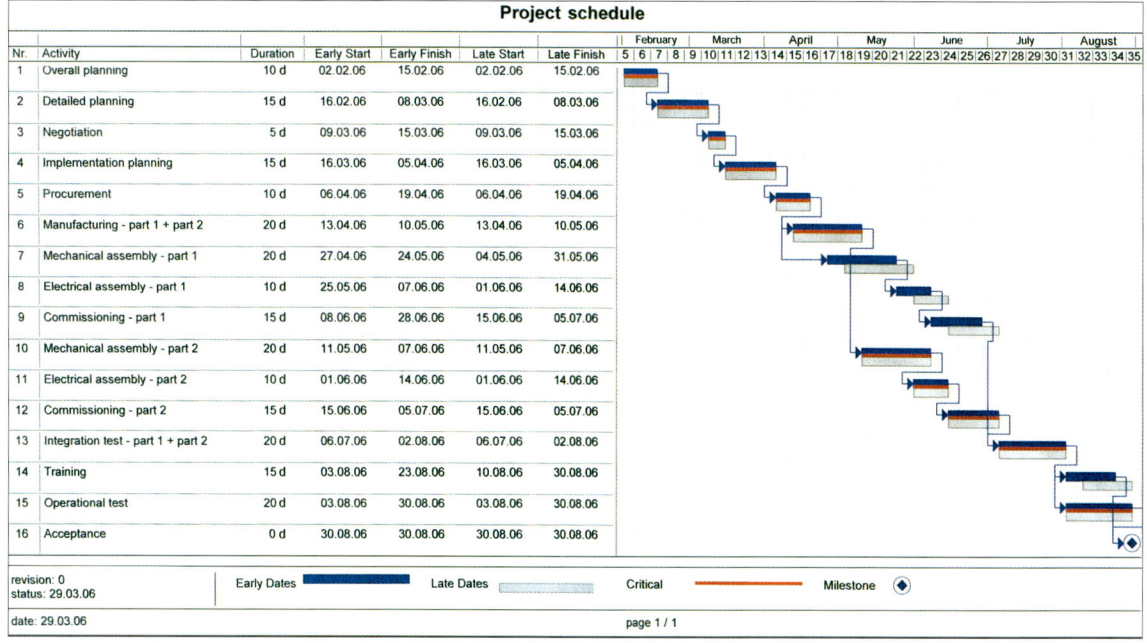

Figure C5-18 'Networked bar chart' display format

Self-assessment questions for each certification level

No.	Question	Level				Self-assessment
		D	C	B	A	
C5.1	In what order should project time scheduling be realised?	2	3	3	4	☐
C5.2	What is a project network diagram?	2	2	2	1	☐
C5.3	What results do forward-pass and backward-pass calculations deliver for network diagrams?	3	2	2	1	☐
C5.4	What types of float exist?	2	2	2	2	☐
C5.5	What steps and methods can be used to create a network diagram?	3	2	2	1	☐
C5.6	How much detail should a network diagram contain?	2	2	2	2	☐
C5.7	What are subnets used for?	2	2	2	2	☐
C5.8	How and why are standard network diagrams developed?	1	2	2	2	☐

C6 COST AND RESOURCE PLANNING

What resources does a project need? With what costs (ICB Element 16) will it be associated? Inadequate resource planning (ICB Element 15) can result in unnecessary costs and deadline-related problems. Not only do cost overruns jeopardise the project, but often also the organisation´s basis for existence. Project managers, therefore, need to accord special priority to this aspect of project management. This chapter explains cost budgeting methods, the resource planning procedure and common mistakes. It also describes project logistics and the methods used for project-specific cost monitoring.

1 Estimating resource requirements and project costs

Media coverage of project scandals often focuses on cost overruns rather than missed deadlines. Public sector construction projects, such as the Allgemeine Krankenhaus (general hospital) construction project in Vienna and the Klinikum Aachen (the city clinic) project (→ Chapter A2) are two notorious examples. Recently, taxpayer-funded construction projects in which the costs vastly exceeded the original budget have made negative headlines. Most of the criticism comes from central and regional government auditing authorities. Private-sector enterprises, on the other hand, tend not to disclose these kinds of management blunders. They fear the loss of image associated with failed projects.

Cost overruns also often jeopardise the organisation´s other projects and objectives. For example, if the budget for a public-sector road construction project is overrun, there will be a lack of funds for other construction projects. In this case, the other projects will either be delayed or terminated. Organisations face the same problem. If project managers overrun the budget for their project, there will be a shortage of funds for concurrent or planned projects. Escalating project costs can also threaten an organisation´s existence if the order is large relative to turnover. Cost overruns – especially in internal projects – are often the reason why organisations fail to meet profitability targets (→ Chapter C3).

Impact on other projects

Most cost types can be quantified in easily-recognised amounts. For example, personnel and material costs are quantified in terms of the number of person hours or units of material consumed. This is why most cost budgeting methods deliver information about the anticipated quantities rather than direct cost values. The commercial project team members then use the relevant cost rates to convert quantities into costs.

Specification of inputs

Cost budgeting is traditional in projects. Most textbooks on the subject of cost budgeting include sections about bid costing and the various methods of preliminary costing that are used in industries where the process of producing goods and services is project-based. For example, many national associations such as the German VDMA [1] have also published a traditional procedure for overhead calculation.

1.1 Cost budgeting methods

In recent decades, several new methods of cost budgeting have been developed for project management. They are classified as follows by Brockhoff [2]:
1. Cost budgeting methods in which the cost drivers are not specified.
2. Cost budgeting methods in which the cost drivers are specified.

Classification of cost budgeting methods

The first category includes, first and foremost, the various types of expert surveys. The second category includes
- cost income ratios and cost income ratio systems on the basis of standard structures (cost databases) and
- parametric budgeting models.

Expert opinions are useful if an organisation is implementing a highly innovative project and has no previous experience of similar projects. Cost databases are used extensively in the construction industry, although they were recently introduced in the IT sector. They can be used for estimating costs if a project or specific components of a project are not especially innovative. Parametric budgeting models are widely used in the weapons industry and in IT projects. Parametric budgeting models and cost income ratios are based on a systematic evaluation of cost data pertaining to completed projects.

1.2 The use of work breakdown structures in cost budgeting

Engineering estimates

Cost budgeting with the assistance of work breakdown structures that are prepared for a specific project is often considered to be a stand-alone method. It is described as a bottom-up method or an engineering-oriented method of estimating costs in conjunction with the establishment of cost income ratios for individual work packages. The basic assumptions in cost budgeting with the assist-ance of work breakdown structures are that
- it is easier to estimate the cost of the individual elements of a complex task than to estimate the cost of the task as a whole, and
- the estimates become more precise with increasing detail of the individual elements.

Subjective work breakdown structure

A work breakdown structure is absolutely essential in almost all of the methods used to estimate costs. Any expert estimating the costs associated with a project must initially consider the components of the project deliverable. At a minimum he estimates these costs on the basis of a subjective WBS, even though it may still be unsystematic and have very low structural depth. Often, it will not even have been set down in writing.

Prerequisites for use

The systematic use of cost budgeting methods in conjunction with the work breakdown structure is dependent on
- the approval of the WBS by the project management team and departments,
- a precise as possible specification of individual items and work packages,
- identical information for all persons involved in cost estimating, and
- acceptance of the WBS as binding.

Hilpert, Rademacher and Sauter [3] give the following advice about using a work breakdown structure for cost budgeting: `A work breakdown structure-oriented cost estimate appears to be far more suitable [better than the traditional cost budgeting models which are not broken down into sub-tasks and work packages], because only a work breakdown structure shows both the deliveries of goods and services that are related directly to a sub-system and those that are related to the overall system.´

Non-assignable costs

Costs than cannot be allocated to a sub-task, work package or sub-system, but only to the overall system, include
- licenses,
- insurance,

- financing costs, and
- project management costs.

1.3 Cost budgeting on the basis of expert surveys

Experts are needed in order to make each cost estimate. Expert-survey methods are structured methods in which experts are surveyed to obtain cost estimates. In the past many attempts have been made to use the Delphi method as a means of project cost estimating (= an expert survey with several rounds of questioning). This method was not a major success for several reasons:

Delphi method

- It is very difficult to ensure that surveys remain anonymous in organisations.
- The surveys involve several time-consuming rounds of questioning.
- There is no knowledge transfer between the experts surveyed.

According to Boehm´s reports, a variation on the Delphi method called `Wideband Delphi´ is more suitable for cost budgeting in software development projects. One essential characteristic of this method of expert surveys is that it comprises a combination of anonymous estimates and group discussions [4]. Anonymity

- largely excludes bandwagon effects in the estimates, and
- offers the experts the opportunity to revise their forecasts without losing face when new information comes to light.

Bandwagon effects occur when the participants in the round of questioning adopt the opinions of other participants, for example, because it is the easy option or because they lack experience.

Bandwagon effect

1.3.1 Estimate meeting

The estimate meeting method [5], of which many forms exist, has proved effective in cost budgeting. An important element is group discussions; anonymity is not required in any of the process steps. This method, which is often used in development projects, includes several modules that also form a part of other processes and expert survey, e.g. assumption analysis and iterative estimates (= in several rounds) for particularly critical system components. It also consistently adheres to the proven precepts of cost estimating, such as the requirement of transparency.

Assumption-based analysis

Iterative estimates

1.3.1.1 Objectives

The main objective of the estimate meeting is to calculate total project costs as precisely as possible. The estimates relate to the specification of inputs expected to be necessary for the work packages. These estimates are multiplied by cost rates and entered into a computer system to enable project-specific cost management. Systematic surveys of experts help us to achieve a number of secondary objectives:

Secondary objectives of the surveys

- To enable work package-specific, structured communication between project team members.
- To bring to light as many undisclosed assumptions and prerequisites relating to the project as possible (e.g. dependencies on other departments, availability of human resources).
- To assure management and the project team that the project plan is actually workable.
- To develop a common basis of work and communication for all working and status meetings.

An estimate meeting therefore fulfils more or less the same function as a project start-up meeting. However, the focus in this case is budgeting and cost estimates.

1.3.1.2 Participants

Roles

There are four roles in the meeting:
1. Estimator
2. Expert
3. Chairman
4. Keeper of minutes

Internal/external estimators

It is hotly debated whether members of the project team or non-project team employees of the organisation should estimate the specification of inputs. Employees who are also on the project team tend to be more cautious in their estimates than non-project employees. On the other hand, it is possible that the non-project personnel will provide overly optimistic estimates because they are not responsible for adhering to the budget. Another argument in favour of using project team members as estimators is that considerable learning effects can be derived from the team estimate, and if non-project personnel are the estimators, these learning effects also have to be transferred to the project team. This, however, is almost impossible in practice.

1.3.1.3 Prerequisites

The work breakdown structure with the work package descriptions that have been accepted by the project participants should be available in the meeting. If not, they must be developed at the necessary level of detail when preparing the meeting.

Work packages in the estimate

Work packages are the smallest planning and control unit in the work breakdown structure (→ Chapter C4). They define the specific activities that have to be carried out. Hand-over activities, familiarisation periods and follow-up work (e.g. documentation) must also be taken into account. The work package is also an accounting unit in project cost management systems. It is therefore the smallest unit in the WBS that is not only associated with projected costs, but for which actual costs are recorded separately during the project.

1.3.1.4 Estimate meeting procedure

Cost unit

In most cases units of quantity are selected for the estimate. In the case of personnel costs, it can be person hours, days, months or years. Before the estimate begins, the project environment has to be defined in detail. For example, in software development projects, the project manager defines the programming and test systems and the tools that the development team will use. All team members describe the work packages in their spheres of responsibility at the estimate meeting. In some cases, cost units are specified. In the work package `Write a job description for the project manager´, the cost unit would be number of pages that are likely to be written.

The estimators write an estimate for each work package on cards (→ Chapter D2) and display these for all to see. There are various procedures for processing the estimates for each work package. For example, it is possible to calculate the arithmetical mean after elimination of the extreme values (= highest and lowest estimates).

Considerable deviations between estimates

Deviation in percent

Sometimes, the individual estimates to be summarised in an overall estimate differ considerably. In such cases, the participants can establish a fixed percentage of estimates that may not exceed a specific range before the estimates are made. If one estimate differs considerably from the others, it can be eliminated before the mean value is calculated. Otherwise, there is a risk that this outlier will distort the overall result. Differences can occur owing to an estimator´s lack of experience. However, if an estimator's opinion differs wildly and he is the only expert in the team, his estimate should be accepted.

Example
Nine estimators make estimates that fall within a range of two to four person days, and only one person estimates 30 person days. As a result, the mean value is so high that the result is no longer comprehensible or reliable. It is therefore necessary to establish whether the person who estimated 30 person days is the only person in the room who is aware of what the work package in question actually involves. If he is an expert, his estimate is the only one that should be accepted. Otherwise, it should be ignored.

Discussion and repetition
In the next step, the two estimators who provided the highest and lowest estimates explain the reasons for their estimates to the other members of the group. Generally, it is the case that both have based their estimates on different experiences and assumptions, despite the description of the project environment that took place before the estimates were made. These assumptions have to be identified and documented. After this discussion, all experts are requested to make new estimates. The estimates in the second round often fall in a narrower spread. The convergence effect (= alignment) which is the objective of the second estimate therefore occurs. If it is not possible to align the estimates after the discussion, the individual aspects of the work package need to be examined in more detail.

Deviating assumptions

Convergence effect

OVERVIEW: ESTIMATE MEETING PROCEDURE
1. Definition of project environment
2. Explanation of work packages
3. First estimate
4. Deal with outliers
5. Explanation of highest/lowest estimates
6. Clarification and correction of (wrong) assumptions
7. Second estimate
8. Closer inspection of problematic work packages
9. Drafting/updating of the minutes

Estimate meeting procedure

Figure C6-1 Estimate meeting procedure

1.3.1.5 Example of an estimate meeting
In a project aiming to reorganise the processing of customer orders, the project manager and the departments involved in the project have created a work breakdown structure. In an estimate meeting, the six members of the project team then estimate the costs for the individual work packages, which are already described according to a standard format in terms of person hours. The team member responsible for the work package `Interviewing the organisation's departments´ (Estimator 5) explains this in detail, shows a preliminary interview guideline to the other estimators and names all the departments and persons to be interviewed. The chairman then asks all six team members to provide their estimates of the required person hours.

ESTIMATORS		1	2	3	4	5	6
Round 1	Estimate of person hours	140	180	190	220	185	190
Round 2	Revised estimate	175	180	195	187	185	190

Figure C6-2 Estimate of person hours required

Arithmetical mean After Round 1, the arithmetical mean of the estimates is approximately 184 person hours. Since the estimates of Estimator 1 and Estimator 4 lie far apart, the chairman requests both to explain why their estimates are so high or low. Estimator 1 says that, as far as he is aware, most of the departments mentioned have been interviewed by a management consultant two years ago, and it will be possible to use the data obtained from these interviews in the current project. The responsible team member confirms that these interviews did take place, and explains that the questions were different in those interviews. At that time, there were plans to support – but not change – the existing processes by installing a computer program. The interview results are therefore not relevant for the current project.

Estimator 4 explains his high estimate by saying that the systematic evaluation of questionnaires is, in his experience, an extremely time-consuming activity. Estimator 5 admits this. However, he points out that the evaluation is part of the `Summary of the as-is analysis´ work package, although this is not clear from the work package descriptions. He says that he will remedy this ambiguity after the meeting.

New estimate After this discussion, in which it was possible to clarify a number of misunderstandings and incorrect assumptions, a new estimate is made. Some of the estimators make higher or lower estimates. The new mean value is approximately 185 person hours. As a result, the original mean value has hardly changed. However, the individual estimates fall in a much narrower spread. By and large, the estimators have reached consensus.

1.3.1.6 Problems associated with estimate meetings

Estimate meetings for work packages do not always run so smoothly. In many cases, team members are unwilling to provide estimates because they do not believe that they have the appropriate knowledge in a specific field. If only one team member is willing to provide an estimate, the chairman can follow Füting´s [6] advice and ask him to provide
- an optimistic,
- a probable and
- a pessimistic estimate.

In the simplest case, the arithmetical mean of the three estimates is calculated. However, if no team member is willing to provide an estimate owing to lack of experience with similar work packages, the group can call on an expert from the organisation who is not working on the project.

1.4 Cost estimating with cost ratios and code systems

In recent years – particularly in English-speaking countries and Germany – project cost databases have been created as a useful tool for budgeting costs in new projects. They enable organisations to take advantage of valuable experience gained from earlier projects. These systematic cost databases are widely used in the construction and IT sectors [7]. Other sectors of industry are also increasingly using *Project learning* this method – even though terms such as `project learning´ and `knowledge management´ have long been catchphrases.

Cost ratios On the other hand, simple key cost indicators have been used for quite some time now to work out the financial aspects of a bid or in early project phases. Key cost indicators such as
- euros per cubic metre of undeveloped land,
- euros or person months per code line or

- euros per kilogram of machine

are examples of these [8]. One of the methods used by the plant construction industry to work out the financial aspects of a bid is the `cost per kilo´ method [9]. It is based on a simple principle and delivers fast results. However, it can be imprecise and associated with risks - especially when new and unfamiliar technologies are being used. The simple formula for the cost per kilo method is:

Cost per kilo method

$$PCN = \frac{PCB \times WN}{WB}$$

Key:
- PCN   the estimated production costs for the new product
- PCB   the production costs for the basic product
- WN   the weight of the new product
- WB   the weight of the basic product

These undifferentiated indicators, which are systematically calculated on the basis of figures relating to completed projects, only take one cost driver into account, e.g. undeveloped land, the number of code lines or product weight. Caution is also advised when using the resulting cost estimates. They are generally only used in the early stages of the project, when very little information about the planned product is available.

Undifferentiated ratios

On the other hand, cost indicator systems based on standard structures can take numerous cost drivers into account. One example of such a system is a construction cost database based on the cost breakdown specified in the DIN 276 standard [10]. The costs for the individual cost elements are calculated on the basis of completed projects. They are used to summarise the majority of items in the performance specification into a manageable number of elements. One example of such an element is `Foundations, cast-in-place concrete formwork´.

Ratio systems

A suitable indicator is defined (e.g. euros per square metre of façade) for each element. Meyer [11] describes his experience of using cost databases as follows: `If the files are carefully compiled in this way, very useful cost data can be obtained for small buildings … and for very similar buildings (e.g. an organisation´s administrative buildings).´

The task is more problematic if
- very different buildings must be assessed or
- the buildings are to be constructed in very different locations and/or years.

Open-access databases also exist for IT projects [12]. The company´s own data can then be used to supplement the data in the databases.

IT projects

1.4.1 Prerequisites for project cost databases

Anyone planning to introduce a project cost database must ensure that three prerequisites are met [13]:
1. Data on costs in projects that have already been implemented should be defined, collected, stored and updated in such a way that they are available and relevant for future projects.
2. New projects should be structured in such a way that the elements for which cost data was stored in the database form at least part of the planning process.
3. Tools should exist to combine cost data relating to completed projects and the work breakdown structures for new projects to produce a cost budget.

Databases

1.5 Parametric cost estimates

Cost equations

Regression analysis

Parametric cost estimates are carried out using cost equations in which the project costs, sub-project costs or the specification of inputs are shown in relation to cost drivers. The following equation was derived from data relating to completed projects in the aircraft development industry on the basis of regression analysis. It is suitable for the early phases of the project, when little knowledge exists about the system to be developed.

$$E = 0.0609 \times W^{0.631} \times S^{0.820}$$

E is the estimated number of engineer hours required for the development of an aircraft cell. W is the weight of the cell in pounds and S is the maximum speed in knots. If the values for both cost drivers are known, they can be used in the equation to provide a predictive value for the specification of inputs. However, if the aircraft to be developed incorporates new materials, the past experience that is reflected in the equation cannot simply be extrapolated.

Use in the IT sector

Parametric estimating methods are used in the IT sector. The two main cost drivers used are
- the number of instructions in source code and
- the number of function points.

1.5.1 The COCOMO model

In the COCOMO II model, the number of instructions in source code plays an important role. This can be demonstrated using one of the basic equations for this estimating model [14]:

$$\text{Effort} = \text{PC} \times \text{KSLOC}^{CE} \times \text{EAF}$$

PC   Productivity coefficient (= 2.94)
KSLOC   1,000 commented lines of code
CE   Complexity exponent (= 1.1)
EAF   Effort adjustment factor (product of approx. 20 individual cost drivers)

In mid-sized projects, the effort adjustment factor (EAF), which takes a whole range of cost drivers (e.g. analyst's and programmer's experience) into account, is 1. The variables PC and CE are used to quantify the productivity of a software firm. COCOMO provides values for this purpose obtained from the statistical evaluation of around 160 completed projects. Analyses have shown that these values cannot simply be adopted by the organisations for their cost estimates. Instead, the estimate equations are adapted to the organisation's situation by way of another statistical analysis (= calibration).

Calibration

1.5.2 Function point method

Function points

Function points are the key cost drivers in the function point cost budgeting model developed by IBM. It was initially used to estimate software size on the basis of the functions required by the user. Bundschuh [15] believes that the best time to count these for the first time is at the end of the first project phase, when user requirements and data structures are known. They can also be used for cost budgeting. A differentiation is made between five function types when counting:

Function types

1. Internal data structures
2. External interface files

3. External input
4. External output
5. External inquiry

The estimator allocates function points in accordance with the complexity of the individual functions (e.g. input of user data for a computerised library system via the VDU). Adding these points together provides the unweighted function points value. Additional cost drivers are then taken into consideration to yield the final weighted function points [16].

Example
The following example is from Volkswagen [17]. It shows the development costs for a commercial program system based on function points.

$DE = -876 + 9.94 \times FP$	for $300 > FP > 125$
$DE = -550 + 8.5 \times FP + 0.001179 \times FP^2$	for $6{,}000 \leq FP > 300$
DE Development effort in person months	
FP Function points	

The linear estimation equation can be used for smaller programs and the non-linear one for programs with between 300 and 6,000 function points.

Linear estimating equation

Problem: lack of detailed information about the product specification
Impatient customers often expect the project manager to provide reliable cost estimates at a time when the precise features of the project deliverable are still unknown. Providing binding cost estimates at this stage of a project can be negligent and risky. Generally, the reliability of cost estimates improves as the objective definition process progresses. Premature estimates are therefore inadvisable.

Premature assumptions

2 Resource planning

According to the DIN 69 903 standard, resources are personnel, and materials such as machines. When an estimate of the resources required for a project has been made, a specification of inputs only initially exists for the sub-tasks and work packages in the work breakdown structure. The project manager and line managers have to ascertain how these resource requirements are to be distributed over the project lifecycle (= resource usage profile). According to the ICB, `Resource planning includes the identification of required resources and optimised scheduling with respect to all available and procurable resources.´ There are several reasons for such planning:

Usage profile

- The decision makers have to know to what extent available resources will be used over time in existing projects or projects to which the customer has already agreed. They also have to be aware of where potential underusage, usage peaks and bottlenecks could occur since these may have to be compensated by measures such as overtime work or the recruitment of additional personnel. This is the only way to determine realistic milestone and finish dates for the individual projects.
- If the resource usage profile is known, a decision can be made as to whether to commence or postpone further projects.
- Realistic resource planning enables assumptions to be made about the consequences of priority changes. It is then possible to at least roughly calculate, for instance, the effects of the assignment of additional human resources from one project to other projects if these projects are

Arguments in favour of use

competing for the same resources in the organisation. It also provides information about the consequences of project termination.

This chapter assumes that resource planning covers all projects that are being implemented by an organisation.

2.1 The resource planning procedure

Network analysis At first glance, network analysis (→ Chapter C5) appears to be an enticing option for project-specific resource planning. Resources can be allocated to the various activities or work packages in a network diagram. In this process, the required hours or material units can be evenly distributed along the time axis, or allocated on a needs-oriented basis to various workdays or weeks. Since the calendar dates for the start and finish of the various activities and work packages have been calculated, it is possible to distribute the required resources over the calendar axis. The following example assumes that only one project is being implemented.

Example
Three design engineers with similar qualifications are available for a development project in an organisation. Other resource types, such as assembly personnel or machines, are not taken into account. The design engineers work a 40-hour week. They are not available to work on the project for eight of these hours because they have many other responsibilities – such as advising customers and repairing defects in products that have already been delivered. None of the three design engineers is planning a holiday in the period under review. The possibility that one of the design engineers might fall ill is not taken into account. 96 design engineer hours per week are therefore available. The resource usage diagram (→ Figure C6-3) assumes that all activities take place at the earliest dates. It shows that only in Week 3 will the design engineers be unavailable for the required number of hours for Activities 2 and 3.

CALENDAR WEEKS	1	2	3	4	5	6	7
Activities							
Activity 1	85	85					
Activity 2			33				
				33			
Activity 3			70	60			
Activity 4					75	75	
Activity 5							90
Requirements for all activities	85	85	103 (70)	60 (93)	75	75	90
No. of hours for which the design engineers are available	96	96	96	96	96	96	96
Over or undercoverage	11	11	-7 (26)	36 (3)	21	21	6

All figures are stated in hours.
The figures in brackets indicate resource usage after the postponement of Activity 2.

Figure C6-3 Resource usage diagram with the postponement of an activity

One solution to the problem is to postpone Activity 2 for one calendar week. The planned project finish date can still be met and the design engineers are available for a sufficient number of hours in each week. If the postponement of one or more activities is only possible with the result that the project finish date is jeopardised, it would be possible to approve the original finish date on a trial basis. The purpose of approval is to determine the level of resource usage at which the resource limits are no longer exceeded. The project planner therefore attempts initially to postpone activities within the limits of available float and - when this is no longer possible - to keep project finish date overrun to a minimum after its approval.

Several software packages include algorithms for this purpose. However, the solutions that the programs offer should only be viewed as suggestions and not accepted without further verification because algorithms with rigid and often implausible priority rules are not appropriate in every situation. For example, a software program sometimes postpones activities that would probably be brought forward based on common sense. As a result, the project manager has to work with an unacceptable resource usage plan. Therefore it is always important for him to form his own opinion.   *Solutions provided by software*

For example, a project manager should bring a work package forward, even if the program has scheduled it for a later date, if he assumes that an employee will be assigned to other duties in coming months but currently has time to carry out a work package.

There are other ways of reducing capacity peaks. They include, for example, the prolongation, splitting or cancellation of activities.   *Options to reduce capacity peaks*

A similar situation to the one shown in Figure C6-3 would occur if several projects were to be implemented concurrently and use the same resources. Figure C6-4 shows this method of resource planning for several projects. The smaller projects are not divided up into activities.   *Parallel projects*

2.2 Common mistakes

In the first, highly simplified, example, only 80 percent of a design engineer´s working time is allocated to the project. In the second example, the planners have taken into account that the employee frequently has to perform additional duties that are unrelated to the project. They deducted a basic workload and a further time slice for other work. In other words, it is not possible to assume that an employee is able to dedicate 100 percent of his working hours to a specific project.   *Incorrect assessment of availability*

In many cases, team members are fully assigned to new projects, even though they are still involved in other projects. Although these projects have officially ended, they still use resources – for example, for the preparation of outstanding documentation or for defect elimination.

Another common mistake often occurs in research and development projects when the development managers are unfamiliar with the resources that are being used in existing projects and have been assigned to agreed future projects. They allocate teams of a more or less constant size to further projects, even though these people already have high workloads. As a result, the average project turnaround time gets longer and longer.

CALENDAR WEEKS	1	2	3	4	5	6	7	8	9	10	11	12	13	14
Activity or project														
Project 1														
Activity 11	12	12	12	12	12	12								
Activity 12			3	3	3	5								
Activity 13							17	17	17	17	17	13	13	13
Activity 14										4	4	4	4	4
Activity 15														
Activity 16							5	5	5					
Activity 17				7	7	7								
Project 2														
Activity 21	8	8	8	8										
Activity 22		15	15	7	7									
Activity 23						6	6	6	6					
Activity 24						4	4	4	4					
Activity 25		16	16	16	16									
Project 3	250	250	250	250	250	250	250	250	250	250	250	250	250	250
Project 4	230	211	195	177	55	86	118	138	143	167	199	214	216	235
Project resource requirements in hours	500	512	499	480	350	370	400	420	425	438	470	481	483	502
Basic workload	60	60	60	60	60	60	60	60	60	60	60	60	60	60
Other non-project-related work	45	45	45	45	45	45	45	45	45	45	45	45	45	45
Hours required	605	617	604	585	455	475	505	525	530	543	575	586	543	607
Hours available	590	590	590	570	570	570	500	500	500	500	500	510	510	510
Overcoverage or shortfall	-15	-27	-14	-34	115	95	-5	-25	-30	-43	-75	-76	-33	-97

Figure C6-4 Resource plan for several projects

2.3 Network analysis

Expenditure of time and effort in practice

Theoretically at least, network analysis offers an elegant option for the preparation of process and time schedules using available resources. Most of the software programs available for project planning and supervision enable resource planning at activity level. However, in practice, this requires considerable expenditure of time and effort. Scheuring, a leading expert when it comes to resource planning problems, says, `(…) project management tool providers entice customers with advertising slogans that promise integral resource planning from general to detailed plans, though this is really pure fiction´ [18]. He rightly advises against planning in excessive detail: `Resource planning at activity level is not appropriate in most situations.´ [19]

2.3.1 Alternatives

Generalised planning

Since resource planning is essential, we need to find a less detailed alternative to using a full network analysis. Scheuring [20] recommends a more general resource plan for individual project phases.

C6 COST AND RESOURCE PLANNING

Figure C6-5 shows an example of a general resource plan. However, this plan can be even more general, as is shown in Figure C6-6.

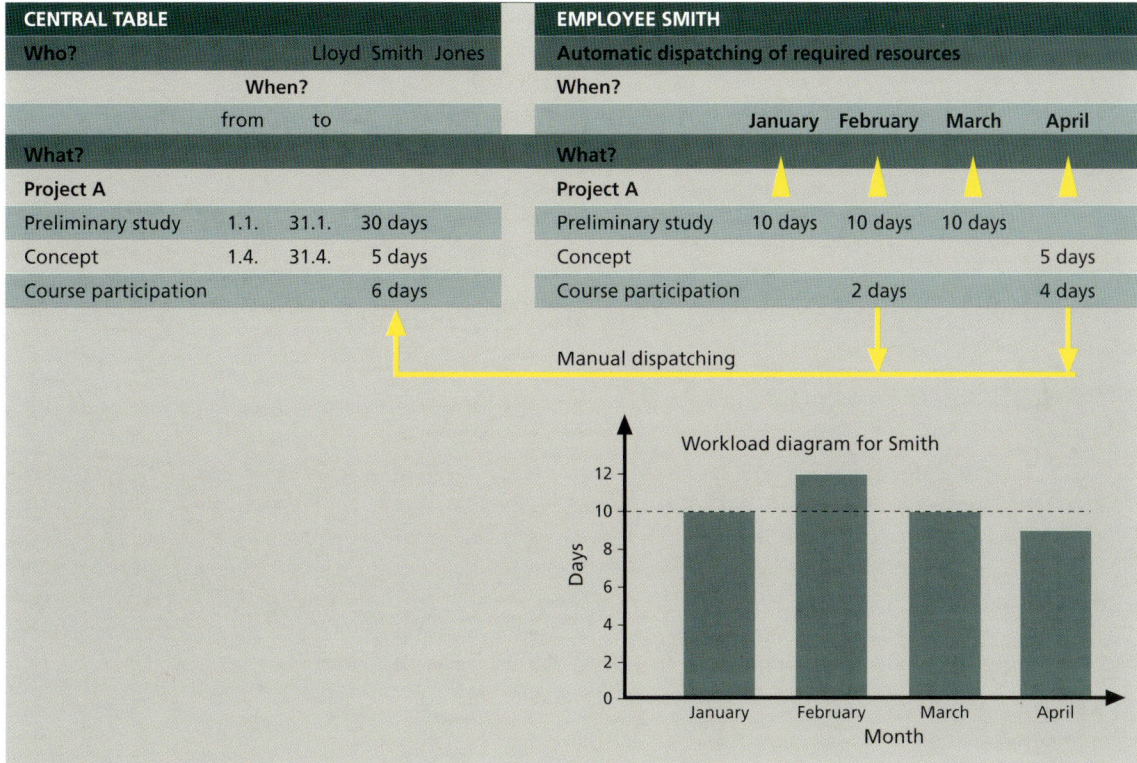

Figure C6-5 Month-by-month resource plan

	Q1				Q2			
Projects	Lab 1	Lab 2	Lab 3	Design office 1	Lab 1	Lab 2	Lab 3	Lab 4
	AE	AE	AE	AE	AE	AE	AE	AE
Project 1	1	2	1	1.5				
Project 2	1	0	0	0				
Project 3	0.5	1.5	3	2				
Project 4	3	3	2	0				
Project 5	0	4	1	1				
...	...	...	...	...	...	...	...	...
Project n	0	1	0	1				
Total current projects	5.5							
Basic workload	1							
AE personnel requirements								
Available	6							
Surplus or deficit	0.5	etc.	etc.					

All figures in AE = employees who charge to the projects

Figure C6-6 Resource planning at quarterly intervals

217

In this case, manpower resource allocation plans are revised regularly at longer intervals. This helps to keep the time and effort expended on planning within acceptable limits. However, the long quarterly planning intervals mean that only major capacity discrepancies are identified. Also, different skill levels of employees in an organisational unit are not taken into account.

2.4 Qualification-oriented resource planning

Availability of specialists

The methods of resource planning described above are purely quantitative. It is assumed that the employees allocated to a project are interchangeable and deliver roughly the same level of productivity. However, this is definitely not the case in many projects. Particularly in software projects, vastly different levels of programmer productivity have been measured. In such cases, the planners must consider separately the time that specialists are allocated to a project and their availability.

2.5 Roles

Matrix organisation

Pure project organisation

The project manager should estimate the requirements of his project in advance and request his line management to make the relevant resources available. In a matrix management structure ($\rightarrow$ Chapter A6), line managers and project managers should elaborate the resource plan jointly, though the former have the final say. In pure (= autonomous) project structures and functional organisation structures, this high level of interaction between the various role holders is not necessary. In pure project structures, the project manager has responsibility; in functional organisation structures, the department manager. Only the department manager can estimate the workloads of his staff resulting from individual projects and routine tasks.

2.6 Opposition to project-specific resource planning

Resource planning often meets with opposition. Line managers are worried about the transparency of their department´s productivity, and that this might lead to stricter controls. Works councils are also often opposed to the assignment of staff to projects. Excessive requirements of planning detail often fuel this opposition.

3 Project logistics

Up to now, this chapter has only dealt with the most important resource – manpower. In many projects, such as software development and organisation projects, labour costs account for the lion´s share of total project costs.

Material goods

On the other hand, investment projects in the construction industry and industrial plant construction projects require many material goods to produce the project deliverable. These include resources such as all kinds of construction machines, pre-fabricated components that are assembled into a complete system at the construction site, numerous component parts and component assemblies, as well as raw materials, consumables and supplies. In large-scale projects, the project manager often has to obtain these resources from numerous sub-contractors and suppliers - production facilities and warehouses in various locations – as the project progresses. An explanation of the specific aspects of project logistics (ICB Element 27) is necessary at this point. Contractual aspects of procurement (→ Chapter A4), the identification and selection of suppliers and the issue of make-or-buy (= decision whether to produce in-house or procure externally) are significant for the project manager.

==According to Schwarze [21], project logistics ensure that the material goods necessary for the implementation of a project are delivered (or in some cases removed) at the right time and in the required quantity and quality.==

The DIN 69 904 standard describes project logistics in somewhat more general terms as the `physical supply of resources allocated to the implementation process´. Comprehensive logistics information systems and telecommunications help to track the goods in transit from their place of origin to the warehouse and to their place of use.

Construction site projects are associated with additional problems that have nothing to do with the procurement of material goods for series and mass production:

Problems in construction projects

- The project implementation locations change frequently. As a result, each time the location changes, the logistics networks have to be rebuilt and, unlike permanent networks, they only remain in place for the duration of the project. This task is often undertaken by specialist logistics firms [22].
- Third-world countries, in particular, tend to have underdeveloped road infrastructures and a great deal of red tape (e.g. restrictive customs formalities) that make it difficult to import material goods.

3.1 Project logistics and network analysis [23]

As a rule, project managers face a conflict: on the one hand, the goods should not arrive at the production site too early, otherwise they cause unnecessary, high warehousing costs. On the other, supply bottlenecks should be avoided so that late deliveries do not cause project delays. It is therefore necessary to schedule carefully the dates on which resources are drawn, dispatched for transportation and available on site. Project process and time scheduling, supported by network analysis (→ Chapter C5) are the best ways of achieving this objective. Among other things, they enable

Benefits of network analysis

- the coordination of the activities of various suppliers and their harmonisation with project requirements,
- the identification of float in the frequently time-critical transport processes,
- the simulation of alternative means of transportation and their impact on the project, as well as
- an analysis of how existing or anticipated missed deadlines can be made up.

4 Cost monitoring during the project

Target costs are calculated, in a process similar to the one used in resource planning, for activities or work packages whose dates are established on the basis of network analysis.

Soon after the development of the network analysis scheduling model, somebody inevitably came up with the idea of combining project cost budgeting and management with network analysis. Target costs are calculated in a similar process to the one used in resource planning for activities or work

Projected costs

packages whose dates are calculated using network scheduling. They are then distributed using various methods over the scheduled duration of the activity.

Linear distribution over the project lifecycle

The simplest method of cost monitoring is to distribute costs on a linear basis over the scheduled duration of an activity or group of activities (work package). The total cost curves over the time axis are added-up from the bottom to the top level of the work breakdown structure. At the point of maximum consolidation, i.e. the project level, the curve representing the projected project costs over the calendar time axis. In actual fact, the planners are provided with two cost curves (= total cost curves): one represents the earliest possible start time for each activity and a second represents the latest possible start time. Figure C6-7 [24] shows the consolidation from the lowest level of the work breakdown structure up to the project level.

Total cost curve

Actual costs

Over the course of the project, the actual costs of the individual work packages are also recorded and compared with the projected costs in a variance analysis. This comparison can be made on a monthly basis, for example.

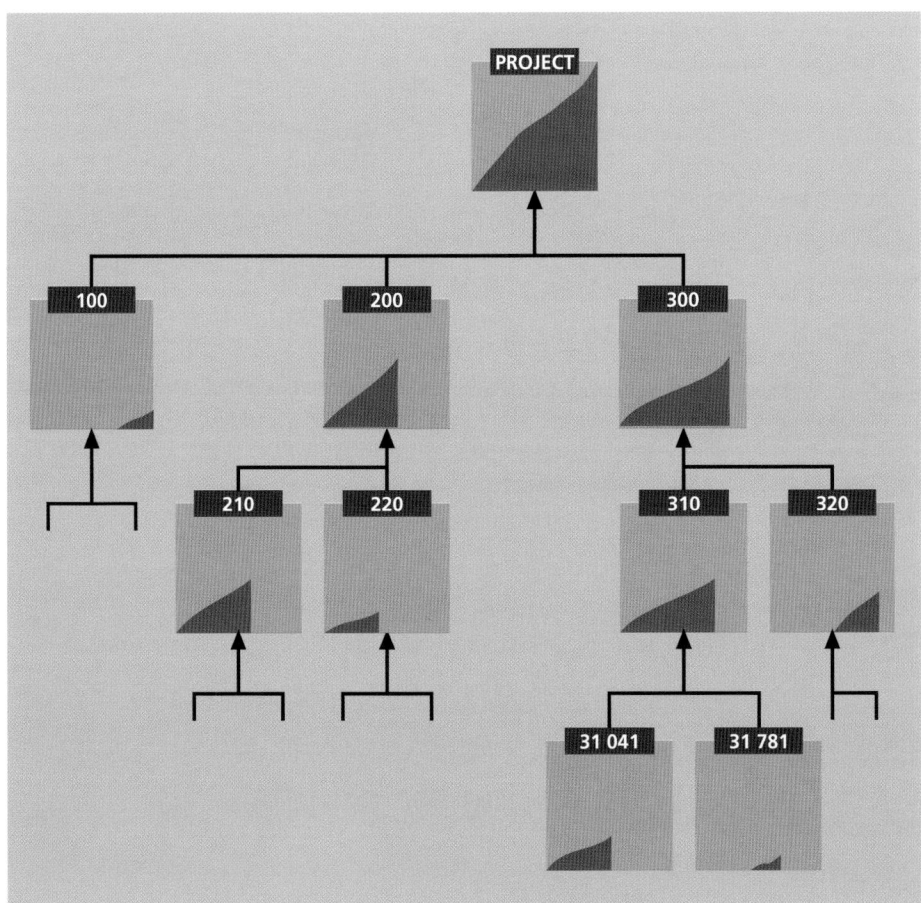

Figure C6-7 Consolidation of cost curves across the elements of the work breakdown structure

4.1 Variants

In practice, variants of the above-described methods of cost budgeting and project-specific cost monitoring have developed over time [25]. Three basic forms, associated with varying levels of complexity, exist. Also, their implementation and use require different amounts of effort. They have one thing in common: they can be used at project, sub-task work package or network analysis activity level. Also, they necessitate the timely recording of the actual costs generated by the elements in the work breakdown structure.

Common features

Variant 1: Basic version
This is the simplest cost monitoring version. It only records actual costs incurred and work/services performed (costs incurred for work/services performed up to the appointed date). A comparison of these costs with the projected costs for the sub-task, work package or project is not particularly informative because it only provides information about the remaining budget. However, periodic reports on actual costs are supplemented by regular cost to complete estimates to provide an early-warning function. The current cost status and the cost to complete estimates are added together to establish cost at completion. This is a forecast of total costs that are likely to be incurred up until the completion of the project.

Cost to complete

This variant is often used in software projects [26]. Figure C6-8 shows basic version cost monitoring in a software development project. It includes cost data at project level. The chart shows the cost to complete estimates but not cost at completion.

R&D COST REPORT – COMPREHENSIVE OVERVIEW					
Division: ORG Z	Financial year: 2003/04	Reporting period: February			
Projects	Costs to date	Cost to complete	Current financial year		Budget utilisation
			Actual	Target	
	End of February 04	March 04 to end of planning period			
Project A	14,381.1	13,330.1	1,435.0	2,643.0	54.9 %
Project B	1,425.3	4,627.0	3,740.0	4,627.0	75.0 %
Project C	20,074.2	1,498.2	586.0	1,498.2	39.1 %
Project D	5,591.8	2,546.1	735.0	1,577.1	48.8 %
Project E	80.0	0.0	0.0	0.0	0.0 %
Project F	8,842.2	20,419.8	2,190.5	6,033.2	36.3 %
Project G	637.0	256.0	245.0	92.0	266.3 %
Project H	1,671.4	0.0	550.0	0.0	
Project I	42,468.9	44,266.1	4,498.5	12,341.9	36.4 %
Project K	3,063.0	153.0	0.0	40.0	0.0 %
Total	98,234.9	87,096.3	13,710.0	28,825.4	47.5 %

Only actual costs and estimated cost to complete are computed.
All figures are stated in EUR '000.

Figure C6-8 Example of Variant 1 in a software development project (evaluation at project level)

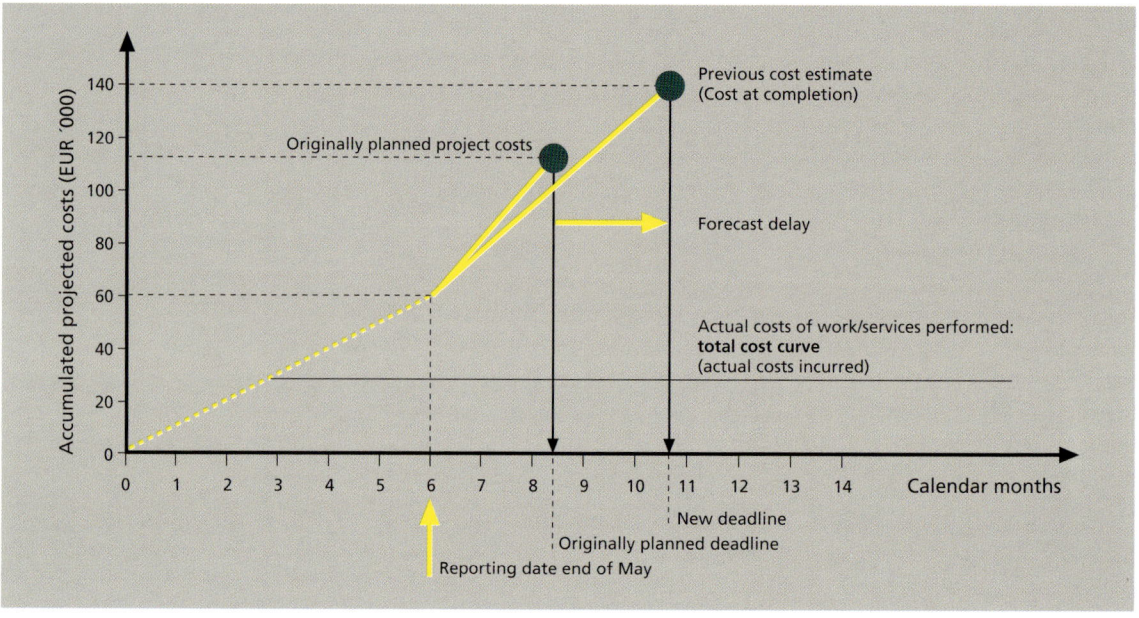

Figure C6-9 Schematic diagram of Variant 1

Some plant construction companies also use a sophisticated version of Variant 1 [27] which records allocated costs relating to the project budget funds that have been made available. For example, budget funds may have been made available for external orders or internal production orders that have not yet been invoiced or do not show up in internal cost centres.

Variant 2: Streamlined de-luxe version

Projected costs of work/services performed

In this version, not only are regular cost to complete estimates made, but also comparisons of actual costs and work/services performed with projected costs and work/services to be performed (`What costs should have been incurred in respect of the work/services performed up to the reporting date?´). Project management literature uses different terms to describe the projected costs of work/services performed, all of which are synonymous:
- Earned value
- Value of work performed
- Budgeted Cost of Work Performed (BCWP)
- Projected cost at completion

Efficiency deviation

The deviation of projected costs for work/services to be performed from actual costs for work/services performed is also called an efficiency deviation. It can only be calculated if it the degree of completion of the project as a whole, a sub-task or a work package can be stated in percentage terms (→ Chapter C9). Therefore, the more reliable the value for work progress is, the more credible the value for efficiency deviation will be.

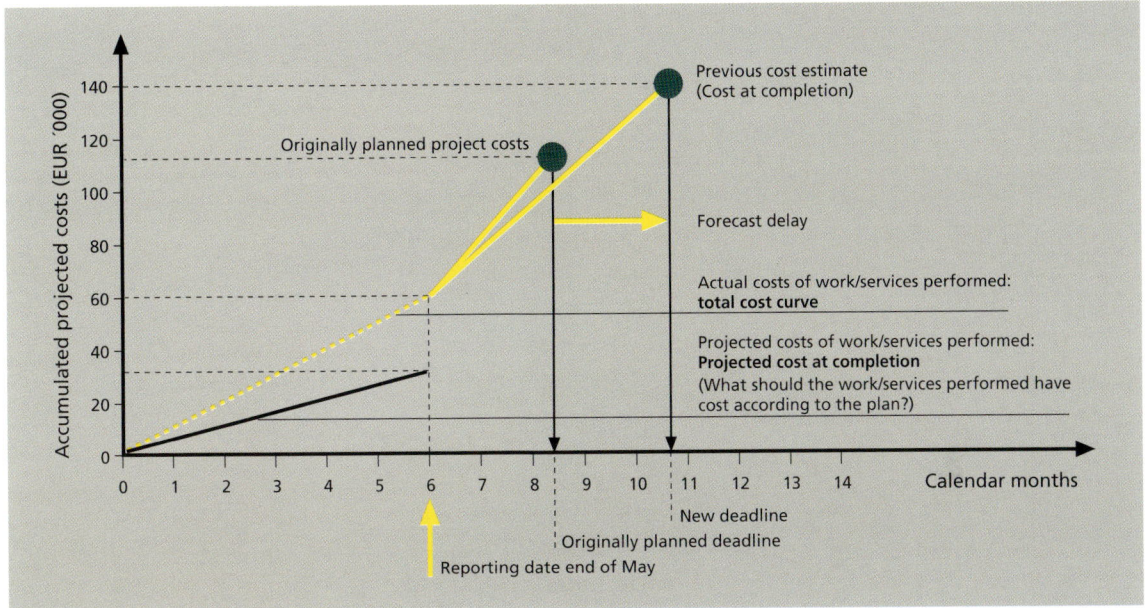

Figure C6-10 Schematic diagram of Variant 2

Variant 3: De-luxe version

Variant 3, which is generally only used in very large-scale and cost-intensive projects, is the most complex form of cost monitoring. In addition to estimated cost to complete, it also ascertains projected costs for work/services to be performed ('What costs should have been incurred by the reporting date for the planned work/services?'), the actual costs of work/services performed and the actual cost to complete. The difference between the projected costs for work/services to be performed and the projected costs for work/services performed is the performance deviation. It shows in terms of costs how far the project is behind its original schedule. If this additional cost category is taken into account, the costs have to be distributed accordingly over the time axis (→ Figure C6-11).

Most complex form of cost monitoring

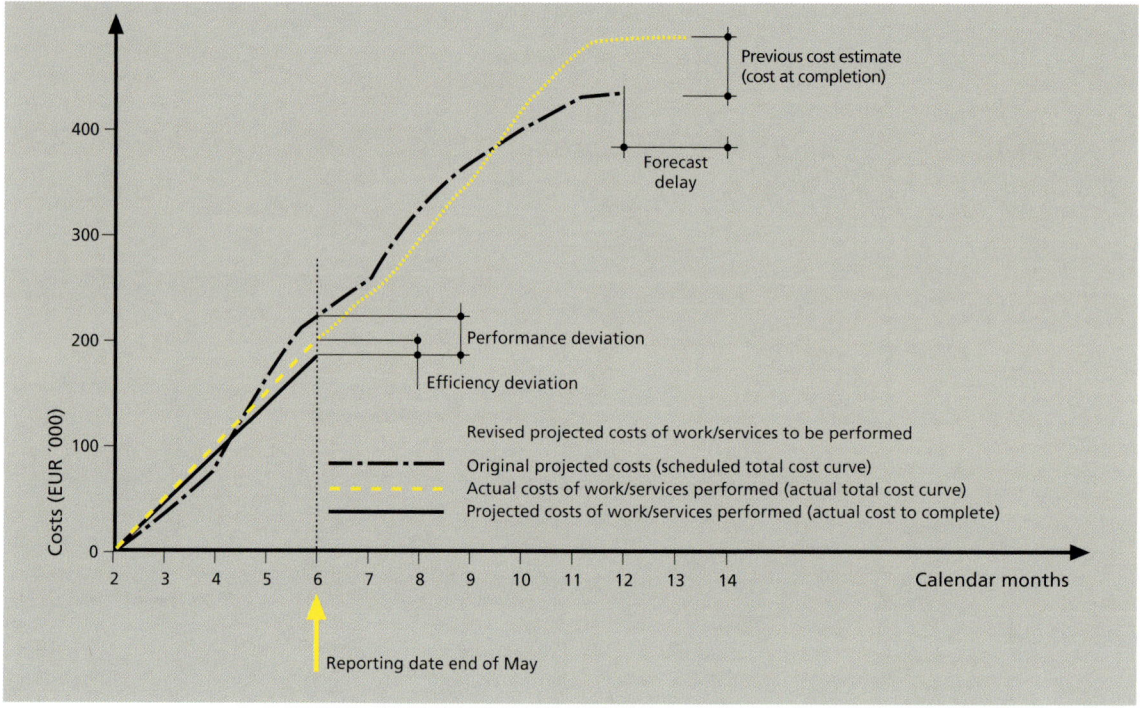

Figure C6-11 Schematic diagram of Variant 3

4.1.1 Selection of the most suitable variant

Variant 1 is associated with the least expenditure of time and effort for planning and data collection, while Variant 3 is associated with the most. However, the establishment of the time relevance of costs (= scheduled total cost curve) provides a vast amount of additional information. This is especially significant if the projected costs are the basis of the contractor's and customer's financing plans. If the distribution of costs over time is known, the dates on which payable costs will occur can be ascertained. However, it is debatable whether the ascertainment of the projected cost at completion does actually provide any additional knowledge.

Financial resource planning

Small-scale projects

In smaller-scale projects with shorter lifecycles, Variant 1 is likely to suffice - especially when cost monitoring extends down to work package level. However, this variant should not be further simplified by dispensing with regular cost to complete estimates.

4.2 Recent developments

Several interesting developments have taken place in recent years in the area of project cost budgeting and monitoring. The most important developments are
- target costing
- activity-based costing and
- the integrative approach suggested by Lachnit, Ammann and Becker.

4.2.1 Target costing

In the target costing process, the costs of a system are not calculated on the basis of the specification and the work breakdown structure. Instead, the question is `What can the project cost?´ According to Seidenschwarz [28], the main purpose of target costing is market-oriented cost management and the management of product costs in the early development phases. This objective takes into account that the opportunities to influence product costs are greatest in the early design phases of the product development process.

Use in earlier project phases

According to the German Ministry of Defence [29], 85 percent of the cost (development, production and subsequent maintenance and operating costs) of military systems is firmly established when the plans for the production of a prototype are finalised. At this stage of the project, no material product exists as yet.

4.2.2 Activity-based costing

At first glance, activity-based costing does not appear suitable for the project-based production of goods and services because it was developed for repetitive activities. However, it is also useful in projects. This type of cost budgeting can provide valuable information in connection with the basic issue of whether a product variant should be developed for a customer or market segment. Unlike the traditional calculation of mark-up, it takes into account the fact that highly complex products necessitate operational functions (e.g. materials scheduling, production control and quality management) and are associated with high workloads for the project management team. As a result, higher costs are budgeted for these products than would be the case for less complex products.

Repetitive activities

Organisations implement product variant development and production projects at the request of the customer or of the sales department. With the assistance of activity-based costing, they can ascertain at the end of the project whether the special orders have generated the profit envisaged and whether the correct overhead rates were charged. Overhead costs are costs that, unlike direct costs, can only be allocated to a product using a key.

Development of product variants

Overhead costs

4.2.3 Integrative approach

The integrative approach suggested by Lachnit, Ammann and Becker [30] unites the processes of project planning and control throughout the project lifecycle and the yearly/monthly performance, balance sheet and financial plans. The project control data are processed so that their effects on the organisation´s operating result are visible and it is possible to make assumptions about the project´s impact on cash flows.

Self-assessment questions for each certification level

No.	Question	Level D	Level C	Level B	Level A	Self-assessment
C6.01	What role does a WBS play in cost budgeting?	2	3	3	4	☐
C6.02	What is the procedure for cost budgeting?	2	3	3	4	☐
C6.03	Who plans the project's resources and how?	2	3	3	4	☐
C6.04	How can project costs be monitored?	2	3	3	4	☐
C6.05	How are cost estimates prepared?	2	2	3	4	☐
C6.06	How is an early warning function implemented during the process of project cost monitoring?	1	2	2	4	☐
C6.07	What methods of planning and monitoring project costs can an organisation use?	1	1	1	4	☐
C6.08	What task does the project office perform as regards project costs?	1	1	1	4	☐
C6.09	What is the purpose of an estimate meeting and who participates?	1	2	3	4	☐
C6.10	What are the advantages/disadvantages of a project cost database?	1	2	2	4	☐
C6.11	What are the most common mistakes in resource planning?	2	2	2	2	☐
C6.12	Why are skills and roles significant in the process of resource planning?	2	2	3	4	☐
C6.13	Why is it practical to use the cost-to-complete method?	2	3	3	4	☐
C6.14	What new developments in the area of project cost budgeting exist?	1	2	2	4	☐

C7 CONFIGURATION AND CHANGE MANAGEMENT

Effective project control depends upon the smooth interaction of the three project management elements of configuration, document and change management (ICB Elements 17 and 21). This chapter describes the various process steps involved in configuration management, from configuration identification to configuration auditing. It also focuses on the requirements for systematic documentation and the significance of a competent approach to change management, which is essential for the monitoring and control of changes.

1 Change control and change management

First of all, it is necessary to differentiate between change control and change management. The former relates to changes in the project or product as described in this chapter. The latter relates to changes in the project environment (→ Chapter A3, F1). Many people use `change management` as a buzz phrase for both, which can lead to misunderstandings.

Project or product
Project environment

2 Significance

In the early 1950s, the US military built missiles in diverse configurations and tested them thoroughly in order to identify the best set-ups. However, many of the around 1,000 missiles tested in various configurations exploded either on launch or in the air; only a few of them exploded on reaching the target. Afterwards, it was impossible to differentiate between the serviceable and non-serviceable missiles. The records kept made it impossible to draw any conclusions about the missiles´ configuration. Minor changes – which often had considerable impact – were not documented. It was therefore neither possible to ascertain why some tests were successful, nor to reproduce the results. This experience prompted the people in charge to introduce the following procedure: effective immediately, changes could only be made to military products if they were recorded in supporting documents [1].

This mishap is considered to mark the birth of configuration management.

Extensive consultation and co-ordination are essential to make a product ripe for mass production, to develop various alternatives for a new IT system or to verify the efficacy of a pharmaceutical drug on the basis of clinical trials. This applies to an even greater extent if many different teams are working together at different locations and at different times. To establish the status after functional changes relative to the reference configuration (= the first product that is described in terms of technical and functional data), developers document the data and facts relating to the product´s development throughout the development process. Supporting documentation is necessary to compare the interim results, achieved in the individual and often overlapping development phases, with the original objectives. If they deviate from the reference configuration, two options are available:
   1. The objective can be modified in favour of another solution.
   2. The budget can be increased and/or end-dates postponed so that the original objective can still be attained.

Reference configuration

3 Interaction of the elements

Project controlling Effective project controlling (time, costs and quality) is only possible on the basis of a functioning configuration, document and change management. These three project management elements only deliver their full impact if they are implemented in conjunction with one another, as seen in Figure C7-1.

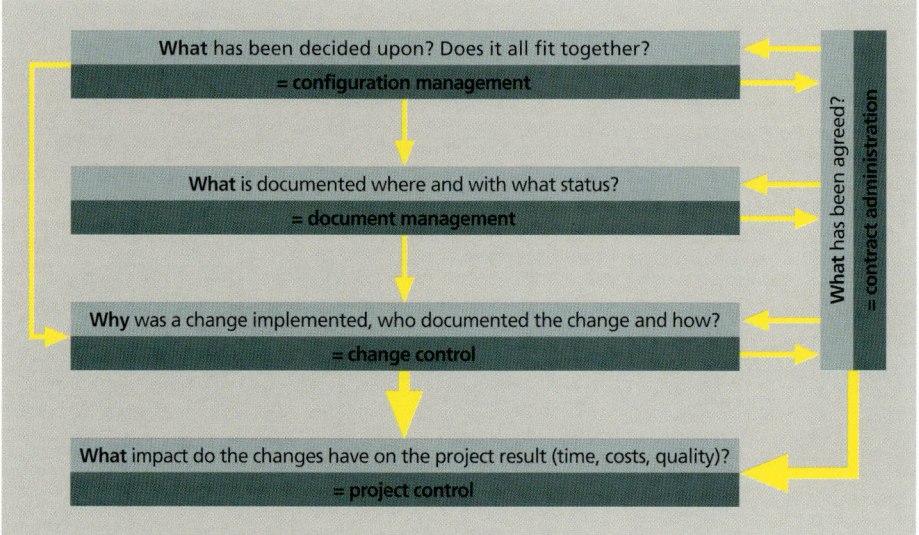

Figure C7-1 Interaction of configuration, document and change management

Data exchange This interaction can be demonstrated using the example of combustion engine development. Since this is a complex process, different car manufacturers install identical engines, developed by one manufacturer, in various car bodies. This enables them to avoid the substantial development costs that they would otherwise have incurred. However, the mountings and connections for each of the different models are specifically designed for the various vehicle bodies. The car manufacturers must therefore initially exchange and co-ordinate data (e.g. engine compartment dimensions) and facts (e.g. shape of connections) in the form of drawings and diagrams. The co-ordination of this process is one aspect of configuration management.

Information carriers Documents – either in paper or electronic format – are generally used as the medium for making these facts and figures available. When a certain volume of project documents exist, it is necessary to administer them, which is where document management comes in.

Modification of interfaces Changes are inevitable over the course of a project, for example when interim results are viewed as unsatisfactory and therefore rejected. In an engine development project, this would be the case if the supply from the fuel tank could not be connected to the fuel pump on the engine block. The dimensions and shapes would have to be changed to ensure this interface. This, in turn, necessitates document changes. Change control provides the framework of procedures used to make these changes.

In practice, the following terms are commonly used:
- Configuration   = as designed
- Change   = how changed
- Documentation   = as built

C7 CONFIGURATION AND CHANGE MANAGEMENT

The elements of configuration, change and documentation are essential for project management if the project staff is working at different times and in different locations.

Project staff working

4 Configuration management

> A configuration is defined as the
> - functions and physical features of a product or service as described in the supporting documents and implemented in the product,
> - detailed and complete compilation and documentation of project results and their systematic updating when project changes are implemented [2].

Configuration management [3] is a management discipline that is applied throughout the entire lifecycle of a product to ensure transparency and guarantee that it incorporates the agreed functional and physical features.

Functional and physical characteristics

The main objective of configuration management is to document the current configuration of a product, as well as the extent to which it satisfies physical and functional requirements and to ensure absolute transparency in these respects. Documentation transparency can be described as the ability to provide a satisfactory answer to any question within a reasonable time. At all phases of a project, all members of a project team should have access to information about the project deliverable and its creation process (= `what´ question) so they can check whether the individual configurations – which are also called design characteristics – can be physically connected to their interfaces. Configuration management also ensures that each project team member uses the correct documentation in all phases of the product´s lifecycle.

Answer to every question

Verifiability

4.1 Tasks

The configuration management process comprises the following activities:
Configuration
- identification
- control
- accounting
- auditing.

The majority of projects have a paper phase (pre-project phase) which precedes the realisation phase. In this early phase of a project, the people involved must reach agreement on project objectives and expected project benefits. The reference configuration data and facts generally originate in this phase. In IT projects this is called the baseline and in plant construction projects it is described as scope. Standard, cross-sector terms and definitions have not been established. However, the terms and definitions that exist are very similar. This chapter predominantly uses the terms referred to by Versteegen and Weischedel [1].

Pre-project phase

4.1.1 Configuration identification

Tasks — Configuration identification comprises the following tasks:
- Definition of the product structure and selection of configuration units, which is also called the reference configuration [4]
- Documentation of the physical and functional characteristics of configuration elements in clearly identified configuration documents
- Establishment and use of rules for numbering configuration elements and sub-elements, as well as for structuring documents, interfaces, changes and approvals during and after realisation (e.g. parts-list structures for the production team or document identification systems)
- Establishment of reference configurations on the basis of formal agreements which, together with the approved changes, constitute the latest version of the agreed and therefore valid configuration

4.1.2 Configuration control

Activities — Configuration control comprises the following tasks:
- Documentation of the cause or reason for changes (e.g. customer request or design defect that had not been previously identified)
- Assessment of the impact of changes (e.g. with/without consequential changes)
- Approval or rejection of changes (with reasons, e.g. additional benefits or costs of the consequential changes are higher than the projected benefit)
- Processing of special approvals before or after implementation (e.g. additional services or features that were only identified as necessary after the first tests were carried out)

At this point, configuration control and change control overlap: Configuration control adapts interfaces in terms of data and shapes, while change control relates to changes in documents [5].

4.1.3 Configuration accounting

Traceability — Configuration accounting ensures the traceability of individual changes (for example, changes that must be approved by state supervisory authorities). In this case, configuration accounting and document management overlap.

4.1.4 Configuration auditing

Types — There are two types of configuration audit [6]:
1. Function-related configuration audit
   Formal audit of a configuration unit to ascertain whether it satisfies the performance and functional characteristics specified in the configuration documents (e.g. acceptance certificate in respect of work performed)
2. Physical configuration audit
   Formal audit of the as-built configuration of an element to ascertain whether it corresponds to the information provided in the configuration documents (e.g. design drawings with the status `as built´)

4.2 Configuration management plan

A configuration management plan informs project team members about the specific content and methods of configuration identification, control, accounting and auditing or change control.

Content

Figure C7-2 shows the typical phases of a project and the associated configuration management tasks [7].

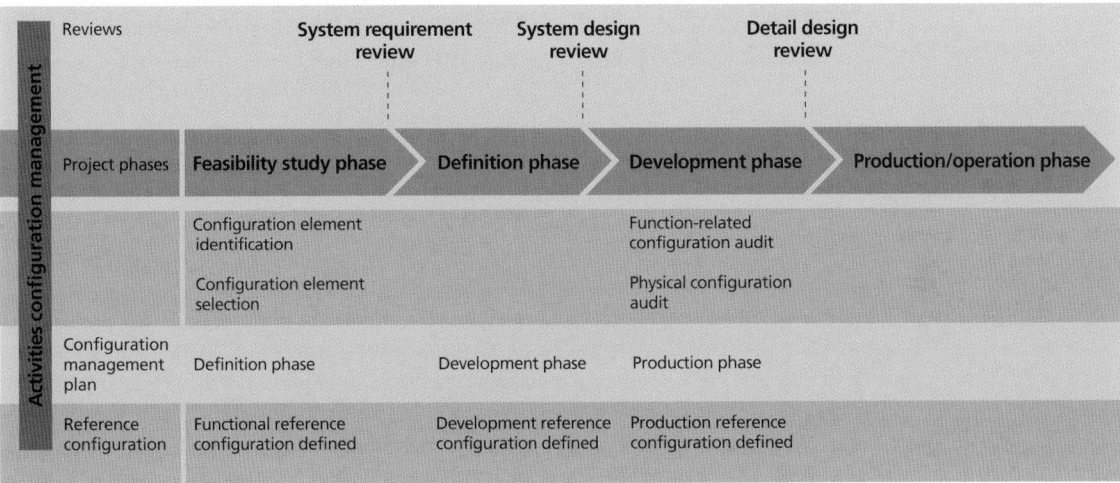

Figure C7-2 Project phases and configuration management activities

Figure C7-3 explains how to prepare a configuration plan in the form of a checklist [8].

Organisation
- Is the organisational structure for the implementation and application of configuration management (= CM) specified?
  - Are the tasks and responsibilities of each department described?
  - Are all CM organisational units (configuration administration, change conference, review committee) taken into account?
  - Are the interfaces to partners (e.g. sub-contractors, customer) specified?
- Has a plan for its introduction been created?

Reference configuration
- Have the reference configurations been defined accurately and are they situation-dependent?
  - If only one reference configuration exists: does this simplification conform to the level of innovativeness and the risks?
  - Does the reference configuration adequately reflect the maturity process?
  - Do the reference configurations conform with the phase structures?
  - Do the reference configurations conform with the technical tests?
- Have the technical tests been accurately defined and are they situation-dependent?

Configuration identification
- Is the specification of documents comprehensive enough – are all necessary document types defined?
- Are the configuration elements (CE) properly formulated? Have the consequences of maintenance and repair been taken into account?
- Is an identification system available?

Configuration control/management – change control
- Are the stages of the change process described precisely?
- Has a procedure for classification and assessment been developed?
- Do change requests and change memos exist?

Figure C7-3 Checklist for the creation of a configuration management plan (1)

> **Configuration accounting – configuration verification**
> - Are status reports specified? Have individual report formats and their recipients been decided?
> - Does the registration and archiving process meet the requirements?
> - Is an IT tool envisaged or already in place? Is there operating experience? Can the application be used efficiently?
>
> **Configuration audit – configuration revision**
> - Do the audits and revisions take place at particular times? Are they related to the reference configurations, technical tests and phase structures?

Figure C7-3 Checklist for the creation of a configuration management plan (2)

5 Document management

Documentation

Documentation is defined as the creation, identification, registration, condensing, editing, updating, distribution, archiving and destruction of data (= formatted information) and facts (= unformatted information), irrespective of the type of information carrier used.

Archive-worthy documents

Document management makes it possible, within reasonable time and effort, to furnish all documents relating to a specific issue. However, the document management team is not responsible for the content of the documents (completeness and correctness). Documents are archive-worthy records that are stored in all kinds of information carriers. A document is archive-worthy if it
- describes future obligations (e.g. contract),
- defines work processes (e.g. job orders),
- contains interim results (e.g. status report with approvals), or
- serves as verification for results achieved (e.g. completion certificate).

Binding effect

The document author's signature makes the content binding. In some cases, the recipient is required to sign the document as confirmation of agreement.

Information carriers

The main types of information carrier are
- paper,
- digital media (e.g. CDs, disks and the punched cards, magnetic tapes and 11-inch diskettes that are still used in some archives) and
- microfilm (which is still used for long-term archiving. Optical enlargement is necessary to read the microfilm).

5.1 Project-specific document instance

Project manager

In smaller projects, it is recommended that all binding project documents are administered by the project manager. On the other hand, experience shows the importance of establishing a project-specific document repository in large-scale projects (e.g. with a duration of more than 2 years and more than 20 project team members) before the project commences. Some companies consider it to be `the nucleus of their know-how and know-why´. The main responsibility of a document repository is to provide, within reasonable time, all documents that are requested in connection with a specific issue. However, the repository is not responsible for the completeness and up-to-dateness of the content. It also performs the following functions:

Identification
- The creation, implementation and application of a standardised and consistent identification

system for all documents that are binding in a project.
- The registration of all project documents, including document administration data (e.g. author, date of creation, distribution list, version, reason for change and date of change). These days, document administration software is often used for this task.
- Monitoring of change control and the systematic distribution of documents when approved changes have been made.
- Establishment and administration of an archiving system (documents are only binding for a project if they are archived in the repository).
- Handover documentation for those receiving the project's results (e.g. customer's department) and the establishment of their own document maintenance teams.

Software

Archiving system

Handover

5.2 Acceptance problems

Documents are still not accorded the significance they deserve - even though they are for many companies and organisations their only product. There are three main reasons for this:
- Documentation is taken for granted by many people and therefore included in the price that is quoted to the customer. However, people forget that, at the end of a project, very few documents still have the same validity in terms of their content as at the outset. Over the course of the project, changes are likely to be necessary and these have to be documented. This generates additional costs.
- Documentation – as the product of intellectual services – is often viewed as less valuable than ´tangible´ products.
- Many people who are involved in projects believe that missing, incomplete and outdated documents can be substituted at any time by a good memory.

Reasons

5.3 Identification and registration of project documents

The planning, creation, checking, approval, distribution and archiving of documents should take place in standardised work processes and in a sensible sequence. A standardised, logical and consistently used identification system for document handling should be developed and implemented. It ought to be structured in accordance with the stages of the document´s lifecycle. This commences with the identification of the product ´document´, and ends when this is archived or no longer required and destroyed.

Manufacturing enterprises that produce physical products often use hierarchical parts lists, IT companies identify program modules and construction firms identify buildings and work packages.

Structured work processes

Lifecycle

5.3.1 Identification standard

Many of today´s document identification systems use the same approach: they distinguish between a minimum and a supplementary identifier. For example, the minimum identifier is the project identifier (e.g. cost centre number or project name), the document content (e.g. the description of the object in the work breakdown structure) and the type of document (e.g. drawing type, test certificate). It is easy to retrieve a document on the basis of this minimum identifier. The supplementary identifier indicates, for example, the document's author, date of creation, recipients, version, status, reason for change and approval of change, as well as supporting documents.

Minimum / supplementary identification

Object identification — The content of the document should be identical with the object description in the work breakdown structure (→ Chapter C4). A WBS with project phases on Level 2 helps the controlling by the project management team. However, a results-oriented breakdown by object is preferable if the project team wants to help those taking-over the project results avoid having to modify the identifier of project-related object documents (e.g. to reflect service or maintenance responsibilities).

Codes — Document type identifiers must include codes for both classical (paper) documents (e.g. circuit diagrams, contracts, records) and for file names (e.g. CAD, graphic, text or tables). Like most object codes, this system is hierarchically structured.

Standard identification systems — Standard coding systems for document content and type, such as DIN EN 6779 (= codes for technical equipment), already exist in some sectors.

5.4 Document requirements matrix

A document requirements matrix [9] is a simple aid for ascertaining document requirements during the course of the project and for preparing handover documentation. It is based on the two dimensions of document content and document type. Owing to the standardisation of work processes and the ensuing documents in repeating projects, this matrix is one of the appendices to the project contract (→ Chapter A4). Figure C7-4 shows that the field for content (car park) and type (drainage plan) can also be used to define responsibilities, completion dates and handover preparations (e.g. file format).

Document content/type

CONSTRUCTION PROJECT PLANS

Objects \ Document types	Site plan	Drainage plan	Foundation drawing	Lighting plan
Office buildings				
Factory buildings				
Car parks		Matrix field		

= address for project management and controlling

Figure C7-4 Document requirements matrix

Minimum identifier — In projects that involve external suppliers, the minimum identifier should be a project-specific, superordinate identifier. In this case, the customer or project sponsor should make the final decision about the identifier because it will remain in place until the end of the project's lifecycle. To ensure that the customer or sponsor is able to correspond with the contractor about maintenance, repairs and sub-

Inventory list — sequent orders of replacement parts, it is necessary to include an inventory list of all documents that have been handed over and the original identifiers of sub-contractor documents together with the project documentation.

6 Change control

Change control is necessary for the monitoring and management of changes that have to be identified, described, classified, assessed, approved, implemented and verified.

Monitoring and control — In some projects, configuration management is not necessary. Change control, however, is an essential aspect of all projects. If data and facts are only contained in one or two documents, an update of one or both of the documents suffices to recognise that a change has been made. Configuration management is only necessary if information is changed in many different documents.

Examples
When a house is being designed, a single-glazed window is replaced by a double-glazed window to improve insulation. Changes are only necessary in the order document.

A wooden door in a hotel corridor is replaced by a fire door. Not only is it necessary to update the order, but also the construction drawings (after approval from the fire service). Documents are also created in respect of fire alarm systems and the automatic closing mechanisms of the new door, including the authorities´ acceptance documentation. This kind of change is very cost-intensive if the requirement for a fire door is only identified shortly before the hotel is due to open.

6.1 Change characteristics

Changes have the following characteristics: They
- are deviations from something that was previously established (reference configuration),
- are triggered by an incident (e.g. defect),
- have a purpose (e.g. to improve utility),
- relate to the content of project objectives (e.g. additional work),
- relate to procedural objectives (e.g. budget cut),
- are necessary owing to   *Causes*
    - one´s own fault (e.g. incorrect calculation),
    - third-party fault (e.g. delayed completion by a supplier),
    - customer request (e.g. for enhanced software performance),
    - statutory requirements (e.g. new safety legislation),
    - new technical developments (e.g. changeover to another operating system by the software provider during an IT project),
- necessitate regulated process structures for traceability purposes,
- generally cause additional costs that cannot be budgeted for in advance. As a result, the acknowledgement of a change is generally associated with a budget increase or additional payment.

6.2 Tasks

Change control must
- identify changes (e.g. why is the change being made?),
- describe the content (what?) and process (how?) of changes,
- classify changes (e.g. what consequential changes will be necessary as a result of this change?),
- assess changes (e.g. what benefits will the change provide? How can they be measured?),
- approve changes (e.g. which hierarchy level approves which changes?),
- implement changes (e.g. which new deadline/budget requirements trigger the change?) and
- verify changes (e.g. has the projected benefit occurred?).

C7 CONFIGURATION AND CHANGE MANAGEMENT

Standard process   Figure C7-5 shows a standard process for implementing changes [10].

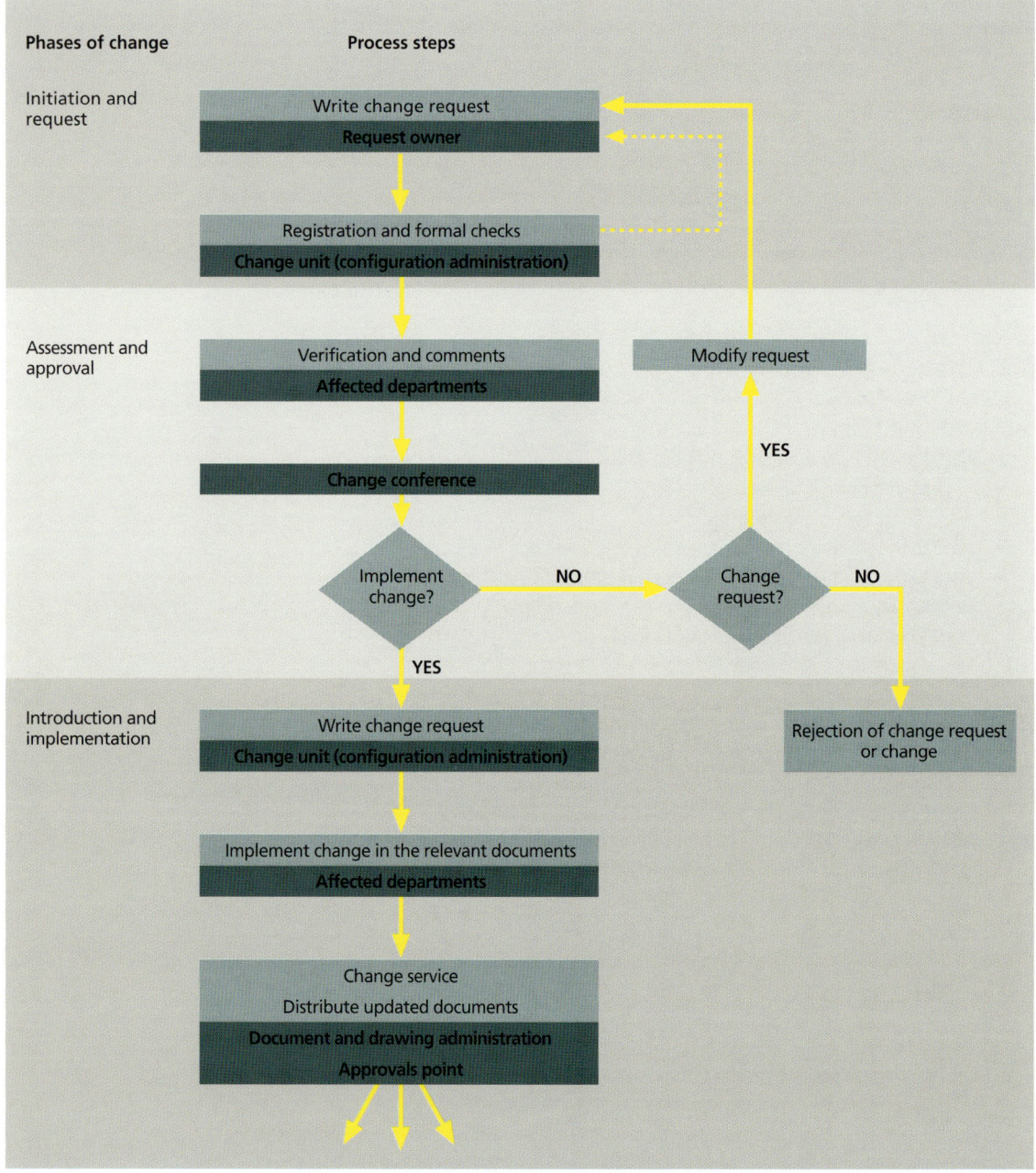

Figure C7-5   Flow chart for a change process

The aforementioned process steps demand a systematic, documented change procedure that records the following information:

Necessary information

- Reason for and content of change
- Changes due to this change
- Risks in the event that the change is not implemented
- Additional risks as a result of the change
- Impact on time, costs and quality
- Approval and assignment of the change
- Updating of the relevant project documents

Figure C7-6 shows a standard change request form that can also be used as a change log during the change process [11].

Standard form

CHANGE REQUEST			
Request owner:		Request no.:	
Component affected			
		Configuration element (CE):	
Drawing no.:	Specification no.:	Part no.:	Designation:
Reason for the change		**Description of the change**	
Reason code		e.g. – exchangeability – performance – delivery deadline – weight – production segment – price	
Documents to be updated		**Equipment and resources to be changed**	
Impact on		e.g. – technical specifications – other modules – efficiency – deadlines and costs	
Change category:		Change priority:	
Comments			
Planned implementation date/change effective as		of:	
Retrofitting to commence on:		for:	
Change request owner: (Name, date, signature)			
Implementation decision/ change conference: (Signature, date)			

Figure C7-6 Change request (example)

6.3 Impact

Changes and change control often have drastic effects on project execution. If the requested change is associated with additional work, it may be necessary to create a new work package for the implementation of the change, and to redefine interim objectives, costs and deadlines. This can result in changes to the contractually-agreed scope of delivery and performance. It is also possible that a change may influence work packages resulting in a claim (→ Chapter A4) that generates additional costs for the customer.

Additional work package

Changes almost always necessitate a fundamental reassessment of costs, deadlines and risks. They therefore influence existing contractual agreements. Systematic claim management is necessary to control the financial impact of changes. Since this is generally associated with considerable time and effort,

Recalculation

Claim management

the project management team should not underestimate the importance of claim management. Rather, it should be treated as an independent activity in a work package or an independent function in a project management structure. The latter measure is often implemented in investment projects that are associated with high risks in the project environment (e.g. projects in other countries). Customers only accept additional costs if they have approved them before changes are implemented and the contractor furnishes complete documentation, including a cost-benefit calculation. Under German law, for example, court cases are almost always won by the customer.

Cost-benefit calculation

Self-assessment questions for each certification level

No.	Question	D	C	B	A	Self-assessment
C7.01	How is the configuration of a product defined?	2	2	2	1	☐
C7.02	When is configuration management used in a project?	2	3	3	1	☐
C7.03	What is the main purpose of configuration identification?	2	3	3	1	☐
C7.04	What are the main tasks of a document repository in a project?	2	3	3	1	☐
C7.05	What is a document requirements matrix used for?	2	3	3	1	☐
C7.06	What constitutes change control in a project?	2	3	3	4	☐
C7.07	When is change control necessary in a project?	2	3	3	1	☐
C7.08	Why are changes sometimes necessary in a project?	2	2	2	1	☐
C7.09	What are the functions of change control in a project?	2	3	3	1	☐
C7.10	How do configuration, documentation and change management tie in with each other?	2	3	3	1	☐
C7.11	What impact does change control have on project control?	2	3	3	4	☐

C8 QUALITY MANAGEMENT

Project management can be defined as a quality management system for the activities that comprise a project. The project manager should be aware of the methods used for the measurement and evaluation of project quality (ICB Element 28), capable of installing a project quality management system and of monitoring its implementation. Total Quality Management (TQM) – as a special extension of quality management –, Continuous Improvement Process (CIP), control systems, standards, audits and the significance of certification are further central aspects of project quality management.

1 Definitions

If one defines performance, time and costs as the quality parameters in a project, then project management can be considered as a quality management system for project work.

In simplified terms, project quality is the conformity of work or services performed to the customer's requirements.

The project manager ensures a clear organisation, clearly defined and allocated tasks, goal-oriented information flows and transparency in project processes. He should be aware of the methods and processes of quality management and select the tools that are appropriate for project management.

A precise description of project processes is crucial for the quality of project work. Quality cannot be assured simply by inspecting component parts or implementing reviews when the project ends. A consistently-applied strategy that is both accepted and carefully-planned, is also essential. Considerable responsibility therefore falls on the project manager and the senior management. The former must remain in contact with the quality management team (= QM) to forge close links between the management, project and quality personnel, and in order to assess the strategic significance for the company. Senior management has to ensure the compatibility of methods used, project personnel and the customer's involvement in the project. Project management quality depends on the extent to which this succeeds.

Universal strategy

Senior management tasks

2 Benefits of a quality management system

Quality management improves the efficiency of internal processes, ensures clear-cut interfaces and enables consistently high product quality. An organisation with a quality management system can make definitive claims about its quality capability and reliability; this has a positive effect on customer relationships. However, the quality management system also helps it to identify any changes that are necessary and define corrective measures.

Non-conformance analyses show that employees are seldom responsible for quality deficiencies. Most non-conformance occurs because of management system deficiencies and is therefore the responsibility of the organisation's middle and upper management. Employees with quality management skills know that the basic framework for quality must be established at management level and they will point out problems or suggest improvements. The management must act upon these suggestions and ensure their consistent implementation.

Causes of non-conformities

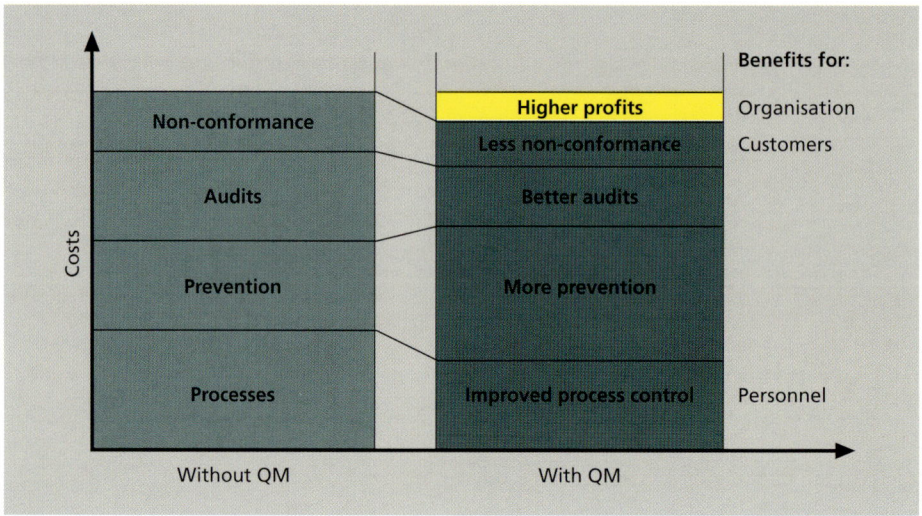

Figure C8-1 Costs and benefits of quality management

Success factors Success factors can be formulated on the basis of the ineffective management practices at many organisations. Any organisation that is planning to install a quality management system must consider these factors:
1. Precisely-defined business objectives
2. A harmonious management team
3. Promotion of innovativeness
4. Speed, quality that is in line with customer requirements, and service orientation
5. Greater flexibility of the corporate infrastructure

Dealing with defects An effective quality management system is distinguished by the methods used to deal with non-conformance (e.g. documentation of non-conformance, root cause analysis). If the concept of quality is a priority in the organisation's business philosophy, QM provides it with a useful means of learning from mistakes (→ Chapter C10) and eliminating weaknesses more effectively. The size of an organisation, measured in terms of employees or turnover, as well as its products, services or projects, play only a subordinate role with regard to the QM system.

Deming's chain Figure C8-2 shows the relationship between quality and economic value added (Deming's chain reaction of quality).

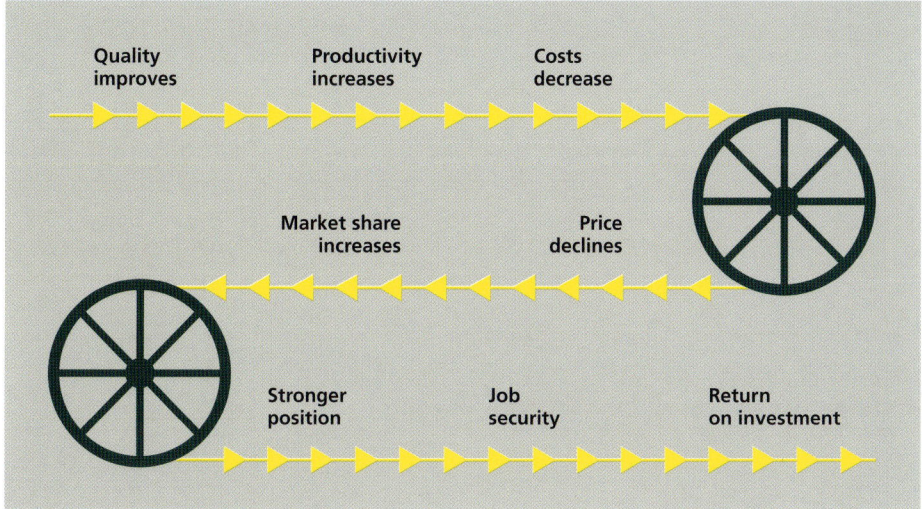

Figure C8-2 The Deming chain reaction of quality

3 Development

Starting from the production-oriented quality control methods of the 1950s and 60s and evolving via process-oriented quality assurance concepts in the 1970s and 80s, Deming and Juran developed a comprehensive quality management system called Total Quality Management (TQM). This concept was originally a response to similar Japanese strategies that provided their companies with considerable competitive advantages in international marketplaces. TQM is about improving all processes and making them more transparent. This leads to a comprehensive process-orientation, including administrative procedures. The aim is to serve customers optimally, from the analysis of the initial situation, through customer support to the conclusion of the work or services to be performed.

Total Quality Management

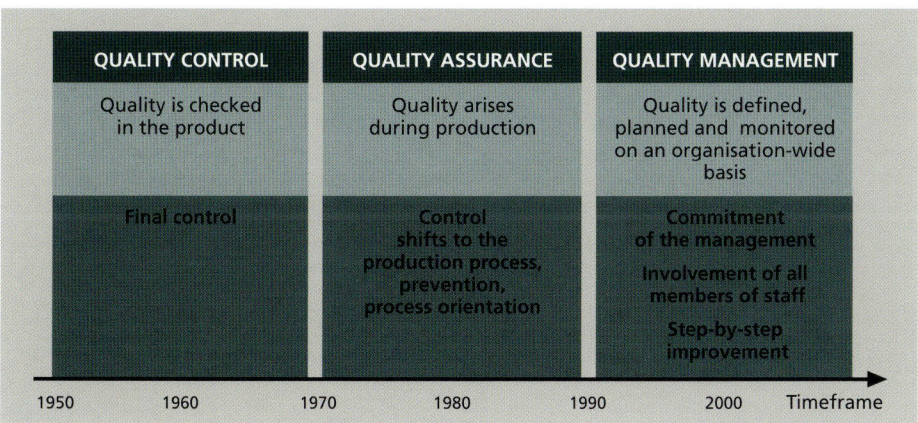

Figure C8-3 Changes to the definition of quality over time

C8 QUALITY MANAGEMENT

Product orientation

In 1950 or thereabouts, quality inspections were made only on the finished product. The organisation was able to improve quality by increasing the number of inspections and/or reducing tolerances. Defects could only be rectified either by reworking the finished product, which is labour and cost-intensive, or by scrapping the product.

Technical process orientation

Since this was extremely cost-intensive, the manufacturers shifted their focus towards quality assurance. They improved quality through preventive measures by incorporating inspections in the development and manufacturing processes. Product orientation was replaced by technical process orientation. Quality assurance was a task for specially-trained staff in the technical departments (development, design, production, assembly and maintenance).

The concept of TQM evolved from an awareness that not only quality assurance officers and their teams, but also the entire management team and all members of staff must be committed to generating value for customers and attaining business objectives.

3.1 External audit

Benefits of certification

These days, external certification bodies evaluate quality management systems, on the basis of the international ISO 9000 standard, for example. Organisations can also apply for quality management awards (e.g. European Quality Award (EQA)). Certification is useful because it involves an external audit of the quality management system and awards are useful because they provide confirmation of self-assessments. Both enable the identification of existing weaknesses and therefore provide the basis for exploiting opportunities for improvement.

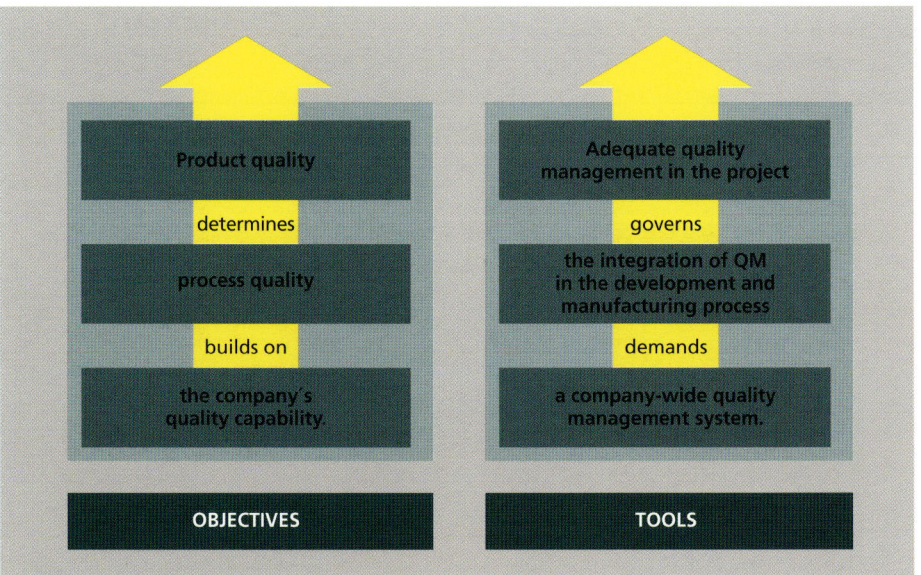

Figure C8-4 The path to quality

4 Standards

These days, not only are basic recommendations on the establishment of a quality management system and minimum requirements defined in standards (general standards such as ISO 9000 and sector-specific standards), but also terms relating to quality assurance and quality management. Organisations can define their objectives, describe and improve processes and subject the management system to internal or external audits on the basis of these standards.

The ISO 9000, 9001:2000, 9004, 19 011 standards play an important role in the establishment and verification of a quality management system. Some standards are internationally valid (standards of the International Standardization Organization (ISO)), some are applicable in Europe (Euronorm (EN)) and some in Germany (the German Institute for Standardisation (DIN)). Strictly speaking, these standards do not lay down rules, but provide guidelines. They provide assistance and key words that enable the establishment of a verifiable quality management system. *Important standards*

An organisation can scrutinise its processes and restructure them if necessary on the basis of standards. A neutral institute can document the result in the form of certification. Certification means that the organisation has successfully installed a quality management system that makes all business processes transparent and comprehensible. It offers the opportunity systematically to evaluate, improve and document quality-relevant facts. *Basis for certification eligibility*

5 Strategic and operational management

An organisation that knows where it wants to go and who its customers are is already on the path to success. First of all, it has to develop a vision. It can do this, for example, by considering the question of 'How do we want our organisation to look in ten years' time?' Based on this vision and on customer requirements, the strategic management team formulates the organisation's quality policy. Measurable objectives are then derived from this policy, and the strategies necessary to attain these objectives are developed. *Vision*

Quality policy and objectives

A comprehensive quality management system is associated with requirements that can only be met by both strategic management and essential operational management functions. The managers have to plan, control and monitor business activities (→ Chapter C9). They mainly focus on the organisation´s turnover, costs and operating profit, its products, projects and technologies, as well as its tendency to invest, and the quality of its products and services. Comprehensive documentation (e.g. in the business, quality, technology and marketing plan, → Chapters C9, D4) is indispensable. *Operational management functions*

6 Process orientation

Quality management must incorporate all processes in an organisation. In terms of a process model, an organisation has two main process types: *Main process types*
- Repetitive processes – which are also called routine activities – with the same or a very similar implementation pattern (e.g. preparation of invoices following completed work or services).
- Processes that are unique and take place within a specific timeframe (e.g. product development projects).

In both main process types, a management system must ensure a structured and goal-oriented workflow. A process-oriented organisation can achieve optimal results for its customers and the company in both routine activities and projects.

Sub-processes

The main process types are associated with upstream sub-processes (e.g. procurement of raw materials, purchasing of project management services) and downstream sub-processes (e.g. delivery of the finished product to the customer, transition from the project to continuous use). Supportive sub-processes also exist (e.g. in-production inspections, reviews during the implementation of the project). Sub-processes are highly significant within the context of process orientation.

7 `Zero defects´ performance standard

Cost of non-conformity

Vast costs are incurred if things are done wrongly (= cost of non-conformity). Nevertheless, people generally remain true to the motto, `We nearly always have the time to repeat a task several times, but we never have the time to get it right the first time´.

Ideally, however, the performance standard should be `zero defects´. In order to attain this standard, an organisation has to do everything right from the outset.

> **Example**
> *If a bricklayer is distracted from his work and constructs a section of wall incorrectly, he will have to rebuild it when the construction manager notices his mistake. If the bricklayer´s mistake costs 1,000 euros to remedy, the construction company´s profit will be reduced by this amount. If the construction company´s profit margin is five percent, it will have to realise additional turnover of 20,000 euros to compensate for the profit shortfall (= total cost of the non-conformity or mistake).*

The interdependencies within a process must also be taken into account to ensure that the costs of non-conformity (e.g. reworking) are transparent.

8 Total Quality Management

The manner in which an organisation´s employees implement processes affects the entire cost and value creation structure. The improvement of processes results in a disproportionately high increase in yield. Higher product quality can considerably increase turnover and market share.

Employees as customers

Customer-supplier relationships

The TQM philosophy is based on a concept of management that permanently changes organisational structures, communication patterns and corporate culture. TQM is a business strategy that puts the emphasis on customer satisfaction in everything people think and do. It has the aim of promoting continuous improvement in the organisation for the benefit of customers, shareholders and employees. According to the definition of TQM, an employee is the customer of the colleague at the next upstream stage of the value chain. When establishing TQM, it is initially necessary to prepare a list of quality principles and define workflows in terms of customer-supplier relationships. TQM markedly reduces the cost of mistakes and improves performance.

Total Quality Management *Benefits*
- improves processes leading to more streamlined workflows,
- boosts profitability thereby making the organisation more flexible,
- integrates customers to enable the more effective satisfaction of customer requirements and
- accelerates processes to reduce the times to market of new products.

According to the TQM philosophy *Philosophy*
- all employees are responsible for their work and the quality of their work,
- everyone who is affected should be involved in the relevant decision and improvement process and
- the quest for perfection is a never-ending process.

The basic requirement of TQM is the continuous improvement of all business activities.

TQM is used with the objective of involving customers, suppliers and all employees, as well as establishing and cultivating internal customer-supplier relationships. This results in integral thinking (= total). *Integral thinking*

TQM also relates to the quality of
- work,
- processes and
- the organisation's performance.

The result is better product and service quality (= quality).

TQM necessitates
- the interdepartmental and interdisciplinary perception of quality as a management function,
- leadership quality (role model function of the management),
- the promotion of teamwork and learning ability,
- perseverance and
- process-oriented rather than department or division-oriented thinking.

This gives rise to the broad-based responsibility of the management. There is a high risk that the TQM process will fail if the management is lax or half-hearted about implementing it. Before an organisation introduces TQM, the executives should be aware of the consequences of this decision, because, in future, the onus will be on them to exemplify the TQM concept by their own actions. Quality therefore becomes the foundation of corporate culture, and this must continually be strengthened. *Management responsibility*

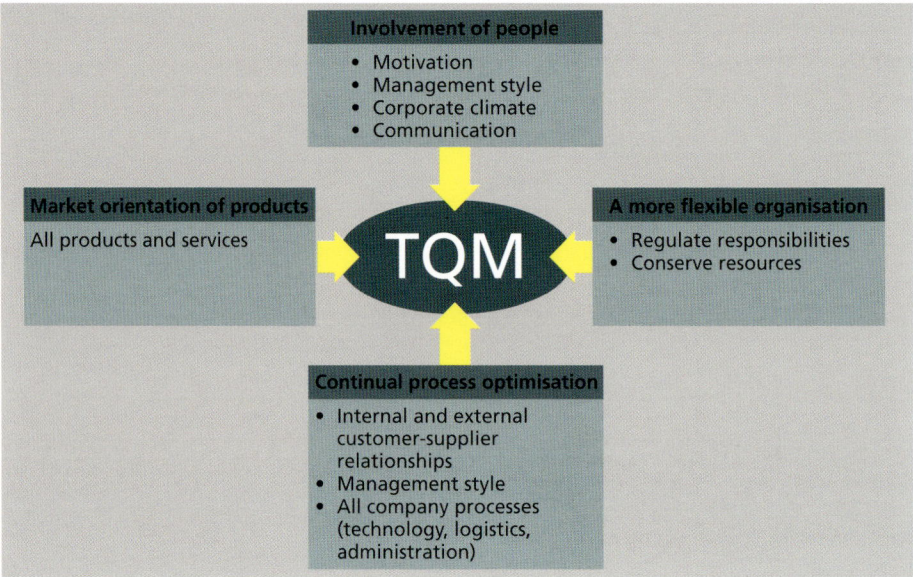

Figure C8-5 The path to TQM

8.1 The EFQM´s TQM model

Awards

The European Foundation for Quality Management (EFQM), which was founded by European corporations, has developed recognised standards for integrated process optimisation. The European Quality Award (EQA), which the EFQM introduced, in conjunction with the EU Commission and the European Organisation for Quality (EOQ), in 1990 is a TQM model that comprises two different types of award:

- the EQA is an annual challenge trophy for the best and most successful TQM implementation and
- the quality awards are for organisations that are committed to quality and quality management.

The EFQM´s EQA awards are presented annually. Candidates are assessed by the jury in a three-stage process:
1. Pre-selection on the basis of the submitted application documents
2. In-situ inspection and audit of the company
3. Decision on the basis of the results

8.1.1 The Business Excellence Model

Eight cornerstones

The EFQM´s TQM model includes various criteria for assessing the progress that an organisation makes. The eight cornerstones of the Business Excellence Model are:
1. Results orientation
2. Customer focus
3. Leadership and constancy of purpose

4. Management by processes and facts
5. People development and involvement
6. Continuous learning, innovation and improvement
7. Partnership development
8. Corporate social responsibility

Organisations can use these criteria for self-assessment and for the identification of strengths and improvement opportunities leading to focused and prioritised planning. To a large extent, the Business Excellence Model enables objective assessment. It makes the organisation´s position clear vis-à-vis other organisations. Specially trained assessors perform these audits and provide valuable input. *Self-assessment*

Assessors

8.2 Continuous improvement process

When a quality management system is installed, a continuous improvement process (CIP) should be set in motion. *CIP*

> Continuous improvement is based on the principle of constantly seeking the root causes of problems so that all of the organisation´s systems (products, processes, activities) can be improved.

Continuous improvement is not a method that is applied to a problem until it is solved. Rather, CIP is all about process-oriented thinking based on a very specific mentality and a fundamental behaviour pattern. This mentality provides the goal and, at the same time, the means to achieve this goal. According to Deming, the basic attitudes that ensure the success of a continuous improvement process are: *Important basic attitudes*
- Every activity can be perceived as a process and therefore improved.
- Problem solving alone is not enough. Fundamental changes are necessary.
- Action must be taken at executive management level. The assumption of responsibility alone is not enough.

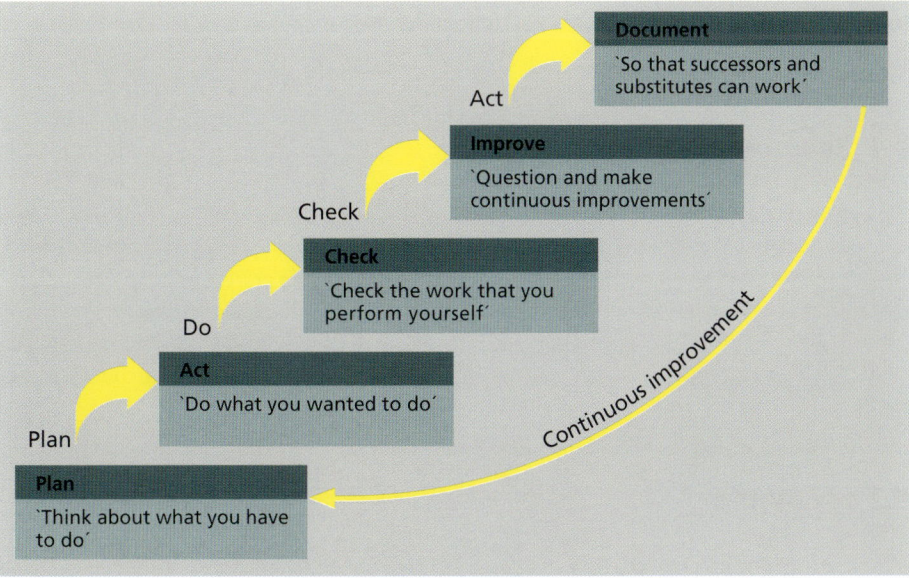

Figure C8-6 The Deming cycle, the basic principle of continuous improvement

The Deming cycle The Deming cycle (plan-do-check-act cycle) of continuous improvement
- Challenges the status quo
- Identifies and attempts to remedy every non-conformity and problem.
- Takes the values attained as the basis for further improvement.

The PDCA cycle also illustrates the principle of continuous improvement. Basically, it shows each activity as a process which, as such, can be gradually improved.

8.2.1 CIP procedure

The responsible staff and managers initially define the improvement strategy. They have to clarify
- the most important results and biggest obstacles,
- the measures that are necessary and
- who is responsible for implementing which measures by when (plan).

In the next step, the plan is implemented. All data necessary to answer the questions in the planning process are collected (**do**).
Then, the impact of changes is monitored and the results are documented and verified (**check**).
Now, the process and documented results are analysed to derive conclusions about opportunities for improvement (**act**).

Narrowing down the problem The PDCA cycle has to be repeated so that the knowledge gained in previous cycles can be used to reduce the problem in each new cycle. It is therefore a continuous process that offers every member of staff the opportunity to make a contribution to continuous improvement.

9 Control systems

Traditional performance indicators are not sufficient to measure progress in, for example, TQM or EFQM initiatives.

9.1 Balanced Scorecard

Intangible parameters

Ratios

The balanced scorecard system is useful in this context because it focuses on an organisation´s performance with regard to finances, customers, internal processes, learning and development. It is based on the organisation´s vision and strategy. From this, in a step-by-step process, key goals, figures, targets and measures can be derived. A scorecard is used to measure intangible values such as customer satisfaction or degree of innovativeness. In each case, the organisation decides upon the most suitable ratios. The main objective is to balance all the organisation´s factors (i.e. employees, customers, suppliers).

9.2 Six Sigma

Many managers believe that the Balanced Scorecard does not go far enough. They prefer Six Sigma, a method for achieving perfect quality as well as preventing errors and wastage in production, services, management and all other business activities. This method combines quality management, data analysis and training for staff at all hierarchical levels. This highly structured process is divided into four steps:

Four steps

- Measure
- Analyse
- Improve
- Check

10 Establishment of a quality management system for project management

In order to satisfy the quality requirements in a project, for example with regard to performance, time and costs, it is necessary to systematically plan and implement the quality concept. The organisation should establish and maintain a project management system that also functions as a quality management system for project work. This task ought to involve all project managers and members of the project teams. In the long run, `lone warrior´ management practices will be ineffective.

Project quality excellence is impossible to attain merely by implementing checks during project work. Rather, the quality framework must be established right at the outset of the project when the objectives are jointly formulated. The organisation should also regularly audit the results of project work and channel them into a project quality improvement programme.

Formulation and review of objectives

When establishing and improving the project management system, the people in charge should restrict themselves to a few, important requirements. If these can be met, the project management system will be founded on a broad and documented basis.

10.1 Interfaces

All interfaces that exist within a project must be perceived as customer-supplier interfaces. This applies to both internal and external relationships. It prevents misunderstandings and problems because the customer and supplier can jointly define their specific requirements (e.g. in contracts, specifications, requirement profiles and work packages) and then provide the relevant work or services. This reduces friction losses and additional work.

Customer-supplier relationships

10.2 Responsibility

The responsibility for the work lies with the person or department performing it. If project work is to be of good quality, it is essential to specify the people responsible for the work packages. Personal encouragement – such as praise, performance-related pay or bonuses for special achievements in a project (e.g. attainment of a milestone) must be provided to reward project team members who attain project quality targets. Involving project team members and acknowledging their achievements is more effective than laying down the law or indiscriminate criticism. Instead of generally-formulated requests, specific targets relating to performance, time and costs must be provided. The attainment of these targets is always measured in terms of the customer or project sponsor´s satisfaction. Specifications and objectives are checked by making a systematic comparison of the status of work with the customer´s expectations.

Personal encouragement

10.3 Personnel

Interviews

Employee orientation is an important aspect of the quality management system. It extends from the recruitment of skilled employees, through continuous skill building, to their inclusion in the workflow. Skilled personnel are needed to attain the ideal of an optimal process implementation that is in line with customer requirements. Managers should regularly interview staff because they are able to provide information about quality non-conformities. The organisation should create job descriptions, identify skill deficits and implement training measures (→ Chapter D3) to match employee skills with requirements.

However, employees can only deliver optimum process results if
- authorities are clearly assigned,
- they are satisfied with their working conditions and
- problems associated with soft factors (e.g. conflicts) are avoided (e.g. through discussions with staff or staff appraisal (→ Chapter D3) or problem-solving methods (→ Chapter D5).

Interdisciplinary working

Project-specific work structures ensure that employees are involved in the entire project process. Working groups assume responsibility for various aspects of the project and project tasks are implemented on an interdisciplinary basis. These working groups have a better overview, a greater understanding of dependencies and a higher awareness of quality than employees who perform work activities that are confined within narrow limits.

Requirements of personnel

Project team members (→ Chapter D3) should have project management training and communication skills. Project managers, on the other hand, require excellent management skills (→ Chapter D1).

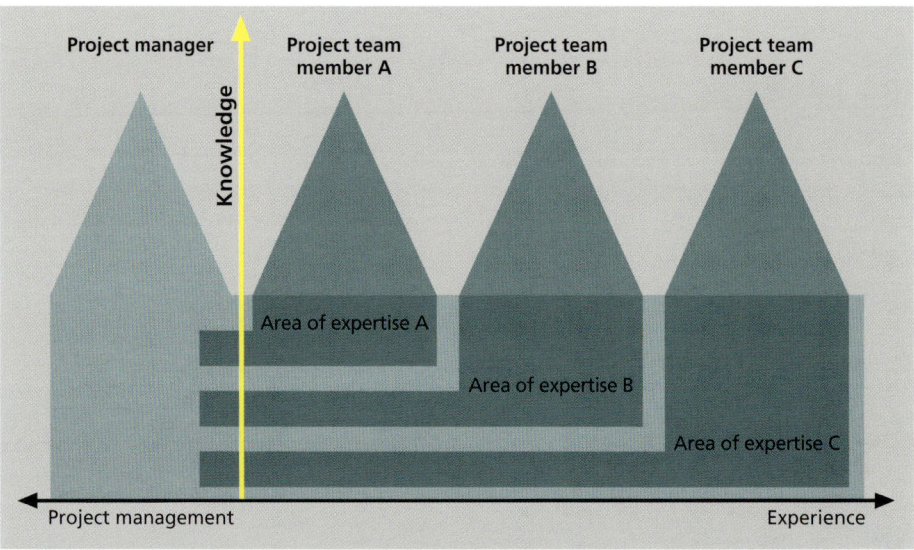

Figure C8-7 Requirement profile for project personnel

10.4 Documentation in the project management manual

To avoid redefining one and the same process in every new project, it is a good idea to
- create instructions and documents in a specific format,
- make them binding for the project organisation,
- summarise them in a project management manual and
- use them as the basis for project work.

Instructions and documents

The project management manual (→ Chapter C9) documents the project management system. It enables the organisation to ensure project management quality. The manual describes the procedures that the organisation uses in projects and defines checklists for systematic project work. It is applicable irrespective of the project type and organisational unit that is implementing the project. It therefore makes no difference whether the project is a development or an organisational project. The project management manual reflects the management's policy on project work and the improvement of project quality.

Project management manual

10.5 Project documentation in the project manual

The project manual summarises project objectives, tasks, organisational structures, planning, (project) plan updates and documentation for each project and is therefore also a quality manual. It is based on the organisation's project management manual. The project manual ensures project quality in terms of the quality parameters of performance, time and costs. When the project has concluded, the project manual is used to record results and experiences that can be used in the future as the basis for planning a similar project or establishing a new project team. Before project work commences, the project team or project manager decides upon the procedure for records, reports, drawings and all other documents to ensure that they are available in the correct format at the right time and at the right place.

Project manual

Documentation and archiving that are adapted to specific situations by way of project records (project-related documents) in the project manual are proof that an effective document management system is in place and that it satisfies the requirements of the projects in question. This also ensures that acquired know-how is available for future projects (→ Chapter C10).

11 Objective evidence on the basis of quality audits

An audit is a systematic, independent examination used to ascertain the conformity of a procedure and its associated results with specifications. It also provides information about whether the planned processes are appropriate for attaining quality objectives.

In project management audits, all aspects of the project management system are scrutinised at regular intervals to check whether the proper management measures have been correctly implemented and whether this can be verified. The aim of such an audit is to optimise the system. The German Association for Project Management's (GPM) PM Delta diagnosis tool supports this process. Each audit is based on the organisation's project management handbook. In large-scale projects, it is also a good idea to link the project management audit with a project review.

PM Delta

Benefits The project management audit shows
- how useful and appropriate the project management system is for the organisation in question, whether it is effective enough and opportunities for improvement,
- whether the project management measures are adequately documented,
- whether the requirements of the project management manual are met and
- any organisational weaknesses that exist.

Based on the audit, organisational measures for system improvement are defined.

11.1 Auditor

Principle of dual control Auditors should always be people who have no direct responsibility for the department being audited. Using the dual control principle, two auditors are responsible for the
- preparation of an audit plan,
- efficient implementation of the audit,
- recording of audit results,
- confidentiality of audit results and
- submission of an audit report.

The auditors must ascertain whether the project team members are familiar with and have access to the organisation's project management manual, instructions and checklists, as well as all other necessary information, whether they understand and apply them and whether the instructions and specifications suffice for the attainment of project objectives. An audit record is used by the project management auditors to document the results of the audit.

11.2 Procedure

Eight audit steps The audited department co-operates with the auditors throughout the audit and furnishes any information that they require. A project management audit involves the following steps:
1. The managers to whom the project management team reports specify the audit framework.
2. First of all, a pre-audit meeting takes place with the project manager and his team. The auditors explain the purpose, procedures and rules for the audit and reporting. Then, the group makes a list of the management processes and documentation to be covered by the audit. It also defines a timeframe and venue for the post-audit meeting. Any project team members who are required for the audit are notified.
3. The auditors examine the project documents and compare them with the underlying project management manual. Non-conformities or omissions can be discovered at this stage. This examination also provides material for in-situ interviews.
4. The auditors collect evidence through in situ interviews. They identify problem areas by inspecting documents and evaluating activities. Those being questioned can avoid misunderstandings by using generally understandable formulations, explanations and through asking questions to clarify points. If a respondent's answer does not conform to the target status, the auditors repeat the answer in their own words. This prevents misunderstandings and confrontations that hinder the progress of the audit and may detract from its success. Aggressive questioning and accusations when non-conformities are identified are not advisable because they poison the audit climate.

5. The auditors should test the results of the interviews through spot checks (= assuring). In most cases, the interviews and spot checks overlap.
6. If the auditors find a non-conformity with the target status, it is recorded in the audit report.
7. They then evaluate the deficiencies that have been identified. Some deficiencies are acceptable. Others, which indicate that the project management objectives are not being met, are not.
8. The auditors summarise the audit results in the post-audit meeting and agree upon improvement measures with the project manager.

11.3 Audit report

The audit report should contain the following information: *Content*
- Scope and objective of the audit
- Names of the auditors
- Date of the audit and the department being audited
- Information about any reference documents used (e.g. project management manual, project manual)
- Non-conformities and deficiencies that are found
- Improvement measures, persons responsible and deadlines
- Auditors' opinion about the status of project management
- Place, date and signatures of the auditors
- Recipients of the audit report

The audit report should be discussed by the auditors and the project manager. If there are any differences of opinion, both opinions should be included in the report.

12 Certification

Certification is the next stage after qualification and is confirmation by an independent body of the conformity of a product, management system or professional qualification. *Conformity*
- When the certification is governed by law, it is issued pursuant to a national statutory regulation or EU directive on the basis of a statutory procedure and
- if it is not governed by law, it is issued in accordance with a standard or other rule on the basis of a voluntary agreement.

Although there are many different motives for obtaining certification, the following are the main ones: *Motives*
- Customers and/or the market require certification. This is often the case in public tendering.
- The company wishes to use the certification for marketing purposes.
- The certification will improve product and process quality and therefore also enhance customer satisfaction.
- The certification serves as the basis for the company's TQM policy.

12.1 Certification of project management personnel

Common level of knowledge

In order to perform complex project management tasks and co-ordinate the actions of project team members in different countries, a common level of theoretical and practical project management knowledge is essential. The International Project Management Association (IPMA) and the GPM, for example, have defined criteria for certification (→ Chapter D3).

12.2 Certification of project management systems

Project management systems can be certified within the framework of ISO 9001 by independent certification companies. The certification and monitoring of the management system by the certification body essentially comprises the following procedure:

Pre-audit
1. Before the certification audit, the certification body offers the company the opportunity to implement a voluntary pre-audit. The pre-audit report offers it the opportunity to eliminate weaknesses in the management system.

Certification audit
2. The certification body audits the organisation´s documents (quality management manual, project management manual, instructions, etc.) either in conjunction with or after the pre-audit.

Control audit
3. The certification audit then takes place. Generally, two certification auditors perform the audit. At least one of them should have several years proven professional experience in the relevant sector of industry.

Re-audit

The certificates that are issued are generally valid for three years. During this time, the organisation is also required to take part in an annual control audit. When the three-year certificate expires, there is a re-audit.

13 Project quality

In order to ensure quality in a specific project, the management methods must include the application of rules and tools (project management manual, project manual) as well as procedures (reviews, audits).

13.1 Project review

The project review is a method of analysing the status of a project in terms of performance, costs and deadline adherence at the time of the review. In the review, the project results are analysed, project progress is evaluated and any problems are discussed. This variance analysis is performed on the basis of project requirements (contracts, specifications), project plans and project records. The project review pinpoints non-conformities and identifies possible control measures.

Control measures

Review times
Project reviews are implemented at fixed dates. Depending on the project type, the reviews can take place on specific weekdays (jour fixe) or once a month. Reviews should also be implemented at transitions from one phase to another. The project review at the end of the project is carried out to provide `rules of thumb´ for future projects.

13.2 The Project Excellence Model for assessing project quality

Every project has several characterising parameters, such as stakeholders (customer, employees, investors), business strategy (growth, stability, liquidity) and facets of the project like objective definition, planning, implementation and attainment of objectives. In 1996, the GPM developed the Project Excellence model as a neutral process for the assessment of project work quality in terms of specific characterising parameters.

Parameters

The Project Excellence assessment holds up a mirror to the project. For example, it identifies and evaluates the attitudes, associations, wishes and expectations expressed by the project participants. It delivers standard questions and assessment criteria for

Standard questions

- excellent procedures and scope of application of project management, as well as
- excellent project results.

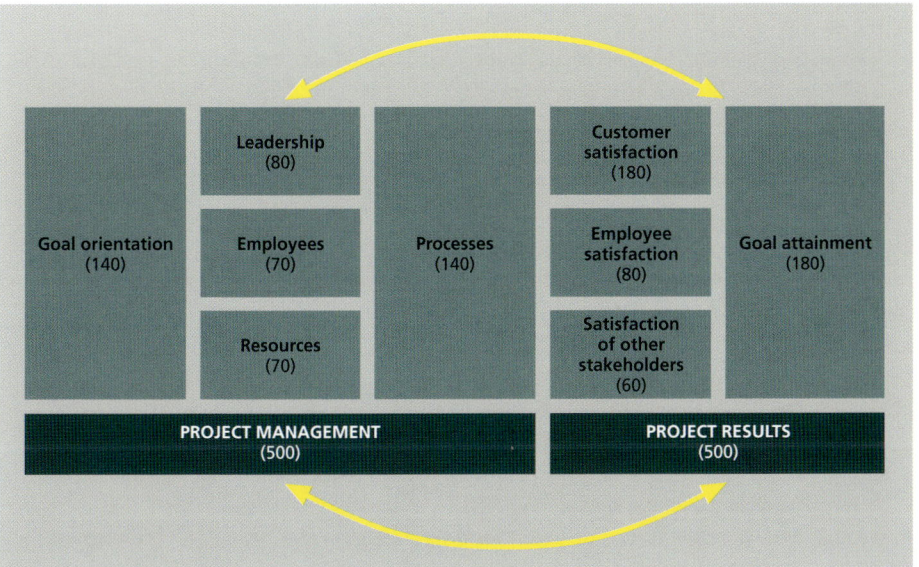

Figure C8-8 The Project Excellence Model and points accorded for each criterion

In the Project Excellence Model, a team of assessors allocates points to nine criteria and 22 assessment fields in the two main areas of

Main areas

- project management and
- project results

on the basis of maximum points. Key points are collected for each assessment field to identify strengths, gather evidence and identify room for improvement. These criteria are the basis for the strategic orientation of project work. They are each evaluated by according assessment points on an ordinal scale. The values provide a project profile that can be represented graphically in a radar diagram.

Criteria and assessment fields

Project profile

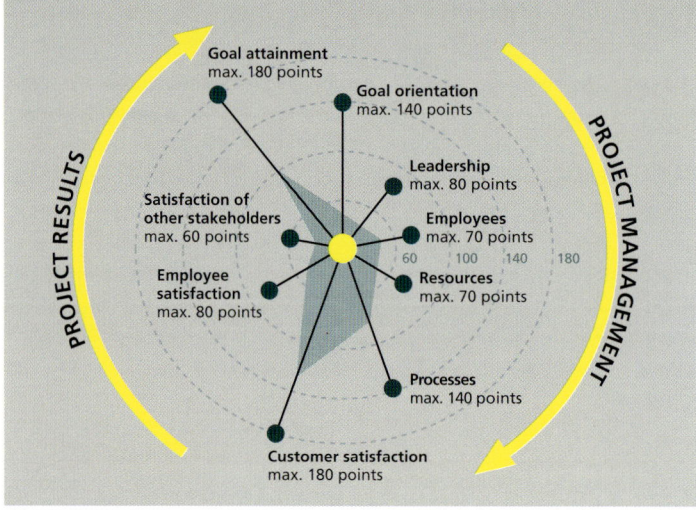

Figure C8-9 Radar diagram of sample project (light-green surface)

Self-assessment

Project assessment

The approach is easy to understand and one can use the model as a project support tool to establish the current status of the project at any time. Project teams can use these nine criteria to implement a self-assessment, identify strengths and weaknesses and plan their further development, if necessary, with the assistance of specially-trained project excellence assessors. The model´s assessment system enables a largely objective evaluation and highlights the project´s status in terms of the required project quality, as well as options for further development.

Assessors

Project Excellence assessors are able to
- assess the status of a project with the aim of achieving project excellence,
- identify strengths and opportunities for improvement,
- bring about team consensus on strengths and areas that require improvement, and on the assessment (based on the system of points),
- audit the available information about the project in terms of coherence and correctness,
- close information gaps,
- formulate detailed feedback for the audited organisation that is comprehensible for the management and staff and useful for the further development of the project and
- assess improvement measures, thereby providing vital input for the further development of the organisation.

13.3 Further methods of evaluating project quality

Further methods of evaluating project quality include
- PM Delta
- Capability Maturity Model (CMM)
- BOOTSTRAP and
- SPICE.

13.3.1 PM Delta

PM Delta, the GPM´s diagnosis tool, is used to analyse projects on the basis of neutral, pertinent standards (→ Chapter F3). A comprehensive catalogue of questions and answers enables the identification of strengths and opportunities in the area of project management. PM Delta differentiates between two types of diagnosis:

Types of diagnosis

1. Diagnosis of project management in the project: This form of diagnosis assesses the application of project management practices in a specific project. Internal project implementation processes can be assessed to derive knowledge for future projects.
2. Diagnosis of the project management system: this diagnosis delivers information about whether the project processes are efficient. As a result, project execution processes can be reproduced.

A project management diagnosis comprises three phases:

Diagnosis phases

1. Entry
2. Implementation
3. Evaluation

In Phase 1, the objectives and the diagnosis schedule are determined. The PM Delta assessors then evaluate the documents that are made available to them. In Phase 2, staff interviews are conducted. The assessors check whether the agreed project management rules are actually being applied. In the evaluation phase, they document the strengths and areas where action must be taken in a summary diagnosis report. The quality of the individual project management processes as described in ISO 10 006 are evaluated on a scale of 1 to 10 to produce a radar diagram.

13.3.2 Capability Maturity Model

The CMM (→ Chapter F2) is a framework containing the key elements of an effective software development process. Although CMM focuses on the optimisation of software development processes, organisations also use this model to optimise internal processes in all types of projects.

All types of projects

13.3.3 BOOTSTRAP

BOOTSTRAP is a standardised process for the analysis and improvement of software development processes. This internationally-recognised method enables an organisation to objectively assess the practice of software development. In a BOOTSTRAP assessment, three to five projects are selected to assess both the requirements for the organisation of software projects and the capability to put them into practice. The results are recorded in an individual action plan that is prepared by experts for the step-by-step improvement and implementation of selected processes. If the organisation consistently implements the recommended improvement measures, it can demonstrably reduce development costs and considerably increase productivity.

Software projects

13.3.4 SPICE

SPICE (Software Process Improvement and Capability Determination), which was developed after CMM and BOOTSTRAP, is a concept for the standardised assessment of software development. It assesses

14 Quality management methods

Over recent decades, many standardised methods in management have become established. At the same time, the various management disciplines (e.g. process management, project management) have developed process models that can be applied in other disciplines.

Benchmarking
1. Benchmarking (→ Chapter F2) can help to markedly improve the quality of project management or project work. One´s own work methods are compared with the methods of other project teams that are known to be extremely efficient.

QFD
2. Quality function deployment (QFD) is useful in the project planning stage to record precisely customer requirements and translate them into a language register that the project team understands. QFD takes place at an early stage of the project.

Cause-and-effect diagram
3 The cause-and-effect diagram (→ Chapter D2) shows the causes and effects of specific circumstances. It is a very effective tool for dealing with problems during the project implementation phase.

14.1 Quality Function Deployment

Incorporation of user requirements in technical objectives
QFD is not a process-oriented approach to quality like CMM, but a methodology that relates directly to the product. In simple terms, it is used to ascertain the requirements of the end-user and to realise technical objectives.

Application in the planning phase
The quality of a project is generally defined in the planning phase. It is therefore necessary to ensure that customer requirements are taken into account in this phase, so that they can be incorporated in the performance specifications. In technical development projects, quality function deployment supports this task. QFD enables the translation of customer requirements into technical language. Its application during the planning phase enables the precise ascertainment of all activities and processes to ensure that the deliverable conforms precisely with the customer's requirements. Since the sig-

Product features
nificance of the defined product features is assessed at an early stage of the project, critical features can be identified in good time.

Design and process characteristics

House of Quality
In the first step, the employees translate customer requirements into measurable product features. In three further phases, they derive design and process characteristics from these features and stipulate work and test instructions. A house of quality (HOQ) is created in each phase. The HOQ provides a graphic illustration of project aspects and ensures structured processes. This method takes quality requirements into account at all times, minimises the risk of mistakes and improves customer orientation.

C8 QUALITY MANAGEMENT

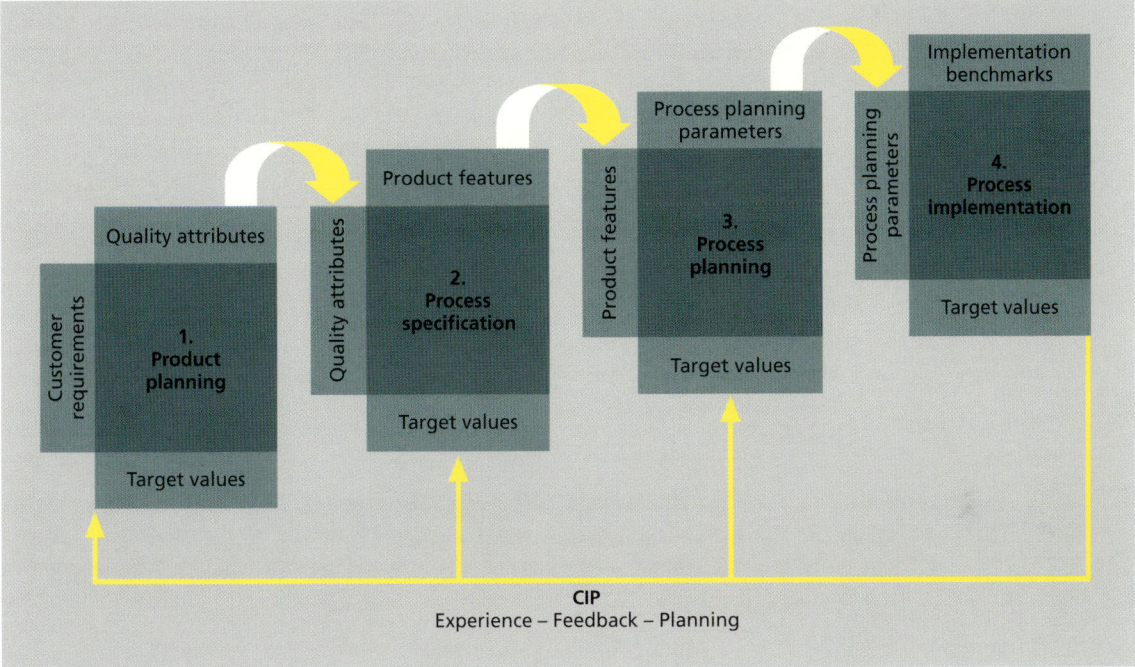

Figure C8-10 QFD planning steps

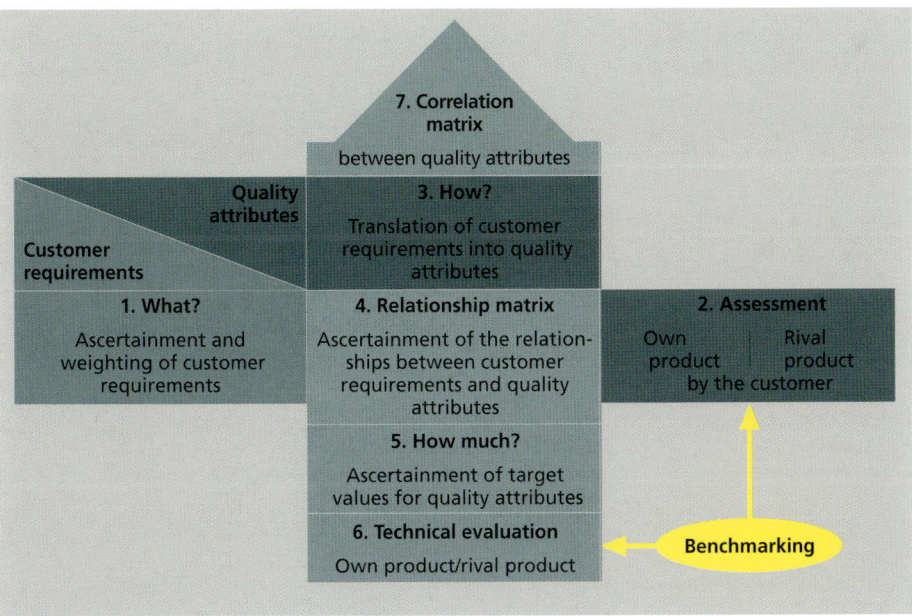

Figure C8-11 House of Quality

To improve communication between the organisation´s departments (e.g. marketing, R&D, quality management, work scheduling, production, customer service) it is initially necessary to appoint an inter-departmental QFD team (five to eight members) and a team leader who is familiar with QFD. This team includes representatives of the company´s various departments. The team leader chairs the

QFD meeting. Teamwork promotes process-oriented thinking among the team members. The clear layout of the HOQ makes it ideal as a form of documentation.

Four phases In each phase, the questions of 'What are the requirements?' and 'How are the requirements met?' are compared. The 'how?' (= result) in one phase serves as the 'what?' (= input data) in the next phase.
- In the first phase of product planning, customer requirements (= what), product features and/or development requirements (= how) are compared.
- In the second phase of process specification, the critical product features (= what) are converted into quality attributes for individual component assemblies or parts (= how).
- In the third phase of process planning, process characteristics and parameters (= what) for process and testing schedules (= how) are derived from the component assembly features.
- In the fourth phase of process implementation, the critical process characteristics (= what) are transferred to work and testing instructions (=how). These instructions are used to implement the process.

The mapping of all four phases in the HOQ is a complex process. It is therefore possible to prepare plans only for individual phases where implementation problems have been experienced in the past. Often, the HOQ only takes place in the first phase because the translation of customer requirements into performance features is what generally causes the most difficulties.

Self-assessment questions for each certification level

No.	Question	D	C	B	A	Self-assessment
C8.1	What are the main functions of TQM in an organisation?	1	1	1	4	☐
C8.2	What are the cornerstones of the EFQM's TQM model?	1	1	1	4	☐
C8.3	How and by what means is project quality assured?	2	2	3	4	☐
C8.4	Where and how is Quality Function Deployment used?	1	1	1	1	☐

By measuring project progress on a regular basis, a project manager can promptly identify undesirable developments and take countermeasures. Performance measurement concepts (ICB Element 19) are therefore a central aspect of project management. The project manager should be aware of the control options (ICB Element 20) which are available to him in the event that the project's progress falls behind schedule. This chapter explains ways to reduce the scope of work or services and costs and increase productivity. These measures are closely associated with documentation and reporting requirements (ICB Element 21).

1 Performance measurement

In the process of project-specific cost monitoring (→ Chapter C6), it is initially assumed that progress monitoring will be unproblematic and that the projected costs of work performed (= earned value, actual cost to complete, value of work performed and budgeted cost of work performed) will be easy to ascertain. Project cost management does not deliver the necessary information unless data about the project's progress is also available.

Cost management

Example
A high-rise building construction project is scheduled to take twelve months. After six months, the degree of completion is 30% and half of the budget has been used up. The project manager has every reason to be concerned because at the stage when 30% of the construction work is finished, only one-third of the budget should have been used up.

The definition provided by the ICB is rather general: 'The continuous measurement of project status is vital for the effective time and cost control.'
The rate of progress (= percent complete) is measured in terms of work or services performed by a specific date relative to the total work or services in a process or project.

It is also possible to monitor the rate of progress – generally expressed as a percentage – for sub-tasks, work packages and individual activities. Both actual percent complete (APC) and budgeted percent complete (BPC) are used.

Progress

1.1 Problems associated with performance measurement

Performance measurement is not without its pitfalls. Various factors can make it difficult to draw objective conclusions about project performance.

1.1.1 Lack of yardsticks

Problems often occur because no suitable yardsticks exist with which the project controller can relate costs incurred to project progress. In investment projects, such as construction projects and plant construction projects, many people assume that it is easy to work out project progress because the work or services performed in the project as a whole – either in sub-tasks, work packages or activities –

C9 PERFORMANCE MEASUREMENT AND PROJECT CONTROL

Measuring, counting and weigthing — can be determined on the basis of measuring, counting or weighing performance variables such as excavated material, installed formwork, concrete consumption or laid pipes. However, an analysis shows that there is no suitable yardstick for measuring progress in many of the work packages of a plant construction project, such as technical planning [1].

Technical planning

R&D projects — Similarly, it is especially difficult to measure performance in R&D projects. It is almost impossible to find suitable yardsticks linking specific work performed to specific portions of the budget.

Example
An engineer and a biochemist are preparing an extensive specification for the development of an innovative medical testing device. Although they have completed a substantial portion of the document by the progress measurement date, both believe that they still have a considerable amount of work ahead of them. Who would like to make a statement about the degree of completion in this case? The quotient of

$$\frac{\text{pages completed}}{\text{estimated total pages}}$$

is definitely not an appropriate measure of progress because the work packages described in the specification may be associated with different degrees of difficulty.

Intangible results — Even in organisational projects with intangible and interim results, performance measurement is often hampered by a lack of suitable yardsticks.

1.1.2 Time-delayed assessment of the fulfilment of objectives

Objectives to be achieved — Let´s take another look at the breakdown of quality objectives ($\rightarrow$ Chapter C2) into
- performance or effectiveness objectives,
- operational objectives,
- design or construction-related objectives and
- production and cost-efficiency objectives or productivity objectives.

Fulfilment only determined when deliverable in operation — In many cases, it is not possible to assess whether these objectives – which are generally expressed in terms of performance indicators and characteristic curves – have been fulfilled until an operational analysis of the project deliverable has been made. This applies especially to certain reliability values required by the customer.

Example
A customer who has requested the development of a new telephone exchange system specifies a maximum cumulative downtime of 60 minutes a year. It is impossible to say whether this objective has been attained until the end of the first year of operation.

In many cases, defects in a product are not discovered until it has left the laboratory and is being used by the customer. Also, it can be assumed that most technical targets in a project will not be approached in a more or less continuous, measurable manner, but rather with occasional jumps. However, the assumption of continuity is implicit in all performance measurement approaches.

The testing of individual components before they are assembled into an overall system is a good example of how inaccurate project progress assessments can be. It is impossible to say, at least in the case of some of the technical variables, whether objectives have been attained until the system test takes place. Often, however, the overall system is not tested until shortly before the scheduled project completion date. If the test results are unsatisfactory, the people who wrote optimistic progress reports on the basis of component tests have to suddenly make radical revisions and work packages that were concluded some time ago have to be reopened. In software projects, the problem is exacerbated by the fact that quality objectives are difficult to measure.

System test

Revised progress reports

1.1.3 Variance analyses with no informative value

The problems relating to project performance measurement also apply without exception to the cost-management variance analyses. The following example shows how uninformative monthly variance analyses of budget cost of work performed (BCWP) or earned value, and the actual cost of work performed [ACWP] can be:

Example
This example is based on the following assumptions:
- *Projected costs of 3.6 million euros [BCWS]*
- *Costs incurred to date of 1.2 million euro [ACWP]*
- *The percent complete stated by the project manager on the as-of date is 40 percent [APC1]*
- *The project manager subsequently reduces the percent complete to 20 percent [APC2]*

Souder [2] questioned nine project managers about the progress of their projects on a monthly basis. They were requested to allocate points representing project progress on a scale of zero to 100, where 100 meant the successful conclusion of the project. Almost two-thirds of the points allocated each month were subsequently revised down by an average of 20 points.
If the following formula is used to calculate the earned value EV for the project as a whole, it is clear how misleading the results of variance analyses can be.

Misleading computations

$$EV = BCWS \times APC \qquad (0\% \leq APC \leq 100\%)$$

In the first case (40 percent completion), the cost deviation is 240,000 euros. In the second case (20 percent completion) it is 480,000 euros.

1.2 Methods of progress measurement in R&D projects

Although it is not possible to make reliable assessments of project status in R&D projects, practitioners still attempt to measure project progress using a relatively simple procedure. They generally use parameters that do not provide any information about work performed. Instead, they simply draw conclusions about project progress or the progress of individual elements of the work breakdown structure on the basis of reference values (e.g. cost data). Although these methods are useful, the project controller should always bear in mind the problems that they are associated with and their limited informative value.

Reference values

Positive values obtained on the basis of project performance measurement should be taken with a pinch of salt. However, negative values are always a warning signal and should therefore be taken seriously. Project controllers with a bookkeeper´s mindset who attempt to calculate the degree of progress to two

Warning signs

decimal places are in the wrong job. They have not grasped the concept of performance measurement, which is all about recognising critical developments in the time-costs-quality relationship.

1.2.1 Performance measurement based on time data

This method is very simple. It is assumed that the percent complete PC is equal to the current elapsed time of the project, T_e, relative to the total project duration, D (latest estimate). The degree of completion for the entire project is thus defined as follows:

$$PC = \frac{T_e}{D} \times 100$$

Limitations

This formula can also be used to calculate the degree of completion of project sub-tasks, work packages or the individual activities in a network diagram. Wehking [3] quite rightly states, however, that it can only be used for work packages if the costs associated with these work packages – such as the task of project management itself – depend on the duration of the project.

1.2.2 Performance measurement based on resource consumption data

Resource consumption, which is often measured in person days or hours, is also used as a reference value. For example, if 150 person hours are scheduled for a work package and 75 have been used by the progress measurement date, it can be concluded that the work package is halfway to completion. However, this approach is risky because it can lead to false conclusions, even in plant construction projects, which become evident during an on-site inspection [4]. Motzel calls this approach the `mortal sin of project management´ because it simply assumes that resource consumption is proportional to project performance. However, in reality, resource consumption is often too high in relation to project performance.

1.2.3 Performance measurement based on cost data

Reasoning errors

Value of work performed approach

The reasoning errors associated with performance measurement on the basis of resource data also apply to cost data. The most well-known method of progress measurement based on cost data is the `value of work performed´ approach, published in the DOD and NASA PERT/Cost Guide (DOD = US Department of Defense) [5]. It initially focuses on ascertaining earned value rather than measuring progress. However, the latter takes place implicitly. If project sub-tasks or work packages have been completed by the status date, earned value is taken to be the most recently valid projected costs of work/services to be performed, i.e. the projected costs for the implementation of the entire work package. However, this assumption is only justified if the planned work/services were actually performed. The controller compares the earned value with the costs that have actually been incurred.

This method cannot be used if the work packages have already commenced but not concluded on the status date (tS). In this case, the formula

$$CPI = \frac{\text{budgeted costs for the work package [BCWS]}}{\text{costs incurred up to the status date } t_s \text{ [ACWP] + remaining cost to complete the work package [RCWP]}}$$

is used, CPI is the Cost Performance Index. The person or unit responsible for the work package must provide an estimate of costs to complete on the status date. In practice, it is often only possible to specify quantities such as person days, which must then be converted into cost units. The projected costs of work performed are calculated by multiplying the actual costs of work performed ACWP by CPI.

Cost to complete

$$BCWP = ACWP \times CPI$$

If CPI = 1, the projected costs of work performed are equal to the actual costs of work performed, i.e. the project is on budget. If, in the most recent estimate, CPI >1, the work package will be associated with fewer costs than assumed at the outset of the project, i.e. the projected cost of the work is higher than the actual costs of the work performed. If Q < 1, the actual cost of work performed is higher than the projected cost of work performed. In other words, a cost overrun is possible.

An example shows that this method of calculation involves the actual degree of completion. If the originally projected cost [BCWS] of a work package is 100,000 euros and costs of 50,000 euros [ACWP] have been incurred, the cost-to-complete [RCWP] is estimated at 150,000 euros and the work package is only one-quarter finished in terms of costs incurred. This can be expressed as a formula:

$$DC = \frac{ACWP}{ACWP + RCWP} \times 100 = \frac{EUR\ 50{,}000}{EUR\ 50{,}000 + EUR\ 150{,}000} \times 100 = 25\%$$

Even if the earned value does not inspire confid- ence for the above reason, the regular cost-to-complete estimates needed for the calculation are a valuable indicator of potential cost overruns and the controller should not dispense with them.

1.2.4 Performance measurement based on performance variables

Performance variables such as excavated material, installed formwork or the length of laid pipes or cables are often used in the plant construction and civil engineering industries. Quantifiable measures are also occasionally used in R&D projects. For example, typical measures in software development projects are the number of code lines written or the number of defined, designed, coded, inspected or tested modules [6]. In the field of electronics development, the number of circuit diagrams that have been created (document count) is occasionally used. In the laboratory development phase, for example, it is possible to calculate the degree of completion on the basis of the formula

Quantifiable measures

$$DC = \frac{\text{number of circuit diagrams created up to the reporting date}}{\text{total circuit diagrams to be created}} \times 100$$

It is also possible to accord different weightings to circuit diagrams, depending on their level of complexity.

Weighting

However, R&D project controllers are seldom able to use performance variables as a measure of project progress with a clear conscience. In some work packages with a low degree of innovativeness (e.g. compilation of parts lists on the basis of existing circuit diagrams), however, quantifiable measures are acceptable.

A more complex performance measure is the number of function points (→ Chapter C6) delivered in a software project. By counting the function points, it is also possible to identify function creep [7]. However, performance measures are also associated with considerable risks, although these are generally ignored. They can result in undesirable adaptation behavioural adjustment responses on the part by project personnel.

Function points

Adaptation responses of personnel

> **Example**
> *The number of finished circuit diagrams is used as a performance measure in a project. The developers started off by drafting the less complex diagrams. They did this so that they could report rapid progress to the project manager, at least in the first stages of development. However, when they decided to create the circuit diagrams in this sequence, they overlooked the fact that some diagrams were associated with higher-level technical components and that an entirely different creation sequence would have been necessary. As a result, considerable time delays occurred in downstream sub-tasks.*

If, for example, only the code lines are counted in a software development project, the employees may neglect other tasks such as test scheduling or user documentation. Seibert [8] therefore quite rightly proposes that these performance indicators should never be used to assess employee performance and that a second performance indicator should be used to `level out the behaviour encouraged by the first metrics´.

Separate performance indicator for staff assessment

1.2.5 Performance measurement based on subjective indicators

In practice, subjective indicators are also sometimes used. Generally, the person responsible for a work package or the project manager makes a direct estimate of work package or project progress, without using units of measurement.

Serious errors of judgement
`90 percent syndrome´

This procedure can result in serious errors of judgement. Weinberg [9] inter alia have demonstrated this in software projects and Souder [10] has reported on it in development projects. Some of these misjudgements are made in good faith. The `90 percent syndrome´, which is mentioned in project management literature in connection with software projects, supports this theory. It implies that many of the people who are responsible for work packages will report continuous progress over a lengthy period of time. However, when they reach a degree of completion of around 90 percent, the positive progress reports suddenly cease. Based on the estimated values reported up to this time, the project has more or less come to a standstill. Yet in actual fact all project personnel are still busy. This indicates that the work packages had not made as much progress as the people responsible for them believed when they prepared their progress reports. They made an overly optimistic assessment of the situation.

1.2.6 Progress measurement based on the milestone technique

Wehking [11] provides a detailed description of this method. Each milestone marks the conclusion of a work package. The degree of completion of the work package is zero until it is completed. Only when the work package is reported as completed is the DC set at 100 percent (0 – 100 method). This method is associated with the disadvantage that a negative efficiency deviation (→ Chapter C6) is reported until the work has been completed because costs are being incurred that are not offset by earned value. This approach is acceptable if the length of a work package does not exceed that of a reporting period – which is usually

0 – 100 method

one month. In this case, the disadvantage is not a problem because no interim values on work progress are recorded.

Lack of progress data

A modification of the above approach, also described by Wehking [12], is the 50 – 50 method. In this case, milestones are set at the start and finish of a work package. When the team starts the work package, the project manager assumes a 50 percent degree of completion. The other 50 percent is credited as soon as the work package is accepted. There are problems associated with this method, though, because no work has been performed at the beginning of the work package, which means that the 50 percent progress is fictive. However, it is a suitable method if the work package is relatively small and its duration is short. Wehking recommends this method for work packages of between one and three months in duration.

50 – 50 method

1.2.6.1 Micro-milestones

If a work package is larger – in terms of costs – and will take a longer period to complete, several milestones can be set. These milestones are also called micro-milestones and should not be confused with the milestones that mark the end of project phases. Wehking [13] recommends this method for work packages with a duration of three or more reporting periods.

1.2.7 Status step method

The micro-milestone method is identical to Motzel's [14] status-step method developed for the plant construction industry. Milestones are set between the beginning and end of a work package. For each milestone reached, the project controller specifies an earned value for the work package.

Example
Completion values, expressed as a percentage, are allocated to the following criteria in the 'engineering' work package for a specific plant component.

STATUS STEP	DEGREE OF PROGRESS
1. Draft prepared	20%
2. Interference test implemented	50%
3. CAD drawing finished	80%
4. Quality assurance inspection implemented	95%
5. Production order issued	100%

Figure C9-1 Degree of completion values within a work package

For example, if a CAD drawing exists, DC is set at 80 percent. This method implicitly assumes that the drawing does not contain any errors, which would mean revisions after the quality inspection.

If this method is used in research and development projects, the controller must ensure that only 100 percent events are defined. One example of this is the milestone description, 'Completion of the inspection of the emergency power supply unit in the climatic chamber as per the process steps specified in the in-house quality management manual.' This helps to counteract the 90 percent syndrome.

100 percent events

1.3 Early warning indicators

Indicators that do not provide reliable information about project progress can nonetheless serve as useful early warning indicators. This is why some authors emphasise the aspect of early warning more strongly than that of precise project measurement, which is often less precise than it appears.

Plateaus

In nine projects, Souder observed that if the points for project progress reported by project managers are not revised, plateaus, i.e. periods of time during which the degree of progress remains more or less constant, often occur. The average duration of these plateaus was 5.5 months. Souder summarised that, if the reported degree of completion in a project changes frequently and considerably, and if lengthy plateau phases occur in conjunction with low measured values, it is extremely likely that the project will fail. In a second study, Souder [15] concluded that subjective monthly information provided by experienced project managers and their direct superiors in respect of project progress is an early warning indicator of project success or failure that should be taken seriously, even if it says little about actual project progress.

Quantitative early warning indicators

Several quantitative early warning indicators have been defined for software projects [16]. They include
- indicators that deadlines will not be met and/or of cost overruns that exceed the float time or cost reserve by ten or more percent,
- an increase of requirements by 50 percent or more per year and
- unscheduled, employee-initiated annual personnel fluctuation of ten percent or more.

Several early warning indicators are also used for project progress measurement in the aerospace industry [17], as shown in Fig. C9-2.

UNITS OF MEASUREMENT	SOURCES	FREQUENCY
No. of requirements (specified, not yet clarified, changes, queries)	Manager	fortnightly
Module (designed, coded, inspected, tested)	Developer	fortnightly
No. of code lines (cumulated)	automated	weekly
Tests (implemented, passed)	Developer	fortnightly

Figure C9-2 Early warning indicators in the aerospace industry

1.3.1 Prerequisites for early warning systems

Statutory regulations

Requirements of indicators

Developing early warning systems for projects in accordance with the European Regulation on the Application of International Accounting Standards (EC 1606/2002) (→ Chapter C3) requires a great deal of empirical work. The indicators used to construct such a system should
- reliably identify risks of failure, even in early project phases,
- be difficult to manipulate and
- be inexpensive and quick to ascertain.

For example, during the development of computers and communication technology systems, the number of laboratory samples rejected in the function test is a good early warning indicator. The number of changes to technical specifications during a project is also considered to be a reliable signal.

2 Project control

The more reliably and promptly a project manager is warned about the possibility of deadlines not being met, cost overruns and the risk of not meeting performance objectives, the more effectively he can implement control measures to keep his project on track for success. In order to do this, he needs information from all relevant persons and systematic documentation that enables him to find what he is looking for at all times. Most job descriptions for project managers clearly specify the duty of project control. He is supported in this function by the project controller (→ Chapter A6).

Information for the project manager

Project controller

The project stakeholders – the departments, the project board and senior managers, for example – should receive regular project status reports from the project manager. That is why the development and updating of a standardised, computer-aided project management information system for all similar project types in an organisation (R&D projects, investment projects, organisational projects) is one of the most important functions of the project controller, the project office or the project management office. Many organisations use standard application software to do this (→ Chapter C11). However, some develop at least some of the components themselves, such as the components for project cost estimates and reports.

Project information system

2.1 Documentation requirements

At the outset of the project, the project manager and controller must decide on the procedure for handling records, reports, agreements, drawings and all other project documents so that they are available at the required time, in the correct form and at the right place. High-quality project work is only possible if
- the project team members have access to relevant documents at all times,
- the documents reflect the project's current status,
- they are easy to find and
- make project progress and results understandable.

Project-related documents can be stored in a project file or a project management information system on a central drive in the corporate Intranet or on the Internet. In practice, the project file is sometimes also referred to as the project data document or project manual (= one manual for each project). In order to prevent it being confused with the project management manual (→ Chapter F1), which contains all of the organisation's project management standards, the term `project file´ is preferable.

Project file

Before project documents are issued, authorised members of staff (e.g. the configuration and control committee, → Chapter C7) check to ensure that they are correct, complete and appropriate (e.g. with regard to the prescribed scope) and then approve them. A list summarising all changes or a document monitoring procedure which identifies the current status of documents ensures that employees do not use invalid or outdated documents.

Authorisation

List summarising all changes

The people within the management structure who are responsible for project records (e.g. the administrator and not the project manager) must establish the retention periods. Some records are subject to statutory retention periods. The project manager must also make the project records available to the customer or his representative for a certain period of time for evaluation purposes if this is contractually agreed.

Retention periods

2.1.1 Project file

An example of project file structure is shown below.

PROJECT FILE FOR PROJECT XY

1 Project requirements and parameters
- 1.1 Contracts
- 1.2 Definition of project objectives
- 1.3 Definition of the project
- 1.4 Specifications

2 Project planning
- 2.1 General plan
  - 2.1.1 Project phases
  - 2.1.2 Milestones
- 2.2 Detailed plan
  - 2.2.1 Results
  - 2.2.2 Costs
  - 2.2.3 Deadlines
  - 2.2.4 Work breakdown structure
  - 2.2.5 Work package descriptions
  - 2.2.6 Interface descriptions
- 2.3 Risk analysis

3 Project management structure
- 3.1 Customer
- 3.2 Steering committee
- 3.3 Project personnel and responsibilities

4 Project reports
- 4.1 Information and document management
- 4.2 Change control
- 4.3 Approvals procedures
- 4.4 Project approval record
- 4.5 Project status reports, including testing and inspection procedures
- 4.6 Project closure record

5 Report on the scope of the project
- 5.1 Result records
- 5.2 Cost updates
- 5.3 Deadline updates
- 5.4 Drawings
- 5.5 Presentation documents
- 5.6 Reports

6 Miscellaneous

Figure C9-3 An example of a project file structure

2.2 Reporting requirements

The project manager and stakeholders should be provided with information via a reporting system that functions efficiently. A central service point should administer this system (e.g. project office or project management office). This prevents each project manager from operating a system that he has designed himself. The service point's activities take into consideration the information requirements of project personnel as defined in the stakeholder communication concept (→ Chapter D4). In particular, it is necessary to ensure that the personnel are provided with the correct quantity of information – enough to give them an idea of what is going on and in a summarised format to ensure that they can retain an overview.

Information requirements of project personnel

Reports to senior managers and steering committees are highly condensed since the recipients, as a rule, are not interested in detailed reports on deadlines and costs. The service point has to ensure that the reporting structures do not get out of hand as a result of too many requests to change the format of reports.

Summarisation of data

PROJECT DATA						
Type of report (selection)	Frequency	Board of management	Steering committee	Departments involved in the project	Project manager	Project controller
Commercial and technical product plan	Created at the beginning of the project and updated at each milestone	x	x	x	x	x
Detailed schedule report (updated network diagram)	weekly			relevant section	x	x
Detailed cost report at work package level	monthly			relevant section	x	x
Summarised cost report at project level (cost at completion)	monthly		x			x
Project status report (cockpit report) including milestone trend analysis	monthly	x	x		x	x
Detailed final report	once only		x	x	x	x
Summarised final report	once only	x				

Figure C9-4 Reporting requirements matrix (excerpt)

2.2.1 Relevance

Project information has to be made available quickly. Information that is several weeks old is no longer of any use to anyone. However, it is often difficult to implement prompt counter-measures when schedule deviations occur since the controller and the project manager first have to analyse the latest data and discuss the necessary counter-measures. Then, the project manager decides upon and implements control measures. Even more time is lost if he has to obtain the approval of the steering committee or senior management before he can implement these measures. Finally, the measures also have to be effective.

Necessary counter-measures

In order to ensure that information can be made available in a timely manner, senior management has to make a fundamental decision to the effect that it is the duty of the employees to deliver information. The project management manual (→ Chapter F1) should therefore include the following text: 'The members of the project group support the project manager in his project management function. They ensure that the information necessary for project-related planning and reporting is promptly delivered to the project manager.'

Duty to furnish information

2.2.2 Spin

Non-specific statements

Written project reports can be given a positive spin. This is why foreseeable project disasters are seldom recorded on paper. The prompt availability of information is also no guarantee that the project manager or next higher reporting level, such as the steering committee or senior management, will receive adequate warning of deviations from the schedule. In particular, non-specific statements about project progress are often absolutely worthless. Here are a few examples of project progress waffle [18]:

TYPICAL STATEMENTS	WHAT THEY REALLY MEAN
We are planning to commence the work.	It is too early to say when the work can commence.
The work started on …	Several employees booked their time against the project …
The delivery of the last part is scheduled for …	It is impossible to finish before …
Delivery is imminent.	We´re still not ready.
The work was finished. However, the results indicate that further tests are necessary.	It didn´t work.

Figure C9-5 Project progress spin

Non-disclosure

Often, project personnel delay disclosing the truth for a long time, for example if a cost overrun has already occurred or is likely to occur.

There are two main reasons for this behaviour:
- They fear sanctions (e.g. reproaches from superiors, career disadvantages).
- They hope that the overruns will be compensated at a later stage of the project.

Filtering and falsification

Even truthful reports by people who are directly involved in the project are no guarantee that higher instances will actually find out about the real status of the project. Information that passes through the various levels of a management structure is often filtered and massaged several times.

2.2.3 Examples of project reports

Overview reports

Several types of project reports have already been explained in Chapter C6. However, the majority of these only provide information about one single planning variable, i.e. specific data on deadlines or costs. These often very detailed reports are obviously necessary. Nevertheless, the project manager, steering committees and senior management prefer to receive a summary of deadlines, costs and project progress. Figure C9-6 [19] shows how an evaluation of several projects can provide such an overview.

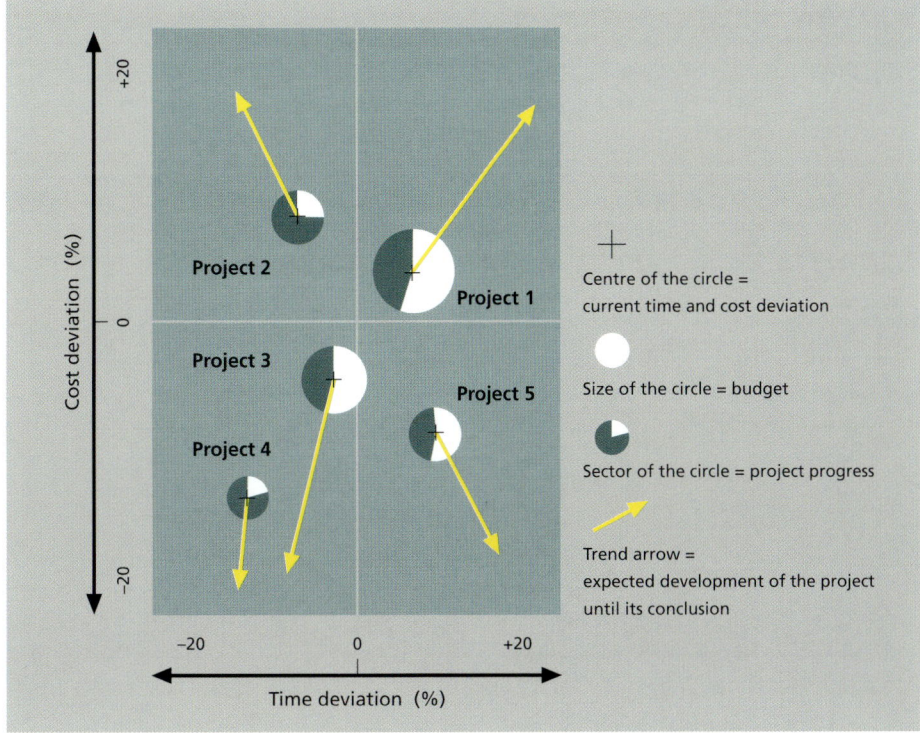

Figure C9-6 Diagram showing time and cost deviations, project progress and trends in several projects

Figure C9-7 shows a 'cockpit report' [20] that contains a milestone trend analysis (MTA) and, in addition to information about deadline adherence and costs, information about the quality of the project deliverable.

Cockpit report

The MTA is an extension of the milestone technique (→ Chapter B). The vertical axis shows the calendar dates of the various milestones and the horizontal axis shows reporting dates. The milestone trend analysis provides an 'at-a-glance' overview of whether the most important project deadlines will be met or not. It is therefore very popular with senior managers. It can be used as a derived (Case 1) or original (Case 2) tool. In Case 1, milestones are set in the network diagram. At each of the regular reporting dates, they are recalculated with the assistance of the updated network diagram. In Case 2, the project personnel who are responsible for meeting deadlines estimate the dates. Milestone dates that are ascertained on the basis of network analysis are preferable to estimated dates.

Milestone trend analysis

Derived or original MTA

The milestones and their dates are generally shown in the form of a right-angled triangle. The vertical and horizontal sides of the triangle are used as time axes. Reporting dates are entered on the horizontal axis and milestone dates on the vertical axis. The date on which the milestones were actually reached is entered on the diagonal. In the example shown (Figure C9-8), the scheduled dates of milestones shift along the axis as they are updated on each reporting date. Only the milestone 'foundation finished' has already been reached.

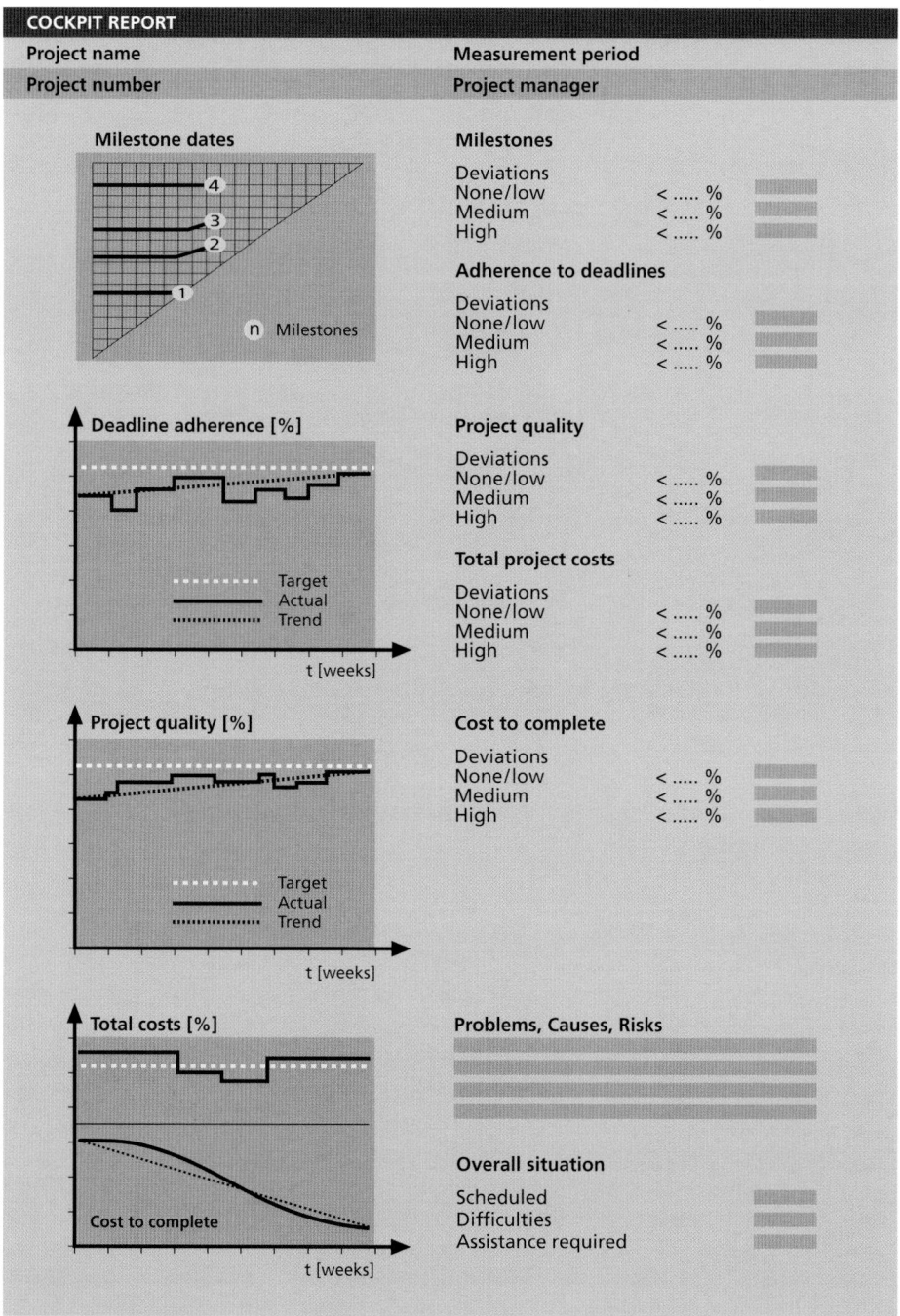

Figure C9-7 Cockpit report

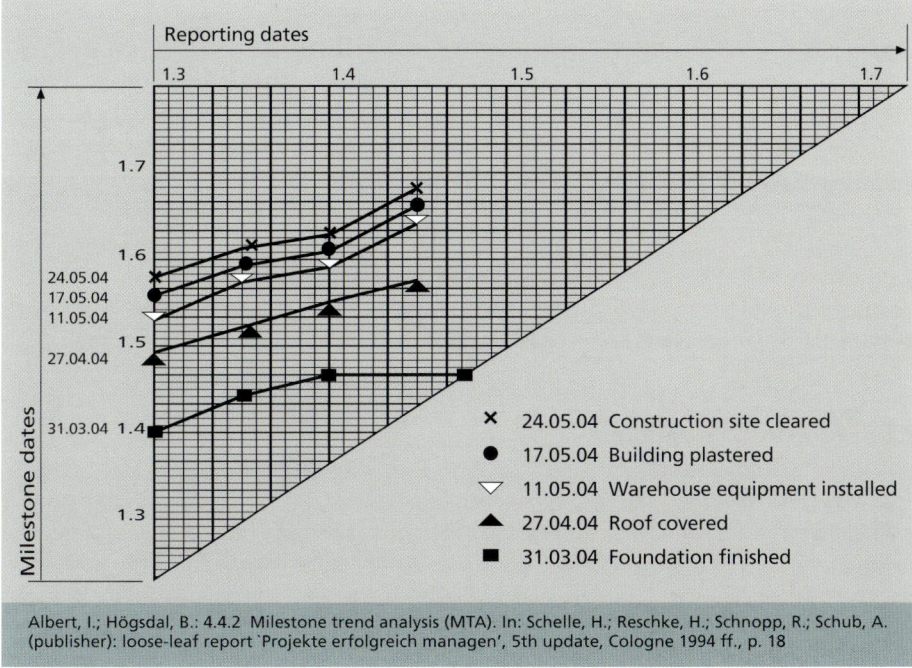

Figure C9-8 Milestone trend analysis

The traffic light report [21] in figure C9-9 uses the colours green, amber and red as project status symbols to provide a highly-simplified overview.

Traffic light report

'TRAFFIC LIGHT REPORT'		
Project name		
Date		
CC		
Created by	PL	
Project status		
	green	everything OK
	amber	some problems
	red	serious problems
Content		
1. Brief description of the project status 2. Completed work packages		
	WP 2.1	'Criteria and key words'
	WP 2.2	'Conduct research'
	WP 2.3	'Summarise results'
	WP 2.4	'Evaluate results'
3. Interim results 4. Cost situation: what costs have been incurred and what is the expected cost to complete? 5. Deadline adherence: are the agreed milestones being reached on schedule? 6. Potential problems and counter-measures 7. Key tasks in subsequent months and revision of plans		

Figure C9-9 Traffic light report

2.2.4 Problems with project reports

Highly condensed reports on project status, such as those shown in Figure C9-3, C9-4 and C9-5, are useful for providing a quick overview and when vast amounts of information exist. They are especially popular with senior managers. However, a note of caution: if they are not based on detailed evaluations such as

- schedules based on network analysis,
- a cost report that includes cost to complete estimates at work package level and
- a detailed review of performance or quality,

Lack of detailed analyses

Manipulation

there is a very high risk that the reports will be tampered with. One project controller said, 'Even though we had regular cost overruns, often missed project deadlines and project progress was behind schedule, the report status was almost always green. It was very rarely amber and never red.'

2.2.5 Face-to-face dialogue

'Soft' information

If the project manager, the project steering committee and senior management want to receive good quality information, they shouldn't trust the reporting system alone. They should initiate face-to-face dialogue with the project personnel as often as possible. This is the only way to obtain 'soft' information, i.e. information about negative sentiment and dissatisfaction in the team, latent conflicts with departments and problems reaching agreement with the customer. Scientific studies on information behaviour show that good managers do not rely on paper reports alone. They attempt, by way of numerous discussions with the project teams and visits, to obtain a realistic picture of the situation.

2.2.6 Regular status meetings

Establishment of status meeting dates at the start-up meeting

There is also direct contact between the project manager, the team members and representatives of the key stakeholders at the project status meetings. However, in just-get-on- with-it projects with obscure objectives and unsystematic project management structures, these meetings are often ad hoc instead of being held at regular intervals. This is an extremely risky approach. Even at the start-up meeting (→ Chapter C1), the project participants should not only establish the form and frequency of formal project reports, but also the dates of the regular status meetings. The rule of thumb is: the shorter the duration of the project, the more frequently these meetings should take place. A specific week day (jour fixe) is recommended.

Crises

This does not prevent the project team from meeting more often if need be (e.g. if a crisis occurs, → Chapter D5). A data variance analysis is made at the regular meetings. Information from the various company departments – for example, about reasons for deviations – is then available immediately and on a first-hand basis. Anything that requires clarification can be discussed at the meeting and counter-measures can be agreed upon.

Compared with a team status meeting, the collection of status information via internal post, Intranet, the Internet or even via video conference is a poor alternative. However, these methods are inevitable if the team members are so widely dispersed that any other option would be too expensive.

2.3 Project control measures

The work breakdown structure is an important tool for setting the project status meeting agendas because deviation analyses and the ensuing project control measures take place at work package level. The following questions [22] are useful at status meetings:

1. Which work packages have been completed since the last status meeting?
2. Which work packages will commence between this and the next status meeting?
3. Which problems have occurred in which work packages?
4. How will the deviations make themselves evident?
5. How can we make sure that fewer deviations occur?
6. Have changes taken place in the work packages? What is the impact of these changes?
7. Have the measures agreed at the last project status meeting been implemented?
8. Are current cost and deadline adherence data available?
9. Is there anything special to report?

Questions about work packages

Project managers can only tackle problems effectively if they have implemented a detailed variance analysis. To do this, they will require the support of the project controller. The project controller's task is to propose control measures and to provide reminders (→ Chapter A6). Figure C9-10 shows possible causes of schedule deviations.

Causes of schedule deviations

The project manager can implement various control measures depending on the cause of the deviation. If there is a capacity shortage, he will consider how to obtain additional personnel as quickly as possible. For example, he could sub-contract the work or transfer employees from less urgent projects.

Control according to cause of deviation

If a deadline has been missed as a result of additional customer requirements, it will be necessary to negotiate with the customer. However, it is a better idea not to agree to additional requirements in the first place unless the customer is willing to accept a delay.

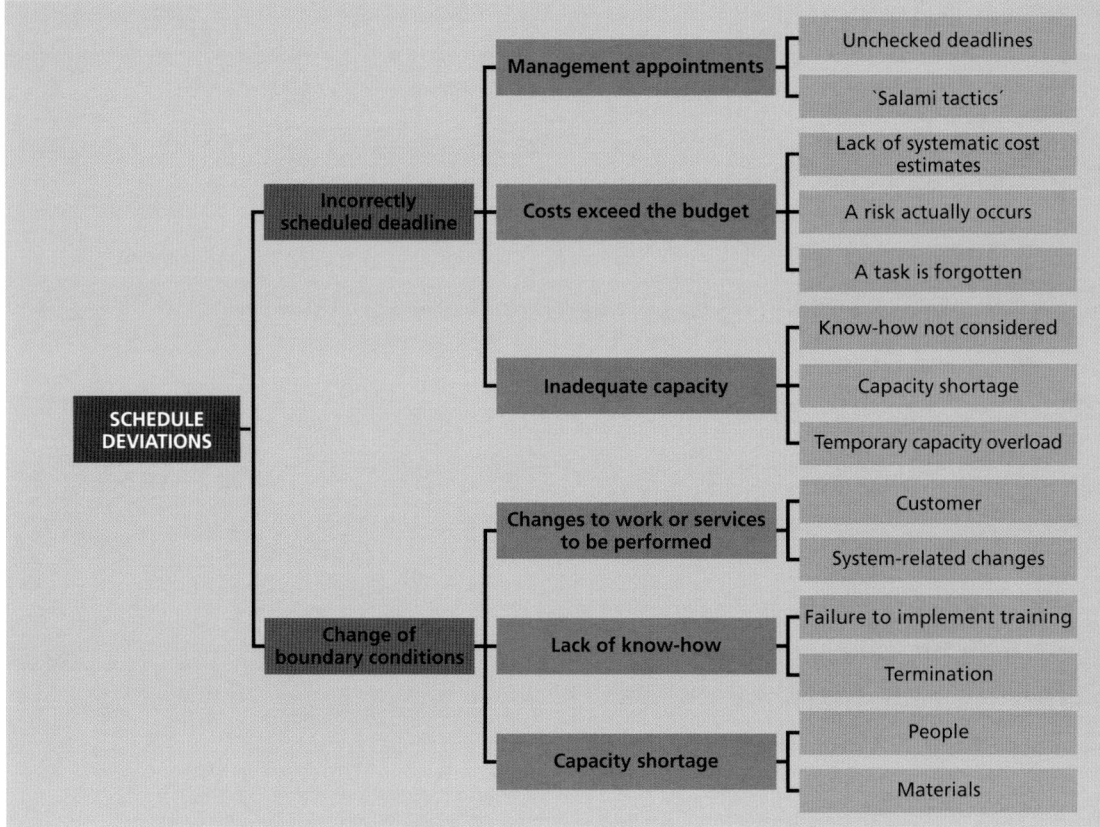

Figure C9-10 Causes of schedule deviations [23]

2.3.1 Obstacles and side-effects

Conflicting objectives

Project objectives often conflict (→ Chapter C2). A controller who is integrated in the project must therefore monitor all project objectives at all times. For instance, additional customer requirements in terms of work or services to be performed can generally only be satisfied at higher cost and/or by extending the project lifecycle. Brooks' Law is an example of one particularly drastic conflict of objectives (→ Chapter C2). Literally, it means that if a project is already behind schedule, bringing in additional team members will only lead to further schedule deviations and higher costs. For example, the new project personnel will require an induction period before they can start work on the project. In this phase, the risk of initial problems is especially high (e.g. misunderstandings, redundant work). This not only applies in software projects, but also in any projects where the project personnel have high communication requirements and require project-specific knowledge.

Brooks' Law

In other words, the project manager should carefully consider each planned control measure with the controller. Figures C9-11 and C9-12 [24] show the most important cost and deadline adherence control measures, obstacles and side-effects, and also point out numerous conflicting objectives.

C9 PERFORMANCE MEASUREMENT AND PROJECT CONTROL

Overview of measures, obstacles, side-effects

MEASURES THAT REDUCE THE SCOPE OF PERFORMANCE	POSSIBLE OBSTACLES AND SIDE-EFFECTS
Reduction of work to be performed	Customer disagreement, the measure is impossible to implement owing to the market situation
Version creation with a temporary reduction of performance	Hidden schedule deviations, higher total cost of the final product
Limitations on the required quality (performance)	Increase in maintenance and operating costs, hidden schedule deviation
Change of performance feature priority	Hidden schedule deviation, product is not accepted by the market or customer
Rejection of change requests	Non-acceptance of the project result, decline in turnover and profits

MEASURES THAT REDUCE COSTS	POSSIBLE OBSTACLES AND SIDE-EFFECTS
Search for technical alternatives	Temporary additional costs and uncertain outcome
Acquisition of licenses and know-how	Dependency, possibility that know-how cannot be transferred for own product development
Purchasing of product components	A suitable supplier must be found, costs relating to definition and acceptance
Alternative suppliers	Effort/time required for the selection and contracting process, supply risk
Process changes	Conversion costs with uncertain outcome
Use of different tools	Initial skill adaptation costs, investment costs
Cancellation of non-urgent work packages	Higher risk, quality impairment
Concurrent implementation of work packages	Increased technical risk

Figure C9-11 Measures to reduce the scope of performance or costs

MEASURES THAT INCREASE CAPACITY	POSSIBLE OBSTACLES AND SIDE-EFFECTS
Recruitment of additional employees	Fixed personnel budget
Redistribution of personnel within the project	Bottleneck displacement
Involvement of additional departments	Increase of coordination costs, induction is necessary
Purchasing of external capacity	Know-how must first be located
Provision of additional resources	Investments are necessary
Change of supplier	Supply risk, quality risk
Outsourcing of work packages	Coordination costs, costs associated with searching for suitable staff, quality risk
Overtime work	Works council approval is necessary, temporary availability
Shift work	Organisational problems
Reduction of other aspects of the project personnel's workload	Deficiencies in other areas

Figure C9-12 Measures to increase capacity (Measures to increase productivity → next page)

MEASURES THAT INCREASE PRODUCTIVITY	POSSIBLE OBSTACLES AND SIDE-EFFECTS
Staff training	No short-term effect, effort
Substitution of specific employees	No alternatives, induction period
Recruitment of employees with specific skills	Specialists are difficult to find, costs
Additional information and communication	Expenditure of time, no short-term effect
Boosting motivation through – individual praise – team spirit – personal responsibility – bonuses and incentives – reducing conflicts – etc.	No short-term effect
Reorganisation of the project	Friction losses, opposition
Ensuring that project personnel do not have to perform administrative tasks	Deficiencies in other areas
Improvement of the project infrastructure	Induction period and costs

Figure C9-12 Measures to increase productivity (Measures to increase capacity → last page)

The project manager should monitor the implementation of the control measures that are decided upon – unless they are included as activities in the process schedule – on the basis of an open issues list and regularly review the impact of project control measures on project objectives at subsequent status meetings.

Open issues list

OPEN ISSUES LIST FOR MONITORING PROJECT MEASURES	
Consecutive no. of the measure	35
Description of the measure	
Implementation of functions in the second version of the program, negotiations with the customer	
The most recent update of the network diagram shows that it will be impossible to deliver the software on the date specified by the customer. The delivery date is non-negotiable because the customer needs the software for a trade fair presentation. It is therefore necessary to talk to the customer and find out which program functions have lower priority and do not need to be implemented until the second version. If the customer agrees, the specification has to be amended and the time schedule adapted.	
Person responsible	Mr Smith
Envisaged date of the agreement	CW 23
Implemented	☐ Yes ☐ No
Comments	

Figure C9-13 Open issues list for monitoring control measures

Self-assessment questions for each certification level

No.	Question	Level				Self-assessment
		D	C	B	A	
C 9.01	What problems are associated with performance measurement?	2	3	3	4	☐
C 9.02	How is earned value calculated?	2	2	2	2	☐
C 9.03	Why is it difficult to measure project performance in R&D projects?	2	2	2	2	☐
C 9.04	How is performance measurement realised using cost to complete?	2	3	3	2	☐
C 9.05	What is the 90 % syndrome?	2	2	2	2	☐
C 9.06	How is progress measured using the milestone technique?	2	3	3	4	☐
C 9.07	What is progress?	2	2	2	2	☐
C 9.08	Which early warning indicators can be used to measure project performance?	1	2	3	4	☐
C 9.09	What are the prerequisites for early warning systems in projects?	2	2	2	4	☐
C 9.10	What is a document requirements matrix used for?	2	3	3	1	☐
C 9.11	Which content and which format should a project report have?	2	3	3	4	☐
C 9.12	How can a project crisis (i.e. project discontinuity) be dealt with?	2	3	3	4	☐
C 9.13	What is the difference between a project management manual and the project manual?	2	3	3	4	☐
C 9.14	What project tasks does a central project office support?	1	2	2	4	☐
C 9.15	What questions can be asked at project status meetings as the basis for further project control?	2	3	3	4	☐
C 9.16	What control measures can the project manager use?	2	3	3	4	☐
C 9.17	What would indicate a project crisis (in the sense of project discontinuity)?	2	2	3	4	☐

C10 PROJECT CLOSE-OUT AND PROJECT LEARNING

Systematic project close-out (ICB Element 11) is essential for many reasons. But when does a project actually finish? What tasks are associated with project close-out? What is a project closure meeting? What should be included in the final report? These are some of the focal issues dealt with in this chapter. This chapter also explains how project experiences can be used in future projects (ICB Element 36). Under the heading of project learning, methods for project analysis on the objective and relationship levels are explained together with recommendations on how to take advantage of learning effects in the project.

1 Definition

When does a project actually finish?

The ICB defines project close-out as 'the completion of project work once the project results have been realised. It combines two processes: first, the commissioning of the project deliverables and their acceptance by the sponsor, and second, [the documentation and forwarding of] all experiences made in the project.'

This definition of project close-out appears plausible at first glance. However, on closer inspection, it turns out to be more problematic, as the following example shows.

A management consultant has been engaged by a medium-sized garment manufacturer to develop and introduce systematic project management. The project objective is to reduce missed deadlines considerably and cost overruns in customer projects (product success → Chapter A5). The management consultant has to consider the issue of when this project actually concludes. Is it when the project manual is handed over to the customer? Or when the key employees have been provided with training and the pilot projects have been selected (implementation success)? Or is it only fin-ished when it is possible to verify whether the objectives of 'improving adherence to deadlines' and 'improving adherence to costs' have actually been achieved – i.e. at a much later date?

The problem of defining project close-out is not exclusive to organisational projects. It also exists in other types of projects. This is why Patzak and Rattay [1] differentiate between the two project close-out events of project handover (= provisional acceptance certificate in international plant construction projects) and project evaluation (= final acceptance certificate). In actual fact, there is also a third project close-out event which occurs between the performance of work and project evaluation: the conclusion of project controlling in the form of an evaluation of the cost, profit and financial situation.

Project handover
Project evaluation

Conclusion
of controlling

The ICB clearly only describes project close-out in terms of the first and third events. It overlooks the fact that the necessary evaluation of experience (= project learning) generally delivers far more valuable information if it is performed at a later date.

Evaluation

If it is accepted that there are three types of project close-out event (conclusion of work and services to be performed, cost evaluation and project evaluation), this inevitably has consequences for the

Formal conclusion

formal project close-out process. Patzak and Rattay propose that when project handover has taken place, the project is provisionally, though formally, closed. This process involves
- a project closure meeting,
- the preparation of a draft final report and
- the dissolution of the project team.

Steering committee

It is a good idea if the steering committee agrees at the outset of the project upon precise criteria which can be used as the basis for establishing when the project can be considered finished.

Example
In a project to develop a new mobile phone to the marketing stage, the point in time when responsibility passes from the project manager to the persons responsible for the product is clearly defined. The project is considered concluded when a previously specified number of mobile phones have been produced and are ready for delivery to the customer.

2 Arguments in favour of systematic project close-out

Acceptance

To ensure systematic project close-out, it is initially necessary to implement an acceptance procedure to clarify whether the project result is acceptable to the customer or whether improvements are necessary. In external projects, the customer has greater scope than in internal projects for imposing sanctions regarding demands for the performance of outstanding services. For example, he can withhold part of the contractually-agreed payment until the contractor has performed all of his obligations. Such sanctions can cause cash flow problems for the contractor and, in some cases, jeopardise the continued existence of his company. Many contractors conclude projects at a loss because the customer withholds a final payment.

A delay in the performance of services by the contractor can cause the customer to incur losses and result in late payments, for example, if the installation of a new IT system is associated with problems or the customer fails to comply with official regulations owing to a delay caused by the contractor.

Examples
An organisation fails to provide the complete set of project documentation that the customer requires to apply for an operating license from a supervisory authority in due time before the conclusion of the project. As a result, production commences later than planned and the customer loses sales.

A software manufacturer has developed call-centre software that is evaluated by the customer as very good. However, the project manager is so busy with the project that he forgets to prepare training documents. When the test run has finished and the software is ready to go live, it becomes evident that the user instructions are inadequate and confusing. As a result, the call centre employees have difficulty in using the system. They often have no idea how to handle customer calls.

If the project manager fails to ensure that the outstanding work is performed properly, the customer may be dissatisfied with what is essentially a successful project (e.g. a system that functions perfectly with an impractical user manual). In this case, the overall project objective has been attained, though with limitations.

2.1 Damage to reputation

Customer dissatisfaction is not always expressed in the form of withheld payment instalments. In the lon grun, dissatisfaction associated with a damaged reputation and a lack of follow-up orders has far more devastating consequences for the organisation. According to Hansel and Lomnitz [2], `The final impression [...] is often decisive for the way people remember the project, i.e. the project´s image. A negative impression made by a project can last for years and even [...] cause major difficulties for the start of a new project.´

2.2 Sudden cost escalations

Sudden cost escalations are a widespread problem in the final phases of a project.
In order to avoid them, the project manager must ensure, in advance of project close-out, that *Counter-measures*
- the project team is officially dissolved and
- all work packages are declared finished.

When this has been done, it is impossible for anyone to generate additional costs and simply charge them to the project or a work package. In practice, team members often continue to work pointlessly on the `old´ project because they have no idea what their next assignment will be. It is especially tempting in internal projects implicitly to prolong a project that has in fact ended, if there are no interesting follow-up orders.

2.3 Mistakes in follow-up projects

A systematic evaluation of the project helps the organisation to save costs and prevent mistakes in follow-up projects.   *Assessment for follow-up projects*

> **Example**
> *An electronics manufacturer has been developing complex, customised systems for various customers for many years. Many of the components, mostly printed circuit boards, differ slightly in terms of function and architecture. In some cases, the engineers had to use the plans for only one predecessor system. In other cases, only minor adaptations to existing developments were necessary. However, the developers started from scratch in each project because they had no classification system or database containing previously built and tested components which the engineers could use as a source of ideas and as samples. New projects derived no benefits whatsoever from predecessor projects.*

3 Tasks at the end of the project

In practice, the systematic conclusion of a project is extremely significant. Hamburger and Spirer [3] allocate the tasks and problems associated with the conclusion of a project to
- an objective level and   *Objective / relationship level*
- a relationship level.

The timely provision of a team to monitor the live operation of a system at the customer´s premises during the first few months and provide training to the customer is an objective task. Measures that counteract a loss of motivation among members of the project team, on the other hand, are allocated to the relationship level. Loss of motivation often occurs in the final stages of the project. Both types of problems can be closely related, as the following example shows.

Example
A medical technology enterprise is requested to develop a special appliance for a clinic in conjunction with a software manufacturer. Numerous technical problems that have jeopardised the success of the project throughout its entire lifecycle have caused the project team's motivation to hit rock bottom shortly before the project is due to conclude. They are more worried about their future assignments than about how best to perform the remaining project work. As a result, the work they deliver is of sub-standard quality, the appliance breaks down at the clinic and the customer refuses to pay the invoice.

3.1 Tasks on the objective level

To-do list

Concluding questions

Although the tasks on the objective level are not generally associated with problems, it is essential that they are performed. It is a good idea to create a regularly updated to-do list to monitor the punctual and complete performance of outstanding work. The project manager and his team should also ask themselves the following questions:

Acceptance procedures, tests and reviews
- Have all the necessary acceptance procedures, tests and reviews been performed?

External/internal assessment

Acceptance can be performed by an external body (e.g. TÜV) or be based on the results of internal tests and inspections. The customer's approval of standard operation can depend on a positive answer to this question.

Performed and outstanding services
- Which services has the contractor still to perform in the project (e.g. delivery of peripherals, documentation, training, customer support during standard operation)?
- With which change requests does the contractor still have to comply?
- Which additional financial claims still have to be invoiced for changes implemented at the customer's request?
- With which obligations do suppliers and sub-contractors still have to comply?

Checklists

In each case, the project manager and customer must check whether the services are actually necessary, how much time they are likely to take and what costs will be incurred as a result. Sometimes, the customer will agree to dispense with specific services if a price discount is granted in return. Checklists can be helpful when analysing the services to be performed. They are prepared in conjunction with the evaluation of concluded projects and archived within the scope of project learning.

Dissolution of key relationships with project stakeholders
- Which tasks still have to be performed by the project team for specific stakeholders (e.g. report for senior management, provision of information to the city council or press)?
- Which tasks have the stakeholder groups still to perform in the project (e.g. user report after the first test run of a software system)?

- How will the relevant stakeholder group be informed about the conclusion of the project (e.g. personal debriefing, circular letter, customer magazine, employee newsletter)?

Cost, profit and financial situation
- What is the final cost, profit and financial situation?

It is the project controller´s responsibility to analyse the cost, profit and financial situation. He does this by determining which instalments the customer still has to pay and which payments the contractor still has to make to suppliers. On the cost side, he has to check if the project costs have been charged to the correct cost centres, the project personnel have charged costs to the correct work packages and whether double charges have been made, e.g. the same costs being charged to two different work packages.

Project controller

Handover
- Has the necessary post-project work (e.g. system support during a transitional period, assignment of responsibility from the project manager to the product manager) been properly transferred to the person or department responsible?
- Were the responsible members of staff adequately prepared? Did they receive all the necessary information (e.g. manuals, drawings, parts lists)?
- Was the customer informed about the transfer of responsibility?
- Have the resources, raw materials and supplies that are no longer required for the project been reallocated?
- Has all the necessary technical data (e.g. power consumption data) been compiled for the customer?

3.2 Tasks on the relationship level

Social psychologists have closely studied the process of group break-up. Geissler [4] details the effects of the extreme situation of group dissolution. He made the following observations about adult education groups: `The process of separation is particularly difficult and stressful if there have been intense group dynamics and a focus on interpersonal relationships over a lengthy period of time.´ The dissolution of project teams is often even more difficult because the conclusion of a project can be associated with major concerns. For example, the project team members may not know whether they will be assigned to a follow-up project or whether they are at risk of losing their job in the organisation, and this suspense can be very stressful for them. This is why project teams often demonstrate a special defence reaction that is not available to groups of students: they implicitly prolong the project work.

Extreme situation

Team dissolution

Common problems on the relationship level include:
- The collective identity of the team gradually weakens and personal interests start to take precedence (e.g. securing a coveted position in a follow-up project). The team gradually loses its identity. This process is exacerbated if team members who are no longer required to work on the project leave the team before the project concludes. New staff are recruited to the team to perform tasks associated with the project´s conclusion or to be trained to provide system support. Often, team members are reassigned to line management or transferred to other projects before the official conclusion of their own project.
- Sometimes, the project team continues to work on a project for longer than necessary because

Loss of identity

its members believe that they have no other prospects in the organisation. In many cases, they are not sure what they will be doing when the project ends. Further motives for unnecessarily extending project work include:

Unnecessary prolongation

- The new assignments are not particularly appealing.
- The team members are worried about having to work on something new.

Voluntary withdrawal

- Team members voluntarily leave the project shortly before its conclusion. In practice, there are various reasons for this phenomenon.
  - The project team members may want to leave the project in good time to join another project.
  - They may prefer not to be identified with a failed project.
  - They may fear that they will be asked to perform menial and boring tasks (e.g. documentation) at the end of the project.

When this happens, the customer and the project manager lose important contacts.

The project manager should be aware of problems that occur on the relationship level when a project team is dissolved and develop an understanding for this type of behaviour. The personnel in question should be offered a specific new position. For example, many problems can be avoided if necessary personnel transfers [5] are planned meticulously in advance by the personnel department and the employees being reassigned. This nips concerns about the future in the bud. The project manager can also take part in these meetings.

Defining a new beginning

Separation rituals

It is important to end the project with a joint experience involving all team members. Various separation rituals and ceremonies exist that are suitable for concluding a project on the relationship level. For example, a close-out party should be held and appropriate tribute paid to the project team – a representative of the organisation´s senior management could attend. Organisational psychologists [6] suggest that awards should be presented to project personnel. The project manager should inform the project team about the planned event well in advance.

Personnel transfers

4 Project closure meeting

The project closure meeting and the report detailing its results are the counterpart to the project start-up meeting. The people attending the meeting analyse and evaluate the

- project results,
- project processes and
- consequences for the post-project phase.

They also document the experience gained in the project and assign the tasks that still have to be performed.

Problematic projects

Unfortunately, these recommendations are difficult to follow, especially in problematic projects. It is never easy to talk about failures. This is why it is possible the project will not be analysed objectively and that the team members will blame each other for the project´s failure. Project closure meetings should therefore be prepared carefully [7].

Discharge

At the project closure meeting, the steering committee generally discharges the project manager and his team from their responsibilities, i.e. they approve all the activities of the project manager and his team (= declaration of acceptance by senior management).

The following issues should be discussed at the project closure meeting:

1. Summing up of the project by the project manager *Agenda*
   – What objectives were attained/not attained?
2. Feedback round: each participant is given the opportunity to speak
   – What went well (= strengths)?
   – What didn´t go well (= scope for improvement)?
3. Discussion of the feedback round
4. Project learning: safeguarding knowledge for future projects
   – What can the team and the entire organisation learn from the project?
   – What measures have been implemented to prevent the repetition of mistakes?
5. Information about the conclusion of the project
   – Who will receive the final report?
   – Who will only receive brief information about the conclusion of the project?
6. Assignment of remaining tasks (e.g. drafting of the final report)
7. Celebration of the project´s conclusion

5 Final report

Project management literature provides numerous suggestions about how to structure final reports (e.g. [8]). However, no one structure is appropriate in all circumstances. The content of the final report depends on the type and scope of the project. Bearing this in mind, the following sections only refer to content that is absolutely essential: *Minimum content*

1. Information about
   • the quality objectives planned at the outset and those that were actually achieved,
   • the originally planned and actual close-out date and
   • the estimated budget and actually incurred costs.
   It may be appropriate to provide reasons for any deviations in all three parameters.

2. The issues of
   • what went particularly well in the team and in relationships with project stakeholders and
   • what didn´t go so well.

3. Information about
   • consequences for future projects that are derived from deviations and
   • a list of tasks that still have to be performed.

6 Project learning

People are the information-channels within a project and between projects, i.e. between current and future projects. To ensure that each team embarking on a new project doesn´t have to reinvent the wheel, every organisation should institutionalise the use of learning from project experience and knowledge sharing. It is a good idea, from a business perspective, to make examples of best practice available for future projects. *Institutionalisation of experience-based learning*

Considering how much money is wasted as a result of parallel developments in different departments, on projects where employees have no idea that their colleagues are performing the same activities, or on work that has to be repeated as a result of mistakes that have already been made in the past, it is clear that the cost of a `project learning´ system (= learning from projects, project knowledge management) that is tailored to the organisation's requirements is a worthwhile investment. It is important to establish a climate in which employees can derive knowledge not only from successful projects, but also from less successful and even failed projects [9].

Learning from mistakes

6.1 Project learning recommendations

Projects are generally only superficially analysed – if at all – at the project closure meeting. In many cases, no detailed analysis is made for the purpose of project learning. There are many reasons for this. Based on these reasons, it is possible for the organisation to draw conclusions about project learning.

1. When the project has officially concluded and project team members are assigned to new tasks, project personnel should still be available to provide a detailed assessment.
2. The company or project management structure should appoint a person to coordinate all learning processes in all projects. This person should have the support of a working group which functions as an interface to the organisation's staff and from which a representative or successor can be recruited. The objective is to sustain the process of project learning when personnel changes take place.
3. Open and constructive criticism, imagination and willingness to experiment should be encouraged (→ Chapter D3). Mistakes should be construed as learning opportunities, otherwise, when projects fail, the people responsible fear that an analysis could reveal mistakes that may jeopardise their careers. The management should therefore install a learning culture that prevents one-off mistakes from being associated with negative consequences.
4. It is the responsibility of the management to ensure that employees are aware of the personal benefits that they will derive from sharing their knowledge with others. Everyone profits from knowledge sharing. In a learning organisation, the principle of `knowledge is power and knowledge sharing means more power´ applies.
5. Project learning is always an official project objective that has to be met (e.g. `collecting and documenting experiences´).
6. Formal processes ensure that project learning objectives are binding. This applies equally to project learning input, status reports and milestones.
7. Management should request regular reports on project learning measures and achievements.
8. Feedback mechanisms (e.g. regular documented reviews, enquiries from the people responsible for project learning) are essential for effective project learning and new, creative ideas.
9. Project teams should not just consider the project in terms of the parameters of costs, time and quality, but also on the basis of experiences relating to the human factor which can be transferred to subsequent projects (e.g. the successful elimination of conflicts).
10. However, if the expenditure for systematic project learning turns out to be higher than initially envisaged, a contact (e.g. project manager, project office, a member of the management team) should be available to absorb frustration and motivate people to continue learning.
11. Considering technical and organisational issues, a project learning system should enable the processing, dissemination and archiving of experiences so that people can specifically look for them and find them (e.g. categorisation of specific project processes or experiences, search terms). It is important to specify the name of a contact. Before an employee leaves the organisation, he should enter the name of a successor (= a person who shares his knowledge) in the system. Documented knowledge provides greater benefits if the authors can also be questioned about it in person.

Appointee

Promoting honesty

The power of knowledge

Formal processes

The human factor

Technical / organisational issues

Contacts

Confidants

12. Employees should receive training so that they can assess whether experiences are worth documenting and in what way they can be useful for the project learning system.
13. At the beginning of each new project, the project personnel should look in the project learning system to see whether the organisation has documented past experiences that are relevant for their project.
14. A coach can provide valuable input. Mentor systems are also practical. Experienced members of staff act as project mentors who answer questions and provide advice. *Coach/Mentor*
15. Whenever possible, successful teams should be assigned to new projects in the same or a similar constellation. However, this is often difficult to realise in practice because staff tend to be requisitioned by their own departments or for other projects soon after the project has finished. *Team-Recycling*
16. The personnel who are assigned to follow-up projects often reject the documented experiences because they were not involved in the predecessor project (`not invented here´ syndrome). It is therefore necessary to create awareness throughout the organisation that, `This is our common pool of knowledge from which we can all profit.´ Cross-project or inter-departmental events and working groups can be helpful in promoting this awareness. A negative image should be attributed to an isolated department mentality. *`Not invented here´ syndrome*

The documented information for the personnel working in follow-up projects must be formulated in a comprehensible way and, if possible, illustrated (e.g. include a sketch), have a context (e.g. project marketing) and suitable depth of detail (not excessively detailed, but without any information gaps). The necessary knowledge can be communicated on the basis of examples in seminars or possibly in cascade training sessions (= a snowball system in which employees train other employees). *Documentation requirements*

7 Project analysis and learning methods

The following sections explain some of the methods used for project analysis which promote project learning.

7.1 Project analysis on the objective level

On the objective level, the following methods can be used.

7.1.1 Calculation of historical costs

The most common method which has been in practical use for many years now is the calculation of historical costs after the conclusion of the project. Historical costs can be taken as the basis for the calculation of costs in a new project, provided that the project is associated with a low degree of innovation. If the originally planned costs are exceeded by far, it is necessary to identify the main cost drivers in a cost variance analysis. It is also important to implement a variance analysis if the project lifecycle is longer than originally envisaged. *Identifying cost drivers*

7.1.2 Project cost databases

Another method, far less frequently used than historical cost calculation, is the creation of cost databases. The construction industry is an exception to this rule (see [10]). This industry systematically evaluates the costs of concluded projects on a relatively frequent basis. These analyses can be used to plan new projects. The construction industry has developed structuring guidelines that enable experts to make an understandable record of cost data and to find information about historical costs. Cross-company cost databases now also exist for software projects.

7.1.3 Performance indicators and performance indicator systems

Key performance indicators

In relatively rare cases, project controllers define performance indicators when the project has concluded. Comprehensive performance indicator systems are used even less frequently, except in the software industry. The performance indicators that are defined for IT projects apply to both the developed product and the process of product development [11].

Key performance indicators include
- adherence to deadlines
- adherence to costs
- frequency of changes in project requirements, and
- number of errors and error rates, which in some circumstances are categorised.

Möller and Paulish developed a simple performance indicator system for software projects [12].

Performance assessment framework

The problem of the absence of a valid performance indicator system for all project types was recently solved by George [13] who designed a performance assessment framework that can be adapted to a specific type of project.

7.1.4 Customer survey

The trend of increasing customer orientation makes it essential to survey this stakeholder group. The following questionnaire [14] was developed for this purpose:

SURVEY OF CUSTOMER SATISFACTION WITH THE PROJECT								
1. In what way were you involved in the project?								
...								
2. How satisfied were you with the project start-up, the definition of objectives and the project plans?								
☺	1	2	3	4	5	6	☹	
Notes								
3. How satisfied were you with the distribution of tasks and competencies, and with the information flow?								
☺	1	2	3	4	5	6	☹	
Notes								
4. How satisfied were you with the project team's performance and work methods?								
☺	1	2	3	4	5	6	☹	
Notes								
5. How satisfied were you with the support that you received from the project management team?								
☺	1	2	3	4	5	6	☹	
Notes								
6. To what extent were the interim/project objectives achieved?								
☺	1	2	3	4	5	6	☹	
Notes								
7. What is your appraisal of the project with regard to time expenditure, costs and the attained or expected result?								
☺	1	2	3	4	5	6	☹	
Notes								
8. What improvements should be made when future projects are implemented?								
...								

Figure C10-1 Questionnaire for a customer satisfaction survey

In practice, it is not always easy to establish who precisely should be surveyed. In a project to install standard user software in an organisation, the customer could be the end users, the IT department or the organisation´s senior manager who commissioned the project. In cases of doubt, it is therefore advisable to survey the satisfaction of several target groups.

Identification of customers

7.2 Project analysis on the relationship level

On the relationship level, the following methods can be used.

7.2.1 Questionnaire

The questionnaire developed by Streich and Marquardt [15] is meant just for the relationship level. It can be used during the project to encourage the team to consider their approach to teamwork.

Questions on the relationship level

C10 PROJECT CLOSE-OUT AND PROJECT LEARNING

CLIMATE IN THE PROJECT TEAM

Please assess the characteristics of your team using the following six-point scale. It is important to provide an honest opinion. Circle the number that best reflects your evaluation.

Openness

Were the members of the team open with one another? Were there secret agreements? Were there any taboo issues for the team? Could team members express themselves openly about others, without wounding?

| The members were open with one another | | | | | | | The members were very cautious |

☺ 1   2   3   4   5   6 ☹

Conformity

Did the team use methods, rituals, dogmas and traditions that hampered their working effectively? Were the opinions of older members taken as law? Were team members freely able to express dissenting or unpopular opinions?

Liberal team, flexible behaviour patterns — Rigid conformity, inflexible behaviour patterns

☺ 1   2   3   4   5   6 ☹

Loyalty

Did the team members all pull together? What happened when one member made a mistake? Did the stronger members look after the ones who had less experience or were less efficient?

High degree of loyalty — Little mutual support in the team

☺ 1   2   3   4   5   6 ☹

Dealing with difficulties

Were difficult or uncomfortable issues discussed? Were conflicts resolved openly or swept under the carpet? Were the members able to express differing opinions with their superiors? Did the group make an effort to resolve problems completely?

Problems were tackled openly and directly — Difficult issues were avoided

☺ 1   2   3   4   5   6 ☹

Willingness to take risks

Did the members feel that they were able to experiment and that they could afford to make mistakes with repercussion? Were individuals encouraged by the team to use their abilities to the full?

It is taken for granted that team members will experiment and check their own work — Willingness to take risks at work was not sought

☺ 1   2   3   4   5   6 ☹

Common values

Did the team members discuss their personal values with each other? Were they aware of both the causes (why?) and the effects (what?)? Did the team have common basic values that the members felt obliged to uphold?

General consensus on values — No common basic values

☺ 1   2   3   4   5   6 ☹

Motivation

Did the team members work hard enough to deepen their relationships with other team members? Was being part of the team stimulating and motivating for the individual members?

The members cared for their team — The members neglected their team

☺ 1   2   3   4   5   6 ☹

Figure C10-2 Questionnaire on the project team climate

7.2.2 Feedback interviews

Feedback interviews between the project manager and his team are a source of information that does not appear in official reports (e.g. about team conflicts). One-to-one interviews are generally more advantageous than group discussions because employees are more likely to express their criticisms and ideas when alone than if other people are present. The disadvantage is that they are time-consuming and management-intensive. The project manager should also hold feedback meetings with the next management level (e.g. the person responsible for project learning in the organisation, a senior manager) to enable the systematic processing and use of experience from the project (e.g. for training junior project managers). The meetings also provide senior management with information about, for instance, which project manager is suitable as a mentor in other projects.

Unofficial advice

One-to-one interviews / group discussions

7.3 Project analysis on the objective and relationship levels

Recently, a whole host of tools for post-project analysis have been developed. Most of them are not specifically designed for one or other of the objective and the relationship levels. They are generally used to analyse both levels.

7.3.1 Project Excellence Model

One of the most informative methods of assessing a concluded project is the Project Excellence Model (→ Chapter C8) [16] developed by the German Association for Project Management (GPM) and based on the concept of Total Quality Management (→ Chapter C8). Using this model, a project can either be assessed by the participants themselves or by external assessors. The results are more objective if independent assessors are used. Since an analysis using the Project Excellence Model is time-consuming, proper planning is essential.

Self- / external assessment

7.3.2 Project personnel questionnaires

The questionnaires are fast and simple to implement. They can be used for analyses at both objective and relationship level. Often, one questionnaire is used to survey both levels. They can be used to survey
- project team members,
- departments involved in the project,
- suppliers or sub-contractors,
- customer representatives,
- potential users or
- other stakeholders.

Target groups

A standardised questionnaire or an interview guideline, that the interviewer uses to question the stakeholders, are commonly used methods. The questionnaire's advantage is that it enables a comparison of different projects. The final project workshop provides a good opportunity for its use. Informal one-to-one interviews allow the interviewer to obtain additional information that a questionnaire cannot collect; ambiguous statements by interviewees can be clarified and they can be prompted if they are obviously withholding information.

Standard questionnaire

Interviews

7.3.3 Project experience databases

The development of project experience databases is even more complex than the construction of project performance indicator systems. These databases are suitable for analysing a project on the relationship level and provide a clearly structured overview of experience gained in earlier projects.

7.4 Process and document-based methods

Schindler and Eppler [17] describe several other methods of project learning. They differentiate between process-based and documentation-based methods.

7.4.1 Process-based methods

Process-based methods record and evaluate the individual processing stages and their order of implementation in the project. Project reviews and audits (→ Chapter C8) are also process-based methods. Post-project appraisals and after action reviews are special variations on these methods, and there are also further variations on these latter two methods.

7.4.1.1 Post-project appraisal
Large organisations such as British Petroleum (BP) use the post-project appraisal method. A special post-project appraisal unit is established to evaluate large-scale projects two years after their conclusion – and the appraisal covers the period from development of the project concept to the time of the assessment. This time interval makes it possible to record project results that do not become evident until after the conclusion of the project. To ensure maximum objectivity, the team of assessors is not involved in the project. Interviews supplement the analyses. A board of assessors then approves the report. All reports are centrally archived as case examples and distributed to the organisation's personnel in the form of manuals, which are regularly updated.

Late identification of project results

7.4.1.2 After action review
The after action review was developed by the US armed forces for military action because this has to be assessed while in progress or immediately afterwards. It enables very fast learning from mistakes and achievements. It can take different forms, from a 20-minute brainstorming session to a discussion lasting several hours. The team has to answer four questions:

Quick assessment

Four questions

1. What was planned?
2. What actually happened?
3. What deviations occurred?
4. What can we learn from this experience?

Companies use this method when fast action is necessary.

7.4.2 Document-based methods

Document-based methods structure the learning content and process it so that it can be archived and promptly made available to interested parties. Examples include the RECALL system, learning histories and micro articles.

7.4.2.1 RECALL
The RECALL method is based on a database that enables project personnel to update their experiences via a web browser. It is part of a NASA project learning programme to simplify and automate the recording of, and access to, experiences. A checklist with questions helps to ensure that the user only inputs relevant information. When he has finished, he is required to answer several more context-related questions.

Input via browser

7.4.2.2 Project learning histories
Project learning histories were developed by the Sloan School of Management at the Massachusetts Institute of Technology (MIT). The author lists the most important events in a project relating to the `human factor´ (e.g. problems in the team) in chronological order. These histories should have a `thread´, like a story. Anonymous direct quotes that only state the person´s function (e.g. member of the R&D team) provide information from the project team member´s perspective in a specific context and offer an advantage compared with keyword-based systems.

The human factor

A learning history is tabulated and divided into several columns. The author enters the interview excerpts in the right-hand column and puts comments as well as additional information in the left-hand column. This makes it possible to put the quotes in context (e.g. a dispute has been going on between employee A and the project manager for several years). There is also a column for details about the project, such as the relevant project phase. The learning history is verified by interviewing the persons involved. It can be used, for example, in workshops.

7.4.2.3 Micro articles
A micro article (based on Willke´s idea) is a text of at most one A4 page written in simple, everyday language that is prepared by each project team member after the conclusion of the project. It is not a literary masterpiece, but merely serves to document project experiences in the most authentic way possible. It offers an advantage compared with keyword-based documentation methods because readers who were not involved in the project find it easier to understand the context. A micro article consists of a heading, a summary, a short breakdown and continuous text. Illustrations and references to other micro articles are also useful and help position the article in a broader context.

Authentic documentation

Self-assessment questions for each certification level

No.	Question	Level				Self-assessment
		D	C	B	A	
C10.1	When does a project actually conclude?	2	2	3	4	☐
C10.2	What tasks have to be performed at the end of the project?	2	3	3	4	☐
C10.3	What issues should be discussed at a project closure meeting?	2	3	3	4	☐
C10.4	What content should be included in the final report?	2	3	3	4	☐
C10.5	Which project learning recommendations should be implemented?	2	3	3	4	☐
C10.6	Which methods of project analysis support project learning?	2	3	3	4	☐
C10.7	Which processes and document-based methods support project learning?	2	3	3	4	☐

C11 IT SUPPORT

In what areas of project management are software tools useful (ICB Element 29)? What are their limitations? Which software should we buy? These are typical questions project managers have to answer. This chapter details the arguments for and against the use of software tools, depending on the purpose for which they are being used, and explains why software is not a blanket solution for the introduction of a project management system. The project manager should be aware of the software categories that exist and how to select the appropriate tools from the increasingly differentiated and confusing range of software products available in the market. He can do this on the basis of a process model.

1 Development history

The emergence [1] of various network analysis techniques in the late 1950s was associated with the rapid development of software tools for batch processing that performed the laborious and error-prone task of manual scheduling. Soon after, software was also available for resource planning, cost budgeting and cost control on the basis of network diagrams. Since most organisations have several projects on the go at the same time which use the same resources (e.g. personnel with specific qualifications), software was soon designed to plan resource requirements for all projects and any number of planning periods.

Batch processing

Network diagrams

Later, software packages that operated in dialogue mode were developed, rendering complex and time-consuming batch processing unnecessary. Finally, an increasing range of PC-based project management software was developed. Once organisations began to use the software, it quickly gained in popularity. User interfaces became increasingly user-friendly and there was a renaissance in network analysis. For a long time, the only systems that were available in the market were based around routines to compute network diagrams. According to Ahlemann's [2] classification, these are planning-oriented multi-project management systems (= PMMS) with comprehensive functions for time and resource scheduling. Microsoft Project is probably the most widely used software tool in this category. Figure C11-1 shows the basic set-up of this category of project management software [3].

PC programs

PMMS

For many years now, project management software tools have been available to support specific functions such as configuration management and risk analysis. However, the IT industry has not yet delivered on its promise to develop expert tools that support project planners (e.g. for cost budgeting or resource planning).

Functional software

Standard desktop software for text processing, spreadsheets and presentations, as well as database software, can also be used for project management. Spreadsheet programs are suitable for both resource planning and for differentiated bid costing in projects. Database software can be used for documentation and to set up a comprehensive project information system. Users often develop their own software, such as tools for the management of project-related costs, because standard application software is often too inflexible for adaptation to the organisation's needs. Lastly, teachware is also available for computer-based personnel training.

Standard desktop software

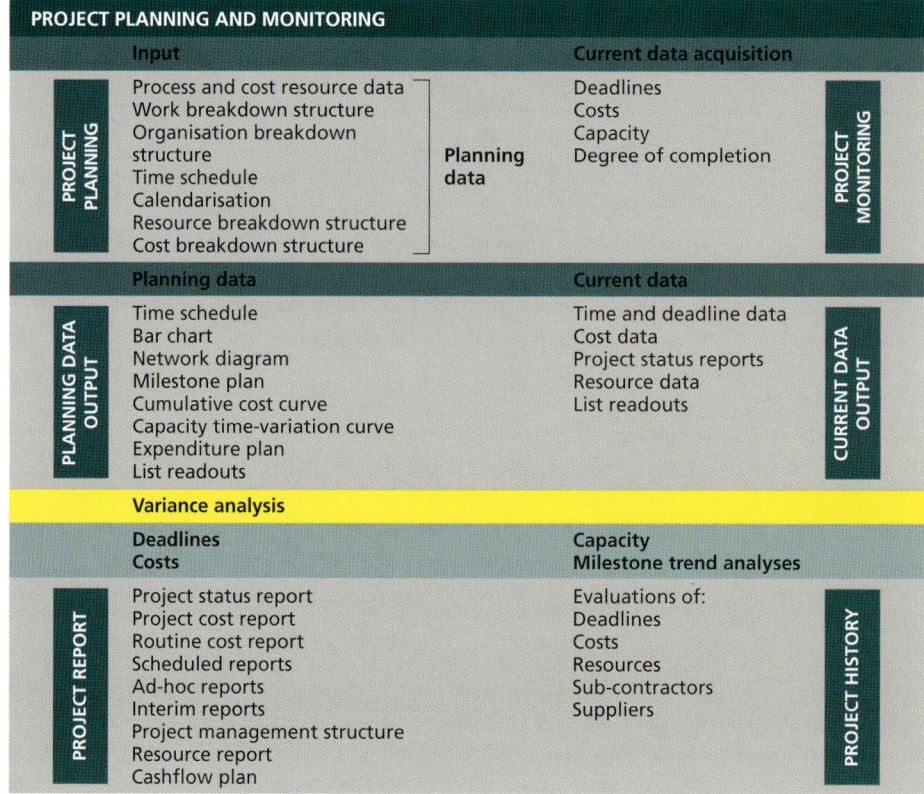

Figure C11-1 Set-up scheme and functions of project management software (planning-oriented multi-project management systems)

2 Trend towards sophisticated software products

Planning-oriented multi-project management systems have dominated the market for many years. Recently, however, the software products available for project management have become more sophisticated.

Software categories Ahlemann differentiates between the following additional categories of software:
- Process-oriented multi-project management systems that focus on quality and process management and, within the framework of largely standardised project management processes, support quality management and workflow.
- Resource-oriented multi-project management systems that focus on resource planning and the administration of a resource pool, the allocation of resources to projects and the control of resource utilisation.
- Global project management systems, such as enterprise project management systems.
- Platforms to support collaboration within the project (project collaboration platforms).

Global PM systems The two latter categories are especially interesting. Global project management systems with a wide array of functions support project management processes throughout the entire project or programme lifecycle - from concept development, through project selection and drafting of the project portfolio to project conclusion.

Platforms are of little use for multi-project management. However, they do enable the collaboration of project teams working at different locations. Many authors currently have high hopes of these software tools because numerous trend forecasts indicate that, in the future, members of project teams will work at different locations and possibly also in different time zones (= virtual teams) [4]. In this situation, face-to-face communication would be time consuming and expensive.

Virtual teams

Schott, Campana and Kuhlmann [5] take Lotus Notes, MS Outlook, Microsoft Office and the Internet as examples of how these platforms can also offer a range of other functions, such as the fast acquisition of project cost data from different locations.

Project cost data

Despite all the optimism based upon existing technology for communication and collaboration, it is necessary to bear Graf and Jordan´s [6] comments in mind: `On the basis of past experience relating to the quality and performance of virtual project teams, it must be assumed that – despite advanced communication technology – personal contact between team members is an essential prerequisite for team efficiency and excellence. The members of virtual teams who are divided by distance need to spend a certain period of time working together at the same location so that they can forge the relationships that are necessary for effective teamwork.´

Personal contact

3 Software purchased as an alibi

Participants in corporate project management seminars are often asked the following question at the outset: `Do you have a documented concept for the planning and development of projects that is tailored to the requirements of your organisation?´ Often, the answer is, `Yes, we use XYZ project management software.´ After further questioning, it turns out that the organisation actually has installed the software. However, in many cases it has not been used once the initial euphoria wore off. Heed should therefore be given to the warning that purchasing software without having a comprehensive project management concept which is tailored to the requirements of the organisation is simply a waste of money.

Many organisations purchase project management software without analysing the organisation-specific requirements that the software package has to meet. They are deceived into thinking that in buying a software package and manual, they have introduced a project management system. Software retailers are happy to reinforce this belief in the hope of making a quick sale. The following claim appeared in an advertisement for a well-known – and perfectly efficient – software package and expresses the typical expectations that developers have of project management software: `Now, at last, you can retain an overview of your projects. You´ll know what, when and where things are happening. You´ll be able to control every aspect of your project.´

Analysis of requirements

Misleading claims

The advertising copywriters have deliberately omitted to mention that this claim is only true if a series of prerequisites are met. For example, the organisation must have clearly-defined and generally-accepted rules governing when specific employees have to report project planning and monitoring data to the project manager.

4 Software – yes or no?

It is difficult to provide a definitive answer to the question of whether software is necessary for successful project management. Scheuring [7], who is also a project management software developer, says, `The development departments of vehicle manufacturing companies would be lost without tool support. And medium-sized engineering firms whose commercial success depends almost exclusively on customer orders for solid waste incineration and sewage treatment plants would be ``flying blind´´ without transparent and timely control data relating to all projects. Sales departments at retail organisations that occasionally implement small-scale organisation projects are at the other end of the scale. These departments can easily control the projects without the assistance of software tools.´

Organisation size and number of projects

In other words, whether and to what extent project management software is necessary depends to a great extent on the scale and number of projects that the organisation is implementing. The necessity of IT-support in many project management tasks, such as risk management, is debateable.

4.1 Realistic assessment of benefits

The significance of software for successful project management is aptly expressed by the US saying, `A fool with a tool is still a fool.´ A survey of 23 experts in eleven countries on the subject of future project management practices [8] revealed that the majority of project management experts attribute low significance to software tools as an aspect of project management in the future, and they do not believe them to be absolutely essential.

Low weighting at IPMA/PMI

This low significance is also reflected in the two standard publications of the International Project Management Association (IPMA) and the Project Management Institute of America (PMI). The IPMA´s International Competence Baseline only devotes one sentence to the subject and the PMI´s Guide to the Project Management Body of Knowledge 2000 Edition does not mention it at all. This is not to give readers the impression that the use of software is unnecessary but to prevent them from according it too high a priority.

4.2 The advantages of IT in project management

Avoiding mistakes

In many circumstances, project management software can provide considerable advantages. For example, the manual preparation of network diagrams and calculation of relative deadlines and calendar dates are extremely painstaking tasks. Even network analysis experts often make mistakes in the process.

Output options

Another argument in favour of using IT tools is that the input data and the data computed by the program can easily be printed out in many different formats as graphs and charts. Most can also provide summarised reports for the various management levels and enable the recipient-oriented selection of data without any problem. Also, the obligatory use of project management software ensures some degree of standardisation of the organisation´s project management processes. Systematically archived data relating to concluded projects can also be useful for planning new projects (→ Chapter C10).

5 Selection

Establishing the most suitable software for an organisation is just as difficult as establishing the best car to suit an individual's needs. It is only possible to find an answer if the organisation has a precise knowledge of the customer's requirements for the project.

Defining customer requirements

Although the range of software available two decades ago was not particularly extensive, it is now difficult even for an expert to retain an overview. Ahlemann analysed 45 products in a survey and provided brief profiles for an additional eight tools. He also listed providers of around 140 other software packages. A database developed by the GPM's Project Management Software team, together with the Institute for Project Management and Innovation at the University of Bremen, contains detailed information about some 120 software packages. Most programs are regularly upgraded, and the range of software available continues to grow.

GPM database

Rather than being helpful in the selection of suitable software, the numerous product comparisons in trade journals and other publications tend to be confusing. Potential buyers often have to sift through catalogue comparisons that include more than 600 criteria. Many of the comparisons overrate program features that are of no practical use. For example, it is irrelevant to the user whether an activity in the network diagram can be allocated to ten, 20 or 30 resource types if it can be assumed – as Scheuring says – that process-oriented resource planning is ineffective (→ Chapter C6).

Unnecessary functions

The option of selecting a different calendar for each process is also irrelevant. Ahlemann therefore took a different approach in his survey. He dispensed with extensive feature lists and used broadly-defined criteria. For example, when analysing network analysis functions, he asked – in simplified terms – whether only standard sequences are possible or whether all four types of precedence relationship (→ Chapter C5) with time weighting are supported.

5.1 Software selection process model

Ahlemann designed the following process model for software selection [9].

1. **Development of a project management concept**
   Initially, the customer must provide the project manager with a concept that is tailored to his organisation's needs and accepted by the key stakeholders. It is only possible to establish software requirements if the project management processes are specified in detail.

   Defining processes

2. **Decision about IT support**
   When the processes have been defined, it is possible to ascertain which processes require IT support. This should be a joint decision involving the most important potential users, such as project manager, project controller, members of the steering committee (e.g. in workshops).

   User workshops

3. **Documentation of requirements**
   When the requirements have been defined, they have to be documented. The documentation should contain the following information.
   - A prioritised list of the necessary features
   - Examples of important evaluations that the tool should be capable of performing.
   - Examples of specific processes and project data.
   - Requirements of services from the provider (e.g. implementation and training support).

4. Initial selection
The initial selection should not include more than ten to 15 providers.

5. Shortlist
When the initial selection has been made, the number of providers should be reduced to a maximum of five. Relatively generalised catalogues of criteria, such as those provided by Ahlemann or the GPM-IPMA working group, make it easier to match the available features with the functions contained in the lists described in Step 3.

6. Presentation
The selected providers are requested to provide product presentations.

7. Selection of the best two systems
After the product presentations, the customer selects the two systems that best reflect his needs for an acceptance test. Ahlemann omits to mention another criterion, in addition to the system features, which should be taken into consideration: will the provider be able to provide maintenance and upgrades in respect of the delivered version in the future? In the past, a whole host of relatively small software developers offered good products. However, despite the high quality of their products, the companies soon disappeared from the market.

Future-proofing

8. Acceptance test with key users
The acceptance test further reduces the procurement risk and promotes acceptance among end-users.

9. Preliminary decision
When the findings of the user test have been evaluated, the customer selects the best provider.

10. Test installation
The software that the customer has chosen is now installed in test mode. Test mode operation enables him to check whether the program can cope with the required volume of data and how stable it is in regular operation.

Test mode

11. Final decision
After the test run, the customer makes the final decision.

Self-assessment questions for each certification level

No.	Question	Level D	Level C	Level B	Level A	Self-assessment
C11.1	Which categories of software exist for IT support in project management?	2	3	4	4	☐
C11.2	What should the organisation take into consideration when purchasing PM software?	2	2	3	4	☐

BLOCK D

PEOPLE IN PROJECTS

D1 PROJECT MANAGER

The project manager plays a key role in the project (ICB Chapter C) and is responsible for its success (or failure). He is a contact point, the project´s spokesman and team leader. This chapter provides information about the project manager´s functions and the expectations that he has to meet. It explains the challenges associated with his work – extending from the different perspectives from which the project participants view the project manager´s role to a lack of decision-making powers. The selection and assessment procedures used for the recruitment of project managers are also detailed. This chapter also aims to provide an awareness of possible solutions to problems associated with project manager recruitment.

1 Significance

Problematic projects, such as Toll Collect in Germany, show that even organisations highly-experienced in project management principles can also make mistakes. These can occur for many reasons. For example, the project manager may lack management skills, be under-qualified, unable to express the project´s requirements or overcome opposition to them if necessary. The ICB [1] warns that, `It is the project manager´s ability to bring together the project participants and contributors and connect them into an effective project organisation that will achieve the project´s objectives.´

The project manager is `the person responsible for managing the project´. The project management team is `an organisational unit that is established for the duration of a project [...] which is responsible for the planning, control and monitoring of the project´ [2].

This organisational unit consists of staff who perform a management function in the project. Thus, sub-project or technical project managers and project coordinators are also members of the project management team. Often, the customer sets up parallel project organisation structures, which means that there are two project managers in the project – the contractor´s project manager and the customer´s project manager. These structures enable horizontal communication below project management level (e.g. from project office to project office, or sub-project manager to sub-project manager), which reduces the project manager´s workload.

Parallel project organisation structures

Large-scale projects sometimes also have a technical and a commercial project manager. Some organisations will artificially sub-divide a project into marketing, development and production projects. They do this to disguise the fact that these projects are still part of the line management structure and that they don´t actually want to have integrated project management structures.

Sub-division of large-scale projects

1.1 Problematic role

Hansel believes that one of the most problematic aspects of project work [3] is the misunderstandings and conflicts that arise as a result of different perceptions of the project manager´s role. `This is evident by the job title of the person responsible for a project. Although many managers are not or only partially aware of it, there are considerable differences between the roles of project leader, project coordinator and project manager. People generally use these designations without really thinking about them. However, they each express a specific understanding of the project manager´s role.´

Different job descriptions

Different perceptions of roles

Hansel also believes that problems occur when the project participants´ perceptions of the project manager´s role differ. For example, the project manager feels that, as a manager, he has a certain degree of authority and decision-making power. However, the customer merely views him as the person responsible for the project with very limited authority to make decisions. The team members would prefer to accept him only as the project coordinator, i.e. the project `butler´. `If these different perceptions clash, conflicts and frustration are inevitable.´

1.2 Ambivalent attitudes of line managers

Lack of competence and support

Line managers [4] often have a very ambivalent attitude towards the role of the project manager. On the one hand, they believe that project managers are capable of assuming a great deal of responsibility, and transfer this responsibility by placing them in charge of projects that are worth millions of euros. On the other hand, the lack of interest that some organisations show in the selection and qualifications of their project managers demonstrates that they do not yet take this function seriously enough. `If the project manager is not provided with adequate training and support, particular personal traits of the project manager will surface´, said Hansel (→ Chapter A6). Owing to a lack of knowledge about management styles and techniques, the project manager attempts to guide and influence the members of his team without giving the matter adequate thought. `The project manager and his team are often unable to cope as a result because the stress associated with most projects demand professional management practices, i.e. a conscious and well thought-out approach to management.´

2 Problems and solutions associated with project manager recruitment

At some organisations, the project manager´s job carries less weight than that of a line manager. It is very difficult to find good project managers in such organisations.

Unrealistic requirements profiles

Most job advertisements are based on the following ideal profile for a project manager: middle-aged (35 to 45 years), several years of professional experience (e.g. as engineer, business economist), special knowledge of the project field, fluent English, business acumen. Further criteria are social competence and management experience. This profile is based on the assumption that the ideal candidate of this age is likely to have acquired professional experience and wisdom, yet still be flexible, adaptive and mobile.

Lack of choice

However, project managers in many organisations come nowhere close to matching this profile. Often, senior management has to select a project manager from its pool of internal staff when a project is set up. In many cases, they have no choice. Anyone who is familiar with the project field or is not busy at the time will be assigned to the next project. Although experience in similar projects is desirable, it is a requirement that is often ignored owing to personnel shortages. Small and medium-sized enterprises often have only a few members of staff with the aptitude to be project managers. Temporary, external project managers would offer them an alternative. However, instead of buying in external expertise, they often say, `We can do it ourselves´ for cost-related reasons. Since these organisations have such a shortage of qualified project managers, they do not need tools such as requirements profiles or selection criteria [5].

2.1 External versus internal recruitment

Hiring external project managers is often not an option because execution of the project demands extensive knowledge of the organisation and its products. For example, the development of the next generation of medical diagnostics equipment can only be managed by a member of the organisation´s staff.

In contrast to the external recruitment of project managers, personnel managers who recruit project managers from the company´s own ranks often lack the authority, experience, tools and insight to identify suitable candidates. Instead, line managers simply assign members of staff as project managers. In large-scale organisations, however, project management certificates (→ Chapter D3) are often a requirement.

Assignment instead of selection

2.2 In-house training for project managers

Ideally, the organisation implements intensive and systematic training programmes for junior project managers to make up for the lack of qualified staff. Long-term career planning has proven to be effective. It could include the following stages:
1. Entry as a working student in the engineering department
2. Involvement in a project within the framework of the engineering job
3. Assignment to a sub-project as technical manager
4. Sub-project manager
5. Project manager

Career stages

2.3 Overweighting of professional qualifications

In many cases, the job of project manager goes to the person who is most highly qualified, while no assessment is made to ascertain whether he possesses the required managerial skills [6]. This can cause several problems according to Sackmann. On the one hand, the innovative nature and complexity of some projects makes it difficult to establish which specialist field is `the most important´ one although, admittedly, projects like this are very rare. On the other hand, managers with professional qualifications tend to focus on professional contributions and do not pay enough attention to the management tasks. This results in an overloading of the project manager, who feels that the project team members are `disturbing´ his real work.

Sackmann suggests the following rule of thumb [7] for this situation. The significance of a project manager´s management experience and skills increases more or less proportionately to the size of a project and the project team. The more lengthy and complex a project is, and the more project team members and material resources it requires, the more important the project manager´s management functions are compared with the functions relating to his area of expertise.

Rule of thumb for technical / management tasks

3 Tasks

The project manager is responsible for ensuring that project objectives are attained. In other words, he has to make sure that deadlines are met and that costs do not exceed the budget while meeting the customer´s specifications (e.g. product quality). This central task is associated with numerous subordinate tasks (→ Chapter A6). In order to complete these, the project manager has to be familiar with the project management methods, procedures and tools that are customary in his organisation (e.g. cost budgeting, conflict resolution). He should also be aware of his organisation´s management policies (e.g. general management, process management, quality management).

Competence in using management techniques

A project manager should be capable of
- managing the project,
- leading his team and
- acting as a contact point for stakeholders (e.g. the customer, senior management, suppliers).

Tasks

Here is a list of typical tasks, which may vary from company to company (→ Chapter A6):
1. Establishment of project organisation structures
2. Contribution to the definition of the project
3. Management of the objective definition process
4. Coordination of project processes
5. Monitoring of project progress (quality, time, costs) (possibly with the assistance of the project controller)
6. Timely identification of possible schedule deviations and implementation of counter-measures
7. Verification and coordination of changes and their incorporation in project schedules
8. Management of communication structures
9. Conflict management
10. Coordination of reports
11. Representation of the project internally and externally
12. Team development
13. Contract management and negotiations
14. Purchasing and logistics, including supplier management
15. Financial management
16. Staff management (technical and where required – in specific areas or in the project as a whole – disciplinary)
17. Risk and opportunity management
18. Customer and partner management
19. Business development in the current project
20. Relationship management and corporate networking

Integration in the organisation

The project manager´s integration in the organisation can depend on the company (→ Chapter A6). This influences the extent of his responsibility and the scope of his decision-making powers, as well as the degree of support he receives. A project office or project management office (→ Chapter E3) can take on many of the project manager´s tasks (e.g. documentation, organisation).

4 Requirements

The requirements on a project manager are in many respects more complex than those on a line manager. Although he requires a minimum level of technical competence (object-related knowledge, i.e. knowledge of the project deliverable), excessive specialist knowledge can be a disadvantage. However, in smaller projects, such as IT projects, the project manager has to perform many technical functions. For example, the chief programmer concept – a special type of organisation structure – assigns him a great many technical tasks.

Weighting of specialist knowledge

A basic grasp of business management – and contract management in some project types – as well as knowledge of essential work methods are indispensable. Social competence is also important. These days, the ability to use key planning tools is no longer a guarantee of successful project management. A project manager needs to demonstrate technical, methodical, organisational and social competence. Sceptics ask whether social competence can be acquired or whether the sentence taken from Goethe´s Faust applies: `Unless you feel, naught will you ever gain.´ The International Project Management Association believes that critical reflection, feedback and consistent learning will enable the successful development of social competence. This is reflected in the project manager certification programme. However, others believe that that you are either born with social competence – or not.

Four competence areas

In recent years, the opinion has become widespread that a good construction engineer, biologist or advertising professional will not necessarily make a competent project manager. In practice, however, social competence is not accorded due significance as a project manager selection criterion. The ICB [8] quite rightly warns that, `Much emphasis is placed on tools and techniques in managing projects and with the growth of the information technology there has been a great amount of development work on sophisticated scheduling and control systems. [...] However, one must not forget that projects involve people.´

Significance of social competence

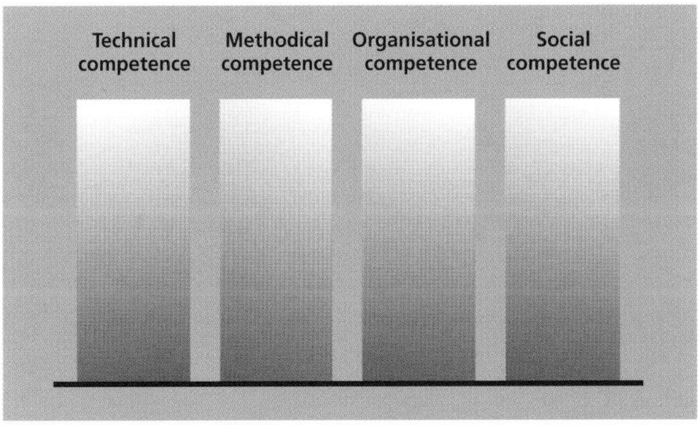

Figure D1-1 The competences required of a project manager

Project management literature provides various requirement checklists according to sector and project type [9]. On the whole, the project manager requires the following:
1. The ability to develop and follow a vision
2. Professional experience/wisdom
3. Determination
4. Motivation
5. An independent approach and business acumen
6. The courage to take calculated risks
7. Strategic, forward-looking thoughts and actions
8. Adaptability (learning from mistakes and achievements, learning from others)
9. Analytical skills (e.g. the ability to understand the complex interrelationships of costs and finances)
10. Critical faculty (including self-criticism)

General requirements

11. Ability to set and adhere to priorities
12. Teamwork skills
13. Management skills (e.g. ability to delegate, ability to make decisions)
14. Authority
15. Integral thinking (project-wide, organisation-wide)
16. Customer orientation

Personnel experts emphasise, however, that these lists of ideal skills are often unrealistic and should only be used as a guideline for HR development measures.

Behaviour in complex situations

Although the formulation of objectives, taking all stakeholders into consideration, and an integrated project planning concept make an important contribution to the success of a project, project managers will always have to deal with unforeseen and complex situations. In order to do this, they have to take an integral and networked approach and have the ability to motivate and `oil the wheels´ of an interdisciplinary team. Strictly speaking, these skills are required at a much earlier stage of the project, for example, when the objectives are being defined.

4.1 Important personal skills and traits

Role model function

The ICB [10] lists the important personal skills and traits that project management personnel should have. Although they apply basically to all project team members, these apply in particular to the project manager who acts as a role model for his staff based on his personal conduct. The ICB lists the skills under the following headings:

- Ability to communicate
- Initiative, engagement, enthusiasm, ability to motivate
- Ability to come into contact, openness
- Sensitivity, self-control, ability to value appreciation, readiness for responsibility, personal integrity
- Conflict solving, argumentation culture, fairness
- Ability to find solutions, holistic thinking
- Loyalty, solidarity, readiness to help
- Leadership abilities (→ Chapter D3)

4.1.1 Practical problems

Measurability

The challenge with using these behavioural traits is to find a way to make these very subjective characteristics measurable. To do this, each one must be described in detail.

Example
Openness means: the person, for example,
- *has a positive basic attitude,*
- *views new things as interesting and a challenge,*
- *builds up trust,*
- *assumes good intentions, and*
- *takes the initiative in approaching others.*

This definition of `openness` is probably insufficient. In this case, an iterative process is necessary to approach the ideal definition. In this example, the term `positive basic attitude´ would need an iterative process of its own.

4.2 Conduct and appearance

Most projects include dealing with people. The project manager deals with customers, the organisation´s senior management, business associates, media representatives and many other stakeholders. He therefore needs good social skills and an agreeable, well-groomed appearance. The objective is to communicate a positive external image for the project and for the project manager to be perceived by others as a discussion or negotiation partner of equal standing who can be taken seriously.

Conduct and appearance

4.3 Management potential

Wildemann identifies three factors which can be used to differentiate between managers who have the potential to succeed and those who are less likely to be successful [11]:
- Disposition (= personality structure of the potential manager)
- Management competence (= broadest and most flexible possible repertoire of skills)
- Career stoppers (= career-damaging behaviour traits)

Potential factors

At this point, it is necessary to highlight the aspect of career stoppers because they constitute a high risk for the people involved. Depending how firmly the person is integrated in the management structure, they can lead to career problems. The more developed these behaviours are, the larger they are in number, and the lower the degree of integration of a person in a department or organisation, the more his career will be jeopardised.

Spin-out tendency

> **Examples of career stoppers**
> *The manager*
> - accords low significance to the personal qualities of staff when selecting team members or putting together his team
> - is diffident or arrogant towards other people
> - doesn´t believe that his team is motivated to perform well
> - gives up too easily, is impatient or has no staying power.

To have management potential means
- to deal successfully with new, complex situations and
- to have the talent and ability to understand the complexities of social systems and identify crucial levers.

Management potential

The development of potential is therefore influenced to a great extent by the frequency and intensity of challenges that a manager encounters in the first phase of his career.

This potential can be defined in terms of five agilities:
1. Mental (ability to deal with complex issues and situations)
2. Personal (confidence in own abilities and interest in hearing feedback, support and encouragement of the success of others)

Behaviour traits of high-potential managers

3. Learning (learning from others)
4. Change (seeking new approaches, experimentation, a dynamic approach to progress)
5. Communication (ability to communicate in the right way with the right people)

Managers without high potential

People who do not show high potential can also develop management skills, although on a much smaller scale. They are efficient in their specialist field, but cannot cope with wider-reaching or entirely new situations in their work.

5 Necessary authority

Senior management responsibility

The formal (decision-making) powers (→ Chapter A6) that are officially accorded to a project manager have proven to be a crucial factor of success. As customer and the highest instance responsible for the project´s success, senior management transfers formal powers to the project manager, whose influence on the constitution of the project team is an organisational prerequisite for the success of project work [12].

Team set-up

Project managers do not always have the opportunity to influence how their project team is put together. Often, staff are simply assigned to their projects. A project is far more likely to be successful if senior management furnishes the project manager with greater authority in this area. A project manager with strong formal authority is important for the success of the project [13]. Organisations should give greater consideration to this fact (→ Chapter A6) [14].

The project manager should have the authority to influence information and communication processes, planning and control activities, conflicts and changes to objectives. The informal authority accorded by the project manager also helps to ensure that the project progresses. According to Lechler, `If, in addition to formal decision-making powers and the authority to issue instructions, the project manager´s technical, administrative, social and leadership skills are taken into account, he will probably have more and, on the whole, stronger influence.´

6 Selection

It is relatively easy to describe the attributes and skills that a project manager needs: how do we find a suitable person for the job? Each candidate differs in terms of his career profile and his current life and work situation, and therefore also in terms of his ability to satisfy project objectives and additional expectations [15].

Certified project managers

Organisations with access to certified project managers have an advantage. In the certification process (→ Chapter D3) the candidates are required to demonstrate both their knowledge of and experience in project management. These are assessed on the basis of concluded or well-advanced projects in which they have been involved or held a management position. A candidate who merely has experience of using certain procedures, methods or software is not eligible for certification.

D1 PROJECT MANAGER

6.1 Requirements profile

Personnel recruitment means advertising for, assessing, selecting and – if approved – hiring staff. Job advertisements are central sources of information, as are the job profiles that are based on these advertisements which specify the type and scope (= complexity) of requirements [16]. These can be created in the form of a matrix (Figure D1-2, simplified, model profile). The HR manager matches the requirements profile with the candidate's skills profile [17].

Type/scope of requirements

Skills profile

If the candidate's skills are too advanced for some of the requirement types, he is overqualified and is better suited to a more demanding position. If the candidate's skills fall short of the requirements profile, further training measures will ensure that the requirements and skills profiles match. However, the requirement types and their level must be matched with particular activities (= operationalisation), otherwise they have only low informative value. The matrix is therefore highly individual and subjective, depending on the requirements of the position to be filled, the candidate, the responsible personnel manager, the company and other factors. To ensure that the recruiter can retain an overview, it should not include too many criteria. One option is to involve all the project participants who will be working with the project manager in the creation of the requirements profile. If they are involved in this process, they are more likely to accept the project manager. However, the disadvantage is that too many opinions may lead to an inflated, diluted result, true to the Dublin proverb: `A camel is a horse designed by a committee.´

Over or under-qualification

Individual requirements matrix

As in Figure D1-2, the person who must select a project manager can list and weight the requirements he believes to be important. This table can then be used as a decision-making aid when selecting the most appropriate candidate. In the example shown, Candidate B has more advanced project management skills, social competence and management abilities than Candidate A. Since the recruiter believes that these aspects are especially important, he selects Candidate B.

CANDIDATE SKILLS – POINTS-BASED EVALUATION						
	Candidate A			Candidate B		
Requirement	1	2	3	1	2	3
Project management competence	X					X
Technical competence			X	X		
General social competence	X					X
Management skills	X				X	
Strategic approach		X			X	
Performance orientation			X		X	
1 Poor 2 Average 3 Very good						

Figure D1-2 Requirements profile for the selection of a project manager

Motzel [18] has developed a table of criteria, shown in Figure D1-3, for the assessment of social skills, suitable for assessing candidates in a certification procedure, based on the ability to make contact.

Social skills assessment criteria

SKILL	+	0	−	OPPOSITE
Builds trust, opens up to other people				Doesn´t communicate with other people, appears inaccessible
Trusts other team members, assumes good intentions				Appears diffident
Takes the initiative in approaching others, is sociable				Waits for others to take the initiative, holds back
Contributes to a pleasant working atmosphere in the team				Causes tension among other team members or in the team
Accepts all team members and is tolerant				Lets others sense his aversions
Accepts the rules for team cooperation				Doesn´t adhere to agreed rules
Tolerates and supports different opinions in the team				Only follows his own convictions, knows everything better
Helps others to be successful				Prevents others from achieving
Accepts and takes minorities into consideration				Orients himself towards the power structures
Tries to fit in with the team				Finds it difficult to adapt to others

Figure D1-3 Social skills assessment criteria based on the example of the ability to make contact (according to Motzel)

6.2 Checklists

Requirements of other project participants

Kessler [19] provides checklists for the selection of a project manager from several internal candidates. They are a decision aid and are designed to take the different functions and perspectives from which other project participants view the project manager into account. For example, customers, multi-project managers, line managers, IT managers, and personnel managers would all prefer to deal with a project manager who caters to their own specific requirements.

Examples
- *The project sponsor wants a project manager who can guarantee that the project will achieve its objectives.*
- *The knowledge manager prefers a candidate who is familiar with and will adhere to the organisation´s own project management standards.*
- *The scientific staff are keen to ensure that their specialist knowledge will be taken into account in the project.*
- *The IT manager wants someone who will use existing IT equipment without making any changes.*
- *The department manager wants to retain his best staff for departmental work.*

7 Assessment

Project-specific decision makers

It is often difficult to assess a project manager´s performance from outside the project. A disciplinary superior (= line manager) generally does not know enough about the activities of those members of his department´s staff who are assigned to a project. Project participants are more aware of what is going on. However, assessments made by project participants have the disadvantage that the assessors may provide a more negative assessment than is necessary owing to rivalry, thus diluting the project manager´s performance. Project decision-makers in the organisation (e.g. steering committee members) are therefore more suitable as assessors.

Staff assessments enable
- decisions on selection (future fields of work, promotion, redundancy etc.),
- the creation of a personal development plan (→ Chapter D3),
- the establishment of salaries and bonus payments,
- the provision of advice to and coaching of staff,
- keeping superiors up–to-date and
- sustaining communication with staff.

Benefits

The assessment covers aspects such as personality traits, achievements and conduct, as well as social and managerial behaviour. Since it is especially difficult to assess behaviour or social competence, standardised, measurable and understandable assessment criteria, which can also be used by an external auditor, must be created and adhered to. This is particularly important if the managers who select project personnel do not know the candidates personally. Otherwise, they will instinctively choose employees whose performance they can themselves assess or who have been recommended to them. As a result, the organisation may fail to identify capable project managers.

External assessment

As part of the PM-Zert [20] certification process (→ Chapter D3), the certification body of the German Association for Project Management (GPM) issues self-assessment sheets (PM Topics Catalogue) that were developed by experienced project managers. The project managers use the self-assessment sheets to evaluate their own knowledge and skills in each of the listed topic areas. These sheets are also suitable for staff assessments since they can be individually adapted by according a higher or lower weighting to specific criteria which are especially important in the project, or omitting insignificant criteria.

Self-assessment sheet

8 Change of project manager

According to the ICB, the project management team can be adapted to the requirements of specific project phases. In other words, the project manager may be changed during the project lifecycle because different phases may demand different skills. In longer projects, some degree of fluctuation is normal because a project manager may leave the company, receive a promotion or leave the project for other reasons. These changes can cause problems if undocumented knowledge results in the loss of valuable contacts – either with the customer or the authorities. Changes should therefore be planned meticulously and discussed well in advance with all relevant stakeholders. Basically, a change of project manager should be avoided if possible, true to the principle of `never change a winning team´.

Problems

Recommendation

D1 PROJECT MANAGER

Self-assessment questions for each certification level

No.	Question	Level D	Level C	Level B	Level A	Self-assessment
D1.1	What skills should a project manager have (requirements profile during the selection process)?	2	2	2	4	☐
D1.2	What requirements must a project manager meet?	2	3	3	4	☐
D1.3	What essential behavioural traits can a project manager be assumed to have?	2	3	3	4	☐
D1.4	How can management potential be recognised?	1	2	2	3	☐
D1.5	What powers and authority should a project manager have?	2	2	2	4	☐

D2 TOOLS FOR THE PROJECT MANAGER

A project manager makes his mark on a project with both his personality and his approach to tackling his tasks. Such tasks (ICB Elements 31 and 32) embrace self-organisation (i.e. time management, setting priorities, the delegation of tasks), decision making, meetings and negotiations. In addition to his project management-specific tasks, he should also be capable of using problem solving, presentation and creativity techniques, and be competent in many other areas. This chapter provides him with specific tools he needs to meet these challenges.

1 Self-organisation

The success of a project is not just dependent on the project manager's personality (→ Chapter D1) but also, to a great extent, on his work style. A successful project manager must be able to keep up to date with his work schedule, ensure that deadlines are adhered to, act professionally, demonstrate decision-making competence and approach his work with the necessary inner calm. `Creative chaos´ is not at all appropriate in the field of project management. Rather, professional (self-)organisation skills are necessary. These include the management of personal resources and also – among other things – the willingness to make an honest evaluation of personal strengths and weaknesses, systematically to define and review objectives, continually to acquire new skills, and the ability to make efficient decisions.

1.1 Management of personal resources

A project manager has both tangible and intangible personal resources [1]. Tangible resources include   *Tangible resources*
   1. Physical constitution
   2. Social environment
   3. Physical fitness
   4. Tools and assets (e.g. money, home, clothing)

The above resources are listed in reverse order of the extent to which they can be changed. The project manager has least influence over his physical constitution, greater influence over his social environment and physical fitness and the most influence over his tools and assets.

Intangible resources include   *Intangible resources*
   1. Time
   2. Personality
   3. Disposition (= the way in which a person presents himself, appearance, stance)
   4. Social competence
   5. Methodical competence
   6. Professional competence

The project manager can also influence these factors to varying degrees. He has least influence over time because it cannot be manipulated (`stopped´ or `turned back´). He can only use the time he has to the best possible advantage by managing it efficiently. By and large, people are born with the personality they have. However, they can work on their disposition and indeed change it. Social competence, on the other hand, can be continually improved – and the best results will be achieved with the assistance of an expert. Compensating for a lack of professional competence should not be a problem, provided that the person in question is willing to make the effort.

1.2 Time management

Cost of inefficient work

Time plays a central role in self-management. Efficient time management not only protects the health of the project manager, it also saves the organisation money because a badly organised member of staff generally works inefficiently. He wastes company time and the associated costs that are generated for the employer are not compensated by services rendered in return. There is a widespread opinion among employees that salaried staff cost the company nothing because `they´re always there anyway´. These hidden costs tend to be regarded as a sort of unavoidable fixed cost.

Success factors

The following three success factors form the basis for efficient time management:
1. Setting priorities
2. The ability to say no
3. The ability to delegate

These skills can be learned and a range of tools enables their effective application.

1.2.1 Priorities

Setting priorities means being able to differentiate between what is essential and what is not. In project management practice, nobody is able to cope with every single task that is theoretically associated with their position. Generally, they only have time to perform absolutely essential tasks. Exaggerated perfectionism tends to get in the way of project work. However, the project manager should have enough experience to be able to decide when a task has been performed thoroughly enough.

Priority-setting matrix: Importance over urgency

Anyone who finds it difficult to set priorities can create a matrix (→ Figure D2-1) and allocate priorities to all tasks per unit of time (e.g. the next day, week or project). It is necessary to ensure that importance takes precedence over urgency. Tasks that are essential for the project´s success should be dealt with before tasks with approaching deadlines which are only designated as urgent for this reason.

> **Example**
> *The manager of a restructuring programme is working on measures which will result in redundancy for many employees. The works council is demanding details so that a redundancy programme can be developed as soon as possible. However, the project manager also has to make a presentation to the managing board about the recruitment of junior managers in a few days time. His decision is obvious: he wants to deliver information to the staff that will be affected by redundancy as soon as possible and prevent the press from finding out about the restructuring measures before the redundancy programme is in place. He therefore accords priority to this task. In contrast, the junior management recruitment programme can wait.*
> *The project manager therefore asks the managing board if he can postpone the date of his presentation.*

TASK	PRIO 1	PRIO 2	PRIO 3
Development of the junior management programme		x	
Complete the restructuring measures	x		
Inform the works council	x		
Elaborate the redundancy programme	x		
Order new photocopiers			x
.....			

Figure D2-1 Priority-setting matrix

1.2.2 Saying no

Many people find it difficult to say no because they fear that, if they do, they will make themselves unpopular with colleagues and superiors. They fail to realise that this ability is critical for their survival. Unless they learn to say no, they will fall prey to burnout syndrome at some time or other. Their body and mind will cease to function effectively and they might even suffer serious physical and psychological damage.

Burnout syndrome

Saying no is not just acceptable, it is a sign of their personal strength. It is important to be polite yet assertive when saying no. Only a brief explanation such as, `I´m afraid I haven´t got time because I have to do X´ is necessary. Ideally, the project manager should suggest an alternative date or colleague to the person who has requested him to perform the additional work.

1.2.3 Delegation

Delegating tasks is not a sign of weakness, but of strong (self-)management and leadership skills. Obviously, people who tend to do everything themselves will on occasions complete the work in less time because they won´t need to provide lengthy explanations or check the work. However, even a well-organised project manager will be unable to cope with the work he has assigned to himself at some point – and the project team members will be frustrated because they feel that he doesn´t trust them to perform the work.

Project managers benefit in many respects from delegation:
- they have more time to perform the tasks that cannot be delegated,
- their team members are motivated and acquire additional skills,
- delegation improves the overall efficiency of the organisational unit (e.g. team, department),
- the sick rate of overworked managers declines, and
- if a manager or knowledge carrier has to take time off work, colleagues can easily perform his work because they are already familiar with it.

Benefits

However, the project manager should not delegate tasks that he cannot cope with himself to colleagues unless they have agreed to perform them because this can result in his team members being just as overworked as he is. The allocation of tasks should therefore be a team activity. The project manager should make it clear to every member of his team that they can refuse additional work without fear of reprisals if they feel that their workload is excessively high. Project managers who delegate tasks that they dislike to subordinate members of staff contradict the principle of fair play.

Saying no without fear of reprisal

Tasks which are suitable for delegation can be identified by supplementing the priority matrix (→ Figure D2-2) with two additional columns.

TASK	PRIO 1	PRIO 2	PRIO 3	DELEGATABLE?	TO WHOM?
Development of the junior management programme			x		
Complete the restructuring measures	x				
Inform the works council		x			
Elaborate the redundancy programme	x				
Order new photocopiers				x	

Figure D2-2 Task delegation matrix

Prerequisites for effective delegation

If the project manager delegates tasks, he must
- provide the member of staff with a precise explanation of the task,
- make clear the purpose and objective of the task,
- ask whether the member of staff has understood everything,
- agree upon a deadline with the member of staff,
- check progress and obtain feedback on agreed dates,
- ensure that the member of staff is aware that he has to deliver status reports (→ Chapter C9) if unscheduled events occur,
- allow the member of staff to incorporate his own methods and ideas when performing the task (the main thing is that the desired outcome is achieved) and
- ensure that the other members of staff are informed that the task has been assigned to this person.

1.2.4 Time inventory

The project manager can use a time inventory [2] to find out how effectively he is really using his time. In most cases, the results of the inventory will deviate from his personal assessment of his time management efficiency. Seiwert [3] suggests the use of a table (→ Figure D2-3):

TIME INVENTORY							
Activity	Start	Finish	Duration	A: Activity necessary?	B: Time required justified?	C: Implementation practical?	D: Point in time practical?
Prepare presentation	9.30	19.30	10 hrs.	Yes	No	No	No
Tidy desk	7.30	9.30	2 hrs.	No	Yes	No	No
Total time required			12 hrs.	Duration of `no´ activities			
				A_{No} = 2 hrs.	B_{No} = 10 hrs.	C_{No} = 12 hrs.	D_{No} = 12 hrs.

Figure D2-3 Time inventory matrix

First, the project manager creates a list of activities to be performed over a realistic period of time (e.g. one week). He then enters `yes´ or `no´ in columns A, B, C, and D of the table shown in Figure D2-3. When this has been done, he calculates the total duration of all activities. He then adds the duration of all activities that have a `no´ entered against them in each of the columns.

The evaluation shown indicates the following: *Evaluation*
1. More than ten percent of all activities (column A) are unnecessary.
    → Changes to the delegation of tasks and setting of priorities should be made!
    Formula: A_{No}/total duration x 100
2. Too much time is required for more than ten percent of activities (column B).
    → Identify the causes!
    Formula: B_{No}/total duration x 100
3. More than ten percent of the activities (column C) are impractical.
    → Review planning and (self-)organisation!
    Formula: C_{No}/total duration x 100
4. More than ten percent of the activities (column D) are performed at an inappropriate time.
    → Change the work schedule!
    Formula: D_{No}/total duration x 100

In each case, the measure that has to be implemented is specified after the arrow. If necessary, simple tables can be used to record the type, causes and duration of problems.

1.2.5 Time scheduling

Seiwert recommends the NERD-F method [4] for time scheduling: *NERD-F method*
- Note down tasks, activities and deadlines.
- Estimate the length (duration) of activities.
- Reserve float time.
- Decide priorities, cutbacks and delegation options.
- Follow-up check (include tasks that were not completed in the next day´s schedule).

1.2.6 Time management tips

The following tips help project managers to effectively manage their working day: *Managing work time*
1. Think first, then act (objective: eliminates the need for `backpeddling´).
2. Set priorities.
3. Take a break, so that you can continue to work productively.
4. Be punctual, so that you can adhere to your appointments schedule.
5. Use a diary with scheduler.
6. Keep your desk tidy so that you can find the information you are looking for quickly.
7. Deal with private matters outside working hours.
8. Start the day early.
9. Complete tasks in small steps instead of thinking about the mountain of tasks ahead of you.
10. Avoid over-researching decisions, so that you can make decisions quickly.
11. Set a time limit for tasks.
12. Plan the next working day the evening before.
13. Allow 40 percent contingency time every day for unforeseeable events and spontaneous activities.
14. Prevent interruptions (e.g. shut the door, divert telephone calls).
15. Create checklists for routine tasks (e.g. preparation of a presentation).

Writing down thoughts

It is generally helpful to write down all the things that one has on one´s mind – pending tasks, solution to a problem, recruiting a new employee or anything else associated with one´s wide range of project responsibilities.

1.3 Definition of objectives

Clarity about objectives

In order to manage personal resources efficiently, it is necessary to be clear about personal objectives. Otherwise, a project manager cannot plan his work autonomously or deal with undesirable developments effectively. The plan-do-check-act principle is not only relevant for project management, but also for self-management. Objectives should be allocated to various timeframes, e.g. a person can have daily, weekly or quarterly objectives, or even a life objective. Setting a life objective is definitely a good idea since it has a strong motivational effect. For example, a life objective could be: `By the age of 60 I want to have retired, be living in Italy and have my own olive grove.´

General advance analysis

To set objectives realistically, a project manager has to consider all aspects of every pending project, and assess the likelihood of these objectives being achieved within the given framework (e.g. whether adequate time and funds exist). Not every project manager is in the cosy position of being able to decide whether or not he will take on a project based on such considerations. Nevertheless, a general pre-project analysis provides a sense of security and a basis for personal time scheduling. It is worthwhile taking the time to make such an analysis because it can prevent unpleasant surprises later in the project (e.g. projects with a schedule that is too tight from the outset).

Control measures when deviations occur

The criteria that apply to project objectives (e.g. clarity, attainability → Chapter C2) also apply to personal objectives. The project manager should also review his personal objectives on a regular basis to check whether they are still practical and what progress he has made towards achieving them. If the current status deviates from the target status, he has to revise his objectives or approach (= control measures).

1.4 Analysis of strengths and weaknesses

Honesty

A project manager can only improve his abilities, if he is aware of his weaknesses. If he knows he can do some things well, he won´t mind discovering that he also has deficiencies. A good method of identifying deficits and skills is a strengths and weaknesses analysis. For this, the project manager needs a piece of paper, a pen and a good dose of honesty. A matrix, such as the one shown in Figure D2-4, is suitable for this purpose:

STRENGTHS		
	What disadvantages do they bring me?	What can I do to counteract them?
Punctuality	Self-discipline after a rebuke from the boss	Setting off earlier for work
...		
WEAKNESSES		
	What disadvantages do they bring me?	What can I do to counteract them?
Untidy desk	It takes too long to find documents	Ask John Smith how his filing system works. His desk is always tidy
...		

Figure D2-4 Analysis of strengths and weaknesses

1.5 Efficient decision making

Project managers have to make decisions every day. Examples of classic project situations requiring a decision include:
- `Should we tell the customer about the cost explosion now or should we wait until the next status meeting?´
- `Should we recruit this project staff member or wait until we find one who is better qualified?´
- `Should we buy the tool from supplier A or B?´

Anyone who can say in all good faith that he has systematically prepared for a decision can cope more effectively with wrong decisions. Insignificant decisions that have no serious consequences if they turn out to be wrong are a good way of practising decision making.

Practising decisions

1.5.1 Procedure

The decision-making procedure comprises eight steps:
1. Justify the necessity for a decision.
2. Describe the alternatives.
3. Reduce each alternative to a clear (written!) statement.
4. List alternatives alongside their consequences (matrix).
5. Weight the consequences (e.g. by allocating school grades according to their difficulty).
6. Make the decision.
7. State the reasons for the decision (in writing!).
8. Document the decision.

Eight steps

It is important to write down the alternatives. This helps the project manager to retain an overview and feel that he has the problem under control. In many cases, all he will need is a two-column table of arguments in favour of and against the decision (→ Figure D2-5). The advantages and disadvantages are then entered below.

Write down alternatives

EXTREMELY URGENT REPLACEMENT PART ORDER				
Subject Area	Alternative A1	Alternative A2	Winner per subject area	Weighting per subject area
Costs	EUR 10,000	EUR 20,000	A1	1 (unimportant)
Delivery period	14 days	Immediately	A2	5 (very important)
Quality	High	Medium	A1	3 (average importance)
...				
Result:	Winning alternative in terms of number of subject areas: A1 Winning alternative in terms of weighting: A2			

Figure D2-5 Decision-making matrix

By substantiating and documenting decisions, the project manager ensures that he need not fear reprisals at a later date for slovenly research or premature decisions.

1.5.2 Talking to the people affected by the decision

In order to make a sound decision, the project manager often has to research a great deal of data and facts, and consider many pros and cons. He should exploit internal and external sources of useful information. However, too much research tends to cause confusion rather be of use! By taking a systematic approach, the project manager is less likely to become disoriented by information overload.

Avoid excessive research

He can avoid problems with the people affected by the decision (e.g. project team members, department managers, works council) if he discusses the decision with them before it is made. He can ask questions such as, `In what way will you be affected by the decision?´, or `What consequences has this decision for you?´ so that his decision is broadly based and he can identify objections to specific options at an early stage. However, the project manager should make it clear that he is the person making the decision and consistently reject all attempts to influence his decision. He has to make it clear that he is discussing the decision with the persons affected as a means of substantiating his decision and that it should not be perceived as a sign of weakness.

Identify resistance

1.5.3 Intuition

`Hard´ facts alone are not a sufficient basis for some decisions. Intuition can be an important indicator of whether a decision is right or not. Sometimes, one solution will simply seem more appealing than another. A systematic analysis of the pros and cons of a decision should definitely be made. This ensures that the decision maker has complied with his duty to exercise diligence. In most cases, he will have to provide verifiable justification of his decision.

> **Example**
> *The project manager has to decide between two project personnel with the same qualifications. His intuition, based on a mixture of professional experience and insight into human nature, tells him that one of the candidates is better suited to the job.*

1.5.4 Non-decisions

Wrong decisions can jeopardise the success of the project and the project manager´s career. Decisions are therefore unpopular and willingly postponed. However, if the project manager postpones the decision for too long, the consequences can be more serious than those associated with a wrong decision because even non-decisions are decisions. A classic non-decision is abandoning the project too late. Projects which are destined to fail but not abandoned are simply a waste of money. In order to understand the widespread practice of `postponitis´ and to prevent it happening in a project, it is necessary to answer two questions [5]:
1. How do individuals and groups benefit from avoiding decisions?
2. How are decisions postponed or avoided?

Arguments of non-decision makers

Lomnitz mentions several advantages of non-decisions from the perspective of the decision-makers:
- averting an uncertain future,
- keeping all options open,
- avoiding negative consequences,

- retaining the advantage of attack: by being able to criticise a decision that somebody else has made through keeping all personal options open, and
- not inflicting harm on others.

Non-decision-makers make many different excuses for their behaviour:
- alleged need for additional information,
- need to examine all the information first,
- the search for safety and orientation in allegedly ambiguous situations (e.g. waiting for a board decision), and
- alleged lack of time.

If the project manager is faced with senior managers who postpone decisions, he should discuss the issue openly as quickly as possible and state the consequences clearly, both orally and in writing (e.g. the consequences for costs, deadlines, quality, other projects or reputation). He should expressly demand a decision, but not in a situation embarrassing for the decision-makers – for example, at a meeting where the customer is present.   *Call for decisions*

Face-to-face discussions or telephone calls are the best way to obtain the support of important individuals before a decision-making meeting. Power brokers (→ Chapter A3), such as a supportive member of the managing board, can help the project manager to put his case to senior management, the customer or suppliers. At the same time, the project manager should clearly state his standpoint.   *Power brokers*

1.6 Motivation

A motivated manager is more productive than a manager who has to force himself to do the work. Motivation is dependent upon the personal benefits that an individual derives from his work (→ Chapter D3). This particularly applies for project managers, because they are role models for their staff.   *Personal benefits*

There are various ways of boosting motivation. A self-management tool that has proven to be particularly effective for documenting success and generating motivation for the future is the success diary. This method can be used by individuals, who keep their own diary, or entire teams (individual and team success diaries).

1.6.1 Success diary

The success diary is a means of consciously recording achievements and adding weight to personal perceptions of these. Obviously, the success diary should not prevent people from reflecting upon and learning from their mistakes (→ Chapter C10).   *Accord greater significance to successes*

Most things can be put in either a positive or negative light, according to the principle of a glass being either 'half empty' or 'half full'. People who learn to derive benefits from negative experiences and view problems as opportunities are able to cope more effectively with difficult (project) situations. With a little training and discipline, it is easy to change personal perceptions. Figure D2-6 shows the structure of a success diary.

Date	Which success?	How did I bring it about?	What would the situation be if this solution hadn´t been implemented?	What positive consequences resulted?
20.12.	Conflict about resource distribution resolved	Face-to-face dialogue with senior management, externally chaired meeting with the relevant department managers	Delays due to a lack of competence jeopardise the project finish date	Allocation of more competent staff, generation of understanding for our project among line managers, project now progressing at a faster pace
21.12.	...			

Figure D2-6 Personal success diary

1.6.1.1 Personal success diary

The personal success diary should accompany its owner at all times, irrespective of whether it is in electronic or paper format. At least three successes should be entered every day, however small or insignificant they may seem (e.g. a successful presentation or a milestone that is achieved on time).

Advantages   The benefits of the personal success diary are:
- the diary's owner develops a positive basic attitude,
- he learns to be motivated by even minor successes,
- he implements personal knowledge management by recording successful strategies which can be used again in the future, and
- his confidence grows because he can prove to himself and others (e.g. at meetings with superiors or finance providers) how successfully he works.

1.6.1.2 Team success diary

All members of the team should have easy access to the team success diary (e.g. it could be kept on the meeting room table or integrated on the project website). Ideally, the project manager should remind the team to enter team achievements in the diary at every meeting. Each member of the team should contribute at least one entry each week. The project manager can also read out entries from the success diary at the beginning of each meeting to create a ritual that the team members will soon learn to appreciate and which reinforces their collective identity.

Promoting collective identity

Advantages   The advantages of a team success diary are:
- short-term enhancement of team atmosphere and motivation (e.g. in difficult projects or crisis situations),
- a positive team sentiment is permanently established. Teamwork becomes more pleasant, which enhances team performance,
- listing successes prevents `off time´ in the team. This can occur, for instance, if a technical problem holds up the project or if a conflict with the customer is on the cards,
- the project manager can get the team on his side with the assistance of a success diary because it helps him to prove that he registers and appreciates even minor achievements, and
- he can present the diary to the customer or senior management at the project handover workshop (→ Chapter C10). It functions as a record, documenting the commitment and efficiency of the team in an unconventional way.

1.7 Self-directed learning

Self-directed learning (→ Chapter D1, D3), which is also an aspect of self-organisation, will not be discussed in detail in this chapter. However, we would like to point out that time spent on training and education is an investment in the future. The higher on´s qualifications, the greater on´s opportunities to choose on´s work and to ensure the success of the organisation´s projects.

Investment in the future

2 Meetings

Meetings are an indispensable tool for the coordination of project work. They are crucial, not only from a professional viewpoint, but also for stakeholder management. In order to get good results quickly, both the person chairing the meeting and the participants must adhere to specific rules (→ Chapter D3) and know what they have to do to ensure the meeting´s success.

2.1 Characteristics of a good meeting

Various indicators provide information about whether a meeting will be worthwhile:
- The meeting has been well-prepared and pursues one or more clear objectives. The participants have received information in advance of the meeting.
- It follows an agenda.
- The only people attending the meeting are the ones who are really needed (e.g. to make decisions).
- Each participant has the opportunity to state his opinion and the chairperson encourages shy participants to speak.
- All participants have equal rights, irrespective of their position in the organisation´s hierarchy.
- The chairperson or a person nominated by him uses a binding speaking order.
- All participants and the contributions they make to the meeting are treated with respect.
- Differences of opinion are resolved immediately at the meeting. If immediate resolution is not possible, a date is fixed for a meeting to resolve these differences of opinion.
- Each participant is able to summarise the results in his own words.
- Each participant can explain the tasks that he has been given at the meeting.
- Each participant leaves the meeting feeling positive.
- Minutes of the meeting are prepared and signed by all participants. It is best to include the comments that are written on flip charts or metaplan walls in the minutes of the meeting.

Establishing advantages

2.2 Preparation

If a meeting is genuinely necessary, answering the following helps the preparations:
1. What items should be included on the agenda?
2. Who will be invited to attend the meeting?
3. What are the participants´ views on the agenda? Are there controversial issues? Is there opposition? Is personally or `politically´ motivated behaviour (e.g. objections from a line manager to a worthwhile project because he doesn´t want his best staff to be assigned to the project) expected?
4. How long should the meeting last?

Dealing with questions

5. Is a suitable meeting room with the appropriate technical equipment available?
6. What information do the participants require in advance?
7. What information do they require at the meeting itself (e.g. document handouts, transparencies for presentations)?
8. Who has to be informed that the meeting is taking place but not invited to attend (e.g. senior managers)?
9. Who will chair the meeting?
10. Who will take the minutes?
11. Who will ensure adherence to the meeting timetable?

2.3 Conduct

Tasks of the meeting chairman

The success of a meeting depends on the chairperson's abilities. He has to

1. Ensure that the meeting commences on time.
2. Clarify who is present and who is absent.
3. Nominate a person to take the minutes and supervise their taking.
4. Lead the introductory part of the meeting, where the participants are requested to state their expectations of the meeting, and explain the agenda to the participants.
5. Ensure that the meeting progresses quickly (e.g. interrupt monologues and discussions) and that it ends at the planned time.
6. Deal with communication problems (e.g. the prevention of an aggressive tone and the inclusion of shy participants).
7. Ensure visual clarity if somebody doesn't understand something (e.g. ask participants to sketch their idea on a metaplan wall or whiteboard).
8. Avert or resolve conflicts.
9. Call for breaks when the participants' concentration starts to wane.
10. Prevent digression from the current topic.
11. Regularly summarise the meeting status (in his own words or on the basis of the minutes).
12. Eliminate items from the agenda if there is not sufficient time to deal with them so that time gained as a result can be used to discuss important items.
13. Arrange a date for the next meeting with participants if items are eliminated from the agenda.
14. Ensure that the minutes contain the persons responsible and deadlines for all tasks assigned at the meeting.
15. Ensure that all persons attending the meeting read and, if appropriate, sign the minutes before they leave.
16. Implement a feedback round.

Recommendations for problematic situations

If anyone attending the meeting has not made adequate preparations, the chairperson can provide a brief summary of the items on the agenda, and politely request the person(s) in question to at least scan over the meeting documents that are sent to them the next time they are invited to attend a meeting. If a participant is late for a meeting, it is a good idea to integrate him in the meeting straightaway. This can be done in the following ways: `Could you give me a hand with the projector?´ Or: `I'm glad you're here. What do you think about project XY?´ In this way, the chairman prevents the latecomer from distracting other participants or taking too long to focus on the content of the meeting. Persons who did not attend the meeting but should be aware of its content or have been assigned tasks should be informed on the same day, if possible, and requested to confirm receipt of the information.

2.3.1 Minutes

The minutes should at least contain the following:
1. Project ID (project name, abbreviation, number)
2. Reason/subject
3. Date, start, finish
4. Venue
5. Participants
6. Absentees who should receive a copy of the minutes (minutes distribution list)
7. Meeting chairperson
8. Minute taker
9. Agenda
10. All results, including tasks and responsibilities
11. Signatures
12. List of appendices and references to relevant documents
13. Deadlines for the distribution of the minutes (e.g. distribution to whom and by when)

Content of the minutes

If disputes or confusion arise at meetings, it is a good idea to include the relevant passages (word for word) in a chronological representation. If the matter is taken to court at a later date, it can be important to have a record of who said what to whom and when. The alternative to a chronological representation is the systemised summary, which only contains important (interim) results.

Chronological representation

There should be enough time left at the end of the meeting for the minute taker to read out the key points of the minutes. It provides participants with the opportunity to check whether everything has been recorded correctly. If necessary, they can ask questions or add further details. This prevents confusion, misunderstandings and conflicts at a later date as a result of different people interpreting the content of the minutes in different ways.

2.3.1.1 Templates
It is always easiest to use a template for the minutes. This reduces the minute taker´s workload because he only has to fill in the appropriate fields and does not have to consider whether all the necessary information has been recorded. If the visual appearance of the minutes is standardised, project personnel will also find it easier to find what they are looking for in the documentation (→ Chapter C9).

Uniform appearance

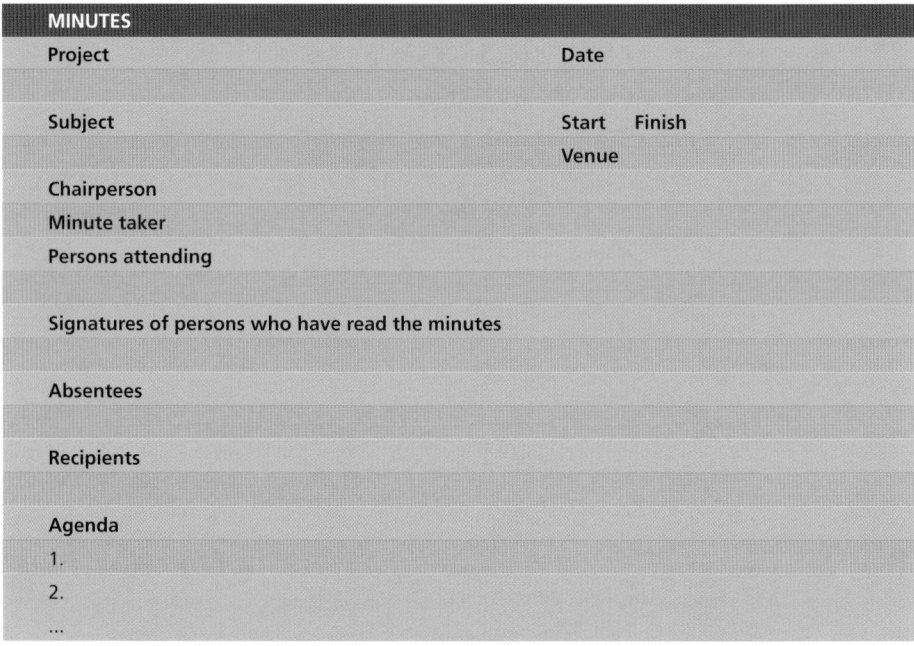

Figure D2-7 Template for the minutes of a meeting

The minutes can be integrated in the following table:

No.	Subject	Result	Type	Who?	By when?
		(Text)	A, D, I		(Deadline)
1.					
2.					
...					
			A Assignment		
			D Decision		
			I Information		

2.4 Follow-up

All meeting attendees should, if possible, receive a copy of the minutes on the day after the meeting. This ensures that they all have the same information and can read about the outcome of ambiguous issues (e.g. `homework´ after the meeting). In practice, an Open Issues List of all jobs assigned at meetings has proven useful.

Open Issues List

2.5 Flow chart

The flow chart shown in Figure D2-8 [6] provides a quick general overview of the planning, implementation and follow-up activities associated with a meeting. It can also be used as a checklist.

Checklist

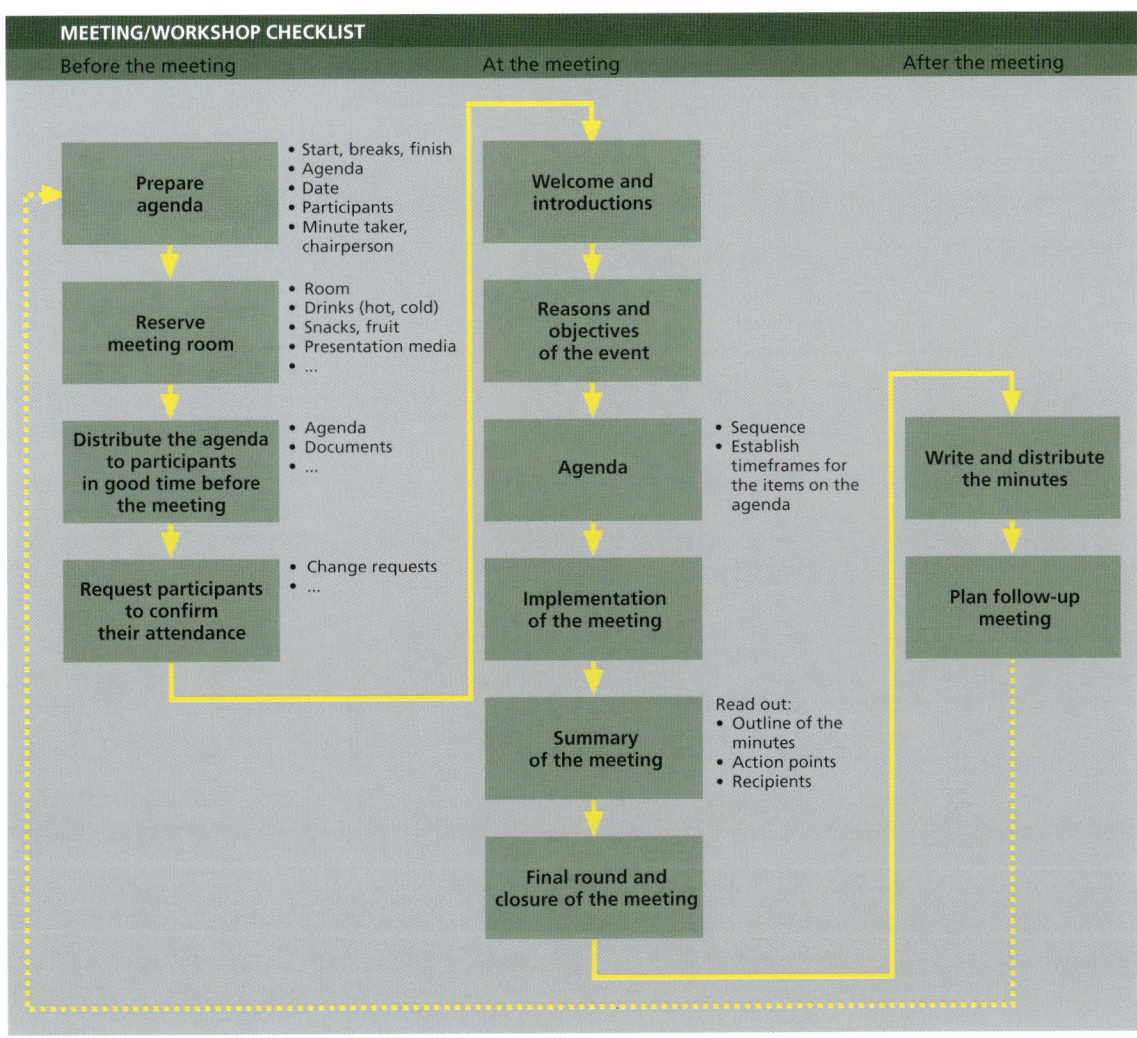

Figure D2-8 Flow chart for a meeting

2.6 Two sets of `Ten Commandments´ for meetings

From the perspective of the initiators, the following `Ten Commandments´ apply to meetings:

1. Only hold meetings if they are necessary.
2. Discuss the date of the meeting with the participants themselves (e.g. not during a works meeting).
3. Only invite persons whose attendance is essential.
4. Make sure that all participants are clear about the objectives of the meeting before it starts.
5. Prepare thoroughly for the meeting and ensure that the participants are also prepared (e.g. send out information material with the invitation).
6. Identify potential conflicts in advance (introductory round where participants are also requested to state their expectations).

Perspective of initiators

7. Cancel a meeting immediately if it is no longer necessary.
8. Stick to the agenda and deal with unforeseen issues under `miscellaneous´.
9. Obtain feedback (implement a feedback round).
10. Ensure that the results of the meeting are used effectively (e.g. in project marketing activities).

Perspective of participants

From the perspective of the participants, the following `Ten Commandments´ apply to meetings:
1. Only attend meetings if your attendance is useful or essential.
2. Prepare for the meeting.
3. Be constructive and cooperate.
4. Dedicate your full attention to the meeting.
5. Make only brief verbal contributions (put forward arguments with brief summary of reasons).
6. Ask questions if you are not clear about something.
7. Express opinions and doubts (→ Chapter D4).
8. Query majority opinions because they are often cases of people merely following the herd.
9. Support the chairperson (e.g. do not chat about irrelevant issues with other participants).
10. Be conscientious about doing homework.

3 Negotiations

Negotiations are a project manager´s daily bread. He has to campaign for budget funds and resources, deadline extensions and follow-up orders, and naturally for his own salary. On the other side of the negotiating table, he conducts staff recruitment interviews with potential employees and price negotiations with suppliers. At meetings with customers, he attempts to secure reasonable project objectives.

Procedure

Negotiating skills are not everything. Much of what makes a person a good negotiator are simply methods that can be learned. The following sections explain possible approaches to negotiations.

3.1 Preparation

Not everyone is a born diplomat. People who are successful in negotiations without having made thorough preparations are generally just lucky. Preparations for negotiations often take longer than the negotiations themselves and comprise several steps.

Step 1 – Obtain information

Anyone who enters negotiations should have obtained as much information as possible about the negotiating partner and his company beforehand. The Internet is a very useful tool for obtaining the relevant information. A good search engine and the company´s website are sources of original information, though information can also be obtained from other sources such as newspaper articles. Information and documents relating to business deals with the same customer in the past which have been archived in the process of knowledge management (→ Chapter C 10) are also useful.

Knowledge management

For example, it is a good idea to find out the negotiating partner´s position in his organisation, his responsibilities and his motives. Is his employer currently implementing redundancies that put him under considerable pressure to succeed? Or will he soon be retiring, which means he is not likely to be concerned about whether the negotiated contract costs the company an extra euro or two?

Personal information can also be very useful. This sort of information is easiest to obtain in informal conversations with people who have already had dealings with the person in question. It provides common ground (e.g. hobbies, acquaintances, subjects studied at university) and promotes a sense of trust.

Step 2 – Define and weight objectives

In the next step, the project manager considers what he actually wants to achieve, what his objectives are. In many cases, brainstorming sessions provide more output than individual cogitation. Finally, he weights the information that he has obtained, either alone or together with his team. This enables him to identify the most important objective, the one he has to focus upon in his further preparations. It also provides him with an opportunity to identify concessions on less important objectives to help achieve the main objective.

Now, it is necessary to ensure that the objectives are realistic, clearly defined, measurable and compatible. This makes it easier to put forward effective arguments and to communicate professional competence and experience to the negotiating partner. Unclear objectives, on the other hand, unnecessarily prolong negotiations because it is impossible to reach specific agreements.

Characteristics of objectives

It is a good idea to document objectives in writing (key points). The project manager can then take this `crib sheet´ with him to the meeting. A list of key points is also indispensable for telephone negotiations.

`Crib sheet´

Step 3 – Clarify the scope for negotiation

The project manager should note down or be aware of the scope for negotiation, or to what extent the negotiation result can deviate from the defined objectives. He identifies his best result and the results that he wants to avoid at all costs. Then, he considers opportunities for compromise and asks himself, `What is my bottom line?´ To evaluate this, he calculates or negotiates internal cost frameworks before entering into price negotiations and requests potential sub-contractors to provide information about prices and delivery periods.

Alternative results

Step 4 – Establish a negotiation strategy

Now, the project manager has to consider how he will structure his arguments. He ensures that he has the necessary arguments, examples, scenarios, etc. to hand at the right stage of negotiations. Nothing is more frustrating than thinking of a good argument when the negotiations have ended. It is important to be able to put yourself in your negotiating partner´s position. Does he view the offer (e.g. price, product, and terms of delivery) as advantageous? How urgently does he need the product? Are other alternatives available to him?

Negotiating partner´s perspective

Step 5 – Prepare the negotiation environment

If the project manager´s organisation is hosting the negotiations, he must ensure that the negotiating partner is made to feel welcome. He should tidy his desk, dust the guest chair, ensure that the floor and toilets are clean, that the glasses do not have fingerprints on them, and that there is always somebody on hand to provide refreshments. These trivialities should not be underestimated. If the negotiating partner is not pedantic about tidiness, you're lucky. However, you should always be prepared. In some negotiations, the choice of a neutral location is crucial.

3.2 Implementation

Avoiding slip-ups Much can go wrong during negotiations. The following points can help to prevent slip-ups.

3.2.1 Always bear objectives in mind

The most important rule is, to bear the objectives in mind throughout the entire meeting. This enables the project manager to respond more quickly if his opposite number attempts to steer the negotiations his way. Notes about important things that are said can serve as an orientation aid in the further course of the negotiations. So can the project manager record what is said during the meeting. It is a good idea to take minutes, even when the negotiations are not particularly important, and request the participants to sign them at the end.

3.2.2 Emphasise common ground

The project manager should introduce common ground, that he has discovered through preparatory research, right at the outset, with the objective of motivating the negotiating partner to listen, since a good result is also based on sympathy. The project manager should make the negotiating partner aware of the fact that he has obtained information about him and his company as a matter of respect and professional courtesy, and convey the impression that he understands him and his motives.

Defining benefits It is always worthwhile highlighting the benefits that both parties will derive from the conclusion of a contract. In the end, there shouldn´t be any losers, just winners (a win-win situation) to ensure that the business relationship will last.

3.2.3 Listen proactively

There are a few basic rules to observe when conducting negotiations. For example, you should always allow the negotiating partner to finish what he is saying. On the other hand, the project manager should also be a proactive listener. Proactive listening [7] means
- One person confirming what the other has said, either by saying `hmm´ or `uh-huh´, or by nodding the head or using appropriate gestures.
- Always maintaining eye contact with the negotiating partner.
- The listener repeating in his own words what the other party has said and supplementing it with his own experiences.
- Only putting forward an argument after listening to the other person´s arguments. This provides a knowledge advantage in the further course of the meeting.
- Asking for clarification if something is not understood. In this way, the negotiating partner knows that the project manager is paying attention.

3.2.4 Include the negotiating partner in the discussion

Open questions It is easiest to include the negotiating partner in the discussion by asking questions, such as, `What improvements do you think should be made to the product?´ Open-ended questions are more suitable than `yes or no´ questions, because these limit the scope for response. Later on in the discussion the questions can be more specifically formulated. For example, `Can you give me binding confirmation of that?´

3.2.5 Body language

Body language sends out messages whose significance should not be underestimated. A negotiator ought to address the other party in a friendly yet confident way. This signalises to the other party that he feels comfortable in his company, yet still knows what he wants. Wide-open eyes signify interest in the other person and what he is saying. Optimism is expressed by looking up. The torso should face the negotiating partner, and the hands should be slightly open. In contrast, holding the arms close to the body is a defensive gesture that means, `I´m holding you at bay.´

3.2.6 Phraseology

Negotiators can only be successful if people understand what they are saying. That´s why they should observe the following rules:

- Be concise and to the point, and avoid long and complicated sentences.
- Use examples and illustrations to explain complex issues.
- Don´t use technical terms that the negotiating partner may not be familiar with – even if, as a result, you have to omit the occasional detail that may be necessary from a technical viewpoint or if you have to provide a more superficial explanation than you would to a technical colleague. The most important thing is to ensure that the key message gets across.
- Speak your negotiating partner´s `language´. This depends, for example, on his level of education, culture and corporate environment.
- Notice the responses of your negotiating partner: Is it possible that he hasn´t understood something? If so, explain it again or ask him `Am I explaining it clearly?´

Understandability

3.3 Follow-up

Document the outcome of the negotiations in writing. It is a good idea to write up the notes that you made during the meeting straightaway while they are still fresh in your mind. If official minutes are taken, it is a good idea to let the negotiating partner read and sign them before he leaves the meeting. This is advantageous for both parties because it prevents future misunderstandings.

4 Problem solving

Projects that never encounter any problems are scarcely imaginable. Such problems, if ignored, can develop into crises. This is why a project manager should be familiar with methods of problem solving.

Crises

The ICB definition [8], `Projects can be considered as the total of a large number of problem solving processes. If each of these processes is done efficiently (at a low cost and in a short time) and effectively (the right problem is solved properly and well), this is a great contribution to the project success. Therefore, the project manager is interested in problem solving´.

The definition of the term 'problem' in project management circles is:

==A problem is a task that cannot be solved by means of existing, standard approaches. The solution is not initially evident, which means that problem solving methods are necessary.==

Team requirements — Problem solving methods do not involve any kind of automatism. Even if a project team uses them, they will not necessarily find a solution immediately. Rather, creativity, analytical skills and the ability to implement are necessary, as well as the determination to solve the problem.

4.1 Problem categories

Problems can be classified into different categories [9].

4.1.1 Analysis problems
When solving analysis problems, it is necessary to identify structures, interrelationships and set procedures.

Example
A project team has to prepare a complex work breakdown structure

4.1.2 Search-related problems
These problems are solved by finding people, objects, terms or structures that satisfy specific criteria.

Example
An employee has to find a research method to obtain information about experiences in similar predecessor projects.

4.1.3 Constellation problems
Here, it is necessary to find new, constructive or conceptual solutions to tasks.

Example
An agency develops an innovative advertising concept for a client. It is to be used as a model for all this client's future advertising campaigns.

4.1.4 Selection problems
Alternatives must be identified to attain a defined objective optimally.

Example
The project manager is looking for an external mechanical engineer who is familiar with the design of certain special-purpose machines. He has to consider ways of finding such an expert.

4.1.5 Linkage problems
These problems arise through compliance with particular laws or rules.

Example
A new production concept requires the preparation of a new work schedule for the affected production employees.

4.2 Problem types

There are two basic types of problem [10]: well-structured and badly-structured problems.

Well or badly-structured problems

4.2.1 Characteristics of well-structured problems
- All elements of the problem are known.
- The problem elements are in a structured relationship to one another.
- The problem solving process is reliable, cogent, systematic and logical.

Example
The project team has to find the optimal output for a new product.

4.2.2 Characteristics of badly-structured problems
- Not all elements of the problem are known.
- Few or no set procedures are evident.
- The problem solving process tends to be unstructured, intuitive and haphazard.

Example
It is necessary to develop a programme for a company anniversary party.

4.3 Obstacles to problem solving

It is more difficult to solve a problem if the project personnel
- fail to recognise it,
- do not understand it,
- misinterpret it,
- do not analyse it or only analyse it superficially or
- if they perceive it differently (e.g. type, severity, impact).

4.3.1 Understanding problems

Problems can only be solved by somebody who understands them. Every team member involved in the process of problem solving must be precisely aware of what the problem is. `W´ questions and graphical representations (e.g. flow charts) are effective tools that help people to understand and tackle problems.

`W´ questions
- What does the problem comprise?
- What are all the different elements of the problem?
- Who is affected?
- What impact will it have – now and in the future?
- When did the problem first occur?
- Which solutions have already been tried out?
- Why didn´t they work?
- What do we have to do to solve the problem?
- What are the consequences if it remains unsolved?

`W´ questions

Graphical representation

In many cases, problematic project processes can be illustrated quickly on the PC with only a few mouse clicks, or on paper. Figure D2-9 shows an example of a simple flow chart.

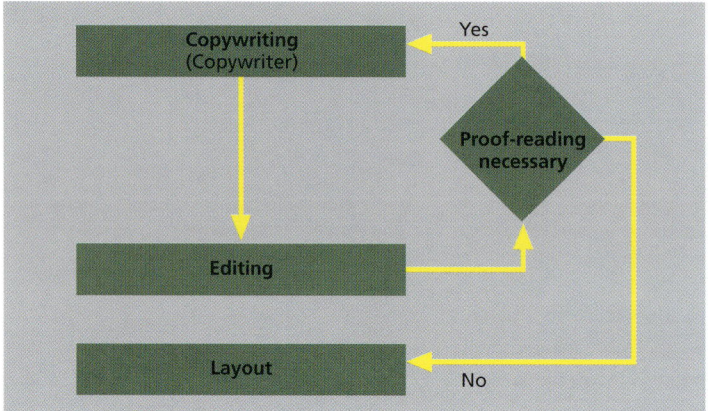

Figure D2-9 Flow chart to illustrate problems relating to the production of an information brochure

Example
The problem in the flow chart shown in Figure D2-9 is that the graphic designers at the agency responsible for brochure layout repeatedly start their work packages too late. The flow chart graphically illustrates the cause of the delay to the editor-in-chief. The quality of the copywritten texts is so poor that the copywriters have to perform an additional process step. This will be eliminated in the future so that the brochures are ready for layout and printing on time. One possible solution would be to use a different team of copywriters. Alternatively, the agency could enlarge the editing team.

4.4 Requirements on problem solving methods

Requirements

Problem solving methods should [11]
- be appropriate for various types of problems,
- support the entire problem-solving process,
- enable the processing of a problem by individuals or groups,
- deliver defined and documented partial solutions so that the problem-solving process can continue after lengthy interruptions,
- permit the use of different techniques to solve individual aspects of the problem,
- be easy to learn, and
- support the work of problem-solving teams working at different locations and times.

4.5 Roles

One usually distinguishes between three problem solving roles:
1. Problem owner: the person who formulates the problem and has the authority to decide on the solution.
2. Problem-solving team: the people who help to elaborate solutions.
3. Supervisor: the person who controls the problem solving process.

4.6 Problem solving methods

According to the ICB, a problem can be solved on the basis of consensus or a decision. Normally, problem solving is a process consisting of several steps. The development of a problem-solving procedure is one of the most important aspects of conducting negotiations. It is a good idea to stick with the chosen method until the process has concluded. Switching over to another method involves the expenditure of time and effort on learning and coordination, with which some smaller project teams are unable to cope. One important aspect of any problem solving process is information procurement, for which there are various methods:

Consensus or decision

Information procurement

- Collection (e.g. studies, statistics, user reports)
- Surveys (interviews, questionnaires)
- Monitoring
- Forecasts
    - intuitive (e.g. survey, Delphi method)
    - analytical (e.g. simulation, extrapolation)

The three basic approaches to solving problems involve the use of either sequential phase models, problem-solving cycles or form-based systems.

Three approaches

4.6.1 Sequential phase models

Sequential phase models consist of several sequential phases in which a problem-solving sub-process takes place. When one phase ends, the next one starts. The project team determines what takes place in each phase. This approach is also suitable for group processes.

Group processes

The problem-solving process could include the following phases:

Phases in the problem solving process

1. Definition of the problem.
2. Description of the actual and target status.
3. Deviation of the actual status from the target status and description of the consequences.
4. Investigation of possible reasons for the deviation.
5. Identification and isolation of the main causes.
6. Elaboration of solution objectives.
7. Elaboration of solution alternatives.
8. Evaluation and prioritisation of solution alternatives.
9. Schedule of measures for the implementation of the favoured solution (including deadlines, responsibilities, resources).
10. Development of criteria for reviewing results and control.

4.6.2 Problem-solving cycle

The problem-solving cycle is nothing other than the sequence of activities (`Deming Cycle´ → Chapter C8):

The Deming cycle

| plan - do - check - act |

Unlike phase models, which are linear, sequential and take place once only, problem-solving cycles continually repeat the above four steps. They are iterative – i.e. repetitive – processes. Each time the cycle is completed, the team comes closer to solving the problem. The starting point of each cycle is the result of the previous cycle.

Iterative process

4.6.3 Form-based systems

Form-based systems are suitable for problems that are being solved by more than one person. Various forms are used throughout the problem-solving process, from the situation analysis, through the problem analysis to the decision and the documentation of the solution. In this standardised procedure, the next step in the process is more or less automatic. The disadvantage of form-based systems is that they tend to be bureaucratic and complex, which means they are not appropriate for small-scale projects.

Suitable for large-scale projects

4.6.4 Cause-and-effect diagram

The cause-and-effect diagram helps the project team to break down the problem and identify possible causes. It is sometimes called the `fishbone diagram´ (due to its shape) or the Ishikawa diagram (after its creator, Kaoru Ishikawa of Japan). The team identifies the possible factors of influence (causes) of a problem (effect), for example, in a brainwriting session. Then, the causes are categorised as main or contributory causes, and entered on the diagram. The subsequent evaluation identifies several key areas that need further investigation.

Breakdown of the problem

The fact that this cause-and-effect diagram is produced in a team enables the combination of different perspectives of the problem. The team focuses only on the specific problem and its solution, and the interests of the individual team members are accorded subordinate importance.

Teamwork

4.6.4.1 Procedure

Creativity techniques (e.g. brainstorming, 635 brainwriting, and morphological boxes) help the team to identify possible causes of the problem. If the team groups these causes in the main boxes, they can use the cause-and-effects diagram to create a structured overview. The diagram also shows the various interdependencies between the different causes. This procedure eliminates the customary restriction to one or two causes and enables a comprehensive overview of the problem.

First of all, the content, time, location and extent of the problem are described. The definition of the problem is written on the right-hand side of the chart by the facilitator. In the next step, the boxes for possible causes are filled. Often, the causes are grouped under the 4M & E categories:

4M-E method

- **M**achine (e.g. tools, equipment, plants)
- **M**ethod (e.g. work method, process)
- **M**aterial (e.g. production materials, raw materials)
- **M**an (e.g. persons involved, degree of familiarity, qualifications)
- **E**nvironment (e.g. work environment, air humidity, temperature)

There is no generally applicable number of categories. The solution can be established in a problem-specific and individual way. All categories are noted on the arrows on the chart (= fish bones). The team then allocates possible causes to these fish bones. The facilitator can ask questions to bring team members´ attention to categories that they have overlooked. Querying individual causes leads to the definition of contributory causes, which adds further branches to the diagram. The question `Why?´ should be asked three times in connection with each cause.

Fish bones

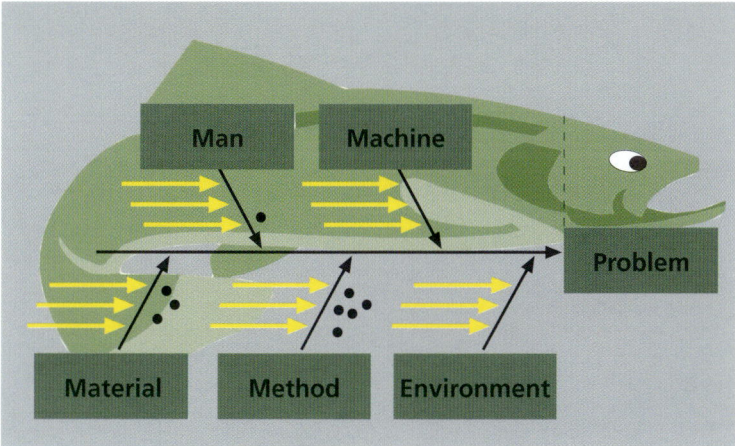

Figure D2-10 Cause-and-effect diagram

When the team finds no further causes, it evaluates those found, for example, by affixing adhesive dots, indicating significance, to them. The causes with the most dots are then investigated further in order to arrive at a solution.

4.6.5 Minimal solution

Anyone who prefers not to use the above, more comprehensive methods, should at least opt for a minimal solution. One very simple yet systematic procedure is
1. Define the problem.
2. Establish the solution requirements.
3. Seek possible alternatives.
4. Assess the advantages and disadvantages of the solutions.

Four steps

If the preferred solution doesn´t work, it is still possible to use the second-best one. The project team should use the following hierarchy and adapt it to their specific needs as necessary.
1. What is the ideal solution?
2. What is the best that we can achieve under the current circumstances?
3. What is the minimum result that we can achieve with our resources?

4.6.6 Solving badly-structured problems

Bergfeld [10] suggests the following approach to solving badly-structured problems:

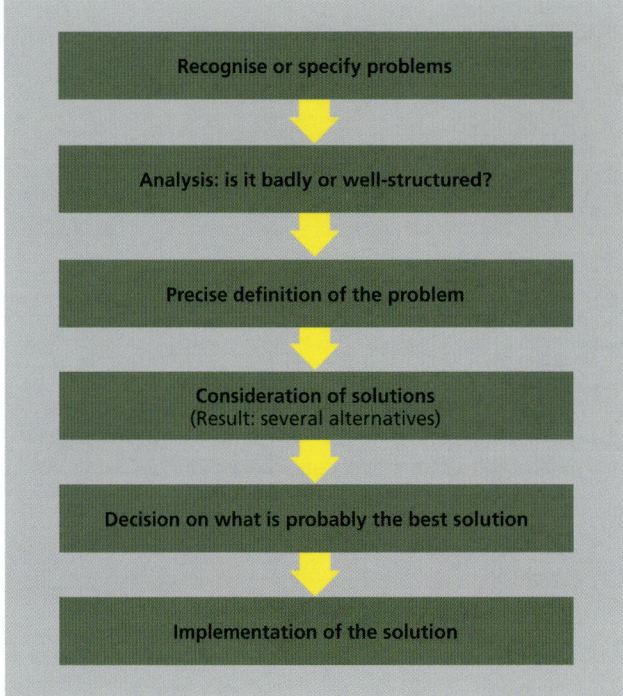

Figure D2-11 Solving badly-structured problems

5 Presentations

Presentations have become an everyday aspect of project managers' work. However, even project managers who routinely make presentations should ask themselves, `Have I thought of everything?´ It is also necessary to ensure that a project presentation is not a boring monologue. It will be far more convincing if it incorporates interactive elements because the presenter wants to get the audience on his side. According to Kellner [12], three key messages should be communicated to the audience´s subconscious:

Three key messages

1. Competence: `Professionals are at work here!´
2. Power/dynamism: `We´ve got the project under control!´
3. Affinity/communication: `We´re nice people and we like talking to you!´

5.1 Environment

Occasion and target group

An environment appropriate to the occasion and the audience is essential for a successful presentation. It includes

- a room where people feel comfortable (suitable location and furniture, temperature, pleasant lighting, cleanliness, tidiness, quiet atmosphere),

- efficiently functioning technology (overhead projector, conventional projector etc.),
- drinks and snacks, as well as
- a presenter, dressed for the occasion, who has well-ordered and smartly-presented documents.

5.2 Time of day

The best times of day for presentations are:
- in the morning between 9 am and lunchtime
- in the afternoon between 2 pm and 5 pm

Many people tend to be still tired at 8 am and unable to assimilate information. After lunch, few people are capable of outstanding mental feats. And after 5 pm, many employees are already mentally on their way home to their evening meal.

5.3 Structure

Here is a typical structure [13] for a project presentation (→ Chapter D4):   *Structure*
1. Project subject
2. Benefits
3. Objectives
4. Means of achieving objectives
5. Discussion and questions
6. Appeal to the audience (e.g. for cooperation)

Alternatively, the presenter can structure the presentation in three steps:
1. `What is the status quo?´ (Description)
2. `Why should we change it?´ (Arguments)
3. `How can we change it so that we are all satisfied?´ (Necessary measures)

These questions are answered in the various sections of the presentation, which has been arranged in a logical sequence by the presenter. He should ensure that a `thread´ runs through the entire presentation. Positive suspense should be gradually built up, and then reduced again towards the end of the presentation. Ideally, the audience should always be curious about the next part of the presentation. In the preparatory phase, the presenter should check after each section that the structure sustains the `thread´ and positive suspense.    *`Thread´*

The first part of the presentation could include an example of project work or a scenario that is slightly exaggerated to grab the audience´s attention. It doesn´t hurt to make them laugh, smile or shake their heads.   *Introductory example*

Graphics and tables that provide a clear overview of facts and figures make a welcome change to overhead transparencies with a lot of text. However, they should be reduced to a clear and immediately obvious key statement, be graphically simple yet professionally presented. It only makes sense to use a chart if the audience can understand it at first glance. The presenter should aim to generate images in the audience´s mind, and not just on the wall.   *Graphics*

5.4 Selection of information

Less is more

Less is often more! This also applies for the content of a presentation. Two or three arguments per issue are sufficient. If the presenter addresses too many or too few points, the essential message loses its significance. Also, too much information confuses the audience. Ad-hoc questions and new aspects that the speaker has to address during the presentation are time-consuming and tax the audience´s attention span.

Benefits for target group

It is easy to ascertain which information the presentation should include by asking the following questions in connection with each point: `Does it interest my audience?´ `How will the audience benefit from the information I am communicating?´ `Will they lack something if the information isn´t provided?´ In the highly likely event that the presenter believes that several points are important, he has to prioritise them. If he still cannot decide which – if any – points are to be omitted, he should at least distribute them on several transparencies. This provides the audience with a better overview. There are several recommendations on the number of transparencies per unit of time, and the common denominator is three to five minutes per transparency. However, a presentation should not include more than 20 transparencies to ensure that the audience is able to assimilate their content.

Number of transparencies

5.4.1 Target group-specific preparation

Technical content must be prepared so that the target audience can understand it. It is necessary to consider whether the audience consists of
- laymen,
- people with an advanced knowledge or
- experts

Knowledge profile

in the field covered by the presentation. When making preparations for a presentation, it is useful to ask colleagues who can assess the audience´s knowledge profile (e.g. `How familiar is the customer with the concept of project control?´). Throughout the preparatory process, the presenter should focus on the intellectual and working environment of the audience members.

To ensure that he can sustain the audience´s attention, it is a good idea to provide tangible objects that can be passed around (e.g. models, prototypes). This forges a closer relationship between the audience and the subject matter of the presentation than listening alone.

The final transparency should summarise the most important points of the presentation (maximum of three) so that the audience remembers them. The presenter should also take several transparencies to the presentation that are not shown to the audience in the main presentation (= back-up). These contain information that will only be used if required (e.g. content of project phase one, even though the project is now in phase three). In this way, he demonstrates his ability and prudence to the audience by obviously being equipped with the right information for all eventualities.

5.5 Design

`Crowded´ pages

A successful presentation is logically structured and the texts are well-spaced so that the audience can remember the content. Transparencies that contain too much text are a waste of time because they bombard the audience with too much information at first glance, which means they don´t make the effort to read it. If the presenter is using transparencies and an overhead projector, he should observe the following rules:

- Type size of at least 18 pt.
- At least single line spacing.
- Maximum of three content statements per transparency.
- Paragraphs with sub-headings should be used.
- Each transparency should have a brief and to-the-point heading.
- Complete yet simple sentences with subject, predicate and object (e.g. `The budget is Euro 10,000.´).
- No passive constructions (e.g. it is better to say `The project manager says´ than … according to the project manager´).
- Highlight important points (e.g. in bold type) and, ideally, only highlight one point per paragraph.
- Use only one or at most two type formats (e.g. normal and bold) and only three type sizes per transparency.
- Arrange the elements so that there is plenty of blank space on the transparency (uncluttered pages).
- Use the same visual aids (e.g. symbols) throughout the presentation.
- Don´t just use text, but also images, charts, diagrams and tables.
- Don´t forget the project logo (→ Chapter D4), positioned in the same place on every transparency.

Structured transparencies

Anyone who is not familiar with the creation and processing of graphics should not use them. Well-structured and properly formatted text blocks are much better than unprofessional graphics.

The presenter should note key points as memory aids when preparing the presentation to ensure that he doesn´t forget anything. It is important to use large handwriting and leave plenty of space between the lines so that the notes are easy to read from a distance.

5.6 Handouts

The audience should be provided with writing pads and pens, as well as handouts to enable them to follow the presentation. In addition to the illustrations, these should provide space for notes. At most three transparencies fit on an A4 page. Space for notes should be provided on the right hand side of each illustration. The audience should be able to pay attention to the presenter. However, formulated texts in the handout will distract them from the presentation. It is therefore better to use bullet points, similar to those on the transparencies themselves, though they should be comprehensive enough so that the reader can understand them.

Handouts

If the audience is provided with handouts, it is a good idea to observe several aspects when creating the transparencies, otherwise they will look `crowded´ and their legibility will suffer.

- Use colours sparingly.
- Use dark type on a pale background.
- Use a few elements only on each transparency (text modules, images, graphics).

Requirements

5.7 Presenter

The success of a presentation depends on the presenter. He should
- appear calm and not make any nervous movements (e.g. continually shifting his weight from foot to foot),
- move slowly, yet energetically and confidently,
- maintain eye-contact with the audience,
- use positive body language and face the audience,
- control gestures and facial expressions (not waving his arms around, because the audience will perceive this as a threat), and
- not use defensive gestures (e.g. never raise his hands to suggest, `I give up´).

5.7.1 Dealing with nerves

Even experienced presenters suffer from nerves. Being nervous before a presentation is nothing to be ashamed of. In fact, it´s entirely normal. Presenters are plagued with fears about [14]
- the unfamiliar situation,
- not being able to satisfy the audience´s expectations,
- being exposed to criticism from other people, and
- being a complete failure.

Recommendations

Wittenzellner recommends the following approaches to dealing with nerves [15]:
- View the situation as an opportunity rather than a threat.
- Use positive thoughts (`Everything´s fine´) instead of negative ones (`I should have prepared more thoroughly´).
- Tone down expectations: nobody is perfect and the audience only expects a well-structured and interesting presentation.
- Remember challenging situations that you have dealt with well in the past.
- Call to mind how the presentation ended successfully and the audience was satisfied.
- When nobody is watching, take two or three deep breaths, ideally at an open window.
- Pace up and down the room, focusing on the task ahead.
- Smile.
- The more practised you become, the less you will suffer from nerves.

5.8 Presentation media

How to select

There are numerous presentation media to choose from, both new as well as tried-and-tested ones. We summarise them briefly in this section[16]. When selecting the appropriate presentation medium, it is necessary to ask
- Which medium is best for communicating the content of the presentation?
- How many people will be in the audience?
- Which rooms and technical equipment are available at the presentation venue?
- Can the room be darkened?
- Which equipment can the presenter bring with him (e.g. mobile devices)?
- Which media is the presenter accustomed to using?

The following media can be used in presentations:

1. **Pinboard, metaplan technique**
   You will need: one or more pinboards, posters, index cards, felt-tipped pens.
   - Suitable for small groups.
   - This offers flexibility in structuring the presentation.
   - This can be used as a visual aid for complex issues because different aspects can be shown on different pinboards - which is not the case when transparencies are used.
   - The sheets that are torn off can be affixed to the walls so that they are in full view of all members of the audience.
   Disadvantage:
   illegible handwriting can make it difficult for the group to follow the presentation.

2. **Flip chart**
   You will need: a stand with paper and felt-tipped pens.
   - Easy-to-use tool for small-scale presentations and meetings.
   - This offers flexibility in structuring the presentation.
   - The sheets that are torn off can be affixed to the walls so that they are in full view of all members of the audience.
   - Suitable for combination with an overhead projector or computer projector.
   Disadvantages:
   when the presenter is writing, the audience cannot see the sheet of paper and he cannot maintain eye contact with the audience.

3. **Overhead projector**
   You will need: projector and accessories (e.g. cable) screen or wall, transparencies.
   - Suitable for large audiences (up to 200 persons).
   - The transparencies can be created easily and flexibly using a PC, or manually during the presentation.
   - The presenter´s hands are free to make gestures that underline what he is saying, and he can maintain eye contact with the audience.
   Disadvantages:
   putting the transparencies on the projector is a laborious and mistake-prone process, and scratches and fingerprints are visible; the room has to be darkened, which makes eye contact with the audience impossible and prevents them from making notes.

4. **Slide and video projector**
   You will need: slide or video projector plus accessories, projection surface.
   - Slide presentations are not often used for presentations, and organisations only produce videos for special occasions.
   - Both are suitable for large-scale presentations.
   - (Moving) images often say more than words and quickly put a message across.
   - Video presentations offer appealing visual effects and are dynamic.
   Disadvantages:
   the equipment can be complicated to operate; the room has to be darkened; it is difficult to highlight or prioritise information in moving images.

5. Multimedia projector/(computer-assisted) projector

You will need: PC, projector and accessories.
- Many people like professional computer-assisted multimedia shows, and they are also suitable for large audiences.
- The information in the diverse storage media can be integrated and combined (text, images, graphics, sound, film).
- Professional image.

Disadvantages:
complex production and, in some cases, professionals have to be called in; it is difficult to highlight and prioritise information in moving images.

5.9 Procedure

Dealing with questions

Ad-hoc questions and interruptions can cause presenters to lose their thread. To prevent such interruptions and discussions occurring during the presentation, the following procedure can be used.

- Important questions from members of the audience who have not understood something can be taken during the presentation, but have to be dealt with in the space of 30 seconds. Otherwise, questions have to wait until after the presentation.
- Questions that the presenter cannot answer should be noted down in view of the audience and he should give his assurance that he will provide an answer at the latest by the following day. The best way to provide the answer is to send a memo to all participants who have provided an e-mail address in the attendance list or who are on the list of recipients for project meeting minutes.
- If the various theme blocks are separated by a brief interlude (e.g. one minute), the audience has time to process what has just been said and make the mental switch to the next theme.

Equipment

To ensure that the presentation goes smoothly, the presenter should take a few precautionary measures beforehand. A replacement lamp for the overhead projector or a spare set of transparencies has saved the day at many a presentation.

5.10 Flow chart

Presentation checklist

The flow chart shown in Figure D2-12 [17] provides a quick overview of the presentation procedure. It can also be used as a checklist.

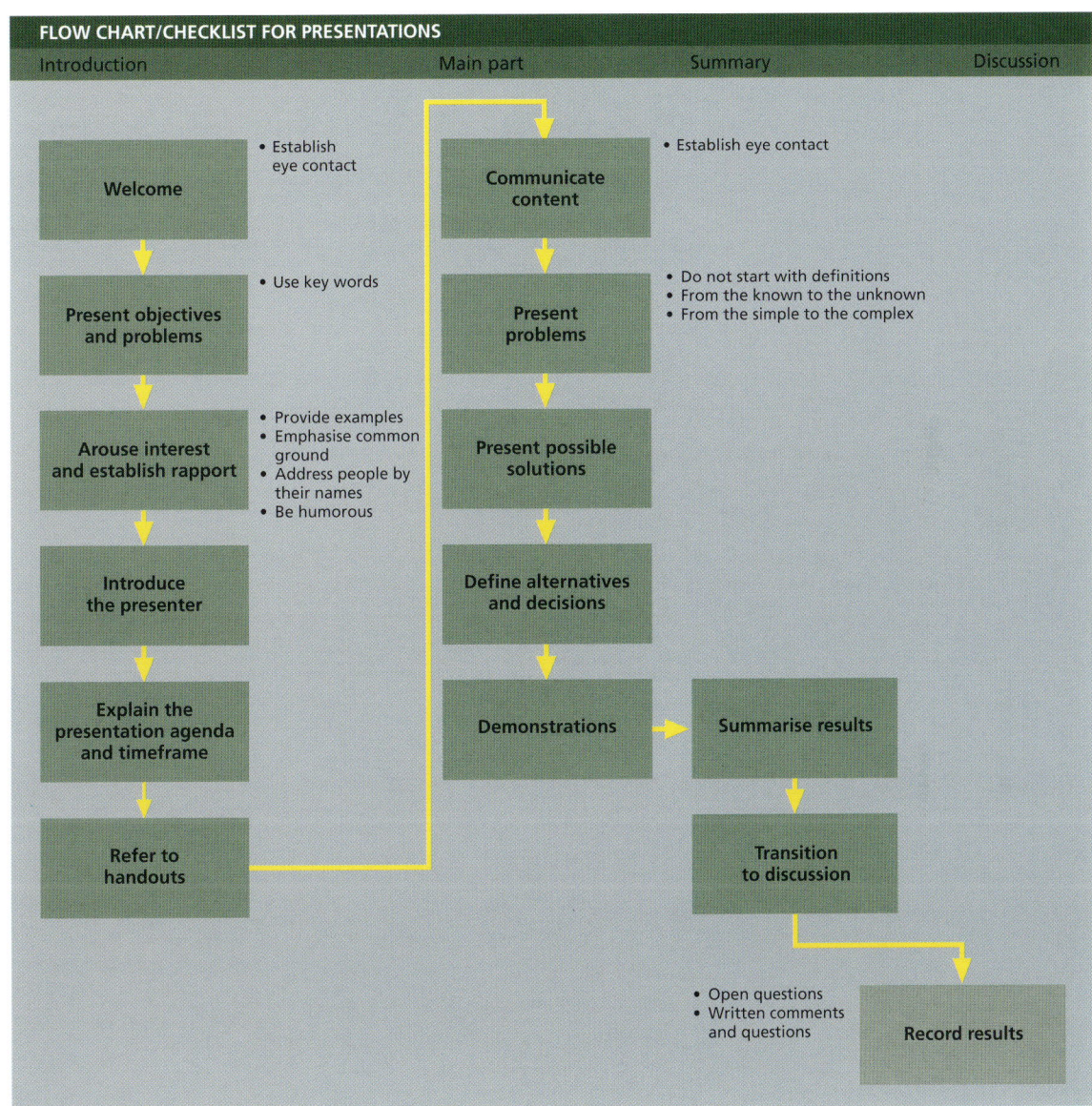

Figure D2-12 Flow chart for a presentation

6 Creativity techniques

Creativity techniques [18] are used to exploit and improve people's potential for creative problem solving. In groups, they are also used to generate synergetic effects and to combine or expand upon individual ideas to arrive at solutions that the individuals themselves would not have come up with on their own. However, the chairman or facilitator has first to eliminate the participants' creativity blocks because entrenched ways of thinking and behaviour as a result of upbringing or experiences at school, in vocational training and at work prevent them from accepting and expressing their own ideas

Stimulate imagination

without fear and prejudice. Negative statements such as, `That won´t work anyway´, or, `We´ve always done it differently´ indicate that they suffer from such inner blocks.

Basically, creativity techniques can be divided into intuitive and analytical (= discursive) categories. Intuitive methods include brainstorming and variants of brainstorming (e.g. discussion 66), brainwriting (e.g. card questioning, method 635) and the Delphi method. Analytical methods include attribute listing and morphological boxes [19]. This chapter explains brainwriting and brainstorming in greater detail, since it is the most popular and widely-used creativity technique in project management. Only a brief outline of the other techniques is provided.

6.1 Brainwriting

Brainwriting and brainstorming are classic creativity techniques. They are often used in project management practice, though in many cases intuitively and without any precise awareness of the ideal procedure. They can be used by individuals or groups to develop creative solutions for very different problems. The aim is for the participants to give their imagination free rein and inspire each other.

Heterogeneity

Brainwriting and brainstorming are techniques that are used in the early stages of a project or design process, since the groups often include representatives from all sorts of departments. Therefore, there are more people to provide interdisciplinary input than later on in the project when there is a higher degree of specialisation. The more heterogeneous the composition of the group (e.g. departments, functions, age), the broader is the range of ideas that will be generated. Unusual ideas are more likely to be voiced in heterogeneous groups than in groups comprising experts only. The ideal group size is between two and twelve persons.

Facilitator

The session should not be longer than one hour, and half an hour is best. The chairperson of the session should ideally be a facilitator. During the entire session, he should prevent the group from digressing and ensure that the ideas are recorded in a structured manner.

6.1.1 Procedure

The following procedure is appropriate for a brainwriting session:
1. The chairperson opens the session and explains the problem or task at hand.
2. The participants write down their ideas on cards.
3. The facilitator affixes the cards one after the other onto a metaplan wall. In order to reduce the length of the subsequent selection process, each time a new card is provided, he asks the group to which category it should be put and which (column) heading is suitable. This process continues until all ideas have been categorised.
4. Then, the suggestions are weighted and prioritised using a points system (e.g. school grades).

The procedure explained in the Section `Efficient decision making´ in this chapter is suitable for setting priorities. After pre-selection, the best ideas can be used in another brainwriting session so they can be adapted to specific needs.

6.1.1.1 Combination of individual and group work
Individual and group work can be combined effectively. For example, the project manager may define

the problem first and ask his staff to find a quiet place and consider possible solutions alone. The group can then combine these solutions. It is also possible to reverse this process and initially to collect group ideas before individually developing a certain number of preferred suggestions (e.g. for the implementation of one of the ideas mentioned).

6.1.1.2 Method 635

Method 635 involves six group members writing three ideas in connection with one problem and then passing them on to the other five members. Each member has a form with three columns and six lines per column. He enters an idea on one of the six lines in each column. Then, the forms are passed on to the other members in a clockwise direction until all the lines have been filled in.

6.2 Brainstorming

Brainstorming is similar to brainwriting. Here is a possible procedure:
1. The facilitator specifies the precise duration and basic rules of brainstorming.
2. The participants are given ten minutes to think about the task at hand and come up with ideas.
3. The facilitator notes all of the participants' ideas in the form of key words on a flip chart or a board. Then, the team sorts the ideas, identifies redundant ones and eliminates them. Related ideas are grouped and sorted until a practical structure has been created.
4. After the meeting, the results are analysed, evaluated and developed, either by the team, or by other members of staff who are responsible for their development.

6.2.1 Basic rules

Group sessions are often misconstrued as meetings. The participants perceive themselves as representatives of, for example, a department or a group of stakeholders. They therefore intuitively attempt to represent the opinions of `their´ group. This goes against the basic principle of brainstorming, which is a process in which the participants provide each other with inspiration instead of imitating discussions and establishing pecking orders. The appropriate attitude and suitable behaviour of all participants is crucial for the success of a brainstorming session.

Creativity rather than discussion

The following basic rules apply:
1. No criticism, assessment or discussion of ideas is allowed during brainstorming sessions. This is because many people will hesitate to make suggestions if they fear criticism. Expressions of anger or annoyance also come under the category of forbidden criticism.

No criticism

2. Self-criticism is also forbidden.
3. As many ideas as possible should be generated (quantity counts). The more suggestions that are made, the higher the probability that one of them will be useful, or that several ideas can be combined.
4. Even ideas that seem impossible are noted down. This is the key to achieving innovative and creative solutions.
5. Ideas should be briefly and precisely formulated. Detailed explanations can be made at a later time.
6. A quiet atmosphere is essential. Chatting about irrelevant things impairs concentration.
7. Everyone should represent himself. Anyone who expresses opinions that already exist in his department or stakeholder group will fail to have any good ideas of his own.
8. No interruptions (e.g. telephone calls).

6.2.2 Tasks of the chairperson

The chairperson or facilitator can do several things to increase participants' productivity:
- Encourage them to use other people's ideas as an incentive for new or further ideas.
- Set the pace of work so that slower colleagues (e.g. those who work especially meticulously) can keep up.
- Ensure pauses of a few seconds in length after each idea is suggested so that all participants can note their own thoughts on it.
- State the rules of behaviour, e.g. `no chatting`.

6.2.3 Versions of brainstorming

Further options for brainstorming include [20]:
- Discussion 66: brainstorming sessions in groups of six, followed by a plenary discussion.
- Anonymous brainstorming: each participant writes down possible solutions to a problem that he was informed about before the session. The facilitator reads out all the ideas, and the group then develops them further.
- Negative brainstorming: a weakness analysis performed in the group, followed by the processing of suggestions for improvement in the group.
- Imaginary brainstorming: in order to encourage the group to be imaginative, the moderator puts the problem in another context or invents an unusual framework (e.g. `Imagine you could read minds´).

6.3 Other creativity techniques

There are many other creativity techniques in addition to brainstorming.

6.3.1 Pro and contra analysis

This method enables the definition of the advantages and disadvantages of a suggestion. The participants consider arguments in two groups and present them to the panel. Then, each group discusses the other group´s suggestions. Both argue against the reasons put forward by the other group. Then, the members of both groups evaluate all arguments.

6.3.2 Delphi method

Long-term expert forecasts

The Delphi method is a structured method of questioning for the preparation of long-term forecasts. Experts in various fields are asked to provide individual forecasts (e.g. forecasts on the development of a specific market). Open-ended questions are used, rather than yes/no questions, so that the person answering has the opportunity to state the reasons for his answer. An assessor then includes the promising results which can be built upon in the next round. Then, each expert provides a more precise forecast based on the input from the other experts. After several rounds, the forecasts will be aligned to such an extent that a recommendation can be derived.

The disadvantage of this method is that it is complex and time-consuming. `Yes men´, who simply agree with the other experts' opinions, are difficult to identify.

6.3.3 Attribute listing

In the analytical method of attribute listing, the team breaks down a problem into its attributes. The status quo and an alternative state are derived for each attribute.

Alternative status quo

6.3.4 Morphological boxes

Morphological boxes are used by the group to initially define, analyse and generalise the problem. In the next step, they define the problem parameters (e.g. colour) and incorporate them in a matrix. They attempt to find alternatives for each parameter (e.g. red, green). Each combination of alternatives is a possible solution. In an iterative process, the group then filters out the realistic solutions.

Problem parameters matrix

6.3.5 Scenario writing

This method is used to prepare medium and long-term forecasts. In phase 1, the group analyses the current situation and the subject matter of the forecast, as well as its components and their inter-relationships with the environment. In phase 2, they elaborate alternative developments and, in phase 3, they define the resulting scenarios.

Medium and long-term forecasts

Self-assessment questions for each certification level

No.	Question	Level D	Level C	Level B	Level A	Self-assessment
D 2.01	What can a strengths and weaknesses analysis be used for?	2	3	3	4	☐
D 2.02	Which of the project manager's resources should be used for self-organisation?	2	3	3	4	☐
D 2.03	What steps are involved in an efficient decision-making process?	2	3	3	4	☐
D 2.04	What is a team success diary used for?	2	3	3	1	☐
D 2.05	Which 'Ten Commandments' apply to meetings from the initiators' perspective?	2	3	3	4	☐
D 2.06	What is the difference between a systematic summary and a chronological representation?	2	2	2	2	☐
D 2.07	What steps are involved in preparing for negotiations?	1	2	3	4	☐
D 2.08	What can help to prevent slip-ups in negotiations?	1	2	3	4	☐
D 2.09	What types of problems can generally occur?	2	2	2	2	☐
D 2.10	What specific types of problems exist in terms of their structure?	2	2	2	2	☐
D 2.11	What can hinder a project team member in the process of problem solving?	2	3	3	4	☐
D 2.12	What problem solving techniques can be used in a project?	2	3	3	4	☐
D 2.13	What basic procedures for problem solving can be applied?	2	3	3	4	☐
D 2.14	How can problems be presented so all team members gain a better understanding of them?	2	3	3	4	☐
D 2.15	Which key messages should a presenter communicate to the audience in a presentation?	2	3	4	4	☐
D 2.16	How should a handout for a project presentation be structured?	2	3	4	4	☐
D 2.17	Which creativity techniques can be used in projects?	2	3	3	3	☐
D 2.18	Where and how would you use the Delphi Method?	1	2	3	3	☐

D3 BUILDING AND MANAGING COMPETENT TEAMS

This chapter focuses upon efficient teams, professional team management and project-oriented personnel management, training and certification (ICB Elements 23, 24 and 35). Social competence is an important aspect of these processes. How do you put a team together?, How do you transform individuals into team players?, What phases does a team go through?, What role does social perception play?, What are the most common management mistakes? are some of the questions project managers need to be able to answer. The subject of occupational health and safety (ICB Element 40) is also briefly outlined.

1 Teamwork

Efficient and highly-motivated teams are essential for the success of a project. Teamwork is the basis of efficient implementation, and project personnel deliver better results if they enjoy and are motivated by working together. A project manager has to understand how to manage a team and ensure that its members enjoy their work. This can´t be done by intuition alone. A project manager has to be capable of putting together an optimum team, be familiar with team building measures, management and training concepts, and have other basic skills in order to exploit effectively their management potential (→ Chapter D1).

1.1 Selection of the project team

A project´s success depends to a great extent on the choice of its team members. This selection generally takes place under difficult circumstances, since projects in which the project manager has the authority to select his own team members are very rare. In many cases, a project manager has to accept staff not required urgently by line managers. In the past, project teams were often used as a parking lot for unpopular or under-qualified members of staff. However, this attitude has changed greatly in recent years.

Problems

These days, the selection of project personnel is not based on an individual´s availability or status within the standard management structures, but on the four areas of technical, methodological, organisational and social competence. Competent members of staff who merely lack project management skills can be trained up in a relatively short period of time so that they are capable of understanding and applying project management terms and methods. Such skills are essential for the performance of project tasks such as time scheduling, progress measurement, documentation, communication and other important activities requiring a systematic approach.

Four competence areas

Project management standards

1.1.1 Social competence

The ability of a team to function efficiently not only depends on professional qualifications and project management skills, but also to a great extent on the social competence of its team members.

D3 BUILDING AND MANAGING COMPETENT TEAMS

'Social competence' is a collective term used in the social sciences to describe a wide range of characteristics demonstrated by human beings in social situations [1].

Aspects of social competence

Social competence can be broken down into a series of individual components:
- Empathy
- Willingness to switch roles (e.g. to perform less prestigious tasks as well)
- Ability to reach consensus
- Ability to resolve conflicts
- Support for team members who don´t fit in
- Concern for group learning (a joint learning process and willingness to share knowledge)

Ability to deliver solutions

According to Ullrich/Ullrich de Muynck [2], social competence is the ability to deliver solutions to problems encountered in specific social situations.

1.1.2 Recommended procedures for team building

Various approaches to building project teams are outlined in this section.

1.1.2.1 Belbin´s model

Belbin´s role model is based on the idea that the different personality traits, knowledge and skills of the individual team members complement each other. Ideally, each team´s members fill nine roles, for which different terms may be used in practice.

Nine roles

1. Inventor/innovator: the ingenious brain of the troop, sometimes lacking in practical relevance.
2. Pathfinder: enthusiastic, sociable, arranges for the implementation of new ideas, although can soon lose interest in them again.
3. Coordinator/integrator: determined, organises situations and people and moulds them into an efficient entity, but is not necessarily intelligent and creative.
4. Implementer: dutiful, hard worker with his feet always firmly on the ground, focuses on facts and not visions.
5. Observer: a keen analyst who tends to stay out of things and is not exactly the driving force in the team.
6. Action man: ambitious, dynamic, encourages other team members, but is always so focused on action that he sometimes overlooks important details.
7. Specialist: a top expert in his field, likes to work in solitude, relatively disinterested in the project work.
8. Networker/teamworker: team-oriented, mediator, unsuitable as a decision-maker in a difficult situation for the team, has difficulty asserting himself.
9. Perfectionist: conscientious and reliable, but worries too much about all kinds of things.

One person with several roles

Most people can perform two or three team roles effectively and fill two further roles if no other team member is available.

1.1.2.2 Team Management System

Margerison & McCann´s Team Management System (TMS) is based on their research into the characteristics of successful teams and is another method of personnel, team and organisation development. TMS presupposes that nine team performance factors are associated with high-performing teams.

These are reflected in the Types of Work wheel model:
1. Advising: gathering and reporting information.
2. Innovating: creating and experimenting with ideas.
3. Promoting: exploring and presenting opportunities.
4. Developing: assessing and testing the applicability of new approaches.
5. Organising: establishing and implementing ways of making things work.
6. Producing: concluding and delivering outputs.
7. Inspecting: controlling and auditing the working of systems.
8. Maintaining: upholding and safeguarding standards and processes.
9. Linking: coordinating and integrating the work of others.

Types of Work wheel

The TMS principle works better in heterogeneous teams. Depending on what the team has to do, specific functions – or the staff who perform these functions – are accorded a greater or lesser weighting in the team building process. The `linking´ function is the team´s hub, the systemic head office of the team. Generally, the project manager performs this function. In more mature teams, the team members sometimes also assume some responsibility for `linking´. Even if the team only lacks one of the above functions, or the function is not performed effectively, efficiency is reduced. According to the TMS principle, the wheel doesn´t turn smoothly because a part is missing or damaged.

Weighting of functions

Figure D3-1 Margerison & McCann´s Types of Work wheel

1.1.2.3 Enneagram

The Enneagram is a personality model, with whose help people can assign themselves to one of nine different personality types. The lines in the symbol indicate how people´s behaviour can change under stress or flow conditions. Some people have a positive and encouraging effect, others a negative effect, on other people. The Enneagram´s structure delivers explanations for team development issues, such as recurring conflicts between particular people.

Reciprocal influence

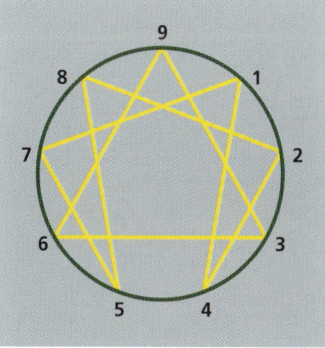

The personality types, for which different names are used in practice, can be described as follows:
1. Perfectionist/reformer
2. Helper/martyr
3. Action man/status type
4. Creative/emotional type
5. Observer/thinker
6. Worrier/networker
7. Enthusiast/adventurer
8. Leader
9. Reserved/harmonious type

Personality types

Figure D3-2 Enneagram

1.1.2.4 Högl´s recommendations for teamwork

Five factors of influence

In two case studies, Högl [3] identified five factors that have a dominant influence on teamwork: social competence, methodical competence, preference for teamwork, relative team size and heterogeneity of the team members´ knowledge and skills.

He recommends:

Social competence
1. Pay attention to social competence
   Social competence is an important prerequisite for open and intensive teamwork.

Methodical competence
2. Ensure methodical competence
   Methodical competence enables several people to work on the same task concurrently, which is an basic aspect of teamwork. It is especially important for project structuring and for the coordination of project work performed by team members and external partners.

Teamwork aptitude
3. Ensure that team members have an aptitude for teamwork
   Team projects should chiefly be staffed by people who are especially motivated by the idea of working on tasks collectively. Extreme individualists can perform specific tasks without being members of the team.

Team size
4. Ensure that the size of the team is appropriate for the project.
   If a team is too small, it will not be able to satisfy the formal requirements of a project. If it is too large, communication, coordination and motivation losses accumulate. Team size should be carefully considered with respect to the task; in some cases individuals´ tasks may be defined as external contributions in order to restrict the size of the team.

Knowledge/skills discrepancies
5. Avoid major differences in the knowledge and skill levels of team members.
   Extreme polarisation between low and high performers has a detrimental effect on teamwork. An attempt should be made to ensure a suitably homogeneous knowledge and skills level within the team.

Individual factors of influence

The individual characteristics and traits of team members, and their differences (= heterogeneity), can have a strong impact on teamwork [4]. These include technical jargon, local organisational cultures (e.g. of a department), professional understanding (e.g. sales vs. development), gender, age, formal qualifications, knowledge and skills, personal values and opinions, socio-economic status and personality. Högl also differentiates between demographic (age, gender, length of employment with the organisation, degree and field of professional qualifications) and performance-related characteristics (knowledge and skills).

In practice, the required extent of a team´s heterogeneity largely depends on its task. In a crisis project, where deadlines have the utmost priority and the tasks to be performed are not complex, a homogeneous team tends to be more effective. The opposite applies in extremely complex projects that demand creative solutions. In this case, a healthy mixture of experts and all-rounders fosters innovative solutions.

1.1.2.5 Sackmann´s recommendations

Structural aspects and management responsibilities

Sackmann not only emphasises the significance of team qualifications, but also takes other criteria into account [5]: `Project teams should not just be built on the basis of the project manager´s and project personnel´s qualifications. Structural aspects and management responsibilities are also important.´ She recommends taking three aspects into consideration [6]:

1. Purely professional skills
   The team must include members with the essential professional skills required throughout the project and that cannot be delivered by non-team experts called in on an ad-hoc basis.

2. Teamwork skills
   Teamwork skills are important because they ensure that staff with different areas of specialisation can incorporate their know-how in the achievement of the project team´s objectives and not merely act in their own or in their department´s interests. Good project team players have the social skills to interact with the other members of the team. This also necessitates some degree of sensitivity towards these people and their interests or needs, as well as about the requirements of a given situation, plus the ability to be reserved or proactive, depending on the circumstances. High-performing team members are neither power-hungry, control freaks nor selfish.
3. Integration in the organisation and representation of interests
   The project manager should specify the level of decision-making power that staff in the organisation´s units (e.g. departments) need in order to be of use to him. A project team is far more effective if its members have the authority to make important decisions in their line organisation unit [7], since this simplifies and accelerates project decision-making processes. It can also be advantageous to include representatives of specific organisational units or stakeholder groups in the project team so that their viewpoints as customers or affected persons can be taken into account.

1.2 Team development process

Once a team has been built, it has to grow together before it can function effectively. This is a process that should be proactively supported by the project manager. In many cases, however, this doesn´t happen. Mayrshofer and Ahrens [8] have observed that, `This process is often not consciously driven, but left to chance.´ This can have severe consequences: `Since the project team members generally specialise in different fields, more often than not come from different levels in the organisation´s hierarchy and sometimes even from different cultures, team coherence and motivation are not clear. This makes communication between the team members problematic at first.´

Active support from the manager

1.2.1 Johari window

In order to guide team development, the project manager should assess the team at the outset of the project. The Johari window [9] offers useful support for this because it helps to visualise the different stages of team development. It shows team members´ different perceptions of each other. As a team develops, some perceptions grow and others fade. In the Johari model, these developments are represented by the relevant quadrant becoming either larger or smaller.

Visualisation of development stages

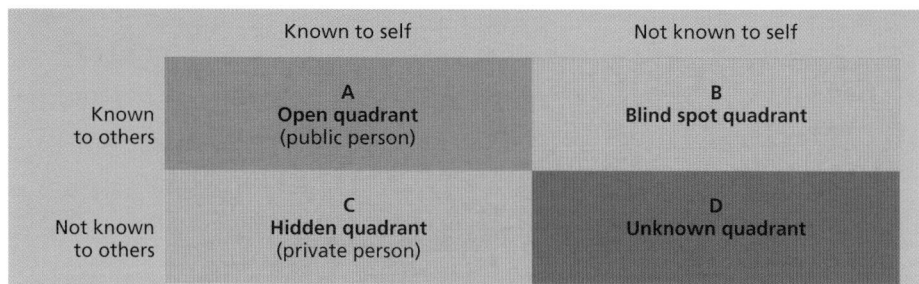

Figure D3-3 The principle of the Johari window

Quadrant A shows the extent to which the behaviour and motives of a team member are known to the person himself and to the other members of the team.

Example
A team member is afraid of making mistakes. Both he and the team are aware of this. The other team members attempt to help him to overcome this fear by being sensitive to it.

Quadrant B shows the extent to which a team member is not aware of his behaviour and motives, even though the other members of the team are.

Example
A team member regularly interrupts other people in discussions. As a result, the other team members would prefer for him to be excluded from meetings. The person in question is aware that something is wrong, but he doesn´t know what.

Quadrant C shows the extent to which a team member wishes to hide his behaviour and motives from the other team members.

Example
A team member finds it difficult to speak a foreign language. He makes various excuses to ensure that other members of the team are assigned to tasks which involve speaking this foreign language. He is even willing to let his colleagues think he is lazy if it means that he doesn´t have to speak the foreign language.

Quadrant D shows the behaviour and motives of which neither the team member nor the other team members are aware.

Example
A team member responds to criticism with stomach problems. However, neither he nor the other team members are aware of the link between the two.

Subconscious behaviour and motives

In the process of team development, the project manager´s objective is to enlarge quadrant A and to shrink quadrants B and C. Shrinking quadrant D is a difficult task for the both the project manager and the team. In this case, an external expert may be able to help by identifying subconscious behaviour and motives.

D3 BUILDING AND MANAGING COMPETENT TEAMS

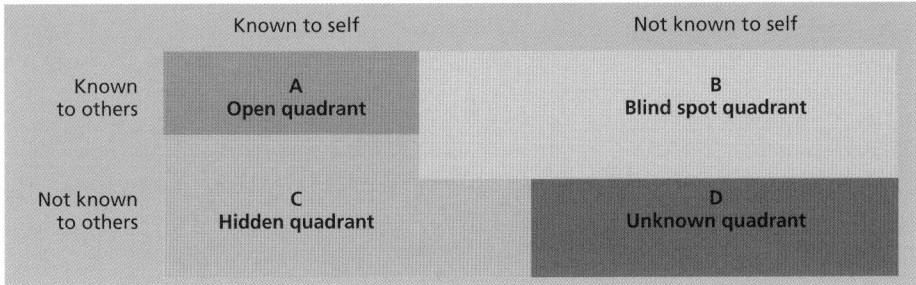

Figure D3-4 Johari window at the beginning of the team development

The sizes of the quadrants relative to one another depend on the criteria and method of decision making used to select team members. In teams where technical selection criteria predominate, B, C and D are relatively large at the outset of team development. In other words, very little spontaneous, open interaction is initially observed during project work. Although the members of the team do keep their eye on each other, their actions depend to a great extent on the project manager. This is not the case in teams that are selected on the basis of soft factors such as affinity and antipathy, similarities and common preferences. These groups have a larger quadrant A than the first group, and the project manager can generally enlarge A even more.

Technical selection criteria

Soft factors

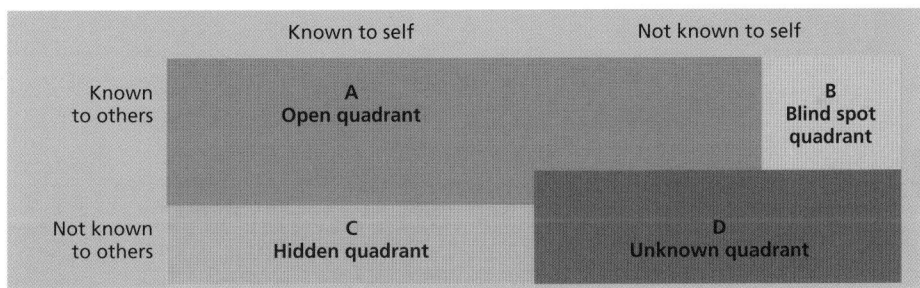

Figure D3-5 Johari window showing successful team development

1.2.2 Phases of team development

Project management literature often divides team development into four ideal phases. Various terms are used to describe these phases. One example is [10]:
  Phase 1: orientation
  Phase 2: disquiet/clarification
  Phase 3: motivation/productivity
  Phase 4: dissolution

In phase one, team members sound each other out and gain their first impressions of one another. They talk about themselves very little to ensure that they do not give away too much about themselves. This behaviour corresponds to quadrant C in the Johari window. It is not yet clear how the team will develop (quadrant D of the Johari window). The project manager can help the team to get to know each other by providing ample opportunities for formal and, especially, informal communication (→ Chapter D4).

Orientation

Disquiet/clarification

In phase two, the team members gradually open up. They express preferences, expectations and criticism, and defend their role and status vis-à-vis other team members. A pecking order, which defines the team members' status within and outside the team, is created. The project manager should allow this phase – even if team members believe that the supposed chaos is caused by his inactivity. This process also has the effect that the team becomes less dependent on the project manager and the members assume responsibility for their work. One-to-one interviews in this phase are not the right way to solve problems because other team members could construe them as collusion, management weakness or team oppression. It is far better if team members discuss any differences of opinion openly. This promotes a sense of team spirit and makes the team less sensitive to external interference.

Personal responsibility

Productivity

In phase three, roles have been assigned and a social structure has emerged. Quadrant A of the Johari window has expanded and the team can work productively.

Dissolution

In phase four, the project is nearing conclusion (→ Chapter C10). The team no longer has a common purpose or reason to exist. Behaviour triggered by the dissolution of the team and the team members' uncertainty about their own future often causes tensions, and the social structure crumbles. It is difficult to reconsolidate the team in this phase. Introducing new team members or changing the team's composition is not a good idea because both mean that the team development process has to begin all over again – which is unrealistic due to the time pressure and lack of motivation in the project's final phase.

Process begins again

The role of the project manager in each of the four phases can be described as follows:
- Phase 1: host
- Phase 2: catalyst
- Phase 3: first among equals
- Phase 4: coach

1.2.2.1 Five-phase model

Team clock

Another model, Tuckman's team development theory (team clock), differentiates between five phases:

1. Orientation phase (= forming)
   The people join the team with different expectations. They sound each other out, routine work (e.g. clarification of the organisational structure) is performed and tasks are allocated. They still feel relatively comfortable and are friendly and polite to each other.
2. Power struggle phase (= storming)
   This phase is all about how to work (together). The first frictions occur (e.g. power struggles, resource conflicts) and team members will sometimes be dissatisfied with the way the team is managed. Conflicts brew.
3. Organisational phase (= norming)
   Conflicts come to a head. The more obstacles are eliminated and conflicts solved, the greater the subsequent team cohesion. Roles are clearly established and team members agree upon rules.
4. Achievement phase (= performing)
   If the team reaches this phase – which is not easy and should by no means be taken for granted – the team as a whole will outperform its individual members. A strong sense of team identity will have developed. Team members will support each other. Achieving the team objective will be the highest priority.
5. Dissolution phase (= adjourning)
   The team is dissolved. Its members leave their tasks, roles, responsibilities and the other team members behind.

In both of the above-described models, it is necessary to emphasise that whenever changes take place (e.g. new team members, changed tasks), the whole process starts again with the first phase (= orientation phase). It is therefore a good idea to keep fluctuation to a minimum. High-performing teams soon return to a previously-achieved performance level.

Impact of changes

1.2.3 Special aspects of the start-up phase

The project manager´s managerial skills are especially important in the start-up phase. His task is to initiate the team-building process and to ensure that
- team members can identify with their project responsibilities,
- they are familiar with and accept the project objectives,
- latent conflicts are brought out into the open and discussed, and
- a positive project culture is created.

Project manager´s responsibilities

In the start-up phase every single project team member needs to be especially creative (e.g. for the definition of project objectives). The project manager is best advised to use a cooperative management style in this phase, i.e. the team members should have the opportunity to contribute knowledge and be involved in decision-making.

Cooperative management style

During this phase, the project manager is responsible for establishing communication channels (→ Chapter D4) with line managers and with the customer to enable proactive stakeholder management. The regular provision of information via formal reporting channels and at status meetings is very important. The project manager should establish a solid basis for efficient informal communication structures. For example, he can set up his workplace close to the workplaces of other team members, or organise team activities.

1.3 Social structures

A social structure evolves in every team, based on roles, status and rules. From the ICB [11]: `Specific roles are transferred onto team members which give expectations. The status of an individual is his reputation in the project team. It depends on his contribution to the development and performance of the team. The ability to function depends on rules which are either defined externally or desired internally.´

1.3.1 Roles

Roles are the expectations that team members have of other team members and of the organisation. They are defined by character and conduct, personal values, position, status and responsibilities. Each team member can have several roles. If the project manager identifies differences in expectations at an early stage of the team development process, conflicts (→ Chapter D5) can be avoided. There are two types of roles: formal and informal roles.

Expectations

Formal roles relate to the functions of individuals. They are already defined in the line organisation (e.g. by a department head) or established on a case-by-case basis (e.g. through a project manager´s authority). By the clarification stage at the latest, the team members should have established which

Role model

expectations each role holder has to fulfil. The aim is to ensure that all team members have a common picture of each role (= role model). If a role holder does not meet these expectations, conflicts are inevitable. Problems also occur if the role holder is not happy about performing a role because not every employee can automatically identify with the formal role that is assigned to him. In such cases, intra-individual and finally inter-individual conflicts (→ Chapter D5) can occur.

Role change

The project manager can also ask the teams to assign roles. However, he should always make it clear that every role is important for the team. Some conflicts can be solved through rotation of the team members' roles (e.g. minute-taker, time keeper, arbitrator).

Psychosocial level

Informal roles, on the other hand, are assumed at psychosocial level during the team development process. For example, many teams have a `ringleader´, a `cheerful soul´, and a `dogsbody´ who has to perform the unpleasant tasks. Since it is impossible to prevent the formation of informal roles, the project manager should attempt to ensure that the process is at least constructive. For example, he can ask an opinion leader with good rhetorical skills to represent the project team at external meetings. He should not, however, leave weaker team members to their own devices, dismissing this as natural role building. Instead, he should give them the opportunity to show what they can do, for example, by assigning them an attractive task.

1.3.2 Status

Formal/informal

Status is the reputation of an individual in the team. It depends, first and foremost, on how the individual performs his role and serves the team, though personality and conduct are also important status factors. A person's formal status is closely associated with his formal role. In contrast, informal status is linked to the individual's behaviour within the team. A person's perception of his own status can differ considerably from that of the team. Formal status often differs considerably from informal status, both positively and negatively. The project manager can support low-status team members by offering them the chance to demonstrate their strengths.

Bullying

Team members with a poor reputation are often subjected to harassment. The other team members systematically attack an unpopular team member, whom they view as inferior, with the objective of excluding him from the group. Project stress and the manager's condoning encourage such aggression. It is often difficult for managers to identify harassment among staff owing to an initial lack of firm evidence. In order to ensure project success, the project manager should attempt to resolve the situation by talking to the team members involved as soon as he notices the first signs of harassment. When he has gathered enough information, he should talk about the problem openly with the team members involved and ask them to help him to identify the causes and work out solutions. This brings the subliminal negativity, typically associated with incidents of harassment, to the surface and out of the taboo zone. In efficient teams, antipathy tends to dissipate as soon as it brought out into the open. However, the project manager should support underdogs in the team to prevent them from being forced into the role of victim.

1.3.3 Rules

Points of negotiation

Teams can only perform well on the basis of rules agreed upon and accepted by the team members. These rules govern the following issues:

- information and data flow,
- conflict-solving methods (e.g. the use of an arbitrator when disputes arise),
- organisation of teamwork (e.g. working hours, breaks, rules on requests for time off, responsibility for materials procurement),
- performance targets and measurement,
- internal and external conduct, and
- external communication rules (→ Chapter D4).

These and many other things have to be negotiated in the clarification phase. For solving conflicts, Mayrshofer and Ahrens [12] recommend: `It is useful to establish transparency throughout the entire conflict phase of natural team development and not to skirt around the issues of what team members have in common, their differences, the power balance and decision-making structures. This requires a high level of social and emotional competence, at least on the part of the project manager.´ The conflict phase corresponds to the disquiet/clarification phase and the power struggle phase in the two models of team development described above.

Creating transparency throughout the development phase

1.4 Team building measures

When building project teams, both formal measures (e.g. start-up meetings, workshops, personnel selection, and training of team members) and informal measures (e.g. promotion and support of teamwork, individual motivation, and social events) come into play [13]. It is the project manager´s task to mould the team members into a cohesive entity. To do this, he has to

- define, with his team, the working rules for the duration of their collaboration.
- ensure that all team members have the same understanding of the project charter and objectives.
- assign responsibilities clearly.
- ensure that all team members back important decisions through explaining to, convincing and communicating between the holders of different opinions.
- ensure that all team members receive the same information.
- create the basis for transparent communication structures (→ Chapter D4).
- provide the team with regular feedback on its performance and development, relating to both work and interpersonal relationships in the team.
- identify conflicts as soon as possible and find constructive solutions (→ Chapter D5).
- foster constructive arguments in which all participants can state their concerns without fear of reprisals from the team [14].

Project manager´s responsibilities

1.4.1 Teamwork rules

The following rules apply to all team members:
- All observe the basic communication rules (→ Chapter D4) (e.g. express perceptions rather than accusations, speak in the first person).
- Team members should provide feedback – especially criticisms – so that the person affected has the opportunity and is motivated to modify his behaviour (e.g. offer specific suggestions, and also refer to the positive aspects of the person being criticised).
- Each individual should regularly inform the other team members about what they are currently working on, the objective of this activity and any possible problems.

Team rules

- All team members should observe the meeting rules (e.g. punctual arrival, minute-taking, acceptance of a binding speaking order, no interruptions when people are speaking, every participant can join in the discussion).
- The team members should provide each other with information (e.g. about organisational and HR-related issues, anything of technical interest) so that they can optimise their work and no one feels left out.
- All team members share responsibility for decisions that are made in accordance with the decision-making process agreed upon by the team.
- Conflicts (→ Chapter D5) and potential conflicts should be discussed openly and the entire team should then develop a solution.
- Every member of the team should try to respect and support team colleagues.
- Everyone takes it in turns to perform unpopular tasks (e.g. typing up the minutes, running errands, cleaning the coffee machine).

1.5 Team dynamics

Individual/teamwork

Group-dynamic effects occur in project teams and can enhance or impair team performance [15]. Some tasks can be performed faster by an individual than by the team. The project manager therefore has to decide which tasks should be performed by individuals and which on the basis of teamwork.

Co-action effect

Overall performance can be improved merely by virtue of several people working together. This phenomenon, which also applies when different people work on different tasks, is called the co-action effect [16].

Performance-enhancing effects

However, co-action effects can only occur under certain circumstances and when specific tasks are being performed [17]:

1. The strengths, knowledge and skills of the team´s members must complement or supplement each other if they are to be more efficient as a team than as individuals. In other words, the team´s additional output must be greater than the input necessary for coordination.
2. If several team members are involved in the process of problem solving, it is possible to construct an `ideal´ solution from their individual suggestions that takes as many different aspects of the problem as possible into account. Team problem solving reduces the likelihood of a unilateral solution due to the cooperation effect [18]. It is necessary to have an objective means of measuring the effectiveness of solutions. Two associated pitfalls are: first, since team members are under some pressure to conform, which means that they may be more easily swayed by other team members´ opinions, important considerations are sometimes ignored and doubts are not voiced. Secondly, teams are more prone to taking risks than individuals. The project manager should explain these pitfalls to his team so that it has the opportunity to reconsider, confirm or change its opinion.

Cooperation effect

Pressure to conform

3. Tasks associated with performance indicators, standards and rules that the team has developed and is responsible for should be performed as a team. The project manager should neither performance indicators, nor check to see whether they have been met. If the project situation changes and new performance requirements come into play, the team should evaluate the situation and decide upon the next steps.

In order to take advantage of these benefits, the team members must respect each other, communicate with each other, have the opportunity to freely contribute their own ideas and be themselves [19].

Mutual respect

1.5.1 Team cohesion

Having a common task (= objective level), conformity of values, interests and expectations, as well as acceptance of team rules and roles (= psychosocial level) promotes team cohesion and differentiates a team from its environment. Members of such teams perceive themselves as part of an entity or unit. Their common history and their sense of belonging, which they often have to work hard to achieve, also consolidate team cohesion.

However, a team´s performance will decline if strong cohesion causes it to ignore external ideas and criticism. This effect can be reduced if several team members remain in contact with the outside world. On the other hand, if the project manager is their only communication channel (= gatekeeper), the team will have fewer ideas and opportunities to benefit from external input.

Gatekeeper

Teams that refuse to consider alternative solutions based on their strong sense of cohesion suffer from groupthink [20]. This risk of having a blinkered mentality is especially high if the team has a strong ringleader. As a result, the team members no longer look right nor left, but exclusively focus on their leader.

Group-minded

That´s why it is important
- regularly to call in external members of the organisation´s staff to provide fresh input and objective criticism,
- occasionally to divide the team into sub-teams which develop their own opinions and solutions and defend them against the other sub-teams, and
- deliberately to encourage a critical review, even if a solution appears at first glance to be ideal.

1.6 Social perception

Social perception is a root cause of interpersonal problems. For example, social perception determines whether individual team members like each other, who gets on well with whom and which colleagues dislike each other intensely.

Perception can be defined as a selection process driven by sensory impressions which takes place actively, but subconsciously [21]. People use their senses to filter out the most important impressions from all the things that are going on around them, to assimilate them on a trial basis, re-filter them, possibly re-assimilate them, and so on, until they make a subconscious decision about whether this `thing´ is worthwhile or not. People prefer to interpret sensory impressions that fit in with their established ideas. This is why they find it difficult to accept information that deviates from these ideas. The team members should be aware of the difference between the perception of and evaluation of a person or situation, otherwise there is a potential for future team conflicts.

Selection of sensory impressions

According to Wittstock and Triebe, simple sensory perceptions are not as important as context-related expectations with regard to our initial impressions of other people. If the other person fits into an existing pattern, we tend to ignore their other characteristics. Therefore, if a person is confronted with a new situation (e.g. a new working environment, a new team), he instinctively seeks

Schema — impressions that resemble past experience. First of all, he registers the objects, people or social constellations with which he is already familiar. Patterns, or networks of interlinked information [22], that he has learned over the course of his life help him to do this.

Assimilation Accommodation — Assimilation and accommodation are relevant terms worth mentioning. Assimilation is the process of dealing with stimuli that do fit our known schemata. Accommodation simply means the creation of new schemata when stimuli don´t fit.

First impression — Our first impression is the most important one. When we see or hug a person for the first time, we leave our `mark´ on them without being able to control this consciously. `That new man is definitely choleric. He looks just like my awful neighbour.´ The person in question finds it difficult to escape this `stigma´ by demonstrating different behaviour. This is a mechanism of which all team members should be aware. Those who are soon realise that first impressions are not necessarily accurate. A colleague whom you dislike at first can turn out to be a nice person who was simply nervous about his first day

Second chance — in a new team. Anyone who gives a new team member a second chance is not only helping him to become part of the team, but also gaining a loyal supporter. At the same time, he is exhibiting a positive and open attitude that fosters team cohesion.

1.6.1 Social aspects of perception

Causal attribution, stereotyping and attitudes are central social aspects of perception.

Causal attribution

Comparison of expectations/ actual behaviour — Causal attribution is a process in which we describe a person´s behaviour in terms of certain causes. The observer compares the observed behaviour with his own expectations. If it deviates from his expectations, he concludes that the person has certain – positive or negative – characteristics. Expectations are shaped by personal experience, socialisation and cultural background.

Stereotypes

A stereotype is an unconfirmed assumption that members of a group have about other group members (e.g. typical behaviour of a certain cultural group). Stereotypes are to social perception what schemata are to general perception. Although these templates are necessary for the classification of

Template — information, they tend to have a negative effect on team development. If the team allocates a role to a person based on a stereotype, frustration, conflicts and wasted potential are likely as a result of the wrong person doing the wrong job. For example, a certain engineer may be assigned to development tasks instead of controlling tasks, even though he has a greater aptitude for controlling tasks.

Prejudice — Stereotypes are therefore also associated with prejudices. These are `unjust, deprecatory or negative attitudes vis-à-vis persons or groups of persons based solely on their membership of certain social groups, irrespective of whether we know the person or not´ [23]. They are not based on collected and evaluated information which disproves the stereotype or can contribute to the creation of a new stereotype. Prejudice is also expressed in the form of remarks such as, `A woman with two children as project manger – are you sure we can really count on her?´ In order to prevent firmly-established stereotypes in the form of prejudices from impairing team development, the project manager should provide his team with adequate opportunity for formal and informal communication so they can get to know each other.

Attitudes

Attitudes are assessments of persons or facts and hold for lengthy periods. People use them to understand the behaviour of others and predict the future.

2 Management

There are so many different management theories that we only outline some of the main terms here. Coordination mechanisms (hierarchy, self-coordination, programmes and rules, as well as planning) have already been discussed [24] and are closely related to team management.

Coordination mechanisms

Management is basically a manager´s influencing of behaviour so that a specific objective is reached. It can be divided into objective functions (e.g. project planning) or personal functions (= people management).

Management is necessary because the staff performing tasks require coordination, both at objective and at personal level. Management style describes the way in which the manager performs his management functions.

Management style / functions

Management techniques are methods, processes and instruments that support management functions (e.g. staff assessments or software).

Management techniques

2.1 Essential management skills

According to the ICB, a manager [25]:
- can delegate tasks and have confidence in others,
- takes over the total responsibility, but also formulates sub-responsibilities,
- allows sufficient freedom for action to subordinates for finding and realising their ways,
- controls the team members´ behaviour in a conscious and constructive way, has discipline and time for communication,
- engages the team members in decisions or has a reason for decisions taken,
- adopts the management style to the specific team and working situation, is open for feedback,
- acts as an example and is acknowledged as a leader, and
- gives direct feedback.

Characteristics of a manager

2.2 Management concepts

The so-called `management by´ approaches are concepts that give managers orientation when performing their management function. The best-known ones are
- Management by objectives
- Management by delegation
- Management by exception

`Management by´ approaches

Management by objectives
This approach is all about management on the basis of jointly-agreed objectives (= target agreement). It is a cooperative management style in which project personnel agree individual objectives with the

Jointly-agreed objectives

project manager. They are more motivated to achieve these objectives because they were involved in their definition and in the decision-making process.

Management by delegation

Authority and responsibility

In this approach, the project manager delegates tasks to staff for a specific period of time. During this time, they are not only authorised to structure their own work, but also to assume responsibility for the timely delivery of results within the agreed budget and to the agreed quality. This provides the project manager with additional time for other tasks, gives team members a sense of responsibility and ensures that they learn new things – both technical skills and soft skills such as decision-making, putting forward opinions and ideas or reporting on the progress of a work package.

Bottleneck

At the same time, delegation prevents the project manager from becoming a bottleneck that impairs the workflow. If he is absent on holiday or on sick leave, other members of the team can assume his responsibilities and keep the project going because the project manager is no longer the sole knowledge carrier.

Management by exception

Reports

This approach is based on the idea that a project manager only intervenes in exceptional cases in the work of a team member to whom he has delegated a task. However, this approach only works if the staff to whom the tasks have been delegated submit reports at the agreed intervals and meet cost, deadline and quality targets. The project manager intervenes if problems occur.

2.3 Management styles

Behaviour patterns

A management style is the pattern of behaviour that a manager demonstrates in management situations. The main styles are
- Authoritarian management style
- Cooperative (= participatory) management style
- Management by the team itself
- Laissez-faire management style

In practice, a mixture of styles is generally used.

Authoritarian management style

A project manager who has an authoritarian management style
- states objectives without asking the opinion of team members,
- issues instructions, and
- checks to ensure that they have been carried out.

Disadvantages

This style puts pressure on the team, and only motivates them superficially. Team members who fear failure or sanctions tend to be less creative. The working climate in organisations with authoritarian management structures is often cool and inhibiting.

Cooperative management style

Compromise between following instructions and autonomy

The cooperative management style is a compromise between the staff following the manager´s instructions and structuring their own work. Although the project manager controls his team, he gives them as much scope as possible to make their own decisions. The objective is to create a motivated and responsible group with a strong sense of team spirit. The cooperative management style is more practical and successful than the authoritarian management style.

Management by the team itself
Each team member assumes responsibility for his area of competence. In this management structure, the team members must be highly competent, have a strong sense of responsibility, have good communication skills, accept each other, support each other and be able to solve conflicts.

Laissez-faire management style
Anyone who uses the laissez-faire style is not managing. He leaves the team to get on with its work in the hope that this freedom will motivate it to perform well. Sometimes, this approach causes team members to lose their orientation. They lose sight of the objectives and put deadlines, costs and quality at risk.

Lack of orientation

Flexible management style: Mixing management styles
A cooperative management style is desirable, though not practical in every situation. It is suitable for project phases where it is important to ensure that the project team members agree and identify with the project, and that they creatively structure the project as a team (e.g. objective definition, risk analysis). In difficult situations – for example, if a technical solution proves to be unsuitable and an alternative solution has to be found quickly – it is more important to have an efficiently functioning team. In this case, a more authoritarian management style is appropriate. There is no time for lengthy discussions and the project manager has to assert his authority and take action.

Difficult situations

2.4 Recommendations for team management

Based on his work, Högl [26] developed recommendations for team management. They are founded on the knowledge that the management variables of objectives and feedback, as well as the equality of all team members, have a significant effect on team performance. These variables can account for almost 70 percent of team performance variance and are therefore an excellent departure point for team management concepts, says Högl.

1. The team objective (→ Chapter C2) should be collectively agreed and binding for all team members (binding team objective, commitment).
   No advantages are gained if the collective project objective is broken down to sub-objectives for individual team members (passed down from the management). It is far more important to ensure that the team members are collectively committed to the customer and to achieving the overall objective. This does not affect project planning and the allocation of tasks within the team. To improve the team´s commitment to its goals, Högl recommends, in addition to goal-setting, instruments based on evaluation (e.g. weighting team performance by individual assessment) and incentives (e.g. project bonuses for the team).

   Binding collective objective

2. The team objective should be clear, manageable in terms of time, realistic in terms of content and constant over time. Goals of high quality promote team commitment and therefore co-operation. The persons responsible should ensure that team objectives, like individual objectives, are associated with quality criteria. Milestones (= interim objectives) are a good way of providing a timeline for achieving objectives in mid to long-term projects, and they offer an excellent opportunity to provide specific, objective-related feedback. It is often necessary to establish consensus among project participants (staff, project manager, line managers) who view performance requirements (objectives) and results´ evaluation (performance) from different perspectives. This is essential for the generation of useful feedback and for team performance-related evaluation and incentive systems.

   Objective quality

   Milestones

Feedback

3. The team should be provided with regular, specific and constructive feedback throughout the project.

This feedback can be provided by external managers, by team members or, most importantly, by the project manager. Team feedback should focus on the issue, not the person, and should include improvement suggestions rather than blame. Feedback should not only be provided if course deviations occur.

In connection with this recommendation, Högl mentions that feedback relating to specific persons can be conducive to team development, but only if the team has reached a certain stage of maturity. Otherwise, objective issues may be addressed when a problem actually exists at relationship level.

Equal status of team members

4. Innovation teams should always use a management model that promotes equality of team members.

Decision-making powers should be distributed as evenly as possible within the team. This is a challenge for both the formal project manager, who needs to share his decision-making powers, and the team members, who need to partake actively in the decision-making process. However, equality does not mean that the decisions have to be made on the basis of complete consensus. This could impair the team´s performance. It is far better to delegate less significant decisions to individual team members or sub-teams.

2.4.1 Ten guidelines for managers

A manager should
1. be at peace with himself,
2. be well organised,
3. enjoy being a manager,
4. have the self- confidence to be a role-model,
5. like his work,
6. like and respect his team,
7. not be afraid of making mistakes,
8. be open and honest when it comes to his own weaknesses and those of his staff,
9. accept criticism with good grace, and
10. promote communication as a matter of course.

Very few people will have all of these characteristics. Schelle [27] comments, `The required traits are in reality seen more as objectives for training and development measures, i.e. they are desirable skills and competences, rather than factors on which the selection of a suitable project manager should be based.´ They should encourage the project manager to continue learning and developing his skills.

2.5 Management problems encountered by project managers

Management problems

Gregor-Rauschtenberger and Hansel [28] have identified management problems that many project managers have to deal with:
1. A project manager is not able to handle his authority.
2. A member of the team has been appointed as project manager.
3. The project manager has insufficient formal authority.
4. The project manager does not acknowledge his (administrative) management tasks or is not

qualified to perform them.
5. The project manager has not yet developed his own management model.
6. The project manager is not prepared for change processes.
7. The project manager predominantly addresses objective matters and ignores emotional and political issues.
8. The project manager registers a lack of or declining project team motivation.

The following recommendations can be formulated based on the above: *Recommendations*
- The project manager should be prepared for taking on responsibility, (e.g. as a member of another project management team, as an assistant manager, through project management training, or coaching) and not be expected to jump in at the deep end. This requires systematic personnel development.
- The organisation's management team should grant adequate formal (decision-making) powers to all project managers (e.g. to have a say in the people who are selected for the teams, involvement in personnel development measures).
- Project managers must be trained in the fields of administration, personnel management and change process management.
- If the project manager has the opportunity to gain project work experience, he will develop a `feel´ for the relationship level.

3 Motivation

Incentives are a prerequisite for goal-oriented and motivated teamwork. Team members must believe in the project and that their involvement offers them personal benefits. These benefits can include job security (because the project will help the company to remain in business), knowledge building, career advancement, a financial bonus, honest praise in the presence of the entire team or a personal tribute from the project manager. It is always best if a project team member can derive personal satisfaction or personal benefits from the success of a project. *Personal benefits*

However, opinions differ as to whether the incentives provided by the manager have a genuine motivating effect. For example, Sprenger [29] doubts whether incentive systems (e.g. bonuses) have a lasting positive effect on the long-term attitudes of employees to their work. Accordingly, sophisticated motivation techniques can mean that the incentives have to be continually increased in order to have a motivating effect on employees, who gradually become more and more immune to them. Other possible side effects of individual incentives are interpersonal problems such as resentment or envy. Ideally, the staff should be personally motivated and the managers should encourage this process. *Disadvantages of incentive systems*

Maslow's needs pyramid represents a needs-based framework of human motivation. It shows that lower needs - one of which is financial security – are fundamental needs. If these lower needs are satisfied, people will turn their attention to higher needs such as recognition and self-esteem – which are motivation factors at a higher level of the pyramid. *Maslow's needs pyramid*

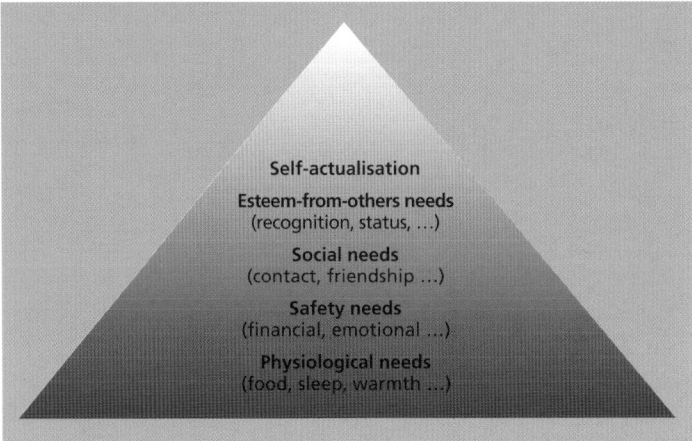

Figure D3-6 Representation of human needs based on Maslow's needs pyramid [30]

3.1 Target agreement

Problems

In his book entitled 'The Motivation Myth', Sprenger explains that the core aspects of human motivation have nothing to do with incentive systems, but with a quest for meaning. A person can only find this meaning if he is involved in the (co-)determination of his objectives. Agreeing targets serves this purpose, although managers have to ensure that certain basic criteria are satisfied. Even experienced managers sometimes find it difficult to introduce more democratic structures that apparently reduce their powers instead of taking an authoritative approach to problem solving. Team managers who are expected to jump in at the deep end without management experience are afraid of the target agreement method.

Rules for project managers

When targets are agreed, the project manager should observe the following eight rules:
1. First discuss the targets with all people affected and then jointly define them.
2. Formulate objectives in a concise and understandable way.
3. Agree, don't dictate – pay attention to the formulation, tone of voice and response of staff.
4. Provide staff with psychological support to cope with their new responsibility.
5. Make it clear that targets have to be met.
6. Encourage staff to voice their opinions.
7. Discuss progress with staff regularly.
8. Identify reasons, when targets are not met.

Coach

It is a good idea to call in a coach who can intervene if the interview doesn't go as planned.

3.2 Motivation problems

Implementation deficiencies

Even organisations that use incentive systems often have staff who are not committed to performance factors and targets. This is because, although these organisations have recognised the significance of staff motivation, they are inconsistent in the implementation of such measures. A bonus that is reduced to next to nothing on the pay slip after tax does not motivate an employee to optimise his work processes. And anyone who, on paper, can set his own working hours but in practice is required to spend the core time in the office, will not focus on developing new products, but grumble about getting stuck in rush hour traffic every evening.

Organisations are still reluctant to introduce genuine changes because they are concerned that these jeopardise power structures and hierarchies. Managers, in particular, tend to avoid disclosing whether they are attaining their targets or not. In addition, few managers will be happy if their top sales employees earn a higher salary than their own because they generate high commission-related sales.

Transparency

3.3 Further methods for boosting motivation

Further methods for boosting motivation are

Job rotation (= rotating staff between similar activities) *Job rotation*

Job enlargement (= enlargement of current activities to include new ones) *Job enlargement*

Job enrichment *Job enrichment*
Planning, preparatory and controlling activities are incorporated in the person´s overall function to increase his scope of responsibility.

(Partially autonomous) group work
Several people working towards one and the same objective, though each with a specific area of responsibility. The participants view themselves as a team, and develop the relevant communication and cooperation structures.

4 Project coaching

Project coaching is increasingly popular in companies. A coach can provide valuable services in a project because, by nature, these have many hidden conflicts and challenges. Typical problems are (resource) conflicts with the line in a matrix organisation (→ Chapter A6), team building problems, a lack of management experience or a lack of project management experience in complex situations.

Hansel [31] describes project coaching, on the one hand, as a tool for training experienced project managers and junior project managers. On the other, it is a specialised and integrated form of project consulting. Coaching is used in the definition, start-up, conflict and concluding phases of a project. It can also support the project by performing a quality assurance function.

In particular, it takes the psychosocial aspects of work situations into account. Coaching is therefore very useful in stressful phases of project work, according to Hansel.

It can also be viewed as a form of training. The coach provides advice to team members or the manager during the project and is available to answer questions or discuss aspects of the project. He supports the project team when problematic situations arise and helps them to identify the causes of certain behaviour, recognise patterns and modify them. The objective is to help the project team members to help themselves.

Tasks

4.1 Selection of a project coach

Competencies

A coach must be able to demonstrate ability in many areas:
- many years of professional and team experience,
- extensive coaching experience,
- good project management knowledge,
- extensive project work and project management experience,
- familiarity with relevant methods (e.g. team building),
- process competence (e.g. special features of project processes in highly innovative projects), and
- social competence (e.g. communication skills)

Mediator and advisor role

A project coach should be able to respond, depending on the circumstances, to changing problems, says Hansel. `The art of coaching is not to develop solutions. These are to be developed by the team. The aim of the coaching process is to identify core problems relating to project management, project work or the project environment relatively quickly.´ When problems occur in connection with the team´s relationships with external departments, the coach often assumes the role of mediator or consultant.

5 Training and certification

Qualified personnel are a vitally important asset to any successful organisation. Often, project management demands special training and certification measures. These are necessary to firmly anchor and make optimum use of the principles of project management in the organisation.

Training and certification should have a common basis so that the learning units and certification process are compatible. At the same time, the International Project Management Association (IPMA) clearly stipulates that the training and the assessment of participants should not be carried out by the same person. The person to be certified can choose whether to apply for certification in conjunction with a training course or without previously taking a course.

5.1 Four-level training and certification system

These days, it is common knowledge that project management offers an additional opportunity to be more successful in a traditional occupation.

Examples
An engineer should be able to organise his own work and the work of his team members.

An IT expert can only adapt and install a new program for his customer if he is able to organise and manage his team´s work and the external work performed by the customer's personnel.

The IPMA´s 4-L-C

Anyone with project responsibility is both a leader and a manager. The more complex the project is, the more management competences are necessary. Based on this knowledge, the IPMA has developed a four-level certification programme (4-L-C) for project management personnel and introduced it worldwide. The national organisations (e.g. GPM German Association for Project Management) are required to organise and implement the activities associated with this programme. The ever increasing number of certified project practitioners and managers clearly demonstrates the certification system´s acceptance. Each year, the IPMA publishes the names of all certificants in its year book and on its website at www.ipma.ch.

5.2 4-level training programme

Preparation for certification should be in accordance with the requirements of 4-L-C. In order to ensure this, the four-level training programme (4-L-T) was developed. Training, in this sense, means that the individual attends a training course. It can consist of basic or advanced education, which enhance knowledge; training, which enriches experience; or coaching, which has a positive effect on personal development.

The 4-L-T

5.2.1 Content of 4-L-T

The various requirements of project management depend on
- the complexity of the project,
- the professional competence of the project participants and
- the project environment.

A successful project manager therefore needs
- a knowledge of applied project management,
- experience gained in completed projects and
- personal charisma as the person responsible for the project and management skills.

Project manager characteristics

The greater the project responsibility, the more project management competence is necessary.

> **Examples**
> *A project management practitioner has a solid basic knowledge of project management. He can apply this knowledge objectively and with guidance, for example*
> - *to create and update a time schedule.*
> - *to monitor project documentation.*
> - *to organise reports.*
>
> *A project leader who has gained initial experience in small-scale projects, and is able to apply this knowledge, can function as a sub-project manager in large-scale projects. He is able to apply the core aspects of project management, e.g. he can*
> - *prepare a basic cost estimate for a project stage,*
> - *monitor deadline adherence and costs,*
> - *monitor project documentation and performance of change management tasks, and*
> - *carry out acceptance and handover procedures for a sub-project.*
>
> *A project manager who is responsible for complex projects needs to be able to*
> - *coordinate the work of all participating sub-contractors, suppliers and sub-systems,*
> - *use all available and necessary project management methods and techniques,*
> - *manage both his own and external project personnel, and*
> - *bear responsibility for deadlines, costs and quality both within the organisation and vis-à-vis customers by way of contract and change management.*

A project director is responsible for all projects in an organisation and performs the following project management functions:
- *establish individual project objectives and align them with the organisation´s overall strategy,*
- *control progress, taking into account the limited availability of resources and specialist personnel,*
- *provide project or programme reports to the organisation´s senior management and external project sponsors,*
- *coach project management personnel, and*
- *implement continuous improvements in project management methods and processes.*

==The content of the certification is the sum of competences in three areas:==
==Competence = Knowledge + Experience + Personality==

ICB

These competence areas apply to all elements of project management as specified by the IPMA in its International Competence Baseline (ICB).

5.3 Procedure in the 4-L-C programme

Three separate areas

Certification is in accordance with the standardised international rules of the IPMA. It comprises three stages:
1. Application for certification (CV and, where applicable, self-assessment, list of projects and references)
2. Tests (knowledge test, workshop where applicable, transfer project report, project summary, project case study and literature conspectus or summary).
3. Questions about the transfer project report or project summary, project case study, literature conspectus, team management skills, personal strengths and potential for improvement.

Assessors

The GPM´s assessors perform the certification process in accordance with the IPMA´s Certification Rules and Guidelines (ICRG) and DIN EN 15 024. The evaluation criteria are assessed on the basis of a points system. This permits an evaluation of the individual assessments. If a candidate achieves a points total within an internationally-agreed range, he is granted certification at the level applied for. The two assessors who perform all aspects of the certification process may not be work colleagues of or related to the certificants.

Validation of the certification bodies

The IPMA audits the certification bodies at its national organisations on a regular basis. This measure has led to the establishment of an internationally-recognised quality standard over recent years.

5.4 Self-assessment

Self-assessment bridges the gap between training and certification. Depending on the certification level, it is the basis upon which
- the trainer ascertains the certificant´s competence deficits and upon which
- the assessor identifies the competences of the certificant.

Trainer

For example, self-assessment can provide the trainer with information about which project management elements are necessary to

- close knowledge gaps,
- compensate lack of experience, and
- improve personal traits through coaching.

In contrast, the assessor
- ascertains whether the certificant's level of project management competence is adequate for the level of certification applied for. He accepts, modifies or rejects the certification application after inspecting the application documents.
- derives monitoring requirements to be verified at the workshop based on the conformity of test results with the self-assessment.
- derives questions, from the self-assessment, for the interview forming the basis for certification.

6 Personnel management

Projects have many personnel management tasks [32]: *Tasks*
- determination and optimisation of personnel requirements,
- recruitment of personnel,
- career planning,
- planning and implementation of training measures,
- application of staff assessment techniques,
- administration of personnel records,
- payroll administration,
- performance-related pay assessments, and
- use of knowledge gained from other departments or projects.

6.1 Determining personnel requirements

When calculating personnel requirements, the department responsible for project personnel determines how many (= quantitative requirements) of which type of (= qualitative requirements) staff are necessary to keep the project operational. A personnel requirements analysis is made to check the variance between available and required personnel. When deviations occur, compensatory measures are defined and implemented. In addition to personnel requirements which do not make allowances for staff absences (e.g. due to holiday or illness), the personnel requirements plan must include the necessary resources (e.g. for coverage or replacement of absent staff).

Quantitative/ qualitative needs

Requirements analysis/ planning

Quantitative personnel requirements
When establishing quantitative personnel requirements (→ Chapter C6) the following aspects should be taken into consideration:
- number of staff needed
- dates when they are required
- length of assignment
- place of assignment

This information can be derived from the
- work breakdown structure (→ Chapter C4),
- time schedule and
- resource breakdown structure.

Qualitative personnel requirements

To ascertain qualitative personnel requirements, it is necessary to clarify two things:
- Work to be performed, with detailed specifications (= target)
- Existing staff and their qualifications (= actual)

This information can be derived from the
- work package descriptions,
- requirements profiles,
- personnel development plans, and
- job descriptions.

6.2 Personnel requirements planning

Requirements matrix Functions / requirements relationship

A simple matrix (→ Figure D3-7) provides an initial overview of personnel requirements. It shows the relationships between them and the project functions. The personnel manager enters in the table the number of required and available members of staff in each department.

	Must be available from		Good skills in		Good skills in		...
	Requirements	Available	Requirements	Available	Requirements	Available	
Project assistant							
Project controller							
Product developer 1							
Product developer 2							
Project communication							

Figure D3-7 Personnel requirements planning matrix

Requirements profile

The matrix, prepared on the basis of the project manager´s requirements profile (→ Chapter D1) is also suitable for other project personnel (→ Figure D3-8).

	Assessment points		
Requirement	1 – weak	2 – average	3 – very good
Project management competence	x		
Professional competence			x
General social competence	x		
Management skills	x		
Strategic approach		x	
Performance orientation			x

Figure D3-8 Requirements profile for project personnel

6.3 Personnel recruitment

The people responsible for the project can either recruit project personnel from within the organisation or externally. If there are constraints on the project budget, they will tend to recruit people who already work in the organisation. Suitable external personnel are best recruited via personnel recruitment agencies that implement specific searches, make a pre-selection and reduce the burden of work falling on their client. However, the disadvantage of using personnel recruitment agencies is that they are expensive.

External staff

Alternatively, job advertisements can be placed in reputable online job markets. Organisations can often recruit external personnel who have already worked on successful projects with them. This provides them with some degree of (planning) security because the organisation´s personnel already know the person. When creating a requirements profile, it is a good idea to use the same procedure as for selecting the project manager (→ Chapter D1).

6.4 Staff assessments

There are dozens of methods of assessing project personnel. They extend from classic job interviews to comprehensive assessments. It is impossible to describe all the methods in detail in this chapter. However, it is possible to provide an introductory overview of these methods. Project staff assessments are based on the same principles as staff assessments by line management. They are used to evaluate achievements, conduct, social skills, personality traits and its development. The GPM and IPMA´s certification systems include specific assessment criteria for project personnel.

PM-Zert [33], the GPM´s certification body uses self-assessment sheets (→ Chapter D1) for the certification of project managers that are also suitable for other project personnel. These sheets are filled in by the staff themselves and provide a record of knowledge and skills in each of the listed thematic areas within the four competence areas of project management fundamentals, interpersonal skills, project management methods and project organisation.

Self-assessment sheet

A basic differentiation is made between general and analytical methods of staff assessment. General assessments take the employee´s overall performance into consideration, whereas analytical methods break the assessment down into achievements, management competence and interpersonal competence [34]. This enables the verification of the completeness and relevance of individual criteria. The assessment results are easier to comprehend, more objective and more reliable. An assessment interview should be held with the member of staff after the assessment. This complies with the statutory requirement for staff to discuss the assessment of their performance with their superior.

General / analytical methods

6.4.1 Responsibilities

Project-specific staff assessments can be performed by members of the organisation´s management or the project management teams. Disciplinary superiors, project management function holders (e.g. project manager or sub-project manager), members of the steering committee and customer representatives can also be involved. One contemporary approach is to involve personnel in their own assessments. As a result, they are more likely to understand and accept them.

Acceptance through involvement

6.5 Personnel development

Task owner

Project staff have to be developed systematically. Some organisations assign personnel to projects as a means of general personnel development. Different task owners are involved in the process of personnel development: Senior management specifies the basic qualifications that the organisation requires and the personnel department ensures that the staff matches these requirements. The personnel department is also responsible for the planning, implementation and monitoring of basic and advanced training measures. The direct superior evaluates staff potential and future perspectives. Even the members of staff themselves are task owners and, as such, participate in personnel development measures.

Career planning/ model

One central element of personnel development is career planning. Many large-scale organisations have career models that can be combined to satisfy the individual requirements of every single member of staff.

6.5.1 People Capability Maturity Model

Benchmarking can be used to compare the performance of project personnel with that of personnel in other organisational structures. The most famous method for assessing and improving the capability of project personnel, as well as for HR management in general, is the People Capability Maturity Model (P-CMM). It is based on the Capability Maturity Model (CMM → Chapter F2), which was developed in the 1980s. Although this model was designed for software development, it is used in many other fields.

The Capability Maturity Model Integration (CMM-I), the successor model to CMM, was introduced in 2002.

6.5.1.1 Maturity levels

Five maturity levels

P-CMM, like CMM, defines five maturity levels that are typical of personnel development processes in organisations:
- Maturity level 1: Initial status (chaotic/ad-hoc approach)
- Maturity level 2: Processes can be repeated
- Maturity level 3: Processes are defined
- Maturity level 4: Processes are managed
- Maturity level 5: Processes are optimised

The following statements are typical of an organisation with level 1 maturity:
- There are no personnel planning and development activities.
- There is no basis for the systematic improvement of professional competence.
- Development options are unknown because there is no way to establish the status quo.
- Employees tend to focus on personal benefits.
- Professional competence stagnates because staff with development potential leave the organisation.

Levels 2 to 4 are associated with very diverse objectives, tasks, methods and personnel development resources, as well as the issues of communication, training, mentoring and many other things, up to and including competence management. At level 5, the management structure is so mature that the competence of its staff and of the organisation itself continually improves.

6.5.1.2 Key processes

The various maturity levels are allocated to key process areas that are necessary for systematic personnel development and should be implemented in accordance with maturity level. All objectives of the key processes must be achieved in several successive projects so that the capabilities defined in these processes are institutionalised. The key processes are divided into four groups, irrespective of maturity level:

Institutionalised competences

Four groups

1. Development of skills
   Identification of weaknesses, improvement of communication skills, development of professional competence
2. Team building
   Improvement of communication, inclusion of personnel in decision-making processes, building of autonomous teams
3. Motivation
   Implementation of career planning, creation of a pleasant working environment, use of incentives
4. Personnel planning
   Realisation of strategic personnel planning, selection of suitable staff

6.5.1.3 Common features

Analogous to CMM, in addition to the maturity levels and key processes, P-CMM has further components that are used in the personnel development process. One such is Common Features. Each key process is sub-divided into five common features:

Sub-division

1. Implementation support: definition of guidelines, support from the management
2. Implementation capability: allocation of resources, establishment of management structures, training
3. Activities to be implemented: definition of key tasks
4. Analysis and assessment: collection of data relating to implementation
5. Verification of implementation by way of quality assurance and management.

6.5.1.4 Key practices

The activities, methods and instructions within key processes are mapped in the form of key practices. They provide information about what is to be done, but not how to do it. Key practices are allocated to a common feature in each key process area.

7 Occupational health and safety

Managers initially associate the issue of occupational health and safety with pressure from the legislators. They also often mentally associate it with heavy manual labour (e.g. on a construction site). However, this perspective is too narrow. Even white collar work can be associated with health risks if the employee is under considerable pressure.

White collar work

Many employees and freelance workers complain about stress and pressure. This can lead to burnout syndrome, which is such a serious condition that insurance companies refuse to insure the people concerned against occupational invalidity. There are many more risks associated with white collar jobs. For example, desk jobs can cause muscular and skeletal disorders.

Burnout syndrome

7.1 Responsibility of the project manager

Risk management

From a project risk management perspective, the project manager is well advised to consider these problems, particularly since it can be taken for granted that healthy and satisfied employees perform better. Sick employees, on the other hand, generate costs and cause project personnel shortages. The project manager should therefore ensure a pleasant environment, an appropriate working climate, efficient work organisation and a balance between work and leisure time for both his staff and himself.

Staff who are stressed and lack concentration, which may simply be due to overwork, work less efficiently. In this case, the project manager should discuss the problem with the employees in question, try to discover the causes, and find solutions. It is important that the project manager is well organised and efficient (→ Chapter D2) so that he can set an example for his staff.

Statutory provisions

It is the project manager´s responsibility to inform himself about and respect the main provisions of employment laws and company regulations concerning working time, health and safety, and employment protection of the countries in which he is managing his project.

D3 BUILDING AND MANAGING COMPETENT TEAMS

Self-assessment questions for each certification level

No.	Question	Level D	Level C	Level B	Level A	Self-assessment
D 3.01	Why is occupational health and safety so important and who is responsible for it?	2	2	3	4	☐
D 3.02	What are the important considerations when building teams?	1	2	3	4	☐
D 3.03	On what principle is the Johari window based and how is it used?	2	3	3	3	☐
D 3.04	Which special tasks should the project manager perform in the start-up phase?	2	3	3	4	☐
D 3.05	Which phases of development does a team normally go through?	2	3	4	4	☐
D 3.06	Which team building measures should the project manager implement?	2	3	4	4	☐
D 3.07	Which rules relating to cooperation should be agreed by the project team members?	2	3	4	2	☐
D 3.08	Which central aspects of social perception are known?	2	2	2	2	☐
D 3.09	Which management skills should a project manager have?	2	3	3	4	☐
D 3.10	Which management concepts are used?	2	3	3	3	☐
D 3.11	Which basic types of management style are used?	2	3	3	4	☐
D 3.12	Which rules should the project manager follow when agreeing objectives?	2	3	3	4	☐
D 3.13	Which methods can be used to boost the motivation of team members?	2	3	3	4	☐
D 3.14	With which management problems should project managers be able to cope?	2	3	3	4	☐
D 3.15	What does 4-L-T consist of?	2	2	2	2	☐
D 3.16	What does certification comprise?	2	2	2	2	☐
D 3.17	What is the 4-L-C procedure according to the IPMA?	2	2	2	2	☐
D 3.18	What is self-assessment used for?	2	2	2	2	☐
D 3.19	Which personnel management tasks are significant in projects?	2	2	3	4	☐
D 3.20	How are personnel requirements ascertained and how is a project personnel requirements plan prepared?	1	2	3	4	☐
D 3.21	How can the 4-L-T and 4-L-C concepts be integrated in career planning?	2	2	2	4	☐
D 3.22	What are the project manager's responsibilities in the areas of occupational safety and health?	2	3	3	4	☐
D 3.23	What information does Maslow's needs pyramid provide?	2	2	2	2	☐

D4 COMMUNICATION

Internal and external project communication (ICB Element 25) should be viewed as a necessity, not a chore. Stakeholders require information and the opportunity to put forward their opinions. Stakeholder dialogue should also be encouraged by the project management so that those affected accept both the project and its consequences. This also applies to small projects with low budgets, for which the necessary communication tools can easily be adapted. The elements of and concepts for good stakeholder communication, project marketing and media work are of central importance for the project and deserve special attention.

1 Significance

Information about project progress, costs, personnel changes and other project news is extremely interesting for stakeholders such as colleagues in the line organisation, other project managers, (potential) customers, authorities, representatives of the media and the general public. If they believe that they are not receiving adequate information, they will soon become opponents of the project, which will result in delays and additional costs. The organisation also risks damage to its reputation if communication measures fail, especially in projects that affect the public. This is why the project management team has to incorporate the stakeholders (→ Chapter A3) in project-related processes of structuring and change (`converting those affected into participants´) right from the outset.

Converting those affected into participants

However, the significance of internal and especially external communication, particularly in small-scale projects, is often underestimated by organisations in both the public and private sectors. They are not aware that potential problems exist because the consequences of deficient communication are initially not measurable in monetary terms. This is why appropriate measures are often rejected as `too complex´ or `too expensive´. In order to encourage an awareness of these potential problems, this chapter focuses mainly on external communication measures.

Awareness of problems

> **Example**
> *Residents living near mobile communications transmitters formed an action group because they were concerned about the harmful effects of electrosmog on their health. Media coverage had sensitised wide sections of the public to this issue and they were fiercely opposed to the installation of new stations. The affected network operators had to respond with marketing initiatives to restore public faith in the safety of the transmitters.*

The significance of communication will continue to grow because a project´s environment is becoming increasingly crucial for success. In the Internet age, information is disseminated extremely quickly. At the same time, corporate enterprises and the public sector have to satisfy higher demands on transparency. Observers (e.g. non-governmental organisations, analysts and the media) are very sensitive to genuine or presumed secret deals. Stakeholders have to receive information about what is happening in the project, and they should also be given the opportunity to ask questions.

Transparency requirements

Conversely, if the project manager proactively provides information to the stakeholders, he increases their acceptance of the project. This is why it is his duty to identify the stakeholders and their information and participation requirements at the start of the project. Proactive stakeholder management is an indispensable risk control measure and adequate budget funds and working time

Information increases acceptance

should be assigned to this task. Stakeholder communication is not effective when only performed as a `sideline´. If projects are associated with delicate issues, stakeholder communication is so essential for acceptance that, measured in terms of work invested in the project deliverable (e.g. power plant construction), it involves extremely high expenditure in terms of time, effort and money.

2 Basic principles

There are many different definitions of `communication´. The common denominator is: communication denotes the exchange of information. It is therefore a specific form of social interaction.

2.1 Objective

Defining benefits

One central objective of project communication should be the consistent clarification of the project´s benefits to the stakeholders and the highlighting of its special aspects compared to other projects. In order to do this, it is necessary to establish communication guidelines for all people who promote the project. Project representatives should present a united front and establish a uniform outward appearance (e.g. project logo and slogan) to provide the project with an identity and ensure high recognition value. These are basic prerequisites for the widespread acceptance of the project among its stakeholders.

Recognition value

2.2 Cost

The cost of project communication should always be in proportion to its benefits. If only three people are working on a project that has only a few stakeholders, a printed project newsletter will be too expensive, although a regular electronic circular would be feasible.

3 How communication works

Interaction

Communication is based on the classic `transmitter/receiver´ model: A transmitter sends a signal which is collected by a receiver; information flows in only one direction. Project communication, on the other hand, is all about interaction. Both sides alternately send and receive information. The objective is to enable the recipient to respond to information rather than simply to acknowledge it without having any opportunity to react. If the sender is able to receive information and the recipient has the opportunity to respond with personal comments about the information he has received, he will be able to influence the future course of the project.

3.1 Possibilities for interpretation

Interpretation and assessment

Misunderstandings

Different people generally interpret information, which may be ambiguous, in different ways. Real information value is achieved by ensuring that it is properly structured and evaluated. Misunderstandings are inevitable if the sender is not able to convey his message so that it is `correctly´ understood by the recipient. Written information is often misunderstood because the sender is not able to support it with gestures, facial expressions and tone of voice. Emotional undertones are therefore difficult to identify.

D4 COMMUNICATION

Ambiguous and flawed communication can cause real conflicts, e.g. arising from misunderstandings when colleagues and partners talk at cross purposes or do not listen to each other properly because hasty accusations and subliminal aggression set the tone [1].

Linguists differentiate between
- denotation (= specific description, ostensible description/statement of the content of an object or matter) and
- connotation (= additional meaning, enigmatic meaning that is read between the lines).

Denotation

Connotation

All information comprises content and relationship elements. The existence of these different information levels – also called the factual and emotional levels - makes it difficult for the recipient to interpret information in the way that the sender intends.

Information levels

One classic example is communication between men and women. Women are generally more skilled at perceiving non-verbal signals and are more capable of interpreting moods. They tend to use relationship language (= emphasis on the emotional level), while men tend to use reporting language (= emphasis on the factual level).

Relationship/ reporting language

Examples
Authors of various self-help books emphasise that men require clear and unambiguous instructions such as, `Please do the washing up now. Be finished in ten minutes.´ Women, on the other hand, tend to be vaguer in expressing their need: `The washing up still hasn´t been done.´ What the woman really means is that she wants the man to do the washing up. However, he isn´t aware that she´s asking him: He hasn´t understood the message `between the lines´.

The statement, `I´m going to the cinema today´ is ambiguous. Is the person talking about a vague plan or a fact? For example, is he on his way to the cinema right now? What is he going to do at the cinema? Is he going to watch a film or does he work there as a popcorn vendor? What sort of a mood is he in? Is he really saying, `I want to do something on my own today´? Or is he sad about not having anyone to accompany him? And so on ...

A dog owner is talking about his dog, whose name is `Tinkerbell´. Based on the name, the person he is talking to initially assumes that it is a small dog. Yet the man then proudly says that Tinkerbell always pulls a sledge with his children on it around the garden in winter. Only then does he mention that the dog is a St. Bernard.

Senders and recipients can also have entirely different assumptions about
- each other,
- the objectives associated with transmitting the information and
- their prior knowledge of the information content.

Different assumptions

Some of the things that these assumptions are based on include
- the sender´s own prior knowledge,
- values and attitudes, as well as
- experiences in situations or involving other people that match the sender and recipients´ own assessment of the situation and the other person.

Example
The project manager's previous controller was careless. He is therefore sceptical about this person's successor. He doesn't yet know that the new controller is always meticulous about supplying correct information.

Context dependency — The way that information is interpreted depends to a great extent on the context in which the sender and recipient view each other.

Example
In a project where low priority is accorded to the time objective (→ Chapter C3), notification that, according to the network diagram, the project finish date will be approximately three weeks later than planned doesn't cause any great concern. However, if the project finish date's delay is associated with a high contractual penalty, it can result in a catastrophic mood in the project.

3.1.1 E-mail problems
E-mail was designed originally as a fast and informal means of communication. However, many project managers prefer to use the telephone if they have to discuss important matters these days because electronic post often causes misunderstandings. The authors of e-mails are often under pressure of time and they don't adequately consider the supplementary information (e.g. mood picture) that they send 'between the lines'. This is why the recipients often assume that the author is being rude. In other words, the sender and recipient interpret the information in different ways.

Supplementary information

Recommendations — In order to prevent such misunderstandings from occurring, it is important to
- be very polite (e.g. `I kindly request that you...´, `Please be so kind as to...´,
- avoid sarcasm,
- explain behaviour that is open to misinterpretation (e.g. `I apologise for sending such a short e-mail, but I have to leave for the airport soon.´)
- never write an e-mail in an emotionally-charged mood (e.g. when angry)
- read through the mail before you finally send it off or – even better – let a colleague proof-read it, and
- sleep on important e-mails.

These measures are especially important if the sender does not personally know the recipient.

3.2 Phraseology

Improving speaking and writing skills — Speaking and writing understandably can be learned. Here are a few helpful tips:
- Use short sentences with subject, predicate and object (e.g. `The project manager praises the staff´)
- Use active rather than passive clauses (e.g. `The project manager informs his staff´ and not `The staff are being informed by the project manager´)
- Avoid foreign words
- Use examples, images and comparisons (e.g. `It's raining cats and dogs´ or `The organisation is distributing funds by giving everyone an equal slice of the cake´)
- Visualise (e.g. draw on a metaplan board when speaking)
- Structure your presentation (e.g. incorporate pauses or start new paragraphs with sub-headings)
- Use varying voice registers, facial expressions and gestures

3.3 Non-verbal communication

Unlike written and oral communication, non-verbal communication focuses on body language. Facial expressions, gestures (= use of the body in conjunction with language), gesticulation (= use of physical gestures independently of spoken language), stance, distance to the other party, external appearance, voice, talking speed, dialect and accent are all forms of expression that enable people to form an opinion about the person they are talking to and provide a context within which information is interpreted.

When dealing with other members of the team, project personnel should therefore make an effort to recognise and control their non-verbal signals, and to observe those of the person they are talking to. Saying `Nice to see you´ with an angry expression on your face will be interpreted as `I don´t want to be at this meeting´. Someone who is sitting at the conference table with a smile on their face and folded arms is indicating defensiveness, disinterest or irony.

Non-verbal signals

3.4 Communication rules

Mayrshofer and Kröger [2] have formulated basic rules for communication in conflict situations. However, they are also generally applicable:
1. Listen attentively (signalise interest)
2. Be aware of the difference between perception, assumption and response
3. Avoid covert communication (`games´)

Additional rules are:
1. Use the first person when speaking (e.g. `I wish …´ instead of `It would be a good idea to …´)
2. Talk about how you feel instead of making accusations (e.g. `I get the impression that you´re edgy´ instead of `You´re very edgy´)
3. Make reference to specific situations (e.g. `I thought you were very aggressive at the time´ instead of `You´re always so aggressive´)

`I´ form

Wolf´s rules
Wolf has formulated different communication rules for senders and recipients [3].

Rules for senders
1. The sender (= speaker) should talk about himself when that is his intention. This prevents misunderstandings. However, it also leaves him more vulnerable and open to attack.
2. He should stick to the subject and avoid digression.
3. He should address the specific situation and the specific behaviour of the person. Aggressiveness and accusations make the recipient feel that he has to justify himself. This results in a ping-pong game and hinders progress.
4. The speaker can use eye contact and gestures to emphasise what he is saying.
5. Speaking volume, clear enunciation and talking speed underline what is being said.

Rules for the sender

Rules for recipients
1. It is important that the listener indicates to the speaker that he has understood what is being said. He can summarise it in his own words and ask specific questions.

Rules for the recipient

2. The listener can nod his head and say things such as 'Really?', 'Oh' and 'Hmm' to emphasise his receptiveness to what is being said.
3. Praise and recognition (e.g. 'I'm glad you mentioned that') encourage the speaker to stay tuned in.

3.4.1 Feedback

Self-image / image perceived by others

According to Mayrshofer and Ahrens [4] feedback is 'voluntary information transfer which enables people to scrutinise their own behaviour and sensitise them to the needs, preferences and expectations of others'. It helps to prevent the impairment of project progress as a result of discrepancies between people's self-image and the image that is perceived by others. 'If no feedback is obtained or provided, both sides will act on the basis of entirely different assumptions or perspectives.'

Recommendations

The following recommendations and guidelines [5] apply to feedback situations.

Receiving feedback
- Other people's perceptions can differ from self-perceptions.
- Feedback is an opportunity to obtain additional information about yourself.
- Feedback is not a request for change.

Giving feedback
- Describe your own experience.
- Describe the effect of the actions ('I' statements), but do not pass judgement or interpret things.
- Formulate feedback concisely and precisely.
- Only mention things that can be changed.

3.5 Communication by way of non-communication

Disadvantages of remaining silent

Proactive communication

It is impossible for human beings not to communicate. Even when they say nothing at all, they are sending out a message. Organisations therefore expose themselves to a significant risk if they believe that remaining silent will shield them from criticism, since, in the event of a problem (event of damage or loss → Chapter A3), the organisation lacks the stable relationships with stakeholders (e.g. the media) needed to minimise damage (to its reputation). Unscheduled events include, for example, mass redundancies, problems in a public sector project or product recalls in the automotive industry. The same applies for 'mini-companies' or 'temporary companies', i.e. for projects. Proactive communication is necessary to ensure that the organisation controls relationships with stakeholders in both good and bad times.

4 Influencing the environment through communiation

Stakeholder communication must be systematic if it is to be effective in the long term. Several unrelated measures do not suffice. Only with a systematic approach can one institutionalise a continuous improvement process and take advantage of the feedback function of stakeholder dialogue. Organisations that already have or plan to install an integrated management system are well advised to link stakeholder communication – and all the other cross-sectional functions (e.g. project, quality or environmental management) – with this system.

Integration in the management system

Stakeholder communication should not be a one-way street. It requires measures that support dialogue between the stakeholders and the project management team (e.g. events). This provides the project management team with opinions and mood pictures on which to base its strategy. The feedback function of stakeholder communication is therefore decisive for project control. Based on this, project teams can continually improve their performance and learn from their mistakes and achievements (→ Chapter C8, C10).

Plan-Do-Check-Act cycle

There are various strategic approaches to influencing the project environment:
- Participative
- Discursive
- Repressive

4.1 Participative approach

A participative approach means that the stakeholders are treated as partners and actively involved in the project. For this the project manager has different possibilities since various levels of participation intensity are possible. Abresch [6] differentiates between three levels, whereby level 1 is the lowest and level 3 the highest.
1. Information/communication
2. Involvement in the project
3. Participation/involvement in the decision-making process

Stakeholders as partners

The extreme case of not involving stakeholders in the project at all would correspond to a level above 1, although this is a highly unrealistic scenario. Additional levels could lie between these main ones. For example, a project would be somewhere between the Levels 1 and 2 if the project manager considers the stakeholders´ opinions, but does not allow them to be involved in the project.

4.2 Discursive approach

Discursive approaches aim to reconcile the various stakeholders´ interests. Project managers who pursue this strategy use negotiating methods (→ Chapter D2) and conflict management methods (→ Chapter D5).

Reconciliation of interests

4.3 Repressive approach

Repressive approaches can be found in many projects. They are based on the concept that the environment can only be influenced by way of pressure, fait accompli, selective information and similar forms of exerting power. Stakeholders are only apparently involved in the project because, in reality, the decisions are made without them. If the project stakeholders are not happy about this strategy, conflicts can soon occur and the project management team will end up fighting a lost cause because it is very difficult to justify repressive behaviour. In this situation, the only opportunity they have to keep the situation under control is to exert more power. They then lose out on the benefits of a proactive, participative strategy. If the exertion of more power does not lead to the desired result, the project management team will be in serious trouble. In these situations, crisis management is necessary (→ Chapter D5), ideally with the assistance of an experienced arbitrator and/ or mediator.

Risk of conflicts

However, there are exceptional cases when a repressive approach can be necessary. One example is the planned merger of two organisations (e.g. major banks). In this case, long discussions are not generally admissible.

4.4 Aspects of effective stakeholder communication

Effective stakeholder communication is
- timely
- regular
- honest
- proactive and
- interactive.

Timely
If the project manager receives relevant information, it is a good idea to pass this information on to the appropriate project stakeholders as soon as possible. For example, if it becomes evident that the project will take four weeks longer than planned to complete, this information should be provided to the stakeholders as quickly as possible. It is important not to give rise to any false expectations. For example, if the project manager communicates a postponed project finish date every few weeks, all the other information that he provides will lack credibility.

Advance planning of communications

Regular
It is not enough merely to provide stakeholders with information at the beginning of a project or when problems occur. They should receive regular information throughout the project lifecycle and when special events occur, and be included in project processes. It is better to provide an early warning that subsequently proves to be a false alarm than to be forced to implement emergency communication measures when a problem occurs.

Early warning and false alarm

Honest
The saying, `Honesty isn´t always the best policy´ has some merits. However, the project manager is better advised honestly to admit mistakes and failures and to communicate them in conjunction with possible solutions. The consequences are far more serious if third parties (e.g. the customer or the media) discover the mistakes themselves. In such a case, a project manager can only react instead of controlling the communication.

Suggesting solutions

D4 COMMUNICATION

Proactive
A project manager should provide information at his own initiative instead of only delivering it in response to project stakeholder requests.

Voluntary information

Interactive
Information flows should be two-way between the project manager and the stakeholders. Responses to an article in the customer newsletter, a telephone call from the mayor and personal feedback from senior management should all be incorporated in further project communications and control measures.

Two-way information

4.5 Communication Concept

At the outset of the project, a project manager and his team develop a stakeholder communication strategy. A communication matrix (→ Figure D4-1), based on the information obtained in the stakeholder analysis (→ Chapter A3), helps them to record the information requirements of project stakeholders. Its structure is similar to that of the reporting schedule (Reports → Chapter C9), and it shows which measures are to be implemented, in what way and when.

Strategy

The stakeholder analysis provides the project manager with information about which stakeholders are important for the project, which could damage the project and which could be of use to him. The team then develops tailor-made communication measures for each stakeholder group.

Stakeholder analysis

In small-scale projects, only one member of staff is usually assigned to the implementation of the measures. In this case, the project manager has to assume responsibility for this task but delegate the work (e.g. writing texts) to his team.

4.5.1 Identifying stakeholder needs

The team should clarify the form in which each stakeholder wishes to receive information and provide feedback. They can use a communication matrix to do this (→ Figure D4-1).

Communication matrix

> **Example**
> *The customer's managing director wishes to be informed about all project schedule deviations and milestones in writing. He wants this information in a format and with a layout that allows him to make a presentable print-out with logo. An e-mail text is therefore unacceptable. This information will have to be provided in the form of an e-mail with an appropriately structured brief presentation in the attachment or as a fax.*

D4 COMMUNICATION

STAKEHOLDER GROUP	CLIMATE/ MOOD + 0 −	MEASURES	CONTENT	FREQUENCY	SCOPE
General management	+	Status meetings	Current status	1 x week	3,500 characters plus graphics
		Face-to-face discussions	Current status, tasks as promotor	Formal: 1 x month	As required
				Informal: as often as possible	
Project team	+	Status meetings	Current status	Every Monday	1 to 1.5 hours
			Current status	When unscheduled events occur	As required
		One-to-one meeting with the project manager	Individual	As required	As required
		Joint undertakings	Culture, meals, sport	1 x month	
Works council	−	Face-to-face discussions	Status, works council concerns, Project manager's issues	1 x month	1 to 1.5 hours or dinner
		Status reports as per the reporting schedule	Current status		
Customer (managing director)	+	Regular personal contact	Informal meal or business meal	1 x month	As required
		Status reports as per the reporting status	Current status		
Customer (technician)	+	Meeting with our technicians	Meetings with a buffet meal	1 x month and as required	Maximum of 3 hours
Local councillors	−	One-to-one meetings	Informal meal	Each of the three councillors every two months	As required
Media	−	Press release		1 x month	See press relations guidelines
				When unscheduled events occur	See press relations guidelines
		Background meeting		1 x month each publication	As required

Figure D4-1 Communication matrix

Non-recurrent development

Standardisation

In order to ensure that communication costs are in proportion to the project scope, a project team should attempt to develop measures that only need to be planned once and can then be used throughout the project. A project newsletter is one example of such a communication measure. When a newsletter is planned, components such as format, layout, content guidelines and distribution structures need only be worked out once, when the first issue is created. As much standardisation as possible is recommended. Text modules for letters and press releases that can be accessed by all the relevant members of staff are one example of this.

Basically, the focus should be on a few essential communication tools for each stakeholder and the optimum use of these tools (quality instead of quantity).

Quality instead of quantity

4.5.2 Communication guidelines

In addition to the communication matrix, the project manager and his team develop communication guidelines. These guidelines specify which communication tools are to be used by project personnel when contacting stakeholders (e.g. organisational tasks) and for what purpose.

Defining the budget

Example
The manager of a film project establishes the following communication guidelines: press enquiries can be responded to via e-mail, office supplies orders must be signed and faxed, while invitations to the premiere have to be sent out on official stationery by post.

5 Elements of stakeholder communication

When communicating with stakeholders, the project team selects the intended methods from a catalogue of measures, which can include a
- project meeting (including telephone and video conference → Chapter D2),
- project report (→ Chapter C9),
- off-the-record conversation,
- project newsletter (project newspaper),
- project presentation,
- website,
- bulletin board,
- project hotline,
- event,
- idea competition, and
- media work (→ Section 8 in this chapter).

Catalogue of measures

5.1 Project meeting

The most effective method of information procurement and dissemination is a meeting – ideally a face-to-face conversation or, alternatively, a telephone conversation. This enables the parties to ask questions straight away if they are not clear about something so that the information is interpreted properly. The complexity of a meeting as an information forum increases in proportion to the size of the project [7]. If several people are involved, the meeting can either be held with all participants present, or as a telephone conference or video conference. The project manager should weigh up the advantages of a personal meeting (e.g. easier to assess moods, and opportunities for informal conversations) against the disadvantages (e.g. travel expenses) on a case-by-case basis.

Face-to face conversation

Although a formal reporting system will deliver facts quickly, it does not enable their evaluation. This can occur at regular meetings of the most important project participants. The meetings enable a fast comparison of current data with target data. The consequences can be considered and suitable measures to remedy deviations can be agreed upon at the meeting itself. The minutes of the meeting can also be used to satisfy formal reporting requirements [8].

Formal reporting

5.2 Project reports

The ICB [9] defines reporting as follows: 'Reporting is a standard kind of communication. It is addressed to specific recipients and may involve different types of reports. [...] As a rule, the project development is documented concurrently with the reporting.'

Reporting schedule

Project reports are not just an intrinsic aspect of project control, but also of stakeholder communication. The reporting schedule (→ Chapter C9) and the communication matrix overlap.

Templates

Every organisation should create a set of standardised report templates (e.g. for quarterly reports, work package reports, ad-hoc reports, phase acceptance reports and the final report).

5.3 Off-the-record conversations

Off-the-record conversations are a method of informal communication. They enable an unofficial exchange of views between one or more stakeholders that are not recorded in minutes or on tape. People tend to be more forthcoming in off-the-record conversations than they are at official meetings. However, it is essential that all parties to the conversation treat it as strictly confidential.

Development of solid relationships

Journalists use off-the-record conversations to obtain information that helps them to gain a better understanding of a subject or the behaviour of their source. They use them as the basis for well-researched articles, yet they do not disclose any confidential information or the source. These conversations can serve the interests of both parties by helping them to establish a stable and trusting relationship and promoting the regular exchange of information about each party's factual argumentations and disposition.

5.4 Project newsletter

Modest effort

A project newsletter (or project newspaper) provides stakeholders with an overview of project processes and keeps them up-to-date. The goal is to interest them in the project and convince them of its benefits. Good results can be achieved inexpensively in terms of time, effort and money. However, many projects still do not take advantage of this opportunity. Newsletters can be published in printed or digital (e.g. e-mail or PDF) format. Neither glossy paper nor expensive advertising agencies are needed to provide interesting information in a compact format.

Advantages of a print version

A print version, which may be suitable for large-scale projects, can be used to address target groups that are not accustomed to using e-mail and the Internet or which do not have Internet access (e.g. production employees). However, even experienced Internet users enjoy reading the printed page. The newsletter can be displayed or distributed at meetings and events, and it can also be sent to customers and the media. The first issue can be used to draw attention to the project – at a works meeting, for example. A print or PDF newsletter is more complex to plan and design than an e-mail version. The additional effort is only worthwhile if the newsletter has a high circulation. Professional external support can be useful when creating information materials.

Obtaining consent

In the case of an electronic newsletter, it is important to obtain the consent of the recipients before the newsletter is sent to them for the first time. Otherwise, it constitutes spam mail which is a criminal offence.

5.4.1 Publication frequency

A newsletter should be published at regular intervals or on specific dates (e.g. when milestones are reached). Since readers are creatures of habit, they want to know when the next issue will be published. If it is published at regular intervals, the project manager indicates that he has the organisation of the project under control and that it is significant for the organisation.

5.4.2 The criterion of benefits

The main criterion for the selection of newsletter topics is reader benefit. Interesting articles *Requirements*
- support the readers' evaluation of project facts (e.g. construction progress report, interview *for contributions*
  with experts),
- promote empathy with project participants (e.g. profile of the project manager or junior managers),
- promote the readers' own careers (e.g. job advertisements, reports on training measures),
- provide useful information (e.g. presentation of software), or
- offer interesting reading matter (e.g. reports about everyday project activities).

Readers should have the chance to respond to articles (e.g. address for readers' letters, or a fax sheet). *Opportunity to respond*

5.4.3 Content

According to an old journalists' saying, `The stories are out there, all you have to do is find them´. *Content*
Possible newsletter content includes
- status reports (e.g. brief reports about milestones, management decisions, meeting results, cost development),
- user reports (e.g. when new software is introduced),
- interviews (e.g. with the managing director about the opportunities for marketing the project deliverable),
- dates, events,
- press feedback,
- customer praise and criticisms,
- job advertisements,
- information and news about education/training,
- staff news (e.g. personnel changes, promotions, anniversaries), and
- best practice tips from readers (e.g. on recycling printer cartridges).

Photos and graphics (e.g. diagrams and map excerpts) make dry facts (e.g. sales figures) more appealing.

5.4.4 Relevance

The topics selected should be comprehensible, and all newsletter articles should be project-related. For each article it is worth considering: `Who is our target group?´ It is worth asking colleagues, `Does *Target group* that belong in our project newsletter?´ If there are any doubts, omit the article. *orientation*

5.4.5 Topicality

Lead time A project newsletter should only include up-to-date articles. Consider the lead time: topics with deadlines could be out of date by publication. However, if the editor wants to address the subject anyway, it is a good idea to include information about where the reader can find out about the latest status (e.g. website, bulletin board, daily newspapers).

5.4.6 Reader involvement

Reflection of project progress The newsletter should mirror the project's progress. This can only happen if the readers are involved in its design. The publication of an article is a good opportunity for project staff to demonstrate their skills.

5.4.7 Negative news

With a little practice, unpleasant news can be diplomatically packaged. For example, it is more diplomatic to say `Project ABC is a success despite the high costs´ than `Cost explosion in Project ABC´. The main thing is to stick to the truth.

6.5 Project presentation

Breakdown Kellner [10] recommends the following structure for project presentations – for example to customers or representatives of licensing authorities:
1. Project task
2. Benefits
3. Objectives
4. Means of achieving objectives
5. Discussion and questions
6. Appeal to the audience (e.g. for cooperation)

Even presentations in small-scale projects should be designed professionally. The charts should be interesting and logically-structured, a computer projector should be used, the speaker should wear smart clothes, the room should be comfortable, and suitably-formulated information should be distributed well in advance of the presentation (→ Chapter D2).

5.6 Websites

Print/online combination A combination of print and online media is ideal for stakeholder communication. The Internet is ideal for the provision of fast, up-to-date information, while printed newsletters are recommended for background articles and reports, photos and graphics. The IT department should reserve several pages on the organisation's website for the project. It can also be presented internally on the Intranet. The advantage of Internet or Intranet solutions compared with printed material is that the creation of new content is a simple and fast process.

5.7 Bulletin board

A high-tech solution is not essential for effective stakeholder communication. Particularly in small-scale projects, where the project personnel work in close proximity to each another, a bulletin board effectively supplements telephone calls, e-mails and video conferences. It should be located at a place which project personnel use regularly (e.g. in the corridor outside the project office or in the meeting room).

Information such as short reports on meetings, status reports, survey results, press articles and project-related job advertisements can be used. Before such items are posted, they should be checked by the member of staff responsible for the bulletin board. This ensures that no critical information is posted and that the content is selected according to standard criteria so that it is of a consistently high quality. Torn, yellowing, and dog-eared sheets of paper are out of place on a bulletin board. Using symbols or colour coding draws attention to new information.

Content

Quality assurance

If the information is visually categorised into sections such as `management news´, `team information´ or `official notices´ (e.g. information from the works council), as it would be in a newspaper, users will soon know exactly where to look for specific information.

Visual separation

5.8 Project hotline

A project hotline is a good idea in larger projects and those that have a central project office or project management office. It offers a point of contact where stakeholders can obtain information about the project and express their concerns. A toll-free telephone hotline is not the only possible communication channel: A `surgery´, an electronic suggestions/complaints box, a project mailbox or an online feedback form can also be used.

5.9 Events

Events do not just serve the purpose of providing information. Their main purpose is to give stakeholders a chance to talk face-to-face with project representatives. They can take the form of panel debates or workshops, where attendees can find out about the project´s current status, as well as the different opinions, concerns and hopes relating to the project.

Being present

> **Example**
> *A local authority holds a panel debate on the planned construction of a local by-pass. Those who live in the village and are hoping for a reduction in the volume of traffic, those who live on the outskirts and are concerned about increased traffic noise, as well as representatives of the roads department and a nature conservation association all have the opportunity to put forward their views. The pressure groups that are for or against the new by-pass, as well as the nature conservation experts have the opportunity to present their work at information stands.*

A survey of people who attend the event is a useful means of obtaining feedback that can be channelled into planning subsequent events. The project team then evaluates the survey results and allocates priorities depending on how significant the improvement suggestions are. This supports a continuous improvement process (CIP → Chapter C8).

Survey of participants

5.10 Idea competitions

Idea competitions are a good opportunity to discover what the stakeholders think about their project, what their expectations are and what problems they envisage. They can be combined with events (e.g. audience votes on results, an awards ceremony, a panel debate, or the opportunity to get to know and talk to each other on an informal basis).

6 Risk communication

The incidents of fraud and balance sheet manipulation that have come to light in recent years have prompted the general public, politicians and the financial markets to demand greater transparency. In the case of certain risks, honesty is not always the best policy. Many project managers are instinctively hesitant to communicate risks instead of systematically filtering risks into critical and non-critical risks for communication purposes. Oechtering [11] defines four categories of risks that are not suitable for publication or should only be disclosed in specific situations.

Risks for limited or no disclosure

1. Risks based on the covert interests of stakeholders which contradict the official project objectives.
2. Risks associated with greater self-disclosure than is customary in a culture.

Example
Not all corporate managers or cultural leaders voluntarily show their hand.

3. Risks that can turn out to be a self-fulfilling prophecy.
   Before making them public, project managers should first investigate the effects of risks if the probability of the worst-case scenario occurring or the consequences of damage would change as a result of their communication.

Example
A member of staff discovers during a risk analysis that the project manager doesn´t consider his performance to be adequate and therefore considers him to be a project risk. As a result, the member of staff feels insecure. He suddenly falls ill on a regular basis. His performance deteriorates and the project manager feels sure that his original assessment was correct.

4. Risks which are caused by the different interests of stakeholders.
   For example, bidders who take part in a call for tenders cannot openly communicate their risks. Otherwise, they may lose out to a rival who has not disclosed his risks. In contracts with fixed prices, customers tend to be cautious about communicating the fact that the cost risk will be assumed by the contractor if they believe that these risks will have an effect on the contractor´s cost estimate.

Political impact

The project manager generally deals with such risks outside the formal risk management process because of their `political´ effects, says Oechtering. Any documentation is always associated with the danger of the disclosure of confidential information. If the formal risk management process only takes risks into account that are easy to communicate, its overall informative value suffers. Only key personalities, who possess all the information, can assess the potential size of a project´s risk. All other project participants are incapable of a complete risk assessment.

If it is decided to disclose the truth, one must act resolutely. Half-heartedness will be interpreted as insecurity and encourage unpleasant questions from interested parties.

Resolute action

7 Project marketing

`Even excellent project management practices are of no use if the project is ineffectively marketed.´ Kellner [12] is talking about a painful, if unexpected, insight for many project managers. Projects need the support of senior management to get funding. They also have to earn the respect of the line managers because they are dependent on them to assign their best staff to the project and they have to earn customer approval to get follow-up orders. Projects also compete with other projects. In this case, the project that makes the most noise attracts the most attention. This is true even if another project is more complex, generates higher profits or is more beneficial to the organisation for other reasons. If a project manager remains silent, he risks going away empty-handed.

Generating attention

The objective of project marketing is to inform the stakeholders of the project´s goals, the approach to achieving these, the consequences (opportunities and risks) and, most importantly, the benefits. It publicises a project and generates maximum acceptance in order to rule out risks due to opposition and information deficits. Project marketing is one aspect of stakeholder communication. In turn, press, media and PR activities are central aspects of project marketing.

Many project managers are not aware of the content and purpose of project marketing. Many have scientific and technical backgrounds and are unfamiliar with a discipline that they simply call `advertising´ because they don´t know any better – and advertising has a negative image. This is one of the reasons why project marketing is often considered to be counterproductive and unnecessary.
However, professional, project-specific marketing is just as important as other central methods of project management such as cost budgeting and financing plans (→ Chapter C6). This is why the project marketing team should have comprehensive knowledge and skills, as well as the appropriate character traits. For example, good interpersonal skills are essential.

Characteristics of marketing staff

7.1 Parallels with corporate marketing

All efficiently managed companies have marketing departments. A project is nothing other than a temporary company, and the stakeholders are the customers. This is why parallels can be drawn between the significance of project marketing and the significance of corporate marketing. Whereas corporate marketing departments build up a company´s corporate identity, the project marketing team is responsible for the establishment and cultivation of a project identity.

Project identity

7.2 System integration

Project marketing is a system that has to function independently or – better – as part of an integrated project management system. It is closely interlinked with other project processes throughout the project lifecycle. The project marketing team has to be familiar with important marketing tools such as as-is analyses, target definition and control, as well as have expertise in the implementation of the various marketing measures. The Plan-Do-Check-Act cycle also applies for project marketing.

Integration in other project processes

7.3 Marketing strategy

The marketing strategy is oriented towards the marketing objectives. It has to fit in with the project´s culture, personnel and objectives. It is based on a stakeholder analysis, in the same way that corporate marketing is based on market research. Authenticity and the identification of the `project ambassadors´ with their project (e.g. the people who develop the project concept or customer representatives) are essential if their marketing strategy is to be credible and convincing.

Project ambassadors

Stakeholder groups

Stakeholders with the same requirements are grouped together, just as they are for stakeholder communication, so that group-specific measures can be decided. Some of these measures can take place on fixed dates and some in conjunction with special events (e.g. damage limitation after project goof-ups). Ideally, the project management team should remain in close contact with the marketing department so that project marketing and corporate marketing activities can be interlinked (e.g. presentation of the project to the customer or at staff events).

Integration with corporate marketing activities

Monitoring competitors

Monitoring competition is another aspect of the marketing strategy. The project personnel should keep tabs on all other projects within and outside the organisation so that they can tap information sources and ensure that project risks and opportunities are promptly identified. Benchmarking methods (→ Chapter C8, F2) can be used to find out which projects will be continued and which will be abandoned by the organisation´s or customer´s decision-makers in case of doubt.

7.4 Operational marketing

Measures level

Measures are the operational level of project marketing and it is these specific measures that enable the implementation of the project marketing strategy. Many possible measures (e.g. information events, presentations of interim results, models and related products, promotional gifts) are mentioned in marketing literature (e.g. in marketing lexicons).

Plan-Do-Check-Act cycle

Within the scope of the Plan-Do-Check-Act cycle, the people responsible for project marketing have to
- Plan
- Do
- Check and
- Act on measures.

Marketing tools

The measures or marketing tools are selected in accordance with the requirements and characteristics of the target groups, the point in time or the degree of project progress. One example is the topping-out ceremony for a shopping centre.

7.5 Project identity

Components

A project identity generally has first to be established. Central aspects are the self-understanding and vision of the project personnel and the corporate design. It is also important to give the project a short and memorable name. A uniform project identity with logo, a letterhead, e-mail signatures and, in larger-scale projects, business cards, is also necessary. A project identity ensures that the stakeholders can differentiate between the project and other projects (= recognition effect). Once they are familiar with and have internalised the project symbols, they are more likely to accept the project.

Recognition effect

A group brainstorming session involving the project participants or a competition are suitable methods to find a project name. One of the very first marketing measures at the beginning of the project is to involve as many stakeholders as possible in finding a name for it. Sometimes, project names are obvious. For example, the lengthy working title `Use of X Technology to Reduce Workloads´ can be abbreviated to the `XT´ project.

7.5.1 A united front

A `united front´ means that the project personnel have internalised the project identity. They are able to answer central questions about the project without hesitation (e.g. `What is your project´s goal?´). To be able to do this, they need to attend at least one workshop at the beginning of the project. Standardised communication rules that apply for all project participants prevent conflicting external communications. The project participants need to be briefed on the most important `W´ questions (e.g. who, what, when, with what and why) and receive regular updates.

Verbal communication rules

Central `W´ questions
- Who are we?
- What is our project called?
- What is the project deliverable?
- What means will we use to achieve our objective?
- What is the current status?
- When do we have to be finished?
- Who will be affected by the result?
- What are the benefits of the project?
- Why can these benefits only be obtained with this specific project?

8 Media relations

The media can function as excellent multipliers in both large-scale projects that affect the public and smaller-scale internal projects. These benefits are often underestimated. An R&D project in which a recently-established biotech enterprise is conducting research into a cancer drug does not directly affect local newspaper readers. However, the positive presentation of a project with a deliverable that the public will view as useful can definitely boost the organisation´s image. Within the organisation, the media coverage motivates employees and financial backers.

Multiplication effect

Media relations should be proactive. Good media contacts have to be established in good times so that they can be sustained in bad times, e.g. when redundancies are necessary.

Good contacts for bad times

8.1 The `Five Commandments´ of media relations

Everything that an organisation publishes must be consistent with
1. the interests of the target group (survey results),
2. the corporate vision or philosophy,
3. the corporate identity (its self-image, desired internal and external impact),
4. the corporate design (e.g. external depiction – logo, house font) and
5. the organisation´s (good) reputation.

8.2 Survey of target group interests

As is generally the case with stakeholder communication, it is necessary to establish the requirements of each medium as regards content, publication frequency and format of project information (= media matrix).

8.3 Time scheduling

Permanent awareness

Sometimes, organisations have to respond quickly to unforeseen events that take place in quick succession. Press relations work in this case involves more than just the distribution of press releases every few weeks and can only be planned to a limited extent. It demands permanent awareness of current internal and external events, commitment, fast responses, continuity and good journalist contacts.

8.4 Internal coordination

Press officer

The project team should never make public communications at their own initiative. They should always obtain advance clearance from the press officer or – in smaller-scale organisations – senior management about
- important issues and deadlines,
- doubts about whether a specific subject should be published in a specific medium, and
- doubts as to whether all five commandments apply to a planned statement.

Checking enquiries

When a media enquiry is received, the press department checks whether
- it is from a reputable source and conducive to promoting the organisation's reputation,
- it is technically/journalistically competent, and
- it addresses relevant target groups.

Authorisation

Some media let organisations proof-read finished articles before they are published. However, the organisation is not legally entitled to insist on this. Legal entitlement only exists in the case of quotations (= authorisation).

8.5 Press releases

Publication frequency

A differentiation has to be made between press releases and press articles. A press release is a text that the organisation distributes to the media, while a press article is a text that is published by the media. Press releases should be issued several times a year, but only on important topics. Otherwise, media interest will wane. The project or organisation's media officers should always ask journalists for feedback about press releases (e.g. information content, text length, frequency). Press releases should
- be at most one page,
- have a short, catchy headline,
- answer the key `W´ questions (who, what, when, where, with what) in the introductory paragraph,
- include names of contacts and people responsible for content in accordance with media law and

- be distributed in good time before the media publication date:
  - Press releases for daily newspapers: at earliest two weeks before the event, otherwise they will be forgotten.
  - Statements on current events outside the organisation (e.g. political decisions): on the same day or one day in advance.
  - Press releases for weekly newspapers: around three weeks before publication.
  - Press releases for monthly publications: at least six weeks before publication because production takes several weeks.

In general, the more concise the press release is, the less likely it is to contain mistakes.   *Short texts*

8.6 Press mailing lists

When creating and updating a press mailing list, the following should be taken into account:
- Before sending out each press release, check whether the contact still exists and whether the address is correct.
- It is better to contact fewer people while making sure that these are the right people.
- Check at least every six months whether the recipients would prefer to receive the press releases via e-mail, as e-mail attachments, by fax or by post.

Many journalists do not accept e-mail attachments. These are impossible to open in some corporate networks, are complicated to handle and can contain viruses. E-mails should always be sent individually or via appropriate software so that the recipients cannot see the names of all the other people on the distribution list. Two sentences personally addressed to the journalist generally suffice to give the impression that the organisation is providing him with a good service.   *E-mail distribution*

Self-assessment questions for each certification level

No.	Question	Level D	Level C	Level B	Level A	Self-assessment
D 4.01	Which media can be used for communication?	2	3	3	4	☐
D 4.02	Which communication rules should be applied?	2	3	4	4	☐
D 4.03	What is a communication matrix and what is it used for?	2	2	2	2	☐
D 4.04	What are the recommendations on (providing/receiving) feedback?	2	3	4	4	☐
D 4.05	Which strategies can be used to influence the project environment via communication?	2	3	4	4	☐
D 4.06	How is effective stakeholder communication practised?	2	3	4	4	☐
D 4.07	Which results should a stakeholder analysis deliver from a communication perspective?	2	3	3	4	☐
D 4.08	How are communication guidelines used in a project and what do they contain?	2	3	4	4	☐
D 4.09	With which elements of stakeholder communication should the project management team be familiar?	2	3	4	4	☐
D 4.10	What should be taken into consideration when communicating risks?	2	3	4	4	☐
D 4.11	What is the purpose of project marketing and what does it involve?	2	2	3	4	☐
D 4.12	What are the main emphases and rules of media work?	2	2	2	4	☐

D5 CONFLICTS AND CRISES

Conflicts between project participants impact project work negatively and, if they are not promptly resolved, often jeopardise the project´s success (ICB Elements 26, 31). Not only does a project manager have to be able to sniff out potential conflicts, he also has to be aware of typical indicators and characteristics of impending and existing conflicts. Knowledge of the main causes and types of conflicts, the significance of the relationship and objective levels and methods of preventing and resolving conflicts is also necessary, as are crisis management skills.

1 Significance

A conflict-free project is an extremely rare phenomenon. Conflicts can still occur even if rules have been agreed upon and contracts concluded because the various project participants almost always have different expectations of the project. Differences of opinion about objectives and procedures, (non-performance of) work, missed deadlines, budget overruns and interpersonal problems can escalate into conflicts. Most conflicts are seriously detrimental to project progress. If they are not promptly addressed and resolved, the conflict-resolution process can be lengthy and costly because conflicts impair work on the project deliverable. The project manager must therefore be aware of the causes of conflicts, be able to recognise impending conflicts and know how to resolve them.

Different expectations

If one examines the various definitions of conflict to ascertain what they have in common, one sees that they are basically characterised by the incompatibility of actions, motives or behaviour.

Incompatible behaviour patterns

The ICB provides the following definition of conflict management [1]: `Conflict management is the art of handling conflicts creatively. […] The act of conflict management is to channel these conflicts so that the result is positive, preferably synergistically so, rather than destructive.´

Sackmann [2] believes that dealing with conflicts is an attribute of a successful project team. `These teams promptly identify, address and constructively resolve potential conflicts and conflicts. This is accepted as a vital aspect of team development. If conflicts are promptly dealt with, they seldom escalate.´

Things that distinguish successful teams

The work of the conflict research expert, Friedrich Glasl, is relevant in this connection. His models demonstrate the dynamic development of conflicts and help people to understand and resolve them. He shows which conflict resolution methods are likely to be successful and at what stage of the conflict escalation process the project manager should obtain external assistance [3].

2 Functions

Conflicts are often considered to be exclusively destructive. However, this viewpoint is too one-sided because conflicts also present opportunities. People can learn from such situations and they also foster personal development. As a result, innovative approaches to resolving conflicts are often found. According to the ICB [4], `Conflicts imply change (symptoms) and may threaten the achievement of project objectives, but they can also improve the project deliverable and project cooperation.´ Figure D5-1 shows the various functions of conflicts.

Opportunity to find innovative solutions

FUNCTION OF CONFLICTS	EXAMPLES
Indicate the changes that are necessary	e.g. conduct, processes, organisational structure
Reveal opportunities	e.g. market opportunities, more efficient organisational structures, improvements to the working climate
'Clear the air' in unpleasant and obstructive situations	e.g. team atmosphere, motivation
Lead to a more mature project culture	e.g. identification with a project-oriented work process
Promote team spirit	e.g. when the project personnel come from rival departments
Enable team solutions	e.g. a standard procedure for elaborating a technical solution
Eliminate confusion	e.g. task distribution, power balance

Figure D5-1 The functions of conflicts

3 Types of conflicts

Basically, there are two types of conflict: intrapersonal and interpersonal.

3.1 Intrapersonal conflicts

Deciding between alternative courses of action

An intrapersonal conflict does not involve several individuals; it is intrinsic to a single person. It can occur, for example, if a project team member finds it difficult to decide which one of several different courses of action to take. This kind of conflict is generally externally manifested in a change of behaviour. The person affected by the conflict may seem edgy, work inefficiently, make mistakes or demonstrate withdrawal symptoms.

In this case, it is up to the project manager and the team colleagues to take action. They should talk to the person on a one-to-one basis in order to discover what his problem is and whether he needs any (decision-making) assistance. The project manager should make sure at the outset of the project that his staff feel confident about approaching him with problems of any kind, even if it relates to the project manager himself. Obviously, the staff should not face any negative consequences (for their career) if they express their criticisms politely.

3.2 Interpersonal conflicts

The term 'system'

An interpersonal conflict exists if two or more parties (persons, groups, organisations, i.e. social systems) pursue (initially or apparently) incompatible objectives or action strategies, view issues from different perspectives or are competing for scarce resources (e.g. production machines, management jobs). The term 'system' means that all elements are related to one another.

Types

There are three types of interpersonal conflict: conflicts between two individuals (= micro-social), two groups (= meso-social) or two large entities such as organisations or countries (= macro-social).

4 Causes

The causes of conflicts [5] are either located at the
- objective level (= factual/content level) or the
- psychosocial level (= emotional or relationship level).

It is necessary to bear in mind that many conflicts that are apparently objective conflicts actually have their root cause at the psychosocial level.

Apparent objective conflicts

4.1 Conflicts at objective level

Conflicts that occur at the objective level can be sub-divided into
1. Objective-related conflicts
2. Assessment-related conflicts
3. Distribution-related conflicts

4.1.1 Objective-related conflicts

If different project participants pursue different objectives in the same project, they are experiencing an objective-related conflict.

> **Example**
> *An environmental protection organisation initiates a project to raise the general public's awareness of the risks associated with genetic engineering. Part of the project group insists on a complete ban of genetically-modified plants, and the other part is in favour of genetically-modified plants to combat starvation in third world countries. The project manager asks the organisation's managing board to mediate. It decides to abandon the project because the group is unable to agree on a uniform external communication policy and is more likely to damage than promote the organisation's image.*

4.1.2 Assessment-related conflicts

Assessment-related conflicts arise in a project when participants differ in their assessment of facts because they perceive and process information in different ways. One aspect of project work that often causes conflicts is the results of estimates (e.g. time required, costs or project risks).

Disputed estimates

> **Example**
> *An organisation launches a new refrigerator on the market.*
> *The manager of the marketing department wants to emphasise its innovative design in advertisements, whereas the head of the R&D department believes that the refrigerator's low energy consumption is more important. Both have different priorities and therefore favour different approaches to consumer marketing. They are involved in a point-blank clash of opinions at a strategy meeting.*

4.1.3 Distribution-related conflicts

Limited resources

Distribution-related conflicts occur when different project participants compete for the same resources.

> **Example**
> *Two project managers complete their sub-projects at the same time. They both have a considerable amount of documentation work to perform. Each one asks the project office for assistance. However, the project office staff are already overworked because one person is off sick. Which project team should they help out first? The two sub-project managers get into a fierce argument.*

4.2 Psychosocial conflicts

Different values and objectives

Social perception

Psychosocial conflicts generally occur when different personalities, values and objectives collide. When a project commences, project team members, who do not initially know each other, have to work together and familiarise themselves with project processes. This is rarely conflict-free. If interpersonal problems are exacerbated by considerable pressure to deliver successful results, the situation will soon become critical. Social perceptions (→ Chapter D3) play an important role in psychosocial conflicts.

> **Example**
> *A project team member complains to the project manager that his management style is too informal. He argues that there were no flexitime working hours, distance working or project excursions in the other projects that he has worked on, and that these projects were disciplined. The project manager doesn´t understand the project team member´s objections. He manages the project team in the way that he believes is appropriate. Based on his experience in other projects, he is not a supporter of the authoritarian management style (→ Chapter D3) that his colleague is demanding.*

4.2.1 Unrecognised psychosocial conflicts

Conflicts at psychosocial level are often not recognised as such, but are assumed to be related to the objective level.

> **Example**
> *The new project controller and a software expert, who had until recently been responsible for project control, argue constantly. Their colleagues are initially satisfied with the obvious explanation that the software expert was reluctant to hand over his responsibilities to the new man. However, the project manager keeps digging and discovers that the two men once worked together in the same department. The controller was promoted, but the software expert wasn´t. This conflict is related to interpersonal problems and has nothing to do with professional differences of opinion.*

External support

When psychosocial conflicts occur, it may be necessary to call in an external expert (e.g. coach, psychologist, mediator). It is difficult for the project manager to identify the covert desires and expectations of project participants. Accordingly, it is just as difficult to solve these kinds of conflicts.

4.3 Causes of conflicts from a process viewpoint

Mayrshofer and Kröger [6] define different process levels in project work to which causes of conflicts can be allocated [7].
1. Product creation process
2. Project management process
3. Team development process
4. Decision-making process

Process levels in projects

4.3.1 Product creation process

In the product creation process, the team works on the project deliverable (e.g. product, service, reorganisation proposal). `It is entirely normal for many disagreements to occur at this level because most projects are interdisciplinary and each participant contributes different knowledge, interests and objectives,´ argue Mayrshofer and Ahrens. It is therefore important to establish a project culture that enables the project team to express openly their different viewpoints.

They also believe that a lack of specialist expertise, or specialist expertise in only one field, can cause conflicts at this process level. Such conflicts can be avoided by ensuring that the right people are assigned to the project team (→ Chapter D3). Professional differences over the course of the project are a natural phenomenon. However, they are often suppressed and relocated to the relationship level. `These apparent relationship conflicts can be avoided if all professional discrepancies are made transparent […] right from the outset´.

Relocation to relationship level

4.3.2 Project management process

One basic problem, according to Mayrshofer and Ahrens, relates to the special way that project work is structured and the incorporation of the project in the organisation. The matrix organisation (→ Chapter A6) can lead to conflicts between project personnel and department personnel. `Responsibilities and authority are not always clearly defined, and it is more difficult to communicate information in project structures than it is in clearly arranged department structures. If the time available to complete the project is short and it is subject to tight budget constraints, power struggles can occur within and outside the project.´ It is therefore important to be aware of the advantages and disadvantages of a project´s organisational structures in order to prevent potential conflicts.

Conflicts can occur during project planning because plans only provide an outline of future developments that never quite happen as envisaged. The project management team will inevitably encounter regular unscheduled deviations. Many project participants could attribute these deviations to planning mistakes and feel the need to blame somebody for them. All project participants should therefore recognise that the project planning process has a kind of action-guiding function that has to be regularly adapted to real-life situations, and should not view it as binding. Distribution-related conflicts and conflicts of interest in the process of resource planning are also typical in the project management process.

Unscheduled deviations

Distribution-related and conflicts of interest

4.3.3 Team development process

Disquiet phase

Every team development process comprises several development phases (→ Chapter D3). During the conflict phase (also known as the disquiet phase), the team members attempt to achieve a viable working relationship. Typical phenomena in this phase include clique formation, discussions about methods or the purpose of teamwork and negotiations to clarify power and decision-making structures.

Mayrshofer and Ahrens recommend that transparency is encouraged in this phase of the natural team building process, and that common ground and differences, power and decision-making structures are dealt with openly. This necessitates a high level of social and emotional competence, at least on the part of the project manager.

4.3.4 Decision-making process

The different ideas held by stakeholders (e.g. customer, committees, members of higher hierarchical levels) about project solutions can trigger conflicts. `Over the course of the project, […] solutions can be developed that they are unable to identify with if they are not or barely involved in the process,´ warn Mayrshofer and Ahrens. These conflicts can be prevented if the project charter is regularly clarified and refined in conjunction with the relevant decision-makers.

Ambiguous decision-making powers

Conflicts arising from ambiguous decision-making powers are also common. They can cause people to act outside the scope of their authority or fail to perform their duties and this leads to different expectations on both sides, emphasise Mayrshofer and Ahrens. It is therefore essential to ensure the transparency of reciprocal expectations and requirements and decision-making scope.

4.4 Potential conflicts as a result of personal conduct

Many conflicts arise due to the personality or personal conduct of project participants. People learn behaviour patterns while they are still children. Those of which others disapprove are more difficult to put right than professional differences of opinion. The past experience of the conflict parties, or their experience of similar situations, greatly influences their perception of the conflict [8] (→ Chapter D4). A person´s outlook on life influences his perception of a situation (→ Chapter D3), even if it occurs in an entirely different context. Mayrshofer and Ahrens recommend that people should learn to distinguish their perception and interpretation of a situation in order to acknowledge that the other party may view the situation differently.

Differentiating between perception and interpretation

> **Example**
> *A young engineer finds it difficult to interact with other people. He is unsure of himself, inhibited and fears criticism. He has believed for quite some time that the project manager doesn´t like him. One day, the project manager – who has no idea how the engineer feels – asks, `When will you have finished the draft?´ The engineer feels affronted and answers, `What exactly have you got against me?´*

5 Indicators

Latent phase

Most conflicts are not spontaneous. They generally build up in the background over a long time (= latent phase). In order to recognise potential problems in this phase, the project manager should be capable of attuning himself to conflict indicators (e.g. the atmosphere in the project environment). This 'antenna' function can, to some extent, be learned. For example, the project manager can learn to identify certain indicators promptly and to find out the cause of the problem. Some of the indicators of potential conflicts are shown in Figure D5-2.

5.1 Project phase-specific conflicts

The causes of some conflicts relate to specific project phases. Whereas the start-up phase is generally associated with disputes between team members about authority and differences of opinion about project objectives, the implementation phase can be associated with conflicts relating to the product design or the most appropriate production process. Towards the end of the project, conflicts are often related to cost-cutting or meeting the project deadline while ensuring that the deliverable is of the quality required by the customer.

INDICATORS	TYPICAL SYMPTOMS
Project participants argue at length about a specific technical problem.	'Why can't you accept that your technical solution won't work?'
Staff are not willing to listen to each other.	'Smith always talks a load of rubbish anyway.'
Managers sell their staff's ideas to customers or senior management as their own.	'I'd like to present my proposed solution to you today.'
Staff dismiss colleagues' suggestions before they can be discussed.	'Forget it, it's not going to work.'
Managers don't accept the proposals that their staff make. These staff then become demotivated.	'Thanks for the well-meant suggestion. But I'm sure the customer would be happier with a conventional solution.'
Former rivalries between individuals or groups resurface.	'You snatched that other project from right under our noses.'
Affinity or antipathy towards opinion leaders cause people to take sides.	'That upstart and his hangers-on have to be told what's what.'
Project participants vie for decision powers that haven't been firmly established in advance of the project.	'If that's your decision, we're not accepting it.'
Staff give colleagues the impression that they are incompetent.	'You're still quite new to our department. Here, let me do it.'
Staff undermine a colleague or superior in the presence of managers.	'His decisions always turn out to be wrong, anyway.'
Staff are not patient enough with their colleagues.	'Come on! Get to the point!'
Project meetings take too long and don't deliver the desired outcomes.	'This is a fundamental decision that we made ages ago. Why are you bringing it up again?'
Staff repeatedly deliver inadequate results.	'How many times have I told you that you have to structure customer presentations differently?'
Staff in a specific department refuse to implement a strategy developed by the interdepartmental project team.	'You can't simply put Department A's problems in the same boat as Department B's.'
The people responsible (e.g. senior management) don't make the necessary decisions or they delay them for too long.	'We can't do anything else until the chairman has looked at our proposals – and he's away on business again.'

Figure D5-2 Conflict indicators

6 Conflict dynamics

Manifest conflict

Conflicts generally build up over a long period, which is also called the latent phase. Action has to be taken, at the latest, when the conflict finally emerges into the open (= manifest conflict). If the people involved in the conflict fail to resolve it once and for all, a conflict cycle commences. Although a manifest conflict can subside back into latency, there remains an ongoing risk that it will manifest itself again at some future point. This cycle continues until the conflict is finally resolved. The conflict can change during this cycle. It can escalate or expand (e.g. to include other persons or issues). Attempts to analyse conflicts should therefore always include past conflict episodes, because they provide a better understanding of the current conflict.

Crisis cycle

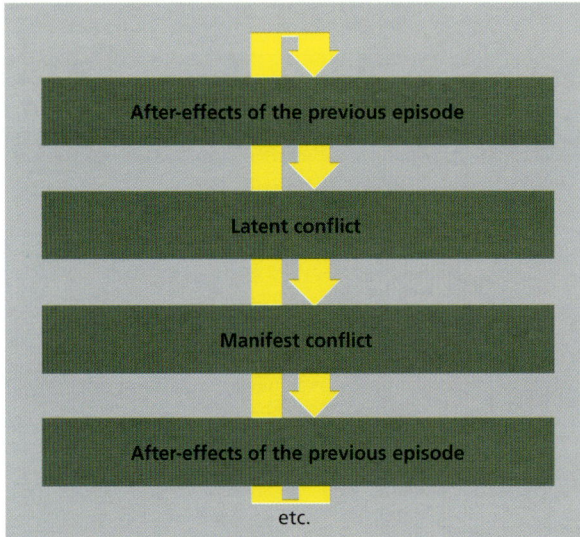

Most options for dealing with conflicts do not result in their final resolution: Adaptation, compromise, disputes/arguments, exerting power and repression generally only provide a temporary respite. At some future point, the conflict manifests itself again and those involved repeat the conflict process.

Figure D5-3 Structure of a conflict episode [9]

7 Conflict escalation

Nine-stage model

Glasl developed a nine-stage model of conflict escalation which can be used to analyse and deal with conflicts. It identifies the following stages [10]:

1. Hardening
   Occasional differences of opinion occur, although the parties are willing to cooperate. They do not yet realise that a conflict is building up.
2. Debate and polemics
   No constructive solution has yet been found. The parties to the conflict now resort to strategies with the aim of convincing the other party of their standpoint. In these debates, the parties give increasingly less consideration to the other side´s interests and attempt to pressurise them. Differences of opinion often escalate into disputes.
3. Actions, not words
   The parties attempt to attain their objectives by way of provocation and pressure. There is little or no communication (e.g. negotiations are broken off) and the conflict escalates at a faster pace.

4. Images and coalitions
   The parties try to enlist allies and form coalitions. This causes the conflict to escalate further. The objective level loses significance. The parties focus on winning the conflict and ensuring that the opponent loses.
5. Loss of face
   The conflict is characterised by defeats and loss of face (e.g. caused by accusations). The aim is to damage the reputation of the other side. All mutual trust is destroyed.
6. Strategies of threat
   The parties issue mutual threats in order to show their ability to set the agenda and to demonstrate their power (e.g. by issuing ultimatums).
7. Limited destructive blows
   In order to reinforce their threats, the parties attempt to neutralise their counterparts´ firepower (e.g. by undermining). They employ tricks and no longer perceive each other as human beings.
8. Fragmentation of the enemy
   The objective at this stage is to destroy the other side.
9. Together into the abyss
   The parties are so strongly driven to annihilate their opponent that they neglect even their self-preservation instinct.

The model is divided into three phases, each with three stages. In the first phase, both sides could potentially win the conflict (= win-win situation). In the second, one party will lose and the other will win (= win-lose situation). In the third phase, both parties lose (= lose-lose situation). This model can be applied to conflicts of varying sizes – from conflicts between project team members to those between nations.

Three stages

8 Approaches to dealing with conflicts

There are different approaches to dealing with conflicts. They all have varying beneficial or detrimental effects on the project. Generally, the sooner and more thoroughly a conflict is resolved, the fewer detrimental effects it has.

Adaptation
Adaptation involves one party in a conflict making concessions to the other. For example, one party may be stronger, and the weaker of the two may fear negative consequences if the conflict escalates. In some cases, a person may act according to the principle of `Discretion is the better part of valour – the project must go on.´

Giving way

Agreement
An agreement is the ideal way to end a conflict, and is the option that will have the most positive effect on the project. The parties agree to an acceptable, permanent solution that cannot be called into question. All conflict parties are satisfied with the outcome. However, resolving a conflict by agreement can be a lengthy process that necessitates perseverance, experience and tact on the part of all persons involved, unless a mediator is used. In an agreement approach, all conflict parties tend to realise that they have to work together if the project is to be brought to a successful conclusion. Agreements have the advantage that they not only motivate the parties to the conflict but also the other project stakeholders.

Ideal way to end a conflict

Compromise

Compromises and advantages

A compromise means that the parties concede some of their original demands after negotiation. At the same time, a compromise offers each of them an advantage. Compromises that the parties only accept reluctantly (e.g. under pressure from superiors or as a result of a lack of time) are generally unstable. People often find insignificant reasons to call the emergency agreement into question, for instance, by attempting to find ambiguities or omissions.

Delegation

Many conflicts can be resolved more quickly if the parties, or a project participant who is interested in an agreement (e.g. the organisation´s management), call in a facilitator. If neither agreement nor compromise is possible, the facilitator makes a decision by which all parties have to abide. This in-

Facilitator´s decision

volves the risk that individual parties to the conflict may not feel obliged to abide by the facilitator´s decision and, when the next dispute arises, they could take it as an excuse to revoke the agreement.

Arguments/disputes

The least effective solution

Fighting to achieve one´s objectives initially seems a logical solution, though it is also the least effective one. On the surface, it produces fast results. However, a confrontational approach causes the other party to feel frustrated or vengeful; the loser broods about reparation or compensation. This is why any solution in which the stronger party wins is generally only short-lived. If one party adopts a confrontational approach without prior consideration, this has a detrimental effect on subsequent negotiations. A confrontational approach can also result in the party being sidelined, because although outsiders may understand his motives, they disapprove of his aggressiveness.

Exercising power

The person with the most power finds it easier to win a conflict (e.g. managers can fire problematic members of staff and customers can cancel orders). Being powerful can also mean

- being able to exploit more lucrative relationships,
- possessing an information monopoly and
- having the suitable means to create a fait accompli.

Repression

Repressing a conflict generally only results in a short-lived respite. If the problem is shelved for too long, it erupts with even greater force later on.

Risk management at the outset of the project

Conflict prevention

Conflict prevention is the best way to ensure that the project is a success. It requires a systematic stakeholder and risk management at the outset of the project (→ Chapter A3, C3).

8.1 Conflict prevention measures

In order to prevent conflicts, you have to look behind the scenes instead of focusing on obvious facts.

> **Example**
> The project manager has forgotten to inform two important members of staff in different departments that the other person is also on the project team. He doesn´t discover that the two men have always disliked each other until the project is already under way. They argue at every possible opportunity.

D5 CONFLICTS AND CRISES

Changes during the project lifecycle (e.g. team composition, customer contact) result in changes to the work and project environments. This, too, could cause conflicts.
One member of staff may suddenly find that he has more work to do because his colleague´s holiday replacement has neither the appropriate qualifications nor the inclination to familiarise himself with the work for such a short period.

The following measures can help to prevent conflicts.
- Open information policy vis-à-vis stakeholders (→ Chapter D4).
- Involving the people affected in important decisions.
- Taking fears and concerns seriously [11].
- Creating a climate of trust.
- Investigating the overt and covert objectives of all the people involved and discussing them openly.
- Clarifying tasks and responsibilities each time the team structure changes.
- Discussing different understandings of processes and work methods.
- Providing and requesting regular feedback, possibly with the assistance of an external feedback coordinator.
- Expelling team members who have a lasting negative effect on the team.

Measures

8.1.1 Professional project start-up

Mayrshofer and Kröger [12] recommend a professional approach to project start-up as a means of preventing conflicts. This involves the following measures:
- Allocate sufficient time to the team building process (→ Chapter D3): around 10 percent of the project duration in projects with a lifecycle of up to three months and at least three days in longer projects.
- Enable the project team to get to know one another.
- Clarify project roles.
- Discuss personal and professional interests.
- Agree upon rules for handling conflicts.

Conflict prevention at the outset of the project

These can be supplemented with the following:
- The team should allocate sufficient time to defining its mutual project objective. It is important that all team members can identify with this objective and are aware of the personal contribution that they can make to its achievement.
- It is a good idea, at the beginning of the project, to work out a standard decision-making procedure or to agree upon a procedure that has already proven to be successful in the past.

8.1.2 Drama triangle

The Karpman drama triangle is one method of conflict prevention. It is a psychological and social model of human action in transactional analysis (TA) which was initially used for psychoanalytical purposes. The players in the drama triangle game (a game involving the three roles of victim, persecutor and rescuer) learn about their mutual dependencies. Afterwards, they are able to draw conclusions about their behaviour in past conflict situations and consider new approaches that they could take in the future. For instance when the drama triangle is used in project teams, it enables team

Conclusions based on interdependencies

members who feel that they have been forced into a role that they don´t want to recognise why this happened and how they can change their behaviour in future (e.g. persecutor or victim in bullying incidents). In this way, it can permanently eliminate conflict situations.

8.1.3 Iceberg theory

Project managers who want to prevent conflicts should also be familiar with the iceberg theory. It was developed by Freud (physician and founder of psychoanalysis). According to him, human consciousness is like an iceberg because only between 10 and 20 percent of it can be directly perceived by us. The other 80 to 90 percent (the subconscious part) lies hidden beneath the surface, which is the interface between the conscious and the subconscious. It prevents us from being directly confronted with the subconscious.

Influence of the relationship level

In a project team environment, this can be interpreted as follows: the soft factors at the relationship level influence project work far more than the hard factors at objective level. When conflicts occur, the project manager therefore always has to look beneath the surface to find out whether an objective conflict actually is one. In some cases, he may find that the conflict really originates at relationship level. The iceberg theory can also be applied in other areas of project management. For example, in project communication (→ Chapter D4), which is closely related to the subject of conflicts, the ratio of `one-seventh objective level to six-sevenths relationship level´ applies.

9 Conflict resolution

Various tools and models are used to resolve conflicts.

9.1 Cooperative conflict regulation model

Figure D5-4 shows Fleischer's [13] cooperative conflict regulation model. The ICB says, `Cooperative conflict regulation requires willingness amongst all parties. It may be moderated via a neutral mediator.´ [14]

Willingness of the parties

COOPERATIVE CONFLICT REGULATION MODEL	
Introduction	
	• The mediator briefs the parties on the causes of the conflict. • The mediator encourages the parties to work at resolving the conflict. • The mediator explains the rules and procedures of mediation.
Diagnosis	
Description of the status quo	• The mediator listens to the different viewpoints. • The mediator breaks the conflict down into components, if necessary, so that they can be processed (possibly individually). • The team members join forces to provide a description of the status quo.
Solution development	
Describe the target situation	• The team defines alternative target situations.
Develop measures	• The team develops a target situation, acceptable to all parties, and a means of achieving it. If the proposal proves to be unfeasible the development process is repeated until a realistic solution, acceptable to all team members, has been found.
Assuring success	
	• The mediator helps each individual to consider what impact the decision will have on him and his behaviour. • The team specifies the `who´, `when´, `where´ and `with what´ for assessing success.

Figure D5-4 Cooperative conflict regulation model

9.2 Standard questions for conflict resolution

The following questions enable a systematic approach to conflict resolution.

Questions

9.2.1 Preparation for conflict resolution

Mayrshofer and Kröger approach the task of conflict resolution by asking a set of questions [15].
1. Who are the people involved?
2. What exactly is it about?
3. How could the conflict benefit the project or organisation?
4. What aspects of the project will be better or more efficient if the conflict is resolved?
5. What aspects of the conflict originated in the project environment and have to be resolved there?

9.2.2 Developing a solution to a conflict

The following questions [16] can be useful when developing a solution to a conflict.
1. Which solutions have already been proposed?
2. How effective were they?
3. What impact will the proposed solutions probably have?
4. What state should be reached after the conflict has been resolved?
5. Who will win/lose?
6. What compensation will the loser(s) receive? Does he/do they accept this?
7. Who has to bring this situation about? Who else has to be involved?
8. Who has to be informed that the conflict has been resolved?
9. What action will be taken if the conflict recurs?
10. What procedure will apply in future conflicts?

9.3 Conflict mediation model

The mediation process

According to Redlich, a conflict mediation model can include the following steps [17].
1. Agreement between the project manager and mediator about the assignment.
2. Preliminary discussion with the project manager to assess the problem.
3. Preliminary discussion with the team to build trust.
4. Definition of issues and correction of false expectations.
5. Clarification of viewpoints.
6. Negotiation of compromises.
7. Follow-up and further support.

9.3.1 The advantages of mediation

The use of a mediator in the conflict solving process offers several advantages because he
- views the conflict as an outsider (= objectivity).
- assumes the project manager´s responsibility for the conflict in the conflict resolution process and enables him to focus entirely on resolving the conflict.
- gives the project manager the opportunity to state his position openly as a party in the conflict resolution process.
- has experience in conflict mediation and is aware of which approaches are likely to be successful.

9.4 Arbitration

Advantages

Arbitration (→ Chapter A4) is another means of conflict resolution. This cooperative conflict solving method is often used to resolve conflicts out of court. The conflict parties assume responsibility for resolving the conflict themselves with the assistance of a neutral third party (= arbitrator). Although they always remain in control of the process, they have to adhere to certain rules. The arbitration process often only takes a few days, whereas recourse to an arbitration court can often take several months and involve considerably higher costs. Arbitration focuses on sustaining a workable relationship between the parties.

9.5 Communication rules

If the people involved in a conflict meet to discuss the matter openly, they have to observe basic communication rules (→ Chapter D4). The three most important rules in conflict discussions are:
1. Talk in the first person. Say `I wish...´ and not `It would be easier if...´
2. Talk about how you feel instead of making accusations. Say `I get the feeling that you are very edgy´ and not `You´re very edgy´
3. Come to the point rather than generalising. Say `I noticed that you were confrontational´ and not `You´re always so confrontational´

If these rules are not observed, the other party will not be interested in working constructively to find a solution. Instead, he may feel frustrated, concerned, aggressive or have similar negative feelings. It is difficult to observe all three rules at the same time. A mediator is extremely useful because he can draw the parties´ attention to lapses and intervene if necessary.

In conflict situations, it is important to differentiate between perception, interpretation and evaluation. Before the people involved in the conflict form and express an opinion, they should attempt to consider the complexity of the situation. This prevents hasty judgements and the associated negative effects on the conflict resolution process.

Perception
Interpretation
Evaluation

9.6 Recommendations for constructive conflict management

The following recommendations enable the prompt and effective resolution of conflicts:
- deal with conflicts immediately,
- take warning signs seriously (e.g. staff turnover, brusque tone of voice),
- try to discover the real causes,
- clarify the objectives of those involved,
- ensure that arguments are precisely worded, address the other party directly (e.g. `In future, please give me the documents on the day before the customer appointment´),
- don't cause the other party to lose face,
- accept emotional responses and ensure that your own responses are calm, and
- celebrate together the resolution of the conflict.

9.7 Checklist

The following checklist provides a general overview of the key aspects of conflict resolution:
1. Recognise the conflict.
2. Identify the people involved in the conflict.
3. Talk about the conflict.
4. Analyse the conflict.
5. Visualise the different sides of the conflict.
6. Categorise the conflict (relationship or objective level).
7. Move the conflict from relationship to objective level.
8. Structure the conflict.
9. Consider, evaluate, select and implement possible solutions.
10. Take advantage of the conflict to introduce new approaches.

Important aspects of resolving conflicts

10 Crises

A project crisis is a special kind of conflict that is characterised by `absence of a way out, retreat, blockage or long-range paralysis´ [18]. In some cases, it can cause the project to come to a standstill. According to Neubauer's [19] definition, `If problems escalate to such an extent that it appears impossible to resolve them in the given framework, they can be classified as crises.´

However, it is impossible to say precisely when a conflict escalates into a crisis. Gareis [20] emphasises that, `The existence of project discontinuity cannot be measured in terms of objective criteria. Rather, it has to be defined by a communication process within the project.´ Project discontinuity is tantamount to a project crisis.

10.1 Crisis indicators

The human factor

There are many different crisis indicators. For example, the following indicators are associated with the `human factor´:
- Employee turnover increases.
- Conflicts are impossible to resolve and escalate.
- Employees are unable to get other people to accept their ideas and resort to blocking tactics, boycotts and similar destructive behaviour (e.g. withholding documents).

Hard factors

Other indicators [21] relate to `hard´ factors and require professional project control measures (→ Chapter C9). Examples include
- Considerable forecast or actual project cost overruns, or a substantial forecast or actual postponement of the project finish date. Gareis specifies a crisis threshold of 50 percent in both cases.
- The customer regularly expresses new requirements.

10.2 The stages of a crisis

Fluid transition between phases

The different stages of a crisis can be shown in a model [22]. However, in reality, it is impossible to clearly differentiate between each stage since the transitions are fluid.

Crisis origination

Lack of action

Crises often build up over a long time before they become manifest. If the project manager does not intervene promptly, his lack of action can actually cause a crisis.

Crisis identification

The crisis is identified and the project personnel realise that the problem cannot be easily solved.

Crisis description

Written documentation

The crisis description – which should be written down if possible – explains the crisis situation, what and who it involves. On the basis of this description, the project manager ascertains whether or not a genuine crisis exists. The document can also be used to inform the stakeholders (e.g. senior management or customers) about the crisis, draw their attention to the problem and involve them in any attempts to resolve it.

Crisis resolution

Resolving a crisis is not merely a matter of developing and implementing possible solutions. The project manager or senior management should always initiate emergency measures to prevent the crisis from escalating.

Emergency measures

Learning from crises

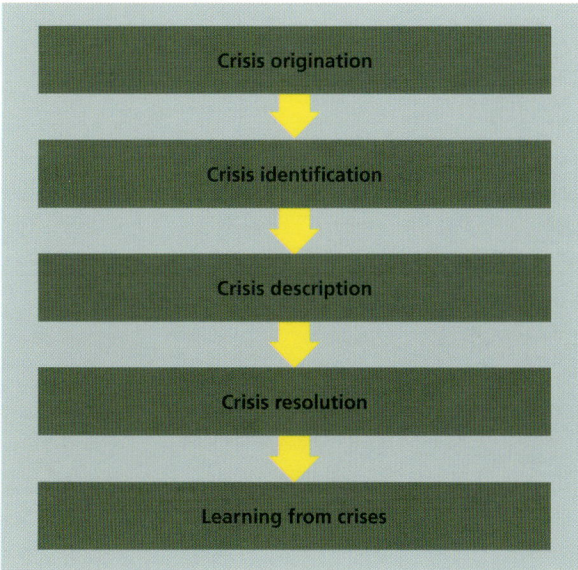

The project manager should take advantage of the experience gained during the crisis and the process of overcoming the crisis to learn things that will benefit the project (→ Chapter C10). It is also necessary to implement measures to improve crisis management (e.g. staff training).

Documenting past experience

Figure D5-5 The stages of a crisis

10.3 Team crises

If teams are no longer able to influence themselves and their situation, this is a sure indication of a crisis. Two widespread forms of team crisis are where a team is impeded by itself or external causes.

10.3.1 A self-impeding team

The absence of a counterparty characterises a group that impedes itself [23]. This can occur when familiar cooperation structures suddenly no longer function. The team and its members have changed without being aware of it.

Changes within the team

Although conflict potential exists, it does not surface. The team gradually senses that `something is wrong´. Teams with a high level of cohesion are prone to this kind of crisis. Out of fear that the team may disintegrate, nobody dares to introduce conflict management measures. The team perceives external attempts to make changes as attacks and attempts to obstruct them. Only the team itself can change the situation (e.g. through restructuring). The longer the team persists in its obstinacy, the more difficult it will be to change the situation.

10.3.2 Externally impeded teams

Detrimental intervention

This kind of crisis is caused by external intervention in the team with the objective of preventing an (assumed) conflict. Where a team is impeded by external causes, it loses its identity, its self-awareness and, finally, any hope of being able to make a difference. Formal procedures to regulate behaviour (evasive manoeuvres) start to take precedence. The parties cease to communicate directly with one another [24].

10.4 Crisis management

External assistance

Neubauer developed a model for managing crises which have escalated [25]. This model focuses on the restatement of problems and altering the perspectives of the people involved in the project. Outside assistance is generally necessary because project personnel often follow their panic instinct and fail to acknowledge new and unconventional problem-solving options.

10.4.1 Neubauer´s model

1. Analyse the problem, with detailed documentation.
2. Ascertain anticipated negative effects.
   All parties involved in the crisis (especially the customer and the contractor) will want to find a solution that costs less than the anticipated negative effects of the crisis.
3. Search for feasible solutions.
   In this phase, creativity techniques can be used.
4. Assess potential negative effects.
   When an acceptable solution has been found, the potential negative effects of the crisis have to be assessed as precisely as possible. The solution should only be implemented if it will cost less than these anticipated negative effects.
5. Present the benefits.
   The benefits of the solution have to be convincingly presented to the project personnel as the new basis for the project.
6. Document agreements reached.

Project abandonment

If the parties cannot resolve the crisis, the project has to be abandoned. In practice, far too few project managers opt for this solution.

10.5 Crisis prevention

Communication

Crisis prevention, both at relationship and objective level, depends to a great extent on communication (→ Chapter D4). The central elements of crisis prevention are:
- Provision of comprehensive information to stakeholders
- Proactive dialogue with stakeholders
- An efficient reporting system (→ Chapter D4, D9)
- An open and trusting project and corporate climate
- A project manager with a cooperative management style (→ Chapter D3)

D5 CONFLICTS AND CRISES

Self-assessment questions for each certification level

No.	Question	Level D	Level C	Level B	Level A	Self-assessment
D 5.01	How can conflicts arise?	2	2	2	2	☐
D 5.02	How can one recognise a conflict?	2	3	4	4	☐
D 5.03	How can conflicts be resolved?	2	3	4	4	☐
D 5.04	What measures can be implemented to prevent conflicts?	2	3	4	4	☐
D 5.05	What functions can conflicts have?	2	2	2	2	☐
D 5.06	Which causes of conflicts can be found on which levels?	2	2	2	2	☐
D 5.07	Which conflicts are specific to certain project processes?	2	3	3	4	☐
D 5.08	How can personal conduct cause conflicts?	2	2	2	2	☐
D 5.09	What options are available for dealing with conflicts?	2	3	4	4	☐
D 5.10	How can conflicts be resolved on the basis of cooperation?	2	3	4	4	☐
D 5.11	Why is a mediator often used in the conflict resolution process?	2	2	2	2	☐
D 5.12	How can conflicts be resolved quickly and effectively?	2	3	4	4	☐
D 5.13	What is the difference between a crisis and a conflict?	2	2	2	2	☐
D 5.14	What kinds of team crises can occur?	2	2	2	2	☐
D 5.15	What is the procedure for crisis management?	2	3	4	4	☐
D 5.16	Which activities are central elements of crisis prevention?	2	3	4	4	☐

D5 CONFLICTS AND CRISES

BLOCK E

SINGLE PROJECTS AND PROJECT ENVIRONMENT

E1 PROGRAMME AND MULTI-PROJECT MANAGEMENT

Organisations that have discovered the advantages of project management and installed the appropriate organisational structures generally implement several projects concurrently (ICB Elements 3, 4, 39). Project managers have to coordinate the projects and allocate scarce resources; they have to set priorities and substantiate them. This brings the terms `programme´ and `portfolio´, which are covered in this chapter, into play. An explanation is provided of the differences between programme management and multi-project management. The roles of programme and multi-project managers are also defined.

1 Parallel projects

To keep things simple, chapters A to D of this textbook assume that only one single project is being planned and implemented. Most organisations concurrently run several projects with many interdependencies. Employees frequently complain, and rightly so, that it is almost impossible to cope with the number of projects being implemented by their organisations (`projectitis´). In many cases it is not even clear which projects take priority. Problems relating to capacity usage and priorities have to be solved by project managers on a case-by-case basis. If several projects are in the pipeline or several customer enquiries have been received, this is particularly significant.

`Projectitis´

When implementing internal projects, it is necessary to clarify the following issues:
- Which projects should we initiate, bearing in mind the scarce resources? This question relates, in particular, to human resources and budget funds.
- How should we prioritise the projects?

Internal customer

The assignment of priorities always goes hand in hand with the allocation of resources. When projects are to be implemented for an external customer, a decision has to be made:
- Is it worthwhile preparing a quotation for this potential customer?

External customer

In many cases, the costs of the often complex process of preparing a quotation are passed on to the potential customer. The probability that the quotation will be accepted and an order placed is low - especially in times of economic recession or in highly competitive markets. The Association of German Engineers (VDI) has observed that [1]: `globalisation of markets and the liberalisation of international trade have led to much tougher competition in the manufacturing sector over recent years […]. As a result, providers in this sector have to prepare more quotations, even though the same number of orders is being placed. This generates substantial advance costs that have to be apportioned among the orders that are actually placed.´ Another problem is that organisations with high order levels are often unable to implement all projects owing to capacity shortfalls.

2 Definitions

Lomnitz [2] clarifies the differences between programme and project portfolios with the following definitions:

Difference Programme/portfolio

A programm is a 'large-scale project with several sub-projects'. A programme manager is responsible for a programme.

A project portfolio comprises several independent projects in one organisation that are being implemented concurrently. Lomnitz calls the task of planning and controlling the projects in the portfolio 'multi-project management'. A multi-project manager has a special role which is not to be confused with that of programme manager.

In some cases, a project portfolio can also include a programme.

Figure E1-1 [3] shows the difference between multi-project management and programme management.

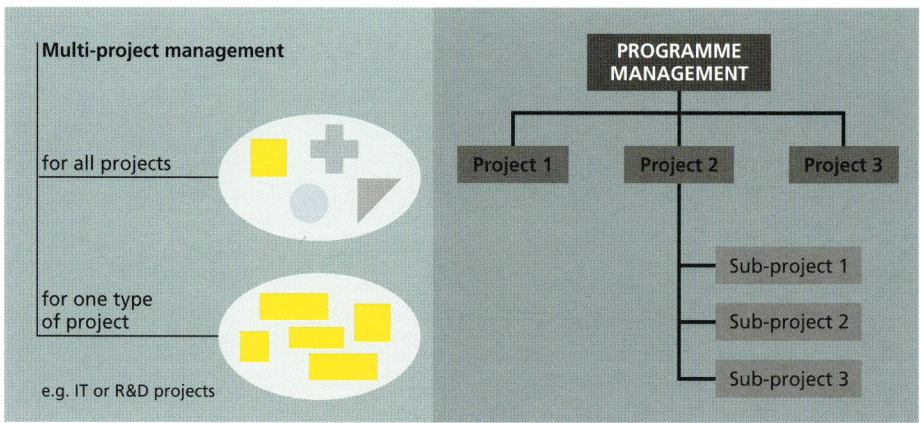

Figure E1-1 Difference between multi-project management and programme management

Different roles and functions

Based on the differentiation between programme and multi-project management, it follows that the people involved have different roles and tasks (→ Chapter E3).

The ICB's definition of programme and multi-project management is similar to that of Lomnitz:

'A programme is a series of specific, interrelated undertakings (projects and additional tasks) which together achieve a number of objectives within one overall strategy. Multi project management coordinates all projects in a company or another organisation during the processes of evaluation and selection, planning, controlling and termination.'

This definition has the following flaws:
- It does not differentiate between the two in terms of their temporary or permanent nature.
- Both a programme and a project portfolio pursue higher-level objectives.

2.1 Programme and project portfolio

Two examples are provided below to illustrate the differences between a programme and a project portfolio.

2.1.1 Programme

Like a project, a programme is a temporary undertaking. The programme manager is released from his duties when the programme ends.

Programme manager

> **Example**
> *The development of a new vehicle model takes place in the form of a main project, which focuses on the development of the new chassis, body and engine, plus several sub-projects that are affiliated to the main project. For example, the automotive company may develop an improved version of an ABS or airbag system in one sub-project, while a supplier works on a more sophisticated navigation system in another. In other sub-projects, the company restructures its sales organisation for the marketing of the new model and launches an advertising campaign. In order to complete all these tasks, senior management sets up a programme. The programme finishes when customers are able to purchase the new model.*

The programme manager has to coordinate the various sub-projects that are affiliated to the main project to ensure that

Sub-project

- the necessary information and physical results from sub-projects are delivered in time for the individual milestones in the main project,
- the numerous technical interfaces between the various projects are properly coordinated and
- the entire programme is implemented within the given time and cost frame, with the required quality and to the satisfaction of the customer.

He also has to ensure that the sub-project deliverables can be used as required in other projects. This helps the organisation to avoid the unnecessary repetition of the same work.

2.1.2 Project portfolio

Unlike programme management, multi-project management is a permanent task. The project portfolio changes regularly, at least in larger organisations, because projects are constantly completed, abandoned and started up. The portfolio itself continues to exist, though its projects will change. The programme manager´s function is temporary whereas the multi-project manager´s function is permanent.

Temporary / permanent function

> **Example**
> *An insurance group always has numerous IT projects in progress at any one time. When one project finishes, a new one is started.*

2.2 Comparison of a programme manager and a multi-project manager

Definition of roles

Lomnitz [4] provides an illustrative though somewhat simplified comparison of the roles of multi-project managers and programme managers.

MULTI-PROJECT MANAGER	PROGRAMME MANAGER
Navigator in the project environment Focus: general coordination of projects	Captain of the programme Focus: programme
Coordination function Analyses and reports problems to the project managers, customer and portfolio board	Management function Must directly intervene in the project if the situation requires this
Has no budget responsibility, but does have to monitor the overall budget	Has budget responsibility
Analyses the human resources situation in the project environment	Has HR responsibility
Permanent function for as long as project environment coordination is necessary	Function ends when the programme finishes
Is often confronted with internal political wrangling, power and his own powerlessness	Often has to deal with angry customers in external projects

Figure E1-2 Definitions of the roles of multi-project manager and programme manager

Self-assessment questions for each certification level

No.	Question	Level D	Level C	Level B	Level A	Self-assessment
E 1.1	What is the main difference between programme management and portfolio management?	1	2	2	3	☐
E 1.2	How can the terms project management, programme management, multi-project management and portfolio management be defined?	1	2	2	3	☐
E 1.3	How can a comparison or differentiation be made between the roles of a programme manager and a multi-project manager?	1	2	2	3	☐
E 1.4	Which manager role in the project environment tends to be temporary and which tends to be permanent?	1	1	1	3	☐

E2 PROJECT SELECTION AND BUSINESS STRATEGY

Enterprises can only survive in the market if they implement the right projects. Yet how do the people responsible for project selection decide which projects are worth implementing? The problem of how to identify suitable projects exists in both internal projects and in projects for external customers. This chapter focuses on the process of project selection. Among other things, it explains the roles of the various decision-making bodies and how the selection methods function (ICB Element 7).

1 Significance

An organisation´s project management and business strategies [1] can be related in two ways. Firstly, the development of a business strategy is a complex project with initially vague objectives, or even a project programme that pursues one single overall objective. However, this chapter only deals with the second aspect of implementing strategies with the assistance of projects.

Strategy implementation with the assistance of projects

Figure E2-1 shows the relationship between an organisation´s business strategy, strategic project management (`implementing the right projects´) and operational project management (`implementing the projects the right way´).

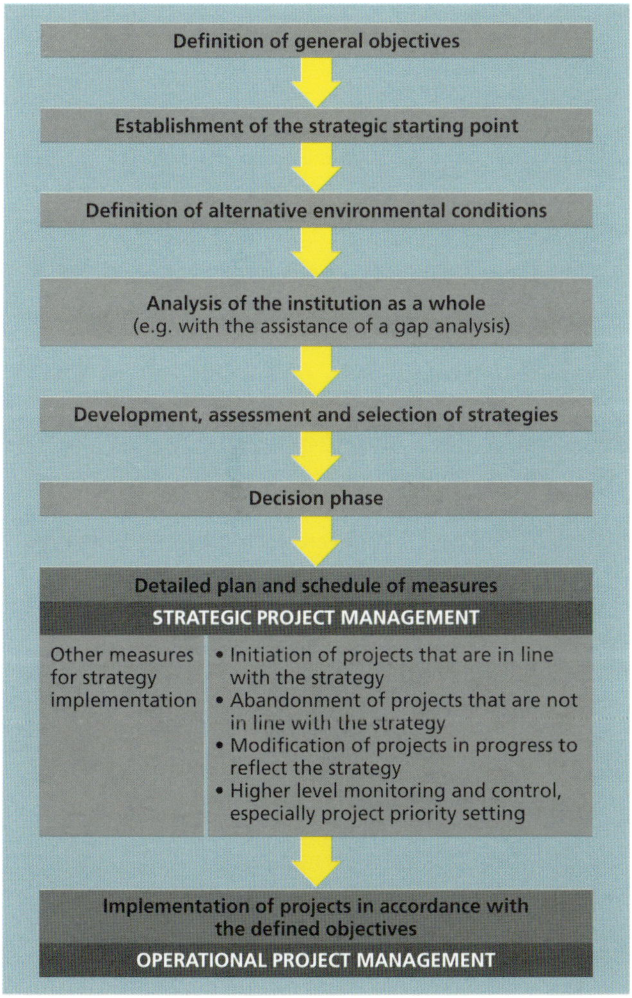

Figure E2-1 Business strategy, strategic and operational project management

2 Operational and strategic project management

A project manager is responsible for operational project management. In other words, he has to ensure adherence to deadlines and the budget, the delivery of the required quality and the implementation of the project to the satisfaction of the key stakeholders.

Strategic project management committees

Strategic project management, on the other hand, is the responsibility of committees established for this specific purpose. They have names such as project board, steering committee or portfolio board. These differ from a steering committee established for one project only (e.g. a reorganisation project) because the latter is mainly responsible for assessing and approving the results delivered by the project team.

Decision-making authority

Members of project boards, steering committees and portfolio boards are generally senior managers – sometimes members of the executive managing board, sometimes at a slightly lower level. These people select the projects to be implemented and, if necessary, ensure their timely abandonment. They also make all the decisions that are outside an individual project manager's authority or require an overview of the entire project/product portfolio and familiarity with the organisation's business strategy. These decisions include
- the approval of the final project definition (specification),
- the allocation of priorities for individual projects,
- important priority changes, and
- approval or rejection of substantial changes to objectives during the project.

They also
- appoint project managers,
- mediate in conflicts between the project managers and line managers and
- are power brokers who support the introduction and development of a project management concept.

2.1 Relationship between business strategy and project selection

When an organisation selects projects, it has to ensure that they are closely aligned with its business strategy and business plans. However, strategic planning is often a process that takes place behind closed doors at executive level. Scheuring [2] quotes a project manager in an organisation's IT department: `I have no idea what our business strategy is. I don´t even know if we have one.´ It is common practice, especially in larger organisations, for the people who are responsible for the formulation of a long-term strategy to have no contact with the people who are responsible for project selection.

Mistakes in practice

King [3] encountered the same phenomenon in his work as consultant. He analysed the existing and planned programmes of a large-scale organisation that operates in diverse business sectors. It was obvious that the existing and planned projects bore no evident relationship to the organisation's business objectives or business strategy. He observed this on many occasions and similar findings have been obtained in more recent studies [4].

Those responsible for business strategy and projects must however deal with extremely complex interrelationships between these two spheres of activity.

E2 PROJECT SELECTION AND BUSINESS STRATEGY

Example

A development project delivers substructures for several products being developed in a business division. The project manager has to consider the issue of how to make a differentiated evaluation of the input from the development project. How can he determine the value of the substructure project to the organisation?

3 Management by projects

Inefficient coordination of strategy definition and project selection is diametrically opposed to the concept of management by projects which an increasing number of organisations are now propagating for the more effective achievement of their objectives.

According to the ICB, management by projects is a `core concept for the management of a permanent organisation, especially of the project-oriented company´. Project-oriented organisations mainly work within project structures. They initiate, implement and conclude many different projects concurrently. `The management by projects enhances organisational flexibility and dynamics, decentralises the operational management responsibilities and improves organisational learning and facilitates organisational change´, says the ICB.

Project-oriented organisations

Management by projects is not just a concept applied to classic projects (for example, projects that are commissioned by a customer, internal investment projects and research & development projects), it can also be used in the organisation´s own restructuring and market research projects. The former, in particular, generally impact on vital employee interests because they are often associated with improving cost effectiveness and cutting jobs.

Possible applications

Gareis [5] summarises the development of an organisation that operates according to the principle of management by projects as follows:

FROM	TO
Order processing, research and development	Order processing, research and development, quotation preparation, PR projects, HR and organisational development projects, investment projects
Few large-scale projects	Many small, medium-sized and large-scale projects
Mainly projects that are commissioned by external customers	Projects for external and internal customers

Figure E2-2 Development into an organisation based on management by projects

Management by projects requires
- an understanding of organisational unit-wide project processes, and
- a willingness to be consistent in delegating temporary responsibility to project managers.

Prerequisites

In times of fast-changing and highly competitive markets, it offers many advantages to the organisation:
- Temporary project structures enable the organisation to respond quickly and flexibly to opportunities and risks.
- Interdepartmental tasks can be performed efficiently, and teamwork and communication can be improved.

Advantages

- Projects give the project personnel the opportunity to distance themselves from line management structures and, to some extent, view problems as an outsider.
- Projects enable the fast implementation of technological and organisational change at the organisation.
- Projects can also be used for the purpose of personnel development. Involvement in projects offers staff new career perspectives and boosts their motivation (`employees as temporary entrepreneurs´)

Authority   However, some organisations are still a long way off consistent project orientation and management by projects. They have greatly to increase their willingness to grant authority and responsibilities to the project manager (→ Chapter A6).

4 Selection of product development projects

The guiding rule for the selection of appropriate product development projects is `select the projects that most effectively enable the organisation to achieve its objectives´. For methodical and other reasons it is not easy to meet this requirement. Often, anyone who attempts to select projects systematically will encounter tough opposition. For example, members of the organisation will fiercely defend their turf.

Difficulties

Example
An executive at an organisation that is involved in many development projects has a successful career as a result of his management of several product development projects and the acquisition of several patents. However, all available forecasts indicate that the underlying technology is likely to be replaced by a more effective one in the near future. It is really high time that the organisation adapted to this trend by implementing development projects with this technology. However, the executive and his team are not familiar with this new technology, object to using it and reject project proposals that are associated with it.

4.1 Success Factors

Product/project profile   One relatively simple method of project selection is to determine the success factors and to create product and project profiles based on these. Such factors are the features of the organisation´s products and its characteristics which, to a great extent, determine its competitive position in the relevant market. Focussing on these factors brings, in addition, the considerable advantage of giving developers criteria for the formulation of product objectives.

Example
Figure E2-2 [6] shows that price is the most important factor of success for Type A electric motors (standard, mass-produced motors). Any development projects in this business sector therefore have to be oriented towards providing this product at a low price. Above all, the research and development activities should focus on improving processes to reduce production costs and designing a product that can be manufactured at low cost.
In Type D products (custom-made motors), customers do not attach as much importance to price. Quality is one of the most important factors of success for this product. Development activities for Type D motors must therefore be oriented, first and foremost, towards product improvements.

Experienced sales and marketing staff are able to assess success factors.

Estimates

PRODUCTION PROJECT TYPES AND SUCCESS FACTORS TAKING THE EXAMPLE OF ELECTRIC MOTORS				
Production project type	A	B	C	D
	Standard motors, mass production, large-scale customers, demand extremely price-elastic	Modified standard motors, mass production, large-scale customers, demand very price-elastic	Modified standard motors, medium production volume, medium-sized customers, demand fairly price-elastic	Custom-made motors, small production volume, small-sized customers, price a secondary consideration
Success Factors				
Price	3	2	2	1
Quality/function	1	2	2	3
Delivery availability	2	2	2	2
Product service	1	1	2	2
Customer support relating to engineering/production	1	2	3	3
Sales network	2	2	2	3
	1 Unimportant	2 Important	3 Very important	

Figure E2-3 Success factors for electric motors

The example shown in Figure E2-4 shows the success factors for car tyres [7] based on the arithmetical conjoint analysis method. It is obvious that road performance is the most important factor in any customer purchasing decision.

Conjoint analysis

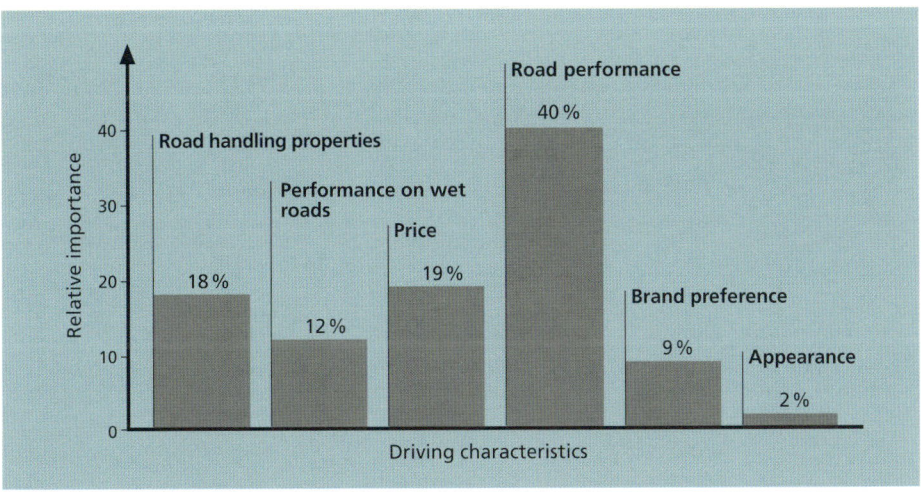

Figure E2-4 Success factors for car tyres

The relatively generalised list of success factors in Figure E2-4 can be further differentiated with the help of the conjoint analysis. Figure E2-5 shows the significance accorded by customers to the various road performance sub-criteria. Most of all, they want tyres that perform well on wet roads and are suitable for year-round use.

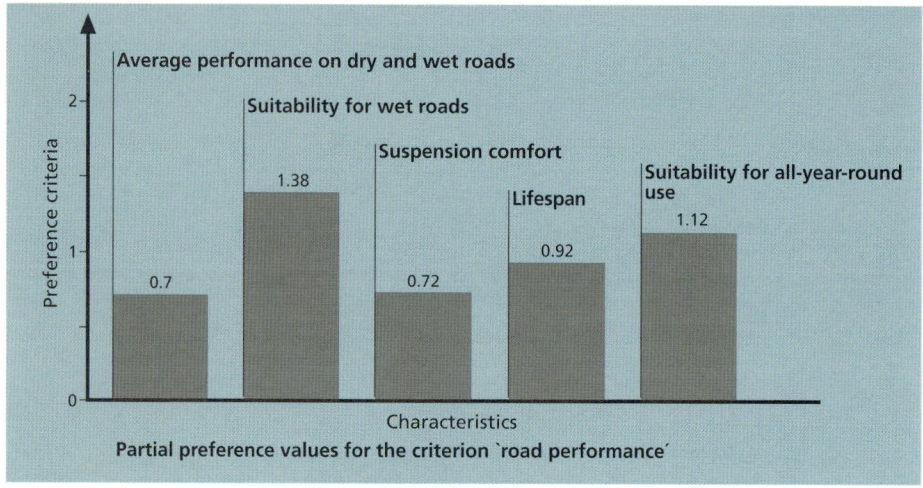

Figure E2-5 Customer weighting of the individual criteria relating to the characteristic 'road performance'

Comparison of alternative projects

The success factors are now applied to the product design and project profiles in order to compare alternative projects. Figure E2-6 shows a highly simplified profile that already includes a generalised comparison with competitors. If points are awarded in the various criteria, it is evident that Project 1 should be given preference over Project 2.

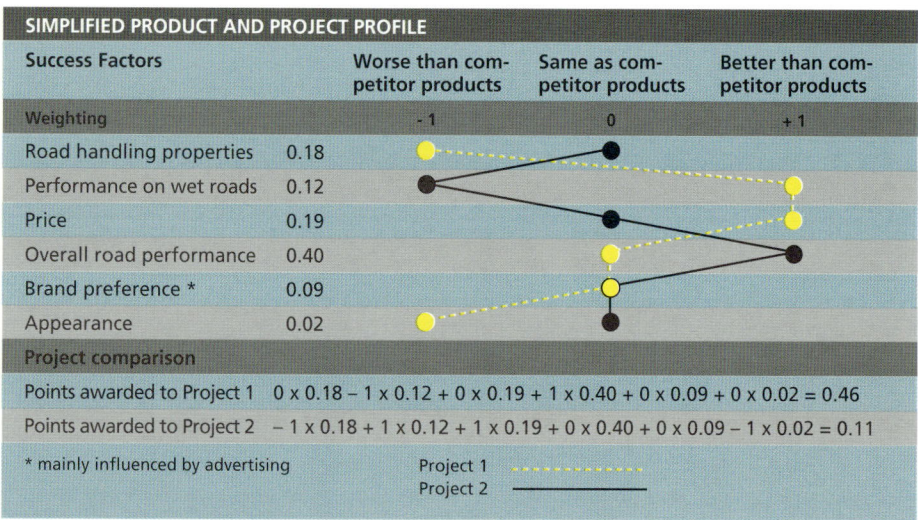

Figure E2-6 Using success factors to define project and product profiles

Decision rules

If the success factors for an organisation's products are known, it is possible to derive simple decision rules for the selection of projects:

1. If price is the main success factor in a market, the majority of projects should focus on reducing production costs and subsequent maintenance and operating costs.
2. If customers attach highest importance to product features, the key quality objectives in the projects should reflect the main success factors. Quality objectives should be defined with the aim of making up deficits or surpassing the quality of the strongest competitor products.

4.1.1 Other parameters

In practice, additional forecast values are considered in addition to the success factors. These include, for instance,
- expected return on investment (= ROI),
- estimated return on sales (= estimated profit that the product will generate),
- projected profit margin (general definition: sales revenue minus variable costs), and
- pay-off time (= estimated time until the expenditure made in respect of the project is recouped).

ROI, return on sales

Pay-off time

These performance indicators can also be combined. Some organisations will not implement project development projects unless they are sure that the expected return on investment and pay-off time will not exceed a specific minimum or maximum value.

4.2 Portfolio method

The portfolio matrix is another tried-and-tested tool. It is used to evaluate potential projects on the basis of two dimensions, such as benefit to the customer or competitive advantage. A third dimension (e.g. anticipated profit) can be shown over the elliptical area representing the project in question.
People are happy to use a portfolio matrix because it is a graphic method. However, a restriction to two dimensions can be risky because projects have more than just two characteristics. That´s why many portfolio matrices with different dimensions are used.

Dimensions

Another popular portfolio method is the competitive advantage/customer benefit portfolio. The projects or products that are to be created in the projects are assessed in terms of
- the competitive advantages that they offer the organisation and
- anticipated benefits for customers.

Competitive advantage/customer benefits portfolio

This is a simplified method because it assumes that the project deliverable is one single product.

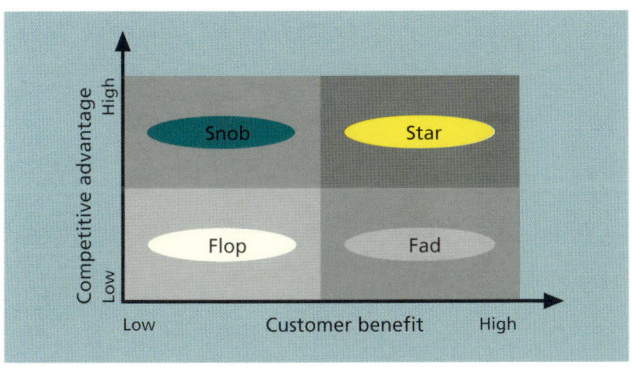

Figure E2-7 Competitive advantage/customer benefit portfolio matrix

The objective must be to select projects
- that will provide the organisation with a major competitive advantage if they are implemented, and
- which develop products that will offer considerable benefit to the customer (= stars).

Stars

Flops, fads, snobs Flops are at the opposite end of the scale. These products are unlikely to generate profits for the organisation. In contrast, `fads´ (high customer benefit, low competitive advantage) can be very successful. An example of a fad is the AIWA walkman, which was marketed at a considerably lower price than the originals by Sony and Sharp. Snobs (high competitive advantage with initially low customer benefit) can sometimes evolve into stars if they are flanked by the right marketing measures or selectively further developed.

5 Selection of investment projects

Accounting parameters Several different methods exist for selecting investment projects [8]. Most are based on accounting principles (costs, performance or revenue, expenditure and income).

People who are considering investment projects ask the same questions as those considering other projects:
- Shall we implement a specific investment project?
- Which investment project should we choose from several available alternatives?

Monetary objectives The main objective is therefore to optimise the investment decision. However, there is one important difference from the methods described above (factors of success and portfolio method): Only monetary objectives are taken into consideration. The issue to be clarified is, what impact will potential investment decisions have on profits?

Non-monetary objectives, such as enhancing the organisation´s reputation, are not taken into account.

Business case analysis The term `business case analysis´, which is also used to describe an appraisal of a potential investment, indicates this. Business case analyses are generally implemented when real investments are planned

Real investments (→ Chapter A2), though they are also suitable for development projects. In real investments, a differentiation is made between
- Replacement investments,
- Rationalisation investments, and
- Expansion investments.

While rationalisation investments and expansion investments increase capacity, replacement investments do not. When replacement investments are made, it is assumed that the income of the organisation making the investment will not increase. In reality, however, replacement and expansion investments are difficult to distinguish from one another.

Unreliable forecasts The different methods of investment appraisal make it possible to evaluate potential investment projects in advance. However, these forecasts are not particularly reliable and the people responsible for investment decisions – and other project decisions – should be aware of this. Often, management accords more objectivity to the calculated figures than they deserve.

5.1 Static and dynamic appraisals

When performing an investment appraisal, a differentiation is generally made between
- static and
- dynamic appraisals.

E2 PROJECT SELECTION AND BUSINESS STRATEGY

Wöhe and Döring [9] provide the following example to simplify the concept for readers with only a rudimentary understanding of business management. To keep things simple, it is assumed that reliable parameters are used in the appraisal. In other words, it is assumed that they will occur precisely as predicted.

Reliable parameters

Example
An investment project is associated with income and expenditure. The expenditure mainly includes the purchase price payment (P_o) and the expenditure (E_t) for wages, materials, repairs and power consumption. The income (I_t) is mainly the sales revenue generated by the investment, though it could also be liquidation proceeds (L_n) resulting from the disposal of the investment object at the end of its useful life.

Investment appraisals generally assume that the expenditure will be incurred and income accrued in the same period. It is also assumed that both expenditure and income can be charged to the investment. However, as Horvath [10] mentions, this assumption is problematic: `It can be assumed that most investments that form part of the business process only deliver operational improvement in conjunction with other investments.´ This means that the investment, on its own, often has no impact at all.

Stand-alone investments

TIME	t_0	t_1	t_2
Purchase price payment (P_0)	– 1,000		
Income (L_t)		+ 500	+ 900
Expenditure (E_t)		– 400	– 200
Liquidation proceeds (L_n)			+ 600
Loan	+ 1,000		
Loan repayment			– 1,000
Interest rate (i)			10%
Investment term (n)			2 years

The figures shown in Figure E2-8 are typical for a planned investment project that is financed exclusively with outside capital.

The values shown in the table can be used to create a payment schedule for this investment project:

TIME	PAYMENT TRANSACTION	AMOUNT
t_0	Inflow of funds from loan	+ 1,000
t_0	Purchase price payment for the investment object	– 1,000
t_0	Balance: Debit (-), Credit (+)	0
t_1	I_1	+ 500
t_1	E_1	– 400
t_1	Loan interest (1)	– 100
t_1	Balance: Debit (-), Credit (+)	0
t_2	I_2	+ 900
t_2	E_2	– 200
t_2	Loan interest (2)	– 100
t_2	Liquidation proceeds	+ 600
t_2	Loan repayment	– 1,000
t_2	Balance: Debit (-), Credit (+)	+ 200

Amounts in EUR

Figure E2-8 Payment schedule for a fictive investment project

If the payments that are actually made when the project is implemented tally with those forecast in the payment schedule, income will cover expenditure. The investing organisation will also be 200 euros in credit. Its equity will have increased by the amount of profit generated by the investment.

5.1.1 Static methods

Simplified methods

Preparing an investment appraisal on the basis of a complete payment schedule is often a complex process because it is necessary to project income and expenditure for every year of the planned investment project. This is why simplified methods were developed for practical use. These methods are also called static investment appraisal methods. They include

- Cost comparison method
  (parameter, costs = value consumption for the production of the deliverable)
- Profit comparison method
  (parameter, costs and work provided = sales proceeds + increase of in-process and finished goods inventories + income from equipment that the organisation produces itself, e.g. the construction of a machine by the trial workshop for the organisation´s own use)
- Profitability calculation
  (parameters, costs and work performed)
- Amortisation calculation
  (parameters, income and expenditure as shown in Figure E2-8).

5.1.1.1 Cost comparison method

Costs per period

In this method of investment appraisal, the controller focuses on assessing whether a replacement investment is worthwhile and choosing the most appropriate of several replacement investment projects with the same objective. He assumes that all the alternatives enjoy the same income. The costs can be calculated for each period. Typically, a period is one year. He compares

- current outlay operating costs (= costs that are reported in the profit and loss account as expenditure)
- imputed depreciation on the investment object and
- imputed interest on the average capital employed. To simplify things, a value of I0/2 is taken for this variable.

Figure E2-9 shows an example of choosing between the two investment projects A and B.

INVESTMENT PROJECT	A	B
Σ fixed costs per year (depreciation, interest payments etc.)	35,000 EUR	42,000 EUR
Σ variable costs per year (materials, production staff wages etc.)	56,000 EUR	62,000 EUR
Period costs per year	91,000 EUR	104,000 EUR

Figure E2-9 Choosing between investment projects

A comparison of the period costs per year shows that Project A is preferable to Project B. The cost comparison method is simple and easy to understand, and the costs of each investment alternative can be calculated relatively quickly. Its disadvantage is that the calculation only covers one representative average period, which can in some cases only be valid for a short time. In other words, it is assumed that the values used will not change within the timeframe of the comparison. This method also gives no indication of whether the achievable income will actually cover costs.

5.1.1.2 Profit comparison method

The profit comparison method is not associated with the above disadvantage. It also provides information about the potential income from any alternative investments with the same functionality. It also takes into account that the income-generating output (= production of goods) of the two investments can differ. This method also calculates profits (= revenue less costs) over a representative time period (= average period). The decision-making rules are:

- Go ahead with a project if the projected profit exceeds the minimum profit required by the decision-maker.
- If there are several projects to choose from, select the project that is expected to generate the highest profit, provided that this profit exceeds the required minimum profit.

Potential revenues

Minimum profit

5.1.1.3 Profitability calculation

The values obtained from a profitability calculation are only comparable if both projects are associated with the same capital expenditure. That's why profit is calculated relative to the average capital employed. This produces the following profitability ratio:

$$\text{Profitability p} = \frac{\text{adjusted profit } (A_P) \times 100}{\text{average capital employed}}$$

Adjusted profit (A_P) is the amount of profit prior to the deduction of loan interest or imputed return on equity. In other words, the calculation also takes into account interest payments on the loan and return on equity. The controller generally assumes that the average capital employed is half of the amount paid for the individual investment objects. If it is only a question of whether an investment project should be implemented or not, p must be larger than the minimum return on investment required by the investor.

Rate of interest

If the controller has the choice between several investment projects, he chooses the project with the highest profitability ratio that also exceeds the required minimum return on investment.

The controller uses a representative period in all three methods – comparison of costs, profit comparison and profitability calculation.

Representative period

5.1.1.4 Amortisation calculation

The amortisation calculation, also called the pay-off calculation, helps the controller to avoid the disadvantages of using a representative period. It also assumes that income and expenditure will be generated. It is used to help the controller calculate how many periods it takes before the return on capital employed (ROCE) exceeds the purchase price payment P_0. These periods can be several years long. ROCE is the amount by which income exceeds expenditure in each period.

Amortisation term

Example
The purchase price payment for a machine tool is EUR 500,000. The annual net cash flow surplus is estimated at EUR 100,000. The amortisation period is therefore five years.

The rule of thumb is: the shorter the amortisation period, the faster the purchase price payment will be recouped and the lower the risk associated with the project. An investment is made if the calculated amortisation period is shorter than the specified target amortisation period.

Example
Several computer manufacturers have specified a target amortisation period of two to three years for the development of new PCs.

E2 PROJECT SELECTION AND BUSINESS STRATEGY

If they have a choice between several projects, they choose the project with the shortest amortisation period, provided that it is shorter than the period specified.

Disadvantage One considerable disadvantage of the amortisation calculation method is that it does not deliver any information about the profitability of a project because the net cash flow surpluses are not accounted for until the end of the amortisation period.

5.1.1.5 Problems with static methods

Distribution of cash flows Anyone who uses a representative individual period is dispensing with the crucial aspect of planning precision [11]. This can lead to wrong decisions since the controller ignores the fact that an alternative investment project may have an entirely different cash flow distribution over the time axis, as illustrated in the example below [12]:

	PERIOD 1	PERIOD 2	PERIOD 3	PERIOD 4	AVERAGE PROFIT
Project 1	EUR 100	EUR 500	EUR 900	EUR 1,300	EUR + 700
Project 2	EUR 1,300	EUR 900	EUR 50	EUR 80	EUR + 695

Figure E2-10 Average profit over four periods

In the above example, the profit for the representative periods was taken as the average profit for periods 1 to 4. Project 1 should therefore be chosen over Project 2. However, if for the sake of simplicity it is assumed that profit is equal to the net cash flow surplus in each period, an investor would opt for Project 2. This would provide him with the highest returns in the first two periods.

Costs and revenues Using the variables costs and revenues is also problematic because
- some costs are not actually expenditure (e.g. depreciation) and
- some revenues are not actually income (e.g. products sold on credit, where the customer is granted an extended time for payment).

5.1.2 Dynamic methods

Projected cash flows When the controller uses dynamic methods, his appraisals are not based on a representative period, but on period-specific data [13]. The business case analysis is based on projected cash flows. The cash flows are attributed to each year of the investment´s useful life (→ Figure E2-8). The problem is that in-coming and outgoing payments made at different points in time are not comparable. For example, they cannot be added up, even though they are all made in the same currency (e.g. euro, US dollar) because they take place at different points on the time axis. Project management literature focuses on the following dynamic methods:
- Net present value method
- Internal rate of return method
- Annuity method

This chapter only deals with the net present value method and the internal rate of return method, since these are commonly used methods.

5.1.2.1 Net present value method

Discounting In order to enable a comparison of cash flows that are likely to take place in different phases of an investment object´s useful life, all cash flows are discounted at a time before the investment is made. This is based on the assumption that the value of money is lower the later it is accrued and that its value is higher the earlier it is available to the investor.

A payment of EUR 10,000 which is due to be made in precisely one year's time, according to the current planning status, has a net present value of t_0.

EUR 10,000 / 1.10 = EUR 9,090.91 at an imputed rate of return (i) of ten percent and
EUR 10,000 / 1.05 = EUR 9,523.81 at an imputed rate of return (i) of five percent.

The higher the imputed rate of return, the lower the present value of the payment. The formula for calculating net present value is:

$$\text{Net present value} = -E_0 + \sum_{t=1}^{n} (L_t - E_t) \times (1+i)^{-t} + L_n(1+i)^{-n}$$

The symbols used here have the same meaning as the symbols used in Figure E2-8. If the figures shown in Figure E2-8 are used in the above formula and the imputed rate of return is assumed to be ten percent, net present value is:

Net present value

$$\text{Net present value} = -1{,}000 + \frac{(500-400)}{1.10} + \frac{(900-200)}{1.10^2} + \frac{600}{1.10^2} = 165.29$$

If this method is used, an investment is worth making if the net present value is > 0. This is true in our example. If net present value is 0, the investment is equal to the rate of return. In the example shown, the required minimum interest rate of ten percent is exceeded. You may now ask why asset growth of +200 and not +165.29 was calculated in Figure E2-8. The answer is simple: the value 165.29 relates to t_0 on the time axis, and the value 200 relates to two periods later. 165.29 multiplied by 1.102 equals 200 euros.

If the controller has a choice of several investment projects, the decision-making rule is: choose the project with the highest positive net present value.

Decision rule

5.1.2.2 Internal rate of return method

The controller uses this method to calculate the rate of interest return on the invested capital. He uses the same equation as in the net present value calculation, sets the net present value to 0 and balances the equation using the required internal rate of return (r).

$$-E_0 + \sum_{t=1}^{n} (L_t - E_t) \times (1+r)^{-t} + L_n(1+r)^{-n} = 0$$

He calculates r using a numerical method. In the example, r is 19.13 percent. This value can be used in the equation to check whether net present value is 0 at this rate of interest. To make an investment decision, r must be compared with the imputed rate of return i. If r > i, the investment is worth making. A controller faced with several alternatives will select the project with the highest internal rate of return, provided that r > i.

Numerical method

The internal rate of return method is strongly criticised in business management literature because it makes several problematic assumptions [14]. That's why it is frequently recommended that the net present value method be used, and that the internal rate of return method is merely used as a supplementary decision-making criterion.

5.2 Choosing between dynamic and static methods

Simple static methods, which are also called 'practitioner methods', are by no means infallible.

Rule of thumb

On the other hand, dynamic methods can be extremely complex to use. It is therefore necessary to ask, when is simplification acceptable and when not? The rule of thumb is: use static methods for small-scale projects and dynamic methods for large-scale projects [15].

A more differentiated view can be obtained taking the example of a vehicle manufacturer who uses the net present value method [16]. The company implements a dynamic performance study in the following circumstances:

- High fluctuation of return on capital employed over time or temporary negative return.
- Return on capital employed is preceded by a lengthy period of financing requirements (investments over several years).
- Two different processes or alternatives (e.g. acquisition type analysis/purchase or lease) are associated with very different payment patterns (cash flows).
- It is necessary to take different tax effects into account.
- The statically calculated return is close to the minimum return on capital employed.

5.2.1 Non-monetary factors

The above-described dynamic and static methods are only used to compute monetary parameters. However, non-monetary influence factors and objectives often also play a role in investment decisions. For example, the people responsible for decisions on foreign investments have to take the following factors into consideration.

Foreign investments

- Stability of the political framework
- Legislation that is relevant for the investor
- The country´s infrastructure (e.g. road and rail infrastructure)
- Availability of qualified and motivated employees
- Probability of natural disasters (e.g. earthquakes, seaquakes, volcanic eruptions)

Value benefit analysis

Generally, it is recommended that a value benefit analysis is additionally made in large-scale projects. This enables the controller to take qualitative factors of influence and objectives into account.

6 Bid review process

Bid review process

In the bid review process, projects are selected from the potential customer´s perspective. When a potential customer makes an enquiry, it is first of all necessary for the contractor to decide whether this is the right project for him. The issue of whether or not to prepare a quotation for the potential customer is based on this decision. This process is not called project selection, but bid reviewing. The organisation must assess, irrespective of the project type, whether it intends to bid for a specific project.

The bid review process is especially significant for large-scale investment projects in the plant construction industry because the cost of a quotation can be up to five percent of the contract value and, if the bidder is up against tough competition, the likelihood that he will be awarded the contract can be extremely low. This is why associations such as the Association of German Engineers (VDI) [17] and the Association of German Machine and Plant Manufacturers (VDMA) advise their members thoroughly to assess every enquiry that they receive.

Attractiveness of enquiries

The procedure shown in Figure E2-11, which is a slight adaptation of the VDMA´s wording, helps the decision-maker to assess the attractiveness of an enquiry. There is a table for each criterion so that the controller can convert the generally quality-oriented statements into point scores.

E2 PROJECT SELECTION AND BUSINESS STRATEGY

		CRITERION	WEIGHTING IN %	
	A 1.1	Entry into new markets		3.0
	A 1.2	Recruitment of a new key customer		2.5
	A 1.3	Enhancement of reputation		2.5
	A 1.4	Inclusion in the delivery programme/learning curve effect		1.0
	A 1.5	Future security through other measures		1.0
A		**Strategic objectives**	**10.0**	
	B 1	Attractive profit margin	10.0	
	B 2.1	Capacity utilisation when quotation is prepared		2.5
	B 2.2	Capacity utilisation when order is processed		4.0
	B 2	Capacity utilisation	6.5	
	B 3	Envisaged date of order placement	3.5	
B		**Operational objectives**	**20.0**	
	C 1.1	Existing capacity/competence within the organisation itself		5.0
	C 1.2	Existing capacity/competence of consortium members		2.5
	C 1.3	Existing capacity/competence of sub-contractors		2.5
	C 1	Existing capacity and competence	10.0	
	C 2.1	Economic risks		3.0
	C 2.2	Time-related risks		3.0
	C 2.3	Technological risks		3.0
	C 2.4	Other risks		3.0
	C 2.5	Warranties		3.0
	C2	Risk assessment	15.0	
C		**Feasibility (technical, time-related, technological)**	**25.0**	
	D 1	Customer´s credit standing	9.0	
	D 2.1	Contractual fidelity		2.5
	D 2.2	Cooperation behaviour		1.5
	D 2.3	Additional/follow-up orders		2.0
	D 2	Other special aspects relating to the customer	6.0	
D		**Customer assessment**	**15.0**	
	E 1	Other providers: type, number	3.0	
	E 2	Pre-quotation activities of competitors	3.0	
	E 3	Own pre-quotation activities	3.0	
	E 4	Previous orders executed by competitors	3.0	
	E 5	Customer assessment of our pre-quotation activities	3.0	
	E 6	Probability of the order being placed	5.0	
E		**Competitive situation**	**20.0**	
	F 1.1	Country-specific laws		1.5
	F 1.2	Currency issues		1.5
	F 1.3	Customs duties and taxes		1.0
	F 1.4	Political trends		2.0
	F1	Country-specific aspects	6.0	
	F2	Ratio of quotation costs to order value/probability	4.0	
F		**Other attractiveness criteria**	**10.0**	

Figure E2-11 Value benefit analysis to evaluate the attractiveness of projects

E2 PROJECT SELECTION AND BUSINESS STRATEGY

	WEIGHTING	SCORE		SCORE		SCORE		SCORE		SCORE		SCORE		KO CRITERION
		10	9	8	7	6	5	4	3	2	1			
D1 Credit standing	9.0	Only excellent experiences in the past		Only good experiences in the past		No past experiences		Could be problematic		Known to be problematic				
E2 Pre-quotation activities of competitors	3.0	No pre-quotation activities		Customer canvassing talk only		Submission of a brief study only		Detailed quotation was prepared		Additional advice provided				

Figure E2-12 Point score for each criterion (example)

		WEIGHTING	CHARACTERISTICS	SCORE	POINTS TOTAL	VALUE
A1	Future security	10.0	Barely visible effects	3	30	
ΣA	Strategic objectives	10.0			30	30%
B1	Attractive profit margin	10.0	Around 18%	3	30	
B2	Capacity utilisation	6.5	Tight deadlines	3	20	
B3	When will the order be placed?	3.5	In around three years' time	3	10	
ΣB	Operational objectives	20.0			60	30%
C1	Existing capacity/competence?	10.0	Possible problems appear to be manageable	5	50	
C2	Risk assessment	15.0	Also incalculable risks (which constitute a KO criterion)	0	0	
ΣC	Feasibility	25.0			50	20%
D1	Customer's credit standing	9.0	Creditworthy	8	72	
D2	Other special customer characteristics	6.0	Could be problematic	3	18	
ΣD	Customer assessment	15.0			90	60%
E1	Other providers: type, number	3.0	Above average competition	4	12	
E2	Pre-quotation activities of competitors	3.0	Brief study submitted	5	15	
E3	Own pre-quotation activities	3.0	No	2	6	
E4	Previous orders executed by competitors	3.0	Quality	4	12	
E5	Evaluation of our pre-quotation activities	3.0	No pre-quotation activities	2	6	
E6	Probability of the order being placed	5.0	0.2	2	10	
ΣE	Competitive situation	20.0			61	31%
F1	Country-specific aspects	6.0	Relatively clear and reliable	5	30	
F2	Ratio of quotation costs to order value/probability	4.0	Fair	5	20	
ΣF	Other attractive aspects	10.0			50	50%
	Total	100.0			341	34%

When the grade and weighting are multiplied, the result is sometimes rounded up or down.

Figure E2-13 Assessment of the attractiveness of a specific project

E2 PROJECT SELECTION AND BUSINESS STRATEGY

The rating and weighting for each criterion are multiplied together to produce a total points score. The degree of fulfilment for each group of criteria can be calculated on the basis of the ratio of effective points score to the maximum possible score. Then, the degree of fulfilment or attractiveness of the project as a whole can be calculated (→ Figure E2-13). This degree of attractiveness can, for example, be compared with the average degree of attractiveness of past projects or other projects that are currently being assessed.

Degree of fulfilment / attractiveness in each group of criteria

The project's attractiveness index is 34 percent. In other words, 341 of a possible 1,000 points were attained. However, because of the associated incalculable risks – which constitute a KO criterion – it should be excluded from the next round of the selection process.

7 Selection process for all project types

The previous sections have described various methods of assistance in the selection of investment and product development projects. However, some organisations also execute IT and organisational projects in areas such as HR management or logistics. It is therefore logical to wonder whether there is an approach that an organisation can use to assess all of its projects. One such approach is described by Lange [18], and by Kühn, Hochstrahs and Pleuger [19].

Lange initially selects general pre-selection criteria, such as the ones shown in the assessment table in Figure E2-14. Only `possible projects´ are included in this preselection. `Must´ projects, i.e. projects that have to be implemented as a result of contractual obligations or to ensure compliance with mandatory statutory provisions are selected right from the outset. These include projects such as conversion to the euro and Y2K projects at the beginning of the millennium. One of the most important assessment criteria is the compatibility of a project with the organisation's corporate philosophy and strategic objectives.

Possible / must projects

Compatibility with philosophy / strategy

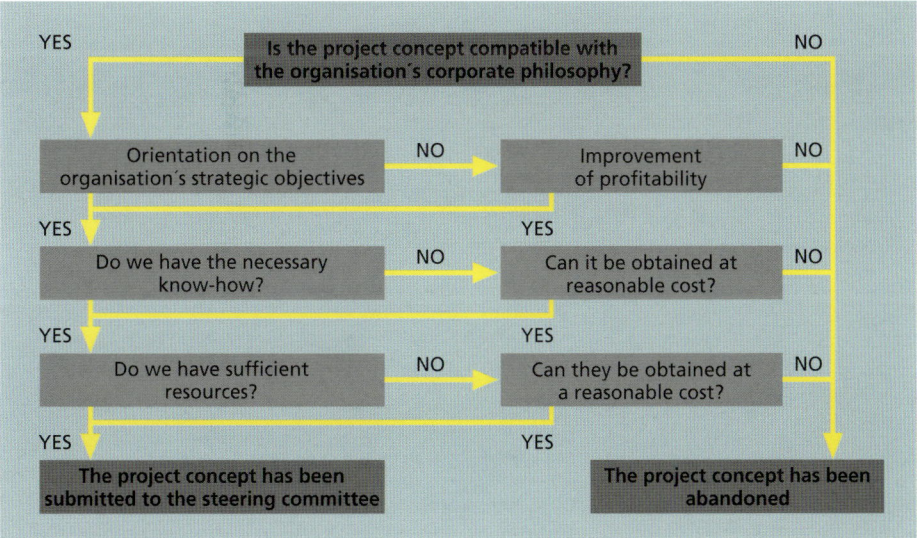

Figure E2-14 Project pre-selection procedure

E2 PROJECT SELECTION AND BUSINESS STRATEGY

Portfolio method with strategic/commercial benefits

In the next step – final selection – the controller uses a portfolio matrix with the dimensions representing strategic benefits and commercial benefits. Strategic benefits can be measured by performing a value benefit analysis to determine the project's contribution to the implementation of the organisation's business strategies. Profitability can be calculated on the basis of the expected net present value of a project or a point value based on a value benefit analysis.

7.1 Contribution of projects to the organisation's business strategy

Projects then have to be assessed in terms of their contribution to strategy implementation (→ Figure E2-15):

- Ranking 0: irrelevant for the strategy
- Ranking 1: beneficial to the strategy
- Ranking 2: important for the strategy
- Ranking 3: crucial for the strategy

PROJECT	BUDGET IN EUROS	CONTRIBUTION TO STRATEGY				STRATEGIC RELEVANCE OF THE PROJECTS		
		Improvement of advice quality	Improvement of brand image	Improvement of delivery availability	Innovation leadership	Total ranking points	Strategic relevance of the projects	Maximum possible points' total
P1 New order-processing system	5,000	1	2	3	0	6 :	12 =	0.50
P2 Switch-over to a new operating system	1,000	0	0	1	0	1 :	12 =	0.08
P3 Reorganisation of logistics	2,800	0	2	3	0	5 :	12 =	0.42
P4 Development of a new product line	6,200	0	2	0	3	5 :	12 =	0.42
Total	15,000							

Figure E2-15 Establishment of the projects' strategic relevance

Computation of strategic relevance

The ranking points total per project is divided by the maximum possible number of points. For example, the strategic relevance of Project 1 is 0.5 (6 divided by 12). In a second step, the value for strategic relevance is considered relative to the budget to ascertain strategic productivity.

Strategic productivity

$$\text{Strategic productivity} = \frac{\text{the project's strategic relevance}}{\text{amount of the project portfolio's total budget allocated to the project}}$$

The higher the degree of strategic relevance and the lower the budget, the better is the result.

PROJECTS WITH BUDGETS AND PROPORTION OF TOTAL BUDGET		BUDGET IN EUR	DEGREE OF STRATEGIC RELEVANCE	PROPORTION OF TOTAL BUDGET	STRATEGIC PRODUCTIVITY
			a	b	a/b
P1	Order processing system	5,000	0.50	0.33 %	1.52
P2	New operating system	1,000	0.08	0.07 %	1.14
P3	Reorganisation of logistics	2,800	0.42	0.19 %	2.21
P4	New product line	6,200	0.42	0.41 %	1.02
		15,000		1.00 %	

Figure E2-16 Establishment of the projects' strategic productivity

The sample calculation of strategic productivity shows that Project P3 has comparatively high strategic relevance at a low budget, followed by P1.

A portfolio matrix with dimensions representing strategic benefits and commercial benefits would look like the one below:

Portfolio chart

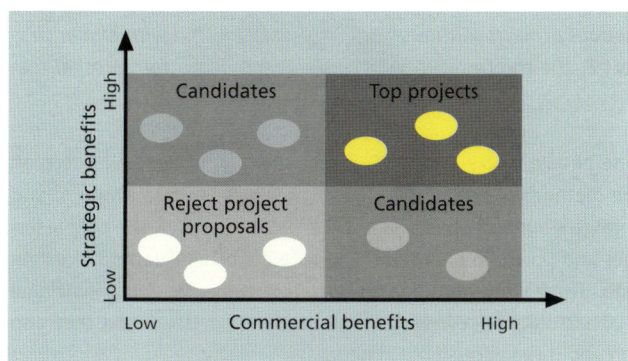

Figure E2-17 Portfolio matrix with dimensions representing commercial and strategic benefits

The most promising candidates for implementation are the projects with high strategic and commercial benefits.

8 Advantages and disadvantages of the methods

The methods described above have two advantages: first, they enable a decision-maker to structure his selection and therefore support the portfolio board. Secondly, they make the selection process more transparent.

Transparent selection decision

However, they also have two main disadvantages: first, portfolio methods tend to simplify the problem considerably by describing the projects available for selection in terms of two dimensions only. Another disadvantage is that the individual project proposals are viewed more or less in isolation. They do not take into account either possible synergetic effects arising from a combination of projects, or the contribution of a project in a field of technology or a business unit that deserves special support.

Problems

Example of a synergetic effect [20]
Both the project `Introduce strategic business division management structures´ and the project `Establish a direct sales organisation´ require the creation of new customer records. If the two projects are realised concurrently, the organisation benefits from important standardisation and synergy effects.

Computer-assisted methods Computer-assisted processes [21] have recently emerged that can take these kinds of project interrelationship into account.

9 Improving selection decisions

Objective-related conflicts There will always be opposition to an objective selection of projects – even if the decision processes are structured and transparent – due to objective-related conflicts.

Example
An organisation´s marketing department representative prefers projects that will enable the organisation to expand its market share. The development director, on the other hand, is more interested in technically ambitious projects. Although Project A is associated with higher strategic productivity than Project B, the chief executive wants B implemented for personal reasons.

Communication Good communication between the people involved in strategic planning, marketing and decision making is just as important as the methods of project selection. Employees must be aware of and understand the organisation´s long-term business objectives. Workshops attended by the people responsible (e.g. the project manager and portfolio board) are one very important method of establishing the best possible project mix. These workshops don´t necessarily have to be about individual projects; they also offer a good opportunity to review the entire project portfolio, and they also enable open and honest discussion about the necessity of abandoning projects.

A multi-project manager (→ Chapter E3) can make an important contribution to improving the project selection process.

E2 PROJECT SELECTION AND BUSINESS STRATEGY

Self-assessment questions for each certification level

No.	Question	Level				Self-assessment
		D	C	B	A	
E 2.01	What function do projects have in organisations?	1	2	2	3	☐
E 2.02	How can the difference between operational and strategic project management be described in one sentence?	1	2	2	3	☐
E 2.03	Who is responsible for strategic project management?	1	2	2	3	☐
E 2.04	What is `management by projects´?	1	2	2	3	☐
E 2.05	What methods can be used for the selection of product development projects and what methods can be used for the selection of investment projects?	1	2	2	3	☐
E 2.06	What methods can be used for the selection of project types?	1	1	1	3	☐
E 2.07	Which non-monetary factors are significant in investment decisions?	1	1	1	3	☐
E 2.08	Which project selection criteria should a contractor take into consideration?	1	2	2	3	☐
E 2.09	What disadvantages can project selection using the project portfolio method have?	1	1	1	3	☐
E 2.10	How can a project portfolio board be positioned in the organisation?	1	2	2	3	☐

E3 OPERATIONAL MULTI-PROJECT MANAGEMENT

An organisation needs a multi-project manager when it implements several interrelated projects concurrently. This chapter focuses on his role and core responsibilities - from planning the project environment to project coordination and the development of an infrastructure for professional project management. It also explains the multi-project manager's position in the organisation and his relationship with the project managers and project management office. In order to understand the complexity of his role, it is necessary to be aware of how the different projects are interrelated.

1 Portfolio board

The portfolio board´s responsibilities have already been detailed in the chapter about strategic project management (→ Chapter E1). Sometimes, the portfolio board and management board are identical because they have the same members. However, this isn´t the case when the organisation has different, specialised project portfolios. For example, it can have one portfolio board for IT projects and another for investment projects.

Many organisations establish the portfolio board one hierarchical level below the managing board to reduce executives´ workload. The portfolio board then reports directly to the managing board, which in some cases, insists on having the final say in significant projects. However, if it repeatedly ignores the portfolio board´s recommendations, it is probably a good idea – as Lomnitz [1] quite rightly suggests – to dispense with the portfolio board.

Position in the organisation structure

2 Multi-project manager

The role of the multi-project manager is crucial for effective multi-project management. Lomnitz [2] provides the most detailed definition: a multi-project manager is necessary when
- an organisation implements several or many projects concurrently and, at least to some extent, these projects are competing for the same resources, and
- when further inter-project dependencies exist.

2.1 Inter-project dependencies

These dependencies can relate to content, social relationships or time.

Dependencies

2.1.1 Content dependencies

Content dependencies exist when projects
- require the same or supplementary know-how, or
- have identical, complementary or contradictory objectives.

Example
The objective 'improvement of product quality' can only be achieved if other projects, such as training programmes or projects to streamline and standardise business processes, are successful [3].

- are implemented in the same or competing business segments.
- have identical customers, suppliers, sub-contractors and other stakeholders.
- enjoy an input-output relationship: one project delivers output for another.

2.1.2 Social dependencies

Social dependencies exist when
- projects have the same stakeholders,
- staff are involved in several projects at the same time, or
- joint reporting and communication structures exist.

2.1.3 Time dependencies

Capacity-related/ technological dependencies

Time dependencies exist, for instance, if a project or project phase cannot start until another project has finished or reaches a specific milestone. These dependencies can result from a resource scarcity (= capacity-related dependency) or an input-output relationship (= technological dependency).

Coordination requirements

These dependencies make it essential to coordinate the various projects effectively. For example, it is necessary to ensure
- the agreement of standard terms and conditions with one supplier for all projects, if possible, and the pooling of purchase orders so that better terms and conditions can be obtained,
- that the customer does not pit the project managers against each other,
- that standardised communication rules (→ Chapter D4) for stakeholder communication are in place and observed,
- the exploitation of synergy effects and
- that detailed time schedules and milestones are linked together.

Risk interrelationships

Multi-project managers also have to be capable of assessing the risks associated with each project in a multi-project context [4]. For example, if an input-output relationship exists, a technical defect in an input project can cause considerable delays in another project.

2.2 Core responsibilities

Project diagnostician

'Project diagnostician' (Lomnitz) is the term that best describes a multi-project manager's function. His core responsibilities [5] are to plan and control the project environment, to develop an infrastructure for professional project management and to provide a pool of staff.

2.2.1 Planning the project environment

A multi-project manager has to prepare a decision for senior management or his portfolio board so that they can set clear and binding priorities in decisions that affect the entire project portfolio. He does this by making reasoned proposals regarding the portfolio's composition. Above all, he has to assess regularly whether running and planned projects are compatible with the organisation's business strategy, and whether it is necessary to abandon any of them.

2.2.2 Multi-project management based on controlling and reporting

This core function is very similar to the function of a project controller (→ Chapter A6). However, a project controller does not work in a multi-project environment. To ensure that the status of all projects is transparent at all times, the multi-project manager has to

Transparent project status

- know which departmental resources – especially personnel – are assigned to project and non-project work,
- provide up-to-date information about deadline adherence, cost and progress of projects,
- be aware of the content, time and human resource dependencies between the various projects. A multi-project manager cannot answer the following questions without this knowledge:
    - How would the reassignment of five development engineers from project A to project B affect the finish date of project A?
    - What consequences will the postponement of the finish date of project C by three months have on milestone M5 (= customer presentation) in project D?
    - Can we implement an engineer-to-order project for customer X, and meet the deadline he has specified, at the current level of resource usage in development departments DD1, DD2 and DD3?
    - What costs have been incurred so far in this financial year in conjunction with all product development projects? Which funds from third-party sponsors have been channelled into these projects? How high are the estimated costs-to-complete in each project?

The project or programme managers cannot answer these questions because they are only familiar with the situation in their own project or programme.

Project manager / programme manager

2.2.3 Development of an infrastructure for professional project management

Lomnitz believes that the development of an infrastructure for professional project management is another core responsibility of the multi-project manager. He should be able to perform the following tasks:

- define processes (e.g. in the context of a process model) and ensure their uniform application,
- design and implement project management standards,
- provide and administer tools (e.g. software),
- train project staff and
- ensure the continuous improvement of project management in the organisation (→ Chapter F2).

Many of these functions are also identical to those of controllers (→ Chapter A6).

2.2.4 Provision of a staff pool

Another task of the multi-project manager is to provide a pool of experienced project managers and consultants.

2.3 Position in the organisation structure

Affiliation with the managing board

It is a good idea if the multi-project manager is the CEO, managing director, or some other senior person in the organisation structure. He should be affiliated to the Project Division, if it exists. If he is only responsible for some of the projects in the portfolio (e.g. for all IT or all R&D projects), he should report to the IT Director or the Chief Technology Officer. Contacts high-up in the organisation structure are recommended because the multi-project manager needs a power broker, especially when he is required to restructure processes and implement standards. Most power brokers are executives.

Power broker

A multi-project manager will probably encounter many things that impair his acceptance. There is also a very real risk that he will come to be viewed as a mega-controller and abuse his authority. This is why it is very important that the person holding this position not only has first-rate project management skills, but also excellent social competence [6].

Social competence

2.3.1 The difference between a project manager and a multi-project manager

A multi-project manager is not a substitute for a project manager. The latter has sole responsibility for operational project management. He performs the functions described in Chapter A6 and provides the multi-project manager with comprehensive, up-to-date and regular information about his project by way of status reports that are coordinated with the multi-project situation and regular meetings.

2.3.2 Multi-project managers and the project office

Project management office

A project office is an institution that project managers are coming to take more seriously. English-language project management literature talks about both the `project office´ and the `project management office´. In recent years, `project management office´ has been the prevailing term in connection with multi-project management. The tasks performed by the project office and project management office differ from organisation to organisation.

The relationship between the multi-project manager and the project office is significant in multi-project management. Campana, Reschke and Schott [7] explain this relationship: `[...] the project office (creates) transparency throughout the entire project portfolio. It is aware of all projects in progress, all resources being used and supports the people responsible for multi-project planning, project coordination and project prioritisation.´ Obviously, this means that the multi-project manager is in charge of the project office or project management office.

E3 OPERATIONAL MULTI-PROJECT MANAGEMENT

Various authors attribute further responsibilities to the project office or project management office, some of which correspond to those of a project controller (→ Chapter A6) and a multi-project manager. These include
- the provision of a pool of project managers,
- the provision of project management training to project staff,
- the standardisation of processes and
- the development and implementation of standards.

The project office or project management office provides services to project and programme managers, project teams, departments, the portfolio board and the executive management team.

Target groups

Project offices or project management offices can also evolve into in-house providers of a comprehensive range of project management services [8]. If an organisation has several business divisions that implement very different types of projects (e.g. investment and organisation projects), it is a good idea to set up separate project offices because of the different areas of expertise required. They need to remain in close contact and regular liaison with each other.

Self-assessment questions for each certification level

No.	Question	D	C	B	A	Self-assessment
E 3.1	What are the connections between project managers and multi-project managers or project managers and programme managers?	1	2	2	2	☐
E 3.2	What functions does a project management office perform?	1	2	2	3	☐
E 3.3	In what way does a project manager benefit from a project management office?	1	2	3	4	☐

BLOCK F

INTRODUCTION AND OPTIMISATION OF PROJECT MANAGEMENT

F1 INTRODUCTION OF PROJECT MANAGEMENT

Efficient project management can only be established in an organisation (ICB Element 2) if the project management team involves the people affected. It won´t work if top management simply decrees it, and there is no point in merely installing project management software. A process model, like the one explained in this chapter, is useful for the introduction of organisational and technical project management structures. A project manager must be capable of dealing with opposition from people in the organisation who are not happy about these changes in their work environment (ICB Element 37). That´s why it is essential to use suitable communication measures.

1 Project management `by decree´

Project management `by decree´ is inevitably ineffective. Nevertheless, many senior managers do just this because it ostensibly provides them with results quickly. The executive board instructs one of the organisation´s departments or an external consultant to develop a concept and put it in a project management manual. Although most employees will be affected by the introduction of such structures, they are not involved in the development of either the concept or the manual. It is not sufficient that selected employees are sometimes interviewed or asked to fill in questionnaires.

One frequent excuse for not implementing more comprehensive measures is, `project management should reduce costs, not drive them up´. This is a very narrow perspective. The cost of introducing project management is soon recouped because, once it is in place, future projects can be implemented more efficiently. Many organisations also believe, quite wrongly, that opposition can be prevented by confronting the workforce with a fait accompli. These organisations assume that systematic project management has been installed once they have sent a memo informing staff that this is the case. `All projects that commence after September 1 this year are to be implemented in accordance with the enclosed manual.´ This approach means that the people affected are likely to reject the concept and be unwilling to use the manual.

Reducing costs

Opposition

In general, those affected will only accept project management if they believe that it offers them personal benefits. Their acceptance can only be guaranteed by implementing timely communication measures (→ Chapter D4) and ensuring that they are involved in the process.

Benefits as a condition of acceptance

1.1 Perspective of the managers

Rosenstiel vividly describes the introduction of project management by decree [1]: `Management deduces that action must be taken since the organisation´s structures and processes […] no longer seem to reflect the conditions of its environment […]. Various concepts that have no bearing on reality are created and organisation charts are drawn up. These documents are then treated as ``strictly confidential´´ and sent to various expert bodies for critical evaluation. One of the options is then selected, for whatever reason, and announced to the other members of the organisation.´

1.2 Perspective of the people affected

Uncertainty

The people affected find it difficult to cope with the uncertainty associated with the lack of communication on the introduction of project management [2]: 'You hear about special directors' or management board meetings and, with a feeling of foreboding, watch men in dark suits with leather briefcases walking through the organisation. Rumours that often have a grain of truth make the rounds.' Then, as if by magic, a new organisation plan and project management manual suddenly appear.

2 Introduction of project management structures through software

False hopes

This option is also ineffective. Some organisations buy a project management software package and organise training for their staff. They believe that they have then introduced project management structures. But they are wrong (→ Chapter C11).

3 Obstacles to acceptance

Figure F1-1 [3] shows the four most common obstacles to the acceptance of project management structures:
1. Information deficits
2. Skill deficits
3. Management support deficits
4. Motivation deficits

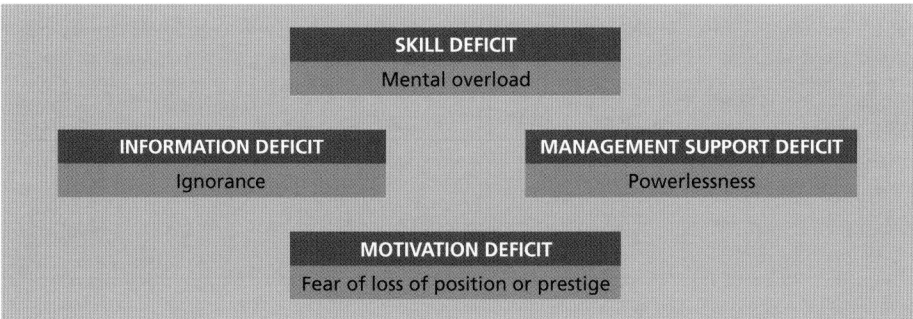

Figure F1-1 Obstacles to introducing project management structures

Communication

Information deficits can be remedied by providing relevant information and skill deficits can generally be eliminated through training measures. A more problematic situation exists when staff support the introduction of project management but are prevented from or not encouraged to do so by authoritarian executives. Senior management support is an important success factor. If this support is not forthcoming, opponents (often middle managers) will gain the upper hand. It will only be possible to implement systematic project management methods if top management is convinced of their benefits. A lack of motivation (→ Chapter D3) is, however, the biggest obstacle that the organisers will face.

Convincing executive managers

3.1 Fear of change

The introduction of project management brings concerns in its wake. Employees who face changes fear that their personal situation will change for the worse. The table in Figure F1-2 shows the disadvantages that are assumed by the people affected [4]:

Disadvantages

Remuneration	Direct income reduction or other indirect financial disadvantages
Security	Compulsory transfer or perhaps even redundancy
Contact	Loss of positive personal relationships with other members of the organisation and being forced to work with unpopular colleagues in future
Recognition	Excessive professional or personal demands in the new work situation
Independence	Loss of decision-making powers or personal scope for action and opportunities to exert indirect influence
Development	Obstacles to learning needs and career ambitions

Figure F1-2 Potential disadvantages from the perspective of those affected

Employees are also initially concerned about the tangible effects of project management on their day-to-day work:

Impact on project work

- Project applications must be well-justified in future. The applicant must forecast a positive net present value for the project and deliver watertight arguments in favour of implementing the project.
- The project managers will have more authority than before. Line managers fear that they will be demoted to mere vicarious agents with no authority. They believe that they will be the losers if changes to the organisation´s structures are made.
- Project-specific resource planning reveals that some departments are not performing as well as they say.
- Cost monitoring at the work package level reveals those departments that are notorious for exceeding their budgets.
- Network analysis identifies the reasons why deadlines are missed.

The following motives can also cause objections to project management:

Other motives

- Idleness
- Lack of willingness to support change
- Anger about being left out of the process of developing the project management concept
- Frustration about not being informed that the concept was being developed

3.2 Forms of opposition and objections

Opposition to new things is only human: `Processes of change trigger opposition´, warn Hansel and Lomnitz [5]. This is particularly true when an organisation makes the sweeping changes to its structures and processes that are associated with the introduction of project management. These authors also explain why people are so dubious about project management [6]: `Many people believe that project management is a fad and fads are always regarded with suspicion.´

Spurious arguments   Employees have a comprehensive range of tools and formulated arguments at their disposal to sabotage project management systematically. The latter are (spurious) arguments which the people affected use to simply reject changes without analysing them. It is difficult to respond to these arguments because they are not substantiated by logic. The arguments that are often encountered in practice are listed below.

The `we don´t do it like that´ argument
Although project management critics admit that project management has been very successful in the telecommunications and aerospace industries, they believe that the framework in their own sector is entirely different. They argue that, because of this different framework, it will be impossible to implement systematic project management methods. However, they don´t specify the reasons in any greater detail.

The `doesn´t work in practice´ argument
One argument that is frequently put forward is, `It all sounds good in theory but, believe me, I´ve been in the business for a long time and it doesn´t work in practice.´ Even though this is probably just a bluff, it should be taken seriously. In the past, many project management concepts have been developed that were impossible to implement in practice. The quality of a project management system is defined by its ability to make processes, structures and issues transparent so that successful aspects of a project can be repeated.

The `we already know how to manage a project´ argument
This objection is similar to the `doesn´t work in practice´ argument. It is generally an objection that is made by staff who feel that they are being indirectly criticised because the methods that they have planned and developed over the years are to be changed. They often make reference to projects that they have implemented successfully without the assistance of systematic project management methods. Of course such projects exist. However, they are usually only successful because the staff made special efforts to ensure this. These projects can cause burnout syndrome (→ Chapter D3) as vividly described by DeMarco [7] and result in a high level of employee fluctuation.

Burnout syndrome

The `success guarantee´ argument
`Can you tell me by how much our adherence to budgets and deadlines will improve in our projects and what impact the new management concept will have on our net profit for the year?´ This is a difficult question to answer. In many cases, the impact of a project management system on the organisation only becomes evident after several years have passed. At the time it is introduced, it is only possible to refer to successful project management systems at other organisations.

The `we can´t afford it´ or `we haven´t got time´ arguments
These objections are valid in the sense that a certain timeframe is necessary to introduce project management. Even when it is in place, the planning and management of individual projects will consume resources. What the opponents of systematic project management fail to consider, however, is that this expenditure of time and resources will pay off. They are arguing like the lumberjack who tried to cut down an oak tree with his pocket knife. When somebody suggested that he ought to buy a chain saw, he answered, `I haven´t got time. I´ve got to cut down this oak tree´.

Deliberately skirting the issue
Opponents of systematic project management like to divert attention from the core issue and embroil the supporters in unnecessary activities. For example, they may demand a detailed inventory of available project management software. This is a waste of time, though, because the market is flooded with products that are continually being replaced by new versions. Focusing on irrelevant issues is another kind of sabotage strategy. For example, one organisation discussed the size of the project office for several months.

Sabotage strategy

The `project management is unfashionable´ argument
Sceptics sometimes say that project management is a fad that has already been replaced by a new trend. For example, they will argue, `project management is out, break-through management is in´. Break-through management can be substituted by any one of the other buzz phrases in management literature (e.g. speed). These assertions initially shift the onus of proof to the organiser. He has to prove that project management is still `trendy´.

Fad

The `we don´t implement projects, we process orders´ argument
This phrase makes project management sound unnecessary, even though orders are often, by nature, novel and one-off undertakings and therefore suitable for management as a project.

Pretending to cooperate
`Our projects are very unpredictable – not only the lead times, but also the process structures. That´s why we need stochastic network analysis.´ This argument is particularly insidious because the person putting it forward is only pretending to cooperate and probably knows very well that stochastic network analysis has only been discussed in textbooks, but never used in practice. If this suggestion is taken up, any projects implemented would probably fail.

3.3 Covert opposition

The above example of feigned cooperation makes it clear that many project management opponents tend to oppose covertly instead of openly. Typical indicators [8] of covert opposition are:

Indicators

- Postponing urgent decisions (e.g. by encouraging endless discussions),
- Failure to attend important meetings,
- Working to rule, and
- Withholding information.

3.4 Dealing with opposition

Executives and those responsible for project management should, in any event, take opposition seriously. Not every critic aims to prevent the introduction of project management. Many practical solutions are only developed because staff do not accept the original suggestions.

Taking opposition seriously

> **Example**
> *The armaments industries in Germany and the USA openly rejected - quite rightly as we know today - the original PERT/COST approach that the German and US defence ministries wanted to introduce (→ Chapter C6), partly because it involved vast amounts of data collection.*

4 Promoting acceptance

Internal marketing

Not only is it important to maintain dialogue with and involve the people affected (= participation) in the development and implementation of project management, it is also necessary to implement effective internal marketing measures (→ Chapter D4). The aim of these measures is to demonstrate to staff the personal benefits that project management offers. A study [9] conducted in the automotive industry about the impact of project management on the satisfaction of the people affected showed that `when the people who are integrated in the project organisation are asked how they feel, [...] the unanimous answer is that they enjoy their work more, are more motivated and have a stronger sense of self worth [...]´. A Siemens study [10] reached a similar conclusion.

Based on a comprehensive empirical analysis, Wahl [11] recommends providing employees with incentives. Many organisations such as Siemens and Deutsche Telekom have incentive systems. They offer bonuses for projects that are brought to a successful conclusion, as well as further training measures and career opportunities in the field of project management [12].

4.1 Making project management the boss´s business

Executive managers as power brokers

Top management has to be involved in the introduction of project management [13]. In the past, however, the people in charge of introducing project management at many organisations have underestimated the crucial role of top management in this process. It was not until recently that a series of studies [14] revealed how important it is to have executives as power brokers (→ Chapter A3). Wahl [15] summarised the outcome of his interviews as follows: `The importance of support from top management was mentioned in practically every interview.´ Witte [16] found that `power brokers contribute to overcoming obstructive attitudes by protecting the people who welcome innovation and blocking their opponents, either by imposing sanctions or vetoing their objections at a higher management level´.

Keeping the system alive

Top managers have to assume responsibility for keeping the installed system alive. Otherwise, opponents may gradually gain the upper hand. They have to
- provide the necessary resources for implementation and regular operations,
- encourage and monitor adherence to rules and standards, and
- request regular, standardised reports about each of the individual projects (→ Chapter C9).

Standard reports

In practice, different project managers provide information to top management in different ways, though this doesn´t necessarily mean that they are going it alone.

Project manager´s authority

The main indicator of how top management takes project management seriously is the authority and powers that it grants its project managers (→ Chapter A6). Some are granted no authority whatsoever to prevent conflicts with the `temperamental´ line department managers. In short, `project management is only successful within organisations where it is understood and supported by top management [17].´

5 Process model

Several process models have been developed for the introduction of project management. Platz's model [18], shown in Fig. F1-3, comprises six phases and is based on the assumption that a comprehensive concept will be created. However, the ICB notes that not every project management concept will be developed from scratch. Sometimes, it is merely necessary to make improvements to an existing concept.

Comprehensive concept

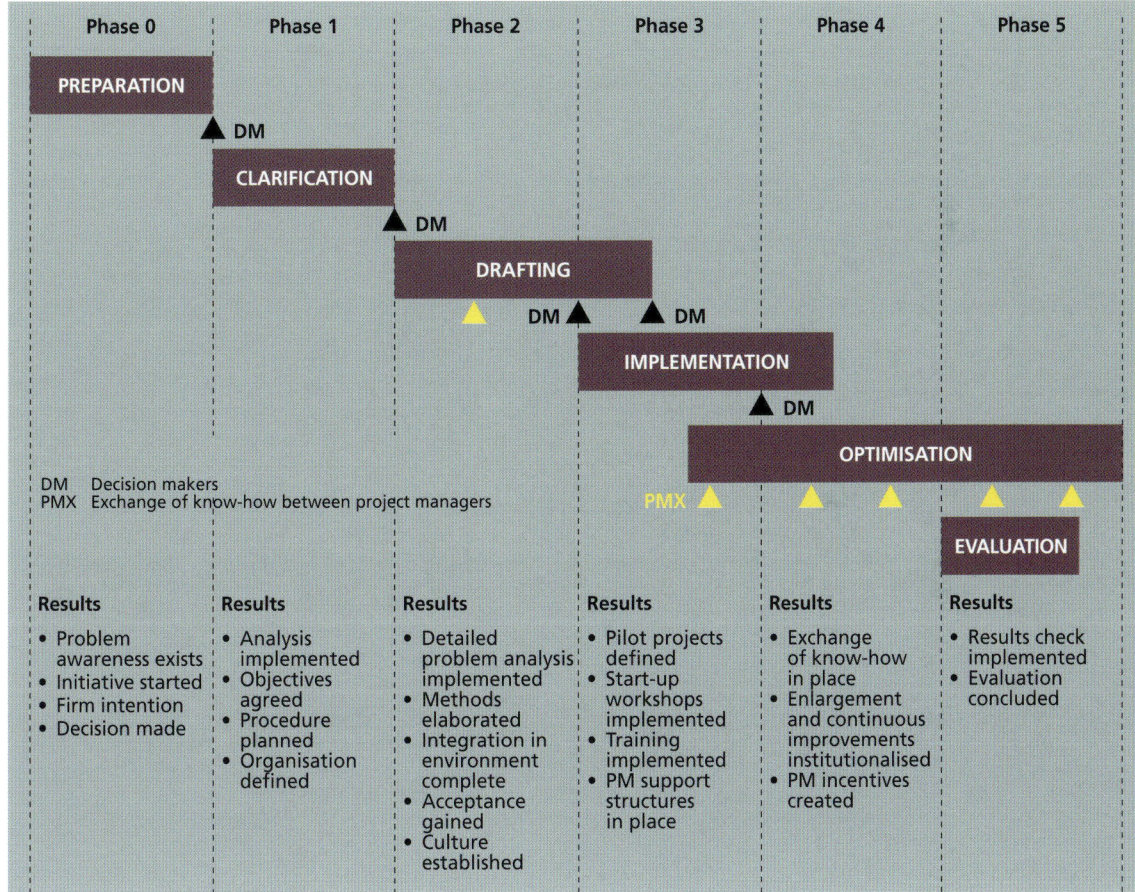

Figure F1-3 Process model for the implementation of project management

5.1 Phase 0: Preparation phase

In the preparation phase it is necessary to develop awareness that the organisation needs a systematic project management. In practice, however, the process of developing this awareness tends to be preceded by a series of failed or relatively unsuccessful projects. The initiative has to come from above, from power brokers. Already in this phase, a power broker needs support from a expert mentor in project management. If the organisation doesn't have someone suitable, top management will have to call in an external expert. Phase 0 ends when the senior management team decides to introduce, or decisively improve, project management.

Power broker / expert mentor

Its introduction should be treated as a stand-alone project. Top management appoints a project manager with adequate project management experience and sets up a project team consisting of representatives from all departments affected [19]. A panel of decision makers will also be needed to approve the results presented by the project team at each milestone and to provide assistance with eliminating obstacles to acceptance.

Decision makers

Promoting acceptance

Even in Phase 0, it is necessary to promote acceptance among those affected. The best way to do this is to hold an information event for the stakeholders about top management´s intentions. In this project, the organisation´s staff and works council are also stakeholders. Top management should avoid criticising past mistakes and managers, because this initiates an unnecessary process of passing the blame.

External speaker

It has proven to be effective if an external speaker is engaged to present the project management concept. A high-ranking executive at a similar organisation that has successfully been implementing the concept for quite some time is a good choice. An organisation that focuses on the planning and processing of research and development projects could invite a speaker from a research-intensive organisation.

5.2 Phase 1: Clarification

The project management team must perform the following tasks in the clarification phase:

Objectives
- Clarification of project objectives
  (e.g. percentage improvement of adherence to deadlines and budgets, reduction of average throughput times, increase in customer satisfaction). If possible, objectives should be formulated in an operational way - i.e. so that they are measurable.

Initial situation
- Analysis of the initial situation
  This involves an examination of existing tools and rules. Many organisations have elements of systematic project management (e.g. processes with on-going cost monitoring) which can be incorporated in the new concept with or without modification. Interviews and possibly a detailed questionnaire will be necessary in Phase 1.

Procedure and dates
- Definition of work packages and milestones for the next steps.
  Most project team members also have line functions and are therefore under time pressure. That´s why it is important to set binding dates for team meetings.

5.3 Phase 2: Drafting

The project team drafts the project management concept in Phase 2. The most important tasks are:
- Selection of necessary methods, such as project structuring, network analysis, risk analysis and reporting, and definition of rules (e.g. on the project manager´s responsibility, tasks and authority).
  These have to be adapted to the organisation´s requirements and culture. There is no such thing as an off-the-peg project management concept. The team should try to avoid perfectionism, i.e. rules that necessitate extremely detailed planning processes or complicated arithmetical processes (e.g. risk analysis), when simple tools would be sufficient. The methods have to be simple and flexible. A process model (→ Chapter B) which was developed for large-scale projects will only

Individual methods that are easy to use

benefit later users if it can be easily adapted for smaller-scale projects. Software ($\rightarrow$ Chapter C11) should not be selected until the concept has been developed and approved by senior management.
- Drafting the project management manual
In practice, comprehensive and theoretical manuals simply collect dust on employees´ shelves. That´s why the following rule applies for project management manuals: `Make it as thick as necessary and as thin as possible.´ It is a good idea to make the manual, project management forms and the proposed work and process methods available on the intranet or internet.

5.3.1 Content of a project management manual

A project management manual comprises `binding guidelines extending from the start to the finish of a project […] that unambiguously explain processes and procedures, tasks and measures. For example, it details the distribution of responsibilities between the steering committee and the project management team´ [20].

Project management manual

A project management manual for plant construction projects, shown in Figure F1-4, provides an idea of the basic content [21]. It is based on a process model with the following phases:
- Clarification
- Quotation
- Order processing
- Project implementation
- Internal acceptance
- On-site commissioning
- Evaluation
- After-sales service

Breakdown

In Phase 2, the decision makers and project team have to continue promoting the acceptance of the PM introduction project among the stakeholders.

F1 INTRODUCTION OF PROJECT MANAGEMENT

STRUCTURE OF PM MANUAL CONTENT	
I. Objectives of the manual	
II. Terms and definitions	
Chapter 1:	**Management structure**
	Responsibilities, tasks and authorities of the project manager, the steering committee and the project controller
Chapter 2:	**Project information**
	Rules on project meetings, workshops, presentations, reports and documentation
Chapter 3:	**Quality assurance**
	Objectives and measures of quality assurance
Chapter 4:	**Clarification**
	Activities to be performed when a customer enquiry is received
Chapter 5:	**Quotation**
	Activities to be performed in this project phase (e.g. technical, commercial and legal aspects of the quotation, planning and cost budgeting)
Chapter 6:	**Order processing**
	Activities relating to the approval of the order for processing, cost, time and quality requirements, including prioritisation, the integration of these in the overall planning process, hand-over of the project to the project manager and project start-up meeting
Chapter 7:	**Project planning**
	Keywords: project file, work breakdown structure, project phase plan, RACI matrix, time and resource scheduling, project documentation, cost estimating and budgeting
Chapter 8:	**Project implementation**
	Rules relating in particular to orders placed internally, purchase orders and information to be provided by the customer (e.g. test data for the project), deadline and cost monitoring and claim management
Chapter 9:	**Internal acceptance**
	Rules relating, among other things, to function tests, supplementary performance, modifications as a result of customer requests and approvals prior to delivery
Chapter 10:	**On-site commissioning**
	Processes for commissioning at the customer´s premises
Chapter 11:	**Evaluation**
	Instructions for systematic project close-out and know-how transfer as the basis for the further development of the project management system
Chapter 12:	**After-sales service**
	Objectives and measures for after-sales service
Chapter 13:	**Glossary**

Figure F1-4 Sample content structure for a project management manual

5.4 Phase 3: Implementation phase

The implementation phase involves
1. the selection of pilot projects to test the concept,
2. staff training and
3. the installation of a support unit (or support point such as a project or project management office).

Since the new concept has not yet been proven effective, organisations initially tend to implement small-scale, low-risk and insignificant projects. This often provokes criticism from opponents, such as, 'we could have done that without project management', and they are probably right. At the other end of the scale, some organisations test the concept in a disaster project that has been running for quite some time already. This is not a good idea because the risk of failure is extremely high – to some extent because the planners are always at least one step behind the current project status. Pilot projects should be projects that are about to commence and are important for the organisation. The project team should receive appropriate training before the pilot projects are implemented. The project management manual is an important training tool.

Pilot project

The project or project management office, whose manager should assume the role of expert mentor, provides support to the project manager and his team, especially in the pilot project implementation phase. The office also continues to develop and optimise project management. Unfortunately, this is an area where many organisations attempt to cut costs. The people responsible for the project hope that the project manager will be able to cope without support. As a result, project management methods are only applied half-heartedly and do not generate the maximum possible benefits for the organisation.

Project management office

5.5 Phase 4: Optimisation

The organisation's project management structures are further developed and optimised in Phase 4. This is only possible with the assistance of a support unit, to some extent because there would not be sufficient resources otherwise. One important source of ideas for optimisation is dialogue between project managers about their own experiences. Project and project management benchmarking (→ Chapter F2) is also useful.

Dialogue
Benchmarking

5.6 Phase 5: Evaluation

In Phase 5, the controller checks whether the objectives defined in Phase 0 have been achieved.

Controlling

6 Communication

When project management is introduced, it is necessary to implement communication and project marketing measures for all employees whose work processes are affected, as well as suppliers, customers, partners and – at some organisations – other project stakeholders. These communication measures should be planned before the project commences.

6.1 Mobilising supporters

The project manager should attempt to mobilise supporters (= power brokers) at an early stage of the project, and to cascade project management throughout the organisation (= via multipliers). Talks with employee representatives are crucial in this phase. Brief information events, preferably with only a few people attending each event, are good places to encourage cooperation. Other measures to be implemented before the project starts are announcements on staff notice boards, on the website or in the staff newsletter (→ Chapter D4).

Multipliers

F1 INTRODUCTION OF PROJECT MANAGEMENT

Communication event

The people affected can be directly involved in the project by way of workshops or a communication event. The latter is especially effective because it enables the people working on the project and the people affected by it to talk to each other. Important interim bulletins, such as information about the project manager´s future authority or a draft process model, are displayed on pin-boards at the events. The stakeholders then walk around in small groups from pin-board to pin-board. Project team members are standing at each board to explain the concept to the stakeholders. The stakeholders also have the opportunity to express criticism and make suggestions. This feedback should be taken seriously because participants will soon realise if the event is a sham. If the first organisational changes have already begun, it is too late to implement this measure because the people affected will feel left out and could become project opponents.

Prompt action

If the project objective is to introduce project management, the organisation will probably not have a project management communication infrastructure (e.g. project management office, project newsletter). In this phase, it is a good idea to use the organisation´s existing infrastructure (e.g. works meetings, department meetings, notices, staff/customer newsletters).

6.2 Dealing with questions from people affected

Working group

It is always best to take a proactive approach. The manager of a project to introduce project management structures should talk to a small, representative group of the people affected and answer their questions. For example, they may ask

- What impact will project management have on our organisation?
- What aspects of my work will change?
- Do I have the appropriate skills? Will I still be needed? Will project management structures put my career or job at risk?
- What do I have to learn?
- Will I have a higher or lower workload?
- Will I be working with new people?

FAQs

The project manager should then formulate clear answers to the working group´s questions and publish them in a brochure, on the intranet or in the project newsletter, like the FAQs that many organisations include on their websites to reduce the number of calls to hotlines and e-mails. The basic idea is that the people affected will look at the FAQs to see whether their question is included and, if it isn´t, they can still call the hotline. This pre-emptive method of information provision demonstrates that top management is proactively providing information, has identified the information requirements of the people affected and is already able to provide the answers.

Self-assessment questions for each certification level

No.	Question	Level				Self-assessment
		D	C	B	A	
F 1.1	What obstacles will an organisation that is introducing project management structures probably encounter?	1	2	2	3	☐
F 1.2	How can opposition to project management be prevented?	1	2	2	3	☐
F 1.3	What is the purpose of the project management manual?	1	2	2	3	☐
F 1.4	According to Platz, what are the phases in the process of introducing project management in an organisation?	1	2	2	3	☐

F2 PROJECT MANAGEMENT OPTIMISATION

Project management optimisation (ICB Elements 2, 37) involves a process of continuous improvement. Benchmarking models, especially maturity models, help those responsible for optimisation to identify the strengths and weaknesses of their project management concept. Comparing best practices with those of other organisations is also a means of evaluating an organisation´s status quo. This chapter focuses on the most important models, e.g. CMM, OPM3, PM Delta – the GPM´s benchmarking model, and their structure. It also explains the advantages and disadvantages of a strictly process-oriented approach.

1 Maturity models

Project management cannot be introduced, embedded and optimised in an organisation at the touch of a button. Anyone who expects this to happen is bound to be disappointed. Project management has to be a step-by-step process of continuous improvement (→ Chapter C8) as is evident by Phases 4 and 5 of the process model described in Chapter F1.

Continuous improvement

Project benchmarking models – especially maturity models – help to reveal the strengths, weaknesses and scope for improvement in an organisation´s project management concept. This chapter includes sections on the Capability Maturity Model (CMM), the Project Management Maturity Model (Kerzner), the Project Management Institute of America´s (PMI) Organizational Project Management Maturity Model (OPM3) and the German Association for Project Management´s (GPM) PM Delta Model.

The GPM´s Project Excellence Model (→ Chapter C8) differs from the above models because it is not designed for the evaluation of project management systems, but of individual projects.

Assessment of individual projects

1.1 Capability Maturity Model

The concept of continuous improvement is clearly evident in the first maturity model, the Capability Maturity Model [1], which is now in widespread use. It was developed by the Software Engineering Institute (SEI) at Carnegie Mellon University in the late 1980s for the US Ministry of Defense´s software projects. CMM differentiates between five maturity levels and helps organisations to improve the quality and efficiency of their software development processes. These days, there is a whole range of CMM models such as the People Capability Maturity Model (P-CMM), which is used to assess capability of personnel (→ Chapter D3).

CMM models

CMM can also be described as a project management benchmarking model for measuring the performance of an organisation´s project management system on the basis of best practices at other organisations. It has many things in common with the sector-independent ISO 9001 standard (→ Chapter C8), although there are some significant differences [2]. CMM places more emphasis on continuous improvement. One thing that both models have in common is that all significant processes have to be documented.

ISO 9001 standard

CMM´s popularity has spread around the globe since it was first developed. It is also an unofficial standard for the certification of software organisations.

1.1.1 Capability levels

Levels CMM´s five capability levels are:
1. Initial (ad-hoc processes). There is no systematic project management at this level. The success of the project depends, to a great extent, on the project team´s commitment.
2. Repeatable
3. Defined
4. Managed
5. Optimising

Key process areas The CMM model identifies the most important processes for the systematic development of software and summarises them in key process areas (KPA). These are allocated to the five maturity levels, as shown in Figure F2-1 [3].

CAPABILITY LEVEL	KEY PROCESS AREA (KPA)	KPA ABBREVIATION
5 Optimising		
	Avoiding mistakes	AM
	Technology change management	TCM
	Process change management	PCM
4 Managed		
	Quantitative process management	QPM
	Software quality management	SQM
3 Defined		
	Organisation-wide process focus	OPF
	Organisation-wide process definition	OPD
	Training programmes	TP
	Integrated software management	ISM
	Software product engineering	SPE
	Group coordination	GC
	Peer review	PR
2 Repeatable		
	Requirements management	RM
	Software project planning	SPP
	Software project management and monitoring	SPMM
	Software quality assurance	SQA
	Software configuration management	SCM
	Software sub-contract management	SSM
1 Initial		

Figure F2-1 CMM maturity levels and key process areas

Key practices Each KPA consists of several key practices. For example, the key process area Software Project Planning includes 25 key practices.

Process, in this context, means a sequence of steps that are necessary to achieve a desired outcome. The basic assumption is that the higher the maturity level of a project, the lower the associated risks and the higher the probability of its success. This is why the US Ministry of Defense (→ Chapter A2) only awards contracts to providers with a maturity level of at least 3 on the basis of an external assessment.

The illustration [4] in Figure F2-2 has been included because CMM´s complexity makes it very difficult to describe it in more detail. It shows the process characteristics and actions that are necessary at each level in order to reach the next level and gives the approximate timeframe that the organisation requires if it wants to move up to the next higher level.

Process characteristics

Timeframe

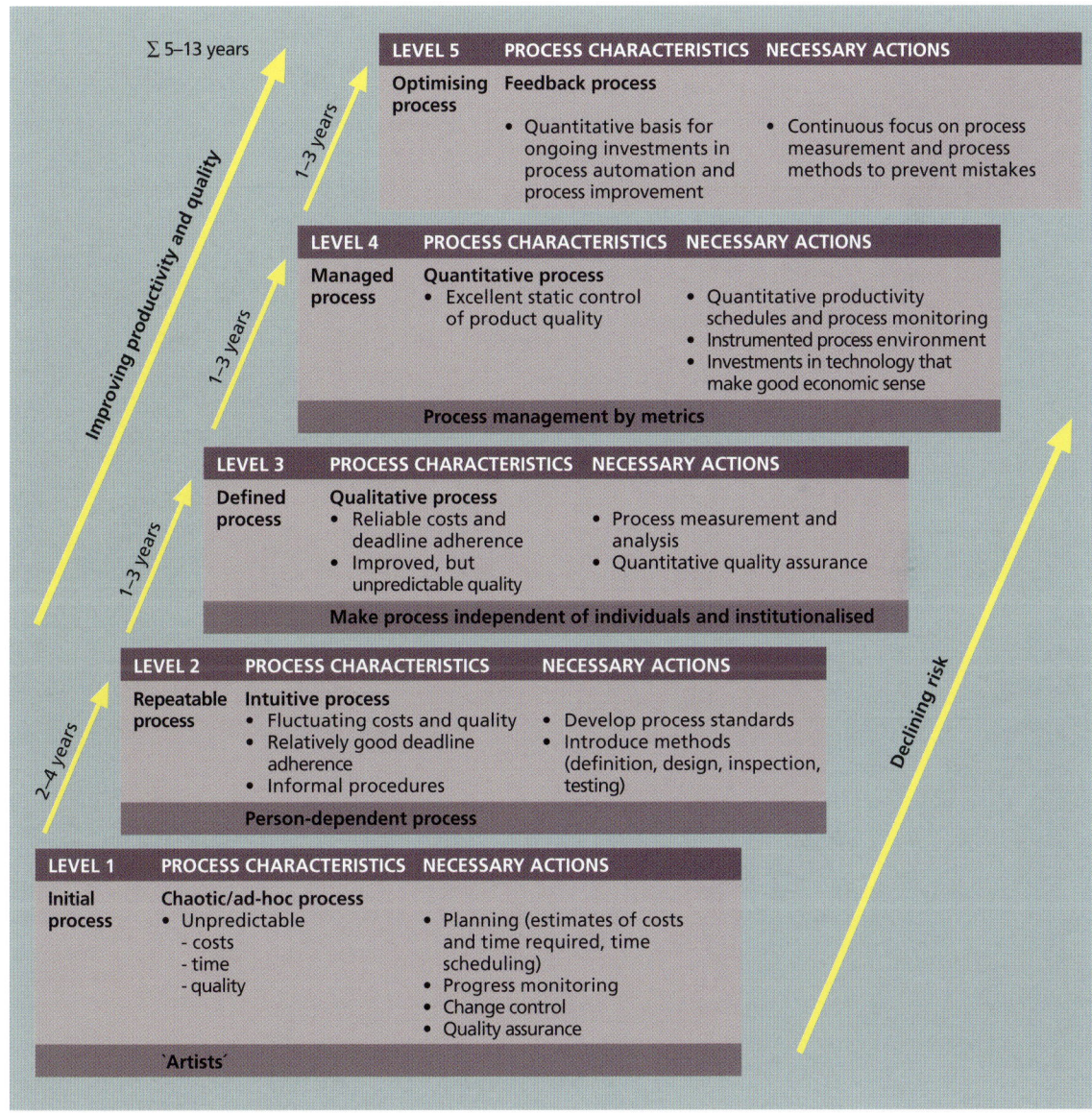

Figure F2-2 An overview of the five CMM capability levels

Today, the original CMM has been replaced by the much more complex CMM-I (I = integration) [5] model. According to SEI, this model is also suitable for the development of physical products, such as machines,

CMM-I

F2 PROJECT MANAGEMENT OPTIMISATION

BOOTSTRAP, SPICE — electrical or electronic products. BOOTSTRAP und SPICE [6] (→ Chapter C8) are other CMM successor models. BOOTSTRAP was developed during an Esprit project with CMM as the reference model. Unlike the CMM developers, though, BOOTSTRAP´s creators based their model on the ISO 9000 standards.

1.2 Sector-independent maturity and assessment models

The maturity models for the software industry were followed by sector-neutral models such as Kerzner´s [7] Project Management Maturity Model and OPM3.

1.2.1 Project Management Maturity Model

Five maturity levels — Like CMM, the Project Management Maturity Model differentiates between five maturity levels. These are shown in Figure F2-3.

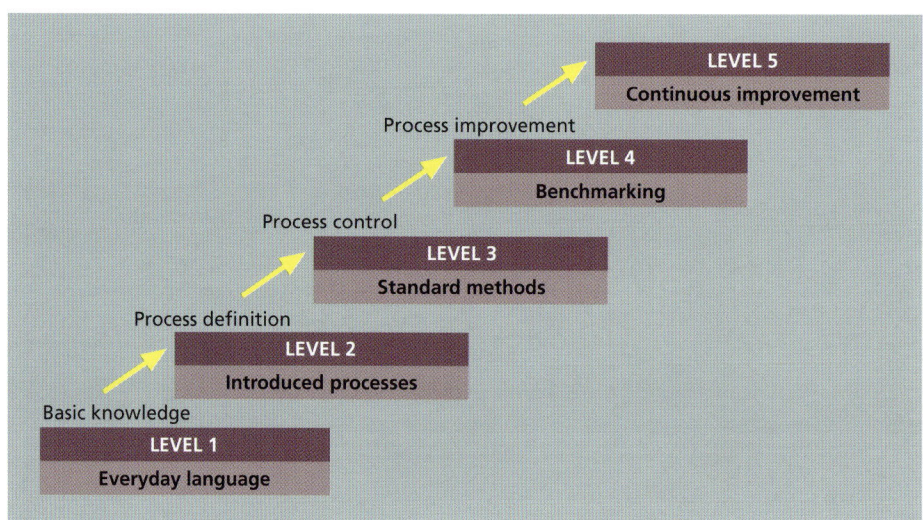

Figure F2-3 Kerzner´s Project Management Maturity Model

Everyday language — At Level 1 (Everyday Language without project management context) the organisation hardly discusses project management at all. There are only a few isolated cases – if any at all – of project management methods being used. Senior managers do not support project management, middle managers are not aware of its benefits and staff have no project management training. There is extensive hierarchical thinking and a resulting underdeveloped understanding of interdepartmental project management.

Opposition — In the transition phase from Level 1 to Level 2, the introduction of project management methods is hampered by several things. Opponents formulate a series of objections (→ Chapter F1) and sabotage the establishment of project management in the organisation. Kerzner recommends that organisations should implement training measures and provide comprehensive information to staff about project management `state of the art´ in order to move up to Level 2.

At Level 2 (Introduced Processes), managers recognise the benefits of project management and the necessity of defining processes and methods. The concept is supported at all management levels. Managers create training curricula that do not just include individual, stand-alone training measures, but measures that are integrated in the project management concept as a whole, and they recognise the need for project-related cost management. To reach Level 3, an organisational culture that fosters project management is required.

Introduced processes

At Level 3 (Standard Methods), processes such as project management, total quality management (→ Chapter C8) and concurrent engineering (→ Chapter B) are integrated. The organisation's prevailing culture is one in which all those involved and affected accept and support project management without any reservations. Training in the soft skills needed for project management is also provided. The benefits derived from the provision of training to staff are measurable.

Standard methods

At Level 4 (Benchmarking) a project or project management office or a centre of excellence exists. The organisation learns from experience in its own and other sectors of business and implements extensive benchmarking (→ Chapter C8).

Benchmarking

At Level 5 (Continuous Improvement) the project office has a mentoring system. The organisation is consistent in the implementation of knowledge management. A detailed analysis (→ Chapter C10) is made after the end of each project. Mentors pass on the experience gained in the project to the staff.

Continuous improvement

Kerzner has developed a long list of multiple choice questions for self or external evaluation of an organisation's maturity level.

List of questions

1.2.2 Organisational Project Management Maturity Model [8]

Like CMM, the Project Management Maturity Model (OPM3) shows what is needed to reach a higher level of maturity. A special feature of this model is its strong emphasis on the relationship between project management and the organisation's business strategy. This is evident by the new concept of 'organisational project management', which is defined as the 'systematic management of projects, programmes and portfolios in alignment with the achievement of strategic goals' [9].

Business strategy

1.2.2.1 Basic outline of the model
Only a basic outline of the model is provided here [10]. It has three structuring dimensions:
- Assessment levels
- Categorisation according to four improvement levels
- Categorisation of project processes

1.2.2.2 Assessment levels
First of all, a differentiation is made between the three assessment domains or levels of
- Project
- Programme and
- Portfolio.

Assessment levels

An organisation's portfolio consists of projects and programmes. The following OPM3 definition of a programme differs from the one provided in Chapter E1: 'Groups of projects sometimes constitute a program, which is a group of related projects managed in a coordinated way to obtain benefits and control not available from managing them individually.' However, this definition does not consider the important distinction that a programme is a temporary undertaking and a portfolio is not.

1.2.2.3 Categorisation according to four improvement levels

Improvement levels

Another categorisation consists of four consecutive levels of improvement in a project management system:
- Standardisation
- Measurement
- Control
- Continuous improvement

The two dimensions of Assessment Levels and Improvement Levels in a project management system are combined in Figure F2-4.

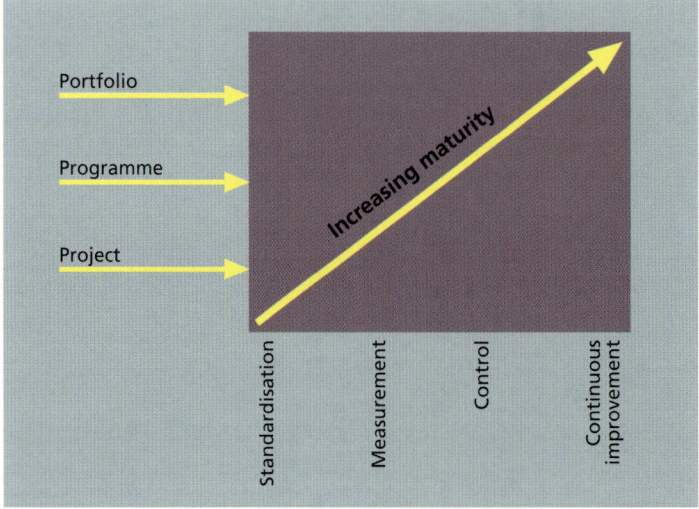

Figure F2-4 Development of maturity according to OPM3

This system has parallels to CMM, even though OPM3 is not a maturity level model, but rather a process of continuous maturity development.

1.2.2.4 Categorisation of project processes

Process categories

A third dimension categorises project management processes into:
- Start-up process
- Planning process
- Implementation process
- Control process
- Conclusion process

1.2.2.5 Assessment of a project management system using OPM3

List of questions

OPM3 uses a list of 151 questions, that reflect the various dimensions to differing extents, for the assessment of an organisation's project management system. The answers can be assessed using special computer software.

F2 PROJECT MANAGEMENT OPTIMISATION

Examples [11]

Question 23
`Does your organisation establish and use standard documented processes at the Project level for the Closing Processes (Contract Close-out, Administrative Closure)?´

Question 26
`Does your organisation have a standard approach for the definition, collection and analysis of project metrics to ensure project data is consistent and accurate?´

Question 60
`Does your organisation establish and use standard documented processes at the Program level for the Initiation Processes (Initiation Process)?´

Question 145
`Does your organisation identify, assess, and implement improvements at the Portfolio level for the Core Planning Processes (Project Plan Development, Scope Planning, Scope Definition, Activity Sequencing, Activity Duration Estimating, Schedule Development, Resource Planning, Cost Estimating, Cost Budgeting, Risk Management Planning)?´

1.2.2.6 Self-analysis

When selected members of the organisation - members of the project office team, for instance – have answered the questions, they can use the software to ascertain the strengths and weaknesses of the organisation´s project management system. The software provides four charts (overall assessment, project level, programme level and portfolio level) to show the relative maturity level of the organisation in percentage terms.

Analysis of strengths and weaknesses

Figure F2-5 shows an example taken from the OPM3 manual [12]:

Project level	Percentage maturity
Standardisation	48 %
Measurement	53 %
Control	50 %
Continuous improvement	89 %
Programme level	**Percentage maturity**
Standardisation	67 %
Measurement	11 %
Control	0 %
Continuous improvement	0 %
Portfolio level	**Percentage maturity**
Standardisation	20 %
Measurement	0 %
Control	0 %
Continuous improvement	0 %

Figure F2-5 Maturity levels in an organisation in percentage terms

F2 PROJECT MANAGEMENT OPTIMISATION

1.2.2.7 Optimisation with OPM3

Best practices directory

When the strengths and weaknesses have been identified as described above, the assessors draft a plan for improving the project management system with the assistance of a Best Practices Directory, which contains a systematic list of around 600 best practices. The directory also differentiates between project, programme and portfolio level, and refers to the four levels of standardisation, measurement, control and continual improvement. This makes it relatively easy to identify the relevant best practices after the analysis of strengths and weaknesses and to use them as the basis for optimising the project management system.

Identification number	Designation	Description	Project	Programme	Portfolio	Standardisation	Measurement	Control	Continuous improvement
1390	Standardisation of administrative project handover processes	Standards exist for the administrative aspects of project handover	x			x			
3120	Standardisation of programme start-up processes	Standards exist for programme start-up		x		x			
6720	Improvement of portfolio composition planning processes	The weaknesses in the process of creating the project portfolio have been assessed. Suggested changes were documented. Changes were implemented				x			x
etc.									

Figure F2-6 Identification of opportunities for improvement with OPM3

1.2.3 The GPM´s PM Delta

Elements instead of levels
List of questions

PM Delta [13], which was developed by the German Association for Project Management (GPM), is also a sector-neutral benchmarking model. Like OPM3, it is not a maturity level model. It consists of 19 project management elements (→ Figure F2-7) and a list of questions which can be enlarged to include organisation-specific questions.

List of strengths and weaknesses

PM Delta can be used to create a catalogue of strengths and weaknesses. This forms the basis of recommendations for optimising the project management system and it also makes an anonymous comparison with other organisations possible.

PM No.	ELEMENTS OF PROJECT MANAGEMENT		
1	Objective definition	11	Resource management
2	Structuring	12	Time scheduling
3	Management structure	13	Multi-project coordination
4	HR management	14	Risk management
5	Contract administration	15	Information and reporting system
6	Claim management	16	Controlling
7	Configuration management	17	Logistics
8	Change management	18	Quality management
9	Costing	19	Documentation
10	Cost management		

Figure F2-7 The PM Delta project management elements

These are a few of the questions contained in the comprehensive list:

Sample questions

Objective definition
- Which processes and rules exist to establish and document the definition of objectives?
- How is it ensured that units of measurement are defined for the achievement of objectives?
- In what way are stakeholders involved in the objective definition process?

HR management
- How are staff selected?
- What are the criteria for setting up a project team?
- How are the project team members reintegrated in the organisation´s structures when the project has finished?

Contract administration
- How is contractual performance monitored?
- What processes and rules exist for the analysis, structuring, conclusion and amendment of contracts?
- How are the interfaces to claim management, change management and configuration management defined?

Claim management
- What mechanisms ensure the identification, verification and assertion of claims arising from breach of contract?
- How are decisions on whether to assert claims made?

1.3 The course of an assessment process

Using PM Delta as an example, Figure F2-8 shows the course of an assessment process. The assessors conduct interviews and assess documents. Often, there is a considerable gap between the written rules and their application in practice. It has also been observed during the application of CMM, among others, that the results of self-assessments are always more positive than external assessments.

Discrepancy theory – practice

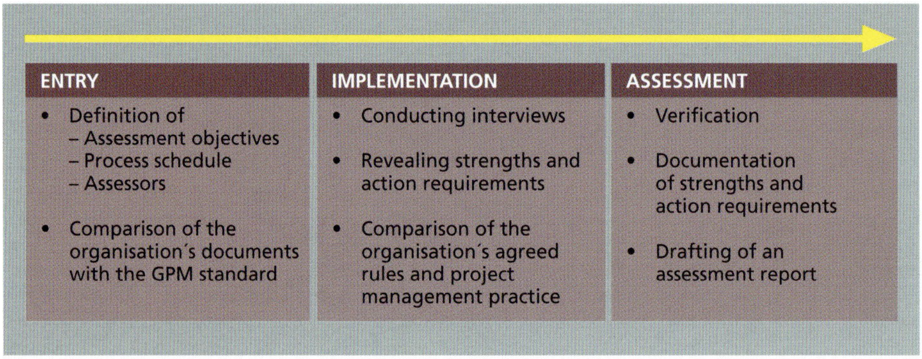

F2 PROJECT MANAGEMENT OPTIMISATION

ENTRY	IMPLEMENTATION	ASSESSMENT

• Definition of
  – Assessment objectives
  – Process schedule
  – Assessors
• Comparison of the organisation's documents with the GPM standard
	• Conducting interviews
	• Revealing strengths and action requirements
	• Comparison of the organisation's agreed rules and project management practice
		• Verification
		• Documentation of strengths and action requirements
		• Drafting of an assessment report

Figure F2-8 PM Delta assessment process

Example

The example shown in Figure F2-9 [14] is just a small excerpt of the assessment process for auditing risk management structures (→ Chapter C3).

Strengths
- The risks are documented with the Risk Mitigate tool and then checked by a controller.
- There is an informative checklist for risk analysis.
- Priority risks (comprising more than five percent of the order value) are reported to the management.

Weaknesses
- A proper risk evaluation (risk workshop) only takes place in the project start-up phase. In practice, it is not possible to continually update the risk assessment during the course of the project (e.g. changes in probability of occurrence or impact).

Recommendations
- Application of project risk management processes for the entire project lifecycle.
- Documentation and continuous (re-)assessment of potential problems and project opportunities, including the establishment of appropriate measures and their implementation status.

Figure F2-9 Assessment process to enable risk management

Prioritising recommendations The assessors have to prioritise the recommendations. Senior management is responsible for ensuring that the recommendations are implemented and should obtain regular information about the implementation status. Figure F2-10 [15] shows an example of prioritisation.

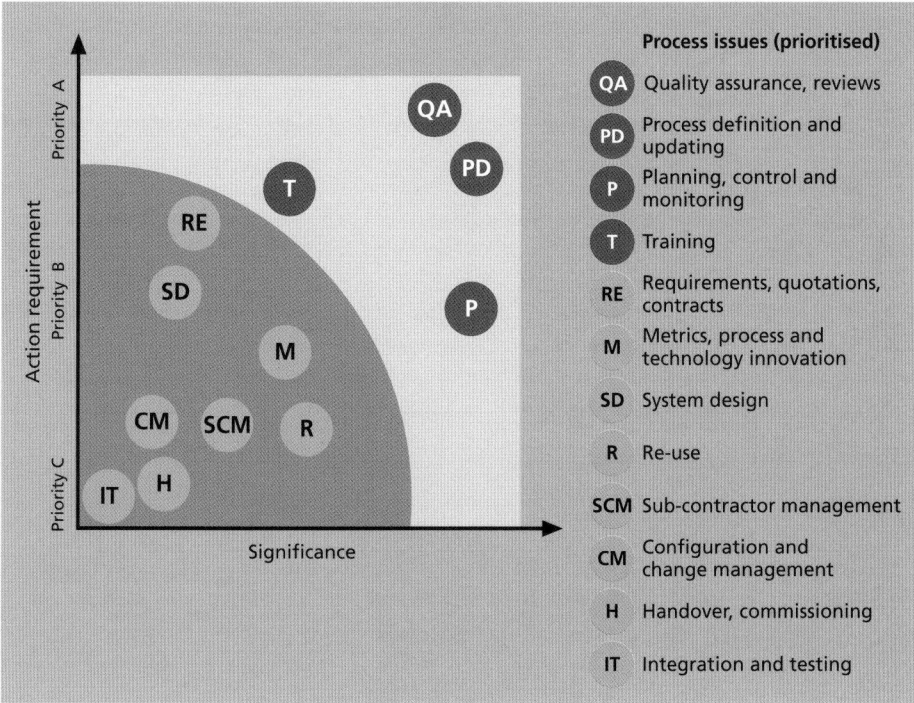

Figure F2-10 Priorities for optimisation measures in a project management system

2 Critical appraisal of maturity models

There are so many benchmarking models for project management that it is almost impossible to retain an overview. In 2002, there were 30 registered models [21]. No comparison of their common features and differences has been made. There isn´t even a neutral, critical appraisal of the various approaches and recommendations on the suitability of specific models for specific purposes. It is unlikely that standardisation similar to ISO 9000 will be introduced.

CMM, BOOTSTRAP, SPICE, OPM3 and PM Delta are extremely process-oriented. They do not focus on the project deliverable, but on the processes that lead to its creation. Generally, a differentiation is made between
- ad-hoc processes that are spontaneous, individual and not controlled [16], and
- systematic processes that are clearly defined and are adhered to by personnel.

Process orientation

By systemising processes, it is possible to standardise project procedures. The objective is to ensure that project success is less dependent on individual people and more predictable. The systemisation and documentation of processes also provides indications of where process improvements can be made. The underlying assumption is that good processes lead to good products.

In the end, the customer is interested in the quality of the product or service and not the quality of the process. Glinz [17] found that an almost exclusive focus on processes carries risks:

Risks associated with process orientation

- Tasks which are not associated with defined processes may be neglected.
- Following all prescribed processes to the letter results in project bureaucracy.
- Processes that are extremely complex to define can become obsolete simply because nobody is willing to assume responsibility for modifying them.
- If the focus is on processes, soft factors such as the project manager's ability to deal with conflicts are neglected.

Soft factors It is important to remember that project work depends not only on processes, but also on people. Ruskin [18] said that meticulous descriptions of the processes in an organisation are of no use if the people affected are not able to implement them competently.

Flexibility Maturity and benchmarking models have to be more flexible so that they can be adapted to the specific requirements of an organisation. If this were possible, they would be a useful tool for the systematic improvement of project management practices.

Self-assessment questions for each certification level

No.	Question	Level D	Level C	Level B	Level A	Self-assessment
F2.1	What is the main difference between the maturity models and the Project Excellence model?	1	2	2	3	☐
F2.2	Between what levels does Kerzner's Project Management Maturity Model differentiate?	1	2	2	3	☐
F2.3	Which tasks should be performed by the project management office according to Kerzner's project management maturity model?	1	2	2	3	☐
F2.4	What is benchmarking?	1	2	3	4	☐
F2.5	Which maturity and benchmarking models exist to optimise project management structures?	1	2	3	4	☐
F2.6	What are the criticisms of the main maturity and benchmarking models?	1	1	2	2	☐

F3 PROJECT MANAGEMENT STANDARDS

1 Significance

One of the main reasons why standards [1] and regulations are necessary is to simplify communications within and between organisations. In the 1960s, project management language, or network analysis language to be more precise, caused considerable confusion. For example, several terms (such as slack, float, and buffer) were used to describe the phenomenon of time margins in projects. Every time negotiations took place, it was necessary to define what each negotiating partner meant by the terms they used. Even this relatively minor problem demonstrates the need for standardised terminology. This terminology set has been greatly expanded by experts in German-speaking countries and this chapter details the current status.

2 Terminology standards in German-speaking countries

DIN 69 900 Part 1: Project work, project network techniques, concepts (August 1987)
This standard particularly focuses on network analysis methods, network diagram types, display and procedural elements as well as structuring and time scheduling concepts.

DIN 69 900 Part 2: Project work, project network techniques, methods of presentation (August 1987)
This standard includes information about the manual or machine-assisted creation of network diagrams (charts). It describes the basic display elements and how they are used to represent procedural elements, network diagram labelling, general rules for graphic representation, graphic simplification and special identifiers (e.g. for the critical-path method of planning).

DIN 69 901: Project work, project management, concepts (August 1987)
This standard not only covers the basic concepts of project, project management and project work, but also the subjects of project structuring (e.g. work breakdown structure), personnel management structures and management information.

DIN 69 902: Project work, resources, concepts (August 1987)
After the basic definitions, this standard deals with the concepts of resource scheduling, utilisation and management.

DIN 69 903: Project work, cost and efficiency, financial resources, concepts (August 1987)
This standard only deals with project-related investment and efficiency analyses, and financial resource planning.

DIN 69 904: Project work, project management systems, elements and structures (November 2000)
This standard provides advice about structuring project management systems and explains 19 elements of project management: definition of objectives, structuring, organisation, HR management, contract administration, claim management, configuration management, change management, budgeting, cost management, resource management, time scheduling, multi-project coordination, risk management, information and reporting system, controlling, logistics, quality management and documentation.

The standard also defines rules for project processes and refers to the use of experience and expert knowledge.

DIN 69 905: Project work, project development, concepts (May 1997)
This standard covers the general terminology that occurs during the course of a project, such as project initiation, offer, order, customer specification and supplier specification.

Draft DIN 69 906: Logistics, basic concepts (December 1990)
This standard defines concepts in logistics. The terminology is not exclusive to projects.

Another DIN standard for project management is:
DIN 19 246 Measurement and control; procedure of projects

3 Foreign standards

Switzerland has not published its own standards and uses the German ones as required. A standards board in Austria has focused on standardising network analysis terminology. Standard specifications are published in the UK by the British Standards Institute. These standards are recommended in the Netherlands. Several terminology standards also exist in France.

There are no comparable standards in the USA. Nevertheless, the Project Management Institute (PMI) has published the comprehensive Guide to the Project Management Body of Knowledge (PMBoK) [2], which is now in its fourth edition and approved as a standard by the American National Standards Institute (ANSI). PMBoK is also used in Canada. The 2000 edition was translated into several languages, including German.

The International Project Management Association´s (IPMA) Competence Baseline (ICB) also serves as a project implementation standards guideline for project managers within the national associations. The ICB provides information about the elements of project management in English, German and French in three adjacent columns to provide international project teams with a standard communication platform. The ICB is also used by the national certification companies as the basis for the certification of project personnel (4-Level-Certification, 4-L-C → Chapter D3).

F3 PROJECT MANAGEMENT STANDARDS

3.1 International standards

There are no binding global or European standards at the moment.

3.2 International Standards Organization (ISO) standards

ISO has no standard for project management. However, the Technical Committee ISO/TC 176 `Quality Management and Quality Assurance´ did publish a supplementary guideline to standard ISO 10 006, `Quality management, Guidelines to quality in project management´, as part of the ISO 9000 family of quality management standards in December 1997. This standard includes useful information for project managers. ISO 10 006 is currently in the process of being revised. When this standard was originally being developed, a corresponding ISO standard for configuration management was drafted and translated by the German Institute for Standardisation in 1997 and published as DIN EN ISO 10 007, `Quality management systems – Guidelines for configuration management´. This is also currently being revised.

F3 PROJECT MANAGEMENT STANDARDS

CASE STUDY

INTRODUCTION OF PROJECT MANAGEMENT

at a consumer electronics manufacturer

1 Preliminary remarks

This case study comprises three sections:

Section 1: The introduction of project management at an organisation (→ Chapter F1) is a project in its own right and should therefore be planned and implemented according to the rules of project management.

Section 2: Instruments have to be designed and rules established in this project.

Section 3: In the process of concept development and introduction, a series of situations arise for which the project manager is required to propose appropriate solutions.

In practice, most of the activities in this project require teamwork. However, you can develop your solutions individually in the case study.

2 Initial situation

A consumer electronics manufacturer develops and mass manufactures a variety of products (CD players, TV sets, Playstations, Walkmen, etc.) for distribution through retail outlets. In the past, a number of its projects have been flops. Some products were launched too late compared to products from strong competitors, while others had excessively high development and production costs which meant the project profit margin wasn´t reached. Quality didn´t always meet expectations. As a result, many products were returned by angry retailers after customer complaints.

The company has never used systematic project management methods. Instead, each project manager implements `his´ project as he sees fit. In an assessment, an external consultant has identified that the organisation has a project management maturity level of 1 (`chaotic´) in the Capability Maturity Model (CMM or CMM-I). In other words, the organisation has no standards and rules, and project success depends solely on the hard work put in by the project team. The organisation has two managing directors, one with a commercial background and one with an engineering background. They both decide on the basis of the analysis findings and in face of growing pressure from the competition to introduce project management for all projects subject to their approval.

CASE STUDY

Assume the following: you are manager of the central development department and have been requested to manage this project. The necessary resources are placed at your disposal. The directors also ensure that the employees assigned to your team for the duration of the project are relieved of some of their line department responsibilities. You can employ one specialist to provide expert support. The directors send a circular to all members of staff and the works council informing them about the project and requesting them to support you. After discussing the matter with your development colleagues, you know that other department managers don´t think much of systematic project management because they believe that it constrains the developers´ creativity. Opinions are mixed in the other central departments. The production departments take a positive view of the whole thing. They have had a sophisticated production scheduling and control system for quite some time now and they know that it is to be incorporated in the project management system.

Since the sales department has often suffered as a result of development project delays in the past, it is likely to be positively disposed towards the introduction of project management. It hopes that it can regain lost market shares as a result. The designers are likely to be in favour of project management, too. Like the sales team, they have to deal with the consequences of the development team´s `misdemeanours´. The commercial administration department is likely to be neutral. The conservative manager of the accounts department will probably not support new methods such as project-specific cost monitoring at work package level. The chief controller hopes that his status will be enhanced by additional responsibility for project control. The opinions of the central department managers are not known. They generally object to organisational changes, except for the central sales department manager.

You can expect covert or open resistance to your project, despite having the support of the two managing directors. Plan in advance how you intend to cope with this resistance. Incorporate the measures that you intend to use to promote widespread acceptance in your work breakdown structure.

ORGANISATION PLAN

The organisation is structured as follows:

Managing directors

CD purchasing and warehousing
Department 1 (Purchasing)
Department 2 (Warehouse Administration)

CD Development*
Development department 1
Development department 2
Development department 3
Testing

CD Design*
Design department 1
Design department 2
Design department 3

CD Production*
Production scheduling 1
Production scheduling 2
Production scheduling 3
Production department 1
Production department 2
Production department 3

Sales*
Market research
Sales 1
Sales 2
Sales 3
Customer service

Commercial administration
Finances
Accounts
Controlling
Organisation, data processing, auditing
General administration

CD central department
* structured according to product groups

CASE STUDY

3 Tasks

3.1 Task group 1

1. Prepare an agenda for the kick-off event.
2. Prepare an agenda for the start-up meeting. Who are you going to invite to the start-up meeting?
3. Prepare the following planning documents for the project management introduction project:
    - Detailed objectives, differentiating between implementation and product success.
      To define implementation success, ask yourself how you will measure the success of the project when project management has been in place for a while.
    - Work breakdown structure (WBS)
    - Milestone plan with milestone results
    - Table of contents for the subsequent creation of project management guidelines
4. Perform risk and stakeholder analyses. Based on the stakeholder analysis, develop a concept for dealing with the most important project stakeholders. Hint: if you are not sure whether the various stakeholder groups are positively or negatively disposed towards the project management concept, assume that they are negatively disposed to it and consider what proactive measures you can take to deal with them. The concept should be reflected in the work breakdown structure. In other words, integrate work packages and sub-projects in the WBS that you have already prepared.
5. Consider which projects you will select as pilot projects. All you need to do is provide a rough description of the type and scope of the projects, and your reasons for selecting them.

3.2 Task group 2

You have already held the start-up meeting, it was a success, and now you can start work with your team. Create a list of the project results that you want to achieve in conjunction with an external consultant. In order to make this possible, the project team has to perform the following tasks:

1. Prepare a standard agenda for the start-up meeting.
2. Prepare a checklist for the stakeholder and risk analyses.
3. Create a standard work breakdown structure for development projects. Establish which department is responsible for each work package (e.g. development or construction department) and formulate all details of the work packages for the project management team.
4. Design a process model with phases, milestones and results for each phase. Then assign the work packages that you have formulated to the individual phases.
5. Design several templates for standard monthly reports. What are the directors´ likely reporting requirements?
6. Specify a standard agenda for status meetings.
7. Design a form for the final report.
8. Create a catalogue of responsibilities, tasks and authorities for the project portfolio board, the project manager and his team, the line managers and the project management office that is to be established.
9. Develop a requirements profile for project managers.

3.3 Task group 3

1. Set up a project team. Create a profile matrix and enter the following information:
   - The functions that your project team members will perform (e.g. project assistant, controller, etc.)
   - The requirements that the team have to satisfy (e.g. project management know-how, knowledge transfer expertise, and interpersonal skills)

FUNCTION	REQUIREMENT 1	REQUIREMENT 2	REQUIREMENT ...
Project assistant	Project management knowledge	Knowledge transfer expertise	...
Project controller	Interpersonal skills	...	...
...	...		

Requirements matrix for the project team

By filling in the matrix fields (or leaving them empty) you can find out which function has to satisfy which requirements. Based on this, you can search for suitable staff within the organisation. What ways have you to find these people?

2. You will have to employ a sub-project manager to set up and manage an organisation-wide project management office. What skills will he need to do this? Extend the profile matrix to find out which skills (e.g. project management skills, management competence) you believe to be important for a sub-project manager.

3. Soon afterwards, this matrix will have helped you to select three possible candidates from the organisation´s own ranks. Their profiles are so similar that you find it difficult to make a decision. How will you make your final choice?

4. What body, other than the project team, will you require for your project? Where in the hierarchy should its members be located?

5. In your function as project manager, you have organised an initial meeting for representatives of various hierarchical levels within the accounting department (e.g. department manager, desk officer, secretary, student employee). They are all affected by the changes in the organisation and use the opportunity to discuss openly opportunities and voice concerns at the meeting. An experienced commercial administrator, who has a neutral opinion of the project, chairs the meeting.
You have withdrawn to play the role of observer. You want to identify the project supporters and opponents, and to use the information that you gain to plan your communication and project marketing strategy. You make notes about the arguments put forward at the meeting and the way people behave. What are you looking out for? Consider the basic rules for conducting negotiations and your knowledge about group dynamics, roles, perceptions, prejudices, etc.

6. Create a communication matrix and a project marketing plan. What information do you need for this? Refer to Task Group 1, Point 4.

7. The directors have granted you authority to issue instructions for the duration of the project with regard to all aspects of the introduction of project management vis-à-vis the central

CASE STUDY

department managers, even though they are your superiors in the line management structure. You are obliged to ensure that your instructions are carried out in the central departments. You are aware that this is problematic for some central department managers from an interpersonal viewpoint. What management style will you choose? What reactions are you likely to encounter? How will you deal with these reactions?

8. Within the scope of the project management introduction project, you intend to introduce a standardised organisation-wide reporting system for all projects. You have to convince the central department managers of your idea by putting across persuasive arguments in a presentation. You will only use your authority from the directors as a last resource. First, you attempt to win over the people affected. To what do you have to pay attention when preparing and implementing the presentation?

9. Two central department mangers were not convinced by the ideas for the standardised reporting system that you presented. They are determined to keep their own reporting structures in place. However, you manage to persuade them to attend a meeting with you to discuss the issue again. Your objective is to persuade both of them to accept your point of view, because such a system is absolutely essential for standard, organisation-wide project management. Prepare a negotiation strategy. To what do you have to pay attention during the meeting – concerning yourself and them?

10. How can you ensure that the central sales department manger, who supports you, is even more strongly integrated in the project so that you can use his positive attitude to benefit the project? What is the technical term for the function that he will perform?

11. The managers of the sales and accounts departments dislike each other intensely. People aware of the problem said during the stakeholder analysis that it is only a matter of time before the two argue about the new project management system. The sales department manager is in favour of the project, the accounts department manager against. This constitutes a project risk. Bearing this in mind, you decide to request both the men to attend a meeting. You are aware that this conflict cannot be resolved at objective level (= pros and cons of project management), but that you have to get to its roots (= relationship level) in order to put an end to it. What approach to conflict resolution do you take?

12. You have to work with external service providers. This relationship has to be governed by a contract. Create a list of possible contractual partners and contracts and ask yourself what problems are likely to occur in connection with
    - designing the contract and
    - the contractual partners.

    How can these problems be dealt with or resolved?

AUTHORS

Heinz Schelle

Heinz Schelle studied political economics in Munich. After graduating, he worked as a research assistant before obtaining his Ph.D. in 1968. From 1969 to 1975 he was employed by Siemens in the Central Research and Development Division, where he headed a laboratory team that was involved in projects relating to management consulting and project management methods. In 1975 he was appointed to the Chair of Business Economics with Special Emphasis on Project Management at the Faculty of Computer Science of the University of the Armed Forces in Munich. In 1979, he founded the German Association for Project Management (GPM) with Professor Hasso Reschke and Roland Gutsch, and was a director of the GPM for 19 years. During this time, he was responsible for the agendas of around 25 congresses and symposia, and published some 60 books and essays on project management. He was appointed Honorary Chairman of the GPM in 1998. He is author of Chapters A1-3, A5-6, B, C1-4, C6, C9, C10 (Part 1), C 11, E1-3, F1 (Part 1), F 2-3, the case study, the glossary and is expert consultant to the book.
E-mail: h.schelle@GPM-IPMA.de

Günter Rackelmann

Günter Rackelmann has a degree in business administration. After graduating, he worked at the Friedrich Alexander University of Erlangen – Nuremberg for several years as Assistant to the Chair of Computer Science and Business Information Systems. He is co-founder and Managing Director (since 1979) of GCA projektmanagment + consulting GmbH in Nuremberg. He has worked as project manager, project controller and project consultant in large-scale, publicly-funded industrial projects in the building and aviation industries, in plant construction, power station construction, railway and road construction as well as in urban development, and he has also been involved in software development projects. He specialises in the conception, development and introduction of project management systems, time scheduling and cost management in large-scale projects and training courses for senior managers, project managers and project teams. He obtained project management trainer certification in 1993 and joined the GPM board in 1996. He is also the author of several publications on the subject of project management. He is author of Chapter C5.
E-mail: g.rackelmann@GPM-IPMA.de

Kurt E. Weber

Kurt E. Weber is a lawyer and chartered engineer who has studied chemical engineering and law. He worked as a project engineer and project manager in the industrial plant construction industry until 1981, when he was admitted to practice as a lawyer. In 1983 he founded his own law firm in Munich that specialises in civil law. Today, he is mainly involved in contract design and providing legal advice for building and industrial plant construction contracts, contract controlling (contract management), claim management and the settlement of disputes arising from construction and engineering contracts. He is author of Chapter A4.
E-mail: k.weber@GPM-IPMA.de

Astrid Pfeiffer

Astrid Pfeiffer is a political science graduate who worked as a journalist at the Süddeutsche Zeitung newspaper while still at university. After completing a post-graduate IT/internet course in 1998, she worked as a journalist and editor of business magazines and trade publications (print and online), and for the Die Welt broadsheet. In recent years, she has specialised in project management, IT and business. She has also been working as a communications and media consultant to businesses since 2001. Today, she is mainly involved in the production and management of project management publications and in sustainable management, working with forward-looking companies that proactively unite economic, ecological and social requirements in their risk-control strategies. She is a certified Project Management Practitioner (GPM). She is author of Chapters D, C10 (Part 2), F1 (Part 2), the chapter summaries, the case study, and responsible for the editing.
E-mail: a.pfeiffer@GPM-IPMA.de

Roland Ottmann

Roland Ottmann studied mechanical engineering, management and economics, and graduated as a Master of Business Administration (MBA) from Henley-on-Thames (UK). He has been working since 1985 as a project manager, project management/quality management consultant, coach and trainer. Since 1992, he is Managing Director of Ottmann & Partner GmbH Management Consulting. He was Chairman of the Project Management Association chapter in the German Association of Management Consulting Firms (BDU). For several years, he represented Germany as member of the Council of Delegates of the International Project Management Association (IPMA), as well as being Executive Board Officer and Vice-President of the IPMA. He obtained project management trainer certification in 1993 and project manager level B certification in 1995. He has been a member of the GPM board since 1996 and Board Chairman since 2002. He is the initiator and project manager of the German and International PM Award and the Project Excellence Model, PM Award assessor trainer and member of the PM Award jury. He is author of Chapter C8, contributed to A6, B, C7, D1-3, F2-3, the case study, the glossary, and acted as expert advisor to the book.
E-mail: r.ottmann@GPM-IPMA.de

Klaus Pannenbäcker

Klaus Pannenbäcker started his career at Siemens as a quality expert for company products in industrial plants after graduating from Dortmund University in 1959 with a degree in electrical engineering. When KWU was founded in 1969, he was made responsible for the introduction of project management for the planning and construction of large-scale power stations in Germany and abroad. In 1982 he founded the GABO Anlagentechnik und Prozessmanagement GmbH firm of management consultants. As member of the GPM board (from 1983 to 1994), he developed the Project Management Practitioner course and a franchise model for certified and licensed GPM trainers. The 4-Level Certification Programme (4-L-C) was established under his guidance as President and Chairman of the IPMA (from 1992 to 1998). It is now established as a career model in around 40 countries and some 40,000 project management experts have been certified (as at 2004). Today, he is a project management consultant, certification assessor, IPMA validator and MBA course lecturer in Neu-Ulm and Hanover. He is author of Chapter C7.
E-mail: k.pannenbaecker@GPM-IPMA.de

GLOSSARY

Term	Definition
Accounting system	A system for recording → costs and → financial resources in a business unit. To a great extent, corporate accounting systems are required to conform with (tax) legislation requirements. A wide variety of methods for accounting costs are used in projects.
Activity	A sub-process or work step defined as regards content. In a network diagram: sub-process that takes place within a fixed time, with defined start and end status, and constant resource loading. Some PC software permits both interruptions and changes to resource loading. In a workflow: linear business process that is implemented in an identical or similar manner and for whose implementation valid rules exist.
Actual costs	Actual costs of work performed.
Alternative objectives	Different objectives feasible for one and the same project. The objectives to be achieved are selected in the → project preparation phase because they are decisive for the success or failure of the project.
Antedating time	Refined precedence relationship in a network diagram: time by which a conditional event (e.g. the start of an activity) can antedate the event upon which it is conditional (e.g. end of the predecessor activity). Expressed in terms of a negative time → lag (also called lead time).
Assessment	Evaluation. This term is generally used in conjunction with diagnostic monitoring.
Audit	Systematic, independent investigation to ascertain whether real processes and results conform to the effective description and whether this description is suitable for achieving the intended results.
Auditing	Implementation of an audit.
Authority, Authorisation	The authority to perform (legally effective) acts on behalf of or within the scope of an organisation or project.
Autonomous project organisation	A form of organisation used in large-scale projects. The project manager assumes full responsibility for the project and is the disciplinary superior of the project team members. Also called pure or absolute project organisation.
Bar chart (Gantt diagram)	A chart that shows objects as flat bars ordered chronologically. In process scheduling, the objects could be activities. The timeframe can be taken from the network diagram or it can be intuitive. Invented by the American mechanical engineer, Henry Laurence Gantt (1861 – 1919).
Baseline costs	The scheduled total costs of a project are the total costs budgeted for in the project plan. Generally, baseline costs are production costs as opposed to the contract price of the project. → Lifecycle costs
Basic plan	An approved plan including all approved changes.
Benchmarking	A method for the comparative evaluation of (complex) processes or organisations.
Bid review process	Evaluation of customer enquiries according to specific criteria (e.g. technological risk or customer´s credit rating). It helps the management to decide whether or not to prepare a quotation in response to a customer enquiry.
Brainstorming	A problem-solving technique that involves creating a comprehensive list of related ideas.
Budget	Funds allocated to a → project, → sub-task or → work package.
Budgeting	The allocation of funds for specific purposes.
Call to tender	An invitation to contractors to tender for a work package, sub-task or project. The main content is the → specification of what is to be performed. It also details professional qualification requirements, completion deadlines etc.
Career development plans	Plans relating to the long-term career development of individual members of staff (in large-scale organisations).
Chance	A possibility due to a favourable combination of circumstances.
Change committee	A committee that makes decisions which change project objectives, or whose impact exceeds certain limits. In large-scale projects, it is one of the configuration committee´s or steering committee´s sub-committees. In medium-sized projects, the steering committee also functions as the change committee, and in small-scale projects the people responsible for the project make the decisions relating to changes.

GLOSSARY

Change management	Assessment of all change requests, especially when they affect project objectives. Initiation, monitoring and documentation of changes to the project result.
Change of objectives	A change to the confirmed objectives, at the request of the customer, for instance, or because of changes to the legislative or market framework. → change management.
Change order	Document for the implementation of approved changes (ideally integrated in the → change request). Generally provides both instructions and information for specific recipients.
Change request	Basic document in → change management, generally containing the following information: • Request owner • Aspects of the project affected • Reasons and justification • Impact (on costs, deadlines, technology...) • Documents to be updated • Comments • Decision • Instructions on how to implement the change
Chart of accounts	The organisation sets up a chart of accounts that is closely related to the accounting system and takes its business and project-specific requirements into account.
Circumstances	All conditions under which the project is implemented. These can include the → project sponsor´s financial position, the political framework or prices in the buying and selling markets.
Claim	A claim is made in respect of unscheduled work or work that exceeds the contractually-agreed scope of performance and remuneration.
Claim management (CM)	Aspects of professional project management related to the structuring and prevention of claims. It includes the documentation of all data relevant for the claim, the legal and economic evaluation of this data and the assertion or rejection of claims.
Coding	The identification of an object with a code, establishing an unambiguous relationship between the object and its description. Differentiation is made between • the characters used: numerical, alphabetical, alphanumeric codes, • the structure: unstructured codes or codes with separators (e.g. /, ., -), • the purpose: identification codes as a system of ordering (every element has its code) or as a system of classification (every feature has a code).
Combined WBS	A → work breakdown structure is combined if some of its sub-tasks (at the higher levels) are object-oriented and some are function-oriented.
Communication	A process in which information is exchanged, which makes it a specific form of social interaction. Also: all technical equipment and rules for the use of such equipment to ensure communication between people and processes in a project. → Information service and → reporting for relevant processes
Configuration	Functions and physical features of a product as described in the product´s technical documentation and implemented in the product.
Configuration accounting	A process, supporting configuration management, that includes the registration and archiving of changes and status reports.
Configuration audit	Audit to ascertain whether the actual implementation status conforms to configuration documents at certain times or on certain occasions.
Configuration control	(= change management) Essential aspect of configuration management in which the planned configuration is monitored and intervening action is initiated or advised when necessary.
Configuration documents	Detailed product documentation with identification codes for configuration units and individual parts.
Configuration identification	(= configuration determination) An essential aspect of configuration management: • Breakdown of product into configuration units (CU) • Coding and identification of the CUs and the relevant documents • Description of the CU (including the regulations and processes that apply)

GLOSSARY

Configuration management	Detailed and complete compilation and documentation of project results and their systematic updating when changes in the project take place. Technical and organisational measures for configuration identification, monitoring, accounting and auditing.
Configuration manager	A project management function or position with responsibility for monitoring the target configuration and intervening with appropriate measures whenever necessary.
Configuration structure	Detailed breakdown of a product into configuration units and the systematic. → coding and identification of these units. Product of → configuration identification.
Continuous improvement process (CIP)	One of the basic → quality management methods. Continuous improvement is based on the principle of constantly seeking the root causes of problems so that all of the organisation´s systems (products, processes, activities) can be improved.
Contract	A legally-binding agreement between two parties.
Contract administration	Design, analysis, conclusion and amendment of contracts, taking into consideration interrelationships with change and claim management and the monitoring of contract execution.
Contract analysis	Detailed analysis of a draft contract provided by one party. It forms the basis for agreement on contract design between the parties to the contract, i.e. before contract conclusion.
Contract design	All processes relating to the agreement and formulation of the contract up to contract conclusion. Agreement has to be reached with regard to technical aspects, legal and commercial regulations, financing and budgeting, the incorporation of framework agreements and many other aspects.
Contract execution	All processes relating to the execution and/or amendment of the contract after it has been signed.
Contractor	From the project´s viewpoint, the contractor is the legal entity or natural person who contracts the implementation of a project.
Control	The activity of managing or exerting control over something. Also a mechanism that controls the operation of a machine.
Control charts	Charts and tables showing an order of events for controlling purposes (e.g. → milestone trend or → cost trend analysis).
Controller	(= project controller) The member of the project management team responsible for → Controlling. Generally a position with its own job description. The controller essentially performs a service function. In simplified terms, the controller is responsible for ensuring that the status of individual projects is transparent for all stakeholders at all times. He supports the project manager in his operational project management functions and, if necessary, recommends project control measures. In small projects, the controller is often the project manager.
Controlling	The on-going acquisition of current data relating to time, expenditure/costs and performance/quality (for project control), evaluation of variance analyses and, if necessary, the initiation of measures. Controlling can comprise very different activities, depending on the controller´s → authority.
Controlling measure	Intervention when an unscheduled variance occurs.
Cost	Expenditure of funds for goods or services to produce the deliverable. • Appropriation as: unit cost, overhead cost • Allocated to: → cost unit, → cost centre • Method of generation: → cost type • Time sequence: initial cost, follow-up cost, lifecycle cost
Cost baseline	Chart or table showing costs throughout the project lifecycle (y-coordinate = costs per time interval).
Cost centre	A place where costs are incurred that can be defined in terms of physical parameters or position in the organisation. For example, cost centres can be departments or individual machines. The costs can either be assigned directly to the cost centre (e.g. depreciation of the machines located in the cost centre) or apportioned with the assistance of a formula (e.g. building heating costs). The former are cost centre unit costs, the latter cost centre overhead costs.
Costing	Predetermination of project costs in terms of amount and distribution over time. → cost baseline and → total cost curve

GLOSSARY

Cost management	Determination of costs for individual activities, work packages and the project as a whole as the basis for project financing, budgeting and control.
Cost objectives	Primarily the absolute upper limits for cost in a project and its → work packages. Cost objectives can also be defined for costs that are generated over time or for the distribution of costs by cost type.
Cost rate	Costs per unit; either unit of time (e.g. per hour) or unit of measurement (e.g. per cubic metre).
Cost type	Cost unit defined in terms of method of generation, e.g.: • Personnel cost: wages and salaries, non-wage labour costs • Material expense: materials, machines, buildings • Financing cost: interest payments, charges • Services: energy, consulting • Charges: taxes and levies
Cost units	In project management, the project is always the cost unit. However, sub-tasks/sub-objects and work packages can also function as cost units, and an → object-oriented WBS is ideal as the cost unit structure.
Cost to complete	(= net income value, earned value, projected costs of work performed, budgeted cost of work performed). The costs of an activity or project in terms of its degree of completion. Estimated cost to complete means → projected costs of work/services performed.
Cost trend analysis (CTA)	A CTA is used to obtain information about the future development of → project costs based on → estimate to completion. A realistic CTA can only be made in conjunction with progress measurement. Cost deviations should be viewed as negative if they are associated with performance delays. → cost to complete
Craftsman	A type of resource, common in construction, that is defined in terms of a trade or craft (e.g. painter, bricklayer).
Critical	In project management, critical generally means crucial, decisive or important. The critical path is the longest path and therefore the duration-determining activity chain in the process schedule. Critical resources are those used if bottlenecks occur on the critical path.
Current status documentation	Documentation of the current status.
Customer	The legal entity that commissions, finances, and accepts the project. In smaller projects, this is generally a natural person who is then also the contact. In large-scale projects, it is important that the customer appoints authorised agents as members of a → steering committee.
Customer specification	All of the customer´s requirements in respect of goods or services ordered from a contractor. A list of all the customer´s or user´s requirements of the project (especially objectives, scope of delivery and services, constraints). The customer specification should also be used by the project, as customer, when it subcontracts work.
Definition of objective	The documentation of all interests and objectives relevant to a project, their evaluation, definition, prioritisation, implementation in operational objectives, and monitoring.
Degree to which objectives	Measure of (projected or actual) objective achievement. In practice, the have been attained degreeof completion is determined.
Degree of completion	Ratio of net income value/cost to complete to (budgeted) total project costs. A target and actual degree of completion can be ascertained at any time during the course of the project.
Deliverable	The subject matter of the contract.
Documentation	The systematic compilation of information about the project deliverable (inventory, user or operator documentation) and the process of its creation (development documentation).
Duration (D)	The time from the start to the finish of an activity. The number of time units in a work calendar (e.g. without non-workdays). It not only relates to activities, but also to the → project duration.
Duration of an activity	The total number of time units (e.g. hours, days) required for an activity.
Efficiency variance	The difference between the projected costs of work/services performed (= earned value, actual cost to complete) of a work package or sub-task and the costs that are actually incurred up to the review date (= → actual costs of work/services performed). If progress is accurately recorded, efficiency variance can be used to measure how cost-effectively work packages are being implemented.

GLOSSARY

Escalation	A defined process that is used when incidents occur that cannot be dealt with using conventional project management means. This requires the definition of limits, and may mean involving higher management levels, liquidating reserves and initiating emergency programmes.
Estimate at completion (EAC)	Estimate of total costs at the time of project handover.
Estimate to completion (ETC)	Estimate of anticipated costs up to project handover.
Expenses	Collective term describing the consumption of resources such as funds, working and production time, and materials.
Expense calculation	Determination of the time and resources required for all activities/work packages as the basis for project planning and control processes.
External labour	Sub-tasks/work packages awarded to third parties/sub-contractors or the product of the same. Opposite: Own labour.
Financial resources	Funds available or needed for the remuneration of work and services.
Float	(= total float) The available time, derived from the network plan, by which an activity can be extended or delayed without any impact on the project finish date.
Float, conditional	Total float available for an activity chain, taking other activities into consideration.
Forecast	1. General: obtaining information about future developments by way of surveys, scenario writing, extrapolation, regression etc. 2. In project management: prognosis about the future development of the project. The most important forecasting tools are → milestone trend analyses and → cost trend analyses.
Free float	The amount of float available when all predecessor activities are scheduled for their earliest deadlines.
Function	An area of responsibility or competence defined in terms of its content. → position
Histogram	A type of chart in which the x-axis is time. Variables (such as costs or no. of personnel required for activities in the network diagram) are plotted as y-coordinates at any time point or time interval.
Informal communication	Communication that is not governed by formal rules. Indispensable as a supplement to formal communication to ensure flexibility and ability to develop.
Information	Knowledge that reduces or eliminates uncertainty as regards the occurrence of one of several possible events.
Information flows	Movement of information between the various departments in an organisation. Information flows are an aspect of → information systems.
Information service	Targeted and needs-based provision of information to all project team members about project processes, especially the provision of information to steering committees and for documentation purposes. → report
Information system	All means of providing information and rules relating to communication within the project team and between the project team and its environment.
Institutionalisation	The assignment (of tasks or processes) to certain departments (institutions) in an organisation.
Instructions	Generic term for operational regulations.
Instruments	Material aids such as checklists, computer hard and software, office equipment and presentation technology. This includes methods/processes that are instrumentalised in checklists and software.
Interface	A technical term describing a method or piece of equipment for interconnecting systems or system elements. It is a theoretical concept to ensure that the individual interconnecting components can be clearly described, manufactured and controlled.
Jour fixe	Regular dates for meetings.
Kick-off (meeting)	Official announcement and enactment of project objectives and rules. The kick-off meeting differs from the → project start-up workshop.
Liability	Commercial obligation, an amount owed. A liability generally exists as a result of the conclusion of a contract for work or services.
Lifecycle costs	Costs that include production/initial costs as well as follow-up costs (operating costs, maintenance costs, reconstruction costs, demolition costs etc.). (The project is valued `from cradle to grave´).

GLOSSARY

Line manager	Person in charge of a department or function in the line or base organisation.
Line organisation	The hierarchical relationships between staff and departmental managers, central departmental managers and executive management team members in an organisation. In project management, line organisation refers to the vertical incorporation of project team members in their base organisation versus their horizontal incorporation in the project organisation. → matrix organisation
Logistics	Physical measures which guarantee that the → resources allocated to the implementation processes are supplied. Also refers to maintenance and waste disposal logistics.
Mailing list	A list of recipients of a certain document. In professional → information systems, all document types are assigned a mailing list.
Management agreement	A document detailing specific rules for interrelationships between managers and staff.
Management by projects	A key management concept used by base organisations, especially project-oriented organisations. The latter mainly work through projects. They initiate, implement and conclude many different projects concurrently. Management by projects enhances organisational flexibility and dynamics, decentralises operational management responsibilities, improves organisational learning and facilitates organisational change.
Matrix organisation	Form of project organisation in which all project team members continue to report to their superior in the (vertical) line organisation (e.g. depart-mental manager) while at the same time ensuring that project requirements are satisfied and carrying out instructions issued by the project manager (horizontal). This creates the image of a matrix.
Method	A systematic way of doing something, a planned process. Often used to describe defined algorithms in complex processes. Development of alternative plans so that the appropriate one can be selected.
Milestone	A significant event (e.g. → completion of a sub-task, interim acceptance) during a project.
Milestone trend analysis (MTA)	Systematic monitoring of → milestones to see how they shift over the course of the project. The milestone trend chart is one of the most important project management tools. It has two time axes. Review dates are plotted on the x-axis and projected milestone occurrence times are plotted on the y-axis.
Monitoring	Watching/supervision of processes.
Multi-project coordination	(= multi-project management) Coordination of the deadlines, resource utilisation, objectives etc. in several projects so that synergetic effects can be generated and to prevent the projects from conflicting with each other.
Natural person	In jurisprudence, a natural person is a human being perceptible through the senses and subject to physical laws, as opposed to an artificial person, i.e., an organization that the law treats for some purposes as if it were a person distinct from its members or owners.
Net value	(= value of work performed, actual cost to complete, projected costs of work/services performed, earned value). A substantiated remuneration claim, based on work performed, which is generally calculated as the cost to complete.
Network of contracts	All agreements between the project (as customer) and the line (as contractor) with regard to work and services performed for the project.
Network re-planning	A measure often necessary in scheduling. Also called rescheduling or shortening. If the project is expected to overrun the specified or required finish date, it can be re-planned by: • Overlapping critical activities • Shortening critical activities • Changing process structures
Objective setting	All processes relating to the selection and definition of → project objectives. The main process in objective setting is → the definition of objective.
Object-oriented	An object-oriented work breakdown structure defines the structure of the project result and the product. → process-oriented
Open issues list	A tool for documenting agreements made at project team meetings. It shows who has to perform which tasks and by when.

GLOSSARY

Organisation	The structures and processes in a project which have to be adapted to reflect the project's progress and are incorporated in the base organisation. → project organisation
Organisational chart	The management structure in an organisation or project, generally displayed graphically as a tree chart. A direct link between two positions means that one of the people → reports to the other person (bottom up) or has the right to issue instructions to the other person (top down).
Organisational planning	The development of a → project organisation and → processes.
Organisational structure	All binding rules relating to responsibilities, supervisory authority and reporting obligations which are generally shown in an → organisational chart.
Overhead costs	Costs that cannot be directly allocated to a cost unit which are proportionately distributed over all → cost units or cost centres.
Overlap	Occasional concurrent implementation of two or more activities in a project phase, e.g. as a result of antedating an activity. Overlap can be an effective method for shortening the project lifecycle. Overlapping different work packages can make managing individual processes more difficult.
Own contribution	The project sponsor's contribution of his own resources for the implementation of work packages, for instance.
Part-time project work	In a → matrix organisation, → project team members typically remain in their line unit and dedicate a certain proportion of their time to the project. Complications occur unless clear rules are established.
Performance variance	Difference between the → projected costs of work or services performed (= value of work performed, actual cost to complete, budgeted cost of work performed) and the projected costs of work or services to be performed (= the projected costs scheduled for work and services to be performed up to the review date). The performance variance delivers information about the extent to which the person responsible for a work package or sub-task is behind or ahead of schedule. Cost trends are used to ascertain whether a product or service is behind or ahead of schedule. The informativeness of this performance indicator depends on how reliably progress can be measured.
Portfolio chart	An illustrative chart that enables the two-dimensional project classification. It is used in the project selection process, for instance. Projects that are available for selection are evaluated or classified in terms of two criteria (dimensions). One widely used portfolio chart is the competitive advantage vs customer benefit portfolio (competitive advantage = first dimension, customer benefit = second dimension). Projects or the products that are developed in the projects are evaluated in terms of the competitive advantage that they will offer the organisation and the benefits that they will offer the customer.
Position	In the → organisational structure: an area of responsibility or competence assigned to a person. In the simplest case, each position has one → function allocated to it. In practice, this is seldom possible because, even in small-scale projects, one person often performs several different functions and in large-scale projects certain functions are allocated to several different position holders.
Precedence relationship	Quantifiable dependence between events or activities. The following standardised relationships exist between → activities in a network diagram: standard sequence (finish-to-start), start sequence (start-to-start), finish sequence (finish-to-finish) and jump sequence (start-to-finish).
Prioritisation	Definition or use of priorities in conflict situations, for example, for the • call on project team members by → project and → line, • fulfilment of conflicting objectives, • implementation of activities competing for the same resources
Probability of occurrence	The probability that a certain risk will actually occur. Probability of occurrence, like amount of loss (= impact), is a risk assessment criterion.
Processing capacity	Capacity (e.g. person days or machine hours) which is scheduled for, or consumed, during the implementation of work packages or activities.
Procedural objectives	(= process objectives) Project objectives relating to project processes (i.e. not to the project deliverable or the project result), such as interim results and transitions between phases.
Procedure	Step-by-step definition of a process. This term has several meanings, including a (primitive) pre-stage for a → method or a (complex) framework for specific methods.

GLOSSARY

Process organisation	All the rules and tools for business processes in a project (management system).
Process schedule	A schedule that divides a complex process into sub-processes (activities). It generally includes • the length, volume of work and other parameters for each activity, • precedence relationships between the activities, • earliest and latest dates.
Procurement logistics	A provisioning process initiated by a requisition order that extends as far as the provision of the material or equipment at the place of installation or use. The different procurement processes, such as supplier selection, order placement, transportation and payment are generally only performed by the project manager in an autonomous project organisation.
Product structure	Structure of the product of human activity. In projects, a differentiation is made between two detailed structures. • → work breakdown structure (→ object-oriented), providing a break-down of → work packages • → configuration structure, providing a breakdown of technical details
Programme	Major projects that comprise several individual projects. One example of a programme is the development of a new truck generation in a project that involves the automobile manufacturer and his suppliers (development of the vehicle plus all component parts, set-up of production facilities, establishment of the service network etc.). A programme manager is responsible for a programme. A programme differs from a → project portfolio because – like a project – it is a temporary undertaking. The truck programme ends when the customer is able to purchase the new truck models. The programme manager is then released from his duties.
Project	Undertaking that is characterised by an overall uniqueness of conditions, such as objectives, time, financial, human resource-related and other constraints, difference from other projects and project-specific organisation structures.
Project approval	A business decision to implement a project, the central aspect of the → project start-up.
Project budget	The total amount of funds that are made available to the project.
Project close-out	(= project conclusion) All procedures and documents that are necessary for the proper conclusion of the project, such as acceptance/handover of → project results, final accounts, → controlling, project documentation, project evaluation, → assessment, reporting.
Project control	In general: an area of supervisory responsibility with contractually defined duties and competences (variance analysis) and targeted influencing of project processes. Construction industry: responsibilities or activities that are specifically defined, for example, by the Association of Project Controllers (in Germany) or the Association of Cost Engineers (UK).
Project controller	→ controller
Project costs	Generic term for all costs incurred during the course of a project. → total project costs
Project documentation	A collection of selected, important data relating to configuration, organisation, funding, solutions, procedures and achieved project objectives.
Projected cost of work or services performed	(= value of work performed, actual cost to complete) Value of work performed which is at variance to the projected cost of that work (→ projected cost of work or services to be performed) when the project is behind schedule.
Projected cost of work or services to be performed	Projected cost for work or services to be performed by a specific date. If the work is on schedule, the projected cost for work or services performed is identical to the → projected cost for work or services to be performed. The term 'work performed' sometimes used in project management software, is misleading because work performed does not always relate to a completed activity.
Project implementation	All processes that directly contribute to arriving at a specific target situation. Also includes the (technical) planning process. → project preparation
Project information	Data for the planning, control and monitoring of a project.
Project information system	All equipment and resources, and the interrelationships between such equipment and resources, in the acquisition, processing, evaluation, onward trans-

GLOSSARY

	fer and storage of project information. Standards and data stock are also part of the project information system.
Project lifecycle	The number of time units (e.g. months, years) to implement a project. This is initially estimated, calculated and shortened if necessary, then planned, implemented, monitored, corrected as necessary and documented.
Project management costs	Expenditure of human and financial capital for the management of a project.
Project management, operational	Operational project management (= doing the project right) is the responsibility of the project manager. He has to ensure adherence to deadlines and budgets, that the product or service is delivered in the required quality and that the project is implemented to the satisfaction of the most important stakeholders.
Project management, strategic	Strategic project management (= doing the right project) is generally the responsibility of a body established for this specific purpose, e.g. the → project portfolio board. This body should not be confused with a → steering committee installed for one specific project. The members of a project portfolio board are generally the senior executives in the organisation and are responsible for the proper selection and timely abandonment of projects. They also make decisions that cannot be made by the individual project managers, but only by a body familiar with all the projects in the portfolio and with the organisation's business strategy. These decisions include the decision to approve the project budget.
Project management manual	(= PM manual) A compilation of rules that applies for the planning and implementation of all projects within an organisation.
Project management office	(= project office) The project management office ensures that the project portfolio is transparent (deadlines, resource usage, costs, functional relationships between the projects) and supports the processes of project selection and coordination. In some cases it also provides a pool of project managers, organises project management training for project team members, standardises processes and develops standards. → project controller
Project management process	All processes to be performed by the project management team within the scope of a project, including → project preparation, → project start-up, → project implementation (= management of technical planning and implementation) and → project close-out.
Project management system	(= PM system) A defined entity in the organisation that through the interaction of its units is able to prepare and implement projects.
Project management tools	Term used to describe all project management instruments and resources, especially software.
Project manual	A handbook documenting all the rules and agreements for a project (generally based on the project management manual).
Project objective	A demonstrable result to be achieved within a defined framework for the complete project.
Project objectives	All objectives related to and to be achieved in the project. Differentiation is made between • objectives relating to the project deliverable: quality, cost and time objectives, • objectives relating to the project result: process and result objectives, • process-related objectives: general and → operational objectives, • the degree to which objectives are binding: essential and non-essential objectives. The project manager has to prioritise and approve the project deliverable objectives. → project objective in the sense of product or result
Project organisation	The organisation in a project or PM system. A characteristic feature of a project organisation is its ability to vary headcount and equipment used during the different project phases. → organisation
Project participant	Person or group of people to be involved in a project because they have a vested interest in the project or will be affected by the project. Examples: customer, contractor, project manager, project team member, user of the

GLOSSARY

	project deliverable, local residents, nature conservation societies, press, public authorities. → stakeholder
Project personnel	Generic term for all people working on a project, including project managers and team members.
Project portfolio	A project portfolio comprises several related projects that are being implemented by the same organisation (e.g. all organisation projects or all investment projects). Unlike → programme managers, portfolio managers (= multi-project mangers) hold permanent positions. The project portfolio changes continually because projects are completed or abandoned or new projects are initiated. The portfolio manager does not replace the managers of individual projects in the portfolio. He differs from the programme manager in that he has a controlling function to ensure the transparency of the project portfolio.
Project portfolio board	(= project steering committee) → project management, strategic for the functions of the project portfolio board
Project preparation	All activities and processes to be performed prior to the → project start-up phase, which is when → project implementation commences.
Project prioritisation	Systematic prioritisation in projects. High priority projects generally have preferential access to resources to remove bottlenecks.
Project process	The entire process leading to the delivery of the project result. It consists, firstly, of the → project management process and then many different implementation processes.
Project progress	The project´s → degree of completion, or the number of → milestones reached.
Project release	A business decision approving the use of external services by a project. The term project release is used in different contexts: • As a go-ahead signal to prepare for → project start-up, in this case provisional project release • As a synonym for → project approval • As the go-ahead for project processes if they do not commence immediately after project release, in this case final project release
Project result	Project target situations differ depending on project type. In some cases, deliverable specifically means physical result (e.g. a building), although it is generally used – in organisation projects for instance – to describe a physical result and its environment.
Project review	Review of project progress on a specific reporting date.
Project selection	Choosing projects from a wide selection of proposals according to certain criteria, such as expected profit margin or return on investment.
Project sponsor	Legal entity or → natural person who sponsors the project.
Project staff	All people working on a project, both those who work on core project tasks and those who work on ancillary project tasks.
Project start-up	In essence, the business decision to implement an idea in project form. • The project manager and project team are named. • The → project objectives are confirmed. • The project budget is approved. • The → project manual is brought into operation. • All project files are created. Project start-up usually takes place between the → project preparation and → project implementation phases.
Project start-up workshop	A workshop attended by the project team where project objectives, the project organisation, methods etc. are drafted and agreed.
Project structure	The structure of a → project as shown in the → work breakdown structure.
Project team	A team of → natural persons who are assigned to a project to perform specific tasks.
Project team meeting	A meeting of project team members. Also called → jour fixe, if it takes place regularly on a specific day of the week or month.
Project termination	Premature termination of a project before the main project objectives have been achieved. In project management, it is quite normal to commence a certain proportion of projects where there is no guarantee that project objectives will be achieved. That´s why, in order to minimise losses, it is all the more important to abandon these projects in good time when it becomes clear that the objectives will not be achieved.

GLOSSARY

Promoter	(= project promoter) Expert promoter: a promoter with special professional competence. Power broker: a promoter with special authority.
Quality Function Deployment	(= QFD) A → quality management method that determines end-user requirements and translates them into technical objectives.
Quality	Since it relates to all characteristics/features of a product, quality also means the product itself. Quality can also describe the conformity of the performance delivered to the customer's specifications.
Quality costs	Costs that can be directly attributed to ensuring compliance with quality objectives. They include costs relating to quality assurance plans and audits, prevention and review, as well as reworking and replacements.
Quality management (QM)	All measures and rules for the assurance and documentation of product and process quality. Professional project management is quality management for projects.
Quality objectives	All project objectives that relate to the characteristics or features of the product or the target situation.
Reference base	Documentation to which all further changes are related (in → configuration management: → reference configuration).
Reference configuration	The formally agreed configuration of a product at a certain time that serves as the basis for further activities. A new reference configuration is created either at the end of a project phase or, in certain circumstances, within a project phase when multiple changes have taken place so that the project management team can keep up to date.
Reference project	A project that has been completed or least planned in detail, which is so similar in type or structure that the current project can use it as a source of cost estimates, work etc.
Relationships	According to systems theory: relationship between the individual elements in a system (e.g. in the → work breakdown structure or in a → goal system). Goals can be related to each other in different ways. They can be mutually supportive, exclusionary or neutral in effect. Mostly, however, they compete with each other and compromises have to be found. → interface
Report	A document, containing information about specific objects and timeframes, which is distributed in a specific format to specific recipients. Unlike internal memos, reports are also used to provide project information to superordinate business units, customers, banks etc.
Reporting	All rules and tools for the provision and handling of reports. → report and → information systems
Reporting formats	The form and content of certain document templates.
Reporting obligation	The duty of a position holder (generally specified in the job description) to deliver reports with pre-defined content to specific recipients at specific intervals.
Report types	Generic term for all → reporting formats and → reporting obligations.
Reserve	Time and resources not consumed if the project remains on schedule, but available if problems occur.
Reserve time	The float assigned to an activity to cover disruptions or delays. Reserve times can also be included in network diagrams as → slack time.
Resources	Personnel or materials required for the performance of work packages, for instance.
Resource levelling	A method used in resource planning in which all activities are postponed or extended to ensure that resource requirements are distributed as evenly as possible over time.
Resource limitation	A method used in resource planning which postpones or extends all activities to ensure that the existing resources (capacity) limits are not exceeded.
Resource management	Identification of the resources required, their assignment to the project as a whole and to individual activities, as well as the effective coordination and control of these resources.
Resource plan	An overview of the available or required → resources for the purpose of matching available resources to resource requirements. → Coding resources are important.

GLOSSARY

Result/deliverable	Project target situations differ depending on the project type. A result is work or services performed in a general sense, while deliverable describes the physical result (e.g. a building). In marketing terms both results and deliverables can be products. → project objective
Result objectives	(= system objectives, project deliverable objectives, task objectives) Project objectives that apply to the project target situation such as performance/functional (= quality objectives), financial objectives, socio-political and ecological objectives. Opposite: → procedural or → process objectives.
Risk	A potential event or situation with negative consequences (damage) for the overall project result, for individual planning variables or events that can lead to unexpected or damaging aspects. Project risk: the risk of the project or its objectives being jeopardised. The risk is expressed in terms of the probability of occurrence (as a percentage) multiplied by the damage caused (impact in euros).
Risk exemption	The contractual exemption of risks constitutes an agreement between the parties to the contract on risk apportionment (e.g. the apportionment of liability and insurance risks). It is therefore not a matter of ruling out risks, but of transferring risks to the contract partner or insurance company.
Risk management	The process of safeguarding the project by documenting and evaluating all potential risks and implementing measures to avert, insure, minimise or transfer these risks. It is one of the project manager´s responsibilities to eliminate, avert or minimise project risks. Risk management is based on risk analysis and assessment. Risk managers also promote project opportunities, i.e. opportunities for positive development.
Risk potential	(= risk factor, risk value) The assessment of a risk in terms of potential loss (impact) and probability of occurrence.
Schedule management	Documentation of the (technological) requirements for the project, definition of agreed dates and deadlines, including their optimisation and monitoring.
Scheduling	Documentation of the (technological) requirements for the project, definition of agreed dates and deadlines, including their optimisation. The monitoring of deadline adherence is also often defined as a function of time scheduling.
Slack time	In a network diagram: the time differential between the specified completion date of a task and the date required to meet the critical path. Slack time can be needed for technological reasons or to provide reserve time.
Solution-neutral	A necessary property of objective definition. The project objectives are formulated without (unnecessarily) ruling out potential solutions.
Specification	Detailed (→ operational, technical) description of the product´s characteristics.
Specification of inputs	A list of the quantities of materials or standard components that are required for a project and can be quantified in terms of time or costs.
Sponsor	A person or entity which donates funds or payment in kind for advertising purposes (e.g. to a sports club). In the USA, it is also used to describe the person funding a project.
Sponsoring organisation	A generic term for the organisation, authority, association etc. that commissions, finances and defines a project´s objectives. Synonym: → project sponsor
Stakeholder	A legal or → natural person with a vested interest in the project or its outcome. → project team members
Stakeholder analysis	Systematic documentation of the interests and intervention powers of all stakeholders, their classification in a stakeholder portfolio (e.g. according to influence or degree affected) and the definition of measures for interactions with stakeholders (e.g. communication, information, integration in the project team or the steering committee).
Standard network diagram	A network diagram which can be used for several (similar) projects.
Standards	A term describing two different, but related, terms: 1. All standards, rules and guidelines (some external) valid for a specific field of activity. 2. All work methods, document templates, values etc. that apply within a specific field of activity.
Standard WBS	A work breakdown structure which can be used for several (similar) projects.

GLOSSARY

Steering committee	Committee with authorised members to which project representatives report. For example, its members can be the → customer, investor(s), representatives of official bodies and public agencies. Some organisations differentiate between two kinds of steering committee: one as the project sponsor's internal committee and the other as a committee that also has external partners as members. The number of steering committee members should be kept to the minimum. It serves as a reporting, decision-making and escalation body for the project manager.
Structuring	The establishment of classification systems for products, processes, resources, costs etc. The majority of these are classified in the work breakdown structure, which also enables project definition.
Sub-task	A group of related → work packages in the → work breakdown structure. Sub-tasks can be defined at several levels, whereby each higher-level sub-task comprises a group of related sub-tasks at the next lower level. A task in the work breakdown structure that can be further sub-divided.
Supplier specification	The supplier's strategy for implementing the → customer specification. In most cases, the supplier specification is agreed between the customer and the project (manager), though it is often simply one of the contractor's internal documents.
Support processes	All preparatory and support processes, particularly the supply of materials and equipment, that are necessary for project implementation.
System of objectives	Integral, systematic list of project objectives and their interrelationships.
Time lag	A time value in a → precedence relationship.
Time objective	Latest deadline for the achievement of a project target or specific milestone.
Time required	The units of time required to implement an activity or process.
Total cost curve	Chart or table showing the development of costs over the course of the project (y-coordinate = cumulative costs up to a specific point). The total cost curve is created by adding up the → cost baseline totals.
Total project costs	The total amount of → costs incurred by a → project.
Variance	Difference between planned and realised dates, costs or quality.
WBS code	Classification system for the elements in the → work breakdown structure.
Work breakdown structure (WBS)	Systematic breakdown of a project into → sub-tasks and → work packages. The WBS can be in chart or table form, → object-oriented, → process-oriented, → function-oriented, phase-oriented or → combined.
	Systematic breakdown of the project deliverable into → sub-projects object-oriented (= objects) (e.g. in construction according to → craftsmen's tasks).
	Systematic breakdown of a project into processes (e.g. development, job process-oriented scheduling, production processes).
Work package (= WP)	An aspect of the project that is not broken down any further in the → work breakdown structure (WBS) and can be located at any of the hierarchical levels. Its purpose is to ensure the manageable bundling of tasks relating to → specification/→ call to tender – bid – order/→ contract – implementation – invoicing.
Work package description	A detailed – generally form-based – document produced for each work package that contains information about the work package, the person responsible for the work package, its content, dates and a breakdown of activities.

This glossary is based on the German Association for Project Management's PM Delta project management benchmarking system. It has been adapted and supplemented with key terms.

GLOSSARY

KEY WORDS

0-100 method	266
4-L-C	379
4-L-Q	379
4M & E method	342
5-phase model	364
90 percent syndrome	267
A united front	407
Accent	393
Acceptance	49, 52, 55, 133, analysis 207, fictive, final 66, for project management 468, 472, for project managers 315, preliminary 65, 284, protocol 55, target schedule 198, staff assessment 383
Accommodation	370
Accounting unit	208
Achievement	383
Action	systems 39, context 369
Activity	111, 176, definition 198, list 198, number, duration, description 180, postponement, cancellation, prolongation, splitting 215, start/finish 177, 180
Activity-on-arrow (AOA)	network diagram 177
Activity-on-node (AON)	network diagram 177
Actual costs	208
Actual costs of work/services performed	263
Adherence to scheduled dates and costs	137
Adjusted profit	447
Advance coordination	29
Advance performance	58
Advertising	405
After action review	296
Agile manifesto	122
Alternative projects	442
Amortisation calculation	446
Analysis of strengths and weaknesses	324
Annuity method	448
Antedating time	183, 185
Apparent objective conflict	413
Approval of next phase	113
Arbitration	424
Arbitration tribunal	65, 66
Architect and engineer contract	68
Arithmetical mean	208
Arrow	177
Assessment	255, interview 383, legal 80, process 487
Assignment	63
Assimilation	370
Attitude	371
Attribute listing	355
Audit	in quality management 251, steps 252, protocol, framework 253, control, re-audit 254
Auditor	252
Authenticity of marketing	406
Authorisation of media work	408
Authority	97, formal, informal 98, 314
Back-up transparencies	346
Backward pass calculation	187
Balanced matrix	case study 102
Balanced scorecard	248
Banana principle	121
Bandwagon effect	207
Bar chart	187, 192, 203, networked 181
Base organisation	93, 95
Baseline	229
Basic workload	resources 215
Benchmarking of projects	33, 135, 258, 384, 486
Best practice examples	project close-out 288
Best practices directory	OPM3 485
Bid	49, review 33, 134, 450

KEY WORDS

Blinkered mentality	369
Block creativity	351
Body language	337
BOOTSTRAP	257
Borderline cases	project definition 27
Bottle-neck	372
Brainstorming	150, 353, variants, anonymous, negative, imaginary 354
Brainwriting	352
Breach of patent law	64
Breakdown of phases	various project types 117
Broadband Delphi	207
Brooks´ law	142, 278
Budgeted Cost of Work Performed (BCWP)	222
Budgeting model	parametric 206
Bulletin board	399, 403
Bullying	366
Burnout syndrome	321
Business case analysis	444, static, dynamic 444
Business excellence	assessment model 246
Calculated amortisation period	447
Calculation of historical costs	291
Calendarisation	187, 194
Cancellation of the contract	58, 64
Capability Maturity Model (CMM)	33, 147, 257, 479
Capacity	utilisation 215, discrepancy, increase 279, 280
Capital	employed, return on 447, net present value 114, net present value method 448
Career stoppers	313
Cash flow surplus	447
Cash flows	225
Causal attribution	370
Cause-and-effect diagram	258, 342
Certification	of personnel, of project management systems, certification body audit 253, 378 ff., procedure 316, 317
Change	contract 74, form 78, 83, 228, 235, in the project environment 45, fear of change 469, list summarising all changes 269, log 237, management 69, 227, 234, order 64, process 236, provisions, protocol 75, request 237
Characteristic curve	137
Checklist	conflict management 425, contract content 54, project manager selection 316, risk 148, routine work 323, stakeholder analysis 43
Chief programmer concept	99
Chronological representation	331
Civil law company	62
Claim	75, additional revenue 76, adversarial -s 78, documents 81, notification 77, prevention 82, total volume of claims, total amount of 76, potential 78
Claim management	47, 66, 68, 75, 237, procedure when variance occurs 79, subjective attitudes 78, systematic work processes 79
Claim under the law of tort	65, 207
Classification of projects	37
Classification key	169
Close-out phase	99
Coach	291, 376
Coaching of projects	377
Coaction effect	368
Cockpit report	274
COCOMO model	216
Codes	234
Coding	180
Commencement of large-scale production	128
Commercial project manager	108, commercial team 106
Communication	basic principles, how it works, objectives, requirements 390, guidelines 399, informal 131, 389, introduction of project management structures 477, matrix, measures 397, rules 425
Communication	significance of 389, team 363, verbal 31, verbal, non-verbal, covert 393

KEY WORDS

Comparison methods	cost comparisons, profit comparisons and profitability calculations 446
Competence	areas 357, 383, management 384
Competition	407
Competitive relationships	140
Complementary relationships	140
Completeness check	formal 114
Completion	degree of 223, 263, date 113
Complexity of projects	25
Component structure	162
Computer projector	349
Concept phase	99
Conditional network diagram (CND)	177
Conduct	forms of 367
Confidants	291
Configuration	227, as-built 230, accounting 77, 229, deviations from the contract 77, 116, identification, monitoring, auditing 229, management 227, 229, plan 231
Configuration and change management	35, 83, 141, 227, interaction of elements 228
Conflict	constructive conflict management 425, dynamics, manifest conflicts, episode 418, escalation 418, functions 411, indicators, distribution (project phase-dependent) 417, potential of personal conduct, dealing with conflicts 419, resolution 423, type (intrapersonal/ interpersonal) 366, 412
Conjoint analysis	441
Connotation	391
Consensus	341
Consortial committee	94
Consortium	48, 60, 61, 94
Consortium contracts	62
Construction contract	pursuant to the German Civil Code, risks 67, pursuant to VOB/B 57
Construction lot	62
Construction site daily report	73
Content-related/ relationship-oriented	elements 391
Contingency model	McFarlan 36
Continuous improvement process (CIP)	247, 248, 395
Contract	34, analysis 71, administration phases 70, administration procedures 71, contract-specific terms 52, contractual autonomy 50, contractual changes 69, contractual language 65, contractual penalty 48, 58, 64, contractual relationships 59, definition of parties to the contract 48, execution (instruments) 73, 74, international 48, management 47, 66, 68, reciprocal 49, strategy 71, subject-matter of the contract 50, type 48, 51
Contract activity monitoring	74
Contract awarding procedure	68
Contract for work and services	48, law relating to 51
Contract of sale	48
Contracting rules for award of public works contracts	54
Contractor	as party to a contract 47
Control	171
Control range	96
Controlling	project handover 283, system for quality management 249
Controlling the environment	through communication 395
Convergence effect	209
Cooperation effect	368
Coordination mechanism	371
Coordination	by personal instruction, hierarchical structures, self-coordination 29, programmes and rules, plans/planning 31
Corporate	culture 337, marketing 406
Corporate design	406
Corrective measure	scheduling 173
Cost	budgeting 205, 206, centres 160, cost equation, parametric cost estimates 212, database 160, driver 206, escalation at the end of the project 284, estimate 63, fixed net cost price 136
Cost	linear distribution, actual, target cost 220, objective 136, per period 446, projected costs 168, ratios 206, 211, reimbursement price 136,

KEY WORDS

	target cost, cost control, allocation, management 168, undifferentiated 211
Cost and resource planning	205
Cost-benefit calculation	238
Cost increases	238
Cost monitoring	basic version 221, project-related 219, streamlined de-luxe version, de-luxe version 223
Cost per kilo method	211
Cost ratios	211
Cost to complete	265, estimate 221
Cost unit	208, 261
Counter-performance	49
Creativity techniques	342, 351, 352, intuitive, analytical, discursive 352
Crisis	indicators, stages of 426, kinds of (internal team crises/externally impeded teams) 427, management 396, prevention 428, project 360
Criteria/assessment fields	Project Excellence Model 255
Critical appraisal	of maturity models 489
Critical path	189, 190
Critical Path Method (CPM)	177
Culture	337, cultural background 370
Cumulative costs	113
Customer	as party to a contract 47, internal/external 433, expectations 41, survey 292
Customer specification	129, 142
Customer-supplier relationship	249
Damage	direct 66, compensation 57
Deadline	187, fixed 194, schedule deviation 278, time management 173, time objective 136
Deadline expiry	without performance being rendered 59
Decision	341, event, process 178
Decision making	efficient, matrix 325
Decision rules	project selection 442
Default	interest 58, 59
Defect	consequential damage caused by a defect 66, elimination 123, liability period 56, negligible 66
Definition phase	120
Degree of attractiveness	453
Degree of completion	265
Delegation	320
Deliverables	55
Delphi method	151, 207, 354
Deming cycle	247, 341
Denotation	391
Departmental responsibility	103, 165
Dependencies between projects	459
Design and process characteristics	258
Design verification	115
Design-to-cost approach	136, 141
Detailed network diagram	197
Detailed schedule	202
Development project	169
Dialect	393
Discharge at the project closure meeting	288
Disciplinary superior	26, 99, 316, 383
Discounting	448
Discursive strategy	395
Discussion 66	354
Disposable prototype	120
Disquiet/clarification	363
Dissolution phase	363
Document	119
Document instance	232
Document management	232
Document requirements matrix	234
Documentation	74, acceptance 234, -based methods 297, claim 80, 160, handover 233, requirements 269, 331, supporting 227, 232, tools 69
Document-driven model	119

KEY WORDS

Double charges	287
Drama triangle	421
Drawing list	73
Duration	187
Duty to cooperate	51
Duty to inform	64
Duty to renegotiate	65
Earliest date	172
Early warning function	221
Early warning indicators	268
Earned value	222
Effectiveness check	154
Effect-related objectives	136
Efficiency variance	222
E-mail	392
Engineer	53
Enneagram	359
Entry scenario	345
EST, EFT	188,194
Estimate	engineering-oriented, bottom-up 206, of costs 131, of project lifecycle/costs 137, optimistic, probable, pessimistic 210, time 178
Estimating equation	linear 213
European Foundation for Quality Management (EFQM)	246
Evaluation	at the project closure meeting 284, of messages 390
Event	176, 399, 403
Event-on-node (EON)	network diagram 177
Execution, successful	89, 283
Exemption from liability	63
Expectations	context-related 370
Expenditure and cost estimation	160
Expert surveys	207
Expression	means of expression, gestures etc. 390, phraseology 337
External consortium	61
External integration	35
External procurement	219
External projects	33
Facial expression	390, 393
Factor Criteria Metric (F-C-M) model	138
Factories Act	386
Fault	59
Feasibility study	129
Feedback	394, coordination 29, data 171, interviews 295
Fictive approval or acceptance	66
Final workshop	296
Financial resources	requirements 450, planning 224
Finish sequence	181, 184
First impression	370
First-person form	367, 393
Fixed-price contract	64
Flexible management style	373
Flip chart	349
Float	free 181, 191, free reverse float 192, hidden 172, 187, 190, independent 192, negative float 196, total 181, 190
Force majeure	65
Forecast	intuitive/analytical 341, long-term 354, medium and long-term 355, value 443
Foreign investment	450
Form-based systems	341, 342
Forward pass calculation	187
Fulfilment of objectives	time-delayed assessment of the 262
Function	business unit 159, points 212
Function point method	212
Functional project organisation	97
Gantt diagram	203
Gatekeeper	369

KEY WORDS

General contractor	59
General schedule	197, 202
General terms and conditions	48, 52
German Civil Code (BGB)	48ff
Gestures	390, 393
Graph theory	176
Graphic elements	345
Handout	347
Heterogeneity of the team	360
Homogeneity of the team	360
Honesty	396
House of Quality (HoQ)	258
ICB Taxonomy	17
Iceberg theory	422
Idea competition	399, 404
Identification key	169
Identifiers	minimum/supplementary 234
Image	284
Image perceived by others	394
Immediate-response measure	for stakeholders 45
Impact analysis	42
Impairment of use	64
Implementation phase	99
Implementation times	172
Implied warranty	56
Imputed rate of return	449
Imputed return on equity	447
Incentive system	373
Incentives	373
Incident	77
Increasing revenues	47
Independence	97
Industrial plant contract	67
Information	carrier 228, information and reporting system 107, information level, factual, emotional 390, -object 160, procurement provision 64, selective 396, selection of information for a presentation 346, (un)formatted 232
Infrastructure for project management	461
Infringement of intellectual property rights	64
In-house claim	75
In-house production	219
Innovative nature of projects	25
Innovativeness	93
Instructions	right to issue 104
Instruments	legal 69
Intangible result	262
Integrated Project Team (IPT)	94
Integrated management system	communication 395
Integrative approach	224, 225
Interaction	open 363, 390
Interdisciplinary nature of projects	25
Interested party	39
Interface	between subnets 200, 230, contractual, between deliveries 63, 168, 171, 172, when work or services overlap 63, quality management 249
Internal integration	35
Internal project	33
Internal rate of return method	448
Internal relationships in a consortium	62
Internal structuring	99
Interpretation	390, of sensory impressions 369
Intuition	325
Invalidity of a contract	50
Inventory list of documents	234
Investment	real, replacement, rationalisation, expansion 444, stand-alone 445
Investment project	34, phase breakdown 117, selection of -s 444
Invitation to tender	50
Ishikawa diagram	342

KEY WORDS

IT support	299
Iterative	estimates 207, personal skills and traits 313, process 172, problem solving 342
Job	description 132, enlargement, enrichment, rotation 377
Johari window	361
Jour fixe	254
Jump sequence	181, 184
Key practices	385
Key processes	385
Key statement presentation	345
Key word register for contract management	73
Kick-off meeting	132
Knowledge	advantage 336, carrier 372, management 149, profile 346, transfer 128
Latent phase	416
Latest date	172
Law	choice of law provision 65, chosen law 48, 65, defect in title 52, governing contracts for services 51, governing contracts of sale 51, legal act 55, legal clarity 48, legal consequence 48, 53, 57, liability for defects in title 64, of contracts 47
Lead company	94
Lead member	61
Legal aspects	47
Liability	distribution of 62, exclusion of 56, joint and several 61, limitation of 66
Life cycle costs	135
Line	department 101, organisation 93, 95, 287, manager 316
Line organisation	functional, pure 95
Links	process, rigid, flexible 186
Liquidation proceeds	445
List of strengths and weaknesses	486
List of suppliers	52
Loading profile	213
Loan interest	447
Loss category approach	152
Loss of identity	287
LST, LFT	189, 192
Management	28, by projects 439, competence 313, concepts, style 371, experience 376, functional/institutional 30, `management by´ approaches 371, potential 313, problems, recommendations 374, style 308, style, functions, techniques, skills 371
Management style	cooperative 365, 371, management by the team itself, *laissez-faire* style 372
Manager	characteristics 371, guidelines 374
Margin	76
Marketing tools	406
Maslow´s needs pyramid	376
Mass manufacture	136
Material defect	52
Matrix organisation	97, 100, balanced 102, 218
Maturity	384
Maturity model	33, 147, critical appraisal of 489, risk management 156, 479
Maturity and assessment models	sector-independent 482
Measuring, counting, weighing	35
Media	399, media enquiry, matrix 408, media work, five commandments, target group interests time, scheduling, internal coordination 407
Mediator	396
Meeting	329, minutes, template for the minutes 331, ten commandments 333
Meeting with people present	399
Mentor	291
Metaplan method	199
Metaplan technique	349
Method	switching methods 341, methodical competence 360
Metra Potential Method (MPM)	177
Metrics	138

KEY WORDS

Micro-articles	297
Micro-milestone	168, 267
Milestone	111, deadline 113, meeting 114, plan 132, result 111, 116, scheduling 202, trend analysis 274, 275, well/badly formulated 124
Minimal solution	problem 342
Minimum interest rate	449
Mistakes	119
Misunderstanding	390
Mixed contract	52
Monetary assessment	risks 150
Monetary objectives	444
Morphological boxes	355
Motivation	375, problems, methods to boost motivation 376, techniques 376
Multimedia project	349
Multiple command system	100
Multiplier	477
Multi-project management	433, 434, operational 459
Multi-project manager	436, 456, 459, core responsibilities 460
Must projects	453
Negotiation	334, strategy, result, scope for negotiation 335
NERD-F method	323
Nerves	348
Network analysis	136, 160, 175, 176, 214, 216, project logistics 219
Network diagram	definition of purpose and objective 197, methods of structuring and processing network diagrams 196
Networked bar chart	171
Nodes	176
Non-communication	394
Non-conformity	start-up phase 128, 170
Non-decision	325
Non-monetary factors	450
Non-verbal signal	391
Not invented here syndrome	291
Numbering system	74, 160
Numerical method	internal rate of return 449
Object	159, document 233
Objections	326, 329, 469
Objective	abstract, social 138, clarity of 129, compromise on -s 141, conflict of interests 40, 140, 169, 456, finish event 177, 180, objectiv formulation 128, 249, objectiv agreement 371, objectiv categories, attainment of objectives 140, objectiv definition 324, objectiv definition process 133, priorities 88, target costing 224, 225, 136, 139, variable 135, weighting 41,
Objective conflict	objective, assessment-related and distribution-related conflicts 413
Objective level	conflicts 413
Obligation	breach of 57, contractual 47, 142
Obligation to deliver a result	51
Occupational health and safety	385
Off-the-record conversations	399, 400
Open issues list	for monitoring control measures 280
Open questions	336
Operational marketing	406
Operationalisation	137, 138, 139, 315
Opinion leader	366
Opposition	34, covert 46, 129, dealing with opposition 471, resource planning 219, 469
Order	written 78, confirmation 51
Organisational objectives	94
Organisational project	34, breakdown of phases 117
Organisational Project Management Maturity Model (OPM3)	479, 482 ff.
Orientation	363
Over-/underqualificaiton	requirements profile 315
Overhead calculation	206, 225
Overhead projector	349
Overhead projector transparencies	design, numbers 346
Overlapping	183

KEY WORDS

Paper phase	229
Parallel implementation of phases	118
Parallel projects	433
Parameters	255
Partial autonomy group work	377
Participative strategy	395
Partnership	62, 68, 94
Passing the risk	56, 64
Payoff time	443
Penalties	71
People affected	389
People Capability Maturity Model (P-CMM)	384
Perception	of problems 339, 361
Performance	assessment 316, claim 55, degree of fulfilment 140, 453, 49, deviation 222, impaired 48, 49, 57, 74, 80, indicator 137, 211, 292, 368, quality objective 136, 262, reduction in scope of 279, refusal of 58, specification 81, vicarious agents 61, `zero defects´ standard 244
Performance measurement	time 89, sequence 90
Performance-enhancing effects	368
Personal responsibility	364
Personality	structure 313, 383, type 359
Personnel	deployment 131, management 381, reassignment 288, recruitment 381, selection 101, staff assessment 317, staff pool 462, staff recruitment agencies 382
Personnel requirements	determining (qualitative/quantitative) 381, planning 382
Phase	model 111, overlapping phases 117, repeat previous phase 114, 116, 119, series of phases 118
Physical result	113
Pilot version	121
Pitfalls	contract 48
Plan optimisation	173
Plan-Do-Check-Act cycle	248, 395, 406
Planning	precision 448, variables 29
PM Award	135
PM Delta	257, 486
PM-Zert	383
Portfolio	34, board 459, method, chart, competitive, advantage/customer benefit 443
Position	event/activity 187
Positive suspense	345
Possible projects	453
Post-project appraisal	296
Potential-to-succeed factors	313
Power	exertion of 396, broker 41, 326
Precedence relationship (PR)	176, 181, substitute PR 202
Predecessor	181
Prejudice	370
Pre-project phase	229
Present value method	448
Presentation	344, media 348, questions on what to include in a 346, structure 350
Presenter	347
Press	release, distribution list 409
Pressure to conform	368
Price reduction	58
Prince	111
Principal contract	59
Principle of dual control	252
Priority setting matrix	320
Pro and contra analysis	354
Proactive listening	336
Probability	178
Probability of occurrence	151
Problem	overview, definition 342, types (analysis, search-related, constellation, selection, consequential) 338, understanding problems, obstacles to solving problems 339
Problem solving	337, cycle 341, methods 341, requirements of problem-solving

KEY WORDS

Process	methods, roles 340 activity-based costing 224, 225, coordination 29, model 129, objective qualitative/quantitative 137, orientation 489, processbased methods 296
Process model	advantages 123, and quality management 118, elements of 111, conflict mediation 424, cooperative conflict regulation 423, crisis management 428, critical appraisal of 122, evolutionary, incremental, object-oriented, concurrent 121, IT sector 118, introduction of project management 472, meta/spiral model 121, projects without a suitable process model 123, standard 132
Process schedule	171, combined 177
Process structure	173
Product	committee 129, control of product costs 225, product structure plan 161, selection of product development projects 440, success 89, 283
Productive use phase	135
Productivity	objective 137, different levels 218, increase 280
Profit	136, margin 114, 136, 443
Profitability	447, target 205
Programme	manager 434, 461, management 433, 434
Progress	report 263
Progress measurement	cost information 265, problems 261, R&D projects 263, subjective indicators, milestone technique 266, time information, resource information 264
Project	integration in the base organisation 95, outside the line organisation 93
Project analysis	methods, objective level 291, relationship level 293
Project assistant	106
Project bureaucracy	120, 490
Project close-out	arguments in favour of systematic project close-out 284, definition, formal 283, meeting, final report 284, 289, project closure meeting 288, tasks 285, tasks at objective level 286, tasks at relationship level 287
Project company	94, 99
Project contract	47, 52, 55
Project control	31, 78, 106, 269, measures 278, project board 96, project steering committee 105
Project controller	106, 107
Project coordination unit	98
Project costs	estimating 205, database 166, 292
Project culture	406
Project definition	25, organisation-specific 27
Project environment	39, 227, 389, planning, control 460
Project Excellence Model	87, 89, 255, 295
Project experience database	296
Project file	270, 269
Project handover	283
Project history	128
Project hotline	399, 403
Project identity	406, 406
Project inflation	27
Projectitis	433
Project learning	210, 283, methods 291, recommendations, people responsible, learning culture, knowledge transfer, project objective, formal process, feedback mechanism 288, 289
Project learning history	297
Project lifecycle	122
Project logistics	218, 219
Project logo	347
Project management	agile 122, by software 468, definition 27, introducing PM `by decree´ 467, manual 251, 475, office 106, 462, 471, operative 129, 438, optimisation 479, strategic 438
Project Management Maturity Model	479, 482
Project management structure	93, basic forms 97, pure 98, 131, parallel 307
Project manager	68, 307, assessment of 316, 317, changes 317, conduct, appearance 313, functions 310, in a parallel project organisation 307, necessary authority 314, personal skills and traits, measurability 302, problems associated with recruitment of/solutions 308, requirements 311,

KEY WORDS

	requirements profile 315, role in the team development process 364, selection of 314,
Project manual	71, 251
Project marketing	45, 405
Project meeting	399
Project monitoring	168
Project newsletter	400
Project objective	35, making the project objective measurable 137, graphic representation 140, project manager´s responsibility 102, 129, relationship between different -s 140, relationship to business objectives 142
Project office	106, 462
Project phase	111
Project plan	129
Project presentation	399, 402
Project profile	255, 442
Project progress	measurement of 35
Project quality	249
Project report	399, 400
Project review	254
Project schedule	173
Project selection	34, and business strategy 437
Project service point	106
Project stakeholders	39
Project start-up	127, meeting, workshop 133
Project structuring	159
Project success	87, recommendations for 91
Project team	105, 129, formation of 130
Project tracking	113, 116, 325, 428
Project triangle	87
Project type	33, breakdown of phases 117, contractual risks 67, selection process for all project types 453
Project viability	assessment of 142
Project-based processes	26
Projected cost at completion	223, 263
Projected costs of work/services to be performed 223, 265	
Project-specific management structures	26
Proof	burden of 56, reversal of the onus of 66, evidence of 76
Protective clause	51
Prototyping approach	120
Psychosocial level	conflicts 413
Qualifications	249, 378, 378
Quality	in the project 255
Quality criterion	139
Quality function deployment (QFD)	258
Quality management	35, 69, 84, 123, 239, development 241, in strategic and operational management 243, methods 258, process orientation 243, standards 243
Quality management system	benefits 239, establishment of a QMS for project management 249
Quantity structure	206
Questionnaire	on project team climate 294
Questions for persons affected	by the introduction of project management structures 478
Rapid prototyping	121
Rate of interest	447
Reallocated costs	222
Recalculation	237
RECALL	297
Recognition effect	406
Reconciliation of interests	395
Reference configuration	116, 227, 230
Reference structure	164
Reference value	138
Regression analysis	212
Relationship language	391
Relationship under the law of obligations	65
Remaining silent	394
Reminder	77
Repetitive activity	225

527

KEY WORDS

Repetitive process	of producing goods and services 26
Report	obligatory report 104, 472
Reporting	language 391, problems, face-to-face dialogue, status meetings 276, requirements, requirements matrix 271 schedule 397
Representative period	447
Repressive strategy	396
Requirement	type, complexity, matrix 315, profile 382
Research and development project	34, contractual risks 67, breakdown of phases 117
Reservations	55
Resource	autonomy 97, material, intangible resources 319, pooled resources 142, schedule 216
Resource breakdown structure	216
Resource requirements	estimating 205, planning 213
Resource scheduling	214
Result objective	qualitative/quantitative 137
Retaining lien	58
Retention period	269
Return on investment	443
Return on sales	443
Revision	current status 269, estimates 137
Risk	47, acceptance problems, concealment 156, assessment, list 150, avoidance 84, 154, communication 404, control 389, handling, reduction 84, identification 148, legal risk areas 65, types 146, mitigation 84, 155, monitoring 153, response planning 154, selection 152, transfer, acceptance 155, typical project risks, occurrence 145, value 151
Risk analysis	150, difference between stakeholder analysis and risk analysis 45
Risk management	43, 83, software 155, 386, benefits of systematic 147
Risk response planning	costs 148, prevention plan for stakeholders 45, role definition 307, career stages 309
Role model	function as 319, 327
Roles	114, in the problem-solving process 340, role type, role change 365, role play 46
Routine	nature 27, project 36, work package 164,
Rule of thumb	static/dynamic processes 449
Rules	368
Rules for project team work	131
Rules for the recipient	393
Rules for the sender	393
Sabotage	43
Saying `no´	320
Scenario writing	355
Scenario-planning techniques	43
Scheduling	171, 323, basic aspects of 172, display formats 203, point in time 187
Schemata	370
Scope	229
Second chance	370
Secretiveness	389
Self-assessment	295, sheet 317, 383
Self-directed learning	329
Self-execution	58
Self-organisation	319
Self-perception	394
Self-understanding	406
Sense of belonging together	364
Sensory impression	369
Separability clause	54
Separation ritual	288
Sequential	approach 117, 118, process 96, phase model 341
Sham	478
Signatory	authorised 48
Silent consortia	62
Simulate	alternatives 173
Simultaneous engineering	118, 121
Single command	principle of 100
Six sigma	248

KEY WORDS

Skills	114
Skills profile	315
Social competence	assessment criteria for certification 315, 357, 360
Social perception	369
Social skills	384
Social structure	365
Socialisation	370
Soft factors	490
Software	claim management 80, 175, time scheduling 184, 199, development history 299, trend to sophisticated software products 300, software purchased as an alibi 301, selection 303
Specialist department	101
Specification	52, phase-oriented 197, technical 53, 120, 141
SPICE	257
Sponsored projects	33
Staff	quality management 250, assessment 383
Staff turnover rate	138
Stage-gate model	111
Stakeholder	39, classification 40, dealing with stakeholders 45, objectives 88, 129, proactive stakeholder management 131, policy 41
Stakeholder analysis	39, arguments in favour of 40, difference between risk analysis and stakeholder analysis 45, problems associated with 45
Stakeholder communication	characteristics 396, elements 399
Standard coding system	234
Standard contract	50
Standard form contract	50
Standard network analysis	200
Standard sequence	181, 183, 185
Standard work breakdown structure (WBS)	165
Standards	368, 491
Stars, flops, fads, snobs	443
Start	event 177, 180, time 128
Start phase	40, significance of 127, tasks 130, special features of 365
Start sequence	181, 184
Statistical simulation	151
Status	formal/informal 366
Status step method	267
Statute of limitations	57
Steering committee	438, project specific 97
Stereotype	370
Strategic productivity	454
Strategic relevance	454
Structural aspects	of team building 361
Structuring and change processes	389
Sub-contractor	59
Sub-model	119
Subnet	174, method 199
Sub-process	127
Sub-project	435, 99, 123, sub-project manager 106
Sub-task	159, 172
Success factors	87, project 91
Success factors method	440
Success journal	327
Successor	181
Summaries in contract analysis	71
Summarisation	197
Supplementary order	formal 64
Supplementary performance	58
Supplier specification	113, 129, 160, 438
Switch-over costs	after the project 100
System integration	marketing 406
Systematic	stakeholder communication 395
Systemised summary	331
Talking speed	393
Target costing	136, 224
Target-current variance analysis	108
Team	dynamics 368, -minded, cohesion 369, work 357, building process

KEY WORDS

Team building	131, formation and management, selection 357, development process 361, ability to work in a 361, clock 364 recommendations 358, 360, Enneagram 359, measures, formal/informal 367
Team cohesion	370
Team development	phases 363
Team dissolution	284, 364
Team estimate	207
Team management recommendations	360
Team Management System (TMS)	358
Team recycling	291
Technical project manager	106
Template	370
Termination of the contract	58
Third-party claim	75, 78
Thread	345
Time	management 320, 323, minimum time lag, maximum time lag 181, time inventory 322, time margin 187
Time schedule	171, preliminary, optimised 174
Time schedule updates	regular 173
Top management issue	introduction of project management structures 472
Total cost curve	220, scheduled 224
Total Quality Management (TQM)	84, 244, 295
Traceability	230
Traffic light report	275
Transfer of title	64
Transmitter/receiver model	390
Transparency	389
Tuckman	364
Types-of-Work wheel	359
Unambiguousness of the contract	50
Unavoidable fixed costs	320
Uniqueness of conditions	26
Uniqueness of projects	25
Unreasonableness	59
Validation	120
Value benefit analysis	450, 454
Value of work performed	223, approach 264
Variance analysis	36, 169, 173, 175, 220, 263, 276, legal 75, 79, 80
Verbal communication rules	367, 407
Verification	120
Video projector	349
Vision	407
V-model	119
Voice	392
Waiting time	185
Warning	59
Warranty	56, maintenance 66
Warranty terms	49
Waterfall model	118
Websites	399
Well-/badly-structured problem	339, 344
Win-win situation	336
Withdrawal	voluntary 288
Work	progress 222, sharing 26, tools for the project manager 319
Work breakdown structure (WBS)	132, 159, tasks 160, breakdown 161, drafting 163, rules for drafting a WBS 168, coding 169, mistakes and omissions 170, object-oriented, function-oriented 161, multidimensional, dynamic 164 subjective 206
Work package	159, description 164, oversized 168, 172, form 165, person in charge of 249, work-life balance 386
Worst-case scenario	84, 151

BIBLIOGRAPHY AND FOOTNOTES

A1 PROJECTS AND PROJECT MANAGEMENT
1. Cf. Caupin, G.; Knöpfel, H.; Morris, P.; Motzel, E.; Pannenbäcker, O.: *ICB IPMA Competence Baseline*, Version 2.0, Bremen (1999), Element 1: `Projects and Project Management´, p. 3
2. DIN 69 901
3. Rüsberg, J.H.: *Die Praxis des Project-Managements*, 2nd edition, Munich (1973), p. 20
4. Author´s opinion
5. Dülfer, E.: *Projekte und Projektmanagement im internationalen Kontext. Eine Einführung*, in Dülfer, E. (Ed.): *Projektmanagement-International*, Stuttgart (1982), p. 11
6. Frese, E.: `Ziele als Führungsinstrumente – Kritische Anmerkungen zum ``Management by Objectives´´´ in *Zeitschrift für Organisation* (1971), p. 227 – 238, specifically p. 227
7. Staehle, W.: *Management*, 2nd edition, Munich (1985), p. 43
8. Edited and supplemented for better comprehension
9. Kieser, A.; Kubicek, H.: *Organisation*, Berlin – New York (1977), p. 74 ff.
10. Staehle: *loc. cit.*, p. 436 f
11. Scacchi, W.: *Managing Software Engineering Projects. A Social Analysis*. in *IEEE Transactions on Software Engineering* (January/1984), vol. SE-10, number 1, p. 623 – 642, p. 638
12. Tushman, M. L.: `Managing Communication Networks in R&D Laboratories´ in: *Sloan Managing Review* (Winter/1979), quoting Wilemon, D. L.; Baker, B. N.: `Some Major Research Findings Regarding the Human Element in Project Management´ Cleland, D. I., King, W. R. (Eds.) in: *Project Management Handbook*, New York (1983), p. 623 – 641, p. 638

A2 PROJECT TYPES
1. Cf. ICB Element 1: `Projects and Project Management´, p. 23
2. See Schulz, G.: `Projektarten´ in *Projektmanagement* (1/1991), p. 43 – 46
3. Schulz: *loc.cit.*, p. 44
4. Schulz: *loc.cit.*
5. McFarlan, F. W. `Portfolio Approach to Information Systems´ in *Harvard Business Review*, (September/October, 1981), p. 142 – 150
6. Sizemore House R.: *The Human Side of Project Management*, Reading/Mass. (1988)
7. Grün, O.: *Taming Giant Projects*, Berlin – Heidelberg – New York (2004), p. 182 ff.

A3 STAKEHOLDER ANALYSIS
1. Patzak, G.; Rattay, R.: `4.2.6 Die Projektumfeldanalyse – Das soziale Umfeld eines Projekts (Stakeholder-Analysis)´ in Schelle, H.; Reschke, H.; Schnopp, R.; Schub, A. (Eds.): loose-leaf report *Projekte erfolgreich managen*, 6th update, Cologne (1994) ff., p. 1
2. Patzak, Rattay: *loc.cit.*, p. 5
3. Landesbausparkasse Baden-Württemberg, quoting Schelle, H.: *Projekte zum Erfolg führen. Projektmanagement systematisch und kompakt*, 4th edition, Munich (2004), p. 101 ff.
4. Hansel, J.; Lomnitz, G.: *Projektleiter-Praxis. Erfolgreiche Projektabwicklung durch verbesserte Kommunikation und Kooperation*, Berlin (1987), p. 40
5. Patzak, G.; Rattay, G.: *Projektmanagement. Leitfaden zum Management von Projekten, Projektportfolios und projektorientierten Unternehmen*, 2nd edition, Munich (1997), p. 75
6. Schulz-Wimmer, H.: *Projekte managen. Werkzeuge für effizientes Organisieren, Durchführen und Nachhalten des Projekts*, Planegg near Munich (2002), p. 115
7. Patzak, Rattay: `4.2.6 Projektumfeldanalyse´ Schelle et. al. (Eds.): loose-leaf report *Projekte erfolgreich managen*, Cologne, p. 3 ff.

A4 LEGAL ASPECTS
Further literature
1. Bernstorff, Christoph Graf von: *Vertragsgestaltung im Auslandsgeschäft*, 5th edition, Frankfurt/M. (2002)
2. Eschenbruch, Klaus: *Recht der Projektsteuerung*, 2nd edition, Düsseldorf (2002)
3. Eysel, Hans: *Vertragsrecht für Architekten und Ingenieure*, 2nd edition, Cologne (2004)
4. Girmscheid, Gerhard: *Projektabwicklung in der Bauwirtschaft*, Berlin (2003)
5. Hahn, Hans Peter: *CE-Kennzeichnung leichtgemacht*, 2nd edition, Munich (1996)
6. Heiermann, Wolfgang; Linke, Liane: *VOB Musterbriefe für Auftragnehmer*, 10th edition, Wiesbaden (2003)
7. Heiermann, Wolfgang; Linke, Liane: *VOB Musterbriefe für Auftraggeber*, 5th edition, Wiesbaden (2003)
8. Hoeren, Thomas; Flohr, Eckhart: *Vertragsgestaltung nach der Schuldrechtsreform*, Recklinghausen (2002)
9. Joussen, Peter: *Der Industrieanlagenvertrag*, 2nd edition, Heidelberg (1996)
10. Kapellmann, Klaus D.: *Juristisches Projektmanagement bei der Entwicklung und Realisierung von Bauprojekten*, Düsseldorf (1997)
11. Kapellmann, Klaus D.; Schiffers: *Vergütung, Nachträge und Behinderungsfolgen beim Bauvertrag, Vol. 2: Pauschalvertrag einschließlich Schlüsselfertigbau*, 3rd edition, Düsseldorf (2000)
12. Oppen, Andreas von: *Der internationale Industrieanlagenvertrag, Konfliktvermeidung und Erledigung durch alternative Streitbeilegungsverfahren*, Heidelberg (2001)
13. Piltz, Burghard: *UN-Kaufrecht*, 3rd edition, Heidelberg (2001)
14. Text edition of contracting rules for the award of public works contracts VOB/A and VOB/B. dtv no. 5595. 7th edition, Munich (2004)
15. Weber, Kurt E.: `Vertragsinhalte und -management. 7th edition´ RKW/GPM (Ed.): *Projektmanagement Fachmann Vol.2*, Eschborn (2003), p. 963 – 1005
16. Westphalen, Friedrich Graf von: *Allgemeine Einkaufsbedingungen nach neuem Recht*, 4th edition, Munich (2003)
17. Westphalen, Friedrich Graf von: *Allgemeine Verkaufsbedingungen nach neuem Recht*, 5th edition, Munich (2003)

Magazines and journals
1. *IBR Immobilien- & Baurecht*, id Verlags GmbH, Postfach 10 17 37, 68017 Mannheim
2. *Baurecht*, Werner Verlag, Postfach 10 53 54, 40044 Düsseldorf
3. *projektMANAGEMENT aktuell*, GPM Deutsche Gesellschaft für Projektmanagement e.V., Frankenstraße 152, 90461 Nürnberg

A5 PROJECT PERFORMANCE AND SUCCESS FACTORS
1. Lechler, Th.: *Erfolgsfaktoren des Projektmanagements*, Frankfurt/M. (1997), p. 44
2. Quoting Schelle, H.: *Projekte zum Erfolg führen. Projektmanagement systematisch und kompakt*, 3rd revised and supplemented edition, Munich (2001), p. 121
3. Strohmeier, H.: `Das aktuelle Stichwort: Was ist eigentlich Projekterfolg?´ in *projektMANAGEMENT aktuell (3/2003)*, p. 29 – 32
4. Strohmeier: *loc. cit.*
5. Lechler, Th.: *loc. cit.*, p. 44. Supplemented by the term product success
6. Lechler, Th.: *loc. cit.*, p. 45

BIBLIOGRAPHY AND FOOTNOTES

7   Lechler, Th.: `1.8 Erfolgsfaktoren des Projektmanagements – Handlungsempfehlung aus 448 deutschen Projekten´ in Schelle et. al. (Eds.): loose-leaf report *Projekte erfolgreich managen,* Cologne
8   Lechler, Th.: *loc. cit.*, p. 18 ff.
9   KPMG Strategic and Technology Service Group (Ed.): `What went wrong? Unsuccessful Information Technology Projects 1997´; The Standish Group International Inc. (Ed.): `Chaos (Application Project and Failure January 1995´; KPMG Great Britain (Ed.): `Why do so many projects still fail when we invest so much in training?´ *KWORLD* January (2001) (Daily Telegraph survey). All three works quote Gaulke, M. in *Risikomanagement in IT-Projekten*, Munich – Vienna (2002), p. 35 f.
10 Cf. the separate case studies in: Heilmann, H.; Etzel, H.-J.; Richter, R. (Eds.) *IT-Projektmanagement-Fallstricke und Erfolgsfaktoren-Erfahrungsberichte aus der Praxis*, 2nd edition, Heidelberg (2003)

A6   PROJECT ORGANISATION

1   Kummer, W. A.; Spühler, R. W.; Wyssen, R.: *Projekt Management. Leitfaden zu Methode und Teamführung in der Praxis*, Zurich (1985), p. 48
2   Grün, O.: Article entitled `Projektorganisation´ in Frese, E. (Ed.) *Handwörterbuch der Organisation*, 3rd entirely revised edition, Stuttgart (1992), p. 2102 – 2116
3   Madauss, B.-J.: `6.2.2 Internationales Projektmanagement´ Schelle, H.; Reschke, H.; Schnopp, R.; Schub, A. (Eds.): loose-leaf report *Projekte erfolgreich managen,* 1st update, Cologne (1994) ff.
4   *Ibid.* p. 8
5   Cf. Seibert, S.: *Technisches Management. Innovationsmanagement, Projektmanagement, Qualitätsmanagement*, Stuttgart – Leipzig (1998), p. 294
6   Madauss: *loc. cit.*, p. 5
7   Schröder, H.-J.: *Projekt-Management. Eine Führungskonzeption für außergewöhnliche Vorhaben*, Wiesbaden (1973), p. 27
8   Keyword `steering committee´ (no author). in Specht, D.; Möhrle, M. G. (Eds.): *Gabler Lexikon Technologie Management, A–Z*, Wiesbaden (2001), p. 158
9   ICB Element 22, p. 44
10 Cf. Reschke, H.; Svoboda, M.: *Projektmanagement. Konzeptionelle Grundlagen*, Munich (1984), p. 63 f.
11 Grün: *loc. cit.*, p. 2102 – 2116
12 Frese, E.: *Grundlagen der Organisation*, 4th reviewed edition, Wiesbaden (1988), p. 467
13 *Ibid.* p. 473
14 Cf. Lumbeck, T.: *Struktur-Organisation von DV-Projekten* in Molzberger, P.; Schelle, H. (Eds.): *Software. Moderne Methoden zur Planung, Überwachung und Kontrolle der Entwicklung*, Munich (1981), p. 121 – 14
15 Knöpfel, H.: `6.2.1 Alternativen der Projektorganisation´ in Schelle et. al. (Eds.): loose-leaf report *Projekte erfolgreich managen,* 12th update, p. 32
16 Daenzer, W. F. (Ed.): *Systems Engineering. Leitfaden zur methodischen Durchführung umfangreicher Planungsvorhaben*, Zurich (1976), p. 135
17 Cf. Vasconcelles, E.: `A Model for a Better Understanding of the Matrix Structure´. *IEEE Transactions on Engineering Management.* (EM-26, No. 3, August 1979), p. 56 – 63
18 Staehle, W.: *Management*, 2nd edition, Munich (1985), p. 448
19 Gemünden, H. G.; Lechler, Th.: `Dynamisches Projektmanagement. Grenzen des formalen Regelwerks´ in *Projektmanagement* (2, 1998), p. 8

20 Further details in Hilpert; Rademacher; Sauter, G.: *Projektmanagement und Projektcontrolling im Anlagen- und Systemgeschäft*, 6th edition, Frankfurt/M., p. 37, and Reschke, H.: `8.3 Tätigkeitsbild: Projektkaufmann/-frau´ in Schelle; Reschke; Schnopp; Schub: loose-leaf report *Projekte erfolgreich managen*, 11th update
21 Horvath, P.: *Controlling*, 5th edition, Munich (1994), p. 826
22 Campana, C.; Reschke, H.; Schott, E.: `6.2.3 Project Office-Implementierung und Verankerung im Unternehmen´ in Schelle et. al. (Eds.): loose-leaf report *Projekte erfolgreich managen*, 18th update, Cologne, p. 3
23 Hilpert; Rademacher; Sauter: The authors´ version has been slightly abridged, p. 37
24 Further details in Hilpert; Rademacher; Sauter: *loc. cit.*, p. 37

B   PROCESS MODELS

1 Office of Government Commerce (Ed.): *Managing Successful Projects with Prince 2*, London (2003)
2 Versteegen, G.: *Projektmanagement mit dem Rational Unified Process*, Berlin – Heidelberg – New York (2000), p. 23
3 Cf. Balzert, H.: *Lehrbuch der Software-Technik. Software-Management – Software – Qualitätssicherung – Unternehmensmodellierung*, Heidelberg – Berlin (1998), p. 98 ff.
4 Seibert, S.: *Technisches Management. Innovationsmanagement – Projektmanagement – Qualitätsmanagement*, Stuttgart – Leipzig (1998), p. 301
5 Source: Siemens AG
6 Madauss, B. J.: *Handbuch Projektmanagement*, 5th edition, Stuttgart (1994), p.158
7 Source: Siemens AG
8 Patzak, G.; Rattay, G.: *Projektmanagement. Leitfaden zum Management von Projekten, Projektportfolios und projektorientierten Unternehmen*, 2nd edition, Munich (1997), p. 158 ff.
9 Schmelzer, H. J.; Buttermilch, K. H.: `Reduzierung von Entwicklungszeiten in der Produktentwicklung als ganzheitliches Problem´ in Brockhoff, K. et. al. (Ed.): `Zeitmanagement in Forschung und Entwicklung´ *Zeitschrift für betriebswirtschaftliche Forschung* (special issue 23/1988), p. 43 – 72, p. 61 specifically
10 See Schnopp, R.: `Concurrent (Simultaneous) Engineering und Projektmanagement´ in Schelle, H.; Reschke, H.; Schnopp, R.; Schub, A. (Eds.): loose-leaf report *Projekte erfolgreich managen*, 4th update, Cologne (1994) ff.
11 Schmelzer, H. J.: *Organisation und Controlling von Produktentwicklungen*, Stuttgart (1992), p. 30 ff.
12 In ISO 9001: 2000 the elements still exist. However they are very confusing when it comes to the main processes in the new standard structure. Section 4.4 of the old standard, which covers design management, corresponds to the new standard 7.3. Cf. Schönbach, G.: *Keine Angst vor ISO 9001:2000. Leitfaden für Manager, Beauftragte und Prozesseigner auf die 2. Normenrevision*, Eschborn (2001)
13 The Bavarian Ministry of Economic Affairs, Infrastructure, Transport and Technology (Ed.): *Qualitätsmanagement für kleine und mittlere Unternehmen. Ein Leitfaden zur Einführung eines Qualitätsmanagementsystems*, Munich (1994), p. 12
14 Balzert: *loc. cit.*, p. 97 ff, provides a more detailed overview
15 Hindel, B.; Hörmann, K.; Müller, M.; Schmied, J.: *Basiswissen Software-Projektmanagement. Aus- und Weiterbildung zum Certified Project Manager nach dem iSQI-Standard*, Heidelberg (2004), p. 15
16 Versteegen: *loc. cit.*, p. 29

BIBLIOGRAPHY AND FOOTNOTES

17 For further details see Schaaf, M.: `7.3.3 Vorgehensmodell der Bundeswehr: Aktivitäten, Produkte und Projektstrukturplanung für ein typisches F&E-Projekt mit DV-Anteil´ in Schelle et. al. (Eds.): loose-leaf report *Projekte erfolgreich managen,* 7th update and www.v-modell.iabg.de

18 V-Modell. Entwicklungsstandard für IT-Systeme des Bundes. Vorgehensmodell. Brief description at www.v-modell.iabg.de/prod.htm, p. 5 (1.9.2004)

19 e.g. Balzert: *loc. cit.*, p. 113

20 Details about the prototyping approach and the various kinds of prototypes at Balzert: *loc. cit.*, p. 114 ff.

21 Balzert: *loc. cit.*, p. 122

22 Hindel et. al.: *loc. cit.*, p. 21

23 Weltz, F.: `Softwareentwicklung im Umbruch: Projektmanagement als dynamischer Prozess´ in Balck, H. (Ed.): *Networking und Projektorientierung. Gestaltung des Wandels in Unternehmen und Märkten*, Berlin – Heidelberg – New York (1996), p. 211 – 220, specifically p. 217

24 Steinmetz, A.: `Management von mittleren Softwareprojekten´ in Ottmann, R.; Grau, N. (Eds.): *Projektmanagement-Strategien und Lösungen für die Zukunft,* 17th German Project Management Forum 2000 in Frankfurt/M. and in Berlin (2002), p. 139 – 154

25 www.swikull.com/north/1088.htm (28.2.2001)

26 Grahl, J.; Puchan, J.; Senzenberger, A.: `Systematisches Management eines Jahr-2000-Projekts´ in Etzel, H.-J.; Heilmann, H.; Richter, R. (Eds.): *IT-Projektmanagement – Fallstricke und Erfolgsfaktoren. Erfahrungsbericht aus der Praxis*, Heidelberg (2000), p. 230

C1 PROJECT START-UP

1 Gareis, R.: `Der professionelle Projektstart´ in *Projektmanagement* (3/2000), p. 23 – 29, specifically p. 23

2 Anders, Th.: `2.3 Zielfestlegungen bei Produktentwicklungen´ in Schelle, H.; Reschke, H.; Schnopp, R.; Schub, A. (Eds.): loose-leaf report *Projekte erfolgreich managen*, Cologne (1994), p. 5 ff.

3 Krause, H.: `Erfahrungen mit dem Phasenmodell zur Entwicklung und Beschaffung von Wehrmaterial´ in Schelle, H. (Ed.): *Symposium Phasenorientiertes Projektmanagement*, Cologne (1989), p. 75 – 97, specifically p. 94

4 Representative of many: Thaller, G. E.: *Software-Test-Verifikation und Validation*, 2nd updated and supplemented edition, Hanover (2002), p. 39

5 Möller, K. H.: `Ausgangsdaten für Qualitätsmetriken – Eine Fundgrube für Analysten´ in Ebert, Ch.; Dumke, R. (Eds.): *Software-Metriken in der Praxis. Einführung und Anwendung von Software-Metriken in der industriellen Praxis*, Berlin – Heidelberg – New York, p. 105 – 116, specifically p. 111

6 Lechler, Th.: *Erfolgsfaktoren des Projektmanagements*, Frankfurt/M. (1997), p. 278

7 Schulz, G.: *Der Projektsteuerungsvertrag*, Cologne (1989), p. 23

8 Saynisch, M.: `4.7.1 Konfigurationsmanagement: Konzepte, Methoden, Anwendungen und Trends´ in Schelle et. al. (Eds.): loose-leaf report *Projekte erfolgreich managen*, p. 33

9 Gareis: *loc. cit.*, p. 25

10 Lomnitz, G.: `4.2.4 Der Projektvereinbarungsprozess von der Projektidee zum klaren Projektauftrag: Sage mir, wie Dein Projekt beginnt, und ich sage Dir, wie es endet´ in Schelle et. al. (Eds.): loose-leaf report *Projekte erfolgreich managen*, 5th update, p. 2

11 Platz, J.: `4.2.7 Der erfolgreiche Projektstart´ Schelle et. al. (Eds.): loose-leaf report *Projekte erfolgreich managen*, 9th update, p. 7

12. Lembke, P. M.: *Strategisches Produktmanagement*, Berlin – New York (1980), particularly p. 211 ff.
13. Platz: *loc. cit.*, p. 14
14. Heilmann, H.: `Erfolgsfaktoren des IT-Projektmanagements´ in Heilmann, H.; Etzel, H.-J.; Richter, R. (Ed.): *IT-Projektmanagement – Fallstricke und Erfolgsfaktoren. Erfahrungsberichte aus der Praxis*, 2. revised and supplemented edition, Heidelberg (2003), p. 5 – 39, specifically p. 33
15. Gareis: *loc. cit.*, p. 27
16. Detailed description of the bid process in VDI-Gesellschaft Entwicklung Konstruktion Vertrieb (Ed.): *Angebotsbearbeitung – Schnittstelle zwischen Kunden und Lieferanten. Kundenorientierte Angebotsbearbeitung für Investitionsgüter und industrielle Dienstleistungen*, Berlin – Heidelberg (1999)
17. Cf. Madauss, B. J.: `4.2.5 Projektdefinition´ in Schelle et. al. (Eds.): loose-leaf report *Projekte erfolgreich managen*, 6th update, Cologne

C2 PROJECT OBJECTIVES

1. German Association for Project Management (Ed.): *The International German Project Management Award 2001. Application Brochure*, Nuremberg (2002), p. 3. Brief summary at www.GPM-IPMA.de
2. Cf. Zapletal, I.; Schub, A.: `4.6.8 Lebenszykluskosten und Lebensdauer von baulichen Anlagen´ in Schelle, H.; Reschke, H.; Schnopp, R.; Schub, A. (Eds.): loose-leaf report *Projekte erfolgreich managen*, 5th update, Cologne (1994) ff.
3. Cf. Seidenschwarz, W.; Niemand, S.; Esser, J.: `4.6.6. Target Costing und seine elementaren Werkzeuge´ Schelle et. al. (Eds.): loose-leaf report *Projekte erfolgreich managen*, 10th update
4. Quoting Rüsberg, K. H.: *Die Praxis des Projektmanagements*, Munich (1971), p. 94 ff.
5. Boehm, B. W.: *Wirtschaftliche Software-Produktion*, Wiesbaden (1981), p. 22
6. Wasielewski, v. E.: `Grundzüge einer Projektvergleichstechnik´ in Saynisch, M.; Schelle, H.; Schub, A. (Eds.): *Projektmanagement. Konzepte, Verfahren, Anwendungen*, Munich (1979), p. 372 – 397, specifically 373
7. Chestnut, H.: *Systems Engineering Methods*, New York: Wiley (1967)
8. Balzert, H.: *Lehrbuch der Software-Technik. Software-Management, Software-Qualitätssicherung, Unternehmensmodellierung*, Heidelberg – Berlin (1998), p. 257 ff.
9. Platz, J.: *priv. comm.*
10. Daenzer, W. (Ed.): *Systems Engineering. Leitfaden zur methodischen Durchführung umfangreicher Planungsvorhaben*, Cologne (1976), p. 76
11. Weinberg, G.; Schulman, E.: `Goals and Performance in Computer Programming´ in *Human Factors* (16/1974), p. 70 – 77
    Good tips on goal formulation can be found in Schulz-Wimmer, H.: *Projekte managen. Werkzeuge für effizientes Organisieren, Durchführen und Nachhalten von Projekten*, Planegg near Munich (2002), p. 124 ff.
12. Source: Siemens AG

C3 PROJECT RISKS

1. Versteegen, G. (Ed.): *Risikomanagement in IT-Projekten. Gefahren rechtzeitig erkennen und meistern*, Berlin – Heidelberg – New York (2003), p. 21

BIBLIOGRAPHY AND FOOTNOTES

2   Similar to the US project management bible: Project Management Institute (Ed.):
    A Guide to the Project Management Body of Knowledge, PMBOK Guide 2000 Edition,
    Newton Square, Pennsylvania (2000), p.12
3   Versteegen: *loc. cit.*, p. 3
4   Cf. Gaulke, M.: `4.2.9 Risikomanagement in IT-Projekten´ in Schelle, H.; Reschke, H.; Schnopp,
    R.; Schub, A. (Eds.): loose-leaf report *Projekte erfolgreich managen*, 22nd update Cologne
    (1994) ff.
5   Dymond, K. M.: *CMM Handbuch*, Berlin – Heidelberg – New York (2002), p. 128
6   Webb, S.; Sidler, Ch.; Meermans, R.: `The New Basel Accord and the Impact on Financial
    Information Technology Project Risk Management´ in Ottmann, R.; Grau, N.; Schelle, H. (Eds.):
    Making the Vision Work. Proceedings of the 16th IPMA World Congress on Project Management,
    Berlin (2002), p. 311 – 315
7   Quoting Gaulke: *loc. cit.*, p. 3
8   Steeger, O.: `Trotz ``Quantensprung´´ noch viele Einsparungspotenziale. PM-Benchmarking-
    Studie nimmt Finanzdienstleister unter die Lupe´ in *projektMANAGEMENT aktuell* (4/2003),
    p. 11 – 13, specifically 12, and Kalthoff, Ch.; Kunz, S.: `Projektmanagement bei der Entwick-
    lung kritischer Softwaresysteme. Fraunhofer Institute (IITB) announces survey results´ in
    projekt MANAGEMENT aktuell (2/2004), p. 33 – 35, specifically p. 36
9   Hilpert, N.; Rademacher, G.; Sauer, B.: *Projekt-Management und Projekt-Controlling im Anlagen-
    und Systemgeschäft*, 6th edition, Frankfurt/M. (2001), p. 169
    The checklist has been slightly modified to make it easier for readers to understand.
10 Franke, A.: *Risikobewusstes Projekt-Controlling*, Cologne (1993), Appendix p. 7 (series written
    by H. Schelle and published by the German Association for Project Management)
11 Versteegen: *loc. cit.*, p. 105
12 Füting, U. C.: *Troubleshooting im Projektmanagement*, Frankfurt – Vienna (2003), p. 119 ff.
13 DIN Deutsches Institut für Normung e.V. (Ed.): *Risikomanagement für Projekte – Anwendungs-
    leitfaden*, DIN IEC 62 198: 2002 – 09
14 Franke, A.: `4.2.2. Risikomanagement im Anlagen- und Systemgeschäft´ in Schelle et. al.
    (Eds.): loose-leaf report *Projekte erfolgreich managen*, p. 16 ff.
15 *Ibid.* p. 34
16 Versteegen: *loc. cit.*, p. 108
17 *Ibid.*
18 Etzel, H.-J.; Vollberg, H.: `Sanierung eines IT-Projekts – Einführung einer Standardsoftware
    zur Vertriebsabwicklung´ in Heilmann, H.; Etzel, H.-J.; Richter, R. (Eds.): *IT-Projektmanagement.
    Fallstricke und Erfolgsfaktoren. Erfahrungsberichte aus der Praxis*, 2nd updated and supple-
    mented edition, Heidelberg (2003), p. 315 – 350, specifically 327 f.
19 More details from Versteegen: *loc. cit.*, p. 68 ff.
20 Schelle, H.: *Projekte zum Erfolg führen. Projektmanagement systematisch und kompakt*,
    3rd edition Munich (2001), p. 106 ff.
21 Gaulke: *loc. cit.*, p. 21
22 Kalthoff, Kunz: *loc. cit.*
23 *Loc. cit.*, p. 41
24 DeMarco, T.; Lister, T.: *Waltzing with Bears. Managing Risks on Software Projects*, Dorset
    House (2003)
25 Dymond: *loc. cit.*, p. 129
26 Hall, E.M.: *Managing Risk – Methods for Software Systems Development* Boston (1998),
    p. 178

C4 WORK BREAKDOWN STRUCTURE

1. Cf. detailed explanation of project-specific cost management
2. VDMA (Ed.): *Projekt-Controlling bei Anlagengeschäften*, Frankfurt/M. (1982)
3. Saynisch, M.: *Konfigurations-Management. Entwurfssteuerung, Dokumentation, Änderungswesen*, Cologne (1984), p. 163, Vol. 1 of the series written by H. Schelle and published by the German Association for Project Management
4. Platz mentions an exclusively object-oriented WBS, then also a product structure or object structure, and a performance-oriented WBS. Cf. Platz, J.: Section entitled: `Projektplanung´, Platz, J.; Schmelzer, H. J.: *Projektmanagement in der industriellen Forschung und Entwicklung. Einführung anhand von Beispielen aus der Informationstechnik*, Berlin (1986), p. 144; Platz, J.: `4.3.1 Projekt- und Produktstrukturpläne als Basis der Projektplanung´ in Schelle et. al. (Eds.): loose-leaf report *Projekte erfolgreich managen*
5. Platz: `Projektplanung´, *loc. cit.*, p. 148
6. Platz: `Projektplanung´, *loc. cit.*, p. 149 ff.
7. Peylo, E.: `Neues Verfahren der dreidimensionalen Projektaufgabenstrukturierung´ in Wolff, U. (Ed.): *Projektmanagement-Forum 93 conference documents*, Munich (1993), p. 427 – 434
8. Madauss, B.: *Projektmanagement. Ein Handbuch für Industriebetriebe, Unternehmensberater und Behörden*, Stuttgart (1984), p. 183
9. Hirzel, M.: `Durch Standardisierung Innovationsprojekte beschleunigen´ in Hirzel, Leder & Partner (Ed.): *Speed-Management. Geschwindigkeit zum Wettbewerbsvorteil machen*, Wiesbaden (1992), p. 81 – 101, specifically p. 92
10. Seibert, S.: *Technisches Management. Innovationsmanagement, Projektmanagement, Qualitätsmanagement*, Stuttgart – Leipzig (1998), p. 330
11. Reschke, H.; Svoboda, M.: *Projektmanagement. Konzeptionelle Grundlagen*, Munich (1984), p. 17
12. Andreas, D.; Sauter, B.; Rademacher, G.: *Projekt-Controlling und Projektmanagement im Anlagen- und Systemgeschäft*, 5th edition, Frankfurt/M. (1992), p. 128
13. Reschke, Svoboda: *loc. cit.*
14. Miller, P. F. (Ed.): *Project Cost Databanks. Working Party Report Association of Project Managers in conjunction with DHSS-Directorate of Work Construction Cost Intelligence*, London (1988), p. 40
15. Burghardt, M.: *Projektmanagement. Leitfaden für die Planung, Überwachung und Steuerung von Entwicklungsprojekten*, Munich (1988), p. 204

C5 TIME SCHEDULING

1. DIN 69 900, Part 1, Definition of Network Planning Terms (August/1987)
2. DIN 69 900, Part 2, Definition of Network Planning Presentation Methods (August/1987)
3. Elmaghraby, S. E.: *Activity Networks*, New York – London – Sydney – Toronto (1977)
4. Goldratt, E. M.: *Critical Chain*, Great Barrington, MA (1997) and Goldratt, E. M.: *Die kritische Kette – Das neue Konzept im Projektmanagement,* Frankfurt/M. (2002), German translation and Techt, U.: `Das aktuelle Stichwort: Critical-Chain-Projektmanagement (A New Keyword: Critical Chain Project Management)´ in *projektMANAGEMENT aktuell* (2/2005), p. 14 – 15

Further literature

1. Albert, I.; Högsdal, B.: `4.4.2 Meilenstein-Trendanalyse (MTA)´ in Schelle, H.; Reschke, H.; Schnopp, R.; Schub, A. (Eds.): loose-leaf report *Projekte erfolgreich managen*, 5th update, Cologne (1994) ff.
2. DIN 69 901, *Projektmanagement* (August/1987)
3. Groh, H.; Gutsch R. W. (Eds.): *Netzplantechnik*, Düsseldorf (1982), p. 36

BIBLIOGRAPHY AND FOOTNOTES

4 Müller, D.: `4.4.1 Methoden der Ablauf- und Terminplanung von Projekten´ in Schelle, et. al. (Eds.): loose-leaf report *Projekte erfolgreich managen*
5 Reschke, H.; Schelle H.; Schnopp, R. (Eds.): *Handbuch Projektmanagement, Vol. 1 and 2*, Cologne (1989), Schwarze, J.: *Projektmanagement mit Netzplantechnik*, Herne – Berlin (2001)
6 *Ibid.*, Übungen zur Netzplantechnik

C6   COST AND RESOURCE PLANNING

1 Hilpert, N.; Rademacher, G.; Sauer, B.: *Projektmanagement und Projektcontrolling im Anlagen- und Systemgeschäft*, 6th edition, Frankfurt/M. (2001), p. 79
2 Brockhoff, K.: *Prognoseverfahren für die Unternehmensplanung*, Wiesbaden (1977), p. 63 and 87
3 Hilpert, Rademacher, Sauter: *loc. cit.*, p. 77
4 For further details of the method compare to Boehm, B. W.: *Wirtschaftliche Softwareproduktion*, Wiesbaden (1986), p. 284 f.
5 Cf. Wolf, M. L. J.; Mlekusch, R.; Hab, G.: *Projektmanagement live. Instrumente, Verfahren und Kooperationen als Garanten des Projekterfolgs,* 5th revised edition with CD Renningen (2004), p. 111 ff.
6 Füting, U. Ch.: *Troubleshooting im Projektmanagement* Frankfurt – Vienna (2003), p. 90
7 For IT projects see Bundschuh, M.; Fabry, A.: *Aufwandschätzung von IT-Projekten*, Bonn (2000), p. 280 ff. and for building engineering: Mayer, P. E.: `4.6.2 Kostendatenbanken und Kostenplanung im Bauwesen´ in Schelle, H.; Reschke, H.; Schnopp, R.; Schub, A. (Eds.): loose-leaf report *Projekte erfolgreich managen,* Cologne (1994) ff.
8 Cf. Brandenberger, J.; Ruosch, E.: *Projektmanagement im Bauwesen*, Zurich (1985), p. 136
9 VDI-Gesellschaft Entwicklung – Konstruktion – Vertrieb (Ed.): *Angebotsbearbeitung – Schnittstelle zwischen Kunden und Lieferanten*, Berlin – Heidelberg – New York (1999), p. 124 ff.
10 Hutzelmeyer, H.; Greulich, M.: *Baukostenplanung mit Gebäudeelementen. Vollständige Hochbaukosten nach DIN 276*, Cologne-Braunsfeld (1983)
11 Mayer: *loc. cit.*, p. 19
12 For details refer to Bundschuh; Fabry: *loc. cit.*, p. 280 ff.
13 Miller, P. F. (Ed.): *Project Cost Databanks. Working Party Report. Association of Project Managers in conjunction with DHSS-Directorate of Works Construction Cost Intelligence*, London (1988)
14 Seibert, S.: `Softwaremessung, quantitative Projektsteuerung und Benchmarking. Wie helfen sie dem Software-Projektmanager?´ in *projektMANAGEMENT aktuell* (4/2003)
15 Bundschuh, M.: `4.6.9 Die Function-Point-Methode im praktischen Einsatz bei Softwareprojekten´ in Schelle et. al. (Eds.): loose-leaf report *Projekte erfolgreich managen*, p. 8
16 For details refer to Bundschuh; Fabry: *loc. cit.*, p. 188 ff.
17 Großjohann, R.: `Kostenschätzung von IT-Projekten´, Ebert, Ch.; Dumke, R. (Eds.): *Software-Metriken in der Praxis*, Berlin – Heidelberg – New York (1996), p. 117 – 141
18 Scheuring. H.: *Der www-Schlüssel zum Projektmanagement*, Zurich (2002), p. 171
19 *Ibid.* p. 183
20 Scheuring, H.: `Ressourcenplanung: Sache der Linie´ in *Projektmanagement* (3/1996), p. 25
21 Schwarze, J.: `Projektlogistik´ in Bloech, J.; Ihde, G. B. (Eds.): *Vahlens Großes Logistiklexikon*, Munich (1996), p. 846
22 Gudehus, T.: *Logistik – 1. Grundlagen, Verfahren und Strategien*, Berlin – Heidelberg – New York (2000), p. 37

23 Cf. Ihde, G. B.: *Transport, Verkehr, Logistik. Gesamtwirtschaftliche Aspekte und einzelwirtschaftliche Handhabung*, 2nd entirely revised and supplemented edition, Munich (1991), p. 231 ff.
24 Gewald, K.; Kasper, K.; Schelle, H.: *Netzplantechnik. Methoden zur Planung und Überwachung von Projekten. Vol. 3: Kosten- und Finanzplanung*, Munich-Vienna (1974), p. 68
25 Schelle, H.: `4.6.1 Projektkostenplanung und -kontrolle: Überblick und neuere Entwicklungen` Schelle et. al. (Eds.): loose-leaf report *Projekte erfolgreich managen*, 14th update
26 Burghardt, M.: *Projektmanagement. Leitfaden für die Planung, Überwachung und Steuerung von Entwicklungsprojekten*, Berlin – Munich (1988), p. 297
27 Andreas, D.; Rademacher, G.; Sauter, B.: `7.3.1 Projektcontrolling bei Anlagen- und Systemgeschäften` in Schelle et. al. (Eds.): loose-leaf report *Projekte erfolgreich managen* and Hilpert, N.; Rademacher, G.; Sauter, B.: *Projektmanagement und Projekt-Controlling im Anlagen- und Systemgeschäft*, 6th edition, Frankfurt/M. (2002), p. 88 ff.
28 Seidenschwarz, W.: `Target Costing und Prozesskostenrechnung` IFUA Horvath und Partner GmbH (Eds.): *Prozesskostenmanagement. Methodik, Implementierung, Erfahrungen*, Stuttgart (1991), p. 49 – 70, specifically p. 50
29 Krause, H.: `Erfahrungen mit dem Phasenmodell zur Entwicklung und Beschaffung von Wehrmaterial` in Schelle, H. (Ed.): *Symposium Phasenorientiertes Projektmanagement*, Cologne (1989), p. 75 – 97, specifically p. 94
30 Lachnit, L.; Ammann, H.; Becker, B.: *Controllingkonzeption für Unternehmen mit Projektleistungstätigkeit. Modell zur systemgestützten Unternehmensführung bei auftragsgebundener Einzelfertigung, Großanlagenbau und Dienstleistungsgroßaufträgen*, Munich (1994)
Further literature
A detailed explanation of project logistics with numerous checklists can be found in: Riethmüller, W.; Lamping H.: `3.3 Projektlogistik im Anlagenbau` in Schelle et. al. (Eds.): loose-leaf report *Projekte erfolgreich managen*

C7 CONFIGURATION AND CHANGE MANAGEMENT

1 Versteegen, G.; Weischedel, G. (Eds.): *Konfigurationsmanagement*, Berlin – Heidelberg – New York (2002), p. 2
2 PM-DELTA glossary published by GPM
3 DIN EN ISO 10007. Beuth Verlag, (1996)
4 Saynisch, M.: `Konfigurationsmanagement: Konzepte, Methoden, Anwendungen und Trends` in Schelle, H.; Reschke, H.; Schnopp, R.; Schub, A. (Eds.): loose-leaf report *Projekte erfolgreich managen*, Cologne (1994) ff., p. 6, Fig. 4.7.1-1
5 DIN 69904. Projektwirtschaft – Projektmanagementsysteme – Elemente und Strukturen (11/00)
6 Versteegen: *loc. cit.*, p. 7
7 DIN EN ISO 10007
8 Saynisch: *loc. cit.*, p. 31, Fig. 4.7.1–8
9 Pannenbäcker, K.: *Projektmanagement-Fachmann*, Eschborn (2003), p. 1051, Fig. 4.5 – 13
10 Saynisch: *loc. cit.*, p. 14, Fig. 4.7.1 – 5
11 *Ibid.*, p. 12, Fig. 4.7.1 – 4

C8 QUALITY MANAGEMENT
Further literature
1 Akao, Y.: *QFD – Quality Function Deployment – Wie die Japaner Kundenwünsche in Qualität umsetzen*, Landsberg am Lech (1992)

2   Bechler, K. J.: `Projektmanagement im Unternehmen richtig einführen – eine Herausforderung für Unternehmensleitung und Unternehmensberater´ Lange, D. (Ed.): *Management von Projekten. Know-how aus der Beraterpraxis*, Stuttgart (1995)
3   Clutterbuck, D.; Crainer, S.: *Die Macher des Managements*, Vienna (1991)
4   Crosby, P. B.: *Qualität ist und bleibt frei*, Vienna (1996)
5   DIN (Ed.): *Qualitätsmanagement und Statistik – Anleitung zur Auswahl aus der Normenreihe DIN EN ISO 9000 und den unterstützenden Normen, Normensammlung*, Berlin – Vienna – Zurich (2004)
6   Frehr, H.-U.: *Total Quality Management – Unternehmensweite Qualitätsverbesserung*, Munich – Vienna (1993)
7   Hauser, J. R.; Clausing, D.: `The House of Quality´ in *HBR* (5 – 6/1988), p. 63 – 73
8   Hummel, T.; Malorny, C.: *Total Quality Management – Tips für die Einführung*, Munich (1996)
9   Kamiske, G. F.; Brauer, J.-P.: *ABC des Qualitätsmanagement*, Munich – Vienna (1996)
10 Lümkemann, H.: *Das Capability Maturity Model (CMM)*, Dortmund (2000)
11 Motzel, E.: `Zertifizierung im Projektmanagement – aktueller Stand in der Bundesrepublik Deutschland´ in *Projektmanagement*, Cologne (2/1996)
12 Ottmann, R.: `Qualitätsmanagement mit DIN EN ISO 9000 – Projektmanagement effizient einführen´ in Lange, D. (Ed.): *Management von Projekten. Know-how aus der Beraterpraxis*, Stuttgart (1995)
13 Ottmann, R.: `Projektmanagement, die Mega-Methode zur Krisenbewältigung´ in Feyerabend F.-K.; Grau, N. (Eds.): *Aspekte des Projektmanagements – Eine praxisorientierte Einführung*, Giessen (1995)
14 Theden, P.; Colsman, H.: *Qualitätstechniken – Werkzeuge zur Problemlösung und ständigen Verbesserung*, Munich – Vienna (1996)
15 Zink, K. J.; Voss, W.: *Wettbewerbsvorsprung durch Qualität*, Eschborn (1997)

Websites
1   SPICE – Software Process Improvement and Capability Determination
    Website (http://www.sqi.gu.edu.au/spice/), 23.04.2004
2   BOOTSTRAP
    Website (http://www.synspace.com/D/Assessments/bootstrap.html)

C9 PERFORMANCE MEASUREMENT AND PROJECT CONTROL
1   Motzel, E.: `Fortschrittskontrolle im Anlagenbau´ in Reschke, H.; Schelle H.; Schnopp, R.: *Handbuch Projektmanagement, Vol. I.*, Cologne (1989), p. 509 – 528 (I) and Motzel, E.: `4.9.2 Fortschrittskontrolle bei Investitionsprojekten´ in Schelle, H.; Reschke, H.; Schnopp, R.; Schub, A. (Eds.): loose-leaf report *Projekte erfolgreich managen*, Cologne (1994) ff. (II)
2   Souder, E. E.: `Experiences with a R&D Project Control Model´ in *IEEE Transactions on Engineering Management*, Vol. EM-15 (1968), p. 39 – 49
3   Wehking, F.: `Projektfortschrittsmessung und -berichterstattung bei F&E-Projekten´ in Reschke, H.; Schelle H.; Schnopp, R.: (Eds.): *Handbuch Projektmanagement, Vol I*, p. 493 – 508, specifically p. 501
4   Motzel, E.: *Fortschrittskontrolle im Anlagenbau (I)*, p. 518
5   NASA (Ed.) *DOD and NASA PERT/Cost Guide* Washington (1962)
6   Seibert, S.: `Softwaremessung, quantitative Projektsteuerung und Benchmarking. Wie helfen sie dem Software-Projektmanager?´ in *projektMANAGEMENT aktuell* (4/2003), p. 26 – 34, specifically p. 28
7   For details refer to Bundschuh, M.; Fabry, A.: *Aufwandschätzung von IT-Projekten*, Bonn (2000), p. 179 ff.

8. Seibert: *loc. cit.*, p. 32
9. Weinberg, G.: *The Psychology of Computer Programming*, New York (1971), p. 101
10. Souder: *loc. cit.*
11. Wehking: *loc. cit.*, p. 499. Cf. Rüsberg, K. H.: *Die Praxis des Projektmanagements*, Munich (1971), p. 94
12. Wehking: *loc. cit.*, p. 499
13. *Ibid.*
14. Motzel, E.: *Fortschrittskontrolle I and II*
15. Souder, E. E.: `The Validity of Subjective Probability of Success Forecasts by R&D Project Managers´ in *IEEE Transactions on Engineering Management*, EM-16 (1964), p. 35 – 49
16. Browne, N.: *The Program Manager´s Guide to Software Acquisition Best Practices*, Arlington, VA (1995), quoting Hall, E. M.: *Managing Risk. Methods for Software Development*, Boston (1998), p. 112
17. Quoting Gaulke: *loc. cit.*, p. 33
18. Madauss, B. J.: *Handbuch Projektmanagement*, 5th revised and supplemented edition, Stuttgart (1994), p. 230
19. Wünnenberg, H.: `4.9.3 Die Projekt-Status-Analyse´ Schelle et. al. (Eds.): loose-leaf report *Projekte erfolgreich managen*, 8th update, p. 3
20. Siemens AG
21. Wolf, M. L. J.: `Die Projektstatusbesprechung als Informationsdrehscheibe nutzen´ in Schelle et. al. (Eds.): loose-leaf report *Projekte erfolgreich managen*, 10th update, p. 15
22. *Ibid.* p. 15 f.
23. Platz, J.: `4.9.1 Aufgaben der Projektsteuerung – Ein Überblick´ in Schelle et. al. (Eds.): loose-leaf report *Projekte erfolgreich managen*, Cologne, p. 233 ff.
24. *Ibid.* p. 233 ff.

C10 PROJECT CLOSE-OUT AND PROJECT LEARNING

1. Patzak, G.; Rattay, G.: *Projektmanagement. Leitfaden zum Management von Projekten, Projektportfolios und projektorientierten Unternehmen*, 2nd edition, Munich (1997), p. 380
2. Hansel, J.; Lomnitz, G.: *Projektleiter-Praxis. Erfolgreiche Projektabwicklung durch verbesserte Kommunikation und Kooperation*, New York – Berlin – Heidelberg (1987), p. 194
3. Hamburger, D. A.; Spirer, H. F.: `Project Completing´ in Kimmons, R. L.; Loweree, J. H. (Eds.): *Project Management: A reference for professionals*, New York (1989), p. 587–616
4. Geissler, Kh.: *Schlußsituationen. Die Suche nach dem guten Ende*, Weinheim – Basle (1992), p. 34
5. Sackmann, S.: `6.5.1 Teambildung in Projekten´ in Schelle, H.; Reschke, H.; Schnopp, R.; Schub, A. (Eds.): loose-leaf report *Projekte erfolgreich managen*, 6th update, Cologne (1994) ff., p. 31f.
6. Doujak, A.; Rattay, G.: `Phasenbezogenes Personalmanagement in Projekten´ in Gareis, R. (Ed.): *Projekte und Personal. Projektmanagementtag 1990*, Vienna (1991), p. 109 – 116
7. A very detailed agenda for a project closure meeting can be found in the book by Kerth, N. L.: *Post Mortem. Projekte erfolgreich auswerten*, Bonn (2003)
8. E.g. Wolf, M. L. J.; Mlekusch, R.; Hab, G.: *Projektmanagement live. Instrumente, Verfahren und Kooperation als Garanten des Projekterfolgs*, 5th revised edition, Renningen (2004), p. 213 and Gareis, R.: *Happy Projects*, Vienna (2003), p. 374 f.
9. Schelle, H.: *Projekte zum Erfolg führen*, 4th edition, Munich (2004), p. 282
10. Cf. Mayer, P. E.: `4.6.2 Kostendatenbanken und Kostenplanung im Bauwesen´ Schelle et. al. (Eds.): loose-leaf report *Projekte erfolgreich managen*, Cologne

11 Seibert, S.: `Softwaremessung, quantitative Projektsteuerung und Benchmarking. Wie helfen sie dem Software-Projektmanager?´ in *projektMANAGEMENT aktuell* (4/2003), p. 26 – 34
12 Möller, K.; Paulish, D. J.: *Software Metrics*, London (1993)
13 George, G.: `4.10.4 Kennzahlen und Kennzahlensysteme für das Projektmanagement´ Schelle et. al. (Eds.): loose-leaf report *Projekte erfolgreich managen*
14 Patzak, Rattay: *loc. cit.*, p. 403
15 Streich, R. K.; Marquardt, M.: `Projektteamverfahren´ in Streich, R. K.; Marquardt, M.; Sanden, H. (Eds.): *Projektmanagement. Prozesse und Praxisfelder*, Stuttgart (1996), p. 32 – 58, specifically p. 42 f.
16 Ottmann, R.: `4.10.2 Projektbenchmarking PBM – Analyse der besten Praktiken´ in Schelle, H. et. al. (Eds.): loose-leaf report *Projekte erfolgreich managen*, 10th update, Cologne, p. 15
17 Schindler, M.; Eppler, M. J.: `Harvesting project knowledge: A review of project learning methods and success factors´ in *International Journal of Project Management* (21/2003), p. 219 – 228

C11 IT SUPPORT

1 Dworatschek, S. provides a detailed description: `5.2 Projektmanagement-Software´ in Schelle, H.; Reschke, H.; Schnopp, R.; Schub, A. (Eds.): loose-leaf report *Projekte erfolgreich managen*, Cologne (1994)
2 Ahlemann, F.: Comparative Market Analysis of Project Management Systems. University of Osnabrück, 2nd edition, Osnabrück (2004) (www.pm-studie.de) and Schelle, H. `Benchmarking von PM-Software. Vergleichende Analyse der Universität Osnabrück´ in *projektMANAGEMENT aktuell* (4/2003), p. 35 – 39
3 Hayek, A.: *Projektmanagement-Software. Anforderungen und Leistungsprofile. Verfahren der Bewertung und Auswahl sowie Nutzungsorganisation von Projekt-Software*, Cologne (1993), p. 25 (series written by H. Schelle and published by GPM)
4 Cf. Bartsch-Beuerlein, S.; Klee, O.: *Projektmanagement mit dem Internet. Konzepte und Lösungen für virtuelle Teams*, Munich – Vienna (2001), p. 107 ff. and Schott, E.; Campana, Ch., Kuhlmann, A.: `5.4 Unterstützung des Projektmanagements durch IT-Plattformen´ in Schelle, H. et. al. (Eds.): loose-leaf report *Projekte erfolgreich managen*, 15th and 16th update, Cologne
5 Schott et. al.: *loc. cit.*
6 Graf, G.; Jordan, G.: `Virtuelles Teammanagement im Projekt. Eine neue Herausforderung im Umgang mit Hochleistungsteams – ein Diskussionsansatz´ in *projektMANAGEMENT aktuell* (3/2002), p. 21 – 28, specifically p. 27
7 Scheuring, H.: *Der www-Schlüssel zum Projektmanagement*, Zurich (2002), p. 185 f.
8 The survey was conducted in spring 2002 by Dr. Karsten Hoffmann, Aresh Yalpani and the author on behalf of GPM. All results are published on www.asynchron.de.
9 Ahlemann: *loc. cit.*, p. 63 ff.

D1 PROJECT MANAGER

1 Chapter C, p. 67
2 DIN 69 901
3 Hansel, J.: `6.5.2.4 Mit Projektcoaching schwierige Projektsituationen erfolgreich meistern´ in Schelle, H.; Reschke, H.; Schnopp, R.; Schub, A. (Eds.): loose-leaf report *Projekte erfolgreich managen*, 13th update, Cologne (1994) ff., p. 9
4 *Ibid.* p. 10

BIBLIOGRAPHY AND FOOTNOTES

5. Also refer to: Kuhlmann, U. 'Was ist wichtig bei der Besetzung von Projektleiterstellen?' in *Projektmagazin* (Online), issue 16/02, p. 2
6. Sackmann, S. A.: '6.5.1 Teambildung in Projekten'. Schelle et. al. (Eds.): loose-leaf report *Projekte erfolgreich managen*, 6th update, Cologne, p. 5 f.
7. *Ibid.*
8. ICB: *loc. cit.*, p. 67
9. Hofstetter, H.: '1.5 Der Faktor Mensch im Projektmanagement' in Schelle et. al. (Eds.): loose-leaf report, *Projekte erfolgreich managen*, 3rd update, Cologne, p. 16
10. ICB Chapter C, p. 68 – 75
11. Wildemann, B.: *Professionell führen*, 4th extended edition, Neuwied (1999), p. 51 ff.
12. Lechler, T.: '1.8 Erfolgsfaktoren des Projektmanagements' in Schelle et. al. (Eds.): loose-leaf report *Projekte erfolgreich managen*, 8th update, Cologne, p. 14 f.
13. Lechler: *loc. cit.*, p. 18 f.
24. Knöpfel, H.; Gray, C.; Dworatschek, S.: 'Projektorganisationsformen: Internationale Studie über ihre Verwendung und ihren Erfolg' in *Projekt Management* (1992), No. 1, p. 3 – 14 (see also Chapter A6)
15. Kessler, H.: '9.2 Auswahl und Einsatz von Projektpersonal – Checklisten' in Schelle et. al. (Eds.): loose-leaf report *Projekte erfolgreich managen*, 21st update, Cologne, p. 2
16. Meyer, H.: 'Personalwirtschaft und Projektmanagement' in *Projektmanagement-Fachmann* (GPM/RKW), p. 1223
17. *Ibid.* p. 1224
18. Motzel, E.: '8.2 Qualifizierung und Zertifizierung von Projektpersonal' in Schelle et. al. (Eds.): loose-leaf report etc., 9th update, Cologne, p. 46
19. Kessler, *loc. cit.*, p. 6 ff
20. PM-Zert

D2 TOOLS FOR THE PROJECT MANAGER

1. According to Rohwedder, A.; Milszus, W.: 'Selbstmanagement' Projektmanagement-Fachmann (GPM/RKW), p. 393 ff.
2. *Ibid.* p. 393 ff.
3. According to Seiwert, L.: *Mehr Zeit für das Wesentliche*, Landsberg (1994)
4. According to Rohwedder; Milszus: *loc. cit.*, p. 393 ff.
5. Lomnitz, G. ' "Nicht-Entscheiden" hat System – Ursachen erkennen und richtig reagieren' in *Projekt Magazin (online)*, (issue 17/03)
6. According to an unpublished draft by Ottmann, R., Munich (2004)
7. Gordon, T.: *Managerkonferenz*, 18th edition, New York (1999), p. 67
8. ICB, p. 53
9. According to Pannenbäcker, O.: 'Methoden zur Problemlösung' in *Projektmanagement-Fachmann* (GPM/RKW), p. 841 ff. From: Battelle-Institut (Ed.): *Battelle-Marketing-Compendium – Probleme und Methoden des Marketing in der Produktions- und Investitionsgüterindustrie. Bericht über ein Gruppenprojekt*, Frankfurt (1974)
10. Bergfeld, H.: 'Kreativitätstechniken' in *Projektmanagement-Fachmann* (GPM/RKW), p. 811 ff.
11. According to Pannenbäcker: *loc. cit.*, p. 842
12. Kellner, H.: 'Richtig präsentieren: Drei Kernbotschaften an das Unterbewusstsein steigern Ihren Erfolg' in *Projekt Magazin* (online)
13. Kellner, H.: *Ganz nach oben durch Projektmanagement*, p. 195
14. According to Wittenzellner, C.: *Präsentieren*, Munich (2001), Chapter 27
15. *Ibid.*

16 *Ibid.* Chapter 15 ff.
17 According to an unpublished draft by Ottmann, R., Munich (2004)
18 Bergfeld, H.: `3.9 Kreativitätstechniken´ *Projektmanagement-Fachmann* (GPM/RKW), p. 809 ff.
19 *Ibid.*
20 *Ibid.*

D3 BUILDING AND MANAGING COMPETENT TEAMS
1 GPM/RKW (Ed.): `Soziale Kompetenz´ in *Projektmanagement-Fachmann* (GPM/RKW), p. 269 f.
2 According to Ullrich/Ullrich de Muynck: *Projektmanagement-Fachmann* (GPM/RKW), (1978), p. 270
3 Högl, M.: *Teamarbeit in innovativen Projekten. Einflussgrößen und Wirkungen*, Wiesbaden (1998), p. 164 f.
4 *Ibid.* p. 97
5 Sackmann, S. A.: `6.5.1 Institutionensysteme in Projekten´ in Schelle, H.; Reschke, H.; Schnopp, R.; Schub, A. (Eds.): loose-leaf report *Projekte erfolgreich managen*, 6th update, Cologne (1994) ff., p. 39
6 *Ibid.*, p. 6 ff.
7 Refers to Denison, D. R.; Hart, S.L.; Kahn, J. A.: `From Chimneys to Cross-Functional Teams: Developing and Validating a Diagnostic Model´ in *Academy of Management Journal 1996*, issue 39, no. 4, p. 1005 – 1023.
8 Mayrshofer D.; Ahrens, S.: `6.5.3.3.3 Der Teamentwicklungsprozess´ Schelle et. al. (Eds.): loose-leaf report *Projekte erfolgreich managen*, 13th update, Cologne, p. 6 f.
9 Ingham, H.; Luft, J.: *The Johari window, a graphic model for interpersonal relations. Western Training laboratory in Group Development*, Los Angeles, University of California, Extension Office (1955)
10 Langmaack, B.; Braune-Krickau, M.: *Wie die Gruppe laufen lernt*, 5th edition, Weinheim (1995)
11 ICB, p. 45
12 Mayrshofer; Ahrens: *loc. cit.*, p. 7 f.
13 ICB: *loc. cit.*
14 According to Schelle, H.: *Projekte zum Erfolg führen*, 4th revised edition, Munich (2004), p. 72
15 ICB: *loc. cit.*
16 Baitsch, C. quoted by Denisow, K. in `Soziale Strukturen, Gruppen und Team´ in *Projektmanagement-Fachmann* (GPM/RKW), 1994, St. Gallen, p. 348
17 According to: Hofstätter, P. R.: *Gruppendynamik*, Hamburg (1986)
18 Baitsch: *loc. cit.*
19 According to Hofstätter: *loc. cit.*
20 Baitsch: *loc. cit.*, p. 348
21 According to Wittstock, M.; Triebe, J.: `Soziale Wahrnehmung´ in *Projektmanagement-Fachmann* (GPM/RKW), p. 277 ff.
22 *Ibid.*
23 *Ibid.*
24 Staehle, W.: *Management*, 2nd edition, Munich (1985), p. 436 ff.
25 ICB, p. 75
26 Högl: *loc. cit.*, p. 166 f.
27 Schelle, H.: *Projekte zum Erfolg führen*, p. 67

28 Gregor-Rauschtenberger, B.; Hansel, J.: *Innovative Projektführung*, Berlin – Heidelberg – New York, p. 33 ff.
29 Sprenger, R. K.: *Mythos Motivation. Wege aus einer Sackgasse*, 16th edition, Frankfurt – New York (1999)
30 According to Maslow´s needs´ pyramid (Maslow 1954)
31 Hansel, J.: `6.5.2 Mit Projektcoaching schwierige Projektsituationen erfolgreich meistern´ in Schelle et. al. (Eds.): loose-leaf report *Projekte erfolgreich managen*, 9th update, p. 24
32 ICB, p. 57
33 PM-Zert
34 Meyer, H.: `Personalwirtschaft und Projektmanagement´ in *Projektmanagement-Fachmann* (GPM/RKW), p. 1227

Further literature

1 Palmer, H.: *The Eneagram in Love & Work*, Harper Collins (1995)

D4 COMMUNICATION

1 Müller, G.: `Konflikte vermeiden durch aufrichtiges Kommunizieren´ in *Projekt Magazin* (online)
2 Mayrshofer, D.; Kröger, H.: *Prozesskompetenz in der Projektarbeit: Ein Handbuch für Projektleiter, Prozessberater und Berater mit vielen Praxisbeispielen*, Hamburg (1990), p. 89
3 Wolf, M. L. J.: `4.9.4 Die Projektstatusbesprechung als Informationsdrehscheibe nutzen´ Schelle, H.; Reschke, H.; Schnopp, R.; Schub, A. (Eds.): loose-leaf report *Projekte erfolgreich managen*, 10th update, Cologne, p. 7
4 Mayrshofer D.; Ahrens, S.: `6.5.3 Konflikte im Projekt´ in Schelle et. al. (Eds.): loose-leaf report *Projekte erfolgreich managen*, 13th update, Cologne, p. 15 f.
5 *Ibid.*
6 Abresch, J.-P.: `Projektumfeld und Stakeholder´ in *Projektmanagement-Fachmann* (GPM/RKW), p. 76
7 Wolf: *loc. cit.*, p. 4
8 *Ibid.*
9 ICB 21, p. 43
10 Kellner, H.: *Ganz nach oben durch Projektmanagement*, p. 195
11 Oechtering, R. P.: `Theorie kontra Praxis: Wie offen lassen sich Projektrisiken kommunizieren?´ in *Projekt Magazin* (online), issue 14/03
12 Kellner: *loc. cit.*, p. 191

D5 CONFLICTS AND CRISES

1 ICB 26, p. 48
2 Sackmann, S. A.: `6.5.1 Teambildung in Projekten´ Schelle, H.; Reschke, H.; Schnopp, R.; Schub, A. (Eds.): loose-leaf report *Projekte erfolgreich managen*, 6th update, Cologne, p. 13
3 For example, Glasl, F.: *Confronting Conflict – A first-aid kit for handling conflict*, Hawthorn Press (1999)
4 ICB 26, p. 48
5 Schelle, H.: *Projekte zum Erfolg führen*, 4th edition, Munich (2004), p. 234 ff.
6 Mayrshofer, D.; Kröger, H.: *Prozesskompetenz in der Projektarbeit: Ein Handbuch für Projektleiter, Prozessberater und Berater mit vielen Praxisbeispielen*, Hamburg (1990), p. 29 ff.
7 Mayrshofer D.; Ahrens, S.: `6.5.3 Konflikte im Projekt´ Schelle et. al. (Eds.): loose-leaf report *Projekte erfolgreich managen*, 13th update, p. 4
8 *Ibid.*, p. 9 ff.

BIBLIOGRAPHY AND FOOTNOTES

9. Pondy, L. R.: `Organisationaler Konflikt: Konzeptionen und Modelle´ Türk, K. (Ed.): *Organisationstheorie*, Hamburg (1975), p. 235 – 251
10. According to Glasl: *Confronting Conflict – A first-aid kit for handling conflict*, Hawthorn Press (1999)
11. Kellner, H.: *Projekte konfliktfrei führen*, Munich – Vienna (2000), p. 42
12. Mayrshofer; Kröger: *loc. cit.*, p. 89 (slightly modified)
13. According to Fleischer, T.: *Zur Verbesserung der sozialen Kompetenz von Lehrern und Schulleitern*, Hohengehren (1990), p. 144 f.
14. ICB 26, p. 48
15. According to Mayrshofer, Kröger: *loc. cit.*, p. 89
16. Ibid., p. 90 (slightly modified)
17. According to Redlich, A.: *Konfliktmoderation* Hamburg (1997), p. 3 ff.
18. ICB 26, p. 48
19. Neubauer, M.: `4.9.5 Krisenmanagement in Projekten´ in Schelle et. al. (Eds.): loose-leaf report *Projekte erfolgreich managen*, 14th update, Cologne, p. 1 ff.
20. Gareis, R.: *Happy Projects*, Vienna 2003, p. 361
21. Gareis: *loc. cit.*, p. 362; Schelle: *loc. cit.*, p. 230; Neubauer, M.: *Krisenmanagement in Projekten. Handeln, wenn Probleme eskalieren*, Berlin – Heidelberg – New York (1999), p. 20
22. According to Neubauer, M.: `4.9.5 Krisenmanagement in Projekten´ in Schelle et. al. (Eds.): loose-leaf report *Projekte erfolgreich managen*, 14th update, p. 4 f.
23. Triebe, J. K.; Wittstock, M.: *Konfliktmanagement* (WS p. 441)
24. Glasl, F.: *Confronting Conflict – A first-aid kit for handling conflict*, Hawthorn Press (1999)
25. Neubauer: *loc. cit.*, p. 8

    Further literature
    1. Sparrer, I.; Varga von Kibed, M.: *Ganz im Gegenteil. Tetralemmaarbeit und andere Grundformen Systemischer Strukturaufstellungen*, Heidelberg (2003)
    2. Rosenberg, M. B.: *Nonviolent Communication: A language of life*, Puddledancer Press (2003)

E1 PROGRAMME AND MULTI-PROJECT MANAGEMENT
1. VDI-Gesellschaft Entwicklung – Konstruktion – Vertrieb (Ed.): *Angebotsbearbeitung – Schnittstelle zwischen Kunden und Lieferanten*, Berlin – Heidelberg (1999), p. 7
2. Lomnitz, G.: *Multiprojektmanagement. Projekte planen, vernetzen und steuern*, Landsberg am Lech (2001), p. 22
3. *Ibid.* p. 23
4. *Ibid.* p. 72

E2 PROJECT SELECTION AND BUSINESS STRATEGY
1. Cf. Schelle, H.: `2.2 Projektmanagement und Geschäftsfeldstrategie´ in Schelle, H.; Reschke, H.; Schnopp, R.; Schub, A. (Eds.): loose-leaf report *Projekte erfolgreich managen*, 7th update, Cologne (1994) ff.
2. Scheuring, H.: *Der www-Schlüssel zum Projektmanagement*, Zurich (2002), p. 169
3. King, W. R.: `The Role of Projects in the Implementation of Business Strategy´ in Cleland, D. I., King, W. R. (Eds.): *Project Management Handbook*, 2nd edition, New York (1988), p. 129 – 39
4. Seibert, S.: `Auf dem Weg zum projektorientierten Unternehmen: PM-Experten zur Zukunft des Projektmanagements´ in *projektMANAGEMENT aktuell* (4/2004), p. 3 – 11, specifically p. 4
5. Gareis, R.: `1.4. Management by Projects´ in Schelle, H. et. al. (Eds.): loose-leaf report *Projekte erfolgreich managen*, Cologne, p. 40 ff.

6 Melzer, B.H.; Kerzner, H.: *Strategic Planning: Development and Implementation*. Blue Ridge Summit (1989), p. 253

7 Schubert, B.: *Entwicklung von Konzepten für Produktinnovationen mittels Conjoint-Analysen*, Stuttgart (1991), p. 281

8 Investment appraisal is an extensive subject area in business studies. A lot of time has to be invested in learning how to perform one and it requires financial mathematical skills. We can only provide a very brief introduction in this textbook. Readers who are interested in learning more should take a look at the very well structured and informative book by Grob (see No. 13 in this list).

9 Wöhe, G.; Döring, U.: *Einführung in die Allgemeine Betriebswirtschaftslehre*, 20th revised edition, Munich (2000); Chapter entitled `Investitionsplanung und Investitionsrechnung´, p. 617 ff. The other information about investment appraisals closely follows this chapter.

10 Horvath, P.: *Controlling*, 5th edition, Munich (1994), p. 461

11 Wöhe; Döring: *loc. cit.*, p. 633

12 *Ibid.*

13 Grob, H. L.: *Einführung in die Investitionsrechnung. Eine Fallstudiengeschichte*, Munich (2001), p. 36

14 Cf. Seibert, S.: *Technisches Management. Innovationsmanagement – Projektmanagement – Qualitätsmanagement*, Stuttgart – Leipzig (1998), p. 262 ff.

15 Horvath: *loc. cit.*, p. 461

16 Ruttkamp, P.; Eicker, M.: `Controlling in Aktion´ in *Controller Magazin* (1978), p. 205 – 220, specifically p. 214

17 VDI-Gesellschaft Entwicklung – Konstruktion – Vertrieb (Ed.): *Angebotsbearbeitung – Schnittstelle zwischen Kunden und Lieferanten. Kundenorientierte Angebotsbearbeitung für Investitionsgüter und industrielle Dienstleistungen*, Berlin – Heidelberg – New York (1999), p. 73 ff. and Hilpert, N.; Rademacher, G.; Sauter, B.: *Projekt-Management und Projekt-Controlling im Anlagen- und Systemgeschäft*, 6th edition, Frankfurt/M. (2001), p. 65 ff.

18 Lange, D.: `Projekte frühzeitiger ¨controllen¨ ´ in Lange, D. (Ed.): *Management von Projekten. Know-how aus der Beraterpraxis*, Stuttgart (1995), p. 21 – 45

19 Kühn, F.; Hochstrahs, A.; Pleuger, G.: `Steuerung des Projektportfolios nach Strategiebezug- und Wirtschaftlichkeit´ in Hirzel, M.; Kühn, F.; Wollmann, P.: *Multiprojektmanagement. Strategische und operative Steuerung von Projektportfolios*, Frankfurt/M. (2002), p. 52

20 Abresch, P.; Hirzel, M.: `Synergien in der Projektelandschaft erkennen und nutzen´ Hirzel; Kühn; Wollmann: *loc. cit.*, p. 110 – 116, specifically p. 114

21 Gackstatter, S.; Habenicht, W.: `4.2.8 Projekte auswählen durch ganzheitliche F&E-Programm- planung´ in Schelle, H. et. al. (Eds.): loose-leaf report *Projekte erfolgreich managen*, 11th update, Cologne

E3 OPERATIONAL MULTI-PROJECT MANAGEMENT

1 Lomnitz, G.: *Multiprojektmanagement. Projekte planen, vernetzen und steuern*, Landsberg am Lech (2002), p. 52

2 *Ibid.*, p. 57 ff.

3 Patzak and Rattay: *loc. cit.*, p. 441

4 For more details, refer to Fischer, F. `Korrelationen von Risiken im Projektportfoliomanage- ment. Ein hybrides Entscheidungsmodell für die Selektion alternativer Projektportfolien´ in *Projektmanagement* (3/2004), p. 25 – 33.

5 Lomnitz: *loc. cit.*, p. 24

BIBLIOGRAPHY AND FOOTNOTES

6   For a detailed description of the requirements profile for a multiproject manager, see Lomnitz, loc. cit., p. 72 ff.
7   Campana, Ch.; Reschke, H.; Schott, E.: `6.2.3 Project Office-Implementierung und -Verankerung im Unternehmen` in Schelle, H.; Reschke, H.; Schnopp, R.; Schub, A. (Eds.): loose-leaf report *Projekte erfolgreich managen*, 18th update, Cologne, p. 22
8   Block, T.; Frame, R.; Davidson, J.: *The Project Office. A Key to Managing Projects Effectively*, Menlo Park (CA), (1998)

F1   INTRODUCTION OF PROJECT MANAGEMENT

1   Rosenstiel, L. von: `Verhaltenswissenschaftliche Grundlagen von Veränderungsprozessen´ Reiss, M.; Rosenstiel, L. von; Lanz, A.: *Change Management. Programme, Projekte und Prozesse*, Stuttgart (1997), p. 191 – 212, specifically 197
2   Ibid.
3   Reiss, M.: `Change Management als Herausforderung´ in Reiss et. al.: *Change Management. Programme, Projekte und Prozesse*, p. 5 – 29, specifically p. 17
4   Modified: Doppler, K.; Lautenburg, C.: *Change Management. Den Unternehmenswandel gestalten*, 2nd edition, Frankfurt/M. – New York (1994), p. 207, quoting Wahl, R.: `Die Implementierung von Projektmanagementkonzepten in der Praxis. Eine empirische Analyse´ in *projektMANAGEMENT aktuell* (3/2001), p. 9 – 18, specifically p. 13
5   Hansel, J.; Lomnitz, G.: *Projektleiter-Praxis. Erfolgreiche Projektabwicklung durch verbesserte Kommunikation und Kooperation*, Berlin – Heidelberg – New York (1987), p. 123
6   *Ibid.* p. 125
7   DeMarco, Slack,T.: *Getting past burn-out, busywork and the myth of total efficiency*, Broadway (2002)
8   Hansel; Lomnitz: *loc. cit.*, p. 150 f.
9   Kraus, H.: *Einfluss des angewandten Projektmanagements auf die Arbeitszufriedenheit der in einer Projektorganisation integrierten Personen. Eine Felduntersuchung in der Automobilindustrie*, thesis, Karlsruhe (1995), p. 243
10 Platz, J.: `Projektmanagement erfolgreich einführen´ in *Projektmanagement* (2/1992), p. 5 – 13, specifically p. 12
11 Wahl: *loc. cit.*, p. 16 ff.
12 Cf. Kessler, H.: `8.4 Karriere machen in und durch Projektmanagement´ in Schelle, H.; Reschke, H.; Schnopp, R.; Schub, A. (Eds.): loose-leaf report *Projekte erfolgreich managen*, 19th update, Cologne (1994) ff.
13 Hilpert, N.; Rademacher, G.; Sauer, B.: *Projekt-Management und Projekt-Controlling im Anlagen- und Systemgeschäft*, 6th edition, Frankfurt/M. (2001), p. 139
14 KPMG Strategic and Technology Service Group (Ed.): *What went wrong? Unsuccessful Information Technology Projects 1997;* The Standish Group International Inc. (Ed.): *Chaos Application Project and Failure. January 1995;* KPMG Great Britain (Ed.): *Why do so many projects still fail when we invest so much in training?* KWORLD (January/2001) (Daily Telegraph survey). All three works quote Gaulke, M.: *Risikomanagement in IT-Projekten*, Munich – Vienna (2002), p. 35 f.
15 Wahl, *loc. cit.*, p. 10
16 Witte, E.: *Organisation für Innovationsentscheidungen. Das Promotoren-Modell,* Göttingen (1973), p. 17
17 Platz: *loc. cit.*, p. 18 ff.
18 Ibid.

19 In contrast to Platz, who recommends that the project team is not formed until Phase 1 The author believes that it should take place much earlier.
20 Hindel et. al.: *loc. cit.*, p. 64
21 *Ibid.* p. 181 f.

F2   PROJECT MANAGEMENT OPTIMISATION

1   www.sei.cmu.edu/cmm/cmm.html (16.9.04)
2   Paulk, M. C.: `How ISO 9001 compares with the CMM´ in *IEEE Transactions on Software,* 12th edition (No.1, Januar 1995), p. 74–83
3   Dymond, K. M. *CMM Handbuch. Das Capability Maturity Model für Software* Berlin – Heidelberg – New York (2002), p. 16
4   Balzert, H.: *Lehrbuch der Softwaretechnik. Software Management, Software-Qualitätssicherung, Unternehmensmodellierung,* Heidelberg – Berlin (1998), p. 11
5   http://www.sei.cmu.edu/cmmi.html (1.12. 04)
6   Stienen, H.: *Nach CMM und BOOTSTRAP: SPICE. Die neue Norm für Prozessbewertungen. Informatik. Informatique* (No. 6/1999), p. 16 – 21
7   Kerzner, H.: *Strategic Planning for Project Management Using a Project Management Maturity Model,* New York (2001), p. 4 – 1
8   Project Management Institute (Ed.): *Organizational Project Management Model (OPM3),* Knowledge Foundation, Newton Square, Pennsylvania (2003)
9   *Ibid.* p. 13
10 *Ibid.* p. 37
11 Placed in bold type by the author to emphasise the chosen system.
12 Projektmanagement Institute: *loc. cit.*, p. 44
13 www.GPM-IPMA.de/11-2.htm (7.10.04)
14 Lebsanft, K.; Westermann, F.: `Projektmanagement-Assessment bei Siemens´ in *projektMANAGEMENT aktuell* (4/2003), p. 16–25, specifically p. 22
15 *Ibid.* p. 24
16 Cooke-Davies, T.: `Project Management Maturities Models. Does it make sense to adopt one?´ in *Project Manager Today* (May/2002), p. 16 – 20
17 Glinz, M.: `Eine geführte Tour durch die Landschaft der Software-Prozesse und Prozessverbesserung´, Informatik, Informatique (No. 6/1999), p. 7 – 11
18 *Ibid.* p. 11
19 Ruskin, A. M.: `Project Management Maturity Models´ Duncan, W. R. (Ed.) *PM Network* October (1998), p. 4, quoting Motzel: loc. cit., p. 36

F3   PROJECT MANAGEMENT STANDARDS

1   Cf. Waschek, G.: `1.6 Normen im Projektmanagement´ in Schelle, H.; Reschke, H.; Schnopp, R.; Schub, A. (Eds.): loose-leaf report *Projekte erfolgreich managen,* 18th update, Cologne (1994) ff. Chapter F3 is strongly oriented towards Waschek´s deliberations as Head of the DIN Committee for Network Analysis and Project Management.
Cf. Motzel, E.: `1.9 Standards und Kompetenzmodelle im Projektmanagement, ibid., 18th update´
2   Project Management Institute (Ed.): *A Guide to the Project Management Body of Knowledge,* 3rd Edition (PMBOK Guide), Newton Square Pennsylvania (2004)